Contents

W9-AGE-376

UNIT 1
Pluralist Democracies: Country Studies

Twelve selections examine the current state of politics in the United Kingdom, Germany, France, and Japan.

Part A. The United Kingdom

The concepts in bold italics are developed in the article. For further expansion, please refer to the Topic Guide and the Index.

UNIT 2
Pluralist Democracies: Factors in the Political Process

Ten selections examine the functioning of Western European democracies with regard to political ideas and participation, money and politics, the role of women in politics, and the institutional framework of resprepresentative government.

The concepts in bold italics are developed in the article. For further expansion, please refer to the Topic Guide and the Index.

ANNUAL EDITIONS

Comparative Politics
04/05

Twenty-Second Edition

EDITOR

Christian Søe

California State University, Long Beach

Christian Søe was born in Denmark, studied at the University of British Columbia and the University of Michigan, and received his doctoral degree in political science at the Free University in Berlin. He is professor in political science at California State University in Long Beach, where he teaches courses in comparative politics. His research deals primarily with political developments in contemporary Germany. He visits that country annually to conduct research on political parties and elections. In these and other ways, he attempts to follow shifts in the balance of power and changes in political orientation within Germany as now represented by a new "red-green" coalition and a new generation of leaders in Berlin. The early phase of this transition in German politics is a main topic of the 1999 book, which he co-edited with Mary N. Hampton, *Between Bonn and Berlin: German Politics Adrift?* He is co-editor (with David Conradt and Gerald R. Kleinfeld) of *Power Shift in Germany,* a study of the 1998 Bundestag election. The same team has co-edited another book manuscript dealing with the 2002 Bundestag election and its aftermath. It will be published in the summer of 2004 under the title, *Precarious Victory*. Three other publications are a biographical essay on Hans-Dietrich Genscher, Germany's foreign minister from 1974 to 1992, in *Political Leaders of Contemporary Western Europe;* a chapter on the Free Democratic Party in *Germany's New Politics*; and another chapter on the Danish-German relationship in *The Germans and Their Neighbors*. Dr. Søe is also co-editor of the latter two books. He has been editor of the twenty-two volumes of *Annual Editions: Comparative Politics* since the beginning of this series in 1983.

McGraw-Hill/Dushkin

2460 Kerper Boulevard, Dubuque, Iowa 52001

Visit us on the Internet
http://www.dushkin.com

Credits

1. **Pluralist Democracies: Country Studies**
   Unit photo—© 2003 by PhotoDisc, Inc.
2. **Pluralist Democracies: Factors in the Political Process**
   Unit photo—Emma Lee/Life File/Getty Images
3. **Europe—West, Center, and East: The Politics of Integration, Transformation, and Disintegration**
   Unit photo—Neil Beer/Getty Images
4. **Political Diversity in the Developing World**
   Unit photo—Corbis Images/Royalty Free
5. **Comparative Politics: Some Major Trends, Issues, and Prospects**
   Unit photo—Index Stock/Getty Images

Copyright

Cataloging in Publication Data
Main entry under title: Annual Editions: Comparative Politics. 2004/2005.
1. Comparative Politics—Periodicals. I. Søe, Christian, *comp.* II. Title: Comparative Politics.
ISBN 0–07–286145–2   658'.05   ISSN 0741–7233

Twenty-Second Edition

Cover image © 2005 PhotoDisc, Inc.
Printed in the United States of America   1234567890QPDQPD0987654   Printed on Recycled Paper

Editors/Advisory Board

Members of the Advisory Board are instrumental in the final selection of articles for each edition of ANNUAL EDITIONS. Their review of articles for content, level, currentness, and appropriateness provides critical direction to the editor and staff. We think that you will find their careful consideration well reflected in this volume.

To the Reader

In publishing ANNUAL EDITIONS we recognize the enormous role played by the magazines, newspapers, and journals of the public press in providing current, first-rate educational information in a broad spectrum of interest areas. Many of these articles are appropriate for students, researchers, and professionals seeking accurate, current material to help bridge the gap between principles and theories and the real world. These articles, however, become more useful for study when those of lasting value are carefully collected, organized, indexed, and reproduced in a low-cost format, which provides easy and permanent access when the material is needed. That is the role played by ANNUAL EDITIONS.

This collection of readings brings together current articles that will help you understand the politics of foreign countries from a comparative perspective. Such a study opens up a fascinating world beyond our borders. It will also lead to deeper insights into the American political process.

The articles in unit 1 cover Britain or the United Kingdom, France, Germany, Italy, and Japan in a serial manner. In terms of gross domestic product, these countries all belong with the United States among the top six economies in the world. Each of these modern societies has an individual tradition of politics and governance within a particular institutional framework. Nevertheless, as the readings of unit 2 show, it is possible to point to some comparable patterns of political challenge and response among these and some other representative democracies.

Unit 3 deals with the impact of two major changes that continue to transform the political map of Europe. One of them is the irregular, sometimes halting, but nevertheless impressive growth of the European Union (EU). It has grown to 15 member countries with nearly 300 million people. In 2004, ten more countries are slated to join the EU, and later there will be more. The other and closely related major change involves the political and economic reconstruction of Central and Eastern Europe, including Russia, after the collapse of the Communist regimes in that region between 1989 and 1991. These developments underscore the continuing political importance of Europe.

Unit 4 looks first at the challenge of globalization and then turns to articles dealing with some of the developing countries and regions, including Mexico and Latin America as a whole, South Africa, Nigeria, India, China, and the Muslim world. The articles will give the careful reader a better understanding of the diversity of social and political conditions in these countries.

Unit 5 considers three major trends in contemporary politics from a comparative perspective. First, the past quarter of a century has seen a remarkable spread of democratic forms of government in the world. This recent "wave of democratization," sometimes described as the "third" of its kind in modern history, seems likely to have a lasting effect on the political process in some countries that previously knew only authoritarian governments. But there is no simple way to construct a stable democracy anywhere— least of all in countries that are divided by deep ethnic, economic, religious, and other cleavages.

Second, beginning in the 1980s there has been a major shift in economic policy toward greater reliance on private enterprise and markets, and a corresponding reduction in state ownership and regulation in much of the world, including Communist-ruled China. But there has been a reaction in the advanced industrial societies and in many developing countries against the inequalities, dislocations, and uncertainties associated with the unfettered market economy.

Third, many parts of the world have seen a surge of what has been called "identity politics." This trend has brought group identities more strongly into play when differences are being defined, played out, and resolved in the political arena.

This is an unusually interesting and important time to study comparative politics. The past fifteen years have seen a major restructuring of politics in many countries along with a generational shift in leadership. Even in a time of political transformation, however, there will be significant patterns of continuity as well as change.

This is the twenty-second edition of *Annual Editions: Comparative Politics.* Over the years, the successive editions have reflected the developments that eventually brought about the post-cold war world of today. This present volume tries to present information and analysis that are useful in the quest to understand today's political world and the parameters it sets for tomorrow's developments.

A special word of thanks goes to my own past and present students at California State University, Long Beach. They are wonderfully inquisitive and help keep me posted on matters that this anthology must address. Several of my past students have helped me gather material. As always, I am particularly grateful to Susan B. Mason, who received her master's degree in political science over a decade ago. She continues to volunteer as a superb research assistant. Once again I also wish to thank some other past and present students at Cal State: Linda Wohlman, Erika Reinhardt, Erik Ibsen, Jon Nakagawa, Perry Oliver, Mike Petri, Richard Sherman, and Ali Taghavi. Like so many others, these individuals first encountered the anthology in my comparative politics courses. It is a great joy to have worked with such fine students. Their enthusiasm for the project has been contagious.

I am very grateful to members of the advisory board and McGraw-Hill/Dushkin as well as to the many readers who have made useful comments on past selections and suggested new ones. I ask you all to help improve future editions by keeping me informed of your reactions and suggestions for change. Please complete and return the article rating form in the back of the book.

Christian Søe
Editor

The concepts in bold italics are developed in the article. For further expansion, please refer to the Topic Guide and the Index.

UNIT 3
Europe in Transition: West, Center, and East

Seven selections examine the European continent: the European Union, Western European society, post-communist Central and Eastern Europe, and Russia and the other post-Soviet Republics.

The concepts in bold italics are developed in the article. For further expansion, please refer to the Topic Guide and the Index.

UNIT 4
Political Diversity in the Developing World

Ten selections review the developing world's economic and political development in Latin America, Africa, China, India, and the Muslim world.

The concepts in bold italics are developed in the article. For further expansion, please refer to the Topic Guide and the Index.

UNIT 5
Comparative Politics: Some Major Trends, Issues, and Prospects

Four selections discuss the rise of democracy, how capitalism impacts on political development, and the political assertion of group identity in contemporary politics.

The concepts in bold italics are developed in the article. For further expansion, please refer to the Topic Guide and the Index.

Topic Guide

This topic guide suggests how the selections in this book relate to the subjects covered in your course. You may want to use the topics listed on these pages to search the Web more easily.

On the following pages a number of Web sites have been gathered specifically for this book. They are arranged to reflect the units of this *Annual Edition.* You can link to these sites by going to the DUSHKIN ONLINE support site at *http://www.dushkin.com/online/.*

ALL THE ARTICLES THAT RELATE TO EACH TOPIC ARE LISTED BELOW THE BOLD-FACED TERM.

World Wide Web Sites

The following World Wide Web sites have been carefully researched and selected to support the articles found in this reader. The easiest way to access these selected sites is to go to our DUSHKIN ONLINE support site at *http://www.dushkin.com/online/*.

AE: Comparative Politics 04/05

The following sites were available at the time of publication. Visit our Web site—we update DUSHKIN ONLINE regularly to reflect any changes.

General Sources

Central Intelligence Agency
http://www.odci.gov

Use this official home page to get connections to *The CIA Factbook,* which provides extensive statistical and political information about every country in the world.

National Geographic Society
http://www.nationalgeographic.com

This site provides links to National Geographic's archive of maps, articles, and documents. There is a great deal of material related to political cultures around the world.

U.S. Agency for International Development
http://www.info.usaid.gov

This Web site covers such broad and overlapping issues as democracy, population and health, economic growth, and development about different regions and countries.

U.S. Information Agency
http://usinfo.state.gov/

This USIA page provides definitions, related documentation, and discussion of topics on global issues. Many Web links are provided.

World Bank
http://www.worldbank.org

News (press releases, summaries of new projects, speeches) and coverage of numerous topics regarding development, countries, and regions are provided at this site.

World Wide Web Virtual Library: International Affairs Resources
http://www.etown.edu/vl/

Surf this site and its extensive links to learn about specific countries and regions, to research international organizations, and to study such vital topics as international law, development, the international economy, and human rights.

UNIT 1: Pluralist Democracies: Country Studies

France.com
http://www.france.com

The links at this site will lead to extensive information about the French government, politics, history, and culture.

GermNews
http://www.germnews.de/dn/about/

Search this site for German political and economic news covering the years 1995 to the present.

Japan Ministry of Foreign Affairs
http://www.mofa.go.jp

Visit this official site for Japanese foreign policy statements and discussions of regional and global relations.

UNIT 2: Pluralist Democracies: Factors in the Political Process

Carnegie Endowment for International Peace
http://www.ceip.org

This organization's goal is to stimulate discussion and learning among both experts and the public at large on a wide range of international issues. The site provides links to the well-respected journal *Foreign Policy,* to the Moscow Center, to descriptions of various programs, and much more.

Communications for a Sustainable Future
http://csf.colorado.edu

This site will lead you to information on topics in international environmental sustainability. It pays particular attention to the political economics of protecting the environment.

Inter-American Dialogue (IAD)
http://www.iadialog.org

This is the Web site for IAD, a premier U.S. center for policy analysis, communication, and exchange in Western Hemisphere affairs. The 100-member organization has helped to shape the agenda of issues and choices in hemispheric relations.

The North American Institute (NAMI)
http://www.northamericaninstitute.org

NAMI, a trinational public-affairs organization concerned with the emerging "regional space" of Canada, the United States, and Mexico, provides links for study of trade, the environment, and institutional developments.

UNIT 3: Europe in Transition: West, Center, and East

Europa: European Union
http://europa.eu.int

This server site of the European Union will lead you to the history of the EU; descriptions of EU policies, institutions, and goals; discussion of monetary union; and documentation of treaties and other materials.

NATO Integrated Data Service (NIDS)
http://www.nato.int/structur/nids/nids.htm

NIDS was created to bring information on security-related matters to the widest possible audience. Check out this Web site to review North Atlantic Treaty Organization documentation of all kinds, to read *NATO Review,* and to explore key issues in the field of European security.

Research and Reference (Library of Congress)
http://lcweb.loc.gov/rr/

This massive research and reference site of the Library of Congress will lead you to invaluable information on the former Soviet Union and other countries attempting the transition to democracy. It provides links to numerous publications, bibliographies, and guides in area studies.

Russian and East European Network Information Center, University of Texas at Austin
http://reenic.utexas.edu/reenic/index.html

This is *the* Web site for information on Russia and the former Soviet Union.

UNIT 4: Political Diversity in the Developing World

Africa News Online
http://allafrica.com/

Open this site for extensive, up-to-date information on all of Africa, with reports from Africa's leading newspapers, magazines, and news agencies. Coverage is country-by-country and regional. Background documents and Internet links are among the resource pages.

ArabNet
http://www.arab.net

This home page of ArabNet, the online resource for the Arab world in the Middle East and North Africa, presents links to 22 Arab countries. Each country Web page classifies information using a standardized system of categories.

ASEAN Web
http://www.aseansec.org/home.html

This official site of the Association of Southeast Asian Nations provides an overview of Asian Web resources, Asian summits, economic and world affairs, political foundations, regional cooperation, and publications.

Inside China Today
http://www.einnews.com/china/

Part of the European Internet Network, this site leads to information on China, including recent news, government, and related sites pertaining to mainland China, Hong Kong, Macao, and Taiwan.

InterAction
http://www.interaction.org

InterAction encourages grassroots action and engages government bodies and policymakers on various advocacy issues. The organization's Advocacy Committee provides this site to inform people on its initiatives to expand international humanitarian relief, refugee, and development-assistance programs.

Organization for Economic Cooperation and Development
http://www.oecd.org/home/

Explore development, governance, and world trade and investment issues on this OECD site. It provides links to many related topics and addresses global economic issues on a country-by-country basis.

Sun SITE Singapore
http://sunsite.nus.edu.sg/noframe.html

These South East Asia Information pages provide information and point to other online resources about the region's 10 countries, including Vietnam, Indonesia, and Brunei.

UNIT 5: Comparative Politics: Some Major Trends, Issues, and Prospects

Commission on Global Governance
http://www.sovereignty.net/p/gov/gganalysis.htm

This site provides access to *The Report of the Commission on Global Governance,* produced by an international group of leaders who want to find ways in which the global community can better manage its affairs.

IISDnet
http://www.iisd.org/default.asp

This site of the International Institute for Sustainable Development, a Canadian organization, presents information through links on business and sustainable development, developing ideas, and Hot Topics. Linkages is its multimedia resource for environment and development policymakers.

ISN International Relations and Security Network
http://www.isn.ethz.ch

This site, maintained by the Center for Security Studies and Conflict Research, is a clearinghouse for extensive information on international relations and security policy. Topics are listed by category (Traditional Dimensions of Security, New Dimensions of Security) and by major world regions.

United Nations Environment Program
http://www.unep.ch/

Consult this home page of UNEP for links to critical topics about global issues, including desertification and the impact of trade on the environment. The site leads to useful databases and global resource information.

Virtual Seminar in Global Political Economy/Global Cities & Social Movements
http://csf.colorado.edu/gpe/gpe95b/resources.html

This site of Internet resources is rich in links to subjects of interest in regional studies, covering topics such as sustainable cities, megacities, and urban planning. Links to many international nongovernmental organizations are included.

We highly recommend that you review our Web site for expanded information and our other product lines. We are continually updating and adding links to our Web site in order to offer you the most usable and useful information that will support and expand the value of your Annual Editions. You can reach us at: *http://www.dushkin.com/annualeditions/.*

World Map

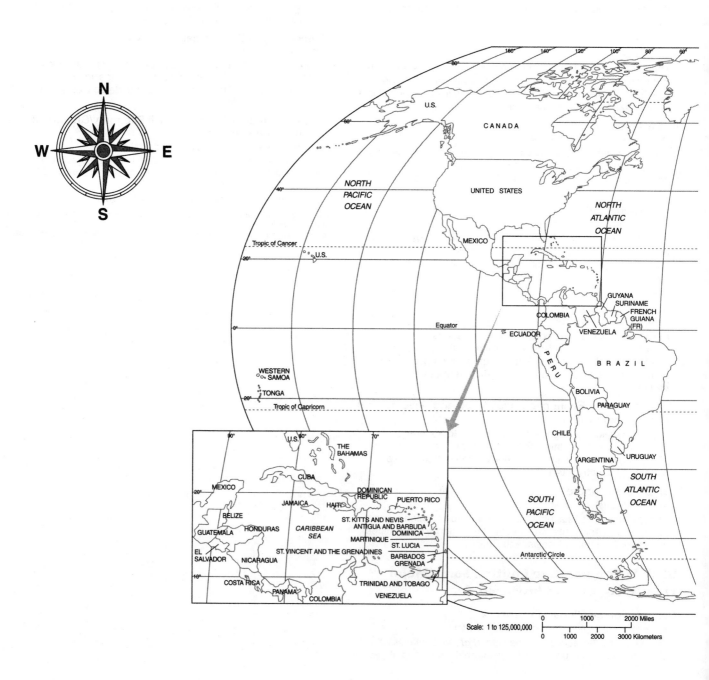

N
W E
S

U.S.

CANADA

NORTH
PACIFIC
OCEAN

UNITED STATES

MEXICO

NORTH
ATLANTIC
OCEAN

Tropic of Cancer

U.S.

GUYANA
SURINAME
FRENCH
GUIANA
(FR)

COLOMBIA

VENEZUELA

Equator

ECUADOR

P E R U

B R A Z I L

WESTERN
SAMOA

TONGA

BOLIVIA

Tropic of Capricorn

PARAGUAY

CHILE

ARGENTINA URUGUAY

SOUTH
ATLANTIC
OCEAN

SOUTH
PACIFIC
OCEAN

Antarctic Circle

U.S.

THE
BAHAMAS

CUBA

MEXICO

DOMINICAN
REPUBLIC PUERTO RICO

JAMAICA HAITI

BELIZE

ST. KITTS AND NEVIS
ANTIGUA AND BARBUDA
DOMINICA

GUATEMALA HONDURAS

CARIBBEAN
SEA

MARTINIQUE
ST. LUCIA

EL
SALVADOR NICARAGUA

ST. VINCENT AND THE GRENADINES

BARBADOS
GRENADA

COSTA RICA

PANAMA

COLOMBIA

TRINIDAD AND TOBAGO

VENEZUELA

Scale: 1 to 125,000,000

| 0 | 1000 | 2000 Miles |
| 0 | 1000 | 2000 | 3000 Kilometers |

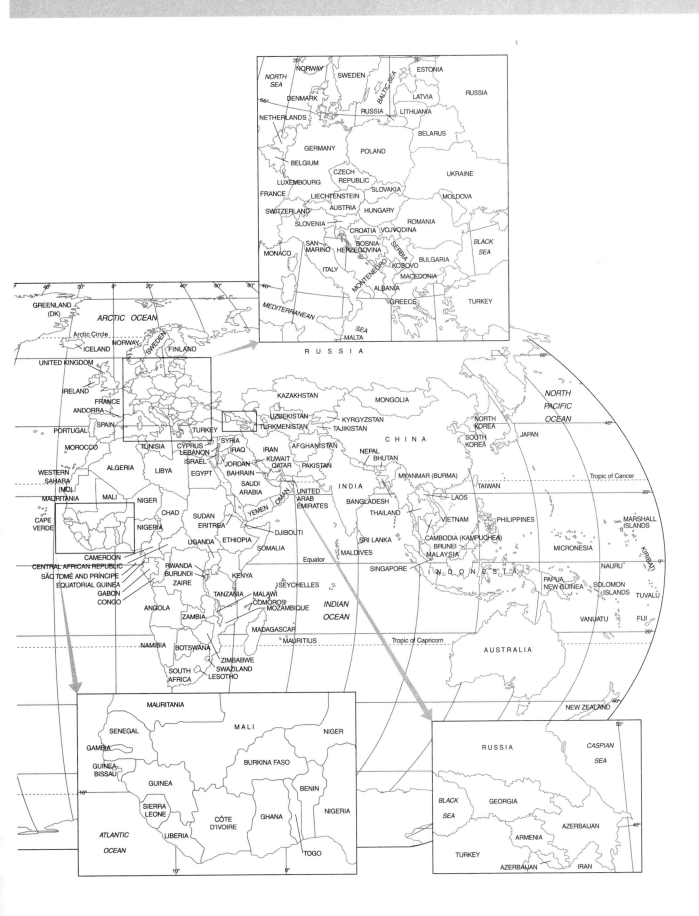

UNIT 1
Pluralist Democracies: Country Studies

Unit Selections

Key Points to Consider

- What are the main items on Prime Minister Blair's constitutional reform agenda, and how far have they become reality by now?

- What were some major factors that helped Tony Blair and Labour win a second term in office in June 2001?

- What is "new" about Labour under Blair's leadership?

- How can his government's policy toward Iraq and public services create difficulties for Blair in his own party?

- What are the political prospects of the other two national parties, the Conservatives and the Liberal Democrats, in the House of Commons?

- Why did Jacques Chirac call an early parliamentary election in 1997, and how did the outcome produce a new form of "cohabitation" in the Fifth Republic?

- What are the signs that French politics have become more centrist or middle-of-the-road for the main political parties?

- How did Lionel Jospin and his government of the Left approach socioeconomic reform in France?

- How did the formula, "first time vote with the heart, next time with the head," boomerang on left-of-center voters in the two-stage French presidential elections of 2004? Name three unusual factors that helped the SPD and the Greens in Germany find new supporters in the parliamentary elections of 2002.

- Why has the perennial debate about the need for a reform of the German social model produced so little real advance?

- How has the federal council (Bundesrat) landed on political reform agenda in Germany?

- Explain why Japan's LDP is jokingly said to be "neither liberal, nor democratic, nor a party." What has been the role of this party in postwar Japanese politics?

- How and why has a would-be reformer like Prime Minister Koizumi begun to resemble his predecessors?

- Why could a reform of the bureaucracy become a major political event in Japan?

- How does the 2003 election provide some hope for the consolidation of the parliamentary opposition in Japan.

 **Links: www.dushkin.com/online/**
These sites are annotated in the World Wide Web pages.

France.com
http://www.france.com

Japan Ministry of Foreign Affairs
http://www.mofa.go.jp

GermNews
http://www.germnews.de/dn/about/

Britain, France, Germany and Italy are the most prominent industrial societies in Western Europe. Their modern political histories vary considerably, but all have developed into pluralist democracies with representative forms of government. None of them is without democratic shortcomings, but each can point to active citizens, competing political parties, assertive interest groups and a free press. The "rule of law" prevails, with government officials and civil servants alike bound by legal rules in their public acts. **Japan** appears to have less pluralist competition, but it too is a representative democracy and occupies a similar position of prominence in Asia. Every one of these five countries has developed a distinctive set of political institutions, defined its own public agenda, and found its own dynamic balance of continuity and change. Their individual traits coupled with important similarities invite cross-national comparison among these and some other representative democracies. A study of comparative politics can usefully begin here.

They all belong in the relatively small category of "**older democracies**," as political scientist Robert A. Dahl refers to the 22 countries—15 of them located in Western Europe—that have continuously maintained democratic forms of governance since at least 1950. Had the starting point for inclusion been set a few years earlier, the list would have been much smaller. It is sobering to remember that in our group of five, only Britain did not interrupt its democratic development at some point in the twentieth century. Three of them (Italy, Japan and Germany) abandoned the democratic road in the period between the two world wars, and France did the same after its defeat and partial military occupation by Germany in 1940. After World War II, these four all started out with new democratic constitutions, whereas Britain continued to function—as it had for centuries—within an evolving framework of basic laws, rules and conventions, often referred to as its "unwritten" or uncodified constitution.

The four West European countries in the group show the impact of some major developments that are changing the political, social and economic map of their continent. This was the birthplace of the **modern nation-state**, and it is now the location where that basic political construct is undergoing a partial and ambiguous transformation. In principle and practice, all of the member nations of **the European Union (EU)** have agreed to an unprecedented dilution of their traditional national sovereignty. For these countries, the fulcrum of much policy-making has been shifting away from the national arena to the EU, particularly in economic matters. As a result, some familiar aspects of their political identity, like national borders or national currencies, have been reduced in importance or entirely replaced.

None of this signals the end of the nation-state or its imminent displacement by a **United States of Europe**. But no student of comparative politics will want to ignore the European Union as a novel political formation that began with six member states in the 1950s and grew to fifteen by 1996. In its next expansion, the EU plans to bring in ten new member states

during 2004. Recognizing that the result had no parallel in the political universe, a former Commission President once referred to the EU as an "unidentified political object" (UPO). One of the big questions is how this regional organization will change as a result of its unprecedented enlargement and diversification.

At the same time, Europeans have begun to examine carefully another of their major contributions to contemporary politics, the **modern welfare state**. In practically every country there are attempts to define a new balance between **economic efficiency and social justice**, as governments and publics are confronted with the increasing costs of a popular and relatively generous system of welfare and service entitlements. If the funding problem were merely a cyclical one, it would lend itself more easily to solutions within the existing policy framework. But there are structural components that seem to require a revamping or "reinvention" of the welfare state. The problem is exacerbated by the overall **ageing of the population** in these societies, with their long life expectancies and low birth rates. This is causing strains on the social budget and its "pay-as-you-go" formula that in practice involves an inter-generational transfer of wealth.

Economically, the five countries have relatively high and fairly similar rankings. They are all members of the Group of Seven (G 7), where they follow the United States in places two (Japan), three (Germany), four (France), five (Britain), and six (Italy) among **the world's largest market economies**. If ranked in terms of their respective **gross national product (GNP) per capita**, the five countries slip somewhat lower as they are passed and become separated from each other by a few smaller but higher performing economies. Even here, they all remain at the high end (in or very near the top tenth percentile) on a World Bank index. They have all arrived at some **"mixed" form of market capitalism**, but their manner and degree of state intervention in the economy varies considerably. Since the "Thatcher Revolution" of the 1980s, Britain has come closer to the relatively open market conditions of the United States, while France and Germany have followed a more organized and regulated form of capitalism. The protected Japanese economy is less competitive and sometimes described as neo-mercantilist. When compared for **disparity in income**, as measured by the gini index, the five countries also show considerable differences. Yet none of them records as high an income gap between the top 10 percent and the lowest 10 percent of the population as the one found in the United States. The income gap is lowest in Japan, followed by Germany, and it is highest—and closest to the U.S. situation—in Britain.

There are some additional developments that underscore the continuing political importance of Europe. For example, it is faced with a **growing ethnic and cultural diversity** brought about by the arrival of many economic migrants and political refugees after the end of the cold war. This influx has had some stimulating economic and cultural effects, but it has also brought issues of **multicultural co-existence and tolerance** back onto the political agenda in a new and intensified form. An example is the current controversy in France (and elsewhere) over a proposed ban on wearing a piece of clothing that could be regarded as a religious symbol, such as a head scarf or a yarmulke, in public schools or other secular institutions.

Even as West Europeans seek to come to terms with this challenge of greater diversity, their politics has been affected by a **growing ecological awareness**. It shows up in widespread support for national and international initiatives to protect the environment, such as the Kyoto Treaty. They are also trying to adjust to the new information technologies and the many challenges of the global market with its opportunities for expansion and its threats of job losses and economic instability. It is clearly **a time of dynamic change and wrenching dislocations** that transcend the traditional boundaries of region and nation. In such a bewildering context, it is not surprising to encounter **manifestations of democratic discontents**, a topic that is further developed in Unit Two.

The events of September 11, 2001 and its aftermath have added a new element of organized violence and unpredictability to our political world. The terrorist attacks on the World Trade Towers and the Pentagon were clearly directed at the United States, but the supportive, clandestine network reached deep into several European countries. Similar strikes could affect them at any time. This awareness has affected the politics of these countries. It helped mobilize their early support for U.S.-led military counter-measures in Afghanistan. But it

soon became clear that there is **no trans-Atlantic consensus** on the most effective strategy for dealing with the new terrorism or our own vulnerability to this type of attack. One crucial assumption of the traditional policy of containment does not apply to this kind of activity, namely that the desire for self-preservation will restrain the actions of potential opponents by making them reluctant to risk retaliation. The primary responsibility of the state, to provide security for its citizens in a dangerous world, has acquired a new dimension in light of the willingness of individual terrorists to risk self-destruction (understood as self-sacrifice). The search for an appropriate and effective response will preoccupy our politics for a long time to come.

This became particularly evident in the controversy about the approach to be taken in dealing with Iraq and its ruler, Saddam Hussein. The U.S. government was determined to move decisively to disarm Iraq of the weapons of mass destruction, which President George W. Bush believed the Baghdad government to be developing and accumulating. In addition, the United States spoke openly of seeking a "regime change," leaving no one in doubt of its readiness to conduct what it presented as a massive preemptive strike to achieve its goals.

Gerhard Schröder and Jacques Chirac, the political leaders of Germany and France, both reacted critically to President Bush's position. Their preference for giving more time to UN weapon inspectors to search for hidden weapons in Iraq ran counter to the official American determination to use military pressure and intervention to force the issue. British prime minister Tony Blair played a markedly different role, in the tradition of his country's "**special relationship**" to the United States. He was largely supportive of President Bush's strategy, even as he stressed that the *casus belli* had been Iraq's failure to meet UN-backed resolutions on weapons inspection. As a result, a significant number of British troops joined the American ones in the invasion and occupation of Iraq in April 2003. Blair ended up having to pay a heavy political price for extending political and military support. In Britain, he ran into an unprecedented barrage of public criticism, much of it from within his own party.

Not surprisingly, the debate has led to reflections on more fundamental political differences between much of continental Europe and the United States. One of the most widely discussed theses has come from the American political writer, Robert Kagan. He concludes that Europe and America are not just separated on this important issue, but that the "older" and weaker continent no longer shares the willingness or propensity of a "younger" and more powerful United States to use military power as a means of foreign policy. In a widely quoted phrase, he sums up his perception of the difference: "Americans are from Mars and Europeans are from Venus." There is little agreement among them, Kagan argues, and less and less understanding. He believes that the deep lying causes are likely to endure. Kagan's thesis has set off a lively discussion, much of it critical of the simple dichotomy he sometimes adopts.

It is important to pay attention to these major changes and new challenges. But we must not lose sight of some equally important if less dramatic aspects of politics. In the stable democracies of Western Europe and Japan, the political process is usually defined by **a relatively mild blend of change and continuity**. Here political agendas are normally modified rather than discarded entirely, and shifts in the balance of power do not take the form of revolutionary displacements of a ruling group. Instead, there are **occasional changes of government** as a result of coalition disagreements or routine elections.

Britain has long been regarded as "the mother" of the parliamentary system of government. In contrast to a presidential system, where the chief executive and legislatures are separately elected by the voters for fixed terms of office, a parliamentary government is often described as based on **the "fusion" of the executive and legislative powers**. Its most distinctive trait is that the prime minister, as head of government, is in some way "chosen" by and from the popularly elected legislature and remains dependent on its sustained majority support or toleration to stay in office. Should the prime minister lose majority support in the legislature, then he or she may be replaced by someone else. The political rupture sometimes finds expression in a formal vote of "no confidence."

There are numerous variations in the institutional workings of parliamentary government over time or from one country to another. In Britain, for example, there is no formal "election" of the prime minister in the House of Commons. Instead, the person who is the recognized leader of the majority party in the House of Commons will be asked by the monarch to form a government. In Germany, on the other hand, the federal chancellor is formally elected by the Bundestag as the result of the formation of a majority based on a coalition of two or more political parties.

In today's British version of parliamentary government, called **the Westminster model**, there is usually one party that wins a majority of the seats in the House of Commons. The result is single-party rule and a form of majoritarian politics in which the main opposition party of "**outs**" plays the adversary role of an institutionalized critic and rival of the government party of "**ins.**" In continental Europe, where elections seldom result in a single party majority in the legislature, the prime minister is normally supported by a parliamentary coalition of parties. Under such power-sharing coalition governments, the political process tends to be less adversary and more inclusive or consensual than in the Westminster system.

Politically, a British prime minister can stay in power between elections as long as he or she continues to receive majority support from the elected legislature. It is possible to lose the prime ministerial office through a **parliamentary vote of no confidence**. Such an overthrow is relatively rare in contemporary British politics, because the electoral system tends to produce a single party majority that is then kept together by political self-interest and other factors that produce a strong party discipline. A motion of no confidence can only threaten a prime minister whose own parliamentary supporters have for some reason become too few to ensure a dependable majority in favor of the government.

A far more likely cause for turnovers in British government is a general election that results in the governing party losing its parliamentary majority. This has happened in seven of the 16 general elections held between 1945 and 2001—compared to seven party alternations in the White House resulting from 14 U.S. presidential elections in the same period. The most recent British example took place in 1997, when Labour defeated the Conservatives and replaced them in office.

It is also fairly common for prime ministers to step down at midterm, voluntarily or as the result of political pressure from members of their own party. Since 1945, there have been five such cases of **early resignation** when a British prime minister has been replaced by a leading member of the same party. The most recent case is that of Margaret Thatcher, who headed a Conservative government for more than eleven years, from May 1979 to 1990. In November 1990, she faced a potential revolt by members of her own parliamentary party, as many Conservatives concluded that she had become a political liability. She stepped down reluctantly, making the way free for another leading Tory, John Major, to succeed her as party leader and prime minister. Such an early resignation is very rare in the U.S. system, where heads of government are elected for fixed terms of office.

Since 1945 Britain can be said to have had **three major reform governments** that greatly altered some key features of British society and politics. The first of these was **Clement Atlee's Labour Government** (1945–51) that came to power immediately after World War II and replaced the wartime coalition government led by Winston Churchill. In a nation weary of war and depression, Labour had won a sweeping victory over the Conservatives. During its first five years in office, Labour established a comprehensive welfare state in Britain, nationalized some key parts of the economy ("the commanding heights"), and took the first major steps to dismantle the large overseas empire by releasing the huge Indian subcontinent. The result was a sea change that turned Britain toward a more egalitarian form of society. Labour scraped through the general election of 1950 with a tiny parliamentary majority, too weak to continue with major new reforms. A year later, it called an early election in a bid to win a "working" parliamentary majority. The stakes were unusually high in 1951, and the result was a milestone election that recorded one of the biggest voter turnouts in British history. Labour won a narrow plurality of the popular vote, but the Conservatives won a majority of the seats in the House of Commons and formed the next government.

During the first five years in office, Atlee's Labour government had taken full advantage of the British political system's capacity for effective, comprehensive yet accountable action. This institutional trait has impressed many U.S. political scientists since Woodrow Wilson. It was much less in evidence during the next quarter of a century. Instead, the British governmental process from 1950 to the late 1970s seemed to be better captured in the phrase "muddling through." Some historians would later refer to these years as an era of "**consensus politics.**"

Having come back to power in 1951 by a whisker, the Conservatives refrained from a "roll back" of the welfare state reforms. They returned some of the nationalized economy to private hands, but they engaged in no major reform program of their own. Decolonization continued and reduced Britain's international presence. When Labour finally returned to government office, between 1964 and 1970, the new government talked a lot about policy innovation but failed like its Tory predecessor to deal effectively with some mounting economic problems. In the regular confrontation between "ins" and "outs" in the House of Commons, the British tradition of **adversary rhetoric** continued to flourish. In practice, however, the differences between the two major political parties seemed often to have been reduced to relatively minor matters.

Specific foreign policy issues continued to provide the occasion for some severe political disagreements that sometimes ran through as well as between the main political parties. In 1956, Conservative Prime Minister Eden tried in collusion with the Fourth French Republic and Israel to wrest control of the nationalized **Suez Canal** from President Nasser's Egypt. The military intervention led to a deep division in British politics and a temporary rift in relations with the United States. Britain's embarrassing withdrawal underscored its decline as a major power. Prime Minister Eden's resignation a few months later was a key element in the resolution of this foreign policy fiasco. He was succeeded by Harold Macmillan, who turned out to be a successful practitioner of consensus politics until he too felt obliged to step down, in his case as the result of a scandal involving a member of the government.

The relationship to the **European Economic Community** (originally EEC, now EU) was the source of another political division. Britain had chosen not to join the original six founding members, who signed the Treaty of Rome at the beginning of 1957. The British government soon came to regret its decision and sought entry in the early 1960s. At this point, however, French President Charles de Gaulle blocked the latecomer who would inevitably have challenged France's political leadership of the Community. Britain finally became a member in 1973, but Labour was deeply divided over the issue. When Labor returned to power the following year, it felt obliged to use a **national referendum**—the first in British political history—to decide whether Britain should stay a member. The decision was affirmative, but there continues until today to be elements in both major parties that are reluctant "Europeans."

By the late 1960s and throughout the 1970s, Britain could no longer be said to live up to its earlier reputation for effective government. Instead, the country became notorious for its **chronic governing problems**. Serious observers spoke of Britain as "**the sick man of Europe**." They diagnosed a sociopolitical infirmity dubbed "**Englanditis**," a condition characterized by such problems as economic stagnation, social malaise, and a general incapacity of elected governments to deal effectively with such evidence of relative deterioration.

There were several attempts to give a macro-explanation of Britain's problems. Some British political scientists, like Anthony King, defined their country's condition as one of "**governmental overload**." According to their diagnosis, British governments had become so entangled by socioeconomic entitlements that the country was on the edge of political paralysis or "**ungovernability**." In the United States, the political economist Mancur Olson developed a more general but in some ways similar explanation of **political "sclerosis"** in advanced pluralist democracies like Britain. He explained it in terms of the clotting effects of a highly developed interest group system that made excessive demands on governments and thereby threatened its ability to perform. In a similar analysis of Western democracies that included the British case, Samuel Huntington detected what he decided to call an "**excess of democracy**," a jarring phrase that critics would not let him forget.

A second cluster of interpretations explained **Britain's relative decline** primarily in terms of **structural inertia** that prevented the country from keeping pace with its European neighbors. From this perspective, the problems were primarily attributed to Britain's tenacious tradition as a **class-divided society and imperial power**. Compared to its more modern European neighbors, supporters of this view argued, the United Kingdom was hampered at home by the remnants of an outmoded and dysfunctional social order. It needed to promote a meritocracy by way of greater equality of opportunity and a general societal "modernization." Abroad, the U.K. needed to disentangle itself from an unproductive legacy of over-commitment or "overstretch" in international affairs. The British-American historian, Paul Kennedy, later pursued the thesis about the paralyzing costs of an imperial over-extension in his widely discussed book on the rise and fall of the great powers.

Yet another explanation of Britain's governing crisis focused on the unusually sharp **adversarial character** of the country's major party politics. It suggested that a major culprit was Britain's famed "Westminster Model" of government by a single majority party. The ritualized parliamentary confrontation of the two major parties served to polarize political discourse, leave the moderate center underrepresented, and disrupt the governmental process when the "ins" were replaced by the "outs." This interpretation, which understandably found support among Liberals, sometimes idealized the broader **power-sharing and consensus-seeking forms of coalition government** that are found in most of the parliamentary systems in Western Europe.

By the mid-1970s, this last explanation gained some plausibility, because the mounting British problems had weakened the grip of consensus politics. The two main parties had again begun to diverge and become more polarized in their search for political answers to Britain's problems. As **Labour** and **Conservatives** moved away from their long held centrist positions, toward the political left and right respectively, some voters in the middle turned to the **Liberals** and thereby helped it revive as a national "third" party. In the early 1980s, British party politics became more complex, when a group of moderates defected from Labour to form a new centrist party. Led by such well-known figures as Roy Jenkins, David Owen and Shirley Williams, this **Social Democratic Party (SDP)** cooperated with the old Liberals in an **electoral alliance**. In this manner, they avoided competing against each other and managed to win about a quarter of the popular vote in 1983 and 1987. Under the plurality election rules of "first past the post," however, the two Alliance parties received only about three percent of the seats in the House of Commons.

The Conservatives, led since 1975 by Margaret Thatcher, were the immediate political beneficiaries of the fragmentation of the non-Conservative vote between Labour, the Liberals, and the Social Democrats. They swept into power in 1979 with 43 percent of the total vote but over 60 percent of the seats, and they went on to win with similar margins in the two general elections of 1983 and 1987. This could hardly have been predicted in the early 1980s, when the prime minister and her party plummeted in popularity as a result of some wrenching economic reform measures. The situation changed in 1982, when Argentina's navy invaded the British-held **Falkland Islands** in the South Atlantic. The move elicited a swift and determined military response from Prime Minister Thatcher. Her success in restoring British control of the distant islands had symbolic significance for many British people who had not accepted a "Little England" role for their country.

This **second major reform government** in Britain since World War II (1979 to 1990) saw itself as an overdue corrective to the general political direction taken by Britain since Clement Atlee's earlier reform government and the consensus politics it had spawned. Prime Minister Thatcher prided herself on being a **"conviction politician"** with policies that were based on sound conservative principles. Thatcher was determined to replace what she saw as a sluggish socialist torpor with a dynamic entrepreneurial spirit. Her policies were designed to stimulate the private sector and the interplay of market forces, weaken the obstructing trade unions, and generally reduce the interventionist role of the government. She stayed in office for over eleven years or about twice as long as Atlee's postwar reform government. Moreover, her successor was another Conservative, John Major, whose additional six and a half years in office (1990 to 1997) served to consolidate the Thatcher legacy.

The prime minister dismissed the centrist path taken by Britain's "consensus politicians," as she referred to her immediate Labour and Conservative predecessors. Her radical rhetoric, non-accommodating style and somewhat less drastic policy changes spawned yet another debate about "the Thatcher Effect." The disagreement was not only about how best to achieve **economic growth** but also about **the kind of polity and society Britain ought to be**. Even among the observers who were impressed by the economic revival of Britain in the mid-1980s, there were many who became disturbed by **some social and political trade-offs**. In particular, the income gap between the highest and lowest 10 percent of the U.K. population grew precipitously, as compared to the West European neighbors. It began to approach the greater U.S. disparity between top and bottom incomes. And in the late 1980s critics could also point to the **return of stagflation**, or sluggish economic performance coupled with fairly high inflation.

The British debate had never been restricted to the economy only. The concerns about an alleged "ungovernability" were now joined by questions about the dislocating consequences of the Conservative government's economic and social policies. In addition, some decried what they saw as emerging authoritarian tendencies in the governance of the country. They cited all manner of high-handed efforts by the national government—such as its imposition of central direction over education at all levels, introduction of greater cost controls in the popular National Health Service, privatization of electricity and water industries, or drastic inroads upon what had long been considered established rights in such areas as local government powers and civil liberties.

In foreign affairs, Prime Minister Thatcher had combined an assertive role for Britain in Europe and close cooperation with the United States under the leadership of Presidents Ronald Reagan and George Bush. As a patriot and staunch defender of both market economics and national sovereignty, Thatcher distrusted the drive toward monetary and greater political union in the European Community. She became known throughout the continent for her unusually sharp public attacks on what she pilloried as tendencies toward bureaucratic intervention or technocratic socialism in Brussels. There were critics in her own party who regarded her "Euro-critical" position

as untenable, also because it isolated Britain and reduced its influence on questions of strategic planning for the EC's future.

For the mass electorate, however, nothing seems to have been as upsetting as Thatcher's introduction of the community charge or **"poll tax."** This was a tax on each adult resident that would replace the local property tax or "rates" as a means of financing local public services. Although the new tax was extremely unpopular from the start, the veteran prime minister resisted all pressure to abandon the project before its full national implementation in early 1990. Not only did such a poll tax appear inequitable or regressive, as compared to one based on property values, it also turned out to be set much higher by local governments than the national government originally had estimated.

The politically disastrous result was that, as a revenue measure, the poll tax was anything but neutral in its impact. It created an unexpectedly **large proportion of immediate losers**, that is, people who had to pay considerably more in local taxes than previously. The immediate winners were people who had previously paid high property taxes. Not surprisingly, the national and local governments disagreed about who was responsible for the high poll tax bills, but the voters seemed to have little difficulty in assigning blame to Margaret Thatcher and the Conservative Party as originators of the unpopular reform. Many voters were up in arms, and some observers correctly anticipated that the tax rebellion would undermine Thatcher's position in her own party and become her political Waterloo.

The feisty prime minister had weathered many previous challenges, but she was now confronted with increasing speculation that the Tories might try to replace her with a more attractive leader before the next general election. The issue that finally triggered such a development was Thatcher's stepped-up attacks on closer European integration during 1990. It led her deputy prime minister and party colleague, Sir Geoffrey Howe, to resign on November 1, 1990, with an unusually sharp public rebuke of her attitude toward the EC. There followed **a leadership challenge** in the Conservative Party that ended with Thatcher's resignation, in advance of an expected defeat by her own parliamentary party.

The transition in power was remarkably smooth. John Major, who was chosen by his fellow Conservatives in Parliament to be Thatcher's successor as party leader and thus prime minister, had long been regarded as one of her closest cabinet supporters. He basically supported her "tough love" approach to economics, which she had often described as **"dry"**—in contrast to the **"wet"** or soft approach of the "consensus" politicians. Although he seemed to prefer a somewhat more compassionate social policy than Thatcher, he followed her general rejection of the Tory tradition of welfare paternalism. Not surprisingly, he abandoned the hated poll tax. Major's governing style was far less dramatic or confrontational than that of his predecessor, and some nostalgic critics were quick to call him dull. During the Gulf War of 1991, he continued Thatcher's policy of giving strong British support for firm and ultimately military measures against the government of Iraq, whose troops had invaded and occupied oil-rich Kuwait.

By the time of Thatcher's resignation, Labour appeared to be in a position to capitalize on the growing disenchantment with the Conservative government. Led by Neil Kinnock, the opposition party had begun to move back toward its traditional center-left position, presenting itself as a politically moderate and socially caring agent of reform. But Labour was now troubled by a new version of the centrist alternative that had helped keep Thatcher in power when it fragmented the non-Conservative camp in the elections of 1983 and 1987. After operating as an electoral coalition or "Alliance" in those years, the Liberals and Social Democrats had finally joined together as a single party, the **Liberal Democrats**.

Under the leadership of Paddy Ashdown and later Charles Kennedy, the Liberal Democrats have sought to overcome the electoral system's bias against third parties by promoting themselves as an attractive alternative to the Conservatives on the right and Labour on the left. Their strategic goal has been to win the balance of power in a **"hung" parliament** and then, as parliamentary **majority-makers**, enter a government coalition with one of the two big parties, presumably Labour. One of their main demands would then be the adoption of some form of **proportional representation** (PR). Such an electoral system, which is used widely in Western Europe, would almost surely guarantee the Liberal Democrats a much larger base in the House of Commons and give them a **pivotal role in the coalition politics** that would ensue in the absence of the single party majorities that Britain's plurality elections tend to produce.

In the general election called by Prime Minister Major for April 9, 1992, the Conservatives delivered a surprise by winning an unprecedented fourth consecutive term of office. The Tories garnered almost the same percentage of the popular vote as in 1987 (about 42 percent), while Labour increased its total share slightly, from 31 to 34 percent. Support for the Liberal Democrats declined to 18 percent. In the House of Commons, the electoral system's bias in favor of the front-runners showed up once again. The Conservatives lost 40 seats but ended up with 336 of the 651 members. Labour increased its number of seats from 229 to 271, while the Liberal Democrats—with half as many voters as Labour—ended up with only 20 seats. As usual, a few remaining seats went to candidates of the small regional parties from Northern Ireland, Scotland, and Wales.

As a result, the Conservatives and Prime Minister Major stayed in office for another five years. But by now the majority party had lost its drive to continue the Thatcher Revolution. The Conservatives were divided, and their new leader was not a dynamic reformer. Nevertheless, John Major's presence as prime minister for six and a half years made a big difference by essentially consolidating his predecessor's controversial reforms. Thatcher would surely have tried to push them further, while Kinnock's Labour would have wanted a partial roll back.

The extended period in opposition had a profound effect on Labour. In the years after the 1992 election, the party came under the increasingly centrist leadership first of John Smith and then, after the latter's sudden death, of Tony Blair. In the public opinion polls, Labour soon took a commanding and continuous lead over the Conservative governing party. John Major therefore had good reason to delay the next election as long as possible, until May 1997. This time there were no surprises, except for the enormous parliamentary landslide that greeted the victor. With just over 43 percent of the British vote (or almost the same share as the Conservatives had won in their four consecutive victories), the Labour Party won a commanding majority of 418 of 659 seats in the House of Commons. The Liberal Democrats saw their share of the vote drop to 17 percent, but widespread **tactical voting** in swing districts more than doubled their number of parliamentary seats to 46, their best showing in about seven decades. Labour had also benefited from such tactical voting aimed at unseating the Conservatives, and so the Liberal Democrats failed once again to reach their strategic goal: They were still not needed to form a majority government.

Labour's victory gave rise to **the third reform government** in Britain since World War II. Unlike prime ministers Atlee or Thatcher, however, Tony Blair did not focus primarily on major social and economic policy changes. Since the mid-1990s, the British economy had once again revived well ahead of those on the mainland in Western Europe. A growing number of observers seemed willing to conclude that Thatcher's "neo-liberal" policies had played a role in stimulating the U.K. economy. It had become more flexible and dynamic, leading to higher growth rates and lower unemployment. But there were serious trade-offs that Blair's government could have been expected to give more remedial attention—above all Britain's growing income disparities and the neglected and dilapidated public service sector.

Instead, Blair's reform agenda gave prominence to the growing demand for **constitutional change** in Britain. In the late 1980s, an ad hoc reform coalition had launched Charter 88, an interest group that called for a bill of rights, electoral reform, and a modernization of the basic "rules of the game" in British politics. The chartists chose the tricentennial of Britain's Glorious Revolution of 1688 to launch their effort. It triggered a broad discussion in the country and several different proposals for constitutional reform.

The Liberal Democrats had been in the vanguard of reform efforts from the beginning. Even some Conservatives entered the fray, primarily to establish citizenship rights against state bureaucracy. Labour's position became crucial after it took office in May 1997. While he was still opposition leader, Tony Blair had identified himself and his party with **institutional modernization**. But he had expressed reservations about abandoning the plurality electoral system for the House of Commons that underpins the Westminster form of government by creating single-party majorities.

In contrast to France, Britain's evolutionary constitutional development and its piecemeal approach to institutional change have produced a remarkable **pattern of asymmetry** in the country's political structures. The Blair reforms fit well into that pattern. This is illustrated by the way the new government dealt with the recurrent demand for setting up special regional assemblies in **Scotland and Wales**. Soon after Labour took power, regional referendums resulted in majority approval of such assemblies—a regional parliament (with very limited powers of taxation) for Scotland, and a weaker assembly for Wales. In both cases, the regional assembly was to be elected by a form of **proportional representation** (PR), even as the United Kingdom continued to elect the House of Commons using a "first past the post" system. The Scottish case turned out to be a textbook example of the political impact of an electoral system: PR resulted in a multiparty regional parliament in Edinburgh, where majorities are only possible by way of two or more parties building a coalition.

The regional problem associated with the six counties that make up **Northern Ireland or Ulster** has long been recognized as far more intractable. It involves the coexistence of two communities of people, who espouse rival identities and in many cases would prefer not to live together. Even if only relatively few took up arms, their paramilitary organizations were responsible for many terrorist actions during the last three decades of the twentieth century. Protestants make up a majority of some 60 percent of the population in Ulster. They vary in the intensity of their political commitment, but they are overwhelmingly Unionist and wish to maintain Northern Ireland's ties to Britain. A very large **structural minority** of close to 40 percent are Catholics. They are overwhelmingly in favor of seeing the six counties unite with the Republic of Ireland that makes up the main part of the island.

The Blair government worked assiduously to broker a deal for Ulster that would be acceptable to the two communities and their leaders. The negotiating process came to include outsiders, with the Irish and U.S. governments playing supportive mediating roles. Former U.S. Senator George Mitchell and a retired Canadian general invested their personal skills and reputations as honest brokers. An agreement was reached in April 1998. In the ensuing referendum, an impressive majority of 71 percent of the voters in Ulster, on a turnout of 81 percent, approved this so-called Good Friday agreement. It also provides for the use of proportional representation in electing a regional assembly along with elaborate measures for **power-sharing** in the regional administration. The goal was to include representatives of the two communities and their several parties.

The settlement soon ran into disputes over its implementation. There followed political confrontations, a temporary suspension of the assembly and later, in 2002, of the regional government. One of the most contentious issues has revolved around the halting progress in disarming the Irish Republican Army (IRA). In view of the paramilitary activities by both sides in the recent past, it is hardly surprising that persistent mutual fear and suspicion continue to hamper relations between the two communities.

In addition to creating these new regional levels of representative institutions, the Labour government has shown interest in another **devolution of power** to existing or newly created local governments, such as that of London. This is a reversal of a shift in the opposite direction that took place under Prime Minister Thatcher. Yet another reform aims at a thorough revamping of the pre-democratic upper house of Parliament, **the House of Lords**, where most of the hereditary peers have now lost their right to vote. The next step in its "modernization" will keep it as an unelected second chamber. It is still unclear how this appointed house will affect the **asymmetrical balance of power** with the elected House of Commons. Here and elsewhere, some critical observers invoke the "law of unanticipated consequences" when they point out that the institutional changes may bring with them some unwanted political trade-offs in terms of a reduced capacity to govern effectively or even to keep Britain together.

In the first article on Britain, Donley Studlar takes stock of these and other institutional reforms as well as the reactions they have triggered until the end of the year 2003. Can one speak of a constitutional revolution in a country we usually associate with change by slow mutation? The author leaves no doubt that the series of reforms since 1997 represent important acts of constitutional engineering, even if Blair's product reflects a selective approach to change and lacks the symmetrical qualities of a complete constitutional blueprint. Clearly these matters would have been approached very differently, *if at all*, under a Conservative government.

What remains less certain is whether these institutional reforms contributed to **Labour's electoral triumph in June 2001**. This recent victory was not free of imperfections. Most serious was the **very low voter turnout**, which had consistently been over 70 percent since World War II but in 2001 sank by more than 10 points to only 59.4 percent. There were hardly any changes in the share of the vote received by each of the parties. The Liberal Democrats again failed to become a balancer, but they won six additional seats for a new high of 52. With close to 41 percent of the popular vote, Labour won 413 of the 659 seats in the House of Commons—another disproportional result that seemed likely to guarantee Labour its first ever full second term in office.

The second article covers various aspects of political change linked to Labour's current stay in power. It shows how Prime Minister Blair's decision to join the military intervention in the Middle East has undermined public confidence in his leadership and his strategy for a major structural reform of the public sector. The disaffection extends to Labour.

Another article examines the dissolute state of the Conservatives after their second electoral debacle in a row. At the end of 2003, they chose their fourth leader since 1997. Michael Howard, a widely respected mainstream Conservative replaced Iain Duncan Smith, who had replaced William Hague, who had replaced John Major. Should the Conservatives fail to revive, the Liberal Democrats stand ready to move into second place under Charles Kennedy. Labour clearly does not need their support at present, and Kennedy began moving the Liberal Democrats toward more independent positions on a number of questions, even before the recent disagreement over policy toward Iraq. Ironically, it was the Liberal Democrats rather than Labour who in the 2001 campaign came out most clearly in favor of higher taxes to fund the somewhat dilapidated public services.

Although Blair's Labour government continues to have a huge majority in Parliament, some observers wonder if he can keep his center-left party united. He seems to sense that he must augment the agenda of institutional modernization with meaningful social reforms. While there is at present no apparent danger from the Conservatives, Labour is itself deeply divided over Blair's Iraq policy and continues to harbor some older factional disputes. A major ideological and strategic cleavage runs between traditional socialists, who favor more emphasis on public service programs, and the more pragmatic modernizers, who wish to continue the centrist policies identified with "**New Labour**." For a long time, Blair seemed impervious when party critics accused him of being lukewarm to traditional Labour concerns. But he is well aware that his government's record in the public service arena has been a lackluster one. There are growing indications that he will try to turn his reform efforts in that direction, if he gets a new lease on life as prime minister.

France celebrated the bicentennial of its 1789 Revolution by preparing major public ceremonies to celebrate that formative event in modern political history. Unexpectedly, the anniversary was partly overshadowed by another great political upheaval, as several Communist regimes in Central and Eastern Europe began to totter before they eventually collapsed. This curious combination of events stimulated a discussion about the costs and benefits of the revolutionary French model for transforming society, in which one heard echoes of Edmund Burke's contemporary advocacy of an alternative British tradition of societal change by slow but steady mutation. In reality, the British experience is not without periods of accelerated and politically driven reform offset by times of consolidation or stagnation. Yet modern French political development has been far more discontinuous than its British counterpart, recording numerous attempts at a fresh start since 1789: For example, historians count between 13 and 17 French constitutions in the first two centuries that followed. French political discourse reflected the sharp ideological cleavages to which the Revolution had given birth.

By now, however, France seems to have found its own form of political stability and continuity. There are radical residues on the far Right and far Left, but moderate center-left and center-right positions have become more prevalent and respectable. The trend toward political moderation has been accompanied by a relative **consolidation of the French party system**. In the Third Republic (1870 to 1940) and Fourth Republic (1946 to 1958), French politics had been notorious for its multiplicity of undisciplined parties and groupings. They provided a weak and unreliable support for prime ministers and their cabinets, resulting in **political paralysis and instability** of the many short-lived governments. In the frequent absence of responsible political direction and oversight, a well-trained civil service maintained **administrative continuity** but was helpless to resolve major political issues. There developed a risky tradition, known in France as **Bonapartism**, of intermittently calling for strong political saviors who were to lead the country out of its recurrent crises. Ironically, it was such a Bonapartist leader who ended up delivering an **institutional solution** to the problem.

In 1958 a political emergency caused by the colonial war in Algeria gave Charles de Gaulle the opportunity to become architect of a new political system. He had already played a Bonapartist role in World War II and later as interim leader of postwar France before the adoption—against his strong warnings—of the constitution of the Fourth Republic. Having long viewed the unruly French parties as beyond reform, de Gaulle decided to prune their power base in the legislature and instead concentrate authority in the executive. In the constitution of the Fifth Republic, the prime minister remains responsible to the National Assembly but enjoys far more prerogatives and is far less vulnerable to legislative power plays than previously. Above all, de Gaulle strengthened the government by adding a politically powerful president in what became known as a **dual executive**. The president is directly elected and has powers that include the appointment and dismissal of the prime minister and the dissolution of the National Assembly. The result is a presidential-prime ministerial system in which the president played the leading role for the first quarter of a cen-

tury. It has found some imitation in the post-Communist political systems set up in Central and Eastern Europe.

There is some additional historical irony in the fact that the political framework of the Fifth Republic has become the setting for a consolidation and moderation of the French party system. The Communists (PCF) were once the main party of the Left, receiving about 20 percent of the vote in parliamentary elections until the late 1970s. They were relatively late to join their colleagues elsewhere in Western Europe in the painful withdrawal from their common Leninist and Stalinist heritage. By now they are a marginal force, less than half their former strength, but they have gained a chance to play a role in coalition politics that was previously denied them. Between 1997 and 2002, they were a small partner in the coalition government dominated by the Socialists, who had overtaken them on the Left in 1978.

On the extreme Right, Le Pen's National Front (FN) seemed in recent years to be weakened by internal splits and rivalries, before it surprised many by capturing 17 percent of the vote in the first round of the presidential election in 2002. The party continues to find right-wing populist support for its authoritarian and xenophobic rhetoric directed primarily against the country's many residents of Arab origin. The apparent electoral appeal of such invective has tempted some leaders of the establishment parties of the more moderate Right to voice carefully formulated reservations about the presence of so many immigrants.

Although it has become increasingly moderate and centrist, French party politics can still be highly volatile. To gain a little perspective, it makes sense to briefly review the electoral politics of the past decade, beginning with **the parliamentary contest of 1993**. Here the Socialists suffered a major setback after 5 years of serving as the main government party. Together, the loosely organized center-right **Giscardists of the Union for French Democracy** (UDF) and the more conservative neo-Gaullists in the **Rally for the Republic** or (RPR) won about 40 percent of the first-round vote. Beginning with that plurality, these two coalition parties ended up with an overwhelming majority of nearly 80 percent of the seats in the 577-member National Assembly.

The **Socialists** (PS) and their close allies were clearly the big losers in this largest electoral landslide in French democratic history. Receiving about 20 percent of the popular vote on the first round, the Socialists plummeted from their previous share of 274 seats to 61 seats or less than one-quarter of their previous parliamentary strength. The Communists, with only 9 percent of the first-round vote, were able to win 24 seats because much of their electoral support was concentrated in a few urban districts where their candidates ran ahead of all others. With a slightly higher share of the total vote, the ultra-right **National Front** won no seats at all, having failed to arrive "first past the post" anywhere.

Socialist president François Mitterrand's second 7-year presidential term lasted until May 1995. After the parliamentary rout of the Socialists in March 1993, he was faced with the question of whether to resign early from the presidency. Alternatively, he could appoint a conservative prime minister for a period of "cohabitation," as after a similar setback in the parliamentary elections of 1986. Mitterrand opted once again for the latter solution, making sure to appoint a moderate Gaullist, Edouard Balladur, to this position.

For a time, the new prime minister enjoyed considerable popularity, and this encouraged him to enter the presidential race in 1995. By declaring his own candidacy, Balladur in effect snubbed Jacques Chirac, the assertive Gaullist leader who had himself served as prime minister in the first period of cohabitation (1986–1988). In 1995, Chirac had expected to be the only Gaullist candidate for the presidency, as he had been 7 years earlier, in 1988, when he lost against the incumbent Mitterrand.

The presidential race in France tends to become highly individualized. Eventually the tough and outspoken Chirac pulled ahead of his more consensual and lackluster party colleague. In the first round of the 1995 presidential election, however, a surprising plurality of the vote went to the main socialist candidate, Lionel Jospin, a former education minister and party leader. In the run-off election, 2 weeks later, Chirac defeated Jospin and thereby ended 14 years of Socialist control of the presidency. He appointed another Gaullist and close political ally, Alain Juppé, to replace the faithless Balladur as prime minister.

The new conservative dominance lasted only until 1997, when France entered into a new version of "cohabitation" as the result of another electoral upset. No parliamentary elections were necessary in France until the end of the National Assembly's 5-year-term in 1998, but President Chirac sensed a leftward drift in the country and decided to renew the legislature 10 months early while the conservative coalition still appeared to be ahead of the Left. As it turned out, Chirac totally underestimated how far public confidence in Juppé's government had already deteriorated. The **two-stage elections for the National Assembly** took place in May and early June of 1997, and the result was a major setback for the neo-Gaullists (RPR) and their increasingly divided neo-liberal allies (mainly the loosely organized UDF). Their combined share of the popular vote dropped to 31 percent, and their parliamentary strength was reduced by 200 seats, to 249. The Socialists quadrupled their strength from 61 to 245 seats, while their non-Communist allies won another 13 seats in the 577-seat National Assembly. In order to form a majority coalition government, they included the small Communist Party, with its 37 seats.

In one respect, the 1997 parliamentary election resembled all the elections to the National Assembly since 1981. Whereas the French voters had elected a conservative majority in elections before that date, they had since then thrown out the incumbent government whatever its orientation. President Chirac now appointed the Socialist leader, Lionel Jospin, as prime minister—the very politician he had narrowly defeated in the presidential race barely 2 years earlier. Thus began France's third and so far longest experiment in cohabitation. It lasted a full parliamentary term of 5 years. The novelty was that this time the president was a conservative serving with a socialist prime minister rather than vice versa.

After three separate periods of cohabitation, between 1986 and 2002, it is possible to conclude that they produce a prime ministerial form of governance that differs from the Gaullist model of a strong presidential leadership. So far, however, the end of cohabitation has always brought a return to the original

dual executive of the Fifth Republic with its strong president dominating a clearly subordinate prime minister—as from 1988 to 1993, from 1995 to 1997, and again since 2002.

In some ways, the latest experiment in cohabitation can be seen as a test of how far the moderate Left and Right in France have really overcome their once very deep ideological differences. During the 1997 election campaign, the political distance between them seemed to have grown. The Socialists sharply criticized neo-Gaullist Prime Minister Juppé's austerity measures and neo-liberal measures of deregulation. Instead, they promised a more traditional program to attack unemployment by priming the economy, creating new public service jobs, and reducing the work week to 35 hours from 39 without lowering pay. Conservative political critics were quick to speak of the socialist platform as one of deceptive smoke and mirrors. Even they could not deny, however, that Jospin's government set off to an excellent start in restoring public confidence.

Meanwhile, the French parties of the Right seem to have been weakened by their internal disagreements on policy and strategy as well as personal rivalries at the leadership level. The UDF, organized by former President Giscard d'Estaing in the 1970s, has always been a loose coalition of disparate political groups and tendencies that differed from the neo-Gaullists by showing a greater support for European integration, civil rights, and economic neo-liberalism. The more conservative and nationally oriented RPR, founded by Jacques Chirac in the 1970s as well, experienced its own internecine battles. Since 2002, when he successfully ran for another term as president, Chirac and some of his followers have attempted to revitalize and modernize their party as a less traditionalist element of the French center-right. It now forms the core of a more inclusive Union for the Political Majority (UMP).

The first article in this section provides many insights on a country that one author describes as a "divided self." Few who know the nation would refer without reservation to "the new France." Instead, contemporary French politics and society combine some traits that reflect a strong sense of continuity with the past and others that suggest a spirit of innovation. One major change is the **decline of the previously sharp ideological struggle between the Left and the Right**. This seems to have resulted in a sense of loss among some French intellectuals who still prefer the political battle to have apocalyptic implications. They seem to find it hard to accept that the grand struggle between Left and Right has been replaced by a more moderate and seemingly more mundane party politics of competition among groups that tend to cluster fairly close to the center of the political spectrum.

In the end, French intellectuals may discover that what they have long regarded as a tedious political competition between those who promise a "little more" or a "little less" can have considerable practical consequences in terms of "who gets what, when, and how." Moreover, such incremental politics need not be without dramatic conflict, since new issues, events, or leaders often emerge to sharpen the differences and increase the stakes of politics. In the last months of 1995 and again in late 1996, for example, French politics took on a dramatic immediacy when workers and students resorted to massive strikes and street demonstrations against a new austerity program introduced by the then conservative government of prime minister Juppé. The proposed cutbacks in social entitlements such as pension rights were perceived by many as unnecessary, drastic, and unfair. They were difficult to explain to the public at large, and many observers saw the political confrontation in France as a major test for the welfare state or "social market economy" that is now being squeezed throughout Western Europe in the name of general affordability as well as international or global "competitiveness."

The loss of the grand ideological alternatives may help account for the mood of **political malaise** that many observers report about contemporary France. But the French search for political direction and identity in a changing Europe has another major origin as well. The sudden emergence of a larger and politically less inhibited Germany next door cannot but have a disquieting effect on France. French elites now face the troubling question of redefining their country's role in a post-cold war world, in which Russia has lost in power and influence while Germany has gained in both. The French resistance to a large American role in Europe adds another source of friction. Together with Germany's Chancellor Schröder, President Chirac has recently gone out of his way to emphasize Franco-German friendship and cooperation. Both have publicly disagreed with what they regard as President Bush's unilateral and militaristic approach in the Iraq Question. They seem to be searching for a distinctive European position on such international problems.

In setting, some observers have even suggested that we may expect a major new cleavage in French politics. It runs between those who favor a reassertion of the traditional French nation-state ideal—a kind of isolationist "neo-Gaullism" that can be found on both the Left and Right—and those who want the country to accept a new European order, in which the sovereignty of both the French and German nation-states would be further diluted or contained by a network of international obligations within the larger European framework.

A persistent question is whether the long-run structural problems of France—similar to those of some of her neighbors—can be handled without a resort to the very market-oriented "therapy" that seems to be alien in spirit to many French voters and political leaders. French capitalism (like its German counterpart) is significantly different from its British and American counterparts. Yet careful observers point out that in his 5 years as prime minister, Jospin engaged in a skillful political sleight of hand by introducing some economic reforms like deregulation and privatization that had the effect of reducing the traditional interventionist role of the French state. Once again, the moderate Left appears to promote a kind of "new centrism" in politics—but with due respect to what is acceptable within a particular national and cultural setting.

The French faced an **electoral marathon in 2002**, when there were two-stage elections for both the presidency and the National Assembly. It was expected in advance that the focus of the relatively short presidential campaign would be on the two veteran warhorses, Chirac and Jospin. The big surprise was the elimination of Jospin in the first stage: He ran a close third behind Chirac, who came first, and the far right candidate, Le Pen, who came second. As in 1995, many people on the Left had apparently voted "with their hearts" in the first round. The result was that the Left vote was split among a multiplicity of candidates, none of whom had a chance of making it into the second round. This time, however, the result was the failure of the main candidate of the Left to make it into the second round, since socialist Jospin gathered slightly fewer votes than nationalist Le Pen. In the run-off between Chirac and Le Pen, the incumbent president won an overwhelming victory by attracting moderate votes from both Right and Left. The electoral statistics can be found in the first article on France.

In the two-stage elections of the National Assembly in June of 2002, the parties of the moderate right-of-center, led by Chirac's neo-Gaullist conservatives, won a major victory over the parties of the Left. Voter turnout was unusually low, as it had been in Britain's general election the year before. President Chirac called on the relatively obscure Pierre Raffarin (DL) to form a new, moderately conservative government in place of the defeated left-of-center government that Jospin had headed for the previous 5 years.

Germany was united in 1990, when the eastern **German Democratic Republic**, or GDR, was merged into the western **Federal Republic of Germany**. The two German states had been established in 1949, 4 years after the total defeat of the German Reich in World War II. During the next 40 years, their rival elites subscribed to the conflicting ideologies and interests of East and West in the cold war. East Germany comprised the territory of the former Soviet Occupation Zone of Germany, where the Communists exercised a power monopoly and established an economy based on Soviet-style central planning. In contrast, West Germany, which had emerged from the former American, British, and French zones of postwar occupation, developed a pluralist democracy and a flourishing market economy, modified by an extensive network of social policy. West Germans generally spoke with approval of their arrangement as a "social market economy." In the 1970s, when the Social Democrats were in power at the federal level and before some structural problems had darkened the economic horizon, the political class began to refer with confidence to *Modell Deutschland*, "the German model." Communist-ruled East Germany lagged far behind, even though it had gained a reputation for being one of the most productive economies within the Soviet bloc. When the two German states were getting ready to celebrate their fortieth anniversaries in 1989, no leading politician was on record as having foreseen that the forced political division was about to come to an end. **In fact, a leading American dictionary published in 1989 defined Germany as a "former country in Central Europe."**

Mass demonstrations in several East German cities and the westward flight of thousands of citizens brought the GDR government to make an increasing number of concessions in the last months of 1989 and early 1990. The Berlin Wall ceased to be a hermetical seal after November 9, 1989, and East Germans began to stream over into West Berlin. Collectors and entrepreneurs soon broke pieces from the Wall to keep or sell as souvenirs, before public workers set about to remove the rest of this symbol of the cold war and Germany's division. Under new leadership, the ruling Communists of East Germany made a last-ditch stand by introducing a form of **power-sharing** with noncommunist groups and parties. They agreed to seek democratic legitimation by holding a **free East German election in March 1990**, in the hope of reducing the westward flight of thousands of people with its devastating consequences for the eastern economy.

The popular demonstrations and the willingness of East Germans to "vote with their feet" had been made possible by two major preconditions. First, the Soviet leader, Mikhail Gorbachev, had abandoned the so-called **Brezhnev Doctrine**, under which the Soviets claimed the right of military intervention on behalf of the established communist regimes in Central and Eastern Europe. And second, the imposed communist regimes of these countries turned out to have lost their will—and ability—to hold on to power at any cost.

At first, the East German Communists only loosened their claim to an exclusive control of power and positions in the so-called German Democratic Republic. The results of the March 1990 election, however, made it clear even to them that the pressure for national unification could no longer be stemmed. An eastern alliance of Christian Democrats, largely identified with and supported by Chancellor Helmut Kohl's party in West Germany, recorded a surprisingly decisive victory, by winning about one-half of the votes throughout East Germany. It advocated a short, quick route to unification, beginning with an early monetary union in the summer and a political union by the fall of 1990. Almost immediately a new noncommunist government was installed in East Germany. Headed by Lothar de Maizière (CDU), it followed the **short-cut to a merger** with the Federal Republic, under Article 23 of the West German Basic Law. The Social Democrats, or SPD, had won only 22 percent of the East German vote. That was widely interpreted as a defeat for their alternative strategy for unification that would have involved the protracted **negotiation of a new German constitution**, as envisaged in Article 146 of the Federal Republic's Basic Law.

During the summer and fall of 1990, the governments of the two German states and the four former occupying powers completed their so-called two-plus-four negotiations that resulted in a mutual agreement on the German unification process. The **monetary union in July** was quickly followed by a **political merger in October 1990**. In advance of unification, Bonn negotiated an agreement with Moscow in which the latter accepted the gradual withdrawal of Soviet troops from eastern Germany and the membership of the larger, united Germany in NATO, in return for considerable German economic support for the Soviet Union. The result was a major shift in both the domestic and international balance of power.

The moderately conservative Christian Democrats repeated their electoral success in the first Bundestag election in a reunited Germany, held in early December 1990. They captured almost 44 percent of the vote, against the long-time low of 33.5 percent for the rival Social Democrats. At the same time, Kohl's small coalition partner of liberal Free Democrats (FDP) did unusually well (11 percent of the vote). The environmentalist Greens, on the other hand, failed to get the required minimum of 5 percent of the vote in western Germany and dropped out of the Bundestag for the next 4 years. Under a special dispensation for the 1990 election only, the two parts of united Germany were regarded as separate electoral regions as far as the 5 percent threshold was concerned. That made it possible for two small eastern parties to get a foothold in the Bundestag. One was a coalition of political dissidents and environmentalists (Alliance 90/Greens), the other was the communist-descended Party of Democratic Socialism. The PDS was able to win about 11 percent of the vote in the East

by appealing to those who felt displaced and alienated in the new order. Its voters included many former privileged party members but also some rural workers and young people. Ironically, the communist-descended party received only weak support among blue-collar workers.

The election results of December 1990 suggested that national unification could eventually modify the German party system and German politics significantly. By the time of the next national election, in October 1994, it became evident that a new **east-west divide** had emerged. This time, the far-left PDS was able to almost double its support and attract 20 percent of the vote in the East, where only one-fifth of Germany's total population lives. At the same time, the PDS won only about 1 percent of the vote in the far more populous West. Its total electoral support in Germany thus fell slightly below the famous "**5 percent hurdle**" established in Germany's electoral law as a minimum for a party to win proportional representation in the Bundestag. The PDS was nevertheless able to keep and expand its parliamentary foothold, because it met an almost forgotten alternative seating requirement of winning pluralities in at least three single-member districts under Germany's double-ballot electoral system. Thus the political descendants of the former ruling Communists were given proportional representation after all. They won seats in the Bundestag for 30 deputies, who presented themselves as a democratically sensitive, far-left party of socialists and regionalists.

Despite a widespread unification malaise in Germany, the conservative-liberal government headed by Chancellor Helmut Kohl won reelection in 1994. His Christian Democrats, who benefited from a widely perceived if only temporary improvement in the German economy, won 41.4 percent of the vote. Their Free Democratic ally barely scraped through with 6.9 percent of the vote. Together, the two governing parties had a very slim majority of 10 seats more than the combined total of the three opposition parties, the SPD (36.4 percent), the revived and united Greens (7.3 percent), and the PDS (4.4 percent).

In the federal upper house, or Bundesrat, the SPD continued to hold a majority of the seats, based on their control of many state governments. This situation gave a united SPD considerable leverage or blocking power in federal legislative politics. The Kohl government charged that the resulting parliamentary gridlock stalled its economic reform initiatives. It would be only a few years before the tables were turned.

Between 1949 and 1999, the seat of government for the Federal Republic had been the small Rhineland town of Bonn. Reunification made possible the move of the government and parliament several hundred miles eastward to the old political center of Berlin. The transfer was controversial in Germany, because of both the costs and symbolism involved. Nevertheless, it had already been approved by the Bundestag in 1991, with a narrow parliamentary majority, and was then delayed until 1999. Observers generally agree that the "**Berlin Republic**" will continue the democratic tradition that has been firmly established in Germany. But they also point to the need for a revamping of the economic and social arrangements that worked so well during much of the Bonn period, if the country is to meet its new obligations within Europe and in the increasingly global market arena.

Unlike their British counterparts, German governments are regularly produced by **coalition politics**. In the multiparty system, based on the country's **modified form of proportional representation**, a single party is unlikely to win a parliamentary majority at the federal level of politics. In some German states, however, single party government has become familiar or is even an embedded tradition, as in Bavaria with its powerful CSU (a Bavarian sister party of the CDU). More remarkable is the fact that between 1949 and 1998 there had never been a complete replacement of a governing coalition in Bonn. Even when there was a change of government, at least one partner of the previous coalition had always managed to hang on as majority maker in the next cabinet. This German pattern of **incomplete power transfers** came to an abrupt end with the clean sweep brought by the Bundestag election of September 1998.

In advance of the contest, it had been widely expected that the outcome once again would be only a partial shift in power, resulting from a "**grand coalition**" of Social Democrats (SPD) and Christian Democrats (CDU/CSU). In such a situation, the chancellorship would go to the leader of the front-running party—most likely the SPD. The result would have been a considerable continuity and, as interpreted by rival scenarios, either a disabling inertia or a newfound strength in the shared responsibility for dealing with Germany's backlog of social and economic reforms.

Instead, the 1998 election made possible **a complete turnover in power**. It brought into office what Germans like to call a "red-green" coalition by giving the Social Democrats, with 40.9 percent of the popular vote, a sufficient margin over the Christian Democrats (35.1 percent) to form a majority coalition with the small party of Greens (6.7 percent). German voters in effect decided it was "time for a change" in their country, similar to the political turnabouts that had taken place in Britain and France a year earlier. As in these neighboring countries, the main party of the Left was very careful to present itself as a moderate reform agent that would provide security along with both "continuity and change." The SPD borrowed freely from both British and American political imagery by proclaiming that it represented a decidedly non-radical "new middle" (*neue Mitte*). It was a successful, if rather vague, political formula.

The complete change in governing parties also brought a generational turnover in the top levels of German government. In the federal chancellery, Social Democrat Gerhard Schröder, born in 1944, replaced Christian Democrat Helmut Kohl, born in 1930. Most of the other leading members of the new government spent their childhood years in postwar Germany. In many cases they had their initial political experiences in youthful opposition to the societal establishment of the late 1960s. By now the "68ers" are well into middle age, but they have ascended to power as successors to Kohl's generation, whose politically formative years coincided with the founding period of the Federal Republic. The new German leaders do not have youthful memories of the Third Reich, World War II, or even, in many cases, the postwar military occupation. They are truly Germany's **first postwar generation in power** as well as its **first left of center governing coalition**.

The larger political system was affected by the shifts in the power balance of the small political parties and their leaders after the milestone election of September 1998. On the far left,

the post-communist PDS managed for the first time to pass the 5 percent threshold, if only barely, by winning 21.6 percent of the vote in eastern Germany, while advancing only slightly to 1.2 percent of the vote in the far more populous West, where approximately 80 percent of the German population lives. Clearly, the PDS is still very much a party rooted in the new federal states that emerged from the communist-ruled East Germany.

The liberal Free Democrats ended up with another close scrape (6.2 percent). In contrast to the PDS, the Liberals now appeared to be a party of the West, where they received 7 percent of the vote as compared to 3.3 percent in the East. After 29 years as junior government party, their struggle for political survival now had to be conducted in the unfamiliar role as a marginal opposition party.

The third small party, the Greens, had also slid back (to 6.7 percent), but this was enough to replace the FDP as majority-maker in the federal government. Like the other small parties, the Greens bore marks of the east-west divide: They received only 4.1 percent in the East versus 7.3 percent in the West.

Germany had in effect arrived at a **slightly more complex party system**. It consisted of **the two major parties** of the moderate center-left (SPD) and the moderate center-right (CDU/CSU) along with **three small parties** that each had a **regional concentration** either in the West (Greens and FDP) or almost exclusively in the East (PDS). Some observers referred to a "**two-and-three-halves**" party system. Each of the three "halves" had an impact on the overall balance of power and what the Germans call the system's "coalition arithmetic," but each was also small enough to be in danger of slipping below the 5 percent mark at any time. Another important result of the 1998 Bundestag election was the continued failure of the parties of the extreme right, with their authoritarian and xenophobic rhetoric, to mobilize a significant support in the German electorate.

For the Greens, the first-time role as junior coalition partner in the national government has not been easy. In fact, some close observers have spoken of an identity crisis of the German Left that includes parts of the Social Democratic Party. It was fed by controversies linked to domestic socioeconomic and environmental issues as well as the German military participation in Kosovo in early 1999. There followed a remarkable political recovery of the SPD in the latter half of that year. The abrupt resignation of the key Social Democrat Oskar Lafontaine, as both finance minister and party leader in March 1999, gave Schröder a welcome opportunity to take over the SPD leadership. The assumption that this move would give him more authority within both the party and the cabinet did not pan out. Instead, the dual set of responsibilities turned out to be very demanding, and the battle weary chancellor soon became known for his repeated threats to resign from one or both positions.

The federal system, which now had 16 states, turned out to be a major obstacle to the new government. The staggered elections in the states had a potential for shifting the balance of power in Berlin as well. In the first year after taking power, the SPD and the Greens suffered a string of serious setbacks in state elections. They were ousted from some state governments, and this led to a loss of their majority control of the federal council or Bundesrat. Beginning in late 1999, the SPD's adverse trend came to a halt. Instead, the Christian Democrats suddenly found themselves in shambles, resulting from the sensational revelations of a major party finance scandal that had taken place under the leadership of Helmut Kohl, the veteran chancellor. Basically the problem stemmed from transfers of huge political contributions, to a slush fund, that were not reported as required by law.

Dubbed "**Kohlgate**," the finance scandal resulted in immediate setbacks for the CDU in several state elections. This had the effect of boosting the FDP, for some disaffected CDU supporters turned to the FDP as an acceptable center-right alternative. The small liberal party went through a significant leadership change, when it chose its former secretary general, the youthful Guido Westerwelle, to become its new head. With this single move, supported by a clever promotion campaign, the party seemed to experience a rejuvenation that boosted its poll standings and brought it well ahead of the Greens in advance of the September 2002 election. In a cocky mood, the FDP announced a year in advance that its election goal would be to attract 18 percent of the vote, at a time when its poll standings had improved to about 8 percent. Suddenly the small party, whose political obituary has been written repeatedly, exuded a new vigor and self-confidence. It appeared as though the FDP could regain its familiar position of balancer in German electoral and coalition politics—a role that before 1998 had made it the most successful small party in West European politics.

As the 2002 election approached, voters shifted their attention to the lackluster economic performance of the Schröder government. The poll standings of the CDU improved and even brought the party ahead of the SPD. The conservative party introduced law and order themes and sometimes played to anti-immigrant sentiments both before and after the September 11 events. At the beginning of 2002, the Christian Democrats decided against nominating as "chancellor candidate" their own leader, Angela Merkel. She is an East German woman who as a newcomer to politics rose rapidly in the party after unification. Untainted by political scandal, she had quickly made it to the top when the CDU needed a facelift.

As chancellor candidate, the Christian Democrats decided in favor of Edmund Stoiber, the governor of Bavaria and leader of the CSU, their more conservative sister party in that large state. Stoiber's main advantage was held to be a strong economic record in his home state, but it surely helped that he was an older male politician from the West with many personal supporters in the CDU/CSU. Some observers wondered whether he was not too right-leaning to attract many voters outside Bavaria. Stoiber trailed Schröder in his individual poll ratings—as did Angela Merkl. But a parliamentary election is also about party support, and here an electoral comeback of the CDU/CSU seemed to be in the making. By the mid-summer of 2002 it was widely believed that the revived Christian Democrats were likely to return to government office in coalition with the recharged FDP. The SPD's weak economic record, most vividly dramatized by a persistent unemployment problem, seemed likely to become its Achilles' heel in the September election.

Once again, **the small parties** were to play a key role in the electoral and parliamentary balance of power established by the 2002 Bundestag election. Until the summer of that year, the Greens had suffered a long string of electoral setbacks at the state level of politics. They had been damaged by their internal quarrels and also lost some of their traditional backing among younger voters, as the founder generation grew older and joined the establishment. Some critical voters now seemed to be attracted by the FDP's self-promotion as the real alternative. The FDP's constant focus on "Project 18" and a "fun" campaign helped maintain the illusion that the Free Democrats were likely to pass the Greens and again become the "third force" in German party politics. The PDS had most reason to tremble at its electoral prospects. It had passed the 5 percent hurdle in only one of the three Bundestag elections since unification, and only barely at that (5.1 percent in 1998). Since then, it had lost some of its previous voters and largely failed to win many new ones. The alternative route to proportional representation in the Bundestag also looked bleak for the PDS: The boundaries of the single-member districts in Berlin had recently been redrawn in a way that diluted the PDS strength and made its capture of three districts less likely.

In the end, the Bundestag election of 2002 did keep the PDS from sharing in the proportional allocation of parliamentary seats. The post-Communists won two single-member districts in eastern Berlin, enough for only two deputies. Had the PDS won a third district, the 5 percent clause would have been set aside, and its 4.0 percent share of the party vote would then have entitled it to about 24 of the 603 seats in the new Bundestag. The PDS may be headed for further marginalization at the sub-national levels as well, but it is also possible that the PDS could instead begin to attract left-wing voters who have become unhappy with Chancellor Schröder and the SPD.

Ironically, it was the near shut-out of the PDS that enabled the red-green government to hold on to power in one of Germany's closest elections ever. The first article on Germany analyzes the outcome in some detail. Both SPD and CDU/CSU won 38.5 percent of the vote, but a quirk in the two-vote electoral law gave the SPD three more seats than its major rival. The SPD had overcome its poor stand in the polls to come within 2.4 percent of its result in 1998. Most observers explain the electoral recovery by referring to points earned by Chancellor Schröder through his performance in the televised debates with Edmund Stoiber, his unusually critical remarks about President Bush's "adventurous" strategy toward Iraq, and his appearance as a decisive leader in dealing with the great floods that ravaged parts of eastern Germany in the month before the Bundestag election. The FDP had lost ground with a controversial campaign since mid-summer. It fell back to 7.4 percent of the vote—an improvement over its previous share of 6.2 percent but far less than its trumpeted goal of 18 percent. The Greens probably benefited from the revival of war fears in connection with Iraq as well as the popularity of their foreign minister, Joschka Fischer. While they continued to perform poorly in the eastern states, where the SPD picked up many former CDU and PDS voters, the Greens benefited from the renewal of ecological concerns in the wake of the August floods.

In the first year after the 2002 election, Germans returned to a discussion of basic structural reform. The two main topics were the country's **federal structure** and its **economic model**. Federalism is a crucial element not only in the country's governance but also in its self-understanding, as reflected in its official name, the Federal Republic of Germany. The founders of the West German state regarded a federal arrangement as a key safeguard against a dangerous concentration and potential abuse of power in the central government. Since then, federalism has set Germany apart from France, which is still fairly centralized even after Mitterrand's regional reforms. Italy and Britain have carried out some regional devolution, but neither comes anywhere close to having a federal system like the one that was projected into the eastern part of Germany at the time of unification. Today there is a growing conviction that federal entanglements may have become an obstacle to effective governance in Germany. One article deals with this issue and reviews some proposed remedies. It does not neglect to point out that there are strong vested interests in keeping the present structures—not least the federal council or Bundesrat, which provides a powerful check on the parliamentary government in Berlin.

It is widely agreed that there is a need for a **basic economic reform** in Germany. In some respects, the discussion resembles that of other advanced countries, but the German version includes some special aspects that have accompanied the challenges and accomplishments of national unification. The task of post-communist reconstruction in eastern Germany goes far beyond the transfer of institutions and capital from the West. The transition to a pluralist democracy and a market economy also requires a measure of social and cultural transformation. Moreover, there are new problems facing the larger and more powerful Germany on the international scene, as it seeks to deal with an ambiguous mixture of expectations and anxieties that this European giant arouses abroad. Not least, there is a growing awareness that Germany's generous social welfare model may have become unsustainable in its present form over the long run, as the country faces the familiar demographic shifts at home and stiff economic competition from abroad. The high unemployment may force the left of center government to bite the bullet and introduce a more flexible labor market.

On the other hand, Germans have traditionally favored a more social form of capitalism than the one that prevails in Britain or the United States. They are unlikely to accept the kind of shock therapy of massive deregulation and other market-oriented reforms that were introduced in the United States and Britain by conservative governments in the 1980s and largely accepted by their left-of-center successors in the following decade. Both the political culture and institutional framework of Germany (and much of mainland Europe) lean far more toward corporatist and communitarian solutions than their British and American counterparts.

At the beginning of 2004, Chancellor Schröder succeeded in mobilizing parliamentary support for much of a comprehensive structural reform package. There followed a public outcry against the government's Agenda 2010, as Germans began to feel the painful reforms. At this point, Schröder decided to concentrate on governing and have a trusted supporter, Franz Müntefering, take over the leadership of the SPD. The party was certainly in need of special attention to quell its protests and stem its massive loss of members. With its many staggered party contests at the local and regional level, the year 2004 had been billed in advance as a "super election year" in Germany. It would inevitably be regarded as a test of whether

the SPD's political tandem would be able to stay upright for long.

Japan has long fascinated comparative social scientists as a country that modernized rapidly without losing its non-Western, Japanese identity. The article, "Japanese Spirit, Western Things," explains how this was possible and why it is important. It begins by recounting the story of Commodore Perry's arrival in Tokyo harbor in the 1850s and his role in forcing the country to "open up." The Japanese rulers decided in effect to learn from the West in order to strengthen Japan and maintain its independence. The special conditions that made the modernization possible have become a staple topic on the social science agenda. About one hundred years later, a few other countries in East and South Asia began taking tentative steps toward what soon became a rapid and self-sustained modernization. Soon known as the "Asian tigers" or "dragons," the New Industrial Countries include South Korea, Taiwan, Singapore, and potentially some others like Thailand and Malaysia.

Japan's tentative move toward a parliamentary form of government after World War I was blocked by a militarist takeover in the early 1930s. After World War II, a parliamentary form of representative democracy was installed in Japan under American supervision. This political system soon acquired indigenous Japanese characteristics that set it off from the other major democracies examined here.

For almost four decades following its creation in 1955, the Liberal Democratic Party (LDP) played a hegemonic role in Japanese politics. The many opposition parties were divided and provided little effective competition for the LDP which, according to a popular saying, was really "neither liberal, nor democratic, nor a party." It has essentially been a conservative political machine that loosely unites several rival and delicately balanced factions. The factions in turn consist mostly of the personal followers of political bosses who stake out factional claims to benefits of office.

In 1993, the LDP temporarily lost its parliamentary majority, when a couple of its factions joined the opposition. This set the stage for a vote of no confidence, followed by new elections in which the LDP lost its parliamentary majority. Seven different parties, spanning the spectrum from conservative to socialist, thereupon formed a fragile coalition government. It was incapable of defining or promoting a coherent policy program and stood helpless as the Japanese economy continued on its course of stagnation that began at the outset of the 1990s after a long postwar economic boom.

Two prime ministers and several cabinet reshuffles later, a revived LDP managed by the summer of 1994 to return to the cabinet by way of a coalition with its former rival, the Socialists. The peculiar alliance was possible because the leadership of both these major parties had adopted a pragmatic orientation at this juncture. By December 1995, the LDP had recaptured the prime ministership. There followed a rapid succession of short-lived governments headed by LDP factional leaders. When the post once again became open in April 2001, there was a surprising number of willing candidates.

The unexpected winner of the leadership contest in the LDP and new prime minister of Japan was Junichiro Koizumi. He was no beginner in Japanese party politics, but he seemed to personify a more unconventional approach than most veteran politicians in Japan. He spoke the language of structural reform, and immediately took some symbolic steps to show that he meant business. His cabinet included five women, including the controversial Makiko Tanaka as head of the foreign ministry. Koizumi soon ran into resistance from conservative elements in the political class, including factional leaders of his own party and members of the high civil service. By January 2002, he dismissed the assertive Tanaka, who had become a favorite target of those who opposed the new political style and possible major policy changes. The move triggered widespread public dissatisfaction. Koizumi countered by appointing another prominent woman, Yoriko Kawaguchi, to head the foreign ministry. By this time, however, his own popularity rating was rapidly falling. It seemed unlikely that his remaining public support provided enough political capital to offset the entrenched foes of a reform of the Japanese economy and fiscal policy. Koizumi now seemed disinclined to try. Some observers argued that the prime minister himself had little realistic understanding of or commitment to the kind of structural change that Japan needed. Thus continuity seemed once again more likely than basic change in Japan.

There now seems to be an emerging understanding that fundamental change must be based on an "opening up" of Japanese society to more competition. From this perspective, the entrenched bureaucratic elites and their cozy relationships with business leaders need to become prime targets of reform. It is remarkable that Japan's prolonged economic stagnation has not resulted in more political protests and electoral repercussions.

It will probably take more than a flamboyant prime minister to revitalize Japanese politics and society, but reform steps are more likely under Koizumi than any of his handful of recent predecessors. A key question becomes whether the fragmented parliamentary opposition will one day take advantage of the situation and become a more coherent, alternative force for reform. There are no clear answers as yet, but the **parliamentary elections of 2003** gave some positive indications.

The immediate result of the 2003 election was that Koizumi remained prime minister. His party had lost ten seats, but the LDP could record exactly one-half of the 480 seats in the House of Representatives after three independents joined its ranks. Together with its two smaller partners, however, Koizumi's ruling coalition commanded a total of 275 seats.

The main change brought by the election lay in its consolidation of the hitherto fragmented opposition. Here the Democratic Party of Japan (DPJ), formed in 1996, gained 40 seats for a total of 177 in all. The young party seemed to have emerged as a major mainstream challenger to the LDP by mopping up voters from other parties. In its assessment, the British *Economist* saw the possible emergence of a two-party system and referred to the DPJ as clear alternative choice for mainstream voters.

The new strength of the DPJ could make it easier for Prime Minister Koizumi to neutralize resistance in his own party and the bureaucracy to the structural reforms that he intermittently advocates. In a sense, he has been given the proverbial second chance.

A Constitutional Revolution In Britain?*

Donley T. Studlar

When the New Labor government led by Tony Blair took office in May 1997, one of its most distinctive policies was its program of constitutional reform. Indeed, few British parties have ever campaigned so consistently on constitutional issues. From its first days of power, Labor promoted its constitutional reform agenda: (1) devolution to Scotland and Wales, (2) an elected mayor and council for London and possibly other urban areas, (3) removal of the voting rights of hereditary peers in the House of Lords, (4) incorporation of the European Convention on Human Rights into British law, (5) a Freedom of Information Act, and (6) electoral reform at various levels of government, including a referendum on changing the electoral system for Members of Parliament. These reforms, plus a stable agreement for governing Northern Ireland, the constitutional implications of membership of the European Union, and the question of modernization of the monarchy will be considered here. This article analyzes the nature of Labor's constitutional proposals, including their inspiration, implementation, and potential impact.

Traditional British Constitutional Principles

The United Kingdom as a state in international law is made up of four constituent parts—England, Scotland, Wales, and Northern Ireland—all under the authority of the Queen in Parliament in London. The constitution is the structure of fundamental laws and customary practices that define the authority of state institutions and regulate their interrelationships, including those to citizens of the state. Although in principle very flexible, in practice the "unwritten" British constitution (no single document) is difficult to change. The socialization of political elites in a small country leads to a political culture in which custom and convention make participants reluctant to change practices which brought them to power.

Even though Britain is under the rule of law, that law is subject to change through parliamentary sovereignty. Instead of a written constitution with a complicated amending process, a simple majority of the House of Commons can change any law, even over the objections of the House of Lords if necessary. Individual rights are protected by ordinary law and custom, not an entrenched Bill of Rights.

Officially Britain remains a unitary state, with all constitutional authority belonging to the central government, rather than a federal state with a formal, even if vague, division of powers between the center and a lower level. Some commentators argue that Britain should be considered a "union-state," since the relationship of the four parts to the central government varies rather than being on the same terms. Although limited devolution has been utilized in the past, especially in Northern Ireland, 1921–1972, central government retains the authority to intervene in lower-level affairs, including local government matters. The voters are asked once every four or five years to choose a team of politicians to rule the central authority through the parliament at Westminster. Under the single member district, simple plurality electoral system, the outcome usually has been a single-party government (prime minister and cabinet) chosen based on a cohesive majority in the House of Commons, a fusion of power between the legislature and the executive. Referendums have been few and are formally only advisory; parliament retains final authority. The judiciary seldom makes politically important decisions, and even then it can be overridden by a parliamentary majority. Thus, in the United Kingdom almost any alteration of the interrelationship of political institutions can be considered constitutional in nature.

Constitutional issues were one of the few on which there were major party differences during the 1997 General Election campaign. Labor and the third party, the Liberal Democrats, had an agreed agenda for constitutional change, developed in consultation over several years. The Conservatives upheld traditional British constitutional principles, including the unwritten constitution, no guarantees of civil liberties except through the laws of Parliament, maintenance of the unitary state, and a

House of Lords composed of hereditary peers and some life peers, the latter appointed by the prime minister.

Other features of the British constitution have also resisted change. British government has been one of the most secretive among Western democracies, with unauthorized communication of information punishable by law. Large cities did not elect their own mayors or even their own metropolitan governing councils. The House of Commons is one of the few remaining legislatures elected by the single member district, simple plurality electoral system, which rewards a disproportionate share of parliamentary seats to larger parties having geographically concentrated voting strength. Thus Britain has continued to have an overwhelmingly two-party House of Commons despite having a multiparty electorate.

Even though the elected Labor government proposed to change some of these procedures and to consider reform in others, there were good reasons to doubt its commitment. Traditionally, constitutional reform has evoked little sustained interest within the party. Like the Conservatives, it has embraced the almost untrammeled formal power that the "elective dictatorship" of British parliamentary government provides for a single-party majority in the House of Commons. Although Labor sometimes voiced decentralist and reformist concerns when in opposition, in government it usually proved to be as centralist as the Conservatives.

Labor's Constitutional Promises

There was general agreement that the most radical aspect of Labor's 1997 election manifesto was constitutional reform. This program was designed to stimulate the normally passive, relatively deferential British public into becoming more active citizens. In addition to parliamentary elections, they would vote for other levels of government with enhanced authority and have enhanced individual rights. More electoral opportunities, for different levels and within the voting process itself, would provide a wider range of choice for citizens.

Tony Blair had for some years advocated an infusion of a more participatory citizenship into British constitutional practices. In *New Britain* (Westview Press, 1997), Blair criticized British government as too centralized, secretive, and containing unrepresentative hereditary peers in the House of Lords. Blair called Labor's constitutional program "democratic renewal," argued that there had been 80 years of erosion of consent, self-government, and respect for rights under governments of both Left and Right, and contended that the mission of a Left-of-center party involves the extension of political rights as well as economic and social equality.

How and Why Labor Developed a Program for Constitutional Change

Several events and trends focused Labor's thinking on constitutional reform as never before. Labor suffered four consecutive general election losses (1979, 1983, 1987, 1992) even though the Conservatives never achieved above 43 percent of the popular vote. Eighteen consecutive years out of government made Labor fearful of ever returning as a single-party government, which made it more attentive to arguments for a more limited central authority.

Groups interested in constitutional reform were not difficult to find. The third party in Britain, the Liberal Democrats, have long been advocating changing the electoral system to have their voting strength better represented in parliament as well as decentralization and increased protection for civil liberties. Since 1988, a nonpartisan lobby group, Charter 88, has not only proposed most of the reforms that Labor eventually embraced but also others, such as a full-scale written constitution and a bill of rights. Other influential thinkers on the moderate left argued that a precondition for social and economic change in an increasingly middle-class Britain was to encourage citizen involvement by limiting central government authority. In Scotland, where the Conservatives had continuously declined as an electoral force, the cross-party Scottish Constitutional Convention encouraged devolution of power. Eventually Labor and the Liberal Democrats [worked together] to form a pre-election commission on constitutional matters, which continued after the election in the form of a special cabinet committee on constitutional reform.

Skeptics have argued that public support for constitutional change is a mile wide and an inch deep. Surveys indicate that the public usually supports constitutional reform proposals in principle without understanding very much about the specifics. Intense minorities, such as Charter 88 and the Electoral Reform Society, have fueled the discussion. During the 1997 election campaign constitutional issues featured prominently in elite discussions of party differences but did not emerge as a critical voting issue, except perhaps in Scotland.

New Labor had multiple incentives in developing an agenda for constitutional change. It provided a clear sense of Labor distinctiveness from the Conservatives, especially important when there were so few differences in social and economic policy between the two parties. It was designed to alleviate threats to Labor support by Scottish and Welsh nationalist parties arguing for more autonomy. There was also the longer-term prospect of possibly realigning the party system by co-opting the Liberal Democrats and their issues into a more permanent government of the center, thereby reducing both the Conservatives and die-hard socialists of the Labor party left wing to permanent minority status. Even with the large majority of parliamentary seats that Labor gained in the May, 1997 election, the government did not abandon constitutional reform.

Constitutional Change after Five Years of Labor Rule

No British government since the early twentieth century has presided over such a large agenda of constitutional reform. There are now new legislatures with devolved powers in

Northern Ireland, Scotland, and Wales. All but 92 hereditary peers have been removed from the House of Lords, and further deliberations have taken place over the second stage of Lords reform. A report from the Independent Commission on the Voting System advocated a change in the electoral system for the House of Commons, but no further government action has been taken. The European Convention on Human Rights has been incorporated into British law through the Human Rights Act. A weak Freedom of Information Act was also passed. In 1998, Londoners approved a proposal for the city to be governed by a directly-elected Mayor and the Assembly, and in 2000 the first election was held. Other cities have now adopted this measure through referendums.

New Labor immediately instituted some elements of its constitutional reform agenda. The referendums held in 1997 showed support for devolution to be stronger in Scotland than in Wales. The Scottish Parliament has more authority over policy and limited taxation powers while the Welsh Assembly has less authority and no taxation powers. Elections for both were held in 1999 under a combination of the traditional single member district, simply plurality electoral system and party list proportional representation, which yielded no clear majority in either legislature. Initially a Labor-Liberal Democrat coalition government was formed in Scotland and a minority Labor government in Wales. The latter was eventually replaced by another Labor-Liberal Democrat coalition. Labor has experienced problems in maintaining its party leaders in both governments; otherwise both have functioned largely as anticipated. No major disagreements on the constitutional allocation of powers have occurred. The second elections for the devolved legislatures will occur in May, 2003. The Welsh Assembly is expected to petition the Westminster government for greater powers, similar to those of the Scottish Parliament.

Eighty percent of the population of the United Kingdom, however, lives in England, which has been treated as a residual consideration in the plans for devolution. Tony Blair has indicated that Labor would be willing to form devolved governments in "regions with strong identities of their own," but, aside from the Northeast, there has been no substantial demand. Finally, in the Queen's Speech in fall, 2002, devolution legislation for English regions, based on a demonstrated willingness for it through a referendum vote, was promised.

The Mayor of London is the first modern directly-elected executive in the United Kingdom. The introduction of party primary elections for mayoral candidates led to less central party control over candidates and a personalization of the contest. The eventual winner was a dissident Labor MP and former London official, Ken Livingstone, who, however, has been relatively conciliatory in office.

Northern Ireland is a perennial problem, a hangover of the separation of Ireland from the United Kingdom in 1922. Six counties in the northern part of the island of Ireland, with approximately two-thirds of the population consisting of Protestants favoring continued union with Great Britain, remained in the United Kingdom. Many Catholics north and south remain convinced that there should be one, united country of Ireland on the island. This fundamental division of opinion concerning to which country the territory belongs led to organized violence by proponents of both sides, especially since the late 1960s. The Irish Republican Army (IRA) was the principal organization fighting for a united Ireland.

The current peace accord in Northern Ireland, the Good Friday Agreement of 1998, has led to new institutions there as well. In December 1999, devolution of power from the Westminster parliament to the Belfast parliament ushered in a period of what the British call "power sharing," or "consensus democracy." This entailed not only joint authority over internal matters by both Protestants (Unionists) and Catholics (Nationalists) through the requirement of super-majorities in the Northern Ireland Assembly and executive, but also some sharing of sovereignty over the territory between the United Kingdom and Ireland. Both countries have pledged, however, that Northern Ireland will remain part of the United Kingdom as long as a majority of the population in the province wishes. According to the latest census, Protestants remain in the majority, by 53 to 44 percent.

Referendums on the Good Friday Agreement passed overwhelmingly in both Northern Ireland and the Irish Republic, which repealed its constitutional claim to the province. As expected, devolved government in Northern Ireland has been rocky. Groups representing formerly armed adversaries, including Sinn Fein, closely linked to the IRA, now share executive power; some dissident factions have refused to renounce violence. The major issues have been continued; IRA terrorist activity in light of its relationship to Sinn Fein, incorporation of Catholics into the police service, and divisions among Protestants about how far to cooperate in the new government. In October, 2002, the Northern Ireland Assembly and government were suspended for the fourth time in three years, and direct rule from London was reinstituted, at least temporarily. The May, 2003 elections for a new assembly remain in place. The Northern Ireland government will continue to have a difficult path in working for peaceful solutions to long-intractable problems.

Britain signed the European Convention on Human Rights in 1951. Since 1966 it has allowed appeals to the European Court of Human Rights at Strasbourg, where it has lost more cases than any other country. Under New Labor, a law was quickly passed incorporating the European Convention on Human Rights into domestic law, but it only went into effect in October 2000. British judges rather than European judges now make the decisions about whether Britain is conforming to the Convention. This enhances the ability of British citizens to raise issues of human rights in domestic courts. Nevertheless, parliamentary sovereignty is maintained because Westminster remains the final authority on whether judicial decisions will be followed.

The tougher questions of constitutional reform—the electoral system for the House of Commons, freedom of information, and the House of Lords—were delayed. Currently the United Kingdom remains one of the most secretive democracies in the world, under the doctrine of executive prerogatives of Ministers of the Crown. The Freedom of Information Act eventually enacted is generally viewed as one which still allows the government to withhold a large amount of information.

Superficially House of Lords reform appears simple since a government majority in the House of Commons eventually can override any objections. Because of the capacity of the Lords to delay legislation, however, reform is difficult to complete in a timely fashion. In fact, discussion of reform of the Lords has been ongoing for 90 years. New Labor pledged to abolish voting by hereditary peers, initially leaving only the prime-ministerially appointed life peers, often senior political figures, as constituting a second chamber. There is fear, however, that the power of the Commons would be enhanced even further if "Tony's Cronies," as critics have dubbed prime ministerial appointees, constituted an entirely patronage-based second chamber. In order to accomplish initial reform, Prime Minister Blair accepted a temporary arrangement in 1999 allowing 92 hereditary peers to remain in the 720-member House of Lords, while eliminating 600 others. He then appointed a Royal Commission on the House of Lords (Wakeham Commission) to consider the second stage of Lords reform.

After the Wakeham Commission reported, in 2001 the government proposed a 600-member chamber, with 60 percent appointed by the prime minister on the basis of party affiliations, 20 percent nonpartisan "cross-benchers" appointed by an independent commission, and 20 percent elected on a regional basis through party list proportional representation. This would occur over a transition period of ten years. The government's plans were greeted with widespread skepticism from all parties, especially because of the low proportion of elected representatives. In an attempt to generate a cross-party consensus, a joint committee of MPs and peers was established to reexamine the question. In December, 2002, the Committee initially reported a list of seven options for further discussion, ranging from a fully elected to a fully appointed second chamber. It is now hoped that agreement on the second stage of Lords reform can be reached by the end of Labor's second term in office.

Although the Prime Minister indicated that he was not "personally convinced" that a change in the electoral system was needed, he appointed an Independent Commission on the Voting System (Jenkins Commission) to recommend an alternative to the current electoral system for the House of Commons. In 1998, the Commission recommended what is called "Alternative Vote Plus." The single-member district system would be retained, but instead of casting a vote for one person only, the electorate would rank candidates in order of preference, thus assuring a majority rather than a plurality vote for the winner. There would also be a second vote for a "preferred party." These votes would be put into a regional pool, with 15–20 percent of the total seats being awarded to parties based on their proportional share of these second votes, a favorable development for smaller parties.

Even such a relatively mild reform, however, generated substantial political controversy, as expected when the very basis on which legislators hold their seats is challenged. The proposed change has been criticized not only by the opposition Conservatives, but also by Labor members because it might make it more difficult for Labor to obtain a single-party parliamentary majority. There are no prospects for enactment of Westminster electoral system reform in the near future.

Some analysts, however, argue that the most significant constitutional change in the United Kingdom has been brought about not by Labor but by three actions of Conservative governments—joining the European Community (now European Union) in 1972, approving the *Single European Act* (1986), and signing the *Maastricht Treaty* (1992). Within the ever-expanding areas of EU competence, EU law supersedes British law, including judicial review by the European Court of Justice. Already one-third of total legislation in the United Kingdom comes from the European Union. Famously, Lord Denning observed that the European Union is an incoming tide which cannot be held back. The current process of the European Constitutional Convention may lead to further government integration among the members.

Britain remains one of only three EU members not to join the new European currency, the euro. If Britain were to join the euro, then control over monetary policy as well would effectively pass into the hands of the European Union. Tony Blair had indicated that this step would only be taken with public support in a countrywide referendum. It is widely expected that the government will call for such a referendum before the end of its second full term of office in 2006.

Although not on the Labor party agenda of constitutional change, the role of the monarchy has also come under increased scrutiny in recent years. The Queen's Golden Jubilee Year, celebrating the first 50 years of her reign (2002), was not a happy one, with two deaths and more scandals in the royal family. A resolution of the Scottish Parliament, supported by some MPs and Lords at Westminster, petitions the government to allow the monarch either to be or to marry a Catholic. Currently this is forbidden by the *Act of Settlement* (1701), passed at the end of a period of religious wars. The heir to the throne, Prince Charles, has proposed removing the monarch's particular tie to the Church of England in favor of the title of a more general "defender of faith" in what is now, despite appearances, a secularized country.

More vaguely, the government has suggested moving toward a "people's monarchy"—a simpler, slimmer, and less ritualized institution, perhaps with a gender-neutral inheritance. This would be more like the low profile "bicycle monarchs" of some other European countries. For the first time since Queen Victoria, there is substantial, if muted, public expression of anti-monarchism (republicanism). Tampering with an established and still widely revered institution such as the monarchy, however, requires extremely careful consideration, as many traditionalists are opposed to all change.

Conflicting Views on the Effects of Constitutional Change

Labor's program of constitutional renewal already has brought about some changes in Britain. Instead of near-uniform use of the single member district, simple plurality electoral system, now there are five different systems in operation: Single Transferable Vote (a form of proportional representation with candidate choice) in Northern Ireland, party list proportional representation for the June, 1999 European Parliament election, alternative member systems (a combination of single member district and party list proportional) for the devolved legislatures in Scotland and Wales and the London Assembly, and a popularly elected executive through the Supplementary Vote (voting for two candidates in order of preference) for London. Plurality elections remain the norm only for the House of Commons at Westminster and English local government elections.

Until 1997, there had been only four referendums in the history of the United Kingdom. Within nine months of taking power, Labor held four additional referendums (in Wales, Scotland, Northern Ireland, and London), with two others promised, on changing the Westminster electoral system and on joining the European single currency.

Broadly, five interpretations of these developments have been voiced by commentators, as outlined below. We might term these the (1) popular social liberalism, (2) lukewarm reform, (3) symbolic politics, (4) the doomsday scenario, and (5) constitutional incoherence. These contending explanations exist at least partially because Labor itself has never outlined a coherent theory behind its constitutional reforms beyond Blair's pre-election formulations. There has been no general constitutional convention; instead there have been a series of *ad hoc* measures.

The well-known American analyst of Britain, Samuel H. Beer, has compared Blair's reforms to the popular social liberalism of the early twentieth century Liberal governments, which included restricting the power of the House of Lords and devolving power to Ireland. After the First World War, however, electorally the Conservatives came to dominate a political Left divided between an insurgent Labor Party and the remaining Liberals. At least in the first term of office, social and constitutional reform served as a substitute for a more traditional Labor program of increased government spending. It is considered important as an element to help establish the long-term political dominance of a revitalized center-left.

Another constitutional scholar, Philip Norton, argues that New Labor's proposals are radical in concept but so far moderate in form and effects, e.g., lukewarm reform. Similarly, Anthony Barnett of Charter 88 claims that the government practices *constitutus interruptus*. Another British academic, Patrick Dunleavy, has suggested that constitutional reform for New Labor represents continuous but financially cheap activity at a time when the government is wary of alienating its middle-class supporters by appearing to be another Labor "tax and spend" administration. This amounts to little substantive change, however, until the two critical questions, electoral reform for the House of Commons and membership of the euro, are faced.

Although there has been grudging acceptance from constitutional conservatives who originally opposed change, they are still fearful of the implications of some reforms. The Conservative former editor of *The Times*, William Rees-Mogg, envisioned Labor's constitutional changes eroding democracy in the United Kingdom through a semi-permanent Labor-Liberal governing coalition in Westminster, Scotland, and Wales, a House of Lords based on patronage, and a more centralized, bureaucratic European superstate. More sanguinely, *The Economist* foresaw a weakening of Westminster's authority through the combined forces of devolution and a more integrated European Union. But by the election of 2001, the Conservative party claimed that it could make devolved institutions work more efficiently as well as maintaining the integrity of an independent House of Lords. However, they continue to oppose a more centralized Europe and a changed electoral system.

Finally, the prominent British political scientist Anthony King has argued that Britain no longer has a coherent set of constitutional principles. Because of the piecemeal constitutional changes over the past quarter century by both Conservative and Labor governments, traditional interpretations of the British constitution no longer adequately describe contemporary practice, but there also is no set of alternative principles as a guide. Britain has moved away from majoritarian democracy without becoming a fully-fledged consensus democracy with proportional representation and coalition governments.

Despite its prominence in the election of 1997 and in New Labor's first term of government, constitutional reform was only a minor feature of the 2001 general election campaign. While the Liberal Democrats, as expected, gave it greater attention, all of the major parties deemphasized constitutional reform in their party manifestos. This was particularly surprising for Labor, which was content to claim that it had delivered on its 1997 commitments. Of Labor's "25 major goals for Britain," the only one touching on constitutional reform was a vague pledge for greater local democracy. Notably absent was any commitment to call a referendum on the Westminster electoral system. While some moves have been made to establish devolved regions in England and to complete Lords reform, as well to deal with the continuing problems in Northern Ireland, overall constitutional reform has been less prominent in Labor's second term of office.

Unintended Consequences Over the Horizon?

Institutional rearrangements often have unanticipated consequences. Although New Labor legislation on constitutional matters claims not to disturb the principle of parliamentary sovereignty, the likelihood is that this constitutional convention will be compromised even more than it already has been under Britain's membership of the European Union. Congruent with the process of decentralization in other European countries, devolution is likely to be entrenched *de facto* if no *de jure*. Some journalists have begun calling British a "federal" political system. Although specific powers are granted to each devolved government, disputes over which level has authority over certain policies are likely to arise. Even without a comprehensive Bill of Rights, incorporation of the European Convention on Human Rights may mean a stronger, more politically active judiciary, a form of creeping judicial review. House of Lords reform, if it is not to be simply an appointed chamber reflecting the wishes of the government of the day, could also lead to a more symmetrical bicameralism.

Incorporation of the European Convention on Human Rights, as well as a limited form of joint authority with Ireland over Northern Ireland and possible membership of the European common currency and central bank, suggest that Britain may be moving into new patterns of international shared authority in areas heretofore considered exclusively within the domain of the sovereign state. Regional policies of the European Union even may be helping stimulate ethnonationalist demands. If the Scottish National Party, still committed to independence for Scotland, ever wins a majority in the Scottish Parliament, the United Kingdom could be faced with a "Quebec scenario," whereby control of a level of government enhances rather than retards its secessionist claims.

The "third way" ideas of Anthony Giddens, influential in the New Labor government, advocate a restructuring of government to promote "subsidiarity" (the taking of decisions at the lowest level possible) and correcting the "democratic deficit" through constitutional reform, greater transparency, and more local democracy. In such a process, Britain would become a more complex polity institutionally. This would demand cultivating habits of conciliation, cooperation, and consent rather than the usual reliance upon parliamentary laws and executive orders. Having additional levels of elected government already has created difficulties for central party organizations attempting to exert control over who becomes the party leader in these jurisdictions.

The electoral system, however, may be the lynchpin of the British parliamentary system as it currently exists. Even the relatively modest changes proposed by the Jenkins Commission might help realign the party system. Because of the fears this arouses within the Labor party, Prime Minister Blair has dealt with electoral reform at Westminster by indefinitely postponing it.

Whatever one's view of the desirability and impact of the changes, New Labor under Tony Blair has pursued and largely fulfilled its 1997 pledges on constitutional reform. Although delays and retreats have occurred on some issues, the implications of these changes will continue to be felt in British politics for some time to come.

Donley T. Studlar is Eberly Family Distinguished Professor of Political Science at West Virginia University, Executive Secretary of the British Politics Group, and author of *Great Britain: Decline or Renewal?* **(Westview Press). This article originated as the 1998 Taft Lecture, delivered to the undergraduate Honors recognition ceremony of the Political Science Department, University of Cincinnati.**

---

*This is a revised version of an article which first appeared in *Harvard International Review,* Spring 1999.

The Blair Moment

When British prime minister Tony Blair took office, he was committed to forging a new European identity for Britain. That great goal is still out of reach, and Blair's support for the United States in the Iraq War may have lost him the public confidence he needs to attain it.

By Steven Philip Kramer

For surely once, they feel, we were,
Parts of a single continent!

—Matthew Arnold

On April 11, 2003, the day Baghdad fell, British prime minister Tony Blair's big gamble seemed to have paid off. Blair had sent British forces into Iraq in defiance of strong popular and parliamentary opposition—and without the UN Security Council resolution he had so desperately sought. But none of the horror scenarios predicted by critics had occurred: no Iraqi use of weapons of mass destruction on the battlefield, no terrorist attacks on coalition cities, no uprisings on the "Arab street." Saddam Hussein's ugly regime had fallen to coalition forces in just three weeks, and with only 31 British casualties among the 45,000 British soldiers and airmen in the Iraq theatre. As in World War II, Britain had proven America's effective and indomitable ally.

Yet what seemed Blair's finest hour was not fated to last—indeed, it posed a mortal threat to the larger goals he had set for himself. He had come to power in 1997 with the mission of transforming modern Britain and reorienting its place in the world. He pledged to end Britain's status as a metaphorical island-nation, and, before Iraq became the central issue of international affairs, he had been pretty successful in making Britain not only an integral part of Europe but one of its leaders. But the Iraq War has done more than delay implementation of Blair's grand strategy. It has threatened to unravel it—and even to bring Blair down. Britain now seems at times more an island than ever.

Of course, Britain is an island nation in the literal sense, but it hasn't always been one in a strategic sense. From the Norman Conquest in 1066 to around the time Queen Elizabeth I took the throne in 1558, Britain's destiny was closely tied to Europe's.

As every reader of Shakespeare's histories knows, Britain was engaged for centuries in a struggle to conquer France. Only in the centuries separating the reign of the current Elizabeth from that of her 16th-century namesake was Britain an island nation in the strategic sense—indeed, an island *empire*.

Four things made Britain an island empire. First, it possessed a superior blue-water navy, which could provide absolute security. Second, it defined its key interests as lying across the seas rather than across the English Channel. Because the empire was the promise and the Continent the threat, British policy toward Europe was largely negative, to prevent the emergence of a potentially hegemonic Continental power. The goal was not to act as a European power from within Europe but as a balancer from without. Third, Britain gave birth to the Industrial Revolution, an engine that in the 19th century made it the world's greatest power, the first great empire based on free trade. Fourth, Protestant Britain felt its very essence to de different from—and better than—the Continent's; its great historical enemies, Spain and France, were Catholic.

Moreover, England followed a different pattern of political development from the 17th century on. While royalist absolutism on the Continent was undermining incipient forms of representative government and customary law, England was overthrowing kings, establishing parliamentary sovereignty, and reaffirming a common-law system. But the nation saw its political system less as a model for the rest of Europe than as a happy exception, based on the special virtues of the English people. The struggles against the Spanish Armada, the France of Louis XIV and Napoleon, and the Germany of the Kaiser and Adolf Hitler were meant to preserve "this other Eden, demi-paradise," "this blessed plot," "against the envy of less happier lands."

Yet even before the coronation of the second Queen Elizabeth in 1952, the underpinnings of British strategic exceptionalism were coming undone. Most obviously, with the rise of submarines and airplanes in the 20th century, Britain's navy could no longer guarantee the nation's security, as Hitler's fearful onslaught showed. Perhaps more important, Britain failed to achieve the "Second Industrial Revolution," which involved the application of science and technology to manufacturing, and so lost its competitive edge by the late 19th century. Having invented the Industrial Revolution, shaped the laissez-faire state, and created a liberal international economic order in the 19th century, Britain by the second half of the 20th century had itself become the economic sick man of Western Europe.

The tragedy of the post-World War II period was that Clement Atlee's government (1945–51), the first Labor government with a strong popular mandate and a majority in Parliament, tried to resolve Britain's social problems without confronting its underlying economic maladies. As historian Correlli Barnett argues, Labor made a grave mistake by choosing this course while attempting to maintain Britain's status as a global power. In contrast, France, while waging costly and ultimately futile colonial wars in Indochina and Algeria, was able to modernize its economy and develop an effective welfare state because, unlike Britain, it put together a coherent program of national economic planning. Its nationalized industries played an integral role in the plan, and the French economy was stimulated by early participation in the European Coal and Steel Community and its successor, the Common Market (which Britain did not join until 1973).

THE GREAT PARADOX OF BRITAIN'S ECONOMIC SITUATION WHEN BLAIR CAME TO POWER WAS THAT THE COUNTRY WAS BOTH WORSE OFF AND BETTER OFF THAN THE CONTINENT.

Britain, a state no longer liberal but not *dirigiste* either, experienced the worst of all worlds. There was no real economic planning, only short term intervention. The increasingly obsolete nationalized industries—such as coal, steel, telephone, gas, electricity, and the railroads—were supported but not modernized, and became a drag on the economy. Segments of the British infrastructure (such as transportation and health care) fell further and further behind their Continental counterparts, as did the educational sector. An unfortunate codependency developed between feckless management and trade unions committed to the preservation of a welter of archaic work rules. Governments, both Labor and Conservative, blessed their unfortunate modus vivendi. But relative economic decline does not make for a happy society, and British politics radicalized in the late 1970s. The Labor Party, taken over by a motley coalition of defenders of the welfare state, opponents of nuclear weapons and NATO, and the "loony Left," went beyond the pale of electability.

Under Prime Minister Margaret Thatcher (1979–90), the Conservative Party, which had lurched to the hard right, engaged in a "class against class" strategy aimed at recreating a classical 19th-century liberal state. Thatcher had some success in encouraging a more entrepreneurial economy, but at great social cost. Her prescription for Britain's chronically ailing manufacturing sector was to privatize nationalized firms and to take the entire sector off government life support. It was sink or swim—and much traditional manufacturing sank. She tried to break the power of the trade unions to create a less restrictive and less expensive labor market. What she could not do was force British manufactures to become entrepreneurial. And while Thatcher seemed determined to force the working class to accept the exigencies of a renewed British economy, she refused to spend on education the money that was needed to create a more skilled work force. Her hapless Tory successor, John Major (1990–97), brought little change to these policies.

The great paradox of Britain's economic situation when Blair came to power in 1997 was that the country was both worse off and better off than the Continent: worse off because it had not enjoyed the high postwar growth rate and renewal of infrastructure achieved across the Channel; better off because Thatcher had freed it from the Procrustean bed of labor market restrictions impeding the transition to a modern information and service economy. Britain was still out of phase with Europe, but that now worked in its favor.

BLAIR AIMED AT NOTHING LESS THAN GIVING BRITAIN A NEW SENSE OF NATIONAL PURPOSE AND ENDING THE AGE-OLD INSULARITY OF BRITISH THINKING AND BEHAVIOR.

It's no exaggeration to call Blair's strategy "grand." He not only wanted to bring the nation into the information economy of the late 20th century, but aimed at nothing less than giving Britain a new sense of national purpose and ending the age-old insularity of British thinking and behavior. His "New" Labor Party proposed a state that promoted economic growth by *not* meddling in the economy but that fought for social justice as well, believing that the social advancement of its citizens would in turn contribute to economic productivity. The new British state was also to reform its archaic political institutions and renegotiate its ties to the non-English areas of the United Kingdom (Scotland, Wales, and Northern Ireland). But most important of all, Blair's Britain would finally accept that its destiny lay with Europe. Europe had to become the promise of Britain's future, not the threat. And by embracing Europe, the prime minister believed, Britain could become one of its leaders.

One key to economic success was fiscal policy. Chancellor of the Exchequer Gordon Brown vowed to exorcise the demons of unsound economic and monetary policies that had haunted Labor (but not only Labor) governments in the past. He immediately granted independence to the Bank of England, giving it freedom comparable to that its U.S. counterpart, the Federal Reserve System. To prove that Labor would pursue sound economic policies, he pledged not to raise taxes or exceed the spending guidelines the Conservatives had set for what would be the first two years of Labor's term. To enforce budget disciple, he extended his control over virtually all government departments. As the economy grew, revenues increased and the government won credibility, and Brown was able to free up new resources for infrastructure and social welfare. By then, however, public patience had worn thin with the lack of obvious improvement in public services, notably transportation and public health. While voters returned Labor to a second term in 2002 (few felt that the Conservative Party's standard-bearer, William Hague, offered a real alternative), there were loud complaints about the state of such services.

A second goal was reform of the work force. "Britain must be the world's number one creative economy," Blair declared in 1997. "We will win by brains or not at all. We will compete on enterprise and talent or fail." A strong and effective state would strive to create a dynamic civil society whose members contributed their skills to the new economy and, in turn, benefited from it. Traditional welfare would be replaced by efforts to help people get jobs. So Blair focused on investing in education and developing programs to increase workforce skills. But in a low-tax economy there's not a lot of money available for education. Thus, an irony: The Tories, wanting to maintain free university education, would restrict expansion of the student body and thereby keep the education a preserve of the upper and middle classes, whereas Blair, seeking to expand working-class enrollment, initiated tuition charges.

On the whole, the Blair government's economic and financial policies were a great success. Britain achieved levels of growth, currency stability, and employment unparalleled in the postwar period, and superior to those of the major Continental counties. Britain no longer faced boom-and-bust crises; the pound was not threatened by currency speculation and devaluation. There was a real sense that everyone was on the same side, and Britain seemed, once again, to be riding the tiger of economic progress. This brought a new sense of self-assurance, with positive consequences for British relations with Europe. Yet the fact that Britain was doing so much better than the Continent raised doubts about whether it was in Britain's interest to surrender control of its currency to a distant, Frankfurt-based European Central Bank. And because Britain's success was based on low taxes and a more fluid labor market, the government was determined to maintain national control over these sectors of economic life as well. Thus, success reinforced island empire old-think.

Another target of Blair's reforms was the British constitution, long seen as embodying everything that was excellent and unique about Britain, a locus classicus of Britain's island mentality. The Revolution of 1688 established the basic principles of parliamentary supremacy, and, after the signing of the Act of Union with Scotland in 1707, a sense of British identity was successfully superimposed on the old national identities of England, Scotland, and Wales, if not that of Ireland. In *Britons*

(1992), historian Linda Colley brilliantly describes the creation of this new identity but concludes that, after World War II, the process reversed itself, and, as elsewhere in Europe, subregional nationalisms returned. So political reality forced Blair to be a constitutional reformer. The result was a system of devolution that gave Scotland its own parliament, with limited powers of taxation, and that accorded a lesser degree of autonomy to Wales. In addition, a constitutional framework had to be developed to resolve the long and deadly conflict in Northern Ireland. In dealing with these immediate problems, Blair could not escape fundamental questions about the nature of the British constitution and British identity.

BLAIR HAS BEEN FORCED TO CONFRONT FUNDAMENTAL QUESTIONS ABOUT THE NATURE OF THE BRITISH CONSTITUTION AND BRITISH IDENTITY.

Since 1688, changes to the constitutional system have never been "across the board" but only fixes (even the great Reform Bill of 1832 fits into this category). Britain's constitution was as full of anomalies and as asymmetrical as its Gothic cathedrals, whereas the constitutions of Continental countries, based on universal principles, resembled neo-classical temples. But the former was made of tough stone that resisted the ages, whereas the latter often turned out to be cardboard palaces. Of the large states of Europe, Britain alone made a peaceful and enduring transition to democracy, thereby giving the impression that the virtue of its system, arising from inherited layers of institutions, laws, and traditions rather than a written document, lay in its uniqueness.

Blair's reforms might have foreshadowed the creation of a federal Britain with three levels: strengthened local government, subnational and regional governments, and the British Parliament at Westminster. The House of Lords might even have been transformed into a chamber of regions, like the German Bundesrat. Such a vision of British governance would have made Britain far more compatible with the rest of the European Union (EU) and, presumably, less terrified by the threat of a federal Europe. Instead, Blair's constitutional reforms dealt with issues piecemeal, and the result is a system more complex than before. Scotland and Wales are both devolved, for example, but they have different models of devolution. There are different forms of proportional representation for the parliaments of Scotland and Wales and the British seats in the EU Parliament, whereas the Westminster Parliament still retains the first-past-the-post system (as in elections for the U.S. House of Representatives, whoever wins the most votes in a district is elected). Scottish members of Parliament at Westminster can vote on strictly English questions, but English MPs cannot do the same for Scottish and Welsh issues. England has no regional government, but areas that seek regional status may attempt to secure it via referendum. London has an elected mayor, but no other large British town has one. The uncompleted House of

Lords reform has produced an incongruous, interim body composed of life peers. There are also 92 hereditary peers chosen by the former hereditary members. The failure of Lords reform explains why Labor's constitutional forays have been faulted for a lack of imagination, vision, and coherence—and for a failure of will, too. Instead of learning from experience, Blair has created a new muddle by an abrupt announcement that he intends to abolish the ancient and much debated post of Lord Chancellor, which combines the powers of chief justice, cabinet member, and MP.

THE BLAIR GOVERNMENT HAS NOT BEEN FRANK WITH THE PUBLIC ABOUT THE SIGNIFICANCE OF THE DRAFT EUROPEAN CONSTITUTION.

Blair's approach to constitutional reform has implications for policy toward Europe. To the extent that the British constitution is seen as the unique product of fortunate circumstances, two conclusions apply: The constitution cannot be exported to or adopted by other countries or the EU, and it would be tragic for Britain to come under the authority of a European constitution, which would surely be inferior to its own. These beliefs have helped perpetuate British ambivalence toward Europe. Nor has the government been frank with the public about the significance of the draft European constitution recently prepared by the European Convention, preferring minimize its importance in order to deflect calls to put it to a referendum. These calls emanate from Tories, who wish the European constitution ill and who would like to put an end to it. But they also come from pro-Europeans who want the British people to make a conscious and educated choice for Europe.

The end of the empire and economic decline reduced Britain's political power. Yet the consciousness of being different from Europe—and better—remained so strong that Britain could not even imagine wanting to become part of the European integration process that began after World War II. Britain supported integration—for the others. Dean Acheson's famous quip that Britain had lost an empire without finding a purpose was all the more unkind for being true. One of Tony Blair's major goals has been to make Britain an integral part of Europe, even a leader. But to embrace Europe, Britain has to reconcile itself with its own nemesis—and frequent ally—France, which, more than any other nation, has shaped European integration.

ONE OF TONY BLAIR'S MAJOR GOALS HAS BEEN TO MAKE BRITAIN AN INTEGRAL PART OF EUROPE, EVEN A LEADER.

In a famous passage of Charles de Gaulle's war memoirs, the general relates a conversation with Winston Churchill, in June 1944, in which Churchill states: "How do you expect us British to take a position different from the United States…? We are going to liberate Europe, but that's because the Americans are with us to do it. For, understand this, every time we must choose between Europe and the open sea, we will always choose the open sea. Every time that I have to choose between you and Roosevelt, I will always choose Roosevelt." Making peace with France thus forces Britain to rethink its relationship with the United States.

In the critical debates of the past 200 years, Britain and France have almost always represented antitheses: reform versus revolution, economic liberalism versus protectionism and statism, empiricism versus rationalism, Shakespeare versus Racine. After 1945, France and Germany, great enemies since 1870, turned their relationship into a privileged partnership. But Britain and France, even though they were allies in the two world wars, remain at loggerheads over the great current debates in Europe, which have been intensified by the Iraq war: What should Europe's role in the world be? And what should its relationship with America be?

Ironically, these debates occur because the two nations now have so much in common. Of the EU states, only Britain and France are seriously involved in global security and think that Europe should be so involved, and only they have the independent military means to support such a role. Their respective conceptions of what the EU should be in institutional terms are no longer very different. Britain was late to enter the EU's forerunner, the Common Market, and remained deeply ambivalent toward an institution that seemed to reflect French predilections (not unnaturally, since integrated Europe was largely a French idea). But today, as demonstrated by the recently completed work of the EU's Constitutional Convention, Britain and France have a common vision of a Europe structured along largely intergovernmental lines (i.e., key decisions are made by top national leaders meeting together in the European Council). What divides the two states is whether Europe should act in partnership with the United States, as the British think, or, in the French view, as a separate pole in a multipolar world, with the capacity and the will to be a countervailing force to the United States.

This difference of opinion stems in large part from the experience of World War II. The collapse of France in 1940 left Britain alone and threatened, and dependent for its survival on U.S. support. The ensuring Anglo-American alliance was the basis of the postwar "special relationship," in which a diminished Britain hoped to influence the new American superpower by playing Greece to its Rome. The United States, forced into a globe role because of France's unexpected collapse, no longer regarded France as a great power, and Franklin Roosevelt disliked what he took to be de Gaulle's delusions of grandeur. De Gaulle—and all presidents of the Fifth Republic— sought to reinforce France's great-power role by standing up to America. He opposed the perpetuation of a bipolar world, which he believed weakened the role of the nation-state, the basic unit of politics. After the end of the Cold War, his successors decried the American-dominated unipolar world and hoped that Europe would play the global role that France no longer could: Europe would be a France writ large.

The symbol of France's aspirations for Europe was the concept of an autonomous all-European military force. After the 1992 Treaty of Maastricht established the legal basis for this so-called European Security and Defense Identity, and often fatuous debate raged about whether such a thing should be created and, if so, how. It got off the ground only when Tony Blair reversed British opposition at the 1998 Saint Malo summit meeting. France and Britain advocated the development under the EU of a military capacity for "autonomous action, backed up by credible force," to act, generally in peacekeeping operations, at times when NATO as a whole was not engaged. A militarily stronger Europe, speaking with one voice, would presumably be taken more seriously by the United States and give Europe more leverage in dealing with America. A fine balance was sought between British wishes to strengthen European capacity but not to undermine NATO, and French wishes to give the EU a more independent role in international security. Starting in 1998, it seemed that a synthesis might take place between British and French conceptions. The debate over Iraq, however, tore asunder the prospect of that synthesis.

> _On the Critical debates of the past 200 years, Britain and France have almost always represented antitheses._

For many years the British supported close transatlantic ties, not only because influencing the United States seemed the best way of affecting global security, but because they believed in a genuine community of values spanning the Atlantic. Some of that belief remains, but since Iraq there is much more doubt. The Iraq War may represent the high-water mark of Anglo-American cooperation. There is a growing belief among policy elites in both Britain and France that the United States is no longer the generally benevolent power it once was, and that Europe must prevent if from doing dangerous things. The British and French remain divided over whether it is better to try influence or to confront the United States.

America does not respond well to French confrontation, but it does not seem prepared to listen much to its friends either. There is intense discussion in Europe about whether Blair's support for American policy in Iraq has given Britain significant influence with the Bush administration. Downing Street asserts that President George W. Bush is far more pragmatic than he is generally portrayed to be, and that Blair enjoys great access and credit; critics insist that Britain has sold its birthright for a mess of pottage. British public opinion was not initially favorable to war, especially without a Security Council mandate, and much of the Labor Party was opposed, even though most Labor MPs reluctantly gave Blair a vote of confidence on Iraq.

But the postwar debate about the existence of weapons of mass destruction and allegations of the misuse of intelligence materials to justify intervention in Iraq have gravely damaged the prime minister. He has faced little real opposition from the inept Tory front bench but serious opposition from Robin Cook, former foreign secretary and more recently leader of the House of Commons, from which position Cook resigned because of government policy on Iraq. Blair's increasing tendency to define foreign policy in terms compatible with U.S. neoconservative thought, and reflections emanating from Downing Street to the effect that it is better to have a Europe divided than one aligned against the United States, do not help relations with his own party. It has become much more common for serious members of the policy establishment to question the special relationship with the United States. There is also a real danger that Britain could relapse to some extent into its pre-1997 situation, when it had close U.S. ties but exerted little influence in Washington, and when its influence in the EU was undercut by its own ambivalence.

If Britain wants to exert maximum influence in the debate over the future of European security and the relationship with the United States, Blair must bring Britain into the European Monetary Union (EMU), which means abandoning the pound for the euro and placing the Bank of England under the European Central Bank. But EMU seems to have suffered collateral damage as a result of the Iraq War. Blair was not prepared to take the risks required to fight an EMU referendum in the fall of 2003, having to face the opposition of the media moguls who harangue against Europe in general and EMU in particular, and to overcome as well the powerful obstruction of Chancellor of the Exchequer Gordon Brown. Curiously, Blair, who professes a deep commitment to EMU, stacked the deck against a referendum by agreeing not to go ahead without Brown's agreement. Brown professes support for the concept of EMU (a profession widely doubted), but claims that he will base his decision to move forward on a series of allegedly objective economic tests that are, in fact, highly subjective. It is certainly legitimate to be concerned that entry into EMU take place under the right economic conditions. No one wants to repeat the monetary debacle that occurred when the government last placed the pound within a European currency framework, only to suffer an onslaught on Sterling in 1993 that forced Britain to leave the system and devalue its currency. This humiliating experience crippled the Major government. But it's not obvious that there ever will be a magic moment to join EMU.

> _It's not obvious that there ever will be a magic moment to join EMU._

On June 9, 2003, Blair and Brown agreed to agree, or agreed to appear to agree, that the time was not yet ripe. They concurred that the sacrosanct tests were not yet satisfied. In truth, this was not the time to contest a referendum. The Continent was suffering from low growth and high unemployment—Sweden's voters would reject EMU in a September referendum—and Blair had only recently been bashing France for its position on Iraq. The two leaders held open the possibility of a referendum before the end of the current Parliament, by 2007 at the latest, but few saw that as more than a fig leaf. They promised to campaign actively for public acceptance of EMU, but signals have been mixed. If EMU is the test of whether Blair has led Britain to the point of abandoning its island identity and truly embracing Europe, he has failed—although, in all fairness, the fault is not his alone. There is something disturbing about a prime minister committed to EMU who cannot manage to bring Britain in despite two smashing electoral victories and an immense majority in Parliament, a politician with conviction who is willing to risk all in war yet us seemingly paralyzed over EMU.

here was Blair moment. It occurred when nostalgia for an island Britain past gave way to a vision of a postmodern Britain. It was based on the notion that progress could be made by co-operation rather than conflict, and that it was time to move beyond archaic ideological and social enmities. Blair was said to be an unconscious Hegelian. His Third Way was a kind of synthesis. Britain could have its cake and eat it, too. This was a notion that was bound to please baby boomers and the young, who, never having experienced an economy of scarcity, do not understand that hard choices must sometimes be made.

Blair and Brown (with the help of the Tories) succeeded in making Labor appear the natural party of government, the guarantor of prosperity and financial responsibility. Blair has also had some success in molding Labor into a broad party whose appeal extends into the middle classes and the City (London's world financial center), a kind of modern version of the 19th-century "New Liberalism," committed to activism and the pursuit of social justice. He consolidated Thatcher's return to liberal economics but eliminated the asversarial edge: Prudent financial management, an end to boom-or bust, and a sound currency were seen as being in everyone's interest. His efforts to strengthen education and equality of opportunity are significant, but they cannot always counter the tendency of modern capitalism to increase inequality. Infrastructure reform has lagged. At times the government's policy seem too doctrinaire in its commitment to private-sector solutions, whether they work or not. To be sure, Britain fell so far behind Europe after World War II that it has not been easy to catch up. As for social services, it is a truism that a nation that chooses low taxes cannot afford social services at the level enjoyed in high-tax states.

The Blair government has declared look the identity questions in the eye, and there's little doubt that in the coming decades the outlines of a new British identity and political system will emerge. Through piecemeal and often pooly thought out reform, the Blair government has destabilized the old system. But it is important that the new political system that emerges be both internally consistent and compatible with a European identity for Britain. This will not happen unless that compatibility is a conscious choice of government—as it should be.

lair seemed well on the way to successful cooperation with France and to acting as a bridge between Europe and the United States. But the rise of a unilateralist United States and the Iraq War made that bridge role improbable. The Iraq War badly damaged British ties with France and undid much of the "confidence building" that had occurred since 1998. Many policymakers in Britain believe that the special relationship with America has reached the end or the road, that it is no longer in Britain's interest, that at the minimum it must become far more conditional. It certainly makes sense to consort with the only global superpower if you can influence it. But if you can't? A Europe that speaks with one voice and acts effectively will have more influence.

Blair crafted a superb grand strategy based on the international context of the last years of the 20th century. The Iraq War has changed the political context and undermined public confidence in his leadership, yet he seems to go on as if nothing has changed, as if he emerged strengthened from Iraq. Even if Blair is politically still very much alive, he should realize that many of his natural supporters don't like where he's heading. He needs to heed *Guardian* columnist Polly Toynbee's message: "It's not another leader we want, it's a better Blair." He needs to rethink his grand strategy, and if he wants a European Britain, he needs to make some tough choices. But unless a "better Blair" emerges soon, his effectiveness as a leader, even his tenure as prime minister, may be ending. And that will defer the day that Britain is truly part of a united Europe.

STEVEN PHILIP KRAMER, a former Wilson Center public policy scholar, is professor of grand strategy at the Industrial College of the Armed Forces, National Defenses University. The views expressed here are the author's and do not neccessarily reflect the official policy or position of the National Defense University, the Department of Defense, or the U.S. government. Copyright © 2003 by Steven Philip Kramer.

From *The Wilson Quarterly*, Autumn 2003, pp. 72-84. © 2004 by Edward O. Wilson.

Coming out smiling:
Blair survives his biggest test as prime minister and promises no wavering on bold policies

*No one expected that the government would be so completely exonerated in an inquiry into how the case for war in Iraq was made. The Labour leader's appetite for power will have been renewed by this week's events writes **James Blitz***

Brian Groom

Tony Blair has survived his most difficult week in politics—as he always said he would. His many detractors inside and outside Britain's ruling Labour party thought this might be the moment that Mr. Blair was finally toppled. But the prime minister is still in Downing Street, and smiling rather more broadly as the end of the week than he was at the start.

For months, there had been an expectation that Mr. Blair could be seriously damaged by a report from Lord Hutton, a leading judge investigating allegations that the prime minister had lied about the case for war with Iraq. When it became clear that Lord Hutton would deliver that report this week on the same day that Mr. Blair faced a knife-edge vote in parliament over his plans to allow Britain's universities to levy higher tuition fees, the prime minister seemed in danger of receiving a devastating double blow.

Some 25 percent of Labour MPs were opposed to the policy on higher education fees, threatening its defeat. That would, for the first time, have impressed upon voters that Labour was internally divided—potentially fatal for Labour just as it was for the Conservative party over its policy towards Europe in the 1990s.

But Mr. Blair won the day on university fees—scraping to victory by just five votes. The following day, to the surprise of nearly everyone in the British political establishment, Mr. Blair and his government were utterly vindicated when Lord Hutton's report was made public. It was the BBC, the world's biggest public service broadcaster—which made the allegations about government duplicity in a radio broadcast by one of its journalists—that was utterly condemned. Within 24 hours, its chairman and chief executive had resigned.

So, at the end of an extraordinary week in politics, it is Mr. Blair's political durability, rather than his mortality, that is uppermost in the minds of MPs. He shows no sign of wanting to give up power. Labour continued to dominate the centre ground of British politics. And, despite acquiring a new leader six months ago, the opposition Conservatives are nowhere near the prospect of winning power at the general election expected in summer 2005.

> In his report the judge came down firmly on the side of the government and against the BBC, which was judged to have a 'defective' editorial system.

However, this has not been a week without difficulty for the prime minister. Tuesday night's wafer-thin Commons victory—one that could so easily have gone the other way—is an embarrassment. For a party with a historic majority of 161 in the 659-seat House of Commons to have to implement important legislation with such a small margin is a humiliation of sorts. There was controversy within the Labour party last year over the war with Iraq. The result of the vote on fees demonstrates more clearly than ever how the prime minister's project to modernize Britain's stretched health and education systems is seriously antagonizing his traditional left-wing supporters. And that, in turn, raises the question about how much longer Mr. Blair wants to stay at Number 10.

At 50, Mr. Blair still dominates the British political landscape. He has been in office for 6½ years—a long time by the standards of British prime ministers. "Because Margaret Thatcher was in power for more than a decade, we tend to forget that six years is actually a very long stint by the standard of most British prime minister," says Vernon Bagdanor, professor of government at the University of Oxford.

But there is no doubting that, if Mr. Blair wants to go on to his third general election victory next year, he will. The Conservatives are on a sounder footing with Michael Howard, their new leader, than they were with Iain Ducan Smith, his predecessor. But a recent opinion poll in The Daily Telegraph suggesting that Mr. Howard is beginning to push the Conservatives ahead in the polls is seriously disputed by Downing Street. Most other polls have shown that a big gap remains.

At its core, Lord Hutton's inquest was into a serous conflict between the government and the BBC over allegations the broadcaster made over how the government had knowingly deployed false information to make the case for war in Iraq. In the course of that conflict David Kelly, a ministry defence scientist who had been the source of the BBC report, killed himself. Mr. Blair—who ordered Lord Hutton's report into the circumstances of Mr. Kelly's death—had been personally involved in decisions relating to Mr. Kelly before his suicide.

But in his several-hundred-page report, the judge came down firmly on the side of the government and against the BBC. While the BBC was judged to have a "defective editorial system, the government was deemed not to have "sexed up" a dossier last September on Iraq's weapons of mass destruction, or to have failed in its duty of care to Mr. Kelly, despite taking action to publicise his name to the press as the likely source of the BBC report.

It was a verdict that yesterday produced some serious questioning in parts of Westminister. So one-sided a judgment from Lord Hutton had not been foreseen. Suddenly engulfed in its biggest crisis in decades, the BBC raised questions about how the law lord had reached his verdict. The front page of The Independent newspaper carried a blank space with one word: "Whitewash". An NOP pol for the London Evening Standard later suggested that 49

percent of people believed that was exactly what it was.

But Mr. Blair can afford to ignore such protestations. For the past seven months he has lived under the cloud of the BBC's allegation that he lied on Iraq. "The allegation that I or anyone else lied to the House or deliberately misled the House by falsifying intelligence on weapons of mass of destruction is itself the real lie," he told the House of Commons this week.

One leading pollster takes the view that this was a big breakthrough for Mr. Blair. "This is a significant moment for him," says Bob Worcester, the chairman of Mori. "All along, the crack in Blair's smooth façade has been the lack of trust. What we saw with Hutton was a re-establishment of the veracity of the prime minister. He was completely vindicated. It will push back the trust problem that has been so corrosive for him for so long."

But the question of whether Mr. Blair enjoys trust is not the defining issue in the run-up to the next general election. The central issue is whether Mr. Blair can press ahead with reforms of public services, akin to those he is trying to push through in universities. His belief is that pouring cash into the public sector is not enough. If the middle classes are to use health and education services they need to be given choice—and that means introducing market mechanisms that deeply unsettle people on the left of the Labour party.

Mr. Blair yesterday acknowledged that he has handled the university tuition fees legislation badly. He accepted that some MPs felt the policy was "sprung on them" with too little explanation. So much time was devoted last year to planning the war on Iraq that Mr. Blair failed to root the reforms in Labour's proclaimed commitment to furthering social justice. There were "lessons to be learnt, bridges to be rebuilt," Mr. Blair said.

But the prime minister also signalled that this was no time to hold back on his radicalism. "There will be no wavering in our political purpose," he said. One Downing Street aide says this is not a surprise. "He believes it is morally wrong to hold power just for the sake of it," says the aide. "It would be unthinkable to him that he could go into the next election without getting out some bold messages."

The prime minister yesterday signalled in his speech what his next big theme would be: it will be to give people at local level a far greater say in how Britain's hospitals, schools and police forces are run, giving them the power directly to elect lo-

cal boards. "The priority for reform… is to put the public at the heart of public services, making 'power to the people' the guiding principle of public sector improvement and reform."

How far Mr. Blair will be able to pursue this radical agenda depends partly on his relations with backbenchers. There are clearly now 60 or 70 MPs who would dearly love to be rid of him. But, more fundamentally, the future of policy depends on his relationship with Gordon Brown, Britain's finance minister and the co-founder of "New Labour".

Both Mr. Blair and Mr. Brown worked closely together to win the tuition fees vote—though when the policy was first mooted a year ago, Mr. Brown was ambivalent about it, believing the reforms were a distraction from Labour's core message that it has heavily invested in public services.

Some of Mr. Brown's allies in the Commons were insisting this week that the finance minister's last-minute intervention had saved the day on the vote on tuition fees. "Nothing can be done in government without his firm say-so," said one Brown-supporting MP. "The prime minister is no longer in as powerful position as he was."

However, Mr. Brown recognized that defeat on the tuition fees bill would have been catastrophic for Labour as a whole, ruining his own chances of succeeding Mr. Blair and keeping the party in power. "The tuition fees win was a team effort," says one of Mr. Brown's senior aides. "Both the prime minister and the [finance minster] have been talking about this hourly for some time."

Whatever the truth, it would be wrong to predict a kind of rift between the two men. Their mutual relationship has significantly improved in recent times. There are also important policy areas now that unite them. For the March 17 finance statement—the Budget—there is a need to keep public spending tight.

New Labour significantly increased public spending on schools and hospitals in 2002. But Mr. Brown now needs to keep spending in check to contain the significant increase in borrowing in recent years and to keep within his self-imposed fiscal rules. Mr. Blair, meanwhile, needs a tough spending round to be able to transfer resources from bureaucratic back-office areas in Whitehall departments to frontline services, where the public feels their impact.

On Europe, too, the two men's positions are converging. Mr. Blair continues to believe that—while maintaining its transatlantic links—the UK must remain at the heart of the European Union. A trilateral summit between Britain, France and Germany next month will underline how Mr. Blair increasingly sees foreign and defense policy through the prism of his relations with Jacques Chirac, president of France, and Gerhard Schröder, Germany's chancellor. Yesterday's announcement that the summit will bring together not only the three heads of government but also a range of ministers is further indication of the deepening three-way relationship.

Mr. Blair and Mr. Brown are also beginning to see eye to eye on the issue of British membership of the euro. In the Budget, Mr. Brown will give his latest report on how close Britain is to entry. But there are growing signs that Mr. Blair has made clear to Mr. Brown that he may be prepared to leave Number 10 without "doing the euro", which had long seemed to be a goal. That has opened up a greater possibility that the prime minister may hand over to Mr. Brown after the election.

When Mr. Blair goes to his country retreat this weekend, it will be with a sense of satisfaction. Lord Hutton's report is a landmark for him. The allegation that Mr. Blair lied to take Britain into war with Iraq has hung over him for seven months. Many in Britain are still unhappy with the failure to find weapons of mass destruction in Iraq. But, for Mr. Blair, a phase of the Iraq war ended this week.

A radical global leader, curbed

The brutality of Britain's political and media culture rarely fails to amaze outsiders. This is the country where the towering figure of Margaret Thatcher was toppled by her party on the eve of the first Gulf war. Now Tony Blair, a similarly strong-minded leader, has been put through a gruelling inquest into his decision to take Britain into a second war against Iraq.

Nowhere has the argument about whether the conflict was justified been more bitter than in the UK. The debate has been conducted not on the broad merits of the case but through the narrow prism of Lord Hutton's inquiry into events leading up to the suicide of David Kelly, the government's Iraq weapons expert.

The BBC's accusation, based on a reporter's conversation with Mr. Kelly, that the government falsified evidence in order to strengthen the case for war marked the nadir in relations between ministers and media critics.

Lord Hutton's emphatic exoneration of Mr. Blair, coupled with a narrow victory in the Commons this week for the prime minster's flagship policy of raising the amount students pay for higher education, will embolden him to aim for a third election victory in 2005 or 2006 and press on with his market-oriented public service reforms.

For the rest of the world—especially for Britain's European neighbours—it raises a broader question: will a reinvigorated Mr. Blair feel encouraged to play a bolder international role?

There is certainly a vacancy for a visionary leader in Europe. The European Union, on the eve of enlargement on May 1 from 15 to 25 member countries, is dangerously adrift. Its attempt to draw up a constitution has been derailed, its institutions are at war over economic management, and its divisions over Iraq have left unanswered questions about the transatlantic relationship.

Many hanker after the late 1980s and early 1990s when Jaques Delors, then president of the European Commission, along with François Mitterrand and Helmut Kohl, the leaders of France and Germany, were driving forward European intergration. Even Baroness Thatcher, for all her deep suspicion of the European enterprise, helped to create the single market.

Today, the commission is weak and, in a troubled economic climate, few EU leaders are prepared to look beyond their narrow national self-interest. Mr. Blair may be the most pre-European British leader since Edward Heath but he has been as hamstrung as other European statesmen in attempting to reconcile his aims with the greater good of the EU.

He has not lacked boldness in international affairs. His decision to stand shoulder to shoulder with President George W. Bush over Iraq will come to be seen as one of the defining moments of modern diplomacy. But he has failed in his aim of uniting the US and Europe in a new approach to international security that will couple US military might with a commitment to peacemaking and nation-building.

Mr. Blair arrived in 1997 determined to play a more central role in European affairs than his Conservative predecessors. Picture bicycling with fellow European leaders at the Amsterdam summit, he signed up for the Maastricht treaty's social chapter and set about proselytizing for his Third Way philosophy bridging the old left and right. It did not last long. A joint *Neue Mitte* initiative with Gerhard Schröder, the German chancellor, fell on stony ground, Other centre-left leaders were ousted. Mr. Blair often found centre-right leaders such as Spain's José María Aznar more congenial.

Euroscepticim at home curbed his ambitions: he failed to create conditions for a referendum on joining the euro. He greeted last month's failure to agree an EU constitution with apparent relief. An accord would have fuelled demands at home for an unwelcome referendum on that issue.

Relations with France's mercurial President Jacques Chirac, and to a lesser extent with Mr. Schröder, have been turbulent. Now he has another chance. Realising that the revived Franco-German motor will not be influential enough in an EU of 25 countries, they have invited Mr. Blair to join their club.

This three-way alliance will no doubt yield results: the three countries have already managed to get the EU's defence policy moving. It has all the hallmarks, though, of a defensive alliance between nations whose interest diverge in any important respects. Taking part in it will be the work of Blair the pragmatist rather than Blair the pragmatist rather than Blair the reborn visionary.

Tories, Even With a New Leader, See Little to Hope For

By Sarah Lyall

Stockton Heath, England—In their six-year struggle to prove that they are not a party of incompetent has-beens, Britain's sad-sack Conservative have nearly everything.

They have hired and fired party strategists and spokesmen. They have introduced and discarded new logos and slogans. They have switched leaders three times, most recently in October, when Michael Howard, a former home secretary, unsurped the chronically hapless Iain Duncan Smith.

But the party has yet to convince voters like Ian Talbott that it presents a plausible alternative to Prime Minister Tony Blair's Labor government, which swept into power 1997.

"Their leaders just aren't strong enough," said Mr. Talbott, 49, a lifelong Tory who looks back with rueful nostalgia on the days when Margaret Thatcher was prime minister and the party seemed to know what it was and what it wanted. Fed up, he voted for the Liberal Democrats in the last election. "The Conservatives don't seem to have many policies, do they?" Mr. Talbott said.

The Conservatives were the dominant force in British politics through much of the 20th century, producing political giants like Mrs. Thatcher, Stanley Baldwin and Winston Churchill, and setting the tone for Britain's view of itself and its place in the world. But after a long period market by damaging struggles for power, internal policy disputes on issues like Europe, an inability to capitalize on missteps by Mr. Blair's government and the steady usurpation of traditional Conservative positions by the newly centrist, even rightist Labor Party, the Conservatives are struggling to find their way.

Much of its problem has been in identifying a leader with the stature to take on Mr. Blair, who has a gravitas that is at times distinctly presidential. None of the post-Thatcher Tory leaders—John Major, lampooned as a colorless nonentity who tucked his shirt into his underpants; William Hague, who never overcame the handicap of looking like an infant Alfred E. Neuman; and Mr. Duncan Smith, who sounded as if he had a chicken bone permanently lodged in his throat—could effectively compete with Mr. Blair.

"Because they're such an elderly, narrowly based party, they've saddled themselves with a variety of incompetent leaders," Robert Harris, the author and political columnist, said in an interview.

But if Mr. Howard is supposed to engineer a Conservative renaissance, it has not happened. When asked if they would vote Conservative in a national election, only 30 percent or so of those surveyed in a recent poll said they would—a figure that has been largely unchanged in recent months, despite the drop in Mr. Blair's approval ratings over issues like crime, the Iraq war, and public services.

"The concerns facing the Conservative Party, I think, are wider and deeper than just the personality of the leader," Nick Gibb, a Conservative member of Parliament, wrote recently in The Guardian. "It goes to the whole direction of our policies. We have policies about hoe people can escape from state services and opt out, but don't really have an agenda or an understanding of what's actually wrong with our comprehensive schools and with out hospitals."

Meanwhile, the party has blundered itself into irrelevance in much of the country. It holds just 163 seats of the 659 in Parliament. It has no parliamentary presence in most of England's northern cities, including Liverpool, Newcastle, Leeds and Bradford. There is only one Tory member of Parliament from Scotland and none from Wales.

Stockton Health, a pretty village of small shops, big houses and pleasantly comfortable people, is classic Tory country. A suburb of Warrington, midway between Manchester and Liverpool, it lies in a parliamentary district that used to be solidly Conservative. But the party lost its seat to Labor by 191 votes in 1992. In the last election, in 2001, the Labor candidate romped in by a margin of 7,397 votes, out of 45,497 cast.

Part of the problem here, as elsewhere, is that Tories are old. Although the party says that its numbers are growing fast among college students, the average age of the country's 250,000 or so dues-paying members is more than 60. "I'm now 60, and I'm still one of the younger ones here," said Mike Haworth, former chairman of the Warrington South Conservative Association.

Many of those older Tories look at the 1980's as the high point of British Conservatism, and they see in Michael Howard, 62, a reassuring link to those days. He served as employment secretary and home secretary in Conservative governments.

But hi strengths—his experience, command of his material, tough debating skills and his natural appeal to the right based on his record—are weaknesses in today's altered political landscape. He represents the old guard at a time it is unclear what relevance the old guard has to the future of the party.

"Howard reminds people of the past," said Vernon Bogdanor, professor of government at Oxford University. "The present opposition is not credible because of the public's memories of the Conservative governments of the 1990's, and because they don't seem to have a coherent theme or set of alternatives."

Mr. Howard says he has changed, becoming more compassionate and a better listener. He has also promised to lead the party from the center and to put a stop to its internecine battles. But whether his message is heartfelt or strategic is anybody's guess.

In Stockton Heath, there is widespread confusion about who the party represents. "The party is trying to move forward and trying to modernize, but the voters—the people who always do vote for us—still revere Mrs. Thatcher, and hanker after the ruling party during its golden age," Mr. Haworth said. "We've got to keep our core supporters and also attract the new."

For Fiona Bruce, who was recently selected as the Tory candidate for the next parliamentary election, which is expected to take place in the next 18 months or so, there is little doubt that the party needs to roll with the times. "We need to communicate to people that the party has changed," she said. "Michael Howard is a listener. Just because he was a member of Thatcher's cabinet does not mean he hasn't accepted that we're a different kind of society, with different problems."

Although she sees herself as a natural Conservative, she is not a traditional Conservative candidate. She is not a man, for one thing—only 14 of the Tories in Parliament are women. Although Mrs. Thatcher broke new ground as prime minister, she did not start a trend. The Tory men in Parliament tend toward the old, "clubable" style—educated in fancy all-male boarding schools, speaking in plummy accents, wearing loud pin-striped suits.

In an effort to broaden the party's appeal, the Tories have begun to put forward non-traditional candidates, including, in several districts, openly gay men. In Wolverhampton South West, where the seat was once held by Enoch Powell, the famously anti-immigrant politician of the 1960's, the Tory candidate for the next election is a woman of Asian descent.

On a national level, Mr. Howard is trying to carve out policies that will distinguish his party from the government. But Mr. Blair's Labor Party has cleverly shifted right, usurping many traditional Conservative positions on issues like crime, social welfare, and immigration, and forcing the Tories to attack policies they once espoused.

"It's an odd situation, because both the liberals and the conservatives are attacking the government from left," Professor Bogdanor said. "There's no opposition from the right,"

Mr. Howard is also trying to press the government on issues where it is vulnerable. They include the unpopular war in Iraq, Mr. Blair's gingerly efforts to pursue closer ties with Europe while maintaining his special relationship with Europe-wary America, the sorry state of public services like health care and transportation and Labor's proposal to allow universities to raise undergraduate tuition.

Back in Stockton Health, Paul McIntyre, 60, another long-time Conservative voter who said at what had happen to the party, said the reasons for its decline were clear, although he was loath to explain why. Finally he did. "I don't think the party has a natural leader," he said. "There's nobody, excluding Tony Blair, who has the stature to lead this country."

A divided self:
A Survey of France

France has an identity problem. It needs to find the courage
to redefine itself, says John Andrews

"I HAVE heard and understood your call: that the republic should live, that the nation should reunite, that politics should change." On a cold evening in early May, Jacques Chirac found the right words for the moment. He had just been re-elected president of the French republic, with 82% of the vote, in a run-off with Jean-Marie Le Pen, the leader of the extreme-right National Front. Two weeks earlier, in the first round of the election, Mr Le Pen had eliminated the Socialist candidate (and incumbent prime minister), Lionel Jospin, from the contest. For left-leaning voters, Mr Chirac was clearly the lesser evil, so in the run-off they joined forces with Mr Chirac's centre-right to humble Mr Le Pen. Hence Mr Chirac's carefully chosen words: his victory may have been sweet, but it was hardly unqualified.

Doubtless that is why as prime minister of his "government of mission", Mr Chirac appointed Jean-Pierre Raffarin, a pudgy and amiable former senator from the Poitou-Charentes region. Mr Raffarin's motto is *la France d'en bas*, grassroots France, which is supposed to mean not only a government closer to the people but a government that comes from the people.

So six months later, is the nation "reunited"; has politics changed; is the republic "alive"? The answers are horribly muddled, mainly because the French themselves are muddled: over France's place in Europe, over the impact of globalisation and, at root, over what it means to be French. In their hearts they want precious little to change; in their heads they suspect change is inevitable.

If it is, their worry is not just what the change will be, but how and when it will come. On June 17th, the day after a parliamentary election in which Mr Chirac's supporters (most of them members of the newly assembled and aptly named Union for the Presidential Majority) won 399 of the National Assembly's 577 seats, the headline of the conservative *Le Figaro* proclaimed: "Five years to change France". Given that there will be no significant elections before the next presidential and parliamentary polls, due in 2007, the opportunity is there. But if change does come, many will not like it: the leftist *Libération*'s headline sarcastically predicted "A five-year sentence".

Whatever the headlines say, for most of France's 59m people not much has changed since the bout of elections in the spring. Around 9% of the workforce is still without a job; the rest troop off to their offices and factories just as before, cosseted by laws that protect them from quick lay-offs, provide them with one of the world's shortest working weeks—just 35 hours—and give them holiday entitlements Americans can only dream of. Meanwhile, their country remains as beautiful and seductive as ever, and the two-hour lunch is alive and well. Add trains that run fast and on time, modern motorways in good repair, and a med-

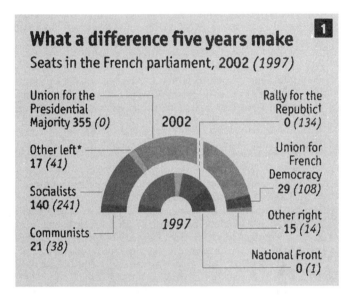

What a difference five years make

Seats in the French parliament, 2002 *(1997)*

Union for the Presidential Majority 355 *(0)* — 2002

Other left* 17 *(41)*

Socialists 140 *(241)*

Communists 21 *(38)*

1997

Rally for the Republic† 0 *(134)*

Union for French Democracy 29 *(108)*

Other right 15 *(14)*

National Front 0 *(1)*

*Includes Radical Party of the Left, 7 *(12)*; Greens, 3 *(7)*
†In 2002 it was absorbed into the Union for the Presidential Majority
Sources: French interior ministry; *The Economist*

ical system at the top of the World Health Organisation's international rankings. Surely the French have a right to feel pleased with themselves?

Not altogether superior

So why do they feel so insecure? Why do politicians, pundits and philosophers (a breed revered on French television) feel a need to bolster the country's collective morale by pointing out the deficiencies of the "Anglo-Saxon" way, be they fraudulent accountancy practices in America or decrepit private railways in Britain?

One reason is doubtless a dash of *Schadenfreude*. Within the lifetime of its senior citizens, France has been occupied by Germany, rescued by America and Britain, and then divested—bloodily in the case of Algeria and Indochina—of almost all its colonies. Since then English has become the world's common language (so much so that France's own politicians will now

Same bed, different dreams

Better to cohabit than be out in the cold

IS IT sensible for France to have a president from one side of the political divide and a government from the other? Olivier Schrameck, chief of staff to Mr Jospin from 1997 until May this year, devoted much of a recent book, "Matignon Rive Gauche, 1997–2001", to denouncing such "cohabitation" as a waste of energy and a recipe for immobility. Under cohabitation, the government would run the country, but the president, who retains traditional authority over defence and foreign policy (the constitutional authority is rather vague), would be tempted to snipe from the sidelines.

Yet French voters have forced such liaisons on their country three times since the birth of the Fifth Republic in 1958. The first time was when the left was defeated in the parliamentary elections of 1986. The Socialist François Mitterrand, who had been elected president in 1981, had to put up with a centre-right government led by Jacques Chirac as prime minister. In 1988 Mitterrand was re-elected president and dissolved parliament. In the ensuing elections the Socialists returned to power. In 1993, however, the left-wing government was voted out and Mitterrand had to cohabit with the centre-right once again, this time with Edouard Balladur as prime minister. Two years later this cohabitation ended with the election of Mr Chirac as president. But in 1997 Mr Chirac provoked the third cohabitation—much tenser than the first two—by calling early parliamentary elections that the left, led by Mr Jospin, won handsomely.

Such cohabitations could happen because the presidential term was for seven years and that of the lower house of parliament, the National Assembly, for five. But in future there will be less opportunity for these oddball relationships. In September 2000, after an arcane debate between constitutional experts and self-interested politicians, a bemused electorate decided in a referendum (in which only 30% cast a vote) that, beginning with the elections of 2002, the president would have the same five-year term as the parliament.

Since a president might die in office, or might dissolve parliament early, there could still be cohabitations in the future. But as long as President Chirac remains in the post, he is unlikely to call early elections again. For the record, he used to be a fierce opponent of reducing the seven-year presidential term, but changed his mind. His critics say he feared that voters in 2002 might think him too old for another seven-year term but young enough for five years (he will be 70 later this month). He himself claims he supported the change in order to modernise France.

speak it in public), America has turned into the world's only superpower and Hollywood has come to dominate the world's entertainment industry. For France, a country which believes that its revolution, just as much as America's, bears a universal message, these changes have not been easy to accept. Seeing someone else having a hard time provides some light relief.

But there are also more troubling reasons for this lack of confidence. One is the feeling, especially among industrialists and businessmen, that France's economic formula, involving higher taxes and social charges than in most of the countries its firms compete with, will not work forever. Indeed, it is already fraying at the edges. At the start of the 1990s, France ranked eighth in the world in terms of economic output per person, but by the end of the decade it had slipped to 18th.

The most important reason, however, is a lurking suspicion that French society itself is not working. Go back to the first round of the presidential election on April 21st, with its 16 candidates, and ask a few simple questions. Why did Mr Jospin, arguably France's most effective prime minister in the 44 years of the Fifth Republic, get only 16.2% of the vote? Why, in that round, did Mr Chirac get only 19.9%, the lowest ever for an incumbent president? Why did 13 no-hoper candidates gather up 47% of the vote between them? And why did a record 28.4% of the electorate abstain? Most bothersome of all, why did Mr Le Pen, ostracised throughout his 40-odd years in politics, win 16.9% of the vote and so pass through to the second round?

There are plenty of superficial answers: Mr Jospin lacked charm; Mr Chirac was stained by alleged corruption; the electorate felt free to indulge its whims because it assumed that a runoff between Messrs Jospin and Chirac was pre-ordained; and Mr Le Pen is a brilliant orator. But there is a more fundamental explanation. As one French journalist, Philippe Manière, puts it in a recent book, the first-round result was "the vengeance of the people".

A question of colour, a matter of faith

France must face up to its immigrant problems

JEAN-MARIE LE PEN, at ease in his drawing room, waves an arm as if to state the obvious: "The greatest challenge is demographic. The countries of the north—the world of the white man, or let's say the non-black world—have an ageing population. They are rich, and they are facing a third world of 5 billion people, maybe more tomorrow, who are very young and dynamic. This dynamism will be translated into immigration."

Outside the room, the guard-dogs are asleep. In the urban plain below the Le Pen mansion (inherited from a political admirer) in Saint-Cloud, the Paris evening rush-hour is under way. The National Front leader goes on: "The rise of Islam is more the result of its youth and dynamism than its religious values. It's a demographic problem which will lead to immigration, whose consequences could lead, if nothing is done, to the submersion of our country, our people, our civilisation... No government, whether by ideology or by blindness, has realised the danger."

France's far-right bogeyman gained second place in the presidential election by saying what few other politicians would either want to or dare to: that the French republic has too many immigrants, who in turn have too many children. But that is putting it politely. What the National Front and the National Republican Movement, its rival on the extreme right, really mean is that France has too many inhabitants who are black, brown and Muslim. And lots of them are not immigrants at all, but were born in France and are French citizens.

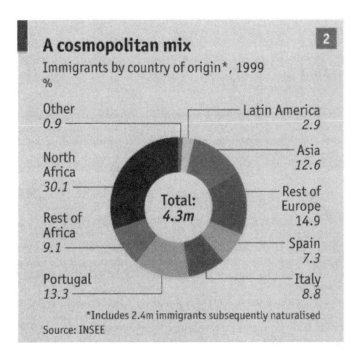

A cosmopolitan mix

Immigrants by country of origin*, 1999
%

Other 0.9
Latin America 2.9
North Africa 30.1
Asia 12.6
Rest of Africa 9.1
Rest of Europe 14.9
Portugal 13.3
Spain 7.3
Italy 8.8

Total: 4.3m

*Includes 2.4m immigrants subsequently naturalised
Source: INSEE

There are plenty of other politicians who have dabbled in the politics of race. Governments of the right have over the years enacted increasingly strong laws to restrict immigration, and governments of the left have for the most part accepted them. Mr Chirac, definitely not a racist himself, found it useful in the 1988 presidential election campaign to refer to the "odours" of immigrant cooking.

What makes Mr Le Pen different is that he has consistently preached the same xenophobic message ever since he entered politics. He became France's youngest member of parliament in 1956, at the age of 27, and first stood for the presidency in 1974. France's ills, he has said all along, are the fault of foreigners, including fellow members of the European Union. The remedy is to keep out foreigners, produce more French children, build more prisons, cut taxes and leave the EU.

The question is why that message suddenly found more resonance with the voters in last spring's presidential election than ever before in Mr Le Pen's political career. Mr Le Pen's previous best score was 14.4% in the first round in 1988, and the only time his party has ever gained more than one seat in the National Assembly was in 1986, when the elections, exceptionally, were held by proportional representation.

The answer is surely not that nearly a fifth of the voters suddenly decided that Mr Le Pen's programme made practical sense, nor that all those who cast their ballot for him are anti-Semitic fascists (Mr Le Pen has described the gas chambers as a "detail" of the second world war, and thinks that Maurice Pa-

pon, the Vichy official who in the late 1990s was eventually convicted for crimes against humanity, was innocent). More likely, the voters wanted to jog the governing elite into action. As a former Socialist prime minister, Laurent Fabius, once said, "Le Pen poses good questions and offers bad solutions."

So what might a good solution look like? A useful start would be, literally, to enumerate France's problems. Malek Boutih, the French-born son of Algerian immigrants and now the president of SOS-Racisme, an anti-racism organisation, argued in a recent book that "France is wrong not to publish, as other countries like America do, statistics of criminality by social category, age, place, type of city development and so on. It is even more wrong not to establish a public debate on the question, as though the French are so irrational that they cannot calmly consider the reality of their problems."

Crime matters

But should that mean a debate on crime as well? Polls before the election showed that the subject topped the list of their concerns, ahead of the state of the economy or pensions or even unemployment. Whether crime in France is worse than in other countries is a moot point: criminal statistics are hard to compare, and although one study showed that France in 2000 had proportionately more crimes than America, other studies suggest that it did a little better than, say, Germany or Belgium. However, what matters to French people is what happens in France.

Or more precisely, what they think is happening. Nicolas Sarkozy, the interior minister, has won plaudits for not only identifying crime as a serious problem but being seen to be doing something about it. Barely a week goes by without him being photographed with a smiling collection of police or gendarmes. Mr Sarkozy has secured the money to add another 6,500 police to the 146,000 he took over from his predecessor. And Mr Raffarin has appointed a junior minister in the justice ministry specifically to supervise a building programme that will add 11,000 prison places to the 47,000 already occupied.

In terms of public perception, such measures will help. One poll in September found that the proportion of those questioned who felt they were "often" at risk of crime was 49%—shockingly high in absolute terms but actually slightly less than in the autumn of last year. Mr Sarkozy has been able to trumpet a reduction in reported crime, by 4.5% in August compared with a year earlier, the first such fall for five years. In Paris, where the tourist industry has long complained about the plague of pickpockets, the fall was 11%.

Whether the momentum can be sustained is another matter. In the country that produced the Declaration of Human Rights (in 1789, a satisfying two years before America's Bill of Rights), the new enthusiasm for "zero tolerance" becomes hard to swallow when it means giving the authorities greater powers of arrest and punishment.

According to critics, many of them well placed in the judiciary and the media, the government is eroding the presumption of innocence (never particularly robust in France, which has no Anglo-Saxon protection of *habeas corpus*); it casually treats many young offenders as though they were adults; and it is callously cracking down on France's most marginal residents, from Romanian beggars to African prostitutes. In other words, the critics allege that the Raffarin government—and Mr Sarkozy in particular—is doing the work of Mr Le Pen for him.

Press Mr Boutih on whether criminal statistics should include a breakdown by race or religion, and he immediately says no: "I remain convinced that ethnic origin is less relevant than the level of education and social status." He has a point: a well-educated Arab or black Frenchman with a decent job is unlikely to turn to petty drug-dealing or car-stealing. The trouble, according to Tahar Ben Jelloun, a Moroccan who is one of France's finest writers, is that only 4% of the children of immigrants get to university, compared with 25% of their native contemporaries.

Our ancestors the Gauls

But the main reason for Mr Boutih's resistance is that to collect information by race or religion would offend the very French concept of "republican values", because it would discriminate between citizens rather than treat them as equal. France makes no allowance for cultural differences: "our ancestors the Gauls" applies to schoolchildren of every hue. In this secular republic, the idea of collecting racial and religious statistics is a virtual taboo across the whole of the political spectrum. Such statistics, it is feared, will lead France along the Anglo-Saxon road of "communautarisme" (in which the idea of separate communities within the country as a whole is acceptable). In the words of the constitution, the French republic is indivisible, and having separate communities is seen as automatically leading to divisions.

Yet the sad reality is that France's race relations are no better than anyone else's. Arab and black minorities are as much as ever excluded from the mainstream. In opinion polls in the late 1990s, two-fifths of the respondents admitted to being at least "a little bit" racist (more than in any other European Union country except Belgium), and just over half thought there were "too many Arabs" in France.

The lack of solid figures leads to the sort of guesswork that plays into the far-right's hands. The state statistics office, INSEE, reckons that in 1999 (the year of the most recent census) the total number of foreign-born residents in metropolitan France, including 2.4m who have acquired French nationality, was 4.3m, or 7.4% of the metropolitan population of 58.5m. Of these, 1.3m had come from Algeria, Morocco and Tunisia. But the official figures end with that breakdown by country of origin.

The best estimate for the religious breakdown that INSEE is not allowed to publish comes from a scholarly report presented to the prime minister two years ago by the High Council for Integration, a committee of academics and experts. The report reckoned that France is home to 4m–5m Muslims—defined by culture rather than religious observance—of whom up to half have French nationality. Of the Muslim total, almost 3m are of North African origin or ancestry, with 1.5m from Algeria, 1m from Morocco and the rest from Tunisia. Of the other Muslims, Turks probably number 350,000, sub-Saharan Africans about 250,000, and assorted Middle Easterners (Iranians and Kurds, as well as Arabs) the remainder. So France's Muslims make up at most one in 12 of the population—and its Arabs one in 20.

Yet the media keep repeating that there are at least 6m Arabs in France, and quite possibly as many as 8m, who are regularly accused of crime, vandalism, the abuse of social services and other wrongdoings. It is easy for the elite and the comfortable middle classes to dismiss Mr Le Pen's view of the world, but less so for those—especially *les petits blancs* (poor whites)—who live in crime-ridden working-class neighbourhoods. According to the analysts, in the first round of the presidential election Mr Le Pen won the support of only 8% of those with a college education, but 30% of blue-collar voters and 38% of the unemployed.

Chronic or curable?

Pessimists argue that the situation will get worse before it gets better. France's high rate of unemployment is not about to tumble overnight. Nor are the high-rise public housing blocks built from the 1950s to the 1970s in the *banlieue*, or suburbs, of most French towns. At the time, they were intended to provide affordable housing to the influx of workers from the countryside and from the colonies or ex-colonies. Now they have all too often become virtual ghettoes, each storey dotted with satellite dishes pointed towards the television stations of the Maghreb. But the problem extends far beyond the *banlieue*. The same combination of poverty, race and social exclusion can be found in the medieval villages of Provence, or in some down-at-heel parts of Paris such as the 10th or 19th *arrondissements*.

The passage of time, say the pessimists, is not healing cultural rifts but making them worse. The generation of immigrants from the Maghreb were often illiterate peasants, keen to work hard in a country whose language they could barely understand. By contrast, their children, and now their children's children, are French-born and French-educated, and have lost respect for their immigrant parents or grandparents. That has caused a loss of parental authority, and often a multitude of behavioural problems in the disciplined world of French schools.

How French can you get?

Moreover, being French-born and French-educated does not mean that an Abdel-Karim or a Samira will be treated the same as a Jean-Pierre or a Marianne. To be white and born in France of French parents and grandparents means you are a *Français de souche*—of "French stock". But to be born in France of Arab ancestry makes you a *beur*, a word which for most Arab Frenchmen has no pejorative undertone (there is, for example, the Beur-FM radio station). The word is a kind of inversion of the word *Arabe*, part of an argot of inversion called *verlan* (*l'envers*, or back-to-front), which turns *français* into *cefran* and *café* into *féca*. This is undoubtedly of linguistic interest, but the language is also a sign of exclusion, sometimes self-imposed. *Beur* is now so universal that the new word among the *beurs* is *rebeu*, a *verlan* of a *verlan*.

How to end that exclusion? In America the answer might be affirmative action or positive discrimination, but in France such notions are seen as a threat to a republic which presumes its citizens to be free, equal and brotherly to begin with. When Sciences-Po, an elite university, last year began a special entry programme for a handful of bright students from the "zones of priority education" in the *banlieue* around the cities of Paris and Nancy, current and former students reacted with horror: their beloved meritocratic institution was slipping down the Anglo-Saxon slope.

Mr Boutih understands the gap between republican theory and everyday practice all too well: "The republican model is not a natural one. It exists through political will. Communautarisme is the natural model." So why not adopt the natural one instead? "Because society will explode from within. Each community will define itself against another, as in the United States."

Arguably, that process is already under way. In October last year, at a soccer match in Paris between France and Algeria, young *beurs* greeted the French national anthem with a storm of whistles and later invaded the pitch, brandishing Algerian flags. Young *beurs* are increasingly turning to Islam, not so much as a faith but as a symbol of identity: they fast during the month of Ramadan, insist on religiously correct food in their school canteens and stay at home to mark religious holidays.

A small minority go a lot further, falling under the influence of extremist imams from the Gulf or North Africa. In their fight to dismantle al-Qaeda, Europe's and America's intelligence services have uncovered a disturbing number of French suspects, not least Zacarias Moussaoui, currently on trial in America for his alleged role in the September 11th attacks on America last year. And a number of young *beur* layabouts have used the excuse of the Arab-Israeli conflict to indulge in anti-Jewish violence and vandalism (at over 600,000, France's Jewish minority is Europe's largest).

The *Français de souche* are accomplices in this process, not just in the April 21st vote for Mr Le Pen or in their reluctance to offer Arabs (and blacks) the same job prospects as whites, but also in the open antagonism some of them display towards the Arabs in their midst. To justify their stance, they quote the inferior status of Muslim women, or the dreadful gang-rapes of "easy" Muslim girls that some Muslim boys regard as a rite of passage. It is no accident that Oriana Fallaci's book "The Rage and the Pride", an extremist tirade against Muslims in general and Arabs in particular, spent so many weeks on this year's French bestseller list.

Could the pessimists be wrong? Back in 1998, France rejoiced in the World Cup victory of a French soccer team starring plenty of blacks and *beurs* (including the incomparable Zinedine Zidane, born of Algerian parents in the Marseilles *banlieue*). Sami Naïr, an Algerian-born member of the European Parlia-

ment and formerly an adviser on immigration to the Jospin government, points out that in an earlier wave of immigration into France, in the early part of the 20th century, Roman Catholics from Italy and Poland were accused of "trying to impose religion on our secular state". Yet in the end, he says, the discrimination fades and the newcomers' descendants end up as *Français de souche*: "I think it will be solved in a generation."

Yet there is an obvious difference between the present wave of migrants and previous waves: the *beurs* and their parents are the first minority that can be physically distinguished from the *Français de souche*. Their assimilation cannot be achieved by fading into the background. Instead, Mr Naïr proposes a pact: the government must live up to the values of the republic when dealing with its Arabs—and the *beurs* must accept the duties that go with them, including equality of the sexes. That might be easier if the economy could deliver more jobs.

A new kind of solidarity

France needs more jobs and less state. The two are not unconnected

NOW is not a good time to be prime minister of France, and Jean-Pierre Raffarin knows it only too well. The world economy is in the doldrums, and the French economy is becalmed with it; investor confidence is low; and the trade unions are restive. Last month, for example, thousands of public-sector workers (80,000 according to the unions; 40,000 according to the police) marched through the centre of Paris to defend their privileges as public servants or agents of the state, and to denounce modest plans for privatisation. On the same day, INSEE, the government statistical office, announced that economic growth for this year was now likely to be only 1%, compared with its forecast in June of 1.4% (and the previous government's self-serving prediction of 2.5% before the elections).

If INSEE is right, then the budget for next year presented in October by the finance minister, Francis Mer, becomes an exercise in fiction. It assumes growth of 1.2% this year and 2.5% next, and a budget deficit of 2.6% of GDP. Instead, the deficit could well break through the 3% limit set by the European Union in its collective quest for economic stability. In other words, crisis looms: the EU will want French belts to be tightened, whereas the voters, worried about their jobs and mortgages, want them loosened.

Engraved in the country's political consciousness is the memory of 1995, the last time a centre-right president was elected with a centre-right majority in parliament. The prime minister of the day was the intellectually brilliant but aloof Alain Juppé; he was determined that France should qualify for membership of the euro zone, which meant keeping the franc closely in line with the D-mark while simultaneously cutting the budget deficit (then running at 5% of GDP). This he hoped to do by reforming the public sector, which would restrain public spending. Instead, he saw hundreds of thousands of public-sector workers taking to the streets in a wave of protests and strikes, with the sympathy of most of the population. Two years later, when President Chirac rashly called an early general election to obtain a popular mandate for the EU's single currency, the right was swept from power.

Not surprisingly, Mr Raffarin and his colleagues are keen to prevent history repeating itself. Their strategy is to tread softly, even to speak softly. In opposition, the right accused Lionel Jospin of "immobility". Now the bosses' association, Medef (Mouvement des Entreprises de France), lays the same charge

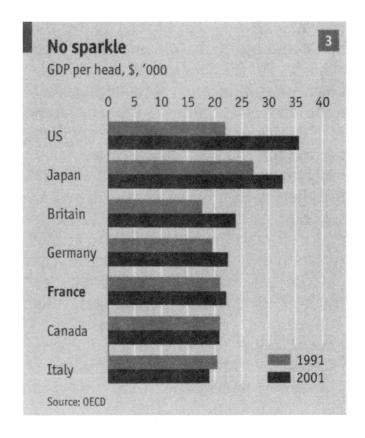

No sparkle

GDP per head, $, '000

Source: OECD

against Mr Raffarin: it accuses him of being too timid in dealing with the consequences of the 35-hour working week, introduced by Mr Jospin (who cut it from 39 hours with no loss of pay), or with the previous government's "Law on Social Modernisation" (which makes it harder than ever for employers to fire people, thus discouraging them from hiring in the first place). The bosses fear that if Mr Raffarin shows the same timidity in other areas, notably slimming down the civil service and reforming pensions, the country will continue its slide down the international scale of GDP per person.

Just as this is a bad time for Mr Raffarin to be prime minister, the previous period was a good time for Mr Jospin. The world economy, powered by America and its dotcom infatuation, was growing strongly, and France, the world's fifth-biggest exporter, reaped the benefits. A series of partial privatisations (or "openings of capital", in the words of Mr Jospin, an ex-Trotskyist well aware of the need to placate the Communists in his coalition) helped to keep the country's finances in excellent shape. Inflation, the public debt and the budget deficit were all low, and economic growth in 1998–2000 averaged 3.3% a year. Successive finance ministers basked in the plaudits of the International Monetary Fund and the OECD.

Growing jobs

All this may have encouraged Mr Jospin to believe that full employment had become a realistic target for France. Certainly a report in December 2000 by Jean Pisani-Ferry, of the Council of Economic Analysis, a body of experts set up by Mr Jospin to give him independent advice, seemed to be suggesting as much. The report noted that in the four years from the start of 1997 France had created 1.6m jobs, "twice as many as during the 1960s and ten times the number created between 1974 and 1996". The drop in the jobless, it said, was "unprecedented".

The government was keen to take the credit. In the run-up to this year's elections, it claimed that the 35-hour week, which came into effect in February 2000 for firms with more than 20 employees (it has yet to be fully applied to small firms), had already created 400,000 jobs. The idea was that to compensate for the shorter week, bosses would have to take on more employees, and could be encouraged to do so through temporary relief on their payroll taxes. The government noted, too, that 320,000 young people had found work since 1997 through the youth employment scheme, under which young people were given five-year contracts in the public sector, for example as school playground assistants or as guards at railway stations and other public buildings. At the beginning of 2001 the government had also taken steps to lessen the poverty trap, in which recipients of state benefits lose out if they take a low-paid job.

A success of sorts

But how much of the credit for all these extra jobs did the Jospin government really deserve? On closer scrutiny, the Pisani-Ferry report reads less like a congratulatory pat on the government's back and more like a warning that things must change. For a start, much of the job creation was simply the result of economic growth. Further, full employment was defined as a jobless rate of 5% or less of the workforce, a rate that in happier days for the world economy would have been considered fairly disastrous in, say, Japan or Singapore. The report also argued that to achieve this target by 2010, the country would have to create at least 300,000 new jobs a year, perhaps as many as 400,000.

That, however, would require large-scale liberalisation, of the sort introduced by Margaret Thatcher, Britain's radical prime minister of the 1980s—and French vested interests are most unlikely to allow that to happen. Besides, there is little sign of a French Lady Thatcher emerging. Only Alain Madelin, of the Liberal Democrats, currently speaks a Thatcherite language of free markets and a minimalist state, and he won a mere 3.9% of the vote on April 21st.

All this puts a different perspective on the labour-market "success" of the Jospin term. True, unemployment fell from the 12.2% of the workforce inherited from the right in 1997, but only

to 9%, getting on for twice as much as in Britain or America—at a time when the economy was booming and employers had jobs they could not fill. The economists concluded that 9%, or a smidgen less, was—and is—France's "structural" rate of unemployment, which can be reduced only by changing the make-up of the economy.

Go to the lovely Place du Capitole in Toulouse, or ride the subway system in Lyons, or watch a game of street-soccer in a Marseilles housing estate, and the economic jargon translates into bored young men whiling away their days doing nothing in particular: no wonder many of them trade drugs to supplement their meagre state benefits. People over 25 receive the RMI (*revenu minimum d'insertion*), created in 1988 to provide a "minimum income for inclusion in society". For a single man with no dependants, this amounts to €406 ($405) a month. In a land of plenty, some 1m of France's 24m households rely on the income of the country's 2.2m *eremistes*.

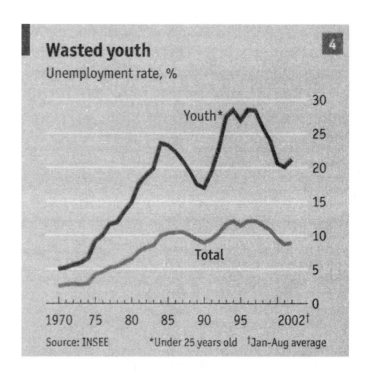

Wasted youth
Unemployment rate, %

Youth*

Total

1970 75 80 85 90 95 2002†

Source: INSEE   *Under 25 years old   †Jan-Aug average

That is a waste of young energy and talent; but a similar waste goes on at the other end of the age range too. In Antibes, a town on the Côte d'Azur sandwiched between Cannes and Nice, men in their 50s and 60s go down to the seafront each afternoon to play *boules*, as do thousands of other perfectly healthy contemporaries throughout the country (albeit perhaps in less pleasant surroundings). In most other industrialised countries, they would still be toiling at the office desk or on the factory floor; in France, they are enjoying a comfortable retirement.

In other words, France's unemployment rate, already bad enough by international standards, is even worse than it looks. In Switzerland, more than 70% of the 55–64 age group are in the labour market; in Japan two-thirds; and in Britain just over half. The average for the OECD group of rich countries is 51%. But in France the share is a mere 37%.

So what, you might say with a Gallic shrug. One of France's many attractive features is that its people work to live, not the other way round (which is what critics say is wrong with the Anglo-Saxon model). Patrick Artus, the chief economist of the Caisse de Dépôts et Consignations, a venerable state-owned bank, makes a joke of it: "No one wants to increase the [labour-market] participation rate except economists over the age of 55.

As the Pisani-Ferry report notes: "Inactivity was viewed in France for many years as an alternative to unemployment." In other words, the government encouraged mothers to stay at home and workers over 50 to retire. This was particularly true for the Mitterrand era of the 1980s and early 90s: legislation to protect workers' rights and the proliferation of payroll charges created an exceptionally illiquid labour market. As a result, *les trentes glorieuses* (the 30 years from 1945 to 1975 when the economy boomed and jobs were there for the taking) were followed by a quarter-century in which high unemployment, especially among the young, became part of the economic landscape.

Embracing business

Could the Raffarin government begin to turn things round? Not in the short term, but at least Mr Raffarin and his team have understood a vital precondition: it is business that must create the jobs of the future, not government. The daily *Le Figaro* went to the trouble of analysing the words used by Mr Raffarin in a recent television programme about his future plans, and found that the second most frequent subject on his lips was "*entreprise*" (business)—surpassed only by the word "France". Compared with Mr Jospin, who spent little time with business bosses during his five-year tenure, Mr Raffarin's interest in *entreprise* seems promising. On the other hand, words are not the same as deeds. For all its alleged antipathy to business, the Jospin government privatised far more of French industry than its centre-right predecessors had done. Mr Raffarin will have to show that he can do better than Mr Jospin.

In part, this will involve more privatisation. Amazingly, there are still around 1,500 companies—compared with 3,500 in 1986—in which the state has a controlling share. In theory, most of the icons of French industry are up for grabs—France Telecom, Air France and even the hitherto sacrosanct Electricité de France (EDF) and Gaz de France (GDF). But at least three things could get in the way.

One is a disinclination on the part of the government to let key industries such as electricity escape from its control, which means that in practice only minority stakes will be sold; a second is union opposition to any loss of pension and other privileges if control goes to the private sector; and the third is the abysmal state of the stockmarket. Air France, 54% owned by the state, may—when market conditions eventually suit the government—be a safe enough bet to fly further into private ownership; France Telecom, 55.5% owned by the state, risks a flop thanks to its debt of around €70 billion.

But the main challenge for Mr Raffarin goes far beyond selling the family silver: it involves lightening the government's hold on the economy in general and the private sector in particular. Government spending accounts for over 53% of GDP, way above the OECD average of 38%. A steeply progressive system of income tax, for example, can claim as much as 60% of an individual's pay-packet, and even the moderately rich have to pay a wealth tax. Virtually every French citizen gripes about taxes or social charges. Admittedly, because of various exemptions, only half of all wage-earners have to pay income tax; the trouble is that the non-paying half are still subject to a variety of payroll charges that make no allowances for income differentials. Value-added tax, levied at 19.6%, also has to be paid by rich and poor alike.

Taxes on business were reduced by the Jospin government, but employers complain that heavy payroll charges still make it hard for them to compete internationally. Medef has calculated that the Jospin government's measures, if they had been fully implemented by their 2003 deadline (in fact some changes will be made), would still have left France bottom out of 14 EU countries. For example, for every €100 an employee takes home, a French employer would still have had to shell out €288, compared with €227 for a German boss and €166 for a British one. Only a Belgian employer would pay more.

Individual taxpayers who are rich and mobile enough vote with their feet. For instance, Laetitia Casta, a model whose face now graces the country's stamps as the national figurehead, Marianne, lives for the most part outside the country; so do virtually all of the French soccer team who won the World Cup for France in 1998 (and lost it so ingloriously in 2002). It is said that up to 300,000 French people now live in south-east England, where the taxes are lower. There is clear evidence that fewer foreigners want to set up business in France, and more French people want to shift their investment abroad.

The government seems to have accepted the need to act. During his election campaign, President Chirac promised to cut income tax by 5% this year and by 30% over his five-year term; to reduce bureaucracy; and to create a million new businesses. Last month Mr Raffarin and his minister for small and medium-sized businesses, Renaud Dutreil, announced that from next autumn the charge for setting up a limited-liability company will be cut from €7,500 to just €1; the company will be able to operate from the entrepreneur's home for up to five years, instead of two (which still raises the question why this kind of restriction should be imposed at all); the tax-exemption limit for capital gains will rise by a third or more; and payment of the first year's social charges can be spread over five years.

French entrepreneurs will be grateful for any lightening of their load. Two years ago the OECD found that France had more business red tape than any other member, and more barriers to entrepreneurs than all but Italy. For example, simply to register a company could take four months.

Let 1m flowers bloom

Will Mr Dutreil's measures meet Mr Chirac's target for 1m new businesses by the next election? At present more than 170,000 companies are created each year, so another 30,000 a year does not look out of the question. It is not as though the country lacked talent and initiative: the Côte d'Azur science park of Sophia-Antipolis is full of high-technology start-ups and foreign investment.

The question is whether France wants that business badly enough. Back in 1925, an American president, Calvin Coolidge, famously declared: "The chief business of the American people is business." It is hard to imagine a French politician ever embracing that sentiment on behalf of his countrymen. In an opinion poll last year, 56% of the respondents said their idea of France was "a country of solidarity and social justice".

They are deluding themselves. According to Timothy Smith, a Canadian historian who specialises in French social policy, "a truly solidaristic society is one which pays the price for its solidarity in the here and now, instead of leaving the bill for future generations, instead of taking raises and an extra month of paid vacation (which is the consequence of the shift from the 39-hour to the 35-hour week) or an expensive pension at 55 years of age, on the backs of 2m-3m unemployed people—most of them under the age of 40." But in France that sort of solidarity still seems a long way off.

The French exception

From agriculture to Europe, France gets away with doing its own thing

THE vineyards bake in the sun of Provence; vast cornfields stretch golden across the plains of Picardy; in Brittany the cattle slowly munch their way from one deep green field to another; in the Dordogne the geese are having their livers fattened for the world's best foie gras. All this is *la France profonde*, that entrancing country of picturesque villages and revered cuisine. No wonder France is by far the world's most popular tourist destination for foreigners. And no wonder the French themselves, not least President Chirac, are determined to preserve it.

Yet the pastoral idyll is in part a myth. The country towns are surrounded by hypermarkets and car-lots; the villages have garish kiosks dispensing videos; and, all too often, the fields and rivers are polluted with pesticides. Meanwhile, the true *paysans* (the word translates better as "country folk" rather than "peasants") are dwindling in number: down to 627,000 in the 1999 census, a drop of 38% on ten years earlier. Their place has been taken by the modern barons of industrialised agriculture (the average farm now is half as large again as in 1988); or the workers who commute to the nearest town; or the Parisians and foreigners who have bought second homes in the country.

Rus in urbe

So why is the myth so important? The answer is a mix of nostalgia, culture and economic self-interest. Only two generations ago, agriculture accounted for one-third of the nation's workforce, which explains why even the most confirmed city types usually still have some rural connection. Mr Chirac once said: "The farmers are the gardeners of our country and the guardians of our memory." But there is rather more to it than gardening: helped by an EU Common Agricultural Policy designed with French farmers in mind, France has become the world's fourth-biggest producer of cereals and meat and pockets a quarter of the CAP's funds.

That does not please José Bové, the pipe-smoking, moustachioed leader of the Confédération Paysanne. Mr Bové, a former student activist turned occasional goat-cheese maker, is demanding a more literal interpretation of the myth. He has become a popular hero by attacking globalisation and the CAP for industrialising agriculture at the expense of the small farmer. Two years ago, when he appeared in court for trashing the site for a new McDonalds restaurant, 30,000 demonstrators gathered in his support. He was briefly imprisoned earlier this year.

By contrast, the politicians think the myth is best served by holding on to the status quo. When the European Commission earlier this year proposed replacing production subsidies for farmers with direct payments geared to their care for the environment, Hervé Gaymard, France's agriculture minister, led the counter-attack. Gathering the signatures of six other EU agriculture ministers, Mr Gaymard sent a letter to several European newspapers, noting: "For us, agricultural products are more than marketable goods; they are the fruit of a love of an occupation and of the land, which has been developed over many generations… For us, farmers must not become the 'variable adjustment' of a dehumanised and standardised world."

Cri de coeur or hypocritical power politics? Perhaps a bit of both. Mr Gaymard's argument is that the CAP has served Europe well, and that its reform should not be rushed, but should involve a debate going back to first principles. Then again, the letter was published on September 24th, to coincide with a meeting of agriculture ministers in Brussels. Moreover, it guaranteed a French victory: the signatories represented a minority big enough to defeat not just the commission's plans but also the wish of several northern countries, particularly Britain, to renegotiate the CAP before the present agreement on the EU's finances expires at the end of 2006.

What kind of Europe?

All this, say the critics, is proof that France, a founder member of the EU, sees it only as a vehicle for its own national interests. But that hardly seems a damning verdict. After all, why join a club if it does not serve your interests? For France, the European club has always served two purposes: to ensure peace with Germany after three wars within a century; and to provide a counterweight to America's power.

Still, the French seem to have a way of bending the club rules to their advantage. For example, back in 1965, when the France of President De Gaulle boycotted Europe's institutions for six months, its "empty chair" policy successfully checked Europe's supranational course, guaranteeing each nation the right to a veto if its vital interests were at stake. And in the early 1990s France held the Uruguay Round of trade negotiations hostage until it won the right to a "cultural exception", allowing it, in effect, to subsidise French films and discriminate against American ones.

In the same vein, Mr Raffarin's finance minister, Francis Mer, blithely told his EU colleagues last June that their "Stability and Growth Pact", a 1997 accord under which all countries had pledged to balance their public-sector budgets by 2004, was "not set in stone." The commission and the other EU members agreed, giving France until 2006 to meet the deadline. But the medium-term budget plans which Mr Mer announced in September show that France will still have a 1% deficit in 2006, prompting open criticism by the commission. Mr Mer seemed unfazed. After a meeting with his EU counterparts last month, he declared: "We decided there were other priorities for France—for instance, increased military spending. Other countries have not taken this kind of decision, but we are still in a Europe where budgetary policy and political decisions are under national control."

It sounds rather like a Europe in which France remains an independent nation-state, choosing for itself when and how to cooperate with the rest of the club. That is one reason why the tie with Gerhard Schröder's federalist-minded Germany has come under strain. However, the tie still holds: last month in Brussels, Mr Chirac, outmanoeuvring—and enraging—Britain's prime minister, Tony Blair, persuaded Mr Schröder that the CAP should remain unchanged until 2006.

Back home, François Bayrou, leader of the Union for French Democracy and a member of the European Parliament, is one of very few French politicians to share the Belgian, Italian or German vision of a powerfully supranational EU. Other visions for the future of the EU, from a confederation of nation-states to a "hard core" of "the willing and the able", all have one thing in common: in essence, France will retain its freedom of action and Europe will serve France's purpose. How else could De Gaulle and his political descendants, including Mr Chirac, have accepted the notion of a communal Europe? Nor are such attitudes confined to Gaullists: the Socialists' François Mitterrand may

High and mighty

France's elite is too clever by half

ALL nations—even those who once believed in Marx—have their elites, so why should France be any different? Philippe Méchet, a well-known opinion pollster, jokes: "We're a very royalist country, and we killed the king. So now we've monarchised the republic."

You can see his point. The American president lives in the White House, but the French president lives in the Elysée Palace, a choice of noun that conjures up a whole retinue of courtiers and uniformed flunkies. Indeed, when the Socialist François Mitterrand inhabited the Elysée, he lavished so much public money on grand schemes for the capital and its monuments that he was often compared to Louis XIV, the "Sun King".

Take the analogy a touch further and you have a modern nobility, products of the *grandes écoles*, a handful of universities—such as Sciences-Po in Paris or the Polytechnique just south of the capital—that are acknowledged to be centres of excellence. In particular, you have the *énarques*, graduates of the Ecole Nationale d'administration (ENA), a postgraduate school established by De Gaulle in 1945 to train a civil service untarnished by the Vichy regime's collaboration with the Nazis.

It has long been fashionable, even among *énarques*, to criticise ENA as being too elitist for the national good. Recruiting through fiercely competitive written and oral exams, the school has an intake of just 120 students a year for its 27-month-long curriculum. Multiply that by the number of years since ENA was established, allow for some natural wastage, and you get a total figure for living *énarques* of perhaps 5,000.

Monarchs of all they survey

That elite, minuscule compared with the massed alumni of Britain's Oxbridge or America's Ivy League, commands most of what matters in France. Mr Chirac is an *énarque*, as is Mr Jospin (but not Mr Raffarin); so too the head of the employers' association, Ernest-Antoine Seillière, and many of the bosses of leading banks and businesses, from Jean Peyrelevade of Crédit Lyonnais to Jean-Cyril Spinetta of Air France.

Is this a good or a bad thing? It depends how you look at it. As one *énarque* at the finance ministry says scathingly, "*Énarques* are pretty smart individually, and pretty dumb collectively." ENA's graduates can hardly help being clever: the meritocratic recruitment process is designed to draw bright children from humble backgrounds into the elite (one example is Hervé Geymard, the agricultural minister). They are also competant: having been groomed for the task of administering the state, by and large they make a good job of it.

The reason that they can be "collectively dumb" is that they all come from the same educational mould, which makes their responses somewhat predictable. Their civil-service instinct is to mistrust the private sector and private initiative. Given their predominance in so many key posts, they have been criticised for holding back France's energy and creativity. But perhaps the dumbest thing they do is to ignore the views of lesser mortals, and assume that they always know best.

have talked of "the European project" and "the European construction", but in his alliance with Germany's Chancellor Kohl he preserved France's role as the architect.

Quite contrary

The same streak of Gaullist independence is evident in the way France so often disagrees in public with the United States, in particular over the Middle East. The most obvious example is the squabbling over what kind of UN resolution to use against Iraq, but there are plenty of others. When President Bush linked Iraq, Iran and North Korea in an "axis of evil", the Socialist foreign minister of the day described the American approach as

"simplistic"—the same adjective Mr Raffarin now uses for America's policy.

All this is fine for France's *classe politique*, trained to deal with the intellectual contortions of being an insider in the rich world's councils yet an outside critic at the same time. Earlier this year, for example, both the Jospin government and the opposition sent representatives to the World Economic Forum in New York—but also sent twice as many to the rival, anti-globalisation summit in Porto Alegre, Brazil.

But what of those lesser mortals who make up the electorate? For them it smacks of double-talk. No wonder so many, either by abstaining or by casting a protest vote, took their revenge in the presidential election last spring. They felt lost, and the elite had not bothered to show them the way.

A magic moment

President Chirac has five years in which to reform France

THE French body politic has had quite a momentous year, but the sense of shock is now fading. The new obsession of the chattering classes is Iraq and American foreign policy (which has catapulted two thoughtful books on French anti-Americanism into the bestseller list). For the political right, the obsession is unity: let the rival parties that coalesced into the Union for the Presidential Majority become a single vehicle to elect the next president in 2007 (Mr Juppé, or Mr

Sarkozy, or—some now whisper—Mr Chirac again?). For the opposition, so much in retreat that the Communist Party, once the largest party of the left, is now struggling to survive with just 21 supporters in the National Assembly, the task is not so much to bind its wounds, but to fight it out until the would-be modernisers of the Socialist Party, such as Dominique Strauss-Kahn and Laurent Fabius, either win or lose.

The government, for its part, talks of "decentralisation". Patrick Devedjian, the "minister of local freedoms", argues that it is time to give power to local officials and to get away from the Napoleonic military logic of a "chain of command" that always leads to Paris. In that way, perhaps a solution could at last be found for Corsica, whose bomb-planting extremists are bent on secession.

But does any of this indicate that the country is facing up to its problems? Sadly, not enough. The *fracture sociale*—a campaign slogan of Jacques Chirac's in his first bid for the presidency, in 1995—still divides the nation; the elites still pontificate at an arrogant distance from *la France d'en bas*; necessary economic reforms still remain a matter of talk rather than achievement; and policy is all to often a consequence of confrontation rather than negotiation. Worst of all, perhaps, is the temptation to seek refuge in a false comfort zone: France as an independent nuclear power, as a permanent member of the UN Security Council, as a member of the G8 club of economic powers—and, of course, as a country that takes culture seriously. France may not match the Anglo-Saxons for Nobel laureates in economics, but in literature it comes top.

Yet there is no need for such a comfort zone. France's engineers are among the best in the world—witness not just high-technology triumphs such as the Ariane rocket programme or the TGV railway system, but also lower-technology successes such as Michelin tyres or the cars of Citroën and Renault (a good enough company to take over Japan's Nissan and return it to profit). The same is true of some of its bankers, insurers and retailers, who successfully compete on the world stage. AXA, for example, will insure your life in America; Carrefour will sell you groceries whether you live in China or Chile.

The disappointment is that such assets are undervalued in the public mind, especially since the fall from grace of Jean-Marie Messier (a graduate both of ENA and the Polytechnique), with his improbable dream of turning a sewage and water company into the Vivendi Universal media giant. Denis Ranque, the boss of Thalès, a French defence and electronics group operating in more than 30 countries, has an explanation: "Popular knowledge of the economy is weak in France. We have important industries, but the French don't like them. They associate them with pollution, not jobs."

Elie Cohen, the economist at Sciences-Po, argues that France has been an ordinary market economy since the mid-1980s, when the folly of Mitterrand's nationalisation programme of 1981–82 became obvious even to the president, but: "The spirit of Gallo-capitalism remains. Each time there's a problem, you appeal to the state." Yet surely an "ordinary" market economy would not go to the lengths France does to resist the liberalising demands of the EU, in particular in the energy market, where EDF is protected at home even as it creates an empire abroad.

Face up to reality

No matter, you might say: France has prospered regardless. Indeed, there is a certain pragmatism behind the rhetoric: criticise globalisation but profit from it too; criticise America but support it at the same time. The problem is that sooner or later this form of self-deception could turn into self-destruction. In 1995, it prevented France's government from getting the popular backing to carry out reforms that have now become all the more necessary.

During his first presidential term, Jacques Chirac's critics had a common taunt: he was a man who knew how to win power, but now how to wield it. But there was a reason: from 1995 he was locked by the voters into cohabitation with his political opponents. For the next five years, he has no such excuse: having promised to reform France, he now has the power to do so. May he use it wisely.

From *The Economist*, November 16, 2002, pp. 3, 4. © 2002 by The Economist, Ltd. Distributed by the New York Times Special Features. Reprinted by permission.

French Secularism Unwraps Far More than Headscarves in the Classroom

ROBERT GRAHAM

New laws have a nasty habit of creating more problems than they pretend to resolve. Could this be the case with President Jacques Chirac's decision this week to use legislation to ban the wearing of "conspicuous" religious symbols in French schools?

By invoking the principles of France as a secular republic, the new law is supposed to be impartial towards Christians Jews and Muslims. Mr. Chirac was careful to say a large cross, a headscarf and skullcap all fall within the category of "conspicuous".

But this cannot hide the context. This is the first time a European head of state has intervened so directly on an issue involving church and state.

Mr. Chirac is anxious to defuse a battle over the Islamic headscarf in the classroom which has highlighted France's failure to integrate its large immigrant community — much of which is made up of Muslims of mainly north African origin.

The move therefore risks being seen as discriminatory: not just against Islamic custom but against Islam itself, now France's second biggest religion.

Using the law to resolve a sensitive religious issue reflects both the current confusion about the wearing of the headscarf and the way the French establishment prefers to hide behind the courts to enforce rules.

Chirac is anxious to defuse a battle that has highlighted France's failure to integrate its large immigrant community. Using the law risks being seen as discriminatory against Islam

---

Mr. Chirac this week even urged a law to prohibit patients in state hospitals from refusing treatment from doctors of the opposite sex.

The roots of the headscarf controversy are common to many European nations trying to assimilate immigrant cultures. But this affair has acquired an intensely French flavour. The drama and debate triggered by the refusal of a relatively small group of girls to remove their headscarves at school is now seen as a threat to two fundamental tenets of the republic.

The first is that of *laicité* or secularism: a rigid separation of the state from organized religion. This harks back to 1905 when the proponents of a secular republic severed all church-state links through a law that prevented the Catholic hierarchy from meddling in politics.

The anti-clerical spirit of 1905 has infused subsequent political thinking. It explains Mr. Chirac's refusal to entertain any reference to Europe's Christian heritage in the text of the proposed European Union constitution.

At another level, secularism has led the national statistics office to exclude any question on religious denomination in its population census. Hence, the generally accepted number of 6m Muslims in France is just a rough estimate.

The second principle under challenge is the indivisible nature of French citizenship shaped around the revolutionary ideal "Liberty, Equality, Fraternity". For immigrants, this means adapting to France rather than France adapting to them.

The authorities discourage any move to retain ethnic identity in the belief it fosters *communitarisme* — literally, trying to establish a "community". The term is political shorthand for refusing to integrate into French society by adhering to traditional customs.

Such is the fear of encouraging *communitarisme* that a recent proposal for affirmative action employment policies put forward by Nicholas Sarkozy, the outspoken interior minister, was immediately shouted down. Affirmative action risked laying bare the fiction of France as a homogenous nation with equal opportunities for all.

These reflexes have become more defensive as the ultra-right National Front successfully exploits fears about France losing its "Frenchness". But at a deeper level, they result from the conservatism of a French political establishment that has been slow to accept an increasingly multi-cultural society where immigrants have difficulty adapting.

The initial 19th-century immigration flows assimilated well - Italians, Armenians, east European Jews, Spaniards and Portuguese. Not so the recent waves from north and sub-Saharan Africa, people who mostly live in outer-city ghettoes and account for the bulk of unemployed youth.

It is therefore unsurprising that politicians and opinion polls generally favour a law banning "conspicuous" religious symbols. This clearly upholds *laicité* and curbs *communitarisem*. Besides, the French president would never have taken the initiative without being assured that public opinion was against allowing the classroom to become a platform for asserting religious identity.

Teachers in particular have been in the firing line, having to mediate between parents, pupils and the state in applying ambiguous legislation on classroom dress codes. Indeed, the Islamic headscarf first surfaced as an issue in the late 1980s, largely due to a constitutional judgment that the wearing of symbols of religious identity was not *per se* "incompatible" with the republic's secular principles.

This allowed a more liberal interpretation of school dress rules, permitting, for example, the wearing of headscarves in school grounds but not in the classroom itself. The appointment in the early 1990s of Hanifa Cherifi, the daughter of Algerian immigrants, as the education ministry mediator in difficult cases has also been a successful palliative. She now deals with about 150 cases a year where girls refuse to remove their headscarves.

"With young girls it is usually under parental pressure that they wear the headscarf; but with teenagers they are often doing it as a gesture against their parents more than the school," she says. What worries Ms Cherifi is the rise of active proselytising by well-organized groups close to Islamic fundamentalist movements.

Other groups, too, including the Christian Churches and the National Muslim Council, argue that a strict headscarf ban will stigmatise Muslims. If girls are ejected from state schools for refusing to remove headscarves, they risk being disadvantaged while the rise of private religious schools is encouraged. And why should obvious religious symbols be banned while prominent clothing brand names such as Nike are tolerated?

Fewer than 10 girls have been expelled from state schools this year for refusing to remove headscarves. Legislation might seem an overreaction if it were not for the many related issues beneath the surface that could now become more visible: religious tolerance, race relations, women's rights and the place of Islam in a modern European society.

In the suburbs of French cities today, a young Muslim girls can be taunted by youth gangs for wearing a headscarf or, if she removes it, threatened by fundamentalists for not being a devout Muslim. No law, however wise, can neatly resolve that dilemma.

The writer is the FT's Paris bureau chief

Iraq Aside, French View the U.S. With a Mixture of Attraction and Repulsion

By ELAINE SCIOLINO

PARIS, Nov. 12—One way of understanding how the French really feel about the United States these days is to ask them not about Iraq but about Arnold Schwarzenegger.

When the Austrian-born actor won the governorship of California, some politicians and commentators said his victory reflected a dangerous American populism.

But many French shared the enthusiasm of Nicolas Sarkozy, France's law-and-order interior minister.

Mr. Sarkozy is said to harbor presidential ambitions, but the fact that he is the offspring of Hungarian immigrants and never went to an elite school puts him at a distinct disadvantage.

In a remarkably confessional interview with RTL radio, Mr. Sarkozy said of Mr. Schwarzenegger: "That someone who is a foreigner in his country, who has an unpronounceable name" can become the governor of the biggest state in the United States, "this is no small thing!"

The current French-American rift, born of differences over Iraq but rooted in deeper post-cold-war friction, is more complex than it may appear. Bitter feelings remain strong on both sides of the Atlantic, and there is a sense that something fundamental in the relationships has failed. In some quarters anti-Americanism—of the kind President Bush will encounter during a visit to Britain next week—is at a high pitch.

But a close look at French attitudes toward America suggests that repulsion and disenchantment are at least equaled by attraction, curiosity and outright envy. The falling-out may be less complete than it seems.

Huge swaths of the relationship—in the realms of business, intelligence and even military affairs—still work. Criticism of the Bush administration, given full voice in the media, is offset by a French business ethic that often lauds the United States and a strong feeling, particularly among the young, that America remains a land of opportunity.

"When someone says, 'I'm going to work for a big corporation in New York for two years,' well, we all want to live that life," said Martin Coriat, 24, a student at a business school.

But many people in France feel they have lost touch with President Bush's America. His certainties in what Washington calls the "war on terror" have little resonance. The French do not feel the same threats that America insists are

so dangerous. Certainly most of them are unconvinced that Iraq was worth invading.

If Sept. 11, 2001, is now the date of reference for America's security outlook, France and all of Europe tend to look more to 1989 and the end of the cold war. Even as the United States feels more threatened, Europe and France feel less so.

These differences often appear to be accentuated by the fact that France still believes, like America, that it has a global mission to spread its concept of democracy and liberty.

But French "republicanism" requires adherence to the notion of the ideal citizen and does not celebrate diversity or ambition. That, says Michele Lamont of Harvard University, "limits possibilities."

So, some young people turn to America as an alternative. At L'E-cole des Hautes Études Commerciales in Jouy-en-Josas, a leafy town 15 miles from Paris, students tend to see the United States as a model.

The goal at this school of business and commerce is to teach students how to compete in a globalized world where American business models set the standard. France's historic unease about discussing money does not exist.

"Profit is the driver," said Bernard Ramanantsoa, the school's dean and a professor of strategy and business policy. "Money is the key."

Here the dream among many students is not to put down roots at home but to sail away—to America—a mythical place, perhaps, but one of boundless energy and possibility.

For Florian Bressand, 23, America offers "the right to fail that does not exist in France. Here we have to stick to a conventional path. In America, if you burn your fingers, you learn from it and start again."

The exodus of young French to the Silicon Valley is so pronounced that it has led to the creation of organizations there like Interfrench, a nonprofit organization of 5,000 French-speaking members. It is devoted to networking, sharing intelligence about work and business and even offering advice about French restaurants in the valley.

The departures reflect a measure of self-doubt. A slim volume titled "The France That Falls" is on the best-seller list. France's troubled economy has set off a fierce debate on the wisdom of a law limiting workers to a 35-hour week and whether the French work hard enough. A recent opinion poll concluded that 63 percent of the French believed that their country was in decline.

Yet such doubts coexist with a French sense of cultural superiority to the United States that often seems overwhelming. Only 24 percent of the French are inspired by the American economic system, 13 percent by American culture, 10 percent by life-style and 8 percent by American foreign policy, a poll by the BVA group found in February.

The disdain for things American is expressed in a variety of ways.

Mayor Bertrand Delanoë of Paris, for example, protested the death penalty in the United States by bestowing honorary citizenship on Mumia Abu Jamal, a former Black Panther sentenced to death for the 1981 murder of a white Philadelphia policeman, giving the medal to the Marxist activist Angela Davis in a ceremony at City Hall in early October.

Such disapproval, even contempt, for the United States is evident in the worker bars just outside a Michelin tire plant in Clermont-Ferrand.

The smell of cigarette smoke masks that of rubber and glue pervading the air of the medieval-turned-industrial city in the heart of France. The conversations about America among assembly line workers just off the night shift tend to focus on the dangers of a world driven by the American quest for profit.

"The United States—many people say it's so good," José Fernandes, 45, a 26-year-veteran at Michelin, said as he sipped a drink of mint syrup with water on ice and smoke Camels at Le Marina bar. "But the bottom line, the only thing that counts, is money. Retired people are forced to go back to work. The lowest workers don't get paid vacations. If your boss doesn't like you, you're fired."

Mr. Fernandes added that Michelin management "would copy the United States if it could."

"But it can't," he said. "Here, we have laws." He was referring to French regulations that often make firing impossible, guarantee six-week vacations and provide comprehensive pensions and health care.

The scene is rather different inside Michelin's corporate headquarters. There, managers use American team-building models and are driven by a fierce competitiveness that has put Michelin—barely—in the position of No. 1 global tire manufacturer.

Michelin may be one of the most secretive companies in France, but it is also one of the most global, with operations in 18 countries. Only about 30,000 of its 130,000 employees work in France. "The culture of Michelin is not to be too French," said Jean Laporte, director of Michelin's internal communications. That means talking about profit all the time, he said, adding, "Maybe it's a little bit of an exaggeration to say that the French never talk about money."

At the height of the Iraq crisis, many French executives and bankers were infuriated not only by the American march to war but also by what they perceived as clumsy French leadership.

At one point a small delegation of bankers and business executives called on President Jacques Chirac to complain that they were losing business. He bluntly told them, "I'll take care of politics; you take care of the economy," according to a French banker familiar with the meeting.

Last spring, in the face of an American campaign to boycott all things French, Michelin itself went to war.

It answered every letter, e-mail message and phone call, informing its potential enemies that Michelin is as American as it is French, that it employs more than 20,000 Americans in 17 American factories and produces tires for United States Army armored personnel carriers.

The public relations offensive worked. The boycott failed, at least at Michelin.

Just as Michelin has gone on selling tires in America, swaths of the France-American relationship have continued to run smoothly. The arrest of Christian Ganczarski—a German Qaeda sympathizer arrested in June by the French police with alleged links to the bombing of a Tunisian synagogue in April 2002 as well as the Sept. 11 attacks—was the result of an American-inspired sting operation with Saudi and French cooperation.

"The cooperation with the C.I.A. and F.B.I. has become even stronger since Sept. 11 when the United States understood, as we did long before, the war against radical Islam," said Pierre de Bousquet, the head of the Directorate for Territorial Surveillance, France's counterintelligence service. "Nothing has changed because of Iraq."

But more than six months after President Bush declared the major combat in Iraq over, the friction with France is not. On a number of issues, from the environment to the death penalty, France and the United States do not share the same values.

The Bush administration remains in an unforgiving mood, French diplomats say. White House officials remind their French counterparts that the relationship is seriously damaged and that they are sorely disappointed that France is refusing to contribute to Iraq's reconstruction.

Aware of the problem, Mr. Chirac has stopped using the expression "multipolar world," which enraged Bush administration officials because it seemed to envision a power to oppose rather than support America.

But privately many of Mr. Chirac's advisers have concluded that they will have to wait for a new American administration before the rift is repaired.

By American and French accounts, when Mr. Bush and Mr. Chirac met in New York in September they had a remarkably cordial chat—until conversation turned to Iraq.

Mr. Chirac said that he knew from "bitter experience" not to underestimate the power of Arab nationalism, and that a swift transfer of sovereignty to the Iraqi people was crucial, said two senior officials familiar with the conversation.

"Jacques, I have listened carefully and I strongly disagree," Mr. Bush was paraphrased as responding.

Mr. Chirac backed off, saying he was making the point as a friend. Then he added ominously, "History will judge."

Germany's general election:

Gerhard Schröder clings on

The incumbent German chancellor has won a cliff-hanging election but with no real mandate for reform

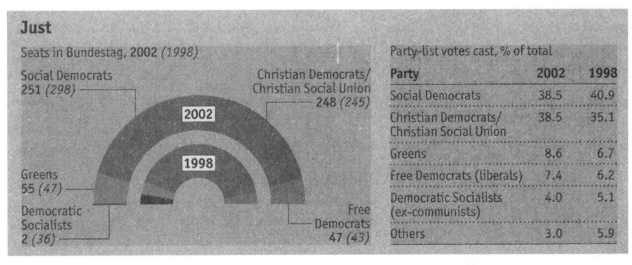

Just		
Seats in Bundestag, 2002 *(1998)*		
Social Democrats 251 *(298)*	Christian Democrats/ Christian Social Union 248 *(245)*	
Greens 55 *(47)*		
Democratic Socialists 2 *(36)*	Free Democrats 47 *(43)*	

Party-list votes cast, % of total		
Party	**2002**	**1998**
Social Democrats	38.5	40.9
Christian Democrats/ Christian Social Union	38.5	35.1
Greens	8.6	6.7
Free Democrats (liberals)	7.4	6.2
Democratic Socialists (ex-communists)	4.0	5.1
Others	3.0	5.9

Source: Bundeswahlleiter

BERLIN

IN ONE of the tightest German elections for half a century, Chancellor Gerhard Schröder's coalition of Social Democrats and Greens managed to cling on to power by its fingertips. Together the pair have 306 seats, a majority of nine in the Bundestag, the lower house of parliament. In the outgoing one, they had a majority of 21, and could usually count on at least the abstention of the 36 ex-communist Democratic Socialists who this time failed to clear the hurdle to obtain any seats by proportional representation and got only two directly elected seats.

Mr Schröder's slim majority will not only make it harder for his government to push through painful reforms but also puts a question-mark over its longevity. Previous governments, notably Helmut Kohl's after 1994, have had equally thin majorities yet have survived; a sitting chancellor can be displaced in mid-term only by a "constructive vote of no confidence", meaning that parliament has to vote for an alternative administration and not just ditch a beleaguered one.

Still, Mr Schröder will find the going tough. Discipline within the left-wing parties is often loose, particularly among the idiosyncratic Greens. The conservative opposition has gained ground. It already controls the Bundesrat, Germany's upper house, where about half of federal legislation has to be passed. And the economy is continuing to stagnate. Edmund Stoiber, the defeated conservative challenger, says he expects the new government's life to be "very, very short".

Charlemagne: Europe marching left, right, left

Why political taboos are being broken in Europe

The Germans invented the word *Zeitgeist,* but anyone hoping that their latest election would confirm a new "spirit of the age" in Europe will have been disappointed. In the past year or so, a clear trend seemed visible. Left-wing governments were ousted by the right in Italy, France, the Netherlands, Denmark, Portugal and Norway. Germany looked like the next and biggest domino to fall. But though Gerhard Schröder's "red-Green" coalition wobbled, it refused to topple. Just the week before Mr Schröder's victory, Sweden's Social Democrats also bucked the trend, easily winning another stint in office. Now Austria's Social Democrats have a chance of regaining power later this year. So much for Europe's inexorable move to the right.

The broader truth, however, is that on the big economic and social issues facing Europe the differences between centre-right and centre-left—between Christian democracy and social democracy—are pretty paltry. Certainly the right is still closer to business, the left to the trade unions. But the resulting differences in policy have more to do with nuance than deep philosophy. In Germany, for example, Edmund Stoiber on the right proposed a top rate of income tax of 40%, while Mr Schröder wants to bring it down to 42%. Mr Stoiber said the state should consume no more than 40% of GDP, Mr Schröder stuck to his own favourite number, 42%. Economists and businessmen may clamour for a drastic revamp of Germany's generous welfare state and for decisive moves to tackle public pensions, but neither candidate was prepared to risk suggesting anything daring. As Mr Stoiber drily remarked, he had not noticed anyone demonstrating for a radical overhaul of social security.

What is true of Germany is true of the rest of Europe. Italy's Silvio Berlusconi admires Margaret Thatcher but has done nothing to tackle Italy's pensions problem and little to free up the labour market. France's new centre-right government has moved cautiously to mitigate the worst effects of its Socialist predecessor's introduction of a 35-hour week but is committed to an extensive welfare state and shows no desire to take on the unions.

Faced with such tiny differences between left and right on the big issues of social and economic management, voters tend to plump for the most appealing personalities. One big reason why Mr Schröder and Sweden's Goran Persson won while Lionel Jospin, a French socialist, lost is that the winning pair are highly effective politicians while Mr Jospin came across as dull and stiff. Tony Blair's mastery of British politics relies at least as much on his personality—and his Schröder-like sense of what people want to hear—as on any particular policies.

It was Mr Blair who made the last real attempt to define a new pan-European (and indeed transatlantic) political *Zeitgeist.* When the centre-left held sway on both sides of the ocean, he earnestly pushed forward his big idea—"the third way". Mr Schröder tried briefly to echo him with cosy talk of a "new middle". But the whole Blairite philosophy was too vague to catch on and much of the European left disliked what little it understood of it, assuming it was code for a kind of soft-edged Thatcherism. Mr Blair has now almost given up talking about the third way. In a recent interview in *Prospect,* a British magazine, he was reduced to claiming that "in parts of Latin America [the third way] is seen as a ground-breaking moment." (They speak of little else in the queues outside Argnetina's banks.)

But while a welfarist consensus may still hold sway across the European Union, consensus politics are fraying around the edges in other ways. The most striking recent trend has been the rise of populist parties openly hostile to immigration. When Austria's People's Party became the first such party to join a governing coalition, there was outrage across the EU. But the rise of politicians making similar appeals elsewhere in other EU countries has muted the outcry. The Pim Fortuyn list in the Netherlands and Umberto Bossi's Northern League in Italy have both joined governing coalitions after campaigns that highlighted the supposedly bad effects of immigration. The new centre-right Danish government relies on the votes of an anti-immigration party. As Bertel Haarder, Denmark's immigration minister, points out, there may be a connection between addiction to welfarism and hostility to immigrants. Partly because of high minimum wages and welfare benefits, there are very few jobs for unskilled immigrants: around 60% of them in Denmark have no job. So they are easily stigmatised as free-loading parasites.

Mainstream politicians have reacted in different ways to the rise of anti-immigration parties. In France the National Front's Jean-Marie Le Pen won close to 20% of the votes in the presidential election but remains firmly beyond the pale. The new French government has nonetheless begun to toughen both rhetoric and actions against illegal immigrants. All across the EU, asylum-seekers are getting a frostier welcome.

Vox populi, a pox on civility?

The rise of anti-immigration populists has demonstrated the political potential of voicing sentiments often heard in the street but rarely in parliamentary chambers. Mr Schröder's campaign was a variation on this theme. Struggling in the polls, he decided to express the anti-Americanism that is a strong current of public opinion in Germany and the rest of the EU. Warning against "adventures" in Iraq and carping at the American economic model was just a mild version of commonplace feelings. Mr Schröder's supporters took the hint—and helped him cling on to power. However, as with the immigration debate elsewhere in Europe, once a political taboo is broken it is hard to control the consequences. German relations with America have nose-dived. And new and queasy-making sentiments are popping out of the closet at home, such as the ill-fated comparison between George Bush and Hitler allegedly made by Mr Schröder's justice minister. Sometimes taboos are there for a reason.

On a night of nerves, with both leaders at different moments claiming victory, the two main formations—the Social Democrats and the combined Christian Democrats and their Bavarian sister party, the Christian Social Union—each got 38.5% of the vote. In the end, the Social Democrats pipped the conservatives, by almost 9,000 votes and three seats. The new Bundestag is expected to have its first sitting in the week that starts on October 14th, with the formal re-election of Mr Schröder as chancellor on the same day or soon after.

With the Social Democrats losing ground since the previous election, in 1998, it was the Greens who kept the ruling coalition afloat. They emerged as the election's only real winners, with 8.6% of the vote, their highest score since they first won seats in parliament in 1983. They are now clearly the country's third force.

Barely a year ago, after a string of electoral setbacks, they seemed tired, bland and on the way out. Mr Schröder had even begun eyeing the Free Democrats, Germany's liberals, as alternative coalition partners. But the combined effect of recent floods in the east (which revived many voters' environmental concerns), of the chancellor's stand against a war in Iraq, and of a strong campaign by Joschka Fischer, the Greens' foreign minister and Germany's most popular politician, helped them bounce back. Mr Schröder can thank the Greens for letting him keep his crown. In turn, they will now expect more influence, and say they will press the chancellor to raise the tempo of reform.

The liberals, despite doing a little better than last time, were the election's losers. Their expectations had been high. Pollsters throughout the campaign had put them ahead of the Greens. Only last month, one poll gave them 13%, double the Greens' projected score. They had begun to assume that no government could be formed without them. But they ended up with a modest 7.4%, a point behind the Greens and a far cry from the 18% they had set themselves. A renewed rumpus over anti-Israeli comments by Jürgen Möllemann was partly to blame. He has now resigned as the liberals' deputy leader. But the "fun party" image projected by their leader, Guido Westerwelle, though attracting young voters, may well have put off many of the party's older, more earnest supporters. Many Germans think Mr Westerwelle lacks gravitas.

Despite failing to hit all three of his proclaimed targets—to have the biggest group in parliament, to win more than 40% of the vote, and to topple the government—Mr Stoiber has emerged beaten but unbowed. His conservatives upped their 1998 vote by more than three percentage points, while the Social Democrats dipped by a couple. In Mr Stoiber's Bavarian homeland, his party's share shot up by 10.9 points to 58.6%, its best score in nearly two decades. Indeed, with 9% of the total national vote, Mr Stoiber's Christian Social Union can claim to be Germany's third biggest party, ahead of the Greens. He says he has no intention of retiring quietly back to his home state but stands ready to take the chancellor's job should the government collapse.

Were it not for last month's floods in the east and the threat of an American-led war in Iraq, Mr Schröder would probably have failed to win a second term. Neither event was of his making, of course. But he exploited them both to his benefit. As a result, says Donald Rumsfeld, the American defence secretary, relations between Germany and the United States have been "poisoned". He refused even to talk to his German counterpart at this week's meeting of NATO defence ministers in Warsaw, and President George Bush failed to send Mr Schröder the customary congratulations. The chancellor is eager for reconciliation and has even asked Britain's Tony Blair to help. But he insists that there will be "no change" in his opposition to Germany's participation in an attack on Iraq, even under a United Nations mandate.

This, says Mr Schröder, is "a difference of opinion" that should be accepted among friends; the relationship, he insists, is "intact". That is not the view in Washington. Matters were not helped last week by the German justice minister, who was accused of lumping Mr Bush with Hitler by saying that the American president has sought to distract voters from problems at home by talk of war—tactics, she is said to have added, that were once used by "Adolf Nazi". She has denied making the remarks, but says she will resign anyway. Relations between the countries, and between Mr Schröder and Mr Bush, who have not talked since June, remain strained.

It is on the home front, however, that Mr Schröder faces his hardest task. Speeding up Germany's dismal growth rate, creating jobs and loosening the country's labour rigidities should be his top priorities. But the election does not suggest that the German people have an appetite for radical reform. Mr Schröder has no mandate for it. Nor would Mr Stoiber, if he had won. That is the election's gloomiest lesson.

Untangling the system

BERLIN

Efforts to cut through the knotty German federal system may not get far

CONSTITUTIONS are like computer-operating systems: the older they get, the clunkier they are-and the more often they crash. Germany's 54-year-old *Grundgesetz,* or Basic Law, is, say critics, ripe for a rewrite. This week a commission comprising members from both legislative chambers, the elected Bundestag and the upper-house Bundesrat, which represents the states or *Länder,* started discussion on "modernising the federal structure".

The commission's deliberations come, fittingly, just as the Bundesrat takes up debate on the government's package of tax and welfare reforms known as Agenda 2010. For the critics say that the biggest problem with German federalism is that levels of government are so intertwined that they often block each other, making any reform exceedingly hard.

The federalism commission is not the first to try to cut the Gordian knot that some call *Politikverflechtungsfalle,* or joint decision-making trap. But never before has there been such demand, right across the political spectrum, for something to be done. Some of the country's leading think-thanks have called for a sweeping reform. Many free-market businessmen are calling for a more competitive federalism.

When Germany first tried (and failed) to give itself a national constitution in 1849, at a convention in Frankfurt, federalists faced a similar challenge to those confronting Europe's constitution-builders today: how to integrate already fully developed states, meaning not just Prussia but also such places as Bavaria and Württemberg. Short of starting another war, getting these states together meant accommodating entrenched political interests.

This initial set-up has put Germany on a unique constitutional path, argues Gerhard Lehmbruch, a political scientist. The Frankfurt convention came up with a concept now called executive federalism: the federal government makes most of the laws, but it leaves their implementation to the states. In 1867 Bismarck established the Bundesrat, a powerful representative body for the states, one function of which was to serve as a negotiating forum.

A similar federal structure was reinstated after the second world war, though this was largely thanks to the allies, who did not want a powerful central government. But they did not impose American-style federalism, which would have meant a directly elected Senate instead of a Bundesrat, partly because the *Länder* had already re-established themselves.

Given that Germany's federalism is more a product of history than of the vision of framers, the system has worked well. But in recent years, it has often come to a grinding halt. One problem is that the Bundesrat now has a say in over 60% of federal legislation, instead of the 10% or so intended when the Basic Law was written. This is partly the result of financial changes in the late 1960s. but it is also because the federal government has extensively exercised its right to legislate, taking power away from states and instead giving them more say at federal level.

Plenty of countries have two powerful chambers, often designed to make legislation harder. But in Germany it can cause near-constipation when combined with Germany's elections. Sixteen *Länder* means as many elections: an average of one every three months. This has had two effects. One is that opposition parties often gain control of the Bundesrat, making change harder. The other is that governments are inhibited from radical reform for fear of an approaching state election.

What is more, the Basic Law ordains a "uniformity of living standards" throughout the country. This explains the complicated redistribution system among the *Länder,* which ensures that tax revenues per head never fall far below the national average. This system of redistribution is increasingly a disincentive to reform and job creation, since the so-called *Finanzausgleich* acts as a tax on success.

Because this slows Germany down just when the need for reform is at its greatest, members of the "Convention for Germany", a new lobby group, favour radical surgery. The poorer *Länder* should be merged into economically more viable entities, says Hans-Olaf Henkel, one of the group's founders and a former IBM executive. If the states were given more areas of responsibility and the right to levy taxes of their own, they could compete with and learn from each other, creating conditions conducive to faster growth.

Such competitive federalism would certainly be an elegant solution, but it stands little chance of being implemented in the foreseeable future. Things would have to get much worse before the poorer *Länder*, especially, agree. Voters dislike mergers, as was shown in 1996 when they rejected one between Brandenburg and Berlin. Less radical adjustments could help, though: holding all state elections on one day of the year only, as in America; giving *Länder* the right to opt out of some federal laws; or disentangling the finances to give *Länder* more power.

The commission is expected to sit for about a year. Any proposed changes it comes up with will require two-thirds majority support in both the Bundestag and the Bundesrat. That points to a timid outcome in which the federal government cedes a few regulatory areas to the *Länder* and they shed some of the Bundesrat's veto power. But so far the federal government has listed only a few insignificant areas in which it is willing to relinquish its legislative rights. An additional complication is that the European Union has taken over many powers, giving rise to fears that it may ultimately supplant one level of government in Germany altogether.

Even if the commission fails to come up with radical changes, it may help to stoke up debates in other countries about the balance between centre and regions, including Spain, France, Austria, Italy and even Britain. Above all, though, it should feed into thinking over the EU's new constitution. If responsibilities between Brussels and national governments are not clearly separated, if subsidiarity-the notion that things are best done at the lowest possible level of government-is not strongly spelt out, and if financial interlinkages are not clarified, the EU could find that it too heads for a system crash.

Schröder's Unfinished Business

Why the Reforms Agreed for Germany's Ailing Economy Leave the Job Half-done

The legislation agreed by parliament, although welcome, should be viewed as only a beginning, many entrepreneurs, investors and economists insist. But the chancellor's appetite for more far-reaching changes may be limited, writes **Bertrand Benoit**

It was an exhausted Gerhard Schröder who rose from the Bundestag's government bench in the week before Christmas to face the lower house of parliament's last plenary session of 2003.

That week, the German chancellor had secured the opposition's backing for the bulk of his Agenda 2010 programme, arguable the most far-reaching economic reforms in Europe since Margaret Thatcher's free market revolution in Britain almost a quarter of a century ago. After nine months of acerbic debate that at times came close to tearing apart the chancellor's ruling coalition of Social Democrats and Greens, the 12 bills making up Mr. Schröder's legislation were about to make it through both houses of parliament.

By and large, German and foreign investors, managers, entrepreneurs and economists have joined the applause that rose from the house's floor that day. But, most warn, further effort and sacrifices will be needed; there is no shortage of problems in need of further attention (see the next steps).

"The giant is moving. Something is happening," says Jürgen Kluge, who runs the German activities of McKinsey, the consultancy. "Now, is it big enough? No. Does it solve our problems? Not for the coming generation. We need bold improvements in the same direction."

As Berlin's political machinery slowly gets in motion for 2004, however, Agenda 2010 is beginning to look less like a work in progress and more like a closed chapter—a bad memory the government is keen to put behind it as fast as possible. At the Social Democratic party's annual gathering in Weimar yesterday, an event that sets the party's agenda for the coming 12 months, there was no

talk of relaxing labour legislation, lengthening store-opening hours, or cutting social security benefits further. Instead, 2004 was proclaimed a "year of innovation", with promises to focus on education, boost research and development and ensure that German excellence in carmaking or machine tools is replicated in newer areas: photovoltaic energy, nanotechnology, biotechnology.

> 'The government is too weak and the opposition has chosen to further its own goals instead of doing the right thing for Germany. I wonder if we are not missing a historic chance to do more'

For several months now, the chancellor's entourage has been playing down the likelihood that, having worked so hard to secure reforms that must count as the most unpopular in recent German history, he would embark on a second such drive in this legislature.

"We have asked a lot from the people; we must give them time to digest," says a close adviser. "Running ahead of the pack waving your flag serves no purpose if no one is following."

With 14 communal, regional and European elections due this year, the SPD badly needs to reverse a trend that has caused it to lose ground in nearly all important ballots since Mr. Schröder's surprise re-election in September 2002.

The Next Steps

Review the role of the state

Business increasingly asks why the public sector should run job centres, television channels, water-purification plants, data-processing centres, airports and opera houses.

The question does not apply only to state-owned entities. Every year, about €2bn flows from the public coffers to the agricultural sector, €5bn into unprofitable coal mining operations, and €125m into shipbuilding.

Since 1961, it has cost more to mine coal in Germany than to buy it abroad. Yet in November the government committed another €16bn to the industry between 2006 and 2012. Meanwhile, plans by the economics ministry for a €500m seed investment fund to help plug a funding gap for very young businesses are still being finalised.

'Despite all the efforts being made to clean up public finances, we should take care not to neglect investments in research, development, and education,' says Ekkehard Schulz, chief executive of ThyssenKrupp, the steel group.

Ease the social security burden

At €26.36 an hour, workers in western Germany are the world's most expensive after the Norwegians. But in a country where 42 per cent of gross pay goes towards social security contributions, lowering labour costs does not necessarily mean cutting wages.

Mr. Schröder's government has addressed non-wage labour costs in its healthcare reform and in adjustments to the pension system that will come before parliament this year. But these will merely stabilise contribution rates. The answer? Breach another taboo.

'The fastest way to beat the demographic challenge is to open up immigration. In the US, 50 per cent of PhDs are foreigners,' says Alexander Dibelius of Goldman Sachs.

A study by Deutsche Bank concludes that, in addition to pushing back retirement age and extending working time, Germany will need 200,000 immigrants a year to keep potential growth from falling below 1 per cent by 2050.

Take a look at the tax system, then leave it alone

Germany's income and corporate tax system, with its countless loopholes, is a bureaucratic monster. Government and opposition have been developing competing models for reforms, some restricted to income tax, others embracing personal and corporate taxation. These measures are certain to be heavily discussed this year.

While companies would welcome a root-and-branch reform, many stress that they want the government to stick to whatever new system emerges.

'We receive new information several times a month about changes in the tax environment,' says Fred Irwin, president of the American Chamber of Commerce in Frankfurt. 'This is why we are not growing, because of uncertainty.'

For Stephan Scholtissek, who runs Accenture in Germany, 'there used to be a time when you could accept lower margins in Germany because it was so predictable: no strikes, no aggressive social experiments and no abrupt changes in tax policies. This is no longer the case.'

Make life easier for the Mittelstand

Few western economies are as reliant on small- and medium-sized companies as Germany, with its 3.3m 'Mittelstand' businesses employing more than 20m people. If job creation is the aim, these companies should be given special treatment, entrepreneurs say.

Under Agenda 2010, restrictions on redundancies, which considerably raises the cost of restructurings, applies to all companies with 10 or more employees.

But according to Klaus Esser, former chief executive of Mannesmann and now head of the General Atlantic private equity house for Germany, 'it is employers, in this segment, who need protection more than employees. By freeing companies with fewer than, say, 80 employees from these shackles you would help curb both the informal economy and the flow of jobs abroad.'

Finance is another issue. An over-abundance of cheap loans until the 1990s has given way to a dearth of funding as unprofitable banks have tightened lending practices. More severe regulation on reserves and a predicted consolidation in Germany's banking sector make a return to the debt-financed economy unlikely. Meanwhile, uncertainty surrounding the tax treatment of venture capital and private equity activities has long made securing equity financing complicated.

The conditions should improve, however, following a ruling by the finance ministry last month. New criteria will ensure that funds can be structured as 'tax transparent' vehicles that do not create additional levies for investors, aligning Germany with the US and the UK.

Make labour attractive again

Agenda 2010 aimed to cut joblessness by forcing the long-term unemployed to take jobs. What Germany needs now, economists say, is a focus on creating new jobs. 'You are seven times more likely to lose your job in the US as in Germany but 10 times more likely to get a new one,' says Elga Bartsch, economist at Morgan Stanley.

Disincentives to hiring are built into Germany's social security system and labour laws, ultimately leading to higher costs. 'The substitution of capital for labour actually fuelled productivity growth in the 1990s,' Ms Bartsch says.

One solution is to extend the working week without full financial compensation, a concept the opposition Christian Democratic Union has been toying with. 'If a religious holiday comes on a Thursday, you need to shut down production for four days because nobody will come to work on Friday,' says Lorne Campbell, of Crédit Agricole Indosuez Cheuvreux. 'Why not move all religious holidays to a Monday?'

Improve corporate governance

While Germany might have been the Wild West for equity investors 15 years ago, with no ban on insider trading and management decisions taking place behind closed doors, standards of corporate governance have improved beyond recognition.

Yet more progress is needed, investors say. Roughly half the recommendations made in July 2001 by a government-appointed commission led by Theodor Baums, a Frankfurt law professor, have been implemented so far.

One proposal, to make it easier for shareholders to claim damages from directors and executives guilty of wrongdoings, has been officially endorsed by the government but not yet put into law.

'There should be easier ways to litigate for shareholders,' says Christian Strenger, supervisory board member at DWS, one of Germany's largest fund management groups. 'As things stand, the law does not provide for you to get your money back even when the state secures a conviction.'

Another proposal would be to review the impact that Mitbestimmung, or workplace co-determination, has on corporate governance. By law, companies with more than 2,000 workers must allocate half their supervisory board seats to employee representatives.

Critics argue that these employee appointees do not speak for foreign workers—a problem for DaimlerChrysler, which has 49 per cent of its staff outside Germany—rarely have the competence required for a directorship, and may at times serve interests in conflict with those of the company.

A ruling by the European Court of Justice in September allows new businesses created in Germany to use legal structures borrowed from other countries, allowing entrepreneurs to circumvent Mitbestimmung altogether.

The political damage wreaked in 2003 was evident in an opinion poll published by the Allensbach institute shortly after Mr. Schröder's reforms had at last been passed. It gave the SPD its lowest score ever.

The protracted negotiations needed to enact the measures also highlighted the extreme fragility of the government. Mr. Schröder has had to rely on the opposition-controlled Bundesrat, or upper chamber, to pass the bills while fighting numerous critics in his own camp. With a majority of just four in the lower chamber, and having emerged as the victor this time, he may not want to put his fate in the hands of opponents a second time in two years.

"The problem is that the government is too weak and the opposition has chosen to use this situation to further its own goals instead of doing the right thing for Germany," says Lorne Campbell, who heads the German operations of Crédit Agricole Indosuez Cheuvreux, the French investment bank. "I wonder if we are not missing a historic chance to do more."

In fairness, the government's weakness would not have been so apparent had the challenges facing the country been less daunting. The multiple checks and balances in Germany's constitutional order, the impossibility of gathering strong majorities that is built into the electoral system and the decentralisation of power inherent in federalism do not lend themselves to swift enactment of controversial measures.

A parliamentary commission now poring over the constitution could come up with proposals that reduce the upper house's considerable blocking power but it will not do so before the end of 2004, too late for a legislature that ends in 2006.

Nonetheless, while admiration for Agenda 2010 runs high among economists, there is agreement that more needs to be done. German economic growth has lagged behind that of its European neighbours for a decade—a relative decline that recalls the experience of the UK in the 1970s.

Economists' recommendations include measures that would be so politically controversial for the SPD that they make Agenda 2010 look like shameless populism. One of these regards the way business federations and trade unions are allowed to set wage levels and working time for entire industries at regional level, which results in one-size-fits-all deals for vastly different companies.

"If I were the CEO of one of these huge German companies, not being able to negotiate with my employees would drive me nuts," says Christiane zu Salm, who runs Euvia Media, a Munich-based television group that is not party to a tariff agreement. "We need a massive disempowerment of trade unions."

While the unions still oppose a significant relaxation of collective wage bargaining, some entrepreneurs admit that the rapid decline in trade union membership, the massive exodus of companies from the business federations and the increasing number of illegal deals struck at company level suggest the time is ripe to scrap the system and let employers and employees bargain directly at company level.

"The labour market must be deregulated, and this is particularly true of the tariff cartel," says Hans-Joachim Körber, chief executive of Metro, Germany's largest retailing group.

So is business bound for a disappointment as it calls for a sequel to Agenda 2010? Not necessarily. Reform advocates have powerful allies, such as Frank Steinmeier, head of the federal chancellery, and Wolfgang Clement, economics minister. And the historically strong links between the SPD and trade unions have been considerably weakened by the latter's strident opposition to Agenda 2010.

The export-led economic rebound expected for this year, meanwhile, could improve the political parameters.

"If we have growth north of 1.5 per cent and there is no outright collapse in the dollar, the public will link it to the reforms," says Alexander Dibelius, co-head of Goldman Sachs for Germany. "This, in turn, could make the next wave of measures possible."

In other words, by boosting US demand for German goods, President George W. Bush's massive budget deficit and ensuing fiscal stimulus could end up making further reforms palatable to the German public. This would be a welcome boost.

But, as Fred Irwin, president of the American Chamber of Commerce in Frankfurt, points out, government and the state cannot be held solely responsible for the slow pace of reform. "Something needs to happen before any further reform is implemented: there must be a broad realisation in the public that without dramatic change, the exodus of brains and companies away from Germany will continue. There is a growing appetite for change, but not enough that it is forcing politicians to act yet."

Opinion polls suggest voters are ambivalent about reform. While they welcome the concept as an abstract notion, they tend to oppose specific measures. Yet implementation of Agenda 2010 should confirm the old truth: reforms are seldom as painful—or as efficient—as expected.

One implication, Mr. Campbell points out, is that sacred cows can be slaughtered. The government made this clear last January when it ended the prohibition on shops staying open on Saturday afternoons; and again in the autumn, when it introduced the first cut in pension benefits since the second world war.

The second implication, however, and one Germans and their political leaders will have to come to terms with soon, is that a lot of cows must be killed for the sacrifices to have any effect. Too little pain can mean no gain at all.

From *Financial Times*, January 7, 2004. © 2004 by Financial Times Syndication. Reprinted by permission.

The vices and virtues of old Germany's 'model' economy

MICHAEL PROWSE

Novelists often exploit our appetite for improbable role reversals. We sit up when the rich boy swaps positions with his poor cousin, the master with his servant, the gamekeeper with a poacher. According to some pundits, a comparably startling inversion is occurring in the real-world domain of political economy. Germany, the story goes, has become the "sick man of Europe". And Britain has assumed its erstwhile position as the continent's premier market economy.

For most of my youth and early adult life, British policymakers looked enviously at the then West Germany. In economic terms it had everything that Britain craved but somehow could not attain. Its economy grew rapidly and it dominated high-technology export markets. It enjoyed stable industrial relations and low unemployment. It had the world's most admired central bank, near-zero inflation and a strong currency. Perhaps most miraculous, it also offered more generous social benefits than most of its competitors.

> Britain has assumed Germany's position as Europe's premier market economy; yet if the UK had shouldered a comparable financial burden, it too might be staggering

If you want to discover how to combine capitalist vigour with a social conscience, I was told in the late 1980s, make a pilgrimage to Bonn. As it turned out I went to Washington, DC, instead, and learnt some rather different lessons. But even in the US, Germany then had many admirers. When Bill Clinton ran for president in 1992, one of his economic proposals was to introduce a German-style apprenticeship programme for US workers. The assumption, at least in Democratic circles, was that America could learn a great deal from the German "social market" economy.

Today, as Gerhard Schröder, the German chancellor, struggles to cut taxes and enact his "Agenda 2010" reforms, aimed at deregulating German labour markets and scaling back welfare promises, the German model looks less appealing. In fact, Ludwig Erhard, the free-market architect of its postwar "economic miracle", would be appalled by its recent record. The German economy has stagnated for the past three years, and grown by an annual average of little more than 1 per cent since the mid-1990s. Having fallen slightly recently, the jobless rate is still 10.5 per cent.

Britain has grown more than twice as fast over the same period and has a far lower unemployment rate. And, given the flaws in the European Central Bank's terms of reference, for the first time in decades Britain can perhaps claim to enjoy a superior monetary regime to Germany's.

German officials have visited Britain to find out how its job centres get the unemployed back to work. Roland Koch, the conservative prime minister of Hesse, wants to let the wages of low-skilled workers fall to market levels and top them up, in Anglo-American style, with social benefits. Meanwhile, German entrepreneurs, frustrated by domestic regulations, are incorporating new ventures in the UK because they regard the British "Limited" legal form as more flexible, and globally better known, than the traditional German "GmbH". It is no wonder that Gordon Brown, Britain's finance minister, brags not only that the UK is Europe's most dynamic economy but also that it is making the most strenuous efforts to update the social market ideals of the postwar German reformers.

Although a degree of role-reversal is undeniable, it would be foolish to exaggerate either Britain's apparent virtues or Germany's apparent flaws. For those who must use Britain's inefficient railways, its congested roads, its overstretched hospitals and retirement homes and its still-failing inner-city comprehensive schools, and for those who rely on its public-sector pensions, the concept of Britain as a beacon for the rest of Europe is laughable. Mr. Brown's "enterprise culture" is partly the product of two unsustainable trends: a chronic run-down of public services, now being expensively reversed, and an explosive growth in consumer debt.

Germany may have spent too heavily in some of these areas but at least it does not face the challenge of making good decades of underinvestment. Nor does it have as yobbish a public culture as the UK, or as many neighbourhoods that are blighted by violent crime.

And, although critics may be correct in arguing that Germany's main problems are structural rigidities, an insufficiently entrepreneurial business ethos and unaffordable welfare promises, these are not the only causes of its sluggish growth. In two respects, Germans are paying a predictable price for policies that were better intentioned than they were designed. Unification and the rebuilding of the former East Germany imposed a huge burden on profitable German business, especially as the architect, Helmut Kohl, the former chancellor, had little grasp of economics and insisted on a one-for-one conversion of Ostmarks into D-Marks. If Britain had shouldered a comparable financial burden in the past decade, it too might be staggering.

Germans were also altruistic in agreeing to give up the D-Mark for the euro. The euro is the right policy for the longer term and it could not have happened without German backing. Yet the immediate effect has been to transfer wealth from Germany to the poorer states on the periphery of the European Union, such as Ireland. They have had lower interest rates and faster growth than would otherwise have been possible. Corporate Germany, by contrast, has had to endure a tighter monetary policy and a higher real exchange rate than even the inflation-averse Bundesbank would have considered necessary.

From a British perspective, Mr. Schröder's reforms may seem relatively modest. Yet the direction of change is significant. And some of the changes, such as the proposed flat-rate, as opposed to income-related, unemployment benefit for those jobless for more than 12 months, are radical in the German context. The impact of reforms on German growth may be greater than expected, partly because demand now seems to be recovering in the eurozone economy and partly because Germany has hitherto attempted so little reform. As with anything else, the marginal benefits from reform tend to decline over time. After two decades Britain could be described as "reformed out". But in Germany the process has just begun, so a lot is still possible.

In any case, a nation should not be judged by narrow economic criteria alone. The German social model has offered stability, security, fairness and a civilised, even tranquil, lifestyle. These are social goods that many people value at least as highly as a few extra euros of national income. They should not be surrendered lightly.

Japanese spirit, western things

When America's black ships forced open Japan, nobody could have predicted that the two nations would become the world's great economic powers

OPEN up. With that simple demand, Commodore Matthew Perry steamed into Japan's Edo (now Tokyo) Bay with his "black ships of evil mien" 150 years ago this week. Before the black ships arrived on July 8th 1853, the Tokugawa shoguns had run Japan for 250 years as a reclusive feudal state. Carrying a letter from America's president, Millard Fillmore, and punctuating his message with cannon fire, Commodore Perry ordered Japan's rulers to drop their barriers and open the country to trade. Over the next century and a half, Japan emerged as one of history's great economic success stories. It is now the largest creditor to the world that it previously shunned. Attempts to dissect this economic "miracle" often focus intently on the aftermath of the second world war. Japan's occupation by the Americans, who set out to rebuild the country as a pacifist liberal democracy, helped to set the stage for four decades of jaw-dropping growth. Yet the origins of the miracle—and of the continual tensions it has created inside Japan and out—stretch further back. When General Douglas MacArthur accepted Japan's surrender in 1945 aboard the battleship Missouri, the Americans made sure to hang Commodore Perry's flag from 1853 over the ship's rear turret. They had not only ended a brutal war and avenged the attack on Pearl Harbour—they had also, they thought, won an argument with Japan that was by then nearly a century old.

America's enduring frustration—in the decades after 1853, in 1945, and even today—has not been so much that Japan is closed, but that it long ago mastered the art of opening up on its own terms. Before and after those black ships steamed into Edo Bay, after all, plenty of other countries were opened to trade by western cannon. What set Japan apart—perhaps aided by America's lack of colonial ambition—was its ability to decide for itself how to make the process of opening suit its own aims.

One consequence of this is that Japan's trading partners, especially America, have never tired of complaining about its economic practices. Japan-bashing reached its most recent peak in the 1980s, when American politicians and businessmen blamed "unfair" competition for Japan's large trade surpluses. But sim-

ilar complaints could be heard within a few decades of Commodore Perry's mission. The attitude was summed up by "Mr Dooley", a character created by Peter Finley Dunne, an American satirist, at the close of the 19th century: "Th' trouble is whin the gallant Commodore kicked opn th' door, we didn't go in. They come out."

Nowadays, although poor countries still want Japan (along with America and the European Union) to free up trade in farm goods, most rich-country complaints about Japan are aimed at its approach to macroeconomics and finance, rather than its trade policies. Japan's insistence on protecting bad banks and worthless companies, say its many critics, and its reluctance to let foreign investors help fix the economy, have prevented Japanese demand from recovering for far too long. Once again, the refrain goes, Japan is unfairly taking what it can get from the world economy—exports and overseas profits have been its only source of comfort for years—without giving anything back.

While these complaints have always had some merit, they have all too often been made in a way that misses a crucial point: Japan's economic miracle, though at times paired with policies ranging from protectionist to xenophobic, has nevertheless proved a huge blessing to the rest of the world as well. The "structural impediments" that shut out imports in the 1980s did indeed keep Japanese consumers and foreign exporters from enjoying some of the fruits of that miracle; but its export prowess allowed western consumers to enjoy better and cheaper cars and electronics even as Japanese households grew richer. Similarly, Japan's resistance to inward investment is indefensible, not least because it allows salvageable Japanese companies to wither; but its outward investment has helped to transform much of East Asia into a thriving economic region, putting a huge dent in global poverty. Indeed, one of the most impressive aspects of Japan's economic miracle is that, even while reaping only half the potential gains from free trade and investment, it has still managed to do the world so much good over the past half-century.

Setting an example

Arguably, however, Japan's other big effect on the world has been even more important. It has shown clearly that you do not have to embrace "western" culture in order to modernise your economy and prosper. From the very beginning, Japan set out to have one without the other, an approach encapsulated by the saying "Japanese spirit, western things". How did Japan pull it off? In part, because the historical combination of having once been wide open, and then rapidly slamming shut, taught Japan how to control the aperture through which new ideas and practices streamed in. After eagerly absorbing Chinese culture, philosophy, writing and technology for roughly a millennium, Japan followed this with 250 years of near-total isolation. Christianity was outlawed, and overseas travel was punishable by death. Although some Japanese scholars were aware of developments in Europe—which went under the broad heading of "Dutch studies"—the shoguns strictly limited their ability to put any of that knowledge to use. They confined all economic and other exchanges with Europeans to a tiny man-made island in the south-western port of Nagasaki. When the Americans arrived in 1853, the Japanese told them to go to Nagasaki and obey the rules. Commodore Perry refused, and Japan concluded that the only way to "expel the barbarians" in future would be to embrace their technology and grow stronger.

But once the door was ajar, the Japanese appetite for "western things" grew unbounded. A modern guidebook entry on the port city of Yokohama, near Tokyo, notes that within two decades of the black ships' arrival it boasted the country's first bakery (1860), photo shop (1862), telephone (1869), beer brewery (1869), cinema (1870), daily newspaper (1870), and public lavatory (1871). Yet, at the same time, Japan's rulers also managed to frustrate many of the westerners' wishes. The constant tension between Japan's desire to measure up to the West—economically, diplomatically, socially and, until 1945, militarily—and its resistance to cultural change has played out in countless ways, good and bad, to this day. Much of it has reflected a healthy wish to hang on to local traditions. This is far more than just a matter of bowing and sleeping on futons and tatami, or of old women continuing to wear kimonos. The Japanese have also clung to distinct ways of speaking, interacting in the workplace, and showing each other respect, all of which have helped people to maintain harmony in many aspects of everyday life. Unfortunately, however, ever since they first opened to the West, anti-liberal Japanese leaders have preferred another interpretation of "Japanese spirit, western things". Instead of simply trying to preserve small cultural traditions, Japan's power-brokers tried to absorb western technology in a way that would shield them from political competition and protect their interests. Imitators still abound in Japan and elsewhere. In East Asia alone, Malaysia's Mahathir Mohamad, Thailand's Thaksin Shinawatra, and even the Chinese Communist Party all see Japan as proof that there is a way to join the rich-country club without making national leaders or their friends accountable. These disciples of Japan's brand of modernisation often use talk of local culture to resist economic and political threats to their power. But they are careful to find ways to do this without undermining all trade and investment, since growth is the only thing propping them up.

Japan's first attempt to pursue this strategy, it must never be forgotten, grew increasingly horrific as its inconsistencies mounted. In 1868, while western writers were admiring those bakeries and cinemas, Japan's nationalist leaders were "restoring" the emperor's significance to that of an imaginary golden age. The trouble, as Ian Buruma describes in his new book, "Inventing Japan" (see article), is that the "Japanese spirit" they valued was a concoction that mixed in several bad western ideas: German theories on racial purity, European excuses for colonialism, and the observation from Christianity that a single overarching deity (in Japan's case the newly restored emperor) could motivate soldiers better than a loose contingent of Shinto gods. This combination would eventually whip countless young Japanese into a murderous xenophobic frenzy and foster rapacious colonial aggression.

It also led Japan into a head-on collision with the United States, since colonialism directly contradicted America's reasons for sending Commodore Perry. In "The Clash", a 1998 book on the history of American-Japanese relations, Walter LaFeber argues that America's main goal in opening Japan was not so much to trade bilaterally, as to enlist Japan's support in creating a global marketplace including, in particular, China. At first, the United States opened Japan because it was on the way to China and had coal for American steamships. Later, as Japan gained industrial and military might, America sought to use it as a counterweight to European colonial powers that wanted to divide China among their empires. America grew steadily more furious, therefore, as Japan turned to colonialism and tried to carve up China on its own. The irony for America was that at its very moment of triumph, after nearly a century of struggling with European powers and then Japan to keep China united and open, it ended up losing it to communism.

A half-century later, however, and with a great deal of help from Japan, America has achieved almost exactly what it set out to do as a brash young power in the 1850s, when it had barely tamed its own continent and was less than a decade away from civil war. Mainland China is whole. It has joined the World Trade Organisation and is rapidly integrating itself into the global economy. It is part of a vast East Asian trade network that nevertheless carries out more than half of its trade outside the region. And this is all backed up by an array of American security guarantees in the Pacific. The resemblance to what America set out to do in 1853 is striking.

For both Japan and America, therefore, the difficult 150-year relationship has brought impressive results. They are now the world's two biggest economies, and have driven most of the world's technological advances over the past half-century. America has helped Japan by opening it up, destroying its militarists and rebuilding the country afterwards, and, for the last 50 years, providing security and market access while Japan became an advanced export dynamo. Japan has helped America by improving on many of its technologies, teaching it new manufacturing techniques, spurring on American firms with its competition, and venturing into East Asia to trade and invest.

And now?

What, then, will the continuing tension between Japanese spirit and western things bring in the decades ahead? For America, though it will no doubt keep complaining, Japan's resistance to change is not the real worry. Instead, the same two Asian challenges that America has taken on ever since Commodore Perry sailed in will remain the most worrying risks: potential rivalries, and the desire by some leaders to form exclusive regional economic blocks. America still needs Japan, its chief Asian ally, to combat these dangers. Japan's failure to reform, however, could slowly sap its usefulness.

For Japan, the challenges are far more daunting. Many of them stem from the increasing toll that Japan's old ways are taking on the economy. Chief among these is Japan's hostility towards competition in many aspects of economic life. Although competitive private firms have driven much of its innovation and growth, especially in export-intensive industries, Japan's political system continues to hobble competition and private enterprise in many domestic sectors.

In farming, health care and education, for example, recent efforts to allow private companies a role have been swatted down by co-operatives, workers, politicians and civil servants. In other inefficient sectors, such as construction and distribution, would-be losers continue to be propped up by government policy. Now that Japan is no longer growing rapidly, it is harder for competitive forces to function without allowing some of those losers to fail.

Japan's foreign critics are correct, moreover, that its macroeconomic and financial policies are a disgrace. The central bank, the finance ministry, the bank regulators, the prime minister and the ruling-party politicians all blame each other for failing to deal with the problems. All the while, Japan continues to limp along, growing far below its potential as its liabilities mount. Its public-sector debt, for instance, is a terrifying 140% of GDP.

Lately, there has been much talk about employing more western things to help lift Japan out of its mess. The prime minister, Junichiro Koizumi, talks about deregulatory measures that have been tried in North America, Europe and elsewhere. Western auditing and corporate governance techniques—applied in a Japanese way, of course—are also lauded as potential fixes. Even inward foreign direct investment is held out by Mr Koizumi as part of the solution: he has pledged to double it over the next five years. The trouble with all of these ideas, however, is that nobody in Japan is accountable for implementing them. Moreover, most of the politicians and bureaucrats who prevent competitive pressures from driving change are themselves protected from political competition. It is undeniable that real change in Japan would bring unwelcome pain for many workers and small-business owners. Still, Japan's leaders continue to use these cultural excuses, as they have for 150 years, to mask their own efforts to cling to power and prestige. The ugly, undemocratic and illiberal aspects of Japanese traditionalism continue to lurk behind its admirable elements. One reason they can do so is because Japan's nationalists have succeeded completely in one of their original goals: financial independence. The desire to avoid relying on foreign capital has underlain Japan's economic policies from the time it opened up to trade. Those policies have worked. More than 90% of government bonds are in the hands of domestic investors, and savings accounts run by the postal service play a huge role in propping up the system.

Paradoxically, financial self-reliance has thus become Japan's curse. There are worse curses to have, of course: compare Japan with the countless countries that have wrecked their economies by overexposing themselves to volatile international capital markets. Nevertheless, Japan's financial insularity further protects its politicians, who do not have to compete with other countries to get funding.

Theories abound as to how all of this might change. Its history ought to remind anyone that, however long it takes, Japan usually moves rapidly once a consensus takes shape. Potential pressures for change could come from the reversal of its trade surpluses, an erosion of support from all those placid postal savers, or the unwinding of ties that allow bad banks and bad companies to protect each other from investors. The current political stalemate could also give way to a coherent plan, either because one political or bureaucratic faction defeats the others or because a strong leader emerges who can force them to cooperate. The past 150 years suggest, however, that one important question is impossible to answer in advance: will it be liberalism or its enemies who turn such changes to their advantage? Too often, Japan's conservative and nationalist leaders have managed to spot the forces of change more quickly than their liberal domestic counterparts, and have used those changes to seize the advantage and preserve their power. Just as in the past, East Asia's fortunes still greatly depend on the outcome of the struggle between these perennial Japanese contenders.

UNIT 2

Pluralist Democracies: Factors in the Political Process

Unit Selections

Key Points to Consider

- How do you explain the apparent shifts toward the political center made by parties of the moderate Left and moderate Right in recent years?

- What are the main sources of electoral support for the far-right political parties?

- Why are women so poorly represented in Parliament and other positions of political leadership?

- In what way has this begun to change, where, and why?

- What became of France's interesting experiment with legislating gender parity for party nominations of political candidates?

- How can institutional arrangements, such as the winner-takes-all election systems, help or hinder an improvement in this situation?

- Would you agree with the inventory of democratic essentials as discussed by Philippe Schmitter and Terry Lynn Karl?

- What do you regard as most and least important in their inventory?

- What are some of the major arguments made in favor of the parliamentary system of government?

- Why do you think Christopher S. Allen includes a multiparty system in his discussion of institutional transplantation.

- Why did de Gaulle include a national referendum in the constitution of the Fifth Republic?

- How does the use of judicial review in some other countries compare with our own?

 **Links: www.dushkin.com/online/**
These sites are annotated in the World Wide Web pages.

Carnegie Endowment for International Peace
http://www.ceip.org

Communications for a Sustainable Future
http://csf.colorado.edu

Inter-American Dialogue (IAD)
http://www.iadialog.org

The North American Institute (NAMI)
http://www.northamericaninstitute.org

Observers of contemporary Western societies frequently refer to the emergence of a new politics in these countries. They are not always very clear or in agreement about what is supposedly novel in the political process or why it is significant. Although no one would dispute that some major changes have taken place in these societies during the last three decades or more, affecting both political attitudes and behavior, it is very difficult to establish clear and comparable patterns of transformation or to gauge their impact and endurance. Yet making sense of continuities and changes in political values and behavior must be one of the central tasks of a comparative study of government.

In two of the most important lines of comparative inquiry, political comparativists have examined the rise and spread of a new set of **"postmaterial" value** and, more recently, the growing signs of **political disaffection** in both "older" and "newer" democracies. The articles in this reader also explore some other trends with major impacts on contemporary politics. Very high on the list is the recent **wave of democratization**—that is, the uneven, incomplete, and unstable but nevertheless remarkable spread of democratic forms of governance to many countries during the last three decades. An important place must also go to the highly controversial "paradigm shift" toward a greater reliance on some kind of **market economics** in much of the world. This move, which has created its own problems and conflicts, also comes in different forms that span the gamut from partial measures of deregulation and privatization in some countries to the practical abandonment of central planning in others. Finally, political scientists recognize the important rise or revival of various forms of "identity politics." This shift has intensified the political role of ethnicity, race, gender, religion, language, and other elements of group identification that go beyond more traditional social, economic, and ideological lines of political division.

Since the early 1970s, political scientists have followed Ronald Inglehart and other careful observers who first noted a marked increase in what they called **postmaterial values**, especially among younger and more highly educated people in the skilled service and administrative occupations in Western Europe.

Such voters showed less interest in the traditional material values of economic well-being and security, and instead stressed participatory and environmental concerns in politics as a way of improving democracy and the general "quality of life." Studies of postmaterialism form a very important addition to our ongoing attempt to interpret and explain not only the so-called youth revolt but also some more lasting shifts in lifestyles and political priorities. It makes intuitive sense that such changes appear to be especially marked among those who grew up in the relative prosperity of Western Europe, after the austere period of reconstruction that followed World War II.

It is possible to find countervailing trends such as the apparent revival of material concerns among some younger people, as economic prosperity and security seem to have become less certain. There are also some indications that political reform activities evoke considerably less interest and commitment than they did earlier.

None of this should be mistaken for a return to the political patterns of the past. Instead, we may be witnessing the emergence of a still somewhat incongruent new mix of material and post-material orientations, along with "old" and "new" forms of political self-expression by the citizenry. Established political parties appear to be in somewhat of a quandary in redefining their positions, at a time when the traditional bonding of many voters to one or another party seems to have become weaker, a phenomenon also known as **dealignment**. Many observers speak about a widespread condition of political malaise in advanced industrial countries, suggesting that it shows up not only in opinion polls but also in a marked **decline in voter participation** and, on occasion, a propensity for voter revolt against the establishment parties and candidates.

The readings in this unit begin with three political briefs that present a comparative perspective on public disillusionment and the decline in voter turnout, the partial weakening of the political parties, and the apparent growth of special interest lobbying. These briefs contain a rich assortment of comparative data and interpretation. Political scientists Dalton, Scarrow and Cain include the United States in their longer comparative study of "advanced democracies and the new politics." They show how the much discussed decline of confidence in representative government has been accompanied by a shift toward other forms of political expression, including more direct democracy and "advocacy democracy." Their discussion also covers the trade-offs involved in this shift.

Without suggesting a simple cause-effect relationship, the British observer Martin Jacques has pointed to possible connections between electoral malaise or **"dealignment"** and the vague rhetoric offered by many political activists and opinion leaders. He believes that the end of the cold war and the collapse of communism in Europe have created a situation that demands a reformulation of political and ideological alternatives. In light of the sharpened differences between much of Europe and the United States over how to approach the Middle East and some other topics such as the Kyoto Accords, some observers wonder whether the end of the cold war will also mean the permanent weakening of the familiar trans-Atlantic relationship. At this point, events are still in flux.

Most established parties seem to have developed an ability to adjust to change, even as the balance of power within each party system shifts over time and occasional newcomers are admitted to the club—or excluded from it. Each country's party system remains uniquely shaped by its political history, but it is possible to delineate some very general patterns of development. One frequently observed trend is toward a narrowing of the ideological distance between the moderate Left and Right in many European countries. Because of this partial convergence, it now often makes more sense to speak of the **Center-Left** and **Center-Right** respectively.

There are still some important ideological and practical differences between the two orientations. Thus **the Right** is usually far more ready to accept as "inevitable" the existence of social or economic inequalities along with the hierarchies they reflect and reinforce. The Right normally favors lower taxes and the promotion of market forces—with some very important exceptions intended to protect the nation as a whole (national defense and internal security) as well as certain favorite groups and values within it. In general, the Right sees the state as an instrument that should provide security, order, and protection for an established way of life. **The Left**, by contrast, traditionally emphasizes that government has an important task in promoting opportunities, delivering services, and reducing social inequalities. On issues such as higher and more progressive taxation, or their respective concern for high rates of unemployment and inflation, there continue to be considerable differences between moderates of the Left and Right.

Even as the ideological distance between Left and Right narrows but remains important, there are also signs of some political differentiation within each camp. On the center-right side of the party spectrum in European politics, economic **neoliberals** (who speak for business and industry) must be clearly distinguished from the **social conservatives** (who are more likely to advocate traditional values and authority). **European liberalism** has its roots in a tradition that favors civil liberties and tolerance but that also emphasizes the importance of individual achievement and laissez-faire economics. For European neoliberals, the state has an important but very limited role to play in providing an institutional framework within which individuals and social groups pursue their interests.

Traditional social conservatives, by contrast, emphasize the importance of societal stability and continuity, and point to the social danger of disruptive change. They often value the strong state as an instrument of order, but many of them also show a paternalist appreciation for welfare state programs that will help keep "the social fabric" from tearing apart. For them, there is a conservative case for a limited welfare state that is not rooted in social liberal or socialist convictions. Instead, it is supported by traditional sentiments of "noblesse oblige" (roughly translated as "privilege has its obligations") and a practical concern for maintaining social harmony.

In British politics, Margaret Thatcher promoted elements from each of these traditions in what could be called her own mix of "business conservatism." The result was a peculiar tension between "**drys**" and "**wets**" within her own Conservative Party, even after she ceased to be its leader. In France, on the other hand, the division between neoliberals and conservatives until recently ran more clearly between the two major center-right parties, the very loosely united Giscardist UDF, and the seemingly more stable neo-Gaullist RPR, who were coalition partners in several governments. In Germany, the Free Democrats (FDP) would most clearly represent the traditional liberal position, while conservative elements can be found among the country's Christian Democrats (CDU/CSU).

On the Left, **democratic socialists** and **ecologists** stress that the sorry political, economic, and environmental record of communist-ruled states in no way diminishes the validity of their own commitment to social justice and environmental protection in modern industrial society. For them, capitalism will continue to produce its own social problems and dissatisfactions. No matter how efficient capitalism may be, they argue, it will continue to result in inequities that require politically directed redress. Today, many on the Left show a pragmatic acceptance of the **modified market economy** as an arena within which to promote their reformist goals. Social Democrats in Scandinavia and Germany have long been known for taking such positions. In recent years their colleagues in Britain and, to a lesser degree, France have followed suit by abandoning some traditional symbols and goals, such as major programs of nationalization. The Socialists in Spain, who governed that new democracy after 1982, went furthest of all in adopting some very business-friendly policies before their loss of power in early 1996.

Some other West European parties further to the left have also moved in the centrist direction in recent years. Two striking examples of this shift can be found among the **Greens in Germany** and in what used to be the Communist Party of Italy. The Greens are by no means an establishment party, but they have served as a pragmatic coalition partner with the Social Democrats in several state governments and have gained respect for their mixture of practical competence and idealism. Their so-called realist faction (Realos) appears to have outmaneuvered its more radical rivals in the party's so-called fundamentalist (or Fundi) wing. Despite some loss in voter support, which can be explained by a revival of the party's internal divisions over strategy and goals, the Greens were finally able to enter government at the national level in 1998. In Gerhard Schröder's government of Social Democrats and Greens, the leading "realo" Joschka Fischer is foreign minister and two other cabinet posts are held by fellow environmentalists. Many German Greens have had a difficult time accepting their country's military involvement in the Kosovo conflict in 1999 and, more recently, in Afghanistan. There is a longer list of moves by the new government that are difficult to square with their idealistic and pacifist origins.

Both center-left and center-right moderates in Europe face a challenge from the **populist tendency** on the **Far Right**, who often seek lower taxes and drastic cuts in the social budget as well as a sharp curtailment of immigration. There is sometimes a **neo-fascist or fascist-descended challenge** as well. These two orientations on the Far Right can often be distinguished, as in Italy, where the populist Northern League and the fascist-descended National Alliance represent positions that seem to be polar opposites on such key issues as government devolution (favored by the former, opposed by the latter). Sometimes a charismatic leader can speak to both orientations, by appealing to their shared fears and resentments. That seems to be the case of Jörg Haider, whose Freedom Party managed to attract over one-quarter of the vote in Austria in the late 1990s. The electoral revival of the right-wing parties can be linked in considerable part to the anxieties and tensions that affect some socially and economically insecure groups in the lower middle class and some sectors of the working class.

Ultra-right nationalist politicians and their parties typically eschew a complex explanation of the structural and cyclical problems that beset the European economies. Instead, their simple answer blames external scapegoats, namely the many immigrants and refugees from Eastern Europe as well as developing countries in Africa and elsewhere. These far-right parties can be found in many countries, including some that have an earned reputation for tolerance like the Netherlands and Denmark. Almost everywhere some of the established parties and politicians have been making concessions on the refugee issue, in order to prevent it from becoming monopolized by extremists.

Women in politics is the concern of the second section in this unit. There continues to be a strong pattern of underrepresentation of women in positions of political and economic leadership practically everywhere. Yet there are some notable differences from country to country, as well as from party to party. Generally speaking, the parties of the Left have been readier to place women in positions of authority, although there are some remarkable exceptions, as the center-right cases of Margaret Thatcher in Britain, Angela Merkl in Germany, and Simone Weil in France illustrate. Far-right parties tend to draw markedly less support from female voters, but at least one of them is led by a woman: Pia Kjaersgaard founded and still heads the People's Party of Denmark.

On the whole, the system of proportional representation gives parties both a tool and an added incentive to place female candidates in positions where they will be elected. But here too, there can be exceptions, as in the case of France in 1986 when women did not benefit from the one-time use of proportional representation in the parliamentary elections. Clearly it is not enough to have a relatively simple means, such as proportional representation, for promoting women in politics: There must also be an **organized will** and a **strategy** among decision makers to use the available tool for the purpose of such a clearly defined reform.

This is where a policy of **affirmative action** can become a decisive strategy. The Scandinavian countries illustrate better than any other example how the breakthrough may occur. There is a markedly higher representation of women in the parliaments of Denmark, Finland, Iceland, Norway, and Sweden, where the political center of gravity is somewhat to the Left and where proportional representation makes it possible to set up party lists that are more representative of the population as a whole. It is of some interest that Iceland has a special women's party with parliamentary representation, but it is far more important that women are found in leading positions within most of the parties of this and the other Scandinavian countries. It usually does not take long for the more centrist or moderately conservative parties to adopt the new concern of gender equality, and these may even move toward the forefront. Thus women have in recent years held the leadership of three of the main parties in Norway (the Social Democrats, the Center Party, and the Conservatives), which together normally receive roughly two-thirds of the total popular vote. And the present Swedish government of Social Democrats has an equal number of women and men in the cabinet.

In another widely reported sign of change, the relatively conservative Republic of Ireland several years ago chose Mary Robinson as its first female president. It is a largely ceremonial post, but it has a symbolic potential that Mary Robinson, an outspoken advocate of liberal reform in her country, was willing to use on behalf of social change. In 1998, a second woman president was elected in Ireland. Perhaps most remarkable of all, the advancement of women into high political ranks has now also touched Switzerland, where they did not get the right to vote until 1971. It is equally noteworthy that Prime Minister Koizumi of Japan appointed five women to his cabinet when he assumed office in 2001, an absolute first in that male-dominated society.

Altogether, there is a growing awareness of the pattern of gender discrimination in most Western countries, along with a greater will to do something to rectify the situation. It seems likely that there will be a significant improvement over the course of the next decade if the pressure for reform is maintained. Several countries have now passed the 30 percent level in their national parliaments, regarded by some observers as a "critical mass." In France, it was lack of political will that derailed one of the most remarkable recent attempts at reform, at least on the first try. It took the form of a statute, promoted by the recent socialist-led government of France, which required the country's political parties to field an equal number of male and female candidates for office in most elections. The first major test of this new parity measure came in the French parliamentary elections of 2002, where it was widely flouted, as Megan Rowling reports in her article.

Changes that erode gender inequality have already occurred in other areas, where there used to be significant political differences between men and women. At one time, for example, there used to be a considerably lower voter turnout among women, but this gender gap has been practically eliminated in recent decades. Similarly the tendency for women to be somewhat more conservative in their party and candidate preferences has given way to a more liberal disposition among younger women in their foreign and social policy preferences than among their male counterparts. These are aggregate differences, of course, and it is important to remember that women, like men, do not represent a monolithic bloc in political attitudes and behavior but are divided by other interests and priorities. One generalization seems to hold: namely, that there is much less inclination among women to support parties or candidates that have a decidedly "radical" image. Thus the vote for extreme right-wing parties in contemporary Europe tends to be considerably higher among males.

In any case, there are some very important policy questions that affect women more directly than men. Any careful statistical study of women in the paid labor force of Europe would supply evidence to support three widely shared impressions: (1) There has been a considerable increase in the number and relative proportion of women who take up paid jobs; (2) These jobs are more often unskilled and/or part-time than in the case of men's employment; and (3) Women generally receive less pay and less social protection than men in similar positions. Such a study would also show that there are considerable differences among West European countries in the relative position of their female workers. The findings would support the argument that political intervention in the form of appropriate legislation can improve the employment status of women.

The socioeconomic status of women in other parts of the world is often far worse. According to reports of the UN Development Program, there have been some rapid advances for women in the field of education and health opportunities, but the doors to economic opportunities are barely ajar. In the field of political leadership, the picture is more varied, as the UN reports indicate, but women generally hold few positions of importance in national politics.

The institutional framework of representative government is the subject of the third section of this unit. Here the authors examine and compare a number of institutional arrangements: (1) essential characteristics and elements of a pluralist democracy, (2) two major forms of representative government, (3) the varying use of judicial review, and (4) the use of national and regional referendums as well as other forms of direct democracy.

The topic of pluralist democracy is a complex one, but Philippe Schmitter and Terry Lynn Karl manage to present a very comprehensive discussion of the subject in a short space. Finally, Christopher S. Allen goes further in bringing U.S. politics into our comparative framework. His article can be seen as part of a long tradition of American interest in the parliamentary form of government and, to a lesser degree, in a multiparty system. Allen organizes his argument as a mental experiment in institutional transplantation, in order to explore how a multiparty parliamentary system would change the American political process. His intriguing rearrangement of our familiar political setting serves as a reminder that institutions are not neutral but have important consequences for the political process.

Public Opinion: Is there a crisis?

After the collapse of communism, the world saw a surge in the number of new democracies. But why are the citizens of the mature democracies meanwhile losing confidence in their political institutions? This is the first in a series of articles on democracy in transition.

Everyone remembers that Winston Churchill once called democracy the worst form of government—except for all the others. The end of the cold war seemed to prove him right. All but a handful of countries now claim to embrace democratic ide-

als. Insofar as there is a debate about democracy, much of it now centers on how to help the "emerging" democracies of Asia, Africa, Latin America and Eastern Europe catch up with the established democratic countries of the West and Japan.

The new democracies are used to having well-meaning observers from the mature democracies descend on them at election time to ensure that the voting is free and fair. But is political life in these mature democracies as healthy as it should be?

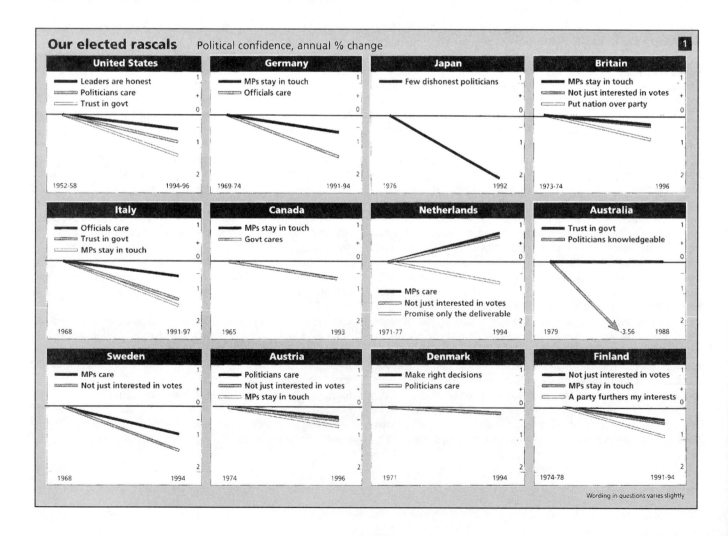

Our elected rascals Political confidence, annual % change

United States
- Leaders are honest
- Politicians care
- Trust in govt

1952-58 — 1994-96

Germany
- MPs stay in touch
- Officials care

1969-74 — 1991-94

Japan
- Few dishonest politicians

1976 — 1992

Britain
- MPs stay in touch
- Not just interested in votes
- Put nation over party

1973-74 — 1996

Italy
- Officials care
- Trust in govt
- MPs stay in touch

1968 — 1991-97

Canada
- MPs stay in touch
- Govt cares

1965 — 1993

Netherlands
- MPs care
- Not just interested in votes
- Promise only the deliverable

1971-77 — 1994

Australia
- Trust in govt
- Politicians knowledgeable

1979 — -3.56 — 1988

Sweden
- MPs care
- Not just interested in votes

1968 — 1994

Austria
- Politicians care
- Not just interested in votes
- MPs stay in touch

1974 — 1996

Denmark
- Make right decisions
- Politicians care

1971 — 1994

Finland
- Not just interested in votes
- MPs stay in touch
- A party furthers my interests

1974-78 — 1991-94

Wording in questions varies slightly

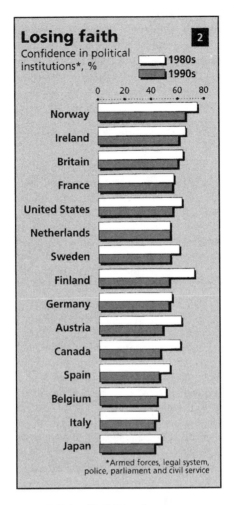

Losing faith

Confidence in political institutions*, %

☐ 1980s
■ 1990s

Norway
Ireland
Britain
France
United States
Netherlands
Sweden
Finland
Germany
Austria
Canada
Spain
Belgium
Italy
Japan

*Armed forces, legal system, police, parliament and civil service

Sources: R. Dalton; World Values Surveys

If opinion research is any guide, the mature democracies have troubles of their own. In the United States in particular, the high opinion which people had of their government has declined steadily over the past four decades. Regular opinion surveys carried out as part of a series of national election studies in America show that the slump set in during the 1960s. The civil-rights conflict and the Vietnam war made this an especially turbulent decade for the United States. But public confidence in politicians and government continued to decline over the next quarter-century. Nor (remember the student unrest in Paris and elsewhere in 1968) was this confined to the United States.

It is hard to compare attitudes toward democracy over time, and across many different countries. Most opinion surveys are carried out nation-by-nation: they are conducted at different times and researchers often ask different sorts of questions. But some generalizations can be made. In their introduction to a forthcoming book "What is Troubling the Trilateral Democracies?", Princeton University Press, 2000) three ac-

ademics—Robert Putnam, Susan Pharr, and Russell Dalton—have done their best to analyze the results of surveys conducted in most of the rich countries.

Chart 1 summarises some of these findings. The downward slopes show how public confidence in politicians seems to be falling, measured by changes in the answers voters give to questions such as "Do you think that politicians are trustworthy?"; "Do members of parliament (MPS) care about voters like you?"; and "How much do you trust governments of any party to place the needs of the nation above their own political party?" In most of the mature democracies, the results show a pattern of disillusionment with politicians. Only in the Netherlands is there clear evidence of rising confidence.

Nor is it only politicians who are losing the public's trust. Surveys suggest that confidence in political institutions is in decline as well. In 11 out of 14 countries, for example, confidence in parliament has declined, with especially sharp falls in Canada, Germany, Britain, Sweden and the United States. World-wide polls conducted in 1981 and 1990 measured confidence in five institutions: parliament, the armed services, the judiciary, the police and the civil service. Some institutions gained public trust, but on average confidence in them decreased by 6% over the decade (see chart 2). The only countries to score small increases in confidence were Iceland and Denmark.

Other findings summarised by Mr Putnam and his colleagues make uncomfortable reading:

• In the late 1950s and early 1960s **Americans** had a touching faith in government. When asked "How many times can you trust the government in Washington to do what is right?", three out of four answered "most of the time" or "just about always". By 1998, fewer than four out of ten trusted the government to do what was right. In 1964 only 29% of the American electorate agreed that "the government is pretty much run by a few big interests looking after themselves". By 1984, that figure had risen to 55%, and by 1998 to 63%. In the 1960s, two-thirds of Americans rejected the statement "most elected officials don't care what people like me think". In 1998, nearly two-thirds agreed with it. The proportion of Americans who expressed "a great deal of" confidence in the executive branch fell from 42% in 1966 to 12% in 1997; and trust in Congress fell from 42% to 11%.

• **Canadians** have also been losing faith in their politicians. The proportion of Canadians who felt that "the government doesn't care what people like me think" rose from 45% in 1968 to 67% in 1993. The proportion expressing "a great deal of" confidence in political parties fell from 30% in 1979 to 11% in 1999. Confidence in the House of Commons fell from 49% in 1974 to 21% in 1996. By 1992 only 34% of Canadians were satisfied with their system of government, down from 51% in 1986.

Staying home

Voter turnout, %

☐ First two 1950s elections
■ Two most recent elections*

Iceland
Italy
Sweden
Denmark
Australia
Belgium
Netherlands
Austria
Norway
New Zealand
Britain
Germany
Finland
Ireland
Japan
Canada
Luxembourg
France
United States
Switzerland

*As of March 1998

Source: Martin P. Wattenberg, University of California, Irvine

• Less information is available about attitudes in **Japan**. But the findings of the few surveys that have been carried out there match the global pattern. Confidence in political institutions rose in the decades following the smashing of the country's old politics in the second world war. Happily for democracy, the proportion of Japanese voters who agree that "in order to make Japan better, it is best to rely on talented politicians, rather than to let the citizens argue among themselves" has been falling for 40 years. However, the proportion who feel that they exert at least "some influence" on national politics through elections or demonstrations also fell steadily between 1973 and 1993.

• Although it is harder to generalize about **Western Europe**, confidence in political institutions is in decline in most countries. In 1985 48% of Britons expressed quite a lot of confidence in the House of Commons. This number had halved by 1995. The proportion of Swedes disagreeing with the statement that "parties are only interested in people's votes, not in their opinions" slumped from 51% in 1968 to 28% in 1994. In 1985 51% expressed confidence in the Rikstad (parliament); by 1996 only 19% did. In Germany, the percentage of people who said they trusted their Bundestag deputy to represent their interests rose from 25% in 1951 to 55% in 1978, but had fallen again to 34% by 1992. The percentage of Italians who say that politicians "don't care what people like me think" increased from 68% in 1968 to 84% in 1997.

Such findings are alarming if you take them at face value. But they should be interpreted with care. Democracy may just be a victim of its own success. It could just be that people nowadays expect more from governments, impose new demands on the state, and are therefore more likely to be disappointed. After all, the idea that governments ought to do such things as protect or improve the environment, maintain high employment, arbitrate between moral issues, or ensure the equal treatment of women or minorities, is a relatively modern and still controversial one. Or perhaps

the disillusionment is a healthy product of rising educational standards and the scepticism that goes with it. Or maybe it is caused by the media's search-light highlighting failures of government that were previously kept in the dark. Whatever the causes, the popularity of governments or politicians ought not to be the only test of democracy's health.

Moreover, there is encouraging evidence to put beside the discouraging findings. However much confidence in government may be declining, this does not seem to have diminished popular support for democratic principles. On average, surveys show, more than three out of four people in rich countries believe that democracy is the best form of government. Even in countries where the performance of particular governments has been so disappointing as to break up the party system itself (such as Japan and Italy in 1993–95), this has brought no serious threat to fundamental democratic principle. It may seem paradoxical for people to express strong support for democracy even while their confidence in politicians and political institutions crumbles. But it hardly amounts to the "crisis of democracy" which political scientists tend to proclaim from time to time.

Nor, though, is it a ringing endorsement, especially given that the evidence of opinion surveys is reinforced by other trends. These include a decline both in the membership of political parties and in the proportion of people who turn out to vote. Numbers compiled by Martin Wattenberg, also at the University of California, show that in 18 out of 20 of the rich established democracies the proportion of the electorate voting has been lower than it was in the early 1950s (see chart 3), with the median change being a decline of 10%. More controversially, some political scientists see the growth of protest movements since the

1960s as a sign of declining faith in the traditional institutions of representative democracy, and an attempt to bypass them. Others reckon that the most serious threat comes from the increasingly professional pressure groups and lobbying organisations that work behind the scenes to influence government policy and defend special interests, often at the expense of the electorate as a whole.

What is to be done? Those who believe that government has over-reached itself call on governments to become smaller and to promise less. Thus, it is hoped, people will come to do more for themselves. But whatever the appropriate size and reach of governments, there is also scope for making the machinery of democracy work better.

Indeed, some commentators see the public's declining confidence in political institutions as an opportunity for democratic renewal. Pippa Norris, at Harvard University's Kennedy School of Government, hails the advent of a new breed of "critical citizens" (in a book of that name, Oxford University Press, 1999) who see that existing channels of participation fall short of democratic ideals and want to reform them.

There are some signs of this. Countries as different as Italy, Japan, Britain and New Zealand have lately considered or introduced changes in their electoral systems. Countries around the world are making growing use of referendums and other forms of direct democracy. Many are reducing the power of parliaments by giving judges new powers to review the decisions that elected politicians make. And governments everywhere are introducing new rules on the financing of politicians and political parties. The rest of the articles in this series will look at some of these changes and the forces shaping them.

Political Parties: Empty vessels?

Alexis de Tocqueville called political parties an evil inherent in free governments. The second of our briefs on the mature democracies in transition asks whether parties are in decline

WHAT would democracy look like if there were no political parties? It is almost impossible to imagine. In every democracy worth the name, the contest to win the allegiance of the electorate and form a government takes place through political parties. Without them, voters would be hard put to work out what individual candidates stood for or intended to do once elected. If parties did not "aggregate" people's interests, politics might degenerate into a fight between tiny factions, each promoting its narrow self-interest. But for the past 30 years, political scientists have been asking whether parties are "in decline". Are they? And if so, does it matter?

Generalising about political parties is difficult. Their shape depends on a country's history, constitution and much else. For example, America's federal structure and separation of powers make Republicans and Democrats amorphous groupings whose main purpose is to put their man in the White House. British parties behave quite differently because members of Parliament must toe the party line to keep their man in Downing Street. An American president is safe once elected, so congressmen behave like local representatives rather than members of a national organisation bearing collective responsibility for government. Countries which, unlike Britain and America, hold elections under proportional representation are different again: they tend to produce multi-party systems and coalition governments.

Despite these differences, some trends common to almost all advanced democracies appear to be changing the nature of parties and, on one view, making them less

influential. Those who buy this thesis of decline point to the following changes:

People's behaviour is becoming more **private**. Why join a political party when you can go fly fishing or surf the web? Back in the 1950s, clubs affiliated to the Labour Party were places for Britain's working people to meet, play and study. The Conservative Party was, among other things, a marriage bureau for the better-off. Today, belonging to a British political party is more like being a supporter of some charity: you may pay a membership fee, but will not necessarily attend meetings or help to turn out the vote at election time.

Running out of ideas

Politics is becoming more **secular**. Before the 1960s, political struggles had an almost religious intensity: in much of Western Europe this took the form of communists versus Catholics, or workers versus bosses. But ideological differences were narrowing by the 1960s and became smaller still after the collapse of Soviet communism. Nowadays, politics seems to be more often about policies than values, about the competence of leaders rather than the beliefs of the led. As education grows and class distinctions blur, voters discard old loyalties. In America in 1960, two out of five voters saw themselves as "strong" Democrats or "strong" Republicans. By 1996 less than one in three saw themselves that way. The proportion of British voters expressing a "very strong" affinity with one party slumped from 44% to 16% between 1964 and 1997. This process of **"partisan de-**

alignment" has been witnessed in most mature democracies.

The erosion of loyalty is said to have pushed parties towards the **ideological centre**. The political extremes have not gone away. But mainstream parties which used to offer a straight choice between socialists and conservatives are no longer so easy to label. In the late 1950s Germany's Social Democrats (SPD) snipped off their Marxist roots in order to recast themselves is a *Volkspartei* appealing to all the people. "New" Labour no longer portrays itself as the political arm of the British working class or trade-union movement. Bill Clinton, before he became president, helped to shift the Democratic Party towards an appreciation of business and free trade. Neat ideological labels have become harder to pin on parties since they have had to contend with the emergence of what some commentators call **post-material issues** (such as the environment, personal morality and consumer rights) which do not slot elegantly into the old left-right framework

The **mass media** have taken over many of the information functions that parties once performed for themselves. "Just as radio and television have largely killed off the door-to-door salesman," says Anthony King, of Britain's Essex University, "so they have largely killed off the old-fashioned party worker." In 1878 the German SPD had nearly 50 of its own newspapers. Today the mass media enable politicians to communicate directly with voters without owning printing presses or needing party workers to knock on doors. In many other ways, the business of winning elections has become more capital-intensive and less labour-intensive, making political donors matter more and political activists less.

Another apparent threat to the parties is the growth of **interest and pressure groups**. Why should voters care about the broad sweep of policy promoted during elections by a party when other organisations will lobby all year round for their special interest, whether this is protection of the environment, opposition to abortion, or the defence of some subsidy? Some academics also claim that parties are playing a smaller role, and **think tanks** a bigger one, in making policy. Although parties continue to draw up election manifestos, they are wary of being too specific. Some hate leaving policymaking to party activists, who may be more extreme than voters at large and so put them off. Better to keep the message vague. Or why not let the tough choices be taken by **referendums**, as so often in Switzerland?

Academics have found these trends easier to describe than to evaluate. Most agree that the age of the "mass party" has passed and that its place is being taken by the "electoral-professional" or "catch-all" party. Although still staffed by politicians holding genuine beliefs and values, these modern parties are inclined to see their main objective as winning elections rather than forming large membership organisations or social movements, as was once the case.

Is this a bad thing? Perhaps, if it reduces participation in politics. One of the traditional roles of political parties has been to get out the vote, and in 18 out of 20 rich countries, recent turnout figures have been lower than they were in the 1950s. Although it is hard to pin down the reasons, Martin Wattenberg, of the University of California at Irvine, points out that turnout has fallen most sharply in countries where parties are weak: Switzerland (thanks to those referendums), America and France (where presidential elections have become increasingly candidate- rather than party-centred), and Japan (where political loyalties revolve around ties to internal factions rather than the party itself). In Scandinavia, by contrast, where class-based parties are still relatively strong, turnout has held up much better since the 1950s.

Running out of members

It is not only voters who are turned off. Party membership is falling too, and even the most strenuous attempts to reverse the decline have faltered. Germany is a case in point. The Social Democrats there increased membership rapidly in the 1960s

and 1970s, and the Christian Democrats responded by doubling their own membership numbers. But since the end of the 1980s membership has been falling, especially among the young. In 1964 Britain's Labour Party had about 830,000 members and the Conservatives about 2m. By 1997 they had 420,000 and 400,000 respectively. The fall is sharper in some countries than others, but research by Susan Scarrow of the University of Houston suggests that the trend is common to most democracies (see chart). With their membership falling, ideological differences blurring, and fewer people turning out to vote, the decline thesis looks hard to refute.

Or does it? The case for party decline has some big holes in it. For a start, some academics question whether political parties ever really enjoyed the golden age which other academics hark back to. Essex University's Mr King points out that a lot of the evidence for decline is drawn from a handful of parties—Britain's two main ones, the German SPD, the French and Italian Communists—which did indeed once promote clear ideologies, enjoy mass memberships, and organise local branches and social activities. But neither of America's parties, nor Canada's, nor many of the bourgeois parties of Western Europe, were ever mass parties of that sort. Moreover, in spite of their supposed decline, parties continue to keep an iron grip on many aspects of politics.

In most places, for example, parties still control **nomination for public office**. In almost all of the mature democracies, it is rare for independent candidates to be elected to federal or state legislatures, and even in local government the proportion of independents has declined sharply since the early 1970s. When state and local parties select candidates, they usually favour people who have worked hard within the party. German parties, for example, are often conduits to jobs in the public sector, with a say over appointments to top jobs in the civil service and to the boards of publicly owned utilities or media organisations. Even in America, where independent candidates are more common in local elections, the parties still run city, county and state "machines" in which most politicians start their careers.

Naturally, there are some exceptions. In 1994 Silvio Berlusconi, a media tycoon, was able to make himself prime minister at the head of Forza Italia, a right-wing movement drawing heavily on his personal fortune and the resources of his television empire. Ross Perot, a wealthy third-party

candidate, won a respectable 19% vote in his 1992 bid for the American presidency. The party declinists claim these examples as evidence for their case. But it is notable that in the end Mr Perot could not compete against the two formidable campaigning and money-raising machines ranged against him.

This suggests that a decline in the membership of parties need not make them weaker in **money and organisation**. In fact, many have enriched themselves simply by passing laws that give them public money. In Germany, campaign subsidies to the federal parties more than trebled between 1970 and 1990, and parties now receive between 20% and 40% of their income from public funds. In America, the paid professionals who have taken over from party activists tend to do their job more efficiently. Moreover, other kinds of political activity—such as donating money to a party or interest group, or attending meetings and rallies—have become more common in America. Groups campaigning for particular causes or candidates (the pro-Republican Christian Coalition, say, or the pro-Democrat National Education Association) may not be formally affiliated with the major party organisations, but are frequently allied with them.

The role of the mass media deserves a closer look as well. It is true that they have weakened the parties' traditional methods of communicating with members. But parties have invested heavily in managing relations with journalists, and making use of new media to reach both members and wider audiences. In Britain, the dwindling of local activists has gone hand-in-hand with a more professional approach to communications. Margaret Thatcher caused a stir by using an advertising firm, Saatchi & Saatchi, to push the Tory cause in the 1979 election. By the time of Britain's 1997 election, the New Labour media operation run from Millbank Tower in London was even slicker.

Another way to gauge the influence of parties is by their **reach**—that is, their power, once in office, to take control of the governmental apparatus. This is a power they have retained. Most governments tend to be unambiguously under the control of people who represent a party, and who would not be in government if they did not belong to such organisations. The French presidential system may appear ideal for independent candidates, but except—arguably—for Charles de Gaulle, who claimed to rise above party, none has ever been elected without party support.

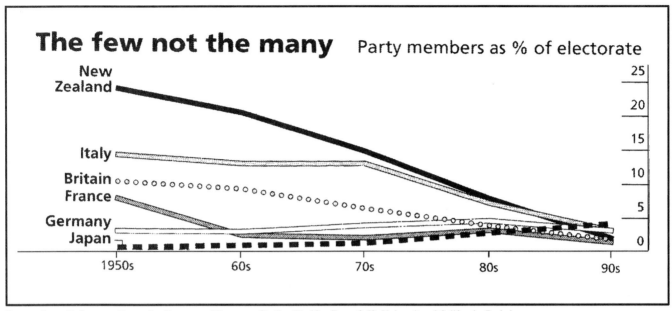

The few not the many Party members as % of electorate

Source: Susan E. Scarrow, Centre for German and European Studies Working Paper 2.59, University of California, Berkeley

The fire next time

Given the cautions that must be applied to other parts of the case for party decline, what can be said about one of the declinists' key exhibits, the erosion of ideological differences? At first sight, this is borne out by the recent movement to the centre of left-leaning parties such as America's Democrats, New Labour in Britain, and the SPD under Gerhard Schröder. In America, Newt Gingrich stoked up some fire amongst Republicans in 1994, but it has flickered out. The most popular Republican presidential hopefuls, and especially George W. Bush, the front-runner, are once again stressing the gentler side of their conservatism.

Still, the claim of ideological convergence can be exaggerated. It is not much more than a decade since Ronald Reagan and Mrs Thatcher ran successful parties with strong ideologies. And the anecdotal assumption that parties are growing less distinct is challenged by longer-term academic studies. A look at the experience of ten western democracies since 1945 ("Parties, Policies and Democracy", Westview Press, 1994) concluded that the leading left and right parties continued to keep their distance and maintain their identity, rather

than clustering around the median voter in the centre. Paul Webb of Britain's Brunel University concludes in a forthcoming book ("Political Parties in Advanced Industrial Democracies", Oxford University Press) that although partisan sentiment is weaker than it was, and voters more cynical, parties have in general adapted well to changing circumstances.

Besides, even if party differences are narrowing at present, why expect that trend to continue? In Western Europe, the ending of the cold war has snuffed out one source of ideological conflict, but new sparks might catch fire. Battered right-wing parties may try to revive their fortunes by pushing the nationalist cause against the encroachments of the European Union. In some places where ideas are dividing parties less, geography is dividing them more. Politics in Germany and Britain has acquired an increasingly regional flavour: Labour and the Social Democrats respectively dominate the north, Conservatives and Christian Democrats the south. Disaffected *Ossis* are flocking to the Party of Democratic Socialism in eastern Germany. Britain, Italy, Canada and Spain have strong separatist parties.

So there is life in the party system yet. But the declinists are on to something. The

Germans have a word for it. One reason given for the rise of Germany's Greens in the 1980s and America's Mr Perot in 1992 was *Parteienverdrossenheit*—disillusionment with mainstream parties that seemed to have abandoned their core beliefs and no longer offered meaningful choices. A "new politics" of citizens' protests appeared to be displacing conventional politics.

In the end, far from undermining the domination of the parties, the German Greens ended up by turning themselves into one and joining the government in an uneasy coalition with the SPD. The balance of evidence from around the world is that despite all the things that are changing them, parties continue to dominate democratic politics.

Indeed, there are grounds for wondering whether their continuing survival is more of a worry than their supposed decline. Is it so very comforting that parties can lose members, worry less about ideas, become detached from broader social movements, attract fewer voters and still retain an iron grip on politics? If they are so unanchored, will they not fall prey to special-interest groups? If they rely on state funding instead of member contributions, will they not turn into creatures of the state? The role of money in politics will be the subject of another brief.

Interest Groups:
Ex uno, plures

The last article in our series on the mature democracies asks whether they are in danger of being strangled by lobbyists and single-issue pressure groups

Previous briefs in this series have looked at the imperfections in democracy as it is currently practised in the rich countries, and at some of the efforts that different countries are making to overcome them. Evidence that all is not well includes declining public confidence in politicians, falling membership of political parties and smaller turnouts for elections. Ideas for improvement range from making greater use of referendums and other forms of direct democracy, to giving more power to courts to check the power of politicians. This article asks a different question: far from being too powerful, are elected politicians in modern democracies too weak?

When Alexis de Tocqueville visited the United States in the 19th century, he was impressed by the enthusiasm of Americans for joining associations. This, he felt, spread power away from the centre and fostered the emergence of democratic habits and a civil society. Until quite recently, most political scientists shared De Tocqueville's view. Lately, however, and especially in America, doubts have set in. At a certain point, say the doubters, the cumulative power of pressure groups, each promoting its own special interests, can grow so strong that it prevents elected politicians from adopting policies that are in the interest of the electorate as a whole.

A hitch-hiker's guide

A key text for such critics was a short book published in 1965 by Mancur Olson, an American economist. Called "The Logic of Collective Action", this took issue with the traditional idea that the health of democracy was served by vigorous competition between pressure groups, with governments acting as a sort of referee, able to choose the best policy once the debate between the contending groups was over. The traditional view, Olson argued, wrongly assumed that pressure groups were more or less equal. In fact, for a reason known to economists as the free-rider problem, they weren't.

Why? Take the example of five car firms, which form a lobbying group in the hope of raising the price of cars. If they succeed, each stands to reap a fifth of the gains. This makes forming the group and working for its success well worth each firm's investment of time and money. If the car makers succeed, of course, motorists will suffer. But organising millions of individual motorists to fight their corner is a great deal harder because it involves coordinating millions of people and because the potential gain for each motorist will be relatively small. Individual motorists will be tempted to reason that, with millions of other people involved, they do not need to do anything themselves, but can instead hitch a "free ride" on the efforts of everyone else.

This simple insight has powerful implications. Indeed, in a later book Olson went on to argue that his theory helped to explain why some nations flourish and others decline. As pressure groups multiply over time, they tend to choke a nation's vitality by impairing the government's ability to act in the wider interest. That, he argued, is why countries such as Germany and Japan—whose interest groups had been cleared away by a traumatic defeat—had fared better after the second world war than Britain, whose institutions had survived intact. With its long record of stability, said Olson, "British society has acquired so many strong organisations and collusions that it suffers from an institutional sclerosis that slows its adaptation to changing circumstances and changing technologies."

Olson's ideas have not gone unchallenged. But they have had a big impact on contemporary thinking about what ails American democracy. In "Demosclerosis" (Times Books, 1994), Jonathan Rauch, a populariser of Olson's work, says that America is afflicted by "hyperpluralism". With at least seven out of ten Americans belonging to at least one such association, the whole society, not just "special" parts of it, is involved in influence peddling.

The result is that elected politicians find it almost impossible to act solely in the wider public interest. Bill Clinton wants to reform the health system? The health-insurance industry blocks him. China's membership in the World Trade Organisation would benefit America's consumers? America's producers of textiles and steel stand in the way. Jimmy Carter complained when he left the presidency that

Americans were increasingly drawn to single-issue groups to ensure that, whatever else happened, their own private interest would be protected. The trouble is, "the national interest is not always the sum of all our single or special interests".

Pressure groups are especially visible in the United States. As Oxford University's Jeremy Richardson puts it ("Pressure Groups", Oxford University Press, 1993), "pressure groups take account of (and exploit) the multiplicity of access points which is so characteristic of the American system of government—the presidency, the bureaucracy, both houses of Congress, the powerful congressional committees, the judiciary and state and local government."

Nevertheless pressure groups often wield just as much influence in other countries. In those where parliaments exercise tighter control of the executive—Canada, Britain or Germany, say—the government controls the parliamentary timetable and the powers of committees are much weaker. This means that pressure groups adopt different tactics. They have more chance of influencing policy behind closed doors, by bargaining with the executive branch and its civil servants before legislation comes before parliament. In this way pressure groups can sometimes exert more influence than their counterparts in America.

Political tribes

Many European countries have also buttressed the influence of pressure groups by giving them a semi-official status. In Germany, for example, the executive branch is obliged by law to consult the various big "interest organisations" before drafting legislation. In some German states, leading interest groups (along with political parties) have seats on the supervisory boards of broadcasting firms.

French pressure groups are also powerful, despite the conventional image of a strong French state dominating a relatively weak civil society. It is true that a lot of France's interest groups depend on the state for both money and membership of a network of formal consultative bodies. But a tradition of direct protest compensates for some of this institutional weakness. In France, mass demonstrations, strikes, the blocking of roads and the disruption of public services are seen as a part of normal democratic politics.

In Japan, powerful pressure groups such as the Zenchu (Central Union of Agricultural Co-operatives) have turned large areas of public policy into virtual no-go areas. With more than 9m members (and an electoral system that gives farming communities up to three times the voting weight of urban voters), farmers can usually obstruct any policy that damages their interests. The teachers' union has similarly blocked all attempts at education reform. And almost every sector of Japanese society has its *zoku giin* (political tribes), consisting of Diet members who have made themselves knowledgeable about one industry or another, which pays for their secretaries and provides campaign funds. A Diet member belonging to the transport tribe will work hand-in-glove with senior bureaucrats in the transport ministry and the trucking industry to form what the Japanese call an "iron triangle" consisting of politicians, bureaucrats and big business.

Pressure groups are also increasingly active at a transnational level. Like any bureaucracy, the European Union has spawned a rich network of interest groups. In 1992 the European Commission reckoned that at least 3,000 special-interest groups in Brussels employing some 10,000 people acted as lobbyists. These range from big operations, such as the EU committee of the American Chamber of Commerce, to small firms and individual lobbyists-for-hire. Businesses were the first to spot the advantages of influencing the EU's law making. But trade unions swiftly followed, often achieving in Brussels breakthroughs (such as regulations on working conditions) that they could not achieve at home.

The case for the defense

So pressure groups are ubiquitous. But are they so bad? Although it has been influential, the Olson thesis has not swept all before it. Many political scientists argue that the traditional view that pressure groups create a healthy democratic pluralism is nearer the mark than Olson's thesis.

The case in favour of pressure groups begins with some of the flaws of representative democracy. Elections are infrequent and, as a previous brief in this series noted, political parties can be vague about their governing intentions. Pressure groups help people to take part in politics between elections, and to influence a government's policy in areas that they care and know about. Pressure groups also check excessive central power and give governments expert advice. Although some groups may flourish at the expense of the common weal, this danger can be guarded against if there are many groups and if all have the same freedom to organise and to put their case to government

Critics of Olson's ideas also point out that, contrary to his prediction, many broad-based groups have in fact managed to flourish in circumstances where individual members stand to make little personal gain and should therefore fall foul of his "free-rider" problem. Clearly, some people join pressure groups for apparently altruistic reasons—perhaps simply to express their values or to be part of an organisation in which they meet like-minded people. Some consumer and environmental movements have flourished in rich countries, even though Olson's theory suggests that firms and polluters should have a strong organisational advantage over consumers and inhalers of dirty air.

Moreover, despite "demosclerosis", well-organised pressure groups can sometimes ease the task of government, not just throw sand into its wheels. The common European practice of giving pressure groups a formal status, and often a legal right to be consulted, minimises conflict by ensuring that powerful groups put their case to governments before laws are introduced. Mr Richardson argues in a forthcoming book ("Developments in the European Union", Macmillan, 1999) that even the pressure groups clustering around the institutions of the EU perform a valuable function. The European Commission, concerned with the detail of regulation, is an eager consumer of their specialist knowledge. As the powers of the European Parliament have grown, it too has attracted a growing band of lobbyists. The parliament has created scores of "intergroups" whose members gain expertise in specific sectors, such as pharmaceuticals, from industry and consumer lobbies.

Governments can learn from pressure groups, and can work through them to gain consent for their policies. At some point, however, the relationship becomes excessively cosy. If pressure groups grow too strong, they can deter governments from pursuing policies which are in the wider public interest. The temptation of governments to support protectionist trade policies at the behest of producer lobbies and at the expense of consumers is a classic example supporting Olson's theories. But problems also arise when it is governments that are relatively strong, and so able to confer special status on some pressure groups and withhold it from others. This puts less-favoured groups at a disadvantage, which they often seek to redress by finding new and sometimes less democratic ways of making their voices heard.

In Germany, for example, disenchantment with what had come to be seen as an excessively cosy system of bargaining between elite groups helped to spark an explosion of protest movements in the 1980s. In many other countries, too, there is a sense that politics has mutated since the 1960s from an activity organised largely around parties to one organised around specialised interest groups on the one hand (such as America's gun lobby) and broader protest and social movements on the other (such as the women's movement, environmentalism and consumerism). One reason for the change is clearly the growth in the size and scope of government. Now that it touches virtually every aspect of people's lives, a bewildering array of groups has sprung up around it.

Many of Olson's disciples blame pressure groups for making government grow. As each special group wins new favours from the state, it makes the state bigger and clumsier, undermining the authority of elected parties, loading excessive demands on government in general, and preventing any particular government from acting in the interest of the relatively disorganised majority of people. By encouraging governments to do too much, say critics on the

right, pressure groups prevent governments from doing anything well. Their solution is for governments to do less. Critics on the left are more inclined to complain that pressure groups exaggerate inequalities by giving those better-organised (ie, the rich and powerful) an influence out of all proportion to their actual numbers.

So what is to be done? A lot could be, but little is likely to be. There is precious little evidence from recent elections to suggest that the citizens of the rich countries want to see a radical cut in the size or scope of the state. As for political inequality, even this has its defenders. John Mueller, of America's University of Rochester, argues that democracy has had a good, if imperfect, record of dealing with minority issues, particularly when compared with other forms of government But he claims that this is less because democratic majorities are tolerant of minorities and more because democracy gives minorities the opportunity

to increase their effective political weight—to become more equal, more important, than their arithmetical size would imply—on issues that concern them. This holds even for groups held in contempt by the majority, like homosexuals. Moreover, the fact that most people most of the

time pay little attention to politics—the phenomenon of political apathy—helps interested minorities to protect their rights and to assert their interests.

Adaptability

This series of briefs has highlighted some of the defects in the practice of democracy, and some of the changes that the mature democracies are making in order to improve matters. But the defects need to be kept in perspective.

One famous critic of democracy claimed that for most people it did nothing more than allow them "once every few years, to decide which particular representatives of the oppressing class should be in parliament to represent and oppress them". When Marx wrote those words in the 19th century, they contained an element of truth. Tragically, Lenin treated this view as an eternal verity, with calamitous results for millions of people. What they both ignored was democracy's ability to evolve, which is perhaps its key virtue. Every mature democracy continues to evolve today. As a result, violent revolution in those countries where democracy has taken deepest root looks less attractive, and more remote, than ever.

ADVANCED DEMOCRACIES AND THE NEW POLITICS

Russell J. Dalton, Susan E. Scarrow, and Bruce E. Cain

Over the past quarter-century in advanced industrial democracies, citizens, public interest groups, and political elites have shown decreasing confidence in the institutions and processes of representative government. In most of these nations, electoral turnout and party membership have declined, and citizens are increasingly skeptical of politicians and political institutions.[1]

Along with these trends often go louder demands to expand citizen and interest-group access to politics, and to restructure democratic decision-making processes. Fewer people may be voting, but more are signing petitions, joining lobby groups, and engaging in unconventional forms of political action.[2] Referenda and ballot initiatives are growing in popularity; there is growing interest in processes of deliberative or consultative democracy;[3] and there are regular calls for more reliance on citizen advisory committees for policy formation and administration—especially at the local level, where direct involvement is most feasible. Contemporary democracies are facing popular pressures to grant more access, increase the transparency of governance, and make government more accountable.

Amplifying these trends, a chorus of political experts has been calling for democracies to reform and adapt. Mark Warren writes, "Democracy, once again in favor, is in need of conceptual renewal. While the traditional concerns of democratic theory with state-centered institutions remain importantly crucial and ethically central, they are increasingly subject to the limitations we should expect when nineteenth-century concepts meet twenty-first century realities."[4] U.S. political analyst Dick Morris similarly observes, "The fundamental paradigm that dominates our politics is the shift from representative to direct democracy. Voters want to run the show directly and are impatient with all forms of intermediaries between their opinions and public policy."[5] As Ralf Dahrendorf recently summarized the mood of the times, "Representative government is no longer as compelling a proposition as it once was. Instead, a search for new institutional forms to express conflicts of interest has begun."[6]

Many government officials have echoed these sentiments, and the OECD has examined how its member states could reform their governments to create new connections to their publics.[7] Its report testifies:

> New forms of representation and public participation are emerging in all of our countries. These developments have expanded the avenues for citizens to participate more fully in public policy making, within the overall framework of representative democracy in which parliaments continue to play a central role. Citizens are increasingly demanding more transparency and accountability from their governments, and want greater public participation in shaping policies that affect their lives. Educated and well-informed citizens expect governments to take their views and knowledge into account when making decisions on their behalf. Engaging citizens in policy making allows governments to respond to these expectations and, at the same time, design better policies and improve their implementation.[8]

If the pressures for political reform are having real effects, these should show up in changes to the institutional structures of democratic politics. The most avid proponents of such reforms conclude that we may be experiencing the most fundamental democratic transformation since the beginnings of mass democracy in the early twentieth century. Yet cycles of reform are a recurring theme in democratic history, and pressures for change in one direction often wane as new problems and possibilities come to the fore. What is the general track record for democratic institutional reforms in the advanced industrial democracies over the latter half of the twentieth century? And what are the implications of this record for the future of democracy?

Three Modes of Democracy

In a sense, there is nothing new about the call to inject "more democracy" into the institutions of representative government. The history of modern democracies is punctuated by repeated waves of debate about the nature of the democratic process, some of which have produced major institutional reforms. In the early twentieth century, for example, the populist movement in the United States prompted extensive electoral and governing-process reforms, as well as the introduction of new forms of direct democracy.[9] Parallel institutional changes occurred in Europe. By the end of this democratic-reform period in the late 1920s, most Western democracies had become much more "democratic" in the sense of providing citizens with access to the political process and making governments more accountable.

A new wave of democratic rhetoric and debate emerged in the last third of the twentieth century. The stimulus for this first appeared mainly among university students and young professionals contesting the boundaries of conventional representative democracy. Although their dramatic protests subsequently waned, they stimulated new challenges that affect advanced industrial democracies to this day. Citizen interest groups and other public lobbying organizations, which have proliferated since the 1960s, press for more access to government; expanding mass media delve more deeply into the workings of government; and people demand more from government while trusting it less.

The institutional impact of the reform wave of the late twentieth century can be understood in terms of three different modes of democratic politics. One aims at improving the process of *representative democracy* in which citizens elect elites. Much like the populism of the early twentieth century, reforms of this mode seek to improve electoral processes. Second, there are calls for new types of *direct democracy* that bypass (or complement) the processes of representative democracy. A third mode seeks to expand the means of political participation through a new style of *advocacy democracy,* in which citizens participate in policy deliberation and formation—either directly or through surrogates, such as public interest groups—although the final decisions are still made by elites.

1) *Representative democracy.* A major example of reform in representative democracy can be seen in changes to processes of electing the U.S. president. In a 30-year span, these elections underwent a dramatic transformation, in which citizen influence grew via the spread of state-level primary elections as a means of nominating candidates. In 1968, the Democratic Party had just 17 presidential primaries while the Republicans had only 16; in 2000 there were Democratic primaries in 40 states and Republican primaries in 43. As well, both parties-first the Democrats, then the Republicans—instituted reforms intended to ensure that convention delegates are more representative of the public at large, such as rules on the representation of women. Meanwhile, legislators introduced and expanded public

funding for presidential elections in an effort to limit the influence of money and so promote citizen equality. If the 1948 Republican and Democratic candidates, Thomas E. Dewey and Harry S. Truman, were brought back to observe the modern presidential election process, they would hardly recognize the system as the same that nominated them. More recently, reformers have championed such causes as term limits and campaign-finance reform as remedies for restricting the influence of special interests. In Europe, populist electoral reform has been relatively restrained by institutionalized systems of party government, but even so, there are parallels to what has occurred in the United States in many European countries. On a limited basis, for example, some European political parties have experimented with, or even adopted, closed primaries to select parliamentary candidates.[10]

> In recent decades, changes in both attitudes and formal rules have brought about a greater general reliance on mechanisms of direct democracy within the advanced industrial democracies.

Generally, the mechanisms of representative democracy have maintained, and in places slightly increased, citizen access and influence. It is true that, compared with four decades ago, electoral turnout is generally down by about 10 percent in the established democracies.[11] This partially signifies a decrease in political access (or in citizens' use of elections as a means of political access). But at the same time, the "amount of electing" is up to an equal or greater extent. There has been a pattern of reform increasing the number of electoral choices available to voters by changing appointed positions into elected ones.[12] In Europe, citizens now elect members of Parliament for the European Union; regionalization has increased the number of elected subnational governments; directly elected mayors and directly elected local officials are becoming more common; and suffrage now includes younger voters, aged 18 to 20. Moreover, the number of political parties has increased, while parties have largely become more accountable—and the decisions of party elites more transparent—to their supporters. With the general expansion in electoral choices, citizens are traveling to the polls more often and making more electoral decisions.

2) *Direct democracy.* Initiatives and referenda are the most common means of direct democracy. These allow citizens to decide government policy without relying on the mediating influence of representation. Ballot initiatives in particular allow nongovernmental actors to control the framing of issues

and even the timing of policy debates, further empowering the citizens and groups that take up this mode of action. In recent decades, changes in both attitudes and formal rules have brought about a greater general reliance on mechanisms of direct democracy within the advanced industrial democracies. The Initiative and Referendum Institute calculates, for example, that there were 118 statewide referenda in the United States during the 1950s but 378 such referenda during the 1990s. And a number of other nations have amended laws and constitutions to provide greater opportunities for direct democracy at the national and local levels.[13] Britain had its first national referendum in 1975; Sweden introduced the referendum in a constitutional reform of 1980; and Finland adopted the referendum in 1987. In these and other cases, the referendum won new legitimacy as a basis for national decision making, a norm that runs strongly counter to the ethos of representative democracy. There has also been mounting interest in expanding direct democracy through the innovation of new institutional forms, such as methods of deliberative democracy and citizen juries to advise policy makers.[14]

How fundamental are these changes? On the one hand, the political impact of a given referendum is limited, since only a single policy is being decided, so the channels of direct democracy normally provide less access than do the traditional channels of representative democracy. On the other hand, the increasing use of referenda has influenced political discourse—and the principles of political legitimacy in particular—beyond the policy at stake in any single referendum. With Britain's first referendum on European Community membership in 1975, for instance, parliamentary sovereignty was now no longer absolute, and the concept of popular sovereignty was concomitantly legitimized. Accordingly, the legitimacy of subsequent decisions on devolution required additional referenda, and today contentious issues, such as acceptance of the euro, are pervasively considered as matters that "the public should decide." So even though recourse to direct democracy remains relatively limited in Britain, the expansion of this mode of access represents a significant institutional change—and one that we see occurring across most advanced industrial democracies.

3) _Advocacy democracy._ In this third mode, citizens or public interest groups interact directly with governments and even participate directly in the policy-formation process, although actual decisions remain in the official hands. One might consider this as a form of traditional lobbying, but it is not. Advocacy democracy involves neither traditional interest groups nor standard channels of informal interest-group persuasion. Rather, it empowers individual citizens, citizen groups, or nongovernmental organizations to participate in advisory hearings; attend open government meetings ("government in the sunshine"); consult ombudsmen to redress grievances; demand information from government agencies; and challenge government actions through the courts.

Evidence for the growth of advocacy democracy is less direct and more difficult to quantify than is evidence

for other kinds of institutional change. But the overall expansion of advocacy democracy is undeniable. Administrative reforms, decentralization, the growing political influence of courts, and other factors have created new opportunities for access and influence. During the latter 1960s in the United States, "maximum feasible participation" became a watchword for the social-service reforms of President Lyndon Johnson's "Great Society" programs. Following this model, citizen consultations and public hearings have since been embedded in an extensive range of legislation, giving citizens new points of access to policy formation and administration. Congressional hearings and state-government meetings have become public events, and legislation such as the 1972 Federal Advisory Committee Act even extended open-meeting requirements to advisory committees. While only a handful of nations had freedom-of-information laws in 1970, such laws are now almost universal in OECD countries. And there has been a general diffusion of the ombudsman model across advanced industrial democracies.[15] "Sunshine" provisions reflect a fundamental shift in understanding as to the role that elected representatives should play-one which would make Edmund Burke turn in his grave, and which we might characterize as a move away from the _trustee_ toward the _delegate_ model.

Reforms in this category also include new legal rights augmenting the influence of individuals and citizen groups. A pattern of judicialization in the policy process throughout most Western democracies, for instance, has enabled citizen groups to launch class-action suits on behalf of the environment, women's rights, or other public interests.[16] Now virtually every public interest can be translated into a rights-based appeal, which provides new avenues for action through the courts. Moreover, especially in European democracies, where direct citizen action was initially quite rare, the expansion of public interest groups, _Bürgerinitiativen,_ and other kinds of citizen groups has substantially enlarged the public's repertoire for political action. It is worth noting that "unconventional" forms of political action, such as protests and demonstrations, have also grown substantially over this time span.

Citizens and the Democratic State

If the institutional structure of democracy is changing, how does this affect the democratic process? The answer is far from simple and not always positive, for democratic gains in some areas can be offset by losses in others, as when increased access produces new problems of democratic governability. In the following pages, we limit our attention to how these institutional changes affect the relationship between citizens and the state.

Robert A. Dahl's writings are a touchstone in this matter.[17] Like many democratic theorists, Dahl tends to equate democracy with the institutions and processes of representative democracy, paying much less attention to other forms of citizen participation that may actually represent more important means of citizen influence over political elites. Thus, while we draw from Dahl's *On Democracy* to define the essential criteria for a democratic process, we broaden the framework to include not only representative democracy but direct democracy and advocacy democracy also. Dahl suggests five criteria for a genuinely democratic system:[18]

1. **Inclusion:** With minimal exceptions, all permanent adult residents must have full rights of citizenship.
2. **Political equality:** When decisions about policy are made, every citizen must have an equal and effective opportunity to participate.
3. **Enlightened understanding:** Within reasonable limits, citizens must have equal and effective opportunities to learn about relevant policy alternatives and their likely consequences.
4. **Control of the agenda:** Citizens must have the opportunity to decide which matters are placed on the public agenda, and how.
5. **Effective participation:** Before a policy is adopted, all the citizens must have equal and effective opportunities for making their views known to other citizens.

The first column of the Table lists Dahl's five democratic criteria. The second column summarizes the prevailing view on how well representative democracy fulfills these criteria. For example, advanced industrial democracies have met the *inclusion* criterion by expanding the franchise to all adult citizens (by way of a long and at times painful series of reforms). General success in this regard is illustrated by the bold highlighting of "universal suffrage" in the first cell of this column.

Nearly all advanced industrial democracies now meet the *political equality* criterion by having enacted the principle of "one person, one vote" for elections, which we have highlighted in the second cell. In most nations today, a majority of citizens participate in voting, while labor unions, political parties, and other organizations mobilize participation to achieve high levels of engagement. Indeed, that noted democrat, the late Mayor Richard Daley of Chicago, used to say that electoral politics was the only instrument through which a working-class citizen could ever exercise equal influence with the socially advantaged. At the same time, certain problems of equality remain, as contemporary debates about campaign financing and voter registration illustrate, and full equality in political practice is probably unattainable. We note these problems in the shaded area of the second cell. Nevertheless, overall the principle of equality is now a consensual value for the electoral processes of representative democracy.

At first glance, it may seem that expanding the number of elections amounts to extending these principles. But increasing the number of times that voters go to the polls and the number of items on ballots actually tends to depress

Table Robert A. Dahl's Democratic Criteria

DEMOCRATIC CRITERIA	REPRESENTATIVE DEMOCRACY	DIRECT DEMOCRACY	ADVOCACY DEMOCRACY
Inclusion	**Universal suffrage provides inclusion**	**Universal suffrage provides inclusion**	Equal citizen acces
			(Problems of access to nonelectoral arenas)
Political Equality	**One person, one vote with high turnout maximizes equality**	**On person, one vote with high turnout maximizes equality.**	Equal opportunity
	(Problems of low turnout, inequality due to campaign finance issues, etc.)	*(Problems of equality with low turnout)*	*(Problems of very unequal use)*
Enlightened Understanding	*(Problems of information access, voter decision processes)*	*(Problems of greater information and higher decision-making costs)*	**Increased public access to information**
			(Problems of even greater information and decision-making demands on citizens)
Control of the Agenda		**Citizen initiation provides control of agenda**	**Citizens and groups control the locus and focus of activity**
	(Problems of control of campaign debate, selecting candidates, etc.)	*(Problems of influence by interest groups)*	
Effective Participation	**Control through responsible parties**	**Direct policy impact ensures effective participation**	**Direct access avoids mediated participation**
	(Principal-agent problems: fair elections, responsible party government, etc.)		

Note: Criteria that are well addressed are presented in **bold,** criteria that are at issue are presented in *italics* in the shaded cells.

turnout. And when voter turnout is less than 50 percent, as it tends to be in, say, EU parliamentary elections-or less than 25 percent, as it tends to be in local mayoral or school-board elections in the United States-then one must question whether the gap between "equality of access" and "equality of usage" has become so wide that it undermines the basic principle of *political equality*. Moreover, second-order elections tend to mobilize a smaller and more ideological electorate than the public at large, and so more second-order elections tend to mean more distortions in the representativeness of the electoral process.

The tension between Dahl's democratic criteria and democratic practice becomes even more obvious when we turn to the criterion of *enlightened understanding*. Although we are fairly sanguine about voters' abilities to make informed choices when it comes to high-visibility (for instance, presidential or parliamentary) elections, we are less so when it comes to lower-visibility elections. How does a typical resident of Houston, Texas, make enlightened choices regarding the dozens of judgeship candidates whose names appeared on the November 2002 ballot, to say nothing of other local office seekers and referenda? In such second- and third-order elections, the means of information that voters can use in first-order elections may be insufficient or even altogether lacking. So the expansion of the electoral marketplace may empower the public in a sense, but in another sense may make it hard for voters to exercise meaningful political judgment.

Another criterion is citizen *control of the political agenda*. Recent reforms in representative democracy have gone some way toward broadening access to the political agenda. Increasing the number of elected offices gives citizens more input and presumably more avenues for raising issues, while reforming political finance to equalize campaign access and party support has made for greater openness in political deliberations. More problematic, though, is performance on the *effectiveness of participation* criterion. Do citizens get what they vote for? Often, this principal-agent problem is solved through the mechanism of party government: Voters select a party, and the party ensures the compliance of individual members of parliament and the translation of electoral mandates into policy outcomes.[19] But the impact of recent reforms on the *effectiveness of participation* is complex. On the one hand, more openness and choice in elections should enable people to express their political preferences more extensively and in more policy areas. On the other hand, as the number of office-holders proliferates, it may become more difficult for voters to assign responsibility for policy outcomes. Fragmented decision making, divided government, and the sheer profusion of elected officials may diminish the political responsiveness of each actor.

How much better do the mechanisms of direct democracy fare when measured against Dahl's five criteria (see column 3 of the Table)? Because referenda and initiatives are effectively mass elections, they seek to ensure inclusion and political equality in much the same way as representa-

tive elections do. Most referenda and initiatives use universal suffrage to ensure inclusion and the "one person, one vote" rule to ensure political equality. However, whereas turnout in direct-democracy elections is often lower than in comparable elections for public officials, the question of democratic inclusion becomes more complicated than a simple assessment of equal access. For instance, when Proposition 98—which favored altering the California state constitution to mandate that a specific part of the state budget be directed to primary and secondary education—appeared on the 1996 general election ballot, barely half of all voting-age Californians turned out, and only 51 percent voted for the proposition. But as a consequence, the state's constitution was altered, reshaping state spending and public financing in California. Such votes raise questions about the fairness of elections in which a minority of registered voters can make crucial decisions affecting the public welfare. Equality of opportunity clearly does not mean equality of participation.

Moreover, referenda and initiatives place even greater demands for information and understanding on voters. Many of the heuristics that they can use in party elections or candidate elections are less effective in referenda, and the issues themselves are often more complex than what citizens are typically called upon to consider in electing office-holders. For instance, did the average voter have enough information to make enlightened choices in Italy's multi-referendum ballot of 1997? This ballot asked voters to make choices concerning television-ownership rules, television-broadcasting policy, the hours during which stores could remain open, the commercial activities which municipalities could pursue, labor-union reform proposals, regulations for administrative elections, and residency rules for mafia members. In referenda, voters can still rely on group heuristics and other cues that they use in electing public officials,[20] but obviously the proliferation of policy choices and especially the introduction of less-salient local issues raise questions about the overall effectiveness of such cue-taking.

The real strengths of direct democracy are highlighted by Dahl's fourth and fifth criteria. Referenda and initiatives shift the focus of agenda-setting from elites toward the public, or at least toward public interest groups. Indeed, processes of direct democracy can bring into the political arena issues that elites tend not to want to address: for example, tax reform or term limits in the United States, abortion-law reform in Italy, or the terms of EU membership in Europe generally. Even when referenda fail to reach the ballot or fail to win a majority, they can nevertheless prompt elites to be more sensitive to public interests. By definition, moreover, direct democracy should solve the problem of effective participation that exists with all methods of representative democracy. Direct democracy is unmediated, and so it ensures that participation is effective. Voters make policy choices with their ballot-to enact a new law, to repeal an existing law, or to reform a constitution. Even in instances where the mechanisms of direct democracy require an elite response in passing a law or a revoting in a later election, the link to policy action is more direct than is the case with the channels of representative democracy. Accordingly, direct democracy seems to fulfill Dahl's democratic criteria of agenda control and effective participation.

But direct democracy raises questions in these areas as well. Interest groups may find it easier to manipulate processes of direct democracy than those of representative democracy.[21] The discretion to place a policy initiative on the ballot can be appealing to interest groups, which then have unmediated access to voters during the subsequent referendum campaign. In addition, decisions made by way of direct democracy are less susceptible to bargaining or the checks and balances that occur within the normal legislative process. Some recent referenda in California may illustrate this style of direct democracy: Wealthy backers pay a consulting firm to collect signatures so as to get a proposal on the ballot, and then bankroll a campaign to support their desired legislation. This is not grassroots democracy at work; it is the representation of wealthy interests by other means.

The expansion of direct democracy has the potential to complement traditional forms of representative democracy. It can expand the democratic process by allowing citizens and public interest groups new access to politics, and new control over political agendas and policy outcomes. But direct democracy also raises new questions about equality of actual influence, if not formal access, and the ability of the public to make fair and reasoned judgments about issues. Perhaps the most important question about direct democracy is not whether it is expanding, but *how* it is expanding: Are there ways to increase access and influence without sacrificing inclusion and equality? We return to this question below.

Formal Access and Actual Use

The final column in our Table considers how new forms of advocacy democracy fulfil Dahl's democratic criteria. These new forms of action provide citizens with significant access to politics, but it is also clear that this access is very unevenly used. Nearly everyone can vote, and most do. But very few citizens file lawsuits, file papers under a freedom-of-information act, attend environmental-impact review hearings, or attend local planning meetings. There is no clear equivalent to "one person, one vote" for advocacy democracy. Accordingly, it raises the question of how to address Dahl's criteria of inclusion, political equality, and enlightened understanding.

"Equality of access" is not adequate if "equality of usage" is grossly uneven. For instance, when Europeans were asked in the 1989 European Election Survey whether they voted in the election immediately preceding the survey, differences in participation according to levels of education were very slight (see the Figure, Social-Staus Inequality in Participations). A full 73 percent of those in the "low education" category said they had voted in the previous EU parliamentary election (even though it is a second-order

election), and an identical percentage of those in the "high education" category claimed to have voted. Differences in campaign activity according to educational levels are somewhat greater, but still modest in overall terms.

A distinctly larger inequality gap emerges when it comes to participation through forms of direct or advocacy democracy. For instance, only 13 percent of those in the "low education" category had participated in a citizen action group, while nearly three times the percentage of those in the "high education" category had participated. Similarly, there are large inequalities when it comes to such activities as signing a petition or participating in a lawful demonstration.

With respect to the criterion of *enlightened understanding*, advocacy democracy has mixed results. On the one hand, it can enhance citizen understanding and make for greater inclusion. Citizens and public interest groups can increase the amount of information that they have about government activities, especially by taking advantage of freedom-of-information laws, attending administrative hearings, and participating in government policy making. And with the assistance of the press in disseminating this information, citizens and public interest groups can better influence political outcomes. By ensuring that the public receives information in a timely fashion, advocacy democracy allows citizens to make informed judgments and hold governments more accountable. And by eliminating the filtering that governments would otherwise apply, advocacy democracy can help citizens to get more accurate pictures of the influences affecting policy decisions, with fewer cover-ups and self-serving distortions. On the other hand, advocacy democracy makes greater cognitive and resource demands on citizens, and thus may generate some of the same inequalities in participation noted above. It requires much more of the citizen to participate in a public hearing or to petition an official than it does simply to cast a vote. The most insightful evidence on this point comes from Jane Mansbridge's study of collective decision making in New England town meetings.[22] She finds that many participants were unprepared or overwhelmed by the deliberative decision-making processes.

Advocacy democracy fares better when it comes to the remaining two criteria. It gives citizens greater control of the political agenda, in part by increasing their opportunity to press their interests outside of the institutionalized time and format constraints of fixed election cycles. By means of advocacy democracy, citizens can often choose when and where to challenge a government directive or pressure policy makers. Similarly, even though advocacy democracy typically leaves final political decisions in the hands of elites, it nevertheless provides direct access to government. Property owners can participate in a local planning hearing; a public interest group can petition government for information on past policies; and dissatisfied citizens can attend a school board session. Such unmediated participation brings citizens into the decision-making process-which ultimately might not be as effective as the efforts of a skilled representative, but greater direct involvement in the demo-

Figure-Social-Status Inequality in Participation

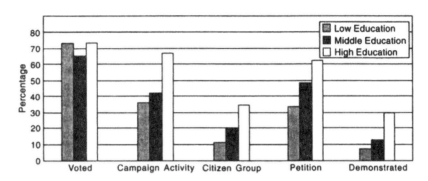

Source: Eurobarometers 31 and 31A conducted in connection with the 1989 European Parliament election. Results combine the 12 nations weighted to represent the total EU population.

cratic process should improve its accountability and transparency (see the bold entries in these last two cells of the Table).

All in all, advocacy democracy increases the potential for citizen access in important ways. It can give citizens and public interest groups new influence over the agenda-setting process, and it can give them unmediated involvement in the policy-formation process. These are significant extensions of democratic participation. At the same time, advocacy democracy may exacerbate political inequality on account of inequalities in usage. New access points created through advisory panels, consultative hearings, and other institutional reforms empower some citizens to become more involved. But other citizens, relatively lacking in the skills or resources to compete in these new domains, may be left behind. In other words, advocacy democracy may in some ways respond to the strength of the claimants, rather than to the strength of their claims. It can even alter the locus of political expertise. While advocacy democracy values know-how and expertise in the citizenry, it devalues those same characteristics among policy makers.

Environmental policy provides a good illustration of this problem. Here, citizens and public interest groups have gained new rights and new access to the policy process. But these are disproportionately used by relatively affluent and skilled citizens, who are already participating in conventional forms of representative democracy, while the poor, the unskilled, and the otherwise disadvantaged tend to get left behind. So while environmentalism is an example of citizen empowerment, it is also a source of increasing inequality.

No form of democratic action is ideal, each having its advantages and limitations. As democratic practice shifts from a predominant reliance on representation toward a mixed repertoire—including greater use of direct and advocacy democracy—a new balance must be struck among democratic goals. It is possible that new institutional arrangements will maximize the benefits of these new modes while limiting their disadvantages—as, for example, the in-

stitutions of representative democracy depend on parties and interest groups. But thus far, the advanced industrialized democracies have not fully recognized the problems generated by the new mixed repertoire of democratic action, and so have yet to find institutional or structural means of addressing them. Democratic reforms create opportunities, but they also create challenges. Our goal should be to ensure that progress on some democratic criteria is not unduly sacrificed for progress on others.

Notes

1. Martin P. Wattenberg, *Where Have All the Voters Gone?* (Cambridge: Harvard University Press, 2002); Susan E. Scarrow, "From Social Integration to Electoral Contestation," in Russell J. Dalton and Martin P. Wattenberg, eds., *Parties Without Partisans: Political Change in Advanced Industrial Democracies* (New York: Oxford University Press, 2000); Russell J. Dalton, *Democratic Challenges, Democratic Choices: The Decline in Political Support in Advanced Industrial Democracies* (Oxford: Oxford University Press, 2004); Susan J. Pharr and Robert D. Putnam, eds., *Disaffected Democracies: What's Troubling the Trilateral Countries?* (Princeton: Princeton University Press, 2000).

2. Russell J. Dalton, *Citizen Politics: Public Opinion and Political Parties in Advanced Industrial Democracies* (New York: Chatham House, 2002), ch. 4; Ronald Inglehart, *Modernization and Postmodernization: Cultural, Economic, and Political Change in 43 Societies* (Princeton: Princeton University Press, 1997); Sidney Verba, Kay Schlozman, and Henry Brady, *Voice and Equality: Civic Volunteerism in American Politics* (Cambridge: Harvard University Press, 1995), 72.

3. James S. Fishkin, *The Voice of the People: Public Opinion and Democracy* (New Haven: Yale University Press, 1995); John Elster, *Deliberative Democracy* (New York: Cambridge University Press, 1998).

4. Mark Warren, *Democracy and Association* (Princeton: Princeton University Press, 2001), 226.

5. Dick Morris, *The New Prince: Machiavelli Updated for the Twenty-First Century* (New York: Renaissance Books, 2000).

6. Ralf Dahrendorf, "Afterword," in Susan J. Pharr and Robert D. Putnam, eds., *Disaffected Democracies: What's Troubling the Trilateral Countries?* 311.

7. OECD, *Government of the Future: Getting from Here to There* (Paris: Organization for Economic Co-operation and Development, 2000).

8. OECD, *Citizens as Partners: OECD Handbook on Information, Consultation and Public Participation in Policy-Making* (Paris: Organization of Economic Cooperation and Development, 2001), 9.

9. Lawrence Goodwyn, *Democratic Promise: The Populist Movement in America* (New York: Oxford University Press, 1976).

10. Susan E. Scarrow, Paul Webb, and David M. Farrell, "From Social Integration to Electoral Contestation," in Russell J. Dalton and Martin P. Wattenberg, eds., *Parties without Partisans: Political Change in Advanced Industrial Democracies;* Jonathan Hopkin, "Bringing the Members Back in: Democratizing Candidate Selection in Britain and Spain," *Party Politics* 7 (May 2001): 343–61.

11. Martin P. Wattenberg, *Where Have All the Voters Gone?*

12. Russell J. Dalton and Mark Gray, "Expanding the Electoral Marketplace," in Bruce E. Cain, Russell J. Dalton, and Susan E. Scarrow, eds., *Democracy Transformed? Expanding Political Opportunities in Advanced Industrial Democracies* (Oxford: Oxford University Press, 2003).

13. Susan E. Scarrow, "Direct Democracy and Institutional Design: A Comparative Investigation," in *Comparative Political Studies* 34 (August 2001): 651–65; also see David Butler and Austin Ranney, eds., *Referenda Around the World* (Washington, D.C.: American Enterprise Institute, 1994); Michael Gallagher and Pier Vincenzo Uleri, eds., *The Referendum Experience in Europe* (Basingstoke: Macmillan, 1996).

14. James S. Fishkin, *The Voice of the People: Public Opinion and Democracy;* Forest David Matthews, *Politics for People: Finding a Responsive Voice,* 2nd ed. (Urbana: University of Illinois Press, 1999).

15. Roy Gregory and Philip Giddings, eds., *Righting Wrongs: The Ombudsman in Six Continents* (Amsterdam: IOS Press, 2000); see also Christopher Ansell and Jane Gingrich, "Re-forming the Administrative State," in Bruce E. Cain, Russell J. Dalton, and Susan E. Scarrow, eds., *Democracy Transformed? Expanding Political Opportunities in Advanced Industrial Democracies.*

16. Alec Stone Sweet, *Governing with Judges: Constitutional Politics in Europe* (New York: Oxford University Press, 2000).

17. Robert A Dahl, *Polyarchy: Participation and Opposition* (New Haven: Yale University Press, 1971); *Democracy and Its Critics* (New Haven: Yale University Press, 1991); *On Democracy* (New Haven: Yale University Press, 1998).

18. Robert A. Dahl, *On Democracy,* 37–38.

19. 1Hans-Dieter Klingemann et al., *Parties, Policies, and Democracy* (Boulder: Westview, 1994).

20. Arthur Lupia, "Shortcuts versus Encyclopedias," *American Political Science Review* 88 (March 1994): 63–76.

21. Elisabeth Gerber, *The Populist Paradox: Interest Group Influence and the Promise of Direct Legislation* (Princeton: Princeton University Press, 1999); see also David S. Broder, *Democracy Derailed: Initiative Campaigns and the Power of Money*

22. Jane Mansbridge, *Beyond Adversary Democracy* (New York: Basic Books, 1980).

Russell J. Dalton *is director of the Center for the Study of Democracy at the University of California, Irvine.* ***Susan E. Scarrow*** *is associate professor of political science at the University of Houston.* ***Bruce E. Cain*** *is Robson Professor of Political Science at the University of California, Berkeley, and director of the Institute of Governmental Studies. This essay is adapted from their edited volume,* Democracy Transformed? Expanding Political Opportunities in Advanced Industrial Democracies *(2003).*

From *Journal of Democracy* 15:1 (2004), 124-138. Copyright © 2004 National Endowment for Democracy and The Johns Hopkins University Press. Reprinted with permission of The Johns Hopkins University Press.

Women
in National Parliaments

The data in the table below has been compiled by the Inter-Parliamentary Union on the basis of information provided by National Parliaments by 29 February 2004. **181 country** are classified by **descending order of the percentage of women in the lower or single House**. Comparative data on the world and regional averages as well as data concerning the two regional parliamentary assemblies elected by direct suffrage can be found on separate pages. You can use the PARLINE database to view detailed results of parliamentary elections by country.

WORLD CLASSIFICATION									
Rank	**Country**	**Lower or single House**				**Upper House or Senate**			
		Elections	Seats*	Women	% W	Elections	Seats*	Women	% W
1	Rwanda	09 2003	80	39	48.8	09 2003	20	6	30.0
2	Sweden	09 2002	349	158	45.3	---	---	---	---
3	Denmark	11 2001	179	68	38.0	---	---	---	---
4	Finland	03 2003	200	75	37.5	---	---	---	---
5	Netherlands	01 2003	150	55	36.7	06 2003	75	24	32.0
6	Norway	09 2001	165	60	36.4	---	---	---	---
7	Cuba	01 2003	609	219	36.0	---	---	---	---
8	Belgium	05 2003	150	53	35.3	05 2003	71	22	31.0
9	Costa Rica	02 2002	57	20	35.1	---	---	---	---
10	Austria	11 2002	183	62	33.9	N.A.	62	13	21.0
11	Germany	09 2002	603	194	32.2	N.A.	69	17	24.6
12	Argentina	10 2001	257	79	30.7	10 2001	72	24	33.3
13	Iceland	05 2003	63	19	30.2	---	---	---	---
14	Mozambique	12 1999	250	75	30.0	---	---	---	---
15	South Africa**	06 1999	399	119	29.8	06 1999	89	17	31.5
16	Seychelles	12 2002	34	10	29.4	---	---	---	---

Rank	Country	Lower or single House				Upper House or Senate			
		Elections	Seats*	Women	% W	Elections	Seats*	Women	% W
17	New Zealand	07 2002	120	34	28.3	---	---	---	---
"	Spain	03 2000	350	99	28.3	03 2000	259	63	24.3
18	Viet Nam	05 2002	498	136	27.3	---	---	---	---
19	Grenada	11 2003	15	4	26.7	11 2003	13	4	30.8
20	Namibia	11 1999	72	19	26.4	11 1998	26	2	7.7
21	Bulgaria	06 2001	240	63	26.2	---	---	---	---
22	Timor-Leste***	08 2001	88	23	26.1	---	---	---	---
23	Turkmenistan	12 1999	50	13	26.0	---	---	---	---
24	Australia	11 2001	150	38	25.3	10 2001	76	22	28.9
25	Switzerland	10 2003	200	50	25.0	10 2003	46	11	23.9
26	Uganda	06 2001	304	75	24.7	---	---	---	---
27	Lao People's Democratic Rep.	02 2002	109	25	22.9	---	---	---	---
28	Saint Vincent & the Grenadines	03 2001	22	5	22.7	---	---	---	---
29	Mexico	07 2003	500	113	22.6	07 2000	128	20	15.6
30	Eritrea	02 1994	150	33	22.0	---	---	---	---
31	Pakistan	10 2002	342	74	21.6	03 2003	100	18	18.0
32	United Rep. of Tanzania	10 2000	295	63	21.4	---	---	---	---
33	Lativa	10 2002	100	21	21.0	---	---	---	---
34	Monaco	02 2003	24	5	20.8	---	---	---	---
35	Nicaragua	11 2001	92	19	20.7	---	---	---	---
36	Canada	11 2000	301	62	20.6	N.A.	105	34	32.4
37	China	03 2003	2985	604	20.2	---	---	---	---
"	Poland	09 2001	460	93	20.2	09 2001	100	23	23.0
38	Bahamas	05 2002	40	8	20.0	05 2002	16	7	43.8
"	Guyana	03 2001	65	13	20.0	---	---	---	---
39	Trinidad and Tobago	10 2002	36	7	19.4	12 2001	31	10	32.3
40	Guinea	06 2002	114	22	19.3	---	---	---	---
"	Slovakia	09 2002	150	29	19.3	---	---	---	---
41	Senegal	04 2001	120	23	19.2	---	---	---	---
42	Portugal	03 2002	230	44	19.1	---	---	---	---
43	Dominica	01 2000	32	6	18.8	---	---	---	---
"	Estonia	03 2003	101	19	18.8	---	---	---	---
44	Bolivia	06 2002	130	24	18.5	06 2002	27	4	14.8
45	Burnudi	06 1993	179	33	18.4	01 2002	53	10	18.9
46	Peru	04 2001	120	22	17.5	---	---	---	---
"	The f.YR. of Macedonia	09 2002	120	22	18.3	---	---	---	---
47	United Kingdom	06 2001	659	118	17.9	N.A.	677	113	16.7

Rank	Country	Lower or single House				Upper House or Senate			
		Elections	Seats*	Women	% W	Elections	Seats*	Women	% W
48	Croatia	11 2003	152	27	17.8	---	---	---	---
"	Philippines	05 2001	214	38	17.8	05 2001	24	3	12.5
49	Suriname	05 2000	51	9	17.6	---	---	---	---
50	Dominican Republic	05 2002	150	26	17.3	05 2002	32	2	6.3
51	Botswana	10 1999	47	8	17.0	---	---	---	---
"	Czech Republic	06 2002	200	34	17.0	10 2002	81	10	12.3
52	Bosnia and Herzegovina	10 2002	42	7	16.7	11 2002	15	0	0.0
"	Luxembourg	06 1999	60	10	16.7	---	---	---	---
"	San Marino	06 2001	60	10	16.7	---	---	---	---
53	Ecuador	10 2002	100	16	16.0	---	---	---	---
"	Singapore	11 2001	94	15	16.0	---	---	---	---
54	Angola	09 1992	220	34	15.5	---	---	---	---
55	Israel	01 2003	120	18	15.0	---	---	---	---
56	Sierra Leone	05 2002	124	18	14.5	---	---	---	---
57	Andorra	03 2001	28	4	14.3	---	---	---	---
"	United States of America	11 2002	435	62	14.3	11 2002	100	13	13
58	Barbados	05 2003	30	4	13.3	05 2003	21	5	23.8
"	Ireland	05 2002	166	22	13.3	07 2002	60	10	16.7
"	Saint Kitts and Nevis	03 2000	15	2	13.3	---	---	---	---
59	Gambia	01 2002	53	7	13.2	---	---	---	---
60	Republic of Moldova	02 2001	101	13	12.9	---	---	---	---
61	Tajikistan	02 2000	63	8	12.7	03 2000	34	4	11.8
62	Chile	12 2001	120	15	12.5	12 2001	49	2	4.1
63	France	06 2002	574	70	12.2	09 2001	321	35	10.9
"	Slovenia	10 2000	90	11	12.2	---	---	---	---
64	Uruguay	10 1999	99	12	12.1	10 1999	31	3	9.7
65	Colombia	03 2002	166	20	12.0	03 2002	102	9	8.8
"	Liechtenstein	02 2001	25	3	12.0	---	---	---	---
"	Syrian Arab Republic	03 2003	250	30	12.0	---	---	---	---
"	Zambia	12 2001	158	19	12.0	---	---	---	---
66	Burkina Faso	05 2002	111	13	11.7	---	---	---	---
"	Jamaica	10 2002	60	7	11.7	10 2002	21	4	19.0
"	Lesotho	05 2002	120	14	11.7	N.A.	33	12	36.4
67	Italy	05 2001	618	71	11.5	05 2001	321	26	8.1
"	Tunisia	10 1999	182	21	11.5	---	---	---	---
68	Cape Verde	01 2001	72	8	11.1	---	---	---	---
"	Saint Lucia	12 2001	18	2	11.1	12 2001	11	4	36.4

Rank	Country	Lower or single House				Upper House or Senate			
		Elections	Seats*	Women	% W	Elections	Seats*	Women	% W
69	Djibouti	01 2003	65	7	10.8	---	---	---	---
"	Morocco	09 2002	325	35	10.8	10 2003	270	?	?
"	Swaziland	10 2003	65	7	10.8	10 2003	30	9	30.0
70	Cyprus	05 2001	56	6	10.7	---	---	---	---
"	El Salvador	03 2003	84	9	10.7	---	---	---	---
"	Romania	11 2000	345	37	10.7	11 2000	140	8	5.7
71	Lithuania	10 2000	141	15	10.6	---	---	---	---
72	Azerbaijan	11 2000	124	13	10.5	---	---	---	---
"	Malaysia	11 1999	191	20	10.5	2003	54	20	37.0
"	Mongolia	07 2000	76	8	10.5	---	---	---	---
73	Kazakhstan	10 1999	77	8	10.4	10 2002	39	2	5.1
74	Belarus	10 2000	97	10	10.3	12 2000	61	19	31.1
75	Mali	07 2002	147	15	10.2	---	---	---	---
76	Kyrgyzstan	02 2002	60	6	10.0	02 2000	45	1	2.2
"	Paraguay	04 2003	80	8	10.0	04 2003	45	4	8.9
"	Zimbabwe	06 2000	150	15	10.0	---	---	---	---
77	Panama	05 1999	71	7	9.9	---	---	---	---
78	Cambodia	07 2003	123	12	9.8	03 1999	61	8	13.1
"	Hungary	04 2002	386	38	9.8	---	---	---	---
"	Russian Federation	12 2003	450	44	9.8	N.A.	178	6	3.4
79	Sudan	12 2000	360	35	9.7	---	---	---	---
"	Venezuela	07 2000	165	16	9.7	---	---	---	---
80	Bhutan	N.A.	150	14	9.3	---	---	---	---
"	Malawi	06 1999	193	18	9.3	---	---	---	---
81	Gabon	12 2001	119	11	9.2	02 2003	91	12	13.2
"	Malta	04 2003	65	6	9.2	---	---	---	---
"	Thailand	01 2001	500	46	9.2	03 2000	200	21	10.5
82	Sao Tome and Principe	03 2002	55	5	9.1	---	---	---	---
83	Ghana	12 2000	200	18	9.0	---	---	---	---
84	Cameroon	06 2002	180	16	8.9	---	---	---	---
85	India	09 1999	543	48	8.8	11 2002	242	25	10.3
86	Greece	04 2000	300	26	8.7	---	---	---	---
87	Brazil	10 2002	513	44	8.6	10 2002	81	10	12.3
88	Congo	05 2002	129	11	8.5	07 2002	60	9	15.0
"	Cote d'Ivoire	12 2000	223	19	8.5	---	---	---	---
89	Guatemala	11 2003	158	13	8.2	---	---	---	---
90	Indonesia	06 1999	500	40	8.0	---	---	---	---

Rank	Country	Lower or single House				Upper House or Senate			
		Elections	Seats*	Women	% W	Elections	Seats*	Women	% W
91	Serbia and Montenegro****	09 2003	126	10	7.9	---	---	---	---
92	Ethiopia	05 2000	547	42	7.7	05 2000	120	10	8.3
93	Togo	10 2002	81	6	7.4	---	---	---	---
94	Benin	03 2003	83	6	7.2	---	---	---	---
"	Georgia*****	10 1999	235	17	7.2	---	---	---	---
"	Uzbekistan	12 1999	250	18	7.2	---	---	---	---
95	Japan	11 2003	480	34	7.1	07 2001	247	38	15.4
"	Kenya	12 2002	224	16	7.1	---	---	---	---
96	Nigeria	04 2003	360	24	6.7	04 2003	109	3	2.8
97	Algeria	05 2002	389	24	6.2	12 2003	144	?	?
98	Samoa	03 2001	49	3	6.1	---	---	---	---
99	Maldives	11 1999	50	3	6.0	---	---	---	---
100	Nepal	05 1999	205	12	5.9	06 2001	60	5	8.3
101	Chad	04 2002	155	9	5.8	---	---	---	---
102	Albania	06 2001	140	8	5.7	---	---	---	---
"	Fiji	08 2001	70	4	5.7	08 2001	32	2	6.3
"	Mauritius	09 2000	70	4	5.7	---	---	---	---
103	Honduras	11 2001	128	7	5.5	---	---	---	---
"	Jordan	06 2003	110	6	5.5	11 2003	55	7	12.7
"	Republic of Korea	04 2000	271	15	5.5	---	---	---	---
104	Antigua and Barbuda	03 1999	19	1	5.3	03 1999	17	2	11.8
"	Ukraine	03 2002	450	24	5.3	---	---	---	---
105	Equatorial Guinea	03 1999	80	4	5.0	---	---	---	---
106	Kiribati	05 2003	42	2	4.8	---	---	---	---
107	Armenia	05 2003	131	6	4.6	---	---	---	---
108	Sri Lanka	12 2001	225	10	4.4	---	---	---	---
"	Turkey	11 2002	550	24	4.4	---	---	---	---
109	Madagascar	12 2002	160	6	3.8	03 2001	90	10	11.1
110	Mauritania	10 2001	81	3	3.7	04 2002	56	3	5.4
111	Haiti	05 2000	83	3	3.6	05 2000	27	7	25.9
112	Belize	03 2003	30	1	3.3	03 2003	13	3	23.1
113	Marshall Islands	11 2003	33	1	3.0	---	---	---	---
114	Egypt	11 2000	454	11	2.4	05 2001	264	15	5.7
115	Lebanon	08 2000	128	3	2.3	---	---	---	---
116	Bangladesh	10 2001	300	6	2.0	---	---	---	---
117	Vanuatu	05 2002	52	1	1.9	---	'	---	---
118	Niger	11 1999	83	1	1.2	---	---	---	---

Rank	Country	Lower or single House				Upper House or Senate			
		Elections	Seats*	Women	% W	Elections	Seats*	Women	% W
119	Papua New Guinea	06 2002	109	1	0.9	---	---	---	---
120	Yemen	04 2003	301	1	0.3	---	---	---	---
121	Bahrain	10 2002	40	0	0.0	11 2002	40	6	15.0
"	Kuwait	07 2003	65	0	0.0	---	---	---	---
"	Micronesia (Fed. States of)	03 2003	14	0	0.0	---	---	---	---
"	Nauru	05 2003	18	0	0.0	---	---	---	---
"	Palau	11 2000	16	0	0.0	11 2000	9	0	0.0
"	Saudi Arabia	05 2001	120	0	0.0	---	---	---	---
"	Solomon Islands	12 2001	50	0	0.0	---	---	---	---
"	Tonga	03 2002	30	0	0.0	---	---	---	---
"	Tuvalu	07 2002	15	0	0.0	---	---	---	---
"	United Arab Emirates	12 1997	40	0	0.0	---	---	---	---
?	Dem. People's Rep. of Korea	08 2003	687	?	?	---	---	---	---
?	Dem. Republic of the Congo	08 2000	500	?	?	08 2003	120	?	?
?	Iran (Islamic Rep. of)	02 2004	290	?	?	---	---	---	---
?	Liberia	10 2003	?	?	?	---	---	---	---
?	Libyan Arab Jamahiriya	03 1997	760	?	?	---	---	---	---

* Figures correspond to the number of seats currently filled in Parliament

** South Africa: the figures on the distribution of seats do not include the 36 special rotating delegates appointed on an ad hoc basis, and the percentages given are therefore calculated on the basis of the 54 permanent seats

*** Timor-Leste: The purpose of elections held on 30 August 2001 was to elect members of the Constituent Assembly of Timor-Leste. This body became the National Parliament on 20 May 2002, the date on which the country became independent, without any new elections

**** For the first time since Yugoslavia ceased to exist and the new State, Serbia and Montenegro, was created, indirect elections were held in the two assemblies of the two member states.

***** Elections were held in November 2003. However, on 25 November 2003, the election results were annuled by the Supreme Court of Georgia. New elections will be held in March 2004.

From *Inter-Parliamentary Union*, February 29, 2004. Copyright © 2004 by Interparliamentary Union (IPU). Reprinted by permission. http://www.ipu.org

EUROPE CRAWLS AHEAD...

By Megan Rowling

As Speaker of the Riksdagen, the Swedish parliament, Birgitta Dahl holds Sweden's second-highest political office. But when she was first elected back in 1969, as a 30-year-old single mother, she was regarded as "very odd."

"To be accepted and respected, you had to act like a bad copy of a man," Dahl recalls of her early years in politics. "But we tried to change that, and we never gave up our identity. Now women have competence in Parliament, and they have changed its performance and priorities."

Back then, women of her generation were eager for change. From the beginning, they based their demands on the right of the individual—whether male or female—to have equal access to education, work and social security. And as politicians, they fought hard to build a legal framework for good childcare and parental leave, for fathers as well as mothers. "We got this kind of legislation through," Dahl says, "even though it took 15 years of serious conflict, debate and struggle."

And their efforts paid off. Sweden now has the highest proportion of women parliamentarians in the world, at 42.7 percent—up from just 12 percent in 1969. Two of its three deputy speakers are also women. Other Nordic countries too have high levels of female representation: In rankings compiled by the Inter-Parliamentary Union (IPU), Denmark takes second place behind Sweden, with women accounting for 38 percent of parliament members, followed by Finland and Norway with around 36.5 percent. (Finland also has one of the world's 11 women heads of state.) These nations' Social Democratic and far-left governing coalitions have made impressive progress toward equality in all areas of society in the past 40 years. But the nature of their electoral systems is also very important.

Julie Ballington, gender project officer at the Stockholm-based International Institute for Democracy and Electoral Assistance (IDEA), points out that the top 10 countries in the IPU ranking all use some form of proportional representation. This kind of voting system, in which parties are allocated seats in multi-member districts according to the percentage of votes they win, Ballington says, "offers a way to address gender imbalance in parliaments." With single-member districts, parties are often under pressure to choose a male candidate. But

where they can contest and win more than one seat per constituency, they tend to be more willing to field female candidates. And by improving the gender balance on their slates, they widen their appeal among women voters.

Most European countries now use proportional representation or a combination of proportional representation and majoritarian voting, the system in use in the United States and the United Kingdom. In Europe, the widespread use of proportional representation has boosted the number of women politicians—particularly in the past three decades. And in the Nordic countries, where left-wing parties have enjoyed long periods in power and feminism has received strong support, the combination of these factors has led to significant progress toward gender parity in politics.

But even within Europe, some countries continue to lag behind. In Britain, which uses a single-member district plurality system, women members of parliament make up just 17.9 percent of the House of Commons. In the general elections of 2001, the ruling Labour Party stipulated that half those on its candidate shortlists be women. But research conducted by the Fawcett Society, a British organization that campaigns for gender equity, showed that some female hopefuls experienced overt discrimination and even sexual harassment when interviewed by local party members during the selection process.

"You are told things like 'your children are better off with you at home'... 'you are the best candidate but we are not ready for a woman.' They would select the donkey rather than the woman," said one candidate. Another complained: "They are absolutely adamant they will not consider a woman.... It was said to me... 'we do enjoy watching you speak—we always imagine what your knickers are like.' It is that basic." In light of such attitudes, it is not surprising that women candidates were selected for only four out of 38 vacant seats.

Thanks to new governmental legislation, however, the party is set to reintroduce the controversial method of all-women shortlists it used in the general election of 1997. The use of these shortlists saw the number of British women MPs double to 120 in that election, which swept

Labour to power with a landslide victory. The technique was later ruled illegal because it was judged to discriminate against men. But in early 2002, the government returned to the idea, passing a bill that will allow political parties to take measures in favor of women when choosing parliamentary candidates—what's often referred to as "positive discrimination."

"Critical mass," or the level of representation above which women make a real difference to the political agenda, is widely judged to be around 30 percent.

Judith Squires, a political researcher at Bristol University, believes that the new legislation got such an easy ride partly because it does not stipulate that parties must take action: "We had expected it to be a hard battle. But there has been a change of mood in the Conservative Party, and the fact that it is permissive, and there is a sunset clause [the legislation expires in 2015], all helped to push it through."

In France, where until the recent election women accounted for only 10.9 percent of National Assembly members, the government opted for a more extreme method: a law aimed at securing political parity between men and women. Now half of all contesting parties' candidates in National Assembly elections and most local ballots must be women. In National Assembly elections, which do not use proportional representation, parties that deviate from the 50 percent target by more than two percent are fined a proportion of their public financing.

The law's first test in the municipal elections of March 2001 saw the percentage of elected women councilors in towns of more than 3,500 almost double, to 47.5 percent. But in June's National Assembly elections, the proportion of women deputies increased by less than 1.5 points, to just 12.3 percent—way below expectations. The main factor behind this disappointing result was the success of right-wing parties that ignored the new law, says Mariette Sineau, research director at the Center for the Study of French Political Life. "The big parties decided it was better to incur the financial penalty than to sacrifice their 'favored sons.' And this was particularly so with parties on the right."

Another problem with the law, Sineau explains, is that it does not apply to regional assemblies, "which is a shame, because most National Assembly deputies are recruited there." And the recent victory of the right suggests that France's ruling—and predominantly male—elite are in no hurry to change the system that has allowed them to hold on to power up until now, law or no law. As Chantal Cauquil, a French deputy at the European Parliament and member of the Workers' Struggle Party, argues, other aspects of French society must change before real

parity can be achieved. "There's no doubt that economic and social conditions—which weigh on women earning the lowest salaries, in the most precarious situations, and with the biggest problems caused by a notable lack of childcare infrastructure—have a negative impact on women's political participation," she says. Moreover, governing parties of both the right and left are influenced by social prejudices and are not inclined to regard women as full citizens. It requires real political will to go against such prejudices and allow women to take on the same responsibilities as men."

Such deep-rooted but hidden obstacles, faced by women everywhere, are precisely why proponents of the use of gender quotas on lists for both party and national elections believe positive discrimination is essential. "Everybody hates quotas, and everyone wishes they weren't necessary," says Drude Dahlerup, professor of politics at the University of Stockholm. "But we have to start from the point that there are structural barriers. Then quotas can be seen as compensation." Currently, political parties in some 40 countries appear to agree, with quota systems in operation from Argentina and India to Uganda.

The use of quotas in Europe varies significantly from country to country and from party to party, but where a quota system is applied, it tends to lead to a rise in women's representation. In 1988, for example, Germany's Social Democrats adopted a system of flexible quotas, under which at least one-third of all candidates for internal party election must be female—and between 1987 and 1990, the number of Social Democratic women in the German parliament, the Bundestag, doubled. In Sweden, parties didn't introduce quotas until the '90s, but the principle of "Varannan Damernas" ("Every Other Seat A Woman's Seat") has been widespread since the '80s. Dahl, the Swedish speaker, argues that "it is not only legislation that changes the world, but convincing people that change is necessary."

Yet, as Dahlerup notes, women in some Scandinavian countries have worked to improve gender equality since the end of World War I, and "other countries are not going to wait that long—they are showing impatience." "Critical mass," or the level of representation above which women make a real difference to the political agenda, is widely judged to be around 30 percent. And in countries such as France and the United Kingdom, where that is still a long way off, measures such as parity laws and all-women shortlists are a way to speed up progress.

Even in countries that are close to achieving political parity, however, women are quick to warn against complacency. Dahlerup emphasizes the case of Denmark, where quotas have been abandoned. "Young women say they don't want and don't need quotas. The discourse is that equality has already been achieved. But I think Denmark could go backward again, and that is dangerous."

Squires of Bristol University also talks about a backlash in Britain's Liberal Democratic Party against what younger women regard as "old-fashioned feminist policies." At the party conference last year, she says, many women in their twenties and early thirties lobbied against any form of positive discrimination, wearing pink T-shirts emblazoned with the words "I'm not a token woman." But Squires suggests that this attitude is somewhat misguided: "All parties [in the United Kingdom] have set criteria that discriminate against women. It is not a supply-side problem, it is a demand-side problem."

"People are waking up and saying that it's not right that there are so few women in politics."

In an attempt to address this "demand-side problem," activists are targeting not only national political institutions, but also those of the European Union. The number of women members of the European Parliament increased from 25.7 percent in 1994 to 29.9 percent in the 1999 elections—not very impressive considering that some countries introduced proportional representation voting, and some parties alternated women and men on their lists to boost women's chances. More worrying perhaps is the gender imbalance in the convention on the Future of Europe, a body charged with the important task of drafting a new treaty for the European Union. Its presidium includes only two women among its 12 members, and the convention itself only 19 out of 118 members.

"The establishment of the convention is a response to the need for transparency and democracy. How can we explain the fact that women are not included?" asks Denise Fuchs, president of the European Women's Lobby. "It is simply not coherent." The EWL has launched a campaign to rectify the problem and is lobbying to achieve parity democracy across all other European institutions as well.

Yvonne Galligan, director of the Belfast-based Center for Advancement of Women in Politics, points out that "there has been a groundswell of support for women in political life across Western Europe, but this has not yet translated into numbers in the United Kingdom, Ireland and the European Union." In May's elections in the Irish Republic, for example, women parliamentarians in Ireland's Dail gained just one seat, and are now at 12.7 percent, according to the IPU.

Galligan is now working with political parties to set targets for Ireland's local elections in a couple of years' time—a tough job, because most parties oppose any form of positive discrimination. Parity in Ireland isn't likely to happen for a long while yet, but Galligan believes the social backdrop is improving. She cites a controversial referendum in March, in which the Irish electorate narrowly voted against a proposal to tighten the country's strict abortion laws even further. "That raised the status of women," she explains. "The underlying question was, how do we perceive the role of women? Now that is carrying over into elections. People are waking up and saying that it's not right that there are so few women in politics."

But where a sea-change in attitudes has not already occurred, it is almost certainly emerging. Naturally, there are fears that the apparent resurgence of the right in Europe could reverse the trend. But most of those interviewed for this article say women have already progressed far enough to prevent a significant decline in representation.

As Linda McAvan, deputy leader of Britain's Labour MEPs, argues: "If we look at how things were 20 years ago, they have changed enormously. Young women are different now. They see what has been done by women politicians before them, and they want to do it too."

From *In These Times*, July 22, 2002. © 2002 by In These Times.

WHAT DEMOCRACY IS... AND IS NOT

Philippe C. Schmitter & Terry Lynn Karl

For some time, the word democracy has been circulating as a debased currency in the political marketplace. Politicians with a wide range of convictions and practices strove to appropriate the label and attach it to their actions. Scholars, conversely, hesitated to use it—without adding qualifying adjectives—because of the ambiguity that surrounds it. The distinguished American political theorist Robert Dahl even tried to introduce a new term, "polyarchy," in its stead in the (vain) hope of gaining a greater measure of conceptual precision. But for better or worse, we are "stuck" with democracy as the catchword of contemporary political discourse. It is the word that resonates in people's minds and springs from their lips as they struggle for freedom and a better way of life; it is the word whose meaning we must discern if it is to be of any use in guiding political analysis and practice.

The wave of transitions away from autocratic rule that began with Portugal's "Revolution of the Carnations" in 1974 and seems to have crested with the collapse of communist regimes across Eastern Europe in 1989 has produced a welcome convergence toward [a] common definition of democracy.[1] Everywhere there has been a silent abandonment of dubious adjectives like "popular," "guided," "bourgeois," and "formal" to modify "democracy." At the same time, a remarkable consensus has emerged concerning the minimal conditions that polities must meet in order to merit the prestigious appellation of "democratic." Moreover, a number of international organizations now monitor how well these standards are met; indeed, some countries even consider them when formulating foreign policy.[2]

WHAT DEMOCRACY IS

Let us begin by broadly defining democracy and the generic *concepts* that distinguish it as a unique system for organizing relations between rulers and the ruled. We will then briefly review *procedures*, the rules and arrangements that are needed if democracy is to endure. Finally, we will discuss two operative *principles* that make democracy work. They are not expressly included among the generic concepts or formal procedures, but the prospect for democracy is grim if their underlying conditioning effects are not present.

One of the major themes of this essay is that democracy does not consist of a single unique set of institutions. There are many types of democracy, and their diverse practices produce a similarly varied set of effects. The specific form democracy takes is contingent upon a country's socioeconomic conditions as well as its entrenched state structures and policy practices.

Modern political democracy is a system of governance in which rulers are held accountable for their actions in the public realm by citizens, acting indirectly through the competition and cooperation of their elected representatives.[3]

A *regime or system of governance* is an ensemble of patterns that determines the methods of access to the principal public offices; the characteristics of the actors admitted to or excluded from such access; the strategies that actors may use to gain access; and the rules that are followed in the making of publicly binding decisions. To work properly, the ensemble must be institutionalized—that is to say, the various patterns must be habitually known, practiced, and accepted by most, if not all, actors. Increasingly, the preferred mechanism of institutionalization is a written body of laws undergirded by a written constitution, though many enduring political norms can have an informal, prudential, or traditional basis.[4]

For the sake of economy and comparison, these forms, characteristics, and rules are usually bundled together and given a generic label. Democratic is one; others are autocratic, authoritarian, despotic, dictatorial, tyrannical, totalitarian, absolutist, traditional, monarchic, obligarchic, plutocratic, aristocratic, and sultanistic.[5] Each of these regime forms may in turn be broken down into subtypes.

Like all regimes, democracies depend upon the presence of *rulers*, persons who occupy specialized authority roles and can give legitimate commands to others. What distinguishes democratic rulers from nondemocratic ones are the norms that condition how the former come to power and the practices that hold them accountable for their actions.

"However central to democracy, elections occur intermittently and only allow citizens to choose between the highly aggregated alternatives offered by political parties..."

The *public realm* encompasses the making of collective norms and choices that are binding on the society and backed by state coercion. Its content can vary a great deal across democracies, depending upon preexisting distinctions between the public and the private, state and society, legitimate coercion and voluntary exchange, and collective needs and individual preferences. The liberal conception of democracy advocates circumscribing the public realm as narrowly as possible, while the socialist or social-democratic approach would extend that realm through regulation, subsidization, and, in some cases, collective ownership of property. Neither is intrinsically more democratic than the other—just *differently* democratic. This implies that measures aimed at "developing the private sector" are no more democratic than those aimed at "developing the public sector." Both, if carried to extremes, could undermine the practice of democracy, the former by destroying the basis for satisfying collective needs and exercising legitimate authority; the latter by destroying the basis for satisfying individual preferences and controlling illegitimate government actions. Differences of opinion over the optimal mix of the two provide much of the substantive content of political conflict within established democracies.

Citizens are the most distinctive element in democracies. All regimes have rulers and a public realm, but only to the extent that they are democratic do they have citizens. Historically, severe restrictions on citizenship were imposed in most emerging or partial democracies according to criteria of age, gender, class, race, literacy, property ownership, tax-paying status, and so on. Only a small part of the total population was eligible to vote or run for office. Only restricted social categories were allowed to form, join, or support political associations. After protracted struggle—in some cases involving violent domestic upheaval or international war—most of these restrictions were lifted. Today, the criteria for inclusion are fairly standard. All native-born adults are eligible, although somewhat higher age limits may still be imposed upon candidates for certain offices. Unlike the early American and European democracies of the nineteenth century, none of the recent democracies in southern Europe, Latin America, Asia, or Eastern Europe has even attempted to impose formal restrictions on the franchise or

eligibility to office. When it comes to informal restrictions on the effective exercise of citizenship rights, however, the story can be quite different. This explains the central importance (discussed below) of procedures.

Competition has not always been considered an essential defining condition of democracy. "Classic" democracies presumed decision making based on direct participation leading to consensus. The assembled citizenry was expected to agree on a common course of action after listening to the alternatives and weighing their respective merits and demerits. A tradition of hostility to "faction," and "particular interests" persists in democratic thought, but at least since *The Federalist Papers* it has become widely accepted that competition among factions is a necessary evil in democracies that operate on a more-than-local scale. Since, as James Madison argued, "the latent causes of faction are sown into the nature of man," and the possible remedies for "the mischief of faction" are worse than the disease, the best course is to recognize them and to attempt to control their effects.[6] Yet while democrats may agree on the inevitability of factions, they tend to disagree about the best forms and rules for governing factional competition. Indeed, differences over the preferred modes and boundaries of competition contribute most to distinguishing one subtype of democracy from another.

The most popular definition of democracy equates it with regular *elections*, fairly conducted and honestly counted. Some even consider the mere fact of elections—even ones from which specific parties or candidates are excluded, or in which substantial portions of the population cannot freely participate—as a sufficient condition for the existence of democracy. This fallacy has been called "electoralism" or "the faith that merely holding elections will channel political action into peaceful contests among elites and accord public legitimacy to the winners"—no matter how they are conducted or what else constrains those who win them.[7] However central to democracy, elections occur intermittently and only allow citizens to choose between the highly aggregated alternatives offered by political parties, which can, especially in the early stages of a democratic transition, proliferate in a bewildering variety. During the intervals between elections, citizens can seek to influence public policy through a wide variety of other intermediaries: interest associations, social movements, locality groupings, clientelistic arrangements, and so forth. *Modern democracy, in other words, offers a variety of competitive processes and channels for the expression of interests and values—associational as well as partisan, functional as well as territorial, collective as well as individual. All are integral to its practice.*

Another commonly accepted image of democracy identifies it with *majority rule*. Any governing body that makes decisions by combining the votes of more than half of those eligible and present is said to be democratic, whether that majority emerges within an electorate, a parliament, a committee, a city council, or a party caucus.

For exceptional purposes (e.g., amending the constitution or expelling a member), "qualified majorities" of more than 50 percent may be required, but few would deny that democracy must involve some means of aggregating the equal preferences of individuals.

A problem arises, however, when *numbers* meet *intensities*. What happens when a properly assembled majority (especially a stable, self-perpetuating one) regularly makes decisions that harm some minority (especially a threatened cultural or ethnic group)? In these circumstances, successful democracies tend to qualify the central principle of majority rule in order to protect minority rights. Such qualifications can take the form of constitutional provisions that place certain matters beyond the reach of majorities (bills of rights); requirements for concurrent majorities in several different constituencies (confederalism); guarantees securing the autonomy of local or regional governments against the demands of the central authority (federalism); grand coalition governments that incorporate all parties (consociationalism); or the negotiation of social pacts between major social groups like business and labor (neocorporatism). The most common and effective way of protecting minorities, however, lies in the everyday operation of interest associations and social movements. These reflect (some would say, amplify) the different intensities of preference that exist in the population and bring them to bear on democratically elected decision makers. Another way of putting this intrinsic tension between numbers and intensities would be to say that "in modern democracies, votes may be counted, but influences alone are weighted."

Cooperation has always been a central feature of democracy. Actors must voluntarily make collective decisions binding on the polity as a whole. They must cooperate in order to compete. They must be capable of acting collectively through parties, associations, and movements in order to select candidates, articulate preferences, petition authorities, and influence policies.

But democracy's freedoms should also encourage citizens to deliberate among themselves, to discover their common needs, and to resolve their differences without relying on some supreme central authority. Classical democracy emphasized these qualities, and they are by no means extinct, despite repeated efforts by contemporary theorists to stress the analogy with behavior in the economic marketplace and to reduce all of democracy's operations to competitive interest maximization. Alexis de Tocqueville best described the importance of independent groups for democracy in his *Democracy in America*, a work which remains a major source of inspiration for all those who persist in viewing democracy as something more than a struggle for election and re-election among competing candidates.[8]

In contemporary political discourse, this phenomenon of cooperation and deliberation via autonomous group activity goes under the rubric of "civil society." The diverse units of social identity and interest, by remaining independent of the state (and perhaps even of parties), not only can restrain the arbitrary actions of rulers, but can also contribute to forming better citizens who are more aware of the preferences of others, more self-confident in their actions, and more civic-minded in their willingness to sacrifice for the common good. At its best, civil society provides an intermediate layer of governance between the individual and the state that is capable of resolving conflicts and controlling the behavior of members without public coercion. Rather than overloading decision makers with increased demands and making the system ungovernable,[9] a viable civil society can mitigate conflicts and improve the quality of citizenship—without relying exclusively on the privatism of the marketplace.

Representatives—whether directly or indirectly elected—do most of the real work in modern democracies. Most are professional politicians who orient their careers around the desire to fill key offices. It is doubtful that any democracy could survive without such people. The central question, therefore, is not whether or not there will be a political elite or even a professional political class, but how these representatives are chosen and then held accountable for their actions.

As noted above, there are many channels of representation in modern democracy. The electoral one, based on territorial constituencies, is the most visible and public. It culminates in a parliament or a presidency that is periodically accountable to the citizenry as a whole. Yet the sheer growth of government (in large part as a byproduct of popular demand) has increased the number, variety, and power of agencies charged with making public decisions and not subject to elections. Around these agencies there has developed a vast apparatus of specialized representation based largely on functional interests, not territorial constituencies. These interest associations, and not political parties, have become the primary expression of civil society in most stable democracies, supplemented by the more sporadic interventions of social movements.

The new and fragile democracies that have sprung up since 1974 must live in "compressed time." They will not resemble the European democracies of the nineteenth and early twentieth centuries, and they cannot expect to acquire the multiple channels of representation in gradual historical progression as did most of their predecessors. A bewildering array of parties, interests, and movements will all simultaneously seek political influence in them, creating challenges to the polity that did not exist in earlier processes of democratization.

PROCEDURES THAT MAKE DEMOCRACY POSSIBLE

The defining components of democracy are necessarily abstract, and may give rise to a considerable variety of institutions and subtypes of democracy. For democracy to thrive, however, specific procedural norms must be followed and civic rights must be respected. Any polity that fails to impose such restrictions upon itself, that fails to follow the "rule of law" with regard to its own procedures, should not be considered democratic. These procedures alone do not define democracy, but their presence is indispensable to its persistence. In essence, they are necessary but not sufficient conditions for its existence.

Robert Dahl has offered the most generally accepted listing of what he terms the "procedural minimal" conditions that must be present for modern political democracy (or as he puts it, "polyarchy") to exist:

1. Control over government decisions about policy is constitutionally vested in elected officials.
2. Elected officials are chosen in frequent and fairly conducted elections in which coercion is comparatively uncommon.
3. Practically all adults have the right to vote in the election of officials.
4. Practically all adults have the right to run for elective offices
5. Citizens have a right to express themselves without the danger of severe punishment on political matters broadly defined….
6. Citizens have a right to seek out alternative sources of information. Moreover, alternative sources of information exist and are protected by law.
7. … Citizens also have the right to form relatively independent associations or organizations, including independent political parties and interest groups.[10]

These seven conditions seem to capture the essence of procedural democracy for many theorists, but we propose to add two others. The first might be thought of as a further refinement of item (1), while the second might be called an implicit prior condition to all seven of the above.

1. Popularly elected officials must be able to exercise their constitutional powers without being subjected to overriding (albeit informal) opposition from unelected officials. Democracy is in jeopardy if military officers, entrenched civil servants, or state managers retain the capacity to act independently of elected civilians or even veto decisions made by the people's representatives. Without this additional caveat, the militarized polities of contemporary Central America, where civilian control over the military does not exist, might be classified by many scholars as democracies, just as they have been (with the exception of Sandinista Nicaragua) by U.S. policy makers. The caveat thus guards against what we earlier called "electoralism"—the tendency to focus on the holding of elections while ignoring other political realities.
2. The polity must be self-governing; it must be able to act independently of constraints imposed by some other overarching political system. Dahl and other contemporary democratic theorists probably took this condition for granted since they referred to formally sovereign nation-states. However, with the development of blocs, alliances, spheres of influence, and a variety of "neocolonial" arrangements, the question of autonomy has been a salient one. Is a system really democratic if its elected officials are unable to make binding decisions without the approval of actors outside their territorial domain? This is significant even if the outsiders are relatively free to alter or even end the encompassing arrangement (as in Puerto Rico), but it becomes especially critical if neither condition obtains (as in the Baltic states).

PRINCIPLES THAT MAKE DEMOCRACY FEASIBLE

Lists of component processes and procedural norms help us to specify what democracy is, but they do not tell us much about how it actually functions. The simplest answer is "by the consent of the people"; the more complex one is "by the contingent consent of politicians acting under conditions of bounded uncertainty."

In a democracy, representatives must at least informally agree that those who win greater electoral support or influence over policy will not use their temporary superiority to bar the losers from taking office or exerting influence in the future, and that in exchange for this opportunity to keep competing for power and place, momentary losers will respect the winners' right to make binding decisions. Citizens are expected to obey the decisions ensuing from such a process of competition, provided its outcome remains contingent upon their collective preferences as expressed through fair and regular elections or open and repeated negotiations.

The challenge is not so much to find a set of goals that command widespread consensus as to find a set of rules that embody contingent consent. The precise shape of this "democratic bargain," to use Dahl's expression,[11] can vary a good deal from society to society. It depends on social cleavages and such subjective factors as mutual trust, the standard of fairness, and the willingness to compromise. It may even be compatible with a great deal of dissensus on substantive policy issues.

All democracies involve a degree of uncertainty about who will be elected and what policies they will pursue. Even in those polities where one party persists in winning elections or one policy is consistently implemented, the possibility of change through independent collective action still exists, as in Italy, Japan, and the Scandinavian social democracies. If it does not, the system is not democratic, as in Mexico, Senegal, or Indonesia.

But the uncertainty embedded in the core of all democracies is bounded. Not just any actor can get into the competition and raise any issue he or she pleases—there are previously established rules that must be respected. Not just any policy can be adopted—there are conditions that must be met. Democracy institutionalizes "normal," limited political uncertainty. These boundaries vary from country to country. Constitutional guarantees of property, privacy, expression, and other rights are a part of this, but the most effective boundaries are generated by competition among interest groups and cooperation within civil society. Whatever the rhetoric (and some polities appear to offer their citizens more dramatic alternatives than others), once the rules of contingent consent have been agreed upon, the actual variation is likely to stay within a predictable and generally accepted range.

This emphasis on operative guidelines contrasts with a highly persistent, but misleading theme in recent literature on democracy—namely, the emphasis upon "civic culture." The principles we have suggested here rest on rules of prudence, not on deeply ingrained habits of tolerance, moderation, mutual respect, fair play, readiness to compromise, or trust in public authorities. Waiting for such habits to sink deep and lasting roots implies a very slow process of regime consolidation—one that takes generations—and it would probably condemn most contemporary experiences *ex hypothesi* to failure. Our assertion is that contingent consent and bounded uncertainty can emerge from the interaction between antagonistic and mutually suspicious actors and that the far more benevolent and ingrained norms of a civic culture are better thought of as a *product* and not a producer of democracy.

HOW DEMOCRACIES DIFFER

Several concepts have been deliberately excluded from our generic definition of democracy, despite the fact that they have been frequently associated with it in both everyday practice and scholarly work. They are, nevertheless, especially important when it comes to distinguishing subtypes of democracy. Since no single set of actual institutions, practices, or values embodies democracy, polities moving away from authoritarian rule can mix different components to produce different democracies. It is important to recognize that these do not define points along a single continuum of improving performance, but a matrix of potential combinations that are *differently* democratic.

1. *Consensus*: All citizens may not agree on the substantive goals of political action or on the role of the state (although if they did, it would certainly make governing democracies much easier).
2. *Participation*: All citizens may not take an active and equal part in politics, although it must be legally possible for them to do so.
3. *Access*: Rulers may not weigh equally the preferences of all who come before them, although citizenship implies that individuals and groups should have an equal opportunity to express their preferences if they choose to do so.

4. *Responsiveness*: Rulers may not always follow the course of action preferred by the citizenry. But when they deviate from such a policy, say on grounds of "reason of state" or "overriding national interest," they must ultimately be held accountable for their actions through regular and fair processes.
5. *Majority rule*: Positions may not be allocated or rules may not be decided solely on the basis of assembling the most votes, although deviations from this principle usually must be explicitly defended and previously approved.
6. *Parliamentary sovereignty*: The legislature may not be the only body that can make rules or even the one with final authority in deciding which laws are binding, although where executive, judicial, or other public bodies make that ultimate choice, they too must be accountable for their actions.
7. *Party government*: Rulers may not be nominated, promoted, and disciplined in their activities by well-organized and programmatically coherent political parties, although where they are not, it may prove more difficult to form an effective government.
8. *Pluralism*: The political process may not be based on a multiplicity of overlapping, voluntaristic, and autonomous private groups. However, where there are monopolies of representation, hierarchies of association, and obligatory memberships, it is likely that the interests involved will be more closely linked to the state and the separation between the public and private spheres of action will be much less distinct.
9. *Federalism*: The territorial division of authority may not involve multiple levels and local autonomies, least of all ones enshrined in a constitutional document, although some dispersal of power across territorial and/or functional units is characteristic of all democracies.
10. *Presidentialism*: The chief executive officer may not be a single person and he or she may not be directly elected by the citizenry as a whole, although some concentration of authority is present in all democracies, even if it is exercised collectively and only held indirectly accountable to the electorate.
11. *Checks and Balances*: It is not necessary that the different branches of government be systematically pitted against one another, although governments by assembly, by executive concentrations, by judicial command, or even by dictatorial fiat (as in time of war) must be ultimately accountable to the citizenry as a whole.

While each of the above has been named as an essential component of democracy, they should instead be seen either as indicators of this or that type of democracy, or else as useful standards for evaluating the performance of particular regimes. To include them as part of the generic definition of democracy itself would be to mistake the American polity for the universal model of democratic governance. Indeed, the parliamentary, consociational, unitary, corporatist, and concentrated arrangements of continental Europe may have some unique virtues for guiding polities through the uncertain transition from autocratic to democratic rule.[12]

WHAT DEMOCRACY IS NOT

We have attempted to convey the general meaning of modern democracy without identifying it with some particular set of rules and institutions or restricting it to some specific culture or level of development. We have also argued that it cannot be reduced to the regular holding of elections or equated with a particular notion of the role of the state, but we have not said much more about what democracy is not or about what democracy may not be capable of producing.

There is an understandable temptation to load too many expectations on this concept and to imagine that by attaining democracy, a society will have resolved all of its political, social, economic, administrative, and cultural problems. Unfortunately, "all good things do not necessarily go together."

First, democracies are not necessarily more efficient economically than other forms of government. Their rates of aggregate growth, savings, and investment may be no better than those of nondemocracies. This is especially likely during the transition, when propertied groups and administrative elites may respond to real or imagined threats to the "rights" they enjoyed under authoritarian rule by initiating capital flight, disinvestment, or sabotage. In time, depending upon the type of democracy, benevolent long-term effects upon income distribution, aggregate demand, education, productivity, and creativity may eventually combine to improve economic and social performance, but it is certainly too much to expect that these improvements will occur immediately—much less that they will be defining characteristics of democratization.

Second, democracies are not necessarily more efficient administratively. Their capacity to make decisions may even be slower than that of the regimes they replace, if only because more actors must be consulted. The costs of getting things done may be higher, if only because "payoffs" have to be made to a wider and more resourceful set of clients (although one should never underestimate the degree of corruption to be found within autocracies). Popular satisfaction with the new democratic government's performance may not even seem greater, if only because necessary compromises often please no one completely, and because the losers are free to complain.

Third, democracies are not likely to appear more orderly, consensual, stable, or governable than the autocracies they replace. This is partly a byproduct of democratic freedom of expression, but it is also a reflection of the likelihood of continuing disagreement over new rules and institutions. These products of imposition or compromise are often initially quite ambiguous in nature and uncertain in effect until actors have learned how to use them. What is more, they come in the aftermath of serious struggles motivated by high ideals. Groups and individuals with recently acquired autonomy will test certain rules, protest against the actions of certain institutions, and insist on renegotiating their part of the bargain. Thus the presence of antisystem parties should be neither surprising nor seen as a failure of democratic consolidation. What counts is whether such parties are willing, however reluctantly, to play by the general rules of bounded uncertainty and contingent consent.

Governability is a challenge for all regimes, not just democratic ones. Given the political exhaustion and loss of legitimacy that have befallen autocracies from sultanistic Paraguay to totalitarian Albania, it may seem that only democracies can now be expected to govern effectively and legitimately. Experience has shown, however, that democracies too can lose the ability to govern. Mass publics can become disenchanted with their performance. Even more threatening is the temptation for leaders to fiddle with procedures and ultimately undermine the principles of contingent consent and bounded uncertainty. Perhaps the most critical moment comes once the politicians begin to settle into the more predictable roles and relations of a consolidated democracy. Many will find their expectations frustrated; some will discover that the new rules of competition put them at a disadvantage; a few may even feel that their vital interests are threatened by popular majorities.

Finally, democracies will have more open societies and polities than the autocracies they replace, but not necessarily more open economies. Many of today's most successful and well-established democracies have historically resorted to protectionism and closed borders, and have relied extensively upon public institutions to promote economic development. While the long-term compatibility between democracy and capitalism does not seem to be in doubt, despite their continuous tension, it is not clear whether the promotion of such liberal economic goals as the right of individuals to own property and retain profits, the clearing function of markets, the private settlement of disputes, the freedom to produce without government regulation, or the privatization of state-owned enterprises necessarily furthers the consolidation of democracy. After all, democracies do need to levy taxes and regulate certain transactions, especially where private monopolies and oligopolies exist. Citizens or their representatives may decide that it is desirable to protect the rights of collectivities from encroachment by individuals, especially propertied ones, and they may choose to set aside certain forms of property for public or cooperative ownership. In short, notions of economic liberty that are currently put forward in neoliberal economic models are not synonymous with political freedom—and may even impede it.

Democratization will not necessarily bring in its wake economic growth, social peace, administrative efficiency, political harmony, free markets, or "the end of ideology." Least of all will it bring about "the end of history." No doubt some of these qualities could make the consolidation of democracy easier, but they are neither prerequisites for it nor immediate products of it. Instead, what we should be hoping for is the emergence of political institutions that can peacefully compete to form governments and influence public policy, that can channel social and economic conflicts through regular procedures, and that have sufficient linkages to civil society to represent their constituencies and commit them to collective courses of action. Some types of democracies, especially in developing countries, have been unable to fulfill this promise, perhaps due to the circumstances of their transition from authoritarian rule.[13] The democratic wager is that such a regime, once established, will not only persist by reproducing itself within its initial confining conditions, but will eventually expand beyond them.[14] Unlike authoritarian regimes, democracies have the capacity to modify their rules and institutions consensually in response to changing circumstances. They may not immediately produce all the goods mentioned above, but they stand a better chance of eventually doing so than do autocracies.

Notes

1. For a comparative analysis of the recent regime changes in southern Europe and Latin America, see Guillermo O'Donnell, Philippe C. Schmitter, and Laurence Whitehead, eds., *Transitions from Authoritarian Rule*, 4 vols. (Baltimore: Johns Hopkins University Press, 1986). For another compilation that adopts a more structural approach see Larry Diamond, Juan Linz, and Seymour Martin Lipset, eds., *Democracy in Developing Countries*, vols. 2, 3, and 4 (Boulder, Colo.: Lynne Rienner, 1989).
2. Numerous attempts have been made to codify and quantify the existence of democracy across political systems. The best known is probably Freedom House's *Freedom in the World: Political Rights and Civil Liberties*, published since 1973 by Greenwood Press and since 1988 by University Press of America. Also see Charles Humana, *World Human Rights Guide* (New York: Facts on File, 1986).
3. The definition most commonly used by American social scientists is that of Joseph Schumpeter: "that institutional arrangement for arriving at political decisions in which individuals acquire the power to decide by means of a competitive struggle for the people's vote." *Capitalism, Socialism, and Democracy* (London: George Allen and Unwin, 1943), 269. We accept certain aspects of the classical procedural approach to modern democracy, but differ prima-

rily in our emphasis on the accountability of rulers to citizens and the relevance of mechanisms of competition other than elections.
4. Not only do some countries practice a stable form of democracy without a formal constitution (e.g., Great Britain and Israel), but even more countries have constitutions and legal codes that offer no guarantee of reliable practice. On paper, Stalin's 1936 constitution for the USSR was a virtual model of democratic rights and entitlements.
5. For the most valiant attempt to make some sense out of this thicket of distinctions, see Juan Linz, "Totalitarian and Authoritarian Regimes" in *Handbook of Political Science*, eds. Fred I. Greenstein and Nelson W. Polsby (Reading Mass.: Addison Wesley, 1975), 175–411.
6. "Publius" (Alexander Hamilton, John Jay, and James Madison), *The Federalist Papers* (New York: Anchor Books, 1961). The quote is from Number 10.
7. See Terry Karl, "Imposing Consent? Electoralism versus Democratization in El Salvador," in *Elections and Democratization in Latin America, 1980–1985*, eds. Paul Drake and Eduardo Silva (San Diego: Center for Iberian and Latin American Studies, Center for US/Mexican Studies, University of California, San Diego, 1986), 9–36.
8. Alexis de Tocqueville, *Democracy in America*, 2 vols. (New York: Vintage Books, 1945).
9. This fear of overloaded government and the imminent collapse of democracy is well reflected in the work of Samuel P. Huntington during the 1970s. See especially Michel Crozier, Samuel P. Huntington, and Joji Watanuki, *The Crisis of Democracy* (New York: New York University Press, 1975). For Huntington's (revised) thoughts about the prospects for democracy, see his "Will More Countries Become Democratic?," *Political Science Quarterly* 99 (Summer 1984): 193–218.
10. Robert Dahl, *Dilemmas of Pluralist Democracy* (New Haven: Yale University Press, 1982), 11.
11. Robert Dahl, *After the Revolution: Authority in a Good Society* (New Haven: Yale University Press, 1970).
12. See Juan Linz, "The Perils of Presidentialism," *Journal of Democracy* 1 (Winter 1990): 51–69, and the ensuing discussion by Donald Horowitz, Seymour Martin Lipset, and Juan Linz in *Journal of Democracy* 1 (Fall 1990): 73–91.
13. Terry Lynn Karl, "Dilemmas of Democratization in Latin America" *Comparative Politics* 23 (October 1990): 1–23.
14. Otto Kirchheimer, "Confining Conditions and Revolutionary Breakthroughs," *American Political Science Review* 59 (1965): 964–974.

Philippe C. Schmitter *is professor of political science and director of the Center for European Studies at Stanford University.* **Terry Lynn Karl** *is associate professor of political science and director of the Center for Latin American Studies at the same institution. The original, longer version of this essay was written at the request of the United States Agency for International Development, which is not responsible for its content.*

From *Journal of Democracy*, Summer 1991. © 1991 by the National Endowment for Democracy and the Johns Hopkins University Press. Reprinted by permission.

Judicial Review:
The gavel and the robe

Established and emerging democracies display a puzzling taste in common: both have handed increasing amounts of power to unelected judges. Th[is] article examines the remarkable growth and many different forms of judicial review.

To SOME they are unaccountable elitists, old men (and the rare women) in robes who meddle in politics where they do not belong, thwarting the will of the people. To others they are bulwarks of liberty, champions of the individual against abuses of power by scheming politicians, arrogant bureaucrats and the emotional excesses of transient majorities.

Judges who sit on supreme courts must get used to the vilification as well as the praise. They often deal with the most contentious cases, involving issues which divide the electorate or concern the very rules by which their countries are governed. With so much at stake, losers are bound to question not only judges' particular decisions, but their right to decide at all. This is especially true when judges knock down as unconstitutional a law passed by a democratically elected legislature. How dare they?

Despite continued attacks on the legitimacy of judicial review, it has flourished in the past 50 years. All established democracies now have it in some form, and the standing of constitutional courts has grown almost everywhere. In an age when all political authority is supposed to derive from voters, and every passing mood of the electorate is measured by pollsters, the growing power of judges is a startling development.

The trend in western democracies has been followed by the new democracies of Eastern Europe with enthusiasm. Hungary's constitutional court may be the most active and powerful in the world. There have been failures. After a promising start, Russia's constitutional court was crushed in the conflict between Boris Yeltsin and his parliament. But in some countries where governments have long been riven by ideological divisions or crippled by corruption, such as Israel and India, constitutional courts have filled a political vacuum, coming to embody the legitimacy of the state.

In western democracies the growing role of constitutional review, in which judges rule on the constitutionality of laws and regulations, has been accompanied by a similar growth in what is known as administrative review, in which judges rule on the legality of government actions, usually those of the executive branch. This second type of review has also dragged judges into the political arena, frequently pitting them against elected politicians in controversial cases. But it is less problematic for democratic theorists than constitutional review for a number of reasons.

Democracy's referees

The expansion of the modern state has seemed to make administrative review inevitable. The reach of government, for good or ill, now extends into every nook and cranny of life. As a result, individuals, groups and businesses all have more reason than ever before to challenge the legality of government decisions or the interpretation of laws. Such challenges naturally end up before the courts.

In France, Germany, Italy and most other European countries, special administrative tribunals, with their own hierarchies of appeal courts, have been established to handle such cases. In the United States, Britain, Canada and Australia, the ordinary courts, which handle criminal cases and private lawsuits, also deal with administrative law cases.

The growth of administrative review can be explained as a reaction to the growth of state power. But the parallel expansion of constitutional review is all the more remarkable in a democratic age because it was resisted for so long in the very name of democracy.

The idea was pioneered by the United States, the first modern democracy with a written constitution. In fact, the American constitution nowhere explicitly gives the Supreme Court the power to rule laws invalid because of their unconstitutionality. The court's right to do this was first asserted in *Marbury v Madison*, an 1803 case, and then quickly became accepted as proper. One reason for such ready acceptance may have been that a Supreme Court veto fitted so well with the whole design and spirit of the constitution itself, whose purpose was as much to control the excesses of popular majorities as to give the people a voice in government decision-making.

In Europe this was the reason why the American precedent was not followed. As the voting franchise was expanded, the will of the voting majority became ever more sacrosanct, at least in theory. Parliamentary sovereignty reigned supreme. European democrats viewed the American experiment with constitutionalism as an unwarranted restraint on the popular will.

Even in the United States, judicial review was of little importance until the late 19th century, when the Supreme Court became more active, first nullifying laws passed after the civil war to give former slaves equal rights and then overturning laws regulating economic activity in the name of contractual and property rights.

After a showdown with Franklin Roosevelt over the New Deal, which the court lost, it abandoned its defence of laissez-faire economics. In the 1950s under Chief Justice Earl Warren it embarked on the active protection and expansion of civil rights. Controversially, this plunged the court into the mainstream of American politics, a position it retains today despite a retreat from Warren-style activism over the past two decades.

Attitudes towards judicial review also changed in Europe. The rise of fascism in the 1920s and 1930s, and then the destruction wrought by the second world war, made many European democrats reconsider the usefulness of judges. Elections alone no longer seemed a reliable obstacle to the rise of dangerously authoritarian governments. Fascist dictators had seized power by manipulating representative institutions.

The violence and oppression of the pre-war and war years also convinced many that individual rights and civil liberties needed special protection. The tyranny of the executive branch of government, acting in the name of the majority, became a real concern. (Britain remained an exception to this trend, sticking exclusively to the doctrine of parliamentary sovereignty. It is only now taking its first tentative steps towards establishing a constitutional court.)

While the goals of constitutional judicial review are similar almost everywhere, its form varies from country to country, reflecting national traditions. Some of the key differences:

• **Appointments.** The most famous method of appointment is that of the United States, largely because of a handful of televised and acrimonious confir-

mation hearings. The president appoints a Supreme Court judge, subject to Senate approval, whenever one of the court's nine seats falls vacant. Political horse-trading, and conflict, are part of the system. Judges are appointed for life, though very few cling to office to the end.

Other countries may appoint their constitutional judges with more decorum, but politics always plays some part in the process. France is the most explicitly political. The directly elected president and the heads of the Senate and the National Assembly each appoint three of the judges of the Constitutional Council, who serve non-renewable nine-year terms, one-third of them retiring every three years. Former presidents are awarded life membership on the council, although none has yet chosen to take his seat.

Half of the 16 members of Germany's Federal Constitutional Tribunal are chosen by the Bundestag, the lower house of parliament, and half by the Bundesrat, the upper house. Appointments are usually brokered between the two major parties. The procedure is similar in Italy, where one-third of the 15-strong Constitutional Court is chosen by the head of state, one-third by the two houses of parliament and one-third by the professional judiciary.

Senior politicians—both before and after serving in other government posts— have sat on all three constitutional courts, sometimes with unhappy results. In March Roland Dumas, the president of France's Constitutional Council, was forced to step down temporarily because of allegations of corruption during his earlier tenure as foreign minister. The trend in all three countries is towards the appointment of professional judges and legal scholars rather than politicians.

• **Powers.** Most constitutional courts have the power to nullify laws as unconstitutional, but how they do this, and receive cases, varies. Once again, the most anomalous is France's Constitutional Council which rules on the constitutionality of laws only before they go into effect and not, like all other courts, after.

The 1958 constitution of France's Fifth Republic allowed only four authorities to refer cases to the council: the president, the prime minister, and the heads of the two houses of parliament. In 1974, a constitutional amendment authorised 60 deputies or senators to lodge appeals with the council as well. Since then, the council has become more active, and most appeals now come from

groups of legislators. Individuals have no right to appeal to the council.

French jurists argue that judicial review before a law goes into effect is simpler and faster than review after a law's promulgation. But it is also more explicitly political, and leaves no room for making a judgment in the light of a law's sometimes unanticipated effect.

No other major country has adopted prior review exclusively, but it is an option in Germany and Italy as well, usually at the request of the national or one of the regional governments. However, most of the work of the constitutional courts in both countries comes from genuine legal disputes, which are referred to them by other courts when a constitutional question is raised.

The Supreme Courts of the United States, Canada and Australia, by contrast, are the final courts of appeal for all cases, not just those dealing with constitutional issues. The United States Supreme Court does not give advisory or abstract opinions about the constitutionality of laws, but only deals with cases involving specific disputes. Moreover, lower courts in the United States can also rule on constitutional issues, although most important cases are appealed eventually to the Supreme Court.

Canada's Supreme Court can be barred from ruling a law unconstitutional if either the national or a provincial legislature has passed it with a special clause declaring that it should survive judicial review "notwithstanding" any breach of the country's Charter of Rights. If passed in this way, the law must be renewed every five years. In practice, this device has rarely been used.

• **Judgments.** The French and Italian constitutional courts deliver their judgments unanimously, without dissents. Germany abandoned this method in 1971, adopting the more transparent approach of the common-law supreme courts, which allow a tally of votes cast and dissenting opinions to be published alongside the court's judgment. Advocates of unanimity argue that it reinforces the court's authority and gives finality to the law. Opponents deride it as artificial, and claim that publishing dissents improves the technical quality of judgments, keeps the public better informed, and makes it easier for the law to evolve in the light of changing circumstances.

Also noteworthy is the growth in Europe of supra-national judicial review. The European Court of Justice in Luxembourg is the ultimate legal authority for the European Union. The court's primary task is to interpret the treaties upon which the EU is founded. Because EU law now takes precedence over national law in the 15 member states, the court's influence has grown considerably in recent years. The European Court of Human Rights in Strasbourg, the judicial arm of the 41-member Council of Europe, has, in effect, become the final court of appeal on human-rights issues for most of Europe. The judgments of both European courts carry great weight and have forced many countries to change their laws.

Despite the rapid growth of judicial review in recent decades, it still has plenty of critics. Like all institutions, supreme courts make mistakes, and their decisions are a proper topic of political debate. But some criticisms aimed at them are misconceived.

Unelected legislators?

To criticise constitutional courts as political meddlers is to misunderstand their role, which is both judicial and political. If constitutions are to play any part in limiting government, then someone must decide when they have been breached and how they should be applied, especially when the relative powers of various branches or levels of government—a frequent issue in federal systems—are in question. When a court interprets a constitution, its decisions are political by definition—though they should not be party political.

Supreme courts also are not unaccountable, as some of their critics claim. Judges can be overruled by constitutional amendment, although this is rare. They must also justify their rulings to the public in written opinions. These are pored over by the media, lawyers, legal scholars and other judges. If unpersuasive, judgments are sometimes evaded by lower courts or legislatures, and the issue eventually returns to the constitutional court to be considered again.

Moreover, the appointment of judges is a political process, and the complexions of courts change as their membership changes, although appointees are sometimes unpredictable once on the bench. Nevertheless, new appointments can result in the reversal of earlier decisions which failed to win public support.

Constitutional courts have no direct power of their own. This is why Alexander Hamilton, who helped write America's constitution, called the judiciary "the least dangerous branch of government." Courts have no vast bureaucracy, revenue-raising ability, army or police force at their command—no way, in fact, to enforce their rulings. If other branches of government ignore them, they can do nothing. Their power and legitimacy, especially when they oppose the executive or legislature, depend largely on their moral authority and credibility.

Senior judges are acutely aware of their courts' limitations. Most tread warily, preferring to mould the law through interpretation of statutes rather than employing the crude instrument of complete nullification. Even the American Supreme Court, among the world's most activist, has ruled only sections of some 135 federal laws unconstitutional in 210 years, although it has struck down many more state laws.

Finally, it is worth remembering that judges are not the only public officials who exercise large amounts of power but do not answer directly to voters. Full-time officials and appointees actually perform most government business, and many of them have enormous discretion about how they do this. Even elected legislators and prime ministers are not perfect transmitters of the popular will, but enjoy great latitude when making decisions on any particular issue. Constitutional courts exist to ensure that everyone stays within the rules. Judges have the delicate, sometimes impossible, task of checking others' power without seeming to claim too much for themselves.

From *The Economist*, August 7, 1999, pp. 43-44. © 1999 by The Economist, Ltd. Distributed by the New York Times Special Features. Reprinted by permission.

Referendums: The people's voice

Is the growing use of referendums a threat to democracy or its salvation? The fifth article in our series on changes in mature democracies examines the experience so far, and the arguments for and against letting voters decide political questions directly.

WHEN Winston Churchill proposed a referendum to Clement Attlee in 1945 on whether Britain's wartime coalition should be extended, Attlee growled that the idea was an "instrument of Nazism and fascism". The use by Hitler and Mussolini of bogus referendums to consolidate their power had confirmed the worst fears of sceptics. The most democratic of devices seemed also to be the most dangerous to democracy itself.

Dictators of all stripes have continued to use phony referendums to justify their hold on power. And yet this fact has not stopped a steady growth in the use of genuine referendums, held under free and fair conditions, by both established and aspiring democracies. Referendums have been instrumental in the dismantling of communism and the transition to democracy in countries throughout the former soviet empire. They have also successfully eased democratic transitions in Spain, Greece, South Africa, Brazil and Chile, among other countries.

In most established democracies, direct appeals to voters are now part of the machinery for constitutional change. Their use to resolve the most intractable or divisive public issues has also grown. In the 17 major democracies of Western Europe, only three—Belgium, the Netherlands and Norway—make no provision

for referendums in their constitution. Only six major democracies—the Netherlands, the United States, Japan, India, Israel and the Federal Republic of Germany—have never held a nationwide referendum.

The volatile voter

Frustrated voters in Italy and New Zealand have in recent years used referendums to force radical changes to voting systems and other political institutions on a reluctant political elite. Referendums have also been used regularly in Australia, where voters go to the polls this November to decide whether to cut their country's formal link with the British crown. In Switzerland and several American states, referendums are a central feature of the political system, rivalling legislatures in significance.

Outside the United States and Switzerland, referendums are most often called by governments only when they are certain of victory, and to win endorsement of a policy they intend to implement in any case. This is how they are currently being used in Britain by Tony Blair's government.

But voters do not always behave as predicted, and they have delivered some notable rebuffs. Charles de Gaulle skil-

fully used referendums to establish the legitimacy of France's Fifth Republic and to expand his own powers as president, but then felt compelled to resign in 1969 after an unexpected referendum defeat.

Francois Mitterrand's decision to call a referendum on the Maastricht treaty in 1992 brought the European Union to the brink of breakdown when only 51% of those voting backed the treaty. Denmark's voters rejected the same treaty, despite the fact that it was supported by four out of five members of the Danish parliament. The Danish government was able to sign the treaty only after renegotiating its terms and narrowly winning a second referendum. That same year, Canada's government was not so lucky. Canadian voters unexpectedly rejected a painstakingly negotiated constitutional accord designed to placate Quebec.

Referendums come in many different forms. **Advisory referendums** test public opinion on an important issue. Governments or legislators then translate their results into new laws or policies as they see fit. Although advisory referendums can carry great weight in the right circumstances, they are sometimes ignored by politicians. In a 1955 Swedish referendum, 85% of those voting said they wanted to continue driving on the left side of the road. Only 12 years later the government went ahead and made the switch to driving on the right without a second referendum, or much protest.

By contrast, **mandatory referendums** are part of a law-making process or, more commonly, one of the procedures for constitutional amendment.

Both advisory and mandatory referendums can usually be called only by those in office—sometimes by the president, sometimes by parliamentarians, most often by the government of the day. But in a few countries, petitions by voters themselves can put a referendum on the ballot. These are known as **initiatives**. Sometimes these can only repeal an already existing law—so-called "abrogative" initiatives such as those in Italy. Elsewhere, initiatives can also be used to propose and pass new legislation, as in Switzerland and many American states. In this form they can be powerful and unpredictable political tools.

The rules for conducting and winning referendums also vary greatly from country to country. Regulations on the drafting of ballot papers and the financing of Yes and No campaigns are different everywhere, and these exert a great influence over how referendums are used, and how often.

The hurdle required for victory can be a critical feature. A simple majority of those voting is the usual rule. But a low turnout can make such victories seem illegitimate. So a percentage of eligible voters, as well as a majority of those voting, is sometimes required to approve a proposal.

Such hurdles, of course, also make failure more likely. In 1978 Britain's government was forced to abandon plans to set up a Scottish parliament when a referendum victory in Scotland failed to clear a 40% hurdle of eligible voters. Referendums have also failed in Denmark and Italy (most recently in April) because of similar voter-turnout requirements. To ensure a wide geographic consensus, Switzerland and Australia require a "double majority", of individual voters and of cantons or states, for constitutional amendments.

The use of referendums reflects the history and traditions of individual countries. Thus generalising about them is difficult. In some countries referendums have played a central, though peripatetic, role. In others they have been marginal or even irrelevant, despite provisions for their use.

Hot potatoes

Although referendums (outside Switzerland and the United States) have been most often used to legitimise constitutional change or the redrawing of boundaries, elected politicians have also found them useful for referring to voters those issues they find too hot to handle or which cut across party lines. Often these concern moral or lifestyle choices, such as alcohol prohibition, divorce or abortion. The outcome on such emotive topics can be difficult to predict. In divorce and abortion referendums, for example, Italians have shown themselves more liberal, and the Irish more conservative, than expected.

One of the best single books on referendums—"Referendums Around the World" edited by David Butler and Austin Ranney, published by Macmillan—argues that many assumptions about them are mistaken. They are not usually habit-forming, as those opposed to them claim. Many countries have used them to settle a specific issue, or even engaged in a series of them, and then turned away from referendums for long periods. But this is mostly because politicians decide whether referendums will be held. Where groups of voters can also put initiatives on the ballot, as in Switzerland and the United States, they have become addictive and their use has grown in recent years.

Messrs Butler and Ranney also point out that referendums are not usually vehicles for radical change, as is widely believed. Although they were used in this way in Italy and New Zealand, referendums have more often been used to support the status quo or to endorse changes already agreed by political parties. Most referendums, even those initiated by voters, fail. In Australia, 34 of 42 proposals to amend the constitution have been rejected by voters. According to an analysis by David Magleby, a professor at Brigham Young University in Utah, 62% of the 1,732 initiatives which reached the ballot in American states between 1898 and 1992 were rejected.

Arguments for and against referendums go to the heart of what is meant by democracy. Proponents of referendums maintain that consulting citizens directly is the only truly democratic way to determine policy. If popular sovereignty is really to mean anything, voters must have the right to set the agenda, discuss the issues and then themselves directly make the final decisions. Delegating these tasks to elected politicians, who have interests of their own, inevitably distorts the wishes of voters.

Referendums, their advocates say, can discipline representatives, and put the stamp of legitimacy on the most important political questions of the day. They also encourage participation by citizens in the governing of their own societies, and political participation is the source of most other civic virtues.

The case against

Those sceptical of referendums agree that popular sovereignty, majority rule and consulting voters are the basic building blocks of democracy, but believe that representative democracy achieves these goals much better than referendums. Genuine direct democracy, they say, is feasible only for political groups so small that all citizens can meet face-to-face—a small town perhaps. In large, modern societies, the full participation of every citizen is impossible.

Referendum opponents maintain that representatives, as full-time decision-makers, can weigh conflicting priorities, negotiate compromises among different groups and make well-informed decisions. Citizens voting in single-issue referendums have difficulty in doing any of these things. And as the bluntest of majoritarian devices, referendums encourage voters to brush aside the concerns of minority groups. Finally, the frequent use of referendums can actually undermine democracy by encouraging elected legislators to sidestep difficult issues, thus damaging the prestige and authority of representative institutions, which must continue to perform most of the business of government even if referendums are used frequently.

Testing any of these claims or counter-claims is difficult. Most countries do not, in fact, use referendums regularly enough to bear out either the hopes of proponents or the fears of opponents. The two exceptions are Switzerland and some American states, where citizen initiatives are frequent enough to draw tentative conclusions on some of these points, although both examples fall far short of full-fledged direct democracy.

Voters in both countries seem to believe that referendums do, in fact, lend legitimacy to important decisions. The Swiss are unlikely now to make a big national decision without a referendum.

Swiss voters have rejected both UN membership and links with the EU in referendums, against the advice of their political leaders. Similarly, American polls show healthy majorities favouring referendums and believing that they are more likely to produce policies that most people want. Polls also show support for the introduction of referendums on the national level.

The claim that referendums increase citizen participation is more problematic. Some referendum campaigns ignite enormous public interest and media attention. Initiatives also give political outsiders a way to influence the public agenda. But in the United States, much of the activity involved in getting initiatives on the ballot, such as collecting signatures, has been taken over by professional firms, and many referendum campaigns have become slick, expensive affairs far removed from the grassroots (so far, this is much less true in Switzerland). Even more surprising, voter participation in American referendums is well below that of candidate elections, even when these are held at the same time. The average turnout for Swiss referendums has fallen by a third in the past 50 years to about 40%. On big issues, however, turnout can still soar.

Many of the fears of those opposed to referendums have not been realised in either country. Initiatives have not usually been used to oppress minorities. A proposal to limit the number of foreigners allowed to live in Switzerland was rejected by two-thirds of voters in 1988. In 1992 Colorado's voters did approve an initiative overturning local ordinances protecting gays from discrimination, but more extreme anti-gay initiatives in Colorado and California have been defeated

by large majorities. Since 1990 voters have consistently upheld certain abortion rights in initiative ballots. Minorities and immigrants have been the targets of initiatives in some states, but voters have generally rejected extreme measures and have often proven themselves no more illiberal than legislators. Most initiatives are, in fact, about tax and economic questions, not civil liberties or social issues, although the latter often gain more attention.

While the frequent use of initiatives has not destroyed representative government, as some feared, it has changed it. Party loyalty among Swiss voters is strong at general elections, but evaporates when it comes to referendum voting. Initiatives, and the threat of mounting one, have become an integral part of the legislative process in Switzerland, as they have in California, Oregon and the other American states where they are most used. Referendums now often set the political agenda in both countries. In the United States they are frequently seen, rightly or wrongly, as a barometer of the national mood. And they can occasionally spark a political revolution. California's Proposition 13, for example, a 1978 initiative lowering local property taxes, set off a tax revolt across America. Elected officials themselves are often active in launching initiatives, and relatively successful in getting their proposals approved, which hardly indicates that voters have lost all faith in their politicians. Initiatives have made legislating more complicated, but also more responsive to the public's concerns.

There is some evidence that American voters, at least, are sometimes overwhelmed by the volume of information coming their way, and cast their vote in

ignorance, as critics contend. Mr Magleby cites studies showing that on several ballots, 10–20% of the electorate mistakenly cast their vote the wrong way. Ballot material dropping through the letterboxes of residents in California is now often more than 200 pages long. According to one poll, only one in five Californians believes that the average voter understands most of the propositions put before him. Quite rationally, this has also bred caution. Californians approve only one-third of initiatives.

Hybrid democracy?

The Swiss and American experience suggests that in the future there is unlikely to be a headlong rush away from representative to direct democracy anywhere, but that, even so, the use of referendums is likely to grow. The Internet and other technological advances have not yet had much impact on referendums, but they should eventually make it easier to hold them, and to inform voters of the issues they are being asked to decide upon.

Representative institutions are likely to survive because of the sheer volume of legislation in modern societies, and the need for full-time officials to run the extensive machinery of government. Nevertheless in an age of mass communication and information, confining the powers of citizens to voting in elections every few years seems a crude approach, a throwback to an earlier era. In a political system based on popular sovereignty, it will become increasingly difficult to justify a failure to consult the voters directly on a wider range of issues.

Reprinted with permission from *The Economist*, August 14, 1999, pp. 45-46. © 1999 by The Economist, Ltd. Distributed by The New York Times Special Features.

The Case for a Multi-Party U.S. Parliament? American Politics in Comparative Perspective

Abstract

This is a "mental experiment" that illuminates the role of institutions in shaping the political process. It is best viewed as part of the long history of American fascination with the parliamentary system and even multiparty politics. The larger hope is to initiate serious dialogue on the respective strengths and weaknesses of majoritarian and consensus systems with scholars of American politics and include American politics in an explicitly comparative perspective.

Christopher S. Allen

INTRODUCTION

Americans revere the constitution but at the same time also sharply and frequently criticize the government. (Dionne, 1991) Yet since the constitution is responsible for the current form of the American government, why not change the constitution to produce better government? After all, the founders of the United States did create the amendment process and we have seen 27 of them in over 200 years.

Several recent events prompt a critical look at this reverence for the constitution: unusual presidential developments, including the Clinton impeachment spectacle of 1998-1999; the historic and bizarre 2000 Presidential election; and the apparent mandate for fundamental change that President Bush inferred from this exceedingly narrow election. In the early 21st century, American politics confronted at least three other seemingly intractable problems: a significant erosion in political accountability; out of control costs of running for public office; and shamefully low voter turnout. More seriously, none of these four problems is of recent origin, as all four have eroded the functioning of the American government for a period of between 25 and 50 years! The core features of these four problems are:

- Confusion of the roles of head of state and head of government, of which the impeachment issue—from Watergate through Clinton's impeachment—is merely symptomatic of a much larger problem.
- Eroding political accountability, taking the form of either long periods of divided government, dating back to the "do nothing" 80th congress elected in 1946, to the recent "gerrymandering industry" producing a dearth of competitive elections. The result is millions of "wasted votes" and an inability for voters to assign credit or blame for legislative action.
- Costly and perennial campaigns for all offices producing "the best politicians that money can buy." This problem that had its origins with the breakdown of the party caucus system and the growth of primary elections in the 1960s; and

When various American scholars acknowledge these shortcomings, however, there is the occasional, off-hand comparison to parliamentary systems which have avoided some of these pathologies. The unstated message is that we don't—or perhaps should never, ever want to—have that here.

Why not? What exactly is the problem with a parliamentary system? Durable trust in government, sense of efficacy, and approval ratings for branches in government have all declined in recent decades. Such phenomena contribute to declining voter turnout and highlight what is arguably a more significant trend toward a crisis in confidence among Americans concerning their governing institutions. So why is institutional redesign off the table?

This article examines these 4 institutional blockages of the American majoritarian/Presidential system and suggests certain features of parliamentary or consensus systems might overcome these persistent shortcomings of American politics.

Less normatively, the article is framed by three concepts central to understanding and shaping public policy in advanced industrialized states with democratic constitutional structures.

First, is the issue of comparability and 'American Exceptionalism'. (Lipset, 1996) The article's goal is to initiate a long-delayed dialogue on comparative constitutional structures with scholars of American politics. Second, the article hopes to participate in the active discussion among comparativists on the respective strengths and weaknesses of majoritarian and consensus systems. (Birchfield and Crepaz, 1998). Third, scandals surrounding money and politics in a number of democratic states (Barker, 1994) should prompt a comparison of parties and party systems and the context within which they function.

This article does not underestimate the quite significant problems associated with "institutional transplantation" (Jacoby, 2000) from one country to another. The more modest and realistic goal is to engage American and Comparative scholars in a fruitful debate about political institutions and constitutional design that (finally) includes American politics in a Comparative orbit.

This article is organized in 5 sections that address: 1) the cumbersome tool of impeachment; 2) eroding political accountability due to divided government and safe seats; 3) the costly, never-ending campaign process; 4) the continued deterioration of voter turnout, and finally, pragmatically; 5) offers a critical analysis of the quite formidable obstacles that initiating a parliamentary remedy to these problems would clearly face.

1. Impeachment: Head of State vs Head of Government

The tool of impeachment is merely a symptom of a larger problem. Its more fundamental flaw is that it highlights the constitutional confusion between the two functions of the US presidency: head of state and head of government.

Americanists have delved deeply into the minutiae of the impeachment process during the past thirty years but comparativists would ask a different question. How would other democracies handle similar crises affecting their political leaders? More than two years transpired from the Watergate break-in to Nixon's resignation (1972–74), the Iran-Contra scandal (1986–87) produced no impeachment hearings; and an entire year (1998–99) transpired from the onset of the Clinton-Lewinsky saga to the completion of the impeachment process. Comparativists and citizens of other democratic polities find this astounding, since in a parliamentary system a fundamental challenge to the executive would take the form of a vote of no confidence, (Lijphart, 1994) and the issue would be politically resolved within weeks. The executive would either survive and continue or resign.

The portrayal of the Clinton impeachment and trial is characterized as his-

toric. For only the second time in American politics, an American president has been impeached in the House and put on trial in the Senate. Yet, the *idea* of using impeachment has been much less rare, having been raised three times in the past thirty years. Yet impeachment hasn't "worked" at all. It is either not brought to fruition (Watergate), not used when it should have been (Iran-Contra), or completely trivialized (Clinton-Lewinsky) when another path was clearly needed. But impeachment itself isn't the real problem; a larger constitutional design flaw is.

The United States has a constitutional structure based on a separation of powers, while most parliamentary systems have a "fusion" of powers in that the Prime Minister is also the leader of the major party in parliament. However, within the American executive itself, there is a "fusion" of functions, which is the exact opposite of Parliamentary regimes.

The US is the only developed democracy where head of state and head of government are fused in one person. The President is the Head of State and, effectively, the Head of Government. In Parliamentary systems these two functions are performed by two different people. (Linz, 1993) Thus impeachment of one person removes two functions in one and likely explained the dichotomy of popular desire for Clinton's retention on the one hand, but also for some form of political censure on the other.

Beyond the impeachment issue, when American presidents undertake some action as head of government for which they are criticized, they then become invariably more remote and inaccessible. For example, Presidents Johnson (Vietnam), Nixon (Watergate), Reagan (Iran/Contra), Clinton (the Lewinsky Affair) and G.W. Bush (Iraq) all reduced their appearances at press conferences as criticism of their policies mounted. In short, when criticized for actions taken in their head of government capacity, they all retreated to the Rose Garden and sometimes created the impression that criticizing the President—now wearing the head of state hat (or perhaps, crown)—was somehow unpatriotic. This was especially the case with George W. Bush, who in the post 9/11 and Iraq war periods, has tried to emphasize the commander in chief aspect of the presidency rather than his role as steward of the economy and domestic politics.

Toward a Politically Accountable Prime Minister and a Ceremonial President

A parliamentary system with a separate head of state and head of government would produce two "executive" offices instead of one. It's odd that the US is so fearful of centralized power yet allows the executive to perform functions that no other leader of an OECD country (France excepted) performs alone. The US Vice President serves many of the functions of heads of state in other countries. But the United States has a comparatively odd way of dividing executive constitutional functions. One office, the Presidency, does everything while the other, the Vice Presidency, does virtually nothing and simply waits until the president can no longer serve. An American parliamentary system would redefine these 2 offices so that one person (the head of state) would serve as a national symbol and preside over ceremonial functions. The second person (the head of government) would function much like a prime minister does in a parliamentary system, namely as the head of government who could be criticized, censured and held accountable for specific political actions without creating a constitutional crisis.

Thus were it necessary to censure or otherwise take action against the head of government (i.e. prime minister), the solution would be a relatively quick vote of no confidence that would solve the problem and move on and let the country address its political business. (Huber, 1996) and unlike impeachment which is the political equivalent of the death penalty, a vote of no confidence does not preclude a politician's making a comeback and returning to lead a party or coalition. Impeachment and removal from office, on the other hand, is much more final.

Prime Ministers, unlike US presidents, are seen much more as active politicians not remote inaccessible figures. In a parliament, the prime minister as the head of government is required to engage—and be criticized—in the rough-and-tumble world of daily politics. In short, the head of government must be accountable. The British prime minister, for example, is required to participate in a weekly "question time" in which often blunt and direct inter-

TABLE 1
Trust in the Federal Government 1964–2002

	'64	'66	'68	'70	'72	'74	'76	'78	'80	'82	'84	'86	'88	'90	'92	'94	'96	'98	'00	'02
None of the Time	0	2	0	0	1	1	1	4	4	3	1	2	2	2	2	3	1	1	1	0
Some of the Time	22	28	36	44	44	61	62	64	69	62	53	57	56	69	68	74	66	58	55	44
Most of the Time	62	48	54	47	48	34	30	27	23	31	40	35	36	25	26	19	30	36	40	51
Just About Always	14	17	7	6	5	2	13	2	2	2	4	3	4	3	3	2	3	4	4	5
Don't Know, Dep.	1	4	2	2	2	2	3	3	2	3	2	2	1	1	1	1	0	1	1	0

PERCENTAGE WITHIN STUDY YEAR

Source: The National Election Studies.

QUESTION TEXT:

"How much of the time do you think you can trust the government in Washington to do what is right—just about always, most of the time or only some of the time?"

Source: The National Election Studies, University of Michigan, 2003

rogatories are pressed by the opposition. (Rundquist, 1991) There is no equivalent forum for the American president to be formally questioned as a normal part of the political process.

But could such a power might be used in a cavalier fashion, perhaps removing the head of government easily after a debilitating scandal? This is unlikely in a well-designed parliamentary system because such cynicism would likely produce a backlash that would constrain partisanship. In fact, the Germans have institutionalized such constraints in the "constructive vote of no confidence" requiring any removal of the head of government to be a simultaneous election of a new one. The context of such a parliamentary system lowers the incentives to engage in the politics of destruction. The political impact of destroying any particular individual in a collective body such as a cabinet or governing party or coalition is much less significant than removing a directly elected president.

A parliamentary head of state is above the kind of criticism generated in no confidence votes and simply serves as an apolitical symbol of national pride. In nation states that have disposed of their monarchies, ceremonial presidents perform many of the same roles as constitutional monarchs such as Queen Elizabeth do, but much more inexpensively. In fact, many of these ceremonial roles are performed by the American vice president (attending state dinners/funerals, cutting ribbons, presiding over the Sen-

ate, etc.) The problem is that the Vice President is often a political afterthought, chosen more for ticket-balancing functions and/or for inoffensive characteristics than for any expected major political contributions. On the other hand, the type of individual usually chosen as a ceremonial president in a parliamentary system is a retired politician from the moderate wing of one of the major parties who has a high degree of stature and can serve as a figure of national unity. In effect, the office of ceremonial president is often a reward or honor for decades of distinguished national service, hardly the characteristics of an American vice president.

In retrospect, one might say that President Clinton was impeached not for abusing head of government functions, but for undermining the decorum and respect associated with heads of state. The separation of head of state and head of government would have a salutary effect on this specific point. Scandals destroying heads of state would have little real political significance since the head of state would not wield real political power. Similarly, scandals destroying heads of government would have significantly less impact than the current American system. The head of government role, once separated from the head of state role, would no longer attract monolithic press and public attention or be subject to extraordinarily unrealistic behavioral expectations.

2. Political Accountability: Divided Government & "Safe Seats"

From the "do nothing" 80th Congress elected in 1946 to the 107th elected in 2002, a total of twenty nine congresses, the United States has experienced divided government for more than two-thirds of this period. In only nine of those twenty nine Congresses has the president's party enjoyed majorities in both houses of Congress. (Fiorina, 1992) Some might observe this divided government phenomenon and praise the bipartisan nature of the American system. (Mayhew, 1991) But to justify such a conclusion, defenders of the bipartisanship would have to demonstrate high public approval of governmental performance, particularly when government was divided. Based on over four decades of declining trust in government, such an argument is increasingly hard to justify

One explanation for the American preference for divided government is the fear of concentrated political power. (Jacobson, 1990) Yet in a search for passivity, the result often turns out to be simply inefficiency.

While the fear of concentrated government power is understandable for historical and ideological reasons, many of the same people who praise divided government also express concern regarding government efficiency. (Thurber, 1991) Yet divided government quite likely contributes to the very

Table 2
The Persistence of Divided Government

	President	House	Senate	Divided/ Unified		President	House	Senate	Divided/ Unified
1946	D Truman	Rep	Rep	d	1976	D Carter	Dem	Dem	u
1948	D Truman	Dem	Rep	d	1978	D Carter	Dem	Dem	u
1950	D Truman	Rep	Rep	d	1980	R Reagan	Dem	Rep	d
1952	R Eisenhower	Rep	Rep	u	1982	R Reagan	Dem	Rep	d
1954	R Eisenhower	Dem	Dem	d	1984	R Reagan	Dem	Rep	d
1956	R Eisenhower	Dem	Dem	d	1986	R Reagan	Dem	Dem	d
1958	R Eisenhower	Dem	Dem	d	1988	R Bush	Dem	Dem	d
1960	D Kennedy	Dem	Dem	u	1990	R Bush	Dem	Dem	d
1962	D Kennedy	Dem	Dem	u	1992	D Clinton	Dem	Dem	u
1964	D Johnson	Dem	Dem	u	1994	D Clinton	Rep	Rep	d
1966	D Johnson	Dem	Dem	u	1996	D Clinton	Rep	Rep	d
1968	R Nixon	Dem	Dem	d	1998	D Clinton	Rep	Rep	d
1970	R Nixon	Dem	Dem	d	2000	R Bush	Rep	Dem*	d
1972	R Nixon	Dem	Dem	d	2002	R Bush	Rep	Rep	u
1974	R Ford	Dem	Dem	d					

* After a 50–50 split (with Vice President Cheney as the tiebreaker), Senator Jeffords (I-VT) switched from the Republican party shortly after the 2000 election, thereby swinging the Senate to the Democrats.

inefficiencies that voters rightfully lament. Under divided government, when all is well, each of the two parties claims responsibility for the outcome; when economic or political policies turn sour, however, each party blames the other. This condition leads to a fundamental lack of political accountability and the self-fulfilling prophecy that government is inherently inefficient.

Rather than being an accidental occurrence, divided government is much more likely to result due to the American constitutional design. For it is constitutional provisions that are at the heart of divided government; 2 year terms for Congress, 4 year terms for the Presidency, and 6 year terms for the Senate invariably produce divided government.

Were it only for these "accidental" outcomes of divided government, political accountability might be less deleterious. Exacerbating the problem, however, is the decline of parties as institutions.

This has caused individuals to have weaker partisan *attachments*—despite the increased partisan *rhetoric* of many elected officials since the 1980s—and has thereby intensified the fragmentation of government. (Franklin and Hirczy de Mino, 1998) Clearly, divided government is more problematic when partisan conflict between the two parties is greater as the sharper ideological conflict and the increased party line congressional voting since the 1990s would suggest. Under these circumstances, divided government seems to be more problematic, since two highly partisan parties within the American political system seems potentially dangerous. Persistent divided government over time will likely produce a fundamental change in the relationship between Presidents and the Congress. Presidents are unable to bargain effectively with a hostile congress-witness the 1995 government shut-

down—leading the former to make appeals over the heads of Congress directly and, hence undermine the legitimacy of the legislative branch. (Kernell, 1997) This argument parallels the one made in recent comparative scholarship (Linz, 1993) regarding the serious problem of dual legitimacy in presidential systems.

A second component of the political accountability problem is the increasing uncompetitiveness of American elections. Accounts of the 2000 Presidential election stressed its historic closeness, settled by only 540,000 popular votes (notwithstanding the electoral college anomaly). And the narrow Republican majorities in the House and Senate apparently indicated that every congressional or senate seat could be up for grabs each election. The reality is something different. (Center for Voting, 2003) Out of 435 House seats, only 10% or fewer are competitive, the outcome of most Senate races is known well in advance, and the Presidential race was only competitive in 15 of 50 states. In the remaining 35, the state winners (Gore or Bush) were confident enough of the outcome to forgo television advertising in many of them. In essence, voters for candidates who did not win these hundreds of "safe seats" were effectively disenfranchised and unable to hold their representatives politically accountable.

For those who lament the irresponsibility—or perhaps irrelevance—of the two major parties, an institutional design that would force responsibility should be praised. Quite simply, those who praise divided government because it "limits the damage" or see nothing amiss when there are hundreds of safe seats are faced with a dilemma. They can not simultaneously complain about the resulting governmental inefficiency and political cynicism that ultimately follows when accountability is regularly clouded.

Political Accountability and the Fusion of Government

A number of scholars have addressed the deficiencies of divided government, but they suggest that the problem is that the electoral cycle, with its "off year" elections, intensifies the likelihood of divided government in non-presidential election years. Such advocates propose as a solution the alteration of the electoral cycle so that all congressional elections are on four year terms, concurrent with presidential terms, likely producing a clear majority. (Cutler, 1989) Yet this contains a fatal flaw. Because there is no guarantee that this proposal would alleviate the residual tension between competing branches of government, it merely sidesteps the accountability factor strongly discouraging party unity across the executive and legislative branches of government.

This suggestion could also produce the opposite effect from divided government, namely exaggerated majorities common to parliamentary regimes with majoritarian electoral systems such as the UK. The "safe seats" phenomenon would be the culprit just as in the UK. The most familiar examples of this phenomenon were the "stop-go" policies of post-World War II British governments, as each succeeding government tried to

overturn the previous election. While creating governing majorities is important for political accountability, the absence of proportional representation creates a different set of problems.

Under a fusion of power system, in which the current presidency would be redefined, the resulting parliamentary system would make the head of the legislative branch the executive, thus eliminating the current separation of powers. Yet if a government should lose its majority between scheduled elections due to defection of its party members or coalition partners, the head of state then would ask the opposition to form a new government and, failing that, call for new elections. This avoids the constitutional crises that the clamor for impeachment seem to engender in the American system.

But what if coalition members try to spread the blame for poor performance to their partners? In theory, the greater the flexibility available to in shifting from one governing coalition to another (with a different composition), the greater potential for this kind of musical cabinet chairs. The potential for such an outcome is far less than the American system, however. A century of experience in other parliamentary regimes (Laver and Shepsle, 1995) shows that members of such a party capriciously playing games with governing are usually brought to heel at the subsequent election.

In other words, the major advantage to such a parliamentary system is that it heightens the capacity for voters and citizens to evaluate government performance. Of course, many individuals might object to the resulting concentration of power. However, if voters are to judge the accomplishments of elected officials, the latter need time to succeed or fail, and then the voters can make a judgment on their tenure. The most likely outcome would be a governing party or coalition of parties that would have to stay together to accomplish anything, thereby increasing party salience. (Richter, 2002) Phrased differently, such an arrangement would likely lead to an increase in responsible government.

Many Americans might react unfavorably at the mention of the word coalition due to its supposed instability. Here we need to make the distinction between transparent and opaque coalitions. Some argue that coalition government in parliamentary systems have the reputation of increased instability. That, of course, depends on the substance of the coalition agreement and the willingness of parties

to produce a stable majority. (Strom et al., 1994) But in most parliamentary systems, these party coalitions are formed transparently before an election so the voters can evaluate and then pass judgment on the possible coalition prior to election day. It's not as if there are no coalitions in the US Congress. There they take the opaque form of ad-hoc groups of individual members of Congress on an issue-by-issue basis. The high information costs to American voters in understanding the substance of such layered bargains hardly is an example of political transparency.

Table 3	
Comparative Coalitions	
American	Parliamentary
Opaque	Transparent
Issue-by-Issue	Programmatic
Back Room	Open Discussion
Unaccountable	Election Ratifies
Unstable	Generally Stable

Finally, for the concerned that the "fusion" of the executive and legislative branches—on the British majoritarian model—would upset the concept of checks and balances, a multi-party consensus parliamentary system produces them slightly differently. (Lijphart, 1984) Majoritarianism concentrates power and makes "checking difficult, while consensus democracies institutionalize the process in a different, and more accountable form. A multi-party parliamentary system would also provide greater minority representation and protection by reducing majoritarianism's excessive concentration of power. A consensus parliamentary system would also address the "tyranny of the majority" problem and allow checking and balancing by the voters in the ballot box since the multiple parties would not likely allow a single party to dominate. Consensus systems thus represent a compromise between the current US system and the sharp concentration of British Westminster systems. Americans who simultaneously favor checks and balances but decry inefficient government need to clarify what they actually want their government to do.

3. Permanent and Expensive Campaigns

The cost to run for political office in the United States dwarfs that spent in any other advanced industrialized democracy. The twin problems are time and money. More specifically a never-ending campaign "season" and the structure of political advertising that depends so heavily on TV money. (Gans, 1993) Listening to the debates about "reforming" the American campaign finance system are bizarre to students of other democratic electoral systems. More than $2 billion was raised and spent (Mann, 1997) by parties, candidates and interest groups in the 1996 campaign, and for 2000 it went up to $3 billion.

The two year congressional cycle forces members of the House of Representatives to literally campaign permanently. The amount of money required to run for a Congressional seat has quadrupled since 1990. Presidential campaigns are several orders of magnitude beyond the House of Representatives or the Senate. By themselves they are more than two years long, frequently longer. Unless a presidential candidate is independently wealthy or willing and able to raise upfront $30–$50 million it is simply impossible to run seriously for this office.

Many of the problems stem from the post-Watergate "reforms" that tried to limit the amount of spending on campaigns which then produced a backlash in the form of a 1976 Supreme Court decision (Buckley vs Valeo) that undermined this reform attempt. In essence, Buckley vs Valeo held that "paid speech" (i.e. campaign spending) has an equivalent legal status as "free speech". (Grant, 1998) Consequently, since then all "reform" efforts have been tepid measures that have not been able to get at the root of the problem. As long as "paid speech" retains its protected status, any changes are dead in the water.

At its essence this issue is a fissure between "citizens" and "consumers". What Buckley vs Valeo has done is to equate the citizenship function (campaigning, voting, civic education) with a market-based consumer function (buying and selling consumer goods as commodities). (Brubaker, 1998) Unlike the United States, most other OECD democracies consider citizenship a public good and provide funding for parties, candidates and the electoral process as a matter of course. The Buckley vs Valeo decision conflates the concepts of citizen and consumer, the logical extension of which is there are weak limits on campaign funding and no limits on the use of a candidate's own money. We are all equal citizens, yet we are not all equal consumers. Bringing consumer metaphors into the electoral process debases the very concept of citizenship and guarantees that the American political system produces the best politicians money can buy.

Free Television Time and the Return of Political Party Dues

Any broadcaster wishing to transmit to the public is required to obtain a broadcast license because the airways have the legal status of public property. To have access to such property, the government licenses these networks, cable channels, and stations to serve the public interest. In return, broadcasters are able to sell airtimes to sponsors of various programs. Unfortunately for campaign costs, candidates for public office fall into the same category as consumer goods in the eyes of the broadcasters. (Weinberg, 1993) What has always seemed odd to observers of other democratic states is that there is no *Quid Pro Quo* requiring the provision of free public airtime for candidates when running for election.

Any serious reform of campaign finance would require a concession from all broadcasters to provide free time for all representative candidates and parties as a cost of using the public airways. Since the largest share of campaign money is TV money, this reform would solve the problem at its source. Restricting the "window" when these free debates would take place to the last two months before a general election would thus address the time dimension as well. Such practices are standard procedure in all developed parliamentary systems. Very simply, as long as "reform" efforts try to regulate the *supply* of campaign finance, it will fail. A much more achievable target would be the regulation of *demand*.

The United States could solve another money problem by borrowing a page from parliamentary systems: changing the political party contribution structure from individual voluntary contributions (almost always from the upper middle class and the wealthy) to a more broad-based dues structure common to parties in other developed democracies. This more egalitarian party dues structure would perform the additional salutary task of rebuilding parties as functioning institutions. (Allen, 1999) Rather than continuing in their current status as empty shells for independently wealthy candidates, American political parties could become the kind of dynamic membership organizations they were at the turn of the 20th century when they did have a dues structure.

4. Low Voter Turnout?

The leading OECD countries have voter turnout ranging from 70% to 90% of their adult population while the US lags woefully behind. Among the most commonly raised explanations for the US deficiency are: registration requirements, the role of television, voter discouragement, and voter contentment (although the latter two are clearly mutually exclusive). None are particularly convincing nor do they offer concrete suggestions as to how it might be overcome.

Table 4
Comparative Voting Turnout— 1945–2000 Average

Country	Turnout %
Italy	92.5
Germany	80.6
Great Britain	74.9
France	67.3
US President	55.1
US Congress "off year"	40.9
US Municipal	21.5

Source: Voter Turnout: A Global Survey (Stockholm: International IDEA, 2004)

The two party system and the electoral method that produces it: the single member district, first past the post, or winner take all system with its attendant "safe seats" often escapes criticism. The rise of such new organizations as the Reform, Libertarian, and Green parties potentially could threaten the hegemony of the Democrats and Republicans. Yet the problem of a third (or fourth) party gaining a sufficient number of votes to actually win seats and challenge the two party system is formidable. The electoral arithmetic would require any third party to win some 25% of the vote on a nationwide basis—or develop a highly-concentrated regional presence—before it would actually gain more than a token number of seats. And failing to actually win seats produces a "wasted vote" syndrome among party supporters which is devastating for such a party. (Rosenstone *et al.*, 1996) Most voters who become disillusioned with the electoral process refer to the "lesser of two evils" choices they face. In such a circumstance, declining voter turnout is not surprising.

The US is a diverse country with many regional, religious, racial, and class divisions. So why should we expect that two "catch all" parties will do a particularly good job in appealing to the interests of diverse constituencies? The solution to lower voter turnout is a greater number of choices for voters and a different electoral system.

Proportional Representation

Under electoral systems using proportional representation, the percentage of a party's vote is equivalent to the percentage of seats allocated to the party in parliament. Comparative analysis shows that those countries with proportional representation—and the multiple parties that PR systems produce—invariably have higher voter turnout. (Grofman and Lijphart, 1986) In other words, PR voting systems provide a wider variety of political choices and a wider variety of political representation.

Eliminating majoritarian single member districts (SMDs) in favor of PR voting would have several immediate effects. First, it would increase the range of choices for voters, since parties would have to develop ideological and programmatic distinctions to make themselves attractive to voters. As examples

in other countries have shown, it would lead to formation of several new parties representing long underserved interests.

Such a change would force rebuilding of parties as institutions, since candidates would have to run as members of parties and not as independent entrepreneurs. The so-called Progressive "reforms" at the turn of the 20th century and the 1960s introduction of primaries—plus TV advertising—plus the widespread use of referenda have all had powerful effects in undermining parties as coherent political organizations. (Dwyre, 1994) In trying to force market-based individual "consumer choice" in the form of high-priced candidates, the collective institutions that are political parties have been hollowed out and undermined.

Table 5
The Advantages of Proportional Representation

- Higher Voter Turnout
- No "Wasted" Votes
- Few Safe, Uncontested Seats
- More Parties
- Greater Minority Representation
- Greater Gender Diversity in Congress
- Greater Ideological Clarity
- Parties Rebuilt as Institutions
- 6% Threshold Assumed
- No More Gerrymandered Redistricting

There are, of course, a wide range of standard objections to PR voting systems by those favoring retention of majoritarian SMD systems.

The first of these, *coalitional instability*, was addressed briefly, but it needs to be restated here. The US has unstable coalitions in the Congress right now, namely issue-by-issue ones, usually formed in the House cloakroom with the "assistance" of lobbyists. Few average voters know with certainty how "their" member of Congress will vote on a given is-

sue. (Gibson, 1995) With ideologically coherent parties, they would.

An American parliament with several parties could produce self-discipline very effectively. Clearly there would have to be a coalition government since it is unlikely that any one party would capture 50% of the seats. The practice in almost all other coalition governments in parliamentary systems is that voters prefer a predictable set of political outcomes. Such an arrangement forces parties to both define their programs clearly and transparently, once entering into a coalition, and to do everything possible to keep the coalition together during the course of the legislative term.

The second standard objection to PR is the *"Too many parties"* issue. PR voting has been practiced in parliaments for almost 100 years in many different democratic regimes. There is a long history of practices that work well and practices that don't. (Norris, 1997) Two countries are invariably chosen as bad examples of PR, namely Israel and Italy. There is an easy solution to this problem of an unwieldy number of parties, namely an electoral threshold requiring any party to receive a certain minimal percentage to gain seats in the parliament. The significant question is what should this minimal threshold be? The Swedes have 4% threshold and have 6 parties in their parliament, the Germans have a 5% threshold and have 5 parties represented in the Bundestag.

The third standard objection to PR voting is *"Who's my representative?"* In a society so attuned to individualism, most Americans want a representative from their district. This argument presumes that all Americans have a member of Congress that represents their views. However, a liberal democrat who lived in House Speaker Tom Delay's district in Texas might genuinely wonder in what way he represented that liberal's interests. By the same token, conservative Republicans living in Vermont have the independent socialist, Bernard Sanders as the state's lone member of Congress representing "their" interests.

Yet if American reformers are still insistent on having individual representatives (Guinier, 1994) the phenomena of "Instant Runoff Voting" (Hill, 2003) where voters rank order their preferences could produce proportionality among parties yet retain individual single member districts.

If there were PR voting in an American parliament, what would the threshold be? The US threshold should be at least 6% and possibly as high as 7%. The goal is to devise a figure that represents all significant interests yet does not produce instability. The "shake out" of parties would likely produce some strategic "mergers" of weak parties which, as single parties, might not attain the 6%–7% threshold. For example, a separate Latino party and an African-American party might insure always attaining a 7% threshold by forming a so-called "rainbow" party. Similarly the Reform Party and the Libertarian Party might find it safer electorally to merge into one free market party.

There are four primary arguments in favor of PR.

The first is *simplicity*, the percentage of the votes equals the percentage of the seats. To accomplish this, the individualistic US could borrow the German hybrid system of "personalized" proportional representation. This system requires citizens to cast two votes on each ballot: the first for an individual candidate; and the second for a list of national/regional candidates grouped by party affiliation. (Allen, 2001) This system has the effect of personalizing list voting because voters have their own representative but also can choose among several parties. Yet allocation of seats by party in the Bundestag corresponds strongly with the party's percentage of the popular vote.

The second advantage to PR is *diversity*. The experience of PR voting in other countries is that it changes the makeup of the legislature by increasing both gender and racial diversity. Obviously, parties representing minority interests who find it difficult to win representation in 2 person races, will more easily be able to win seats under PR. (Rule and Zimmerman, 1992) Since candidates would not have to run as individuals—or raise millions of dollars—the parties would be more easily able to include individuals on the party's list of candidates who more accurately represent the demographics of average Americans. What a multi-party list system would do would provide a greater range of interests being represented and broaden the concept of "representation" to go beyond narrow geography to include representation of such things as ideas and positions on policy issues that would be understandable to voters. Moreover, as for geographic representation on a list system, it would be in the self interest of the parties to insure that there was not only gender balance—if this is what the party wanted—on their list, but also other forms of balance including geography, ideology, and ethnicity, among others.

The third advantage is *government representativeness*. Not only is a consensus-based parliamentary system based on proportional representation more representative of the voting public, it also produces more representative *governments*. (Birchfield and Crepaz, 1998) This study finds that consensus-based, PR systems also produce a high degree of "popular cabinet support," namely the percentage of voters supporting the majority party or coalition.

The fourth advantage to a PR system in the US is that it would *eliminate the redistricting circus*. Until recently, the decennial census occasioned the excruciating task of micro-managing the drawing of congressional districts. Yet, since the 2002 elections, Republicans in Texas have redistricted a second time, creating even "safer" seats by manipulating district lines to their advantage. (Veith *et al.*, 2003) Under PR however, districts would be eliminated. Candidate lists would be organized statewide, in highly populated states, or regionally in the case of smaller states like New England. To insure geographical representation, all parties would find it in their own self-interest that the candidate list included geographical diversity starting at the top of the list.

Getting from Here to There: From Academic Debates to Constitutional Reform?

Clearly, none of these four structural reforms will take place soon. But if they were, what would be the initial steps? Of the four proposals, two of them could be accomplished by simple statute: campaign reform and the voting system. The other two would require constitutional change: head of state/government and divided government. Given the above caveats, it would be easiest to effect campaign reform (the Supreme Court willing) and to alter the voting system.

The largest obstacles to such a radical change in the American constitutional system are cultural and structural. Culturally, the ethos of American individu-alism would have difficulty giving up features such as a single all-powerful executive and one's own individual member of congress, no matter how powerful the arguments raised in support of alternatives. Ideology and cultural practice change very slowly. A more serious obstacle would be the existing interests privileged by the current system. All would fight tenaciously to oppose this suggested change.

Finally, specialists in American politics may dismiss this argument as the far-fetched "poaching" of a comparativist on a terrain that only Americanists can write about with knowledge and expertise. However, the durability of all four of the above-mentioned problems, stretching back anywhere from 25 to 50 years, suggests that Americanists have no monopoly of wisdom on overcoming these pathologies. More seriously, what this comparativist perceives is a fundamental failure of imagination based largely on the "N of 1" problem that all comparativists struggle to avoid. If a single observed phenomenon—in this case, the American political system—is not examined comparatively, one never knows whether prevailing practice is optimal or suboptimal. In essence, those who do not look at these issues comparatively suffer a failure of imagination because they are unable to examine the full range of electoral and constitutional options.

REFERENCES

Allen, Christopher S. (2001) "Proportional Representation," in Krieger, Joel (ed): Oxford Companion to Politics of the World. *Oxford: Oxford University Press.*

Allen, Christopher S., ed. (1999) *Transformation of the German Political Party System: Institutional Crisis or Democratic Renewal?* New York: Berghahn.

Barker, A. (1994) "The Upturned Stone: Political Scandals and their Investigation Processes in 20 Democracies." *Crime Law and Social Change.* 24 1: 337–373.

Birchfield, Vicki and Crepaz, Markus M.L. (1998) "The Impact of Constitutional Structures and Collective and Competitive Veto Points on Income Inequality in Industrialized Democracies." *European Journal of Political Research.* 34 2: 175–200.

Brubaker, Stanley C. (1998) "The Limits of Campaign Spending Limits." *Public Interest*. Fall: 33–54.

Center for Voting and Democracy (2003) "Overview: Dubious Democracy 2003–2004." http://www.fairvote.org/dubdem/overview.htm. June.

Cutler, Lloyd (1989) "Some Reflections About Divided Government." *Presidential Studies Quarterly*. 17: 485–492.

Dionne, E.J., Jr. (1991) *Why Americans Hate Politics*. New York: Simon and Schuster.

Dwyre, Diana (1994) "Disorganized Politics and the Have-nots: Politics and Taxes in New York and California." Polity. 27 (Fall): 25–47.

Fiorina, Morris (1992) *Divided Government*. New York: Macmillan.

Franklin, Mark N. and Hirczy de Mino, Wolfgang P. (1998) "Separated Powers, Divided Government, and Turnout in U.S. Presidential Elections." *American Journal of Political Science*. 42 1 (January): 316–326.

Gans, Curtis (1993) "Television: Political Participation's Enemy #1." *Spectrum: the Journal of State Government*. 66 2: 26–31.

Gibson, Martha L. (1995) "Issues, Coalitions, and Divided Government." *Congress & the Presidency*. 22 2 (Autumn): 155–166.

Grant, Alan (1998) "The Politics of American Campaign Finance." *Parliamentary Affairs*. 51 2 (April): 223–240.

Grofman, Bernard and Lijphart, Arend (1986) *Electoral Laws and Their Consequences*. New York: Agathon Press.

Guinier, Lani (1994) *The Tyranny of the Majority: Fundamental Fairness in Representative Democracy*. New York: The Free Press.

Hill, Steven (2003) *Fixing Elections: The Failure of America's Winner Take All Politics*. New York: Routledge.

Huber, John D. (1996) "*The Vote of Confidence in Parliamentary Democracies.*" American Political Science Review. 90 2 (June): 269–282.

Jacobson, Gary C. (1990) *The Electoral Origins of Divided Government: Competition in U.S. House Elections, 1946–1988*. Boulder, CO: Westview.

Jacoby, Wade (2000) *Imitation and Politics: Redesigning Germany*. Ithaca: Cornell University Press.

Kernell, Samuel (1997) *Going Public: New Strategies of Presidential Leadership*. Washington, DC: CQ Press.

Laver, Michael and Shepsle, Kenneth A. (1995) *Making and Breaking Governments: Cabinets and Legislatures in Parliamentary Democracies*. New York: Cambridge University Press.

Lijphart, Arend (1984) *Democracies: Patterns of Majoritarian and Consensus Government in Twenty-One Countries*. New Haven: Yale University Press.

Lijphart, Arend 1994) "Democracies: Forms, Performance, and Constitutional Engineering." *European Journal of Political Research*. 25: 1–17.

Linz, Juan (1993) "The Perils of Presidentialism," In Diamond, Larry and Plattner, Marc (ed): *The Global Resurgence of Democracy*. Baltimore: Johns Hopkins University Press, 109–126.

Lipset, Seymour Martin (1996) *American Exceptionalism: A Double-Edged Sword*. New York: Norton.

Mann, Thomas, ed. (1997) *Campaign Finance Reform: A Sourcebook*. Washington, DC: Brookings Institute.

Mayhew, David (1991) *Divided We Govern: Party Control, Lawmaking, and Investigations, 1946–1990*. New Haven: Yale University Press.

Norris, Pippa (1997) "Choosing Electoral Systems: Proportional, Majoritarian and Mixed Systems." *International Political Science Review*. 18 3 (July): 297–312.

Richter, Michaela (2002) "Continuity or Politikwechsel?" *Continuity or Politikwechsel? The First Federal Red-Green Coalition*. 20 1 (Spring): 1–48.

Rosenstone, Steven J., Behr, Roy L. and Lazarus, Edward H. (1996) *Third Parties in America: Citizen Response to Major Party Failure*. 2nd Princeton: Princeton University Press.

Rule, Wilma and Zimmerman, Joseph F., eds. (1992) *United States Electoral Systems: Their Impact on Women and Minorities*. New York: Praeger.

Rundquist, Paul S. (1991) *The House of Representatives and the House of Commons: A Brief Comparison of American and British Parliamentary Practice*. Washington, DC: Congressional Research Service, Library of Congress.

Strom, Kaare, Budge, Ian and Laver, Michael J. (1994) "Constraints on Cabinet formation in Parliamentary Democracies." *American Journal of Political Science*. 38 2 (May): 303–335.

Thurber, James A. (1991) "Representation, Accountability, and Efficiency in Divided Party Control of Government." PS. 24 (December): 653–657.

Veith, Richard, Veith, Norma Jean and Fuery, Susan (2003) *Oral Argument*. No. 02–1580, U.S. Supreme Court, Wednesday, December 10.

Weinberg, Jonathan (1993) "Broadcasting and Speech." *California Law Review*. 81 5: 1101–1206.

Christopher S. Allen is Associate Professor of International Affairs at the University of Georgia where he teaches courses in comparative politics and political economy. He is editor of Transformation of the German Political Party System (Berghahn, 2001) and is currently working on a project examining democratic representation in parliamentary and presidential systems.

UNIT 3

Europe in Transition: West, Center, and East

Unit Selections

Key Points to Consider

- What are the major obstacles to the emergence of a more unified Europe?

- Why does it seem likely that further integration of the EU will become more difficult after its 2004 expansion from 15 to 25 members?

- What caused the collapse of the attempt to draft an EU draft constitution?

- What is the evidence that the economic problems of Western Europe are not just cyclical but also structural in origin?

- How would you compare the plight of immigrants to Europe with immigrants to the United States?

- What is "neoliberal shock therapy" for the former Communist-ruled countries, and why is it running into criticism in a country like Poland?

- How do you assess Yeltsin's legacy, and how well is Putin equipped to lead his country to a better future?

- How have the parliamentary elections of December 2003 given President Putin a strong political base for the coming four years?

 **Links: www.dushkin.com/online/**
These sites are annotated in the World Wide Web pages.

Europa: European Union
http://europa.eu.int
NATO Integrated Data Service (NIDS)
http://www.nato.int/structur/nids/nids.htm
Research and Reference (Library of Congress)
http://lcweb.loc.gov/rr/
Russian and East European Network Information Center, University of Texas at Austin
http://reenic.utexas.edu/reenic/index.html

The articles in this unit deal with two major developments that have greatly altered the political map of contemporary Europe. One is the growth and impact on the traditional nation-state and its people of the supranational project known today as the European Union (EU). The other consists of the continuing challenges and responses that have resulted from the collapse of Communist rule in central and Eastern Europe. The year 2004 has linked these two developments more closely, as the EU for the first time admits to membership former Communist-ruled countries in the central and eastern part of the continent. NATO has moved slightly ahead of the European Union in its own eastward expansion, but the EU has very different goals and entry requirements than the defense alliance—in the form of a set of minimum democratic and economic criteria that new members must meet.

The present can be seen as both an important turning point and a crucial testing time for the EU. Its institutional origins go back to 1951, when France, West Germany, Italy, and the three Benelux countries integrated their coal and steel industries. In 1957 the same six nation-states founded the European Economic Community (EEC) that later became the European Union.

Britain declined to join the founders, and the EU did not add new members until 1973, when Britain finally entered along with two close trading partners, Ireland and Denmark. Thereafter the European Community continued to expand incrementally in sets of three newcomers per decade. The former dictatorships, Greece, Portugal and Spain, entered during the 1980s, after having established their credentials as new democracies and market economies. In 1995, soon after the end of the Cold War, three neutral countries—Austria, Finland, and Sweden—joined for a total membership of fifteen.

In 2004 the EU has abandoned this pattern of accretion in favor of a great leap forward. In one swoop, it is expanding the membership by two-thirds to a total of twenty-five countries. This move greatly increases the EU's economic, cultural and political diversity, even as its population moves from 375 million to 480 million people. Of the ten newcomers, eight lie in central or eastern Europe: Poland, Hungary, the Czech Republic, Slovakia, Slovenia, and the three Baltic states, Lithuania, Latvia, and Estonia. All have far less productive economies than is the norm for the older EU members. The remaining two new entrants are the small Mediterranean island nations of Malta and Cyprus that rank last in population among the twenty-five EU members. But that is not all. Several additional countries are applicants who hope for future admission. They include Romania, Bulgaria, several smaller Balkan states, and Turkey. The EU could end up with thirty members before the end of the decade.

The enlargement of the EU will bring changes and challenges not only to the new members of the club but to the supranational body itself as well as its older membership. It cannot be ruled out that the larger and more diverse EU could begin to depart from the founders' vision of "an ever closer union among the peoples of Europe." This evocative phrase is contained in the preamble to the Treaty of Rome, the EU's founding document. Although it echoes the goal of a "more perfect union" announced in the preamble to the U.S. Constitution, it would be a mistake to push the analogy very far. The EU has not become a political union even in the sense of a somewhat loose-knit United States of Europe. Observers like Robert Cottrell think that it is less likely to become one as it expands and diversifies.

Yet the EU is in its own right an impressive political construct that has no close parallel anywhere. It has largely dismantled national barriers to the free movement of people, goods, services and capital among the member nations. Above all, the EU has acquired an institutional presence and authority that go far beyond anything envisaged by NAFTA or other regional free trade arrangements. All member nations have diverted some of their traditional sovereignty to the EU. The appointed Commission uses its supranational executive authority to initiate common policy decisions and oversee their implementation. The independent European Court of Justice makes binding decisions in its adjudication of EU-related disputes. The European Parliament has seen its authority grow over the years, even though it is not a full blown legislature in the traditional sense. The powerful Council of Ministers remains an intergovernmental body, where the national government of every member nation is represented. Each nation has a weighted vote, related to the size of its population. In his article on the recent failure to reach agreement on a draft EU Constitution, John Tagliabue explains some of the intricacies of the weighted votes and the qualified majorities. They can be compared to the far simpler contrivance of the Connecticut Compromise as a way of giving representation to all members without ignoring their considerable differences in size of population. In the case of the supranational EU, the smallest member, Malta, has a population of 400,000, while the largest member, Germany, tops 82 million.

The political process continues unabated in the individual nation-states of Western Europe, as they seek to define their own public agendas. Their relative prosperity rests on a base that was built up during the prolonged postwar economic boom of the 1950s and 1960s. By political choice, a considerable portion of their wealth was channeled toward the public sector and used to develop a relatively generous system of social services and social insurance. Since the early 1970s, however, many West European countries have been beset by economic disruptions or slowdowns offset by periods of cyclical economic upturns. Moreover, it is becoming clear that there are also structural reasons why they no longer can take increasing affluence for granted in a more competitive global economy.

The economic shock that first interrupted the prolonged postwar boom came in the wake of sharp rises in the cost of energy, linked to successive hikes in the price of oil imposed by the Organization of Petroleum Exporting Countries (OPEC) after 1973. In the 1980s, OPEC lost its organizational bite, as its members began to compete against each other by raising production and lowering prices rather than abiding by the opposite practices in the manner of a well-functioning cartel agreement. The exploitation of new oil and gas fields in the North Sea and elsewhere also helped alleviate the energy situation, at least for the present. The resulting improvement for the consumers of oil and gas helped the Western European economies recover, but they did not as a whole rebound to their earlier high growth rates.

The short Gulf War in 1991 did not seriously hamper the flow of Middle East oil, but it once again underscored the vulnerability of Europe to external interruptions in its energy supply. During the year 2000, there were again signs of a petroleum shortage, partly as a result of increased demand, but partly, also, as a result of supply limitations imposed by some of the oil producers. In the fall months of that year, irate citizens demonstrated in several countries, including France, Germany, and Britain, in protest against sharp price hikes in oil and gasoline.

Because of their heavy dependence on international trade, Western European economies are vulnerable to global cyclical tendencies. Another important challenge lies in the stiff competition they face from the new industrial countries (NICs) of East and South Asia, where productivity is sometimes fairly high and labor costs remain much lower. The emerging Asian factor probably contributed to the increased tempo of the European drive for economic integration in the late 1980s. Some observers have warned of a protectionist reaction, in which major trading blocs in Europe, North America, and Eastern Asia could replace the relatively free system of international trade established in recent decades.

Europe still feels the aftershocks from the sudden collapse of Communist rule in Central and Eastern Europe at the end of the 1980s. Here states, nations, and nationalities broke away from an imposed system of central control, by asserting their independence from the previous ruling group and its ideology. In their attempts to construct a new order for themselves, the postcommunist countries have encountered enormous difficulties. Their transition to pluralist democracy and a rudimentary market-based economy turned out to be much rockier than most had anticipated.

The prospect of membership in the EU became a major incentive to continue. Even after they have gained entry to the club, it will be a long time before they can hope to catch up economically. Robert Cottrell reports from a study by the Economist Intelligence Unit that it will take the new entrants to the EU on average more than fifty years to draw level with the old members in average income per person. It is based on the simple assumption of relatively good growth rates of 4 percent for the new EU entrants, and lower growth rates of 2 percent for the older members from Western Europe.

In some areas of the former Soviet bloc, one encounters some nostalgia for the basic material security and "orderliness" provided by the communist welfare states of the past. This should not be understood as a wish to turn back the wheel of history. Instead, it seems to represent a desire to build buffers and safety nets into the new market-oriented systems. Communist-descended parties have responded by abandoning most or all of their Leninist baggage. They now engage in the competitive bidding for votes with promises of social fairness and security. In Poland and elsewhere, such parties have recently gained political leverage. By contrast with the recent past, they must now operate in a pluralist political setting. They have adapted by adopting new strategies and goals. As David Ost reports from

Poland, the democratic Left plays a key role in criticizing a neoliberal market model that has brought instability and sharp inequality with it.

Those who attempt the big move to the "Golden West" resemble in many ways the immigrants who have been attracted to the United States in the past and present. Many Western Europeans are unwilling to accept, however, what they regard as a flood of unwanted strangers. The newcomers are widely portrayed as outsiders whose presence will further drain their generous welfare systems and threaten their economic security and established way of life. Such anxieties are the stuff of socio-cultural mistrust, tensions, and conflicts. One serious political consequence has been the emergence of an anti-immigrant populist politics on the Far Right. In response, the governments in several countries have changed their laws on citizenship, asylum, and immigration.

As Seyla Benhabib points out in his essay, there can be little doubt that the issues of immigration and cultural tensions in Western Europe will continue to occupy a central place on the political agenda in coming years. Some of the established parties have already made symbolic and substantive accommodations to appease protesting voters, for fear of otherwise losing them to extremist ultra-right movements.

It is important to remember that there are also individuals and groups who resist the xenophobic elements in their own societies. Some enlightened political leaders and commentators seek to promote the reasonable perspective that migrants could turn out to be an important asset rather than a liability. This argument may concede that the foreign influx also involves some social costs in the short run, at least during recessionary periods, but it emphasizes that the newcomers can be a very important human resource who will contribute to mid- and long-term economic prosperity. Quite apart from any such economic considerations, of course, the migrants and asylum-seekers have become an important test of liberal democratic tolerance on the continent.

The central and east European countries continue to face the challenge of political and economic reconstruction. When they began their post-Communist journey, there were no ready-made strategies of reform. Much theoretical ink has been spilled on the problems of a transition from a market economy to state socialism, but there was little theory or practice to guide the countries that tried to make a paradigm shift in the opposite direction. Some economists familiar with Eastern Europe, like Sweden's Anders Aslund, argued that a quick transition to a market economy was a preferable course, indeed the only responsible one, even though such an approach could be very disruptive and painful in the short run. They argued that such a "shock therapy" would release human energies and bring economic growth more quickly and efficiently. At the same time, these supporters of a "tough love" strategy warned that compassionate halfway measures could end up worsening the economic plight of these countries. Yet, as David Ost reports from Poland, tough love approaches are likely to meet with rejection, when they are seen as having failed to deliver the promised goods.

Other strategists came out in favor of a more gradual approach to economic reconstruction in these countries. They warned that the neoclassical economists, who would introduce a full-scale market economy by fiat, not only ignored the market system's cultural and historic preconditions but also underestimated the turmoil that was likely to accompany the big transition. As a more prudent course of action, these gradualists recommended the adoption of pragmatic strategies of incremental change, accompanied by a rhetoric of lower expectations.

Experience and the passage of a few more years would probably have given us better insights into the relative merits of each argument. But a pluralist society rarely permits itself to become a social laboratory for controlled experiments of this kind. Moreover, decision makers must often learn on the job. They cannot afford to become inflexible and dogmatic in these matters, where the human stakes are so high. Instead, competitive politics has produced a "mix" of the two approaches as the most acceptable and practical policy outcome.

A similar debate has been carried out in the former Soviet Union. It could be argued that Mikhail Gorbachev, the last Soviet head of government (1985 to 1991), failed to opt clearly for one or the other approach to economic reform. He seems to have been ambivalent about both means and ends of his *perestroika*, or restructuring, of the centrally planned economy. In the eyes of some born-again Soviet marketers, he remained far too socialist. But Communist hard-liners never forgave him for dismantling a system in which they had enjoyed at least a modicum of security and privilege.

Gorbachev appears to have regarded his own policies of *glasnost*, or openness, and *democratization* as essential accompaniments of *perestroika* in what he perceived as his modernization program. He seems to have understood (or become convinced) that a highly developed economy needs a freer flow of information along with a more decentralized system of decision making if its component parts are to be efficient, flexible, and capable of learning and self-correction. In that sense, a market economy has some integral feedback traits that make it incompatible with the traditional Soviet model of a centrally directed, authoritarian economy.

Glasnost and democratization were clearly incompatible with a repressive political system of one-party rule as well. They served Gorbachev as instruments to weaken the grip of the Communist hard-liners and at the same time to rally behind him some reform groups, including many intellectuals and journalists. Within a remarkably short time after he came to power in 1985, a vigorous new press emerged in the Soviet Union headed by journalists who were eager to ferret out misdeeds and report on political reality as they observed it. A similar development took place in the history profession, where scholars used the new spirit of openness to report in grim detail about past Communist atrocities that had previously been covered up or dismissed as bourgeois lies. There was an inevitable irony to the new truthfulness. Even as it served to discredit much of the past along with any reactionary attempts to restore "the good old days," it also brought into question the foundations of the Soviet system under the leadership of the Communist Party. Yet Gorbachev had clearly set out to modernize the Soviet system, not to bring it down.

One of the greatest vulnerabilities of the Soviet Union turned out to be its multiethnic character. Gorbachev was not alone in having underestimated the potential centrifugal tendencies of a Union of Soviet Socialist Republics (USSR) erected on the territory of the old, overland Empire that the Russian tsars had conquered and governed before 1917. Many of the non-Russian minorities retained a territorial identification with their homelands, where they often lived as ethnic majorities. This made it easier for them to demand greater autonomy or national independence, when the Soviet regime became weakened. The first national assertions came from the Baltic peoples in Estonia, Latvia, and Lithuania, who had been forced under Soviet rule in

1940, after some two decades of national independence. Very soon other nationalities, including the Georgians and Armenians, expressed similar demands through the political channels that had been opened to them. The death knell for the Soviet Union sounded in 1991, when the Ukrainians, who constituted the second largest national group in the Soviet Union after the Russians, made similar demands for independence.

In a very real sense, then, Gorbachev's political reforms ended up as a mortal threat not only to the continued leadership role by the Communist Party but also to the continued existence of the Soviet Union itself. Gorbachev seems to have understood neither of these ultimately fatal consequences of his reform attempts until late in the day. This explains why he could set in motion forces that would ultimately destroy what he had hoped to make more attractive and productive. In August 1991, Communist hard-liners attempted a coup against the reformer and his reforms, but they acted far too late and were too poorly organized to succeed. The coup was defeated by a popular resistance, led by Russian President Boris Yeltsin, who had broken with Communism earlier and, as it seemed, far more decisively. After his formal restoration to power following the abortive coup, Gorbachev became politically dependent on Yeltsin and was increasingly seen as a transitional figure. His days as Soviet president were numbered, when the Soviet Union ceased to exist a week before the end of 1991. The dissolution of the Soviet state took place quickly and essentially without armed conflict. It was formally replaced by the Commonwealth of Independent States (CIS), a very loose union that lacked both a sufficient institutional framework and enough political will to keep it together. Almost from the outset, the CIS seemed destined to be little more than a loosely structured transitional device.

There is an undeniable gloom or hangover atmosphere in many of the accounts of post-Communist and post-Soviet Russia. A turn to some form of authoritarian nationalist populism cannot be ruled out. Recent parliamentary and presidential elections give picture of electoral volatility, growing voter apathy or disgruntlement, and widespread authoritarian leanings in a politically exhausted society. They also illustrate how governmental leaders can favor, manipulate or even help create "loyal" political parties.

Duma elections 1993. The first elections of a new Russian Duma after the end of the Soviet Union did not provide a propitious start for post-Communist politics. They came in December 1993 and were preceded by a complete breakdown of relations between President Yeltsin and the parliamentary majority. The Duma had originally supported Yeltsin, but opposition had grown over some sweeping economic reforms pushed by his government. The ensuing political conflict had run the gamut from a presidential dissolution of the legislature, through an impeachment vote by the Duma, to street demonstrations. It ended with Russian soldiers entering the parliament to force out deputies who had refused to leave. Yeltsin used the opportunity to have some political parties and publications outlawed. The powers of the president in the dual executive were constitutionally strengthened.

The electoral result was something of a political boomerang for Yeltsin. It resulted in a fragmented Duma, in which nationalists and Communists occupied key positions. The forces that backed market reforms, above all Yabloko, suffered setbacks. Henceforth Yeltsin seemed to play a more subdued role, and the new government pursued far more cautious reform policies. In 1994, Russia's military intervention in Chechnya, a breakaway Caucasian republic located within the Russian Federation, failed

to give Yeltsin a quick and easy victory that might have reversed his slide into political unpopularity among Russians.

Duma elections 1995. The regular parliamentary elections in December 1995 provided a further setback for the democratic and economic reformers in Russia. However, it was far less their rivals' strength than their own disunity and rivalry both before and after the election that weakened their parliamentary position. Together, the liberal reformers received close to a quarter of the vote. That was slightly more than the Communists, led as before by Gennady Zyuganov, and it was twice as much as the far-right nationalists in Vladimir Zhirinovsky's curiously misnamed Liberal Democratic Party.

Presidential election 1996. Yeltsin still knew how to win elections as he showed in the presidential contest of 1996, albeit in a run-off against the Communist leader, Zyuganov. By this time, ill health and heavy drinking added seriously to his governing problems. His frequent and seemingly erratic replacements of prime ministers did not improve the situation.

Duma elections 1999. Always good for a political surprise, Yeltsin saved two for the end. In the latter half of 1999, he selected a stronger figure for what turned out to be his last prime minister. Vladimir V. Putin, then 47 years old, quickly turned his attention to a tough new military intervention in Chechnya. Within Russia, his strong determination to suppress the breakaway province generated widespread support, based on its presentation and perception as a counterterrorist move. In the Duma elections of December, 1999, the new prime minister's aura of tough leadership probably helped reduce the Communist result to 113 seats, or a quarter of the Duma.

Presidential election 2000. Without warning but with impeccable timing, President Yeltsin announced his resignation on December 31, 1999, just as the century and millennium came to an end. Putin became the new acting president and easily won the presidential election a few months later. Largely due to a favorable oil market for Soviet exports, the new president inherited a much better fiscal balance than Yeltsin or, especially Gorbachev before him.

In his first term as President of Russia, Putin aroused popular support with tough measures against organized crime and political terrorism. This is also true for the judicial action taken against some of the super-rich "oligarchs," who had made huge fortunes when state owned enterprises were privatized. Their ostentatious wealth, gathered quickly in an otherwise poor country, is highly resented by many Russians. The arrest of Mikhail B. Khodorkovsky, reputedly Russia's richest man, in the fall of 2003 met with far more critical reaction abroad than in Russia. During the previous two years, the billionaire had poured money into schemes for building a civil society in Russia. His new interest in political matters had led him to support some of Putin's critics and rivals. It seemed at least politically convenient to have Khodorkovsky out of the way during the parliamentary election of December 2003.

Duma election 2003. The election was memorable in several ways. The voter turnout was low (56 percent), at least by European standards. The democratic middle class parties fared poorly, once again. The Communists received only one-half of their vote share in the previous election (dropping from 24 to

12.7 percent of the vote). And a recently created party, called United Russia. performed better than any party since the end of one-party elections in Russia. Outside observers found evidence of what they considered fraud in the election and cited media favors to United Russia. On the other hand, it seems likely that this party, which the press described as largely defined by its loyalty to President Putin, would have done well in any case.

Presidential election 2004. Putin seemed a sure bet to win the presidential election in March 2004. In advance of the contest, he asserted his authority within the dual executive by dismissing the prime minister and appointing a new one. With the dependable backing of a parliamentary majority, supplied by United Russia and a few independents, the institutional and political basis for a strong presidency until 2008 has been secured. Some Russians are already wondering whether Putin will at that time step aside for someone else, seek to engineer his successor (as Yeltsin did), or seek a third term (a move that would require a change in the Russian Constitution.

Writing several months before the parliamentary and presidential elections, Timothy Colton and Michael McFaul concluded that Russia's political system had quasi-authoritarian tendencies. The Duma election of 2003 is analyzed in the report from *The Economist*. Finally, David Fogelsang and Gordon M. Hahn, in a spirited article written half a year before the one by Colton and McFaul, draw somewhat more optimistic conclusions about Russian politics under President Putin.

When east meets west

Expectantly, and a little nervously, the new members wait to join the European club. Next year's enlargement is welcome, and timely. But there will be some shocks ahead, says Robert Cottrell

THAT humming you can hear from the direction of central Europe is the sound of countries hard at work, catching up with the rest of the continent. It is loudest in the Baltic states to the north, where national incomes will grow by 5-6% this year, seven times faster than in the fat, rich 15 countries of the current European Union. In Poland, Hungary, the Czech Republic and Slovakia (which this survey will call the "Visegrad" countries, after the declaration they signed in 1991) the growth rate will be about 3–4%, as it will be in Slovenia, the bit of the Balkans that works.

In May next year these eight countries will join the European Union, along with the Mediterranean islands of Cyprus and Malta. Bulgaria and Romania will follow in 2007, if they can reform and modernise fast enough. A queue of other hopefuls is forming for the years after that, with Croatia at the head, Turkey and the countries of the western Balkans—Albania, Bosnia, Macedonia, Serbia and Montenegro—some way behind.

This survey considers the impact that next year's European Union enlargement will have on central Europe, and the changes that preparations for enlargement have already wrought there. It wonders, too, what impact enlargement will have on the Union as a whole and its capacity to act. It applauds the ac-

ceptance of the central European countries into the European Union as something necessary, decent and beneficial to Europe as a whole. The preparations for entry have given these countries the motivation and the models they need to entrench or restore democratic institutions and market economies, replacing the communist and socialist ones previously imposed there. Even Eurosceptics in the new member countries should be pleased with this. A country well equipped to join the EU is a country well equipped to make its way in the world otherwise, if it chooses to do so.

As it happens, voters in all the central European countries due to join the EU next year have supported entry, often by large majorities, in referendums over the spring and summer. Now these countries have a last few months to prepare themselves for the shocks and strains, as well as the opportunities and rewards, that lie ahead.

One shock for many people may be the discovery that EU entry does not in itself bring wealth. The countries of central Europe will take a very long time to catch up with their western neighbours. The Economist Intelligence Unit, a sister company of the his newspaper, has calculated that if the 15 countries of the current EU enjoy economic growth of 2% a

year, and the countries joining in 2004 and 2007 (including Bulgaria and Romania) grow by about 4% a year, then it will take the new members, on average, more than 50 years to draw level with the old ones. If the new members manage only 3% growth, it will take them 90 years to catch up.

Of course, growth rates and convergence rates will probably vary widely from country to country. The Baltic countries, though poor today even by the standards of central Europe, could become richer than most current EU countries within 30 years if they maintain annual growth rates of 5% or more, which they look fully capable of doing. Any central European country where the growth rate sags, on the other hand, will find that the pleasures of EU membership turn sour. That country will be saddled with the rules and expenses of a club meant for rich people, while its income per person remains far below the average and may even decline in relative terms.

The central Europeans also face challenges in adjusting to the EU's common visa and border regime, known as the Schengen system. Border controls have already disappeared across most of the EU. They should disappear among the new members too, but only after three or four years. By that time the new

Towards an uncertain future

Enlargement will mean a looser-knit Union

Guided by treaties that scarcely anybody can understand, towards a destination on which nobody can agree, the European Union has survived, and often thrived, for almost half a century. The need for a lasting peace in western Europe gave it early momentum. It offered devastated countries the vision of a supranational order intrinsically more peaceful than the nationalism which had fed Hitler's war. The attractions of this order diminished for nation-states as the memories of war receded. But the collapse of the Soviet empire, and the opportunity to restore and rebuild the eastern half of Europe, gave the EU a new leading role. It offered a vision of freedom and prosperity for which countries hungered after decades under communist rule. This enlargement is the happy outcome of that offer.

History will judge the EU kindly for having done at least two great jobs well. But ask what great job it will do next, and the answer is far from clear. Some further enlargement may take place in 2007 and beyond, but the only truly sinew-stiffening challenge on the agenda there is the admission of Turkey, which remains at best a very distant possibility. Countries led by Germany and France want the EU's next great leaps to take it forward into a common foreign policy and a common defence capability. But these are projects which, if ever seriously pursued, will divide the EU more than unite it. Some older members, notably Britain, hesitate for political or ideological reasons. They dislike the implied threat to national sovereignty, and they fear adventures that might make Europe more a rival to America.

Some new members share these reservations, mixed with more pragmatic ones. It will take them another three years at least to become full members of the Schengen regime; perhaps five or seven years to join the common currency; and ten years or more to master and implement every last rule of the EU as it is today. They do not want the Union to be changing its rules and adding new ones from the moment they join. The new members will be a powerful lobby with the EU for as little change as possible, at least where change means new costs and burdens.

This counts as an unwelcome and even a dangerous situation for those who believe that the Union thrives on a diet of constant change. Big new projects draw governments together in constructive ways. They encourage experimental give-and-take. Inertia, by contrast, leaves governments to come together more in arguments about current policies, be they state aids, excessive deficit procedures, competition law or farm subsidies. Disputes run together easily and erode the general willingness of countries to co-operate at all.

There is real danger here, because the EU is still a fragile thing. It has never won the hearts and minds of all its citizens, the vast majority of whom identify obstinately with their nation-states. Nor does it have much coherence as a political project, now that it has abandoned supranationalism as its final goal without substituting anything else.

The term "political union" survives in EU rhetoric, but without a meaning. Governments are inadvertently demonstrating this point (or lack of it) with their losing battle to capture the Union's aim and scope in a constitutional treaty. They seek to increase the stability and legitimacy of the EU, but risk having the opposite effect. The EU will suffer a big psychological reversal if governments fail to agree on a text, and perhaps a crisis if some countries accept the document while others do not.

Where the EU has succeeded, brilliantly, is as a bureaucratic project. It is shaped, not mainly by its citizens' wishes nor by its founders' intentions, but by the deals done each day between ministers and civil servants in Brussels, usually behind closed doors, endorsed by a parliament to which few outsiders pay heed.

That is not necessarily a bad scheme. The participating countries are well-functioning democracies. Ministers act only within what they judge to be the tolerance of their voters. But enlargement from 15 to 25 countries next year will make the bureaucratic project much harder to manage. A 10% rise in traffic can bring gridlock to the centre of a busy city. A two-thirds rise in membership may bring gridlock to a busy EU. Misunderstandings and disagreements will multiply, even with goodwill on all sides. Two or three actively awkward countries will be enough to guarantee chaos. Other empires have over-extended themselves to the point of collapse, and the EU is at least courting this fate.

The case for optimism rests on the proposition that the EU's workings can adjust quickly and smoothly to a big increase in its size and composition. But a bigger EU will be a more fragmented EU. The countries in it will be far more diverse, whether measured by wealth, history, politics, geography or language. Their interests will be equally diverse. Sub-groups and alliances will form in pursuit of particular policies or priorities. This will be a healthy trend, a source of pluralism and innovation within the Union, so long as the blocks do not become too rigid or too exclusive. If they do become so, the risk will grow of a de facto split within the Union, putting in danger the good functioning of all Union-wide policies and institutions.

A more diverse and fragmented Union will be one that countries leave as well as join. None has left until now (though Greenland, a province of Denmark, did so in 1985), partly because members have bent over backwards to accommodate one another's vital interests. But the more the EU enlarges, the less drama there will be in the loss of a single member, and the less possibility there will be for making all the compromises needed to keep everybody happy. The draft constitutional treaty provides for the possibility of a country's secession, but has nothing useful to say about the transitional arrangements that might be needed.

To say that this enlargement will mean the most uncertain period for the EU since its founding, is not to say that this enlargement was a bad idea. On the contrary, it was the noblest use to which the EU of the 1990s could be put.

The accession countries will take time to find their feet, but they are joining after years of effort and they have motives at least as strong as any older member to make the EU go on working. By that, they mean an EU that goes on working in concrete ways, on things which benefit all its members proportionately: arrangements such as the single market, the Schengen system, perhaps the single currency once its teething troubles are past. They will have less enthusiasm for an EU that expects its smaller and poorer members to subordinate themselves to the ambitions of its bigger and richer ones, and which uses pieties about a political union to cloak that process.

members are expected to have perfected tough border controls of their own against non-EU countries, including friends and trading partners. This prospect worries Poland, which would prefer a more open border with Ukraine; and Hungary, which wants to keep ties with ethnic Hungarian minorities in Serbia and Ukraine; and Romania, which is linked through language and history to Moldova; and Lithuania, which fears for its neighbours, Kaliningrad and Belarus.

Poland is lobbying the EU to keep open the long-term possibility of membership for Ukraine, at least. But any scheme for drawing countries of the Commonwealth of Independent States (put together after the Soviet Union broke up) out of the Russian sphere of influence, and into that of the European Union, will have to include some very good ideas for keeping Russia happy at the same time, and it is not at all clear what those ideas could possibly be.

Russia does not seriously want to join the EU, even if its politicians sometimes flirt with the idea in public comments. It has nothing much to gain from further European integration, having little to sell directly into the European single market except gas, for which it would prefer national markets. If the EU should ever start talking about membership for Ukraine, or Belarus, or Moldova, it is hard to imagine Russia standing by indifferently.

The question of how best to manage relations between the enlarged EU and Russia is one that will recur in this survey, given Russia's propensity to fret about issues such as NATO'S enlargement into the Baltics; the future of Kaliningrad; EU visa regimes; and the vacillation of Ukraine between east and west.

This survey worries, too, about possible tensions between the EU'S older members and those newer ones which have regained their freedom and, in some cases, their independence, relatively recently, after decades spent taking orders from Moscow (or Belgrade, in the case of Slovenia). The currents of nationalism that helped overturn the communist order in central Europe in 1989–91 still run strong there, and not always far from the political mainstream. Central Europeans want an EU in which they and their countries are respected, not one in which they are bossed around casually by top dogs such as France and Germany. President Jacques Chirac's outburst in February—when he said that the central Europeans should have "shut up" instead of supporting United States policy on Iraq—betrayed just the patronising and bullying attitude which the EU'S future members least want to encounter in Brussels. Forewarned by Mr. Chirac, they will enter the Union in a more combative mood, complicating their future relations with France and its increasingly like-minded ally, Germany.

The EU may yet emerge the stronger for all this, if the combative mood of the central Europeans emboldens them to push harder for policies that make the Union work better. As poor countries with threadbare institutions, their interests should like in opposing policies that impose new costs on industry and new regulatory burdens on government. They should insist on the freedom to keep taxes low, public spending down, and labour cheap. Those are also good policies, as it happens, for stagnant rich countries, of which the EU has more than its share.

So the EU'S new members can do everyone a favour by fighting their corner on economic policy, and on foreign policy as well. They are, by and large, pro-American and pro-NATO. This applies especially to Poland, which is already a NATO member, and to the Baltic countries, which will join NATO next year, together with Slovakia, Slovenia, Romania and Bulgaria. Enlargements should favour a stronger pro-American and pro-NATO consensus within the EU, after the vacillations of the past year.

In short, the new members have the chance to show themselves a force for good in the European Union, and to show their voters at home that the EU is a force for good in national life. That means learning the wiles of Brussels, using EU money prudently, getting public spending under control, keeping business happy and keeping the public informed.

European Union Cannot Reach Deal on Constitution

By JOHN TAGLIABUE

Brussels, Dec. 13—The leaders of 25 current and imminent members of the European Union failed to reach agreement on Saturday on a draft constitution, stumbling on a problem familiar to Americans: how to apportion power among large and small states.

At issue was a proposal to discard a voting system agreed upon three years ago that gave Spain, a member of the union, and Poland, which joins next year, almost as much voting weight each as Germany, which has more than twice the population of either.

Klaus Hänsch, a German deputy of the European Parliament, laid the blame for the failed meeting squarely on the two nations' unwillingness to compromise. "I hope that Spain and Poland realize that the failure of the summit is due to them, and that they missed a historic opportunity," he said.

But Italy's prime minister, Silvio Berlusconi, chairman of the talks, defended the Poles. Entering the talks Saturday morning, he told reporters that on Friday he had circulated four different voting formulas among the leaders.

"You cannot make Spain and Poland responsible for an eventual failure," Mr. Berlusconi said. "They are open to other formulas."

Officially, the leaders said they would meet to try again next year. But the failure touched off bitter recriminations, notably between Germans and Poles, underscoring differences between current and imminent members of the union. The war in Iraq also played a part: the bitter divisions in "old" and "new" Europe over whether to go along with the United States' military action contributed to the wedges driving the leaders apart.

The failure prompted reports that some countries—most notably the six founders of the European Union, Germany, France, Italy, Belgium, Luxembourg and the Netherlands—would go it alone in efforts to integrate more closely in areas like foreign and defense policy.

Poland's prime minister, Leszek Miller, left Brussels and was expected to convene a cabinet meeting on Saturday evening to inform the government of the outcome, Polish diplomats said.

The meeting was not without its successes. On Friday, the leaders took a first important step toward striking a deal on the constitution's draft text, the subject of almost two years of discussion, when they agreed unanimously to a common defense policy that included planning abilities independent of NATO.

The constitution is considered crucial in light of the approaching enlargement, by which the union, which began as a customs union of just six countries, will become a 25-member club, bringing most of the former East Bloc states, including Poland, Hungary, the Czech Republic and Slovenia, into its embrace.

"The striking thing is that 95 percent of the issues are largely resolved," said Kevin Featherstone of the European Institute at the London School of economics.

Mr. Featherstone said it was the very fact that agreements had been reached in most areas that had narrowed the room for the usual horse trading that lies at the heart of European compromises. With little else to decide, the voting rights issue became "crystal clear."

But he also said that Mr. Berlusconi's stewardship of the talks may have contributed to the failure. "Berlusconi has this putting-your-foot-in-it tendency," he said.

As with the American leadership in Philadelphia in the 1780's, Europe's leaders are acting because they recognize that the challenges facing an enlarged union require more efficient government structures. Recent moves, including the introduction of the euro and the creation of a central bank, have fueled the drive beyond simple economic integration toward common policies in defense and foreign affairs.

The analogy with the United States, which moved in the 1780's from a confederation to a stronger national government under the Constitution, has not escaped the Europeans. When the former French president Valéry

Giscard d'Estaing, chairman of the convention that framed the draft constitution, left for vacation last summer, he took along a copy of David McCullough's best selling biography of John Adams, the author of the Massachusetts Constitution, the oldest such text still in use.

Mr. McCullough said by phone from his home in Massachusetts that in Philadelphia "all the small states were afraid of the large states, they feared they would take the ball and run with it." To provide equal weight in the councils of power, the founding fathers created the Senate, in which all the states were equally represented. "They called it the balancing wheel," Mr. McCullough said.

Europe's leaders toyed in the past with the idea of a kind of bicameral system, proposing to transform the Council of Europe into a kind of senate. But the idea was discarded in favor of a voting system agreed upon three years ago in Nice that gave mid-sized countries like Poland and Spain almost as many votes each in the European Council as Germany, despite its far greater population.

The discussions here have left Poland and Spain relatively isolated, because the system agreed to at Nice has been jettisoned in favor of an arrangement known as the double majority, which seeks to assure the rights of smaller states by defining a voting majority as at least half of the member states representing at least 60 percent of the total population.

Poland's foreign minister, Wlodzimierz Cimoszewicz, had dug in his heels on Saturday morning.

"If it is not possible to agree on the change today we shall wait," he said before the day's talks began.

Large countries like France, Germany and Britain, who embraced the double majority because of a worry about the risk of giving too much voting power to the smaller states, have also built measures into the constitution that would assure their continued control.

Largely at British insistence, the states will retain veto rights over fiscal matters, leaving the door open to divisive issues like one that erupted recently over decisions by France and Germany, two of the largest nations, to run budget deficits that exceeded limits governing the euro.

Veto rights will also be maintained in matters of foreign and defense policy and changes to European treaties.

For the moment other differences appear to have been overshadowed by the issue of voting weights. Some countries, including Poland, have in the past insisted that the preamble of the constitution evoke Europe's Christian heritage. The draft text refers to Europe's "cultural, religious and humanist heritages."

The French president, Jacques Chirac, addressing reporters Friday, said that Europe's recent history was not a smoothly flowing river, but a "history of crises overcome."

Mr. Featherstone, of the European Institute, said there was not a sense of immediate crisis if the states failed, "but there is a climate of ideas across Europe that something must be done."

In Search of Europe's Borders

The Politics of Migration in the European Union

Seyla Benhabib

On March 11, 1882, the great French scholar Ernest Renan gave a lecture with the provocative title, "What is a Nation?"* Still recovering from the shock of the defeat of France by Prussia in the Franco-Prussian War of 1871, Renan, like many liberal nationalists before and after him, walked a thin line between the affirmation of the individual nation, which he described as "a soul, a spiritual principle," and the celebration of the peaceful plurality of nations. For Renan, nations were not eternal: they emerged through suffering and struggle in the past; they were sustained by the will to live together in the future. Nations had their beginning and their end. One day, he prophesied, "A European confederation will probably replace them. But such is not the law of the century in which we are living."

Twice in the twentieth century nationalist wars convulsed Europe and led to worldwide carnage; the dream of a European confederation that would end such wars has inspired European intellectuals at least since the Napoleonic conquests in the aftermath of the French Revolution. Recent developments within the European Union—the adoption of a common currency by twelve of the fifteen member countries and the launching in February 2002 of a year-long European constitutional convention—have given "Euro-federalists" new hope and energy. Starting from a coal and steel consortium among Germany, France, the Benelux countries, and Italy in 1951, the EU currently encompasses 370 million residents in fifteen member countries. Despite occasional setbacks (Denmark's veto of the Maastricht Treaty, for example) and despite the more serious discord caused by the election of right-wing governments in Austria, Italy, Denmark, and the Netherlands, most Euroskeptics have to admit that the EU is moving inexorably forward. The question no longer is "whether the EU?" but "whither the EU?"

By 2003, the EU intends to expand its current membership to twenty-one countries, including the Czech Republic, Cyprus, Poland, Hungary, Slovenia, and Estonia. An ambitious second expansion by 2007 is intended to bring in Romania, Bulgaria, Lithuania, Latvia, the Slovak Republic, and Malta. Since the Copenhagen accords of 1993, conditions for admission to full membership have been defined very broadly to include (1) a demonstration of a country's commitment to functioning democratic institutions, human rights, the rule of law, and respect for and protection of minorities; (2) a competitive market economy as well as the capacity to cope with competitive pressure; and (3) evidence that the country is able to take on the obligations of membership, including adherence to the aims of political, economic, and monetary union. By focusing on such broad institutional criteria, the EU avoids the much more controversial issues concerning cultural, linguistic, religious, and ethnic identities. The EU supposedly rests on a proven capacity to sustain a set of institutions, which, although originating in the West, are in principle capable of functioning on other soils and in other cultures as well. European identity is not given a thick cultural or historical coating; no exclusionary appeals are made to commonalities of history or faith, language or customs. In Renan's terms, it is the will to live together in the future, and not the fractious past, that defines the new European federation.

Despite these noble wishes to build the EU on "thin" liberal-democratic institutional criteria rather than "thick" cultural identities, a deep conflict between institutional principle and identity is unfolding, both within member states and at their borders. Intense debates range throughout the EU regarding the integration of sizable guest-worker populations and their descendants into their host countries, and many countries are passing new and more restrictive immigration and naturalization bills. These topics have been exploited by right-wing parties and politicians in Austria, Italy, Denmark, the Netherlands, France, and Spain. Social democratic governments in Britain and Germany are also feeling the pressure to cater to more xenophobic sentiments. While the British Labour Party is pushing a restrictive Immigration and Asylum Bill through Parliament, the German coalition government of Social Democrats and Greens has voted for an immigration bill that permits legalized immigration into the country but restricts the rights of asylum and refuge seekers. Despite the signing of the bill into law by President Johannes Rau, the German Christian Democrats, who are favored to win this fall, are threatening to raise objections against the bill in the German Supreme Court.

As has often been the case in European history, xenophobic politics is an easy politics, but the social factors and institutional trends behind European immigration are much more complicated and intractable. Europe's "others," be they guest workers or refugees, asylum seekers or migrants, have become an obvious focus for the anxieties and uncertainties generated by Europe's own "othering," its transformation from a continent of nation-states into a transnational political entity, whose precise constitutional and political form is still uncertain. Will the future EU be a federation of nation-states? A transnational European state in which nation-states are dissolved? Or a post-democratic administrative and bureaucratic conglomerate, bearing more affinities with medieval Europe than with republican traditions of popular sovereignty? These are daunting questions, to which there are no clear answers. As the journalist Joachim Fritz-Vannahme wrote in *Die Zeit*, the only common immigration policy that EU states have is fear itself: "The Europeans are building a fortress against refugees. Each wants to be the architect."

SHORTLY AFTER the Second World War, as Europe entered a period of economic and civil reconstruction, its foreign population stood at 1.3 percent. By 1992-1993 this number had increased to 4.9 percent; the growth stopped in the 1990s, when the countries of the EU began to monitor and control the influx of guest workers, refugees, and asylum seekers into their territories; the current figure is around 5 percent. But these aggregate numbers do not tell the whole story. In many countries the percentage of foreigners in the population is much higher: 9.0 percent in Austria and Belgium; around 8.9 percent in Germany; about 6.3 percent in France. In other EU countries, such as Spain, Denmark, Sweden, and Great Britain, the percentage hovers between 3 percent and 5 percent (note that this figure is well below the 9.7 percent that the U.S. census of 2000 revealed).

Germany and France have been intake countries for longer periods of time than Austria, whose foreign population more than doubled in the 1990s from 4.1 percent to 9 percent. The first *Gastarbeiter* arrived in Germany in the 1950s, and the largest influx of Algerian-born immigrants came to France in 1956–1957. Primary immigration to both Germany and France has slowed down more recently and has been restricted largely to family unification; by contrast over a million and a half "ethnic Germans" from the former Soviet Union and other East European territories were permitted to enter Germany during this period. Great Britain, with its large number of citizens from former colonies as well as ex-colonial British subjects, presents an even more complex picture: according to the *Times* of London "there has been a net loss of British citizens and a net gain of foreign citizens in the past decade." Interestingly, the *Times* reports that immigration of those born in the EU and the old members of the Commonwealth—Canada, Australia, and New Zealand—declined, while net immigration from newer countries of the Commonwealth in Africa and the Asian subcontinent increased. In other words, the face of the 183,000 new Britons is mainly black and brown—an unmentioned fact that is the subtle subtext of the intense debate about immigration in Great Britain.

European societies that once, despite their imperialist history, considered themselves homogeneous nation-states are now experiencing changes in the make-up of their population that they did not foresee and about which they feel deeply ambivalent. Caught among the exigencies of a global economy in which the free movement of cheap labor across national borders is essential to capital expansion, urged by their liberal-democratic consciences to help asylees and refugees from the breakup wars of former Yugoslavia and the third world in general, and preoccupied with their own national histories and cultural legacies, EU countries are struggling with radically new collective self-definitions. Even Greece, Italy, Spain, and Portugal, which had traditionally been sender rather than receiver countries, now have to deal with large numbers of legal and illegal immigrants.

Reflecting these contradictory trends, EU countries have made sure that every step of the European integration process is accompanied by a redefinition of Europe's relation to its "others." Thus the Schengen accord of 1985, which abolished internal border controls between Belgium, the Netherlands, Luxembourg, the former German Federal Republic, and France, was accompanied by some of the harshest restrictions on refugee and asylum policies. The Dublin Convention of June 1990, which followed upon Schengen, stipulated further restrictions upon the movements within the EU of foreigners or third country nationals; that is, foreigners who are not citizens of EU member countries. The Dublin Convention set up an EU-wide data base of asylees and refugees and clarified responsibility for processing asylum seekers who had applied to several EU countries.

Schengen and Dublin had marked consequences. In the mid-1990s, entry into Belgium, Denmark, Finland, and Luxembourg leveled off, and there were sharp falls in entry figures in Germany, France, and Sweden. But the "fortress Europe" that Schengen and Dublin intended to create was a fantasy, and another wave of liberalized entry into the EU—driven primarily by labor markets and the realities of Europe's aging labor force—is now on the European agenda. Even as right-wing parties denounce migrants and foreigners for "invading" their cities and cultures, demographic trends in many of Europe's social democracies as well as the demands of certain industries for specifically qualified workers make it likely that tides of migrant labor will continue to rise.

Throughout the nineteenth century, Europe was a continent of emigration as well as immigration. What accounts for the explosive potential of these issues at the present? The answer lies partly in the great ferment generated by processes of European unification and the difficulties of bringing rapid institutional change and the evolution of collective identities into some kind of compatible pace.

Since the Maastricht Treaty of 1993, citizens of the fifteen European states have acquired EU citizenship. Article 8 of the treaty states, "Citizenship of the Union is hereby established. Every Person holding the *nationality* of a member state shall be a citizen of the Union" [emphasis added]. This article has been the subject of intense debate from the start. Is European citizenship analogous to ancient Roman citizenship, something like membership in an empire, with attendant privileges but with little room for democratic participation? Should European citizenship be conceived principally as social citizenship, eventually entitling everyone who shares this status to an equivalent package of health, retirement, and old age benefits across the union states? Certainly, these problems are not unique to Europe and reflect dilemmas affecting citizenship in liberal democracies everywhere. There is a general concern that contemporary citizenship is defined less by political responsibilities and participation than by the entitlement to social benefits and privileges. Against the background of falling electoral participation rates and the ossification of established party mechanisms, political citizenship appears obsolete. Within the European context, however, the linkage between citizenship and "national" membership expresses a deeper ambivalence about the future of European identity.

EU CITIZENSHIP grants its holders the right to free movement, residence, and employment throughout the EU. Although EU citizens do not have the right to vote in the national elections of their respective host countries, they can vote and run for office in local as well as EU-wide elections. Thus a Dutch resident of London or Dublin can be a candidate for city and county government seats, hold office if elected, and still vote for the Dutch members of the EU Parliament. Although there is skepticism about how rigorously these rights are being claimed and exercised by the EU citizens entitled to them, the Maastricht Treaty delivered a blow to nationalist conceptions of sovereignty and citizenship.

These conceptions are exemplified in a German Supreme Court ruling in 1987 on attempts by Bremen and Hamburg to grant municipal voting rights to foreign residents who had fulfilled certain residency requirements (following the example of Denmark, which gives all foreign residents such rights). The Court barred the grant, claiming that "the people's sovereignty is indivisible." The right of election could only rest upon the sovereignty of a united people, who shared a common past and fate (*"die Nation als Schicksalsgemeinschaft"*). This decision has since been revised to conform to the requirements of the Maastricht Treaty. In a 1997 decision, the Court argued that the possession by non-German citizens of electoral rights did not prejudice the rights of German citizens to political representation through "general, direct, free, equal, and secret" elections. In the case of municipal and district elections, the concept of the sovereign people could be interpreted to include persons "who possess the citizenship of a member-state of the European Union," as well as those who became German citizens in accordance with Article 116 of the German Constitution.

The Court did not explain, as it had done previously, what concept of the people it was now invoking and how it was interpreting popular sovereignty. What political, moral, and juridical principles give certain kinds of people the right of democratic voice while excluding others? Is it only by virtue of its treaty obligations that the democratic franchise can and should be extended to EU citizens? And if the local franchise, why not extend the national one as well? And if to EU citizens, why not to Turks, Moroccans, and Serbians who may have lived and worked in Hamburg or Bremen longer than their Dutch or British neighbors? What is the link between national membership and the democratic franchise?

The EU upholds this link in that access to EU citizenship is based upon national citizenship. But insofar as the active exercise of political rights at local levels no longer requires shared linguistic, ethnic, or religious belonging, but rather is based on interests, affiliations, and associations emerging from a common life in a certain locality, a different conception of democratic citizenship is also becoming visible. The exercise of political citizenship at the subnational level means that the interests of all long-term residents of an electoral district are worthy of equal consideration and respect; therefore democratic participation rights should be extended to all those whose long-term interests would be affected by them. The laws should bind those who can see their own will reflected in them.

Many countries such as Denmark, Netherlands, Sweden, Ireland, and Great Britain, which are EU members, and others such as Norway and Switzerland, which are not, actually extend local and—in some cases—regional political rights to non-EU foreigners resident in their territories. So what is emerging in contemporary Europe is a mixed bag of rights, entitlements, and privileges, distributed quite unevenly across resident populations, in accordance with varying principles.

At the same time, throughout the EU, a great rift has opened between the status of its citizens and that of those foreign residents who are third country nationals. The latter include Turks as well as U.S. citizens, Moroccans as well as Bosnians, Argentinians as well as Chinese. Of course, in every democratic country the rights of citizens are distinct from those of tourists, and those of permanent residents are distinct from both. What is unique about the situation of third country nationals in contemporary Europe is that this category includes large numbers of people who have been guest workers in residence for ten to twenty-five years. It also includes people who are asylees and who will most likely never return to the countries from which they fled, and still others who are refugees, whose fate depends upon changing political conditions in their host countries as well as their countries of origin. The social and political rights and entitlements of these groups differ across the EU; they are dependent upon the national and local legislatures of their countries of residence. Furthermore, the rules governing "naturalization" procedures that would give access to citizenship are distinct for each EU member country. Although the European Convention of Human Rights applies to all residents of the union and not just to EU citizens, third country nationals have limited civil rights in that their freedom of movement, domicile, and employment is strictly regulated by each host country and across the Schengen and Dublin borders. Add to this complex tapestry of identities, entitlements, and rights the urgent need for young migrant laborers, in order to stave off the disastrous effects of low birth-rates upon social security and old age pensions, and the magnitude of Europe's problems in articulating fair and democratic principles of membership becomes evident.

A more precise breakdown of third country nationals shows that their differential juridical status corresponds to significant ethnocultural and religious cleavages. Turks and ethnic Kurds (who are in most cases Turkish citizens) are the largest group of foreigners, not only in Germany but in Western Europe in general. In 1993, they numbered 2.7 million. Of that number, 2.1 million live in Germany and as of 1999 made up 2.8 percent of the population. The second largest group of foreigners is the members of former Yugoslav states, many of whom enjoy either full or temporary refugee status: 1.8 million Croats, Serbians, Bosnian Muslims, and Albanians. Among the EU countries most affected by the breakup wars of former Yugoslavia are the Netherlands, where as of 1998, citizens of former Yugoslavia numbered 47,500; Sweden, where the corresponding figure is 70,900; and Italy, in which 40,800 former citizens of Yugoslavia, as well as 91,500 Albanians, have settled. This picture is complicated by the presence in countries such as France of former colonials. As of the 1990 census, France counted 614,200 Algerian-born individuals among its population and 572, 200 Moroccans.

After the fall of communism in Eastern and Central Europe, a slow but increasing tide of immigration from the former Eastern bloc countries to the EU began. In 1998, 66,300 Poles entered Germany, about 10,400 entered France, and about 14,000 the Netherlands. In 1998, there were 20,500 members of the Russian Federation resident in Finland; Greece is host to about 5,000 Russians, 3,000 Bulgarians, and approximately 2,700 Albanians.

It is obvious that EU expansion, if and when it comes, will do little to alter the legal status of most third country nationals, since neither Turkey nor the former Yugoslav states—with the exception of Slovenia—nor Algeria, Morocco, or Albania will join the EU in the foreseeable future. To the contrary, given that the largest number of third country nationals within the EU are from Muslim countries, it is to be expected that after the attacks of September 11, 2001, there will be less sympathy for their plight and less readiness to bring their juridical status into line with that of other residents. The shift from employing laborers from such predominantly Muslim countries as Morocco, Algeria, Tunisia, and Albania to those from Eastern European countries has already started. In Spain, which is dependent upon large numbers of migrant laborers in its agricultural sector, this displacement has not been missed by the migrants themselves. Rachid Benyaia, a forty-year-old Algerian who has been in Spain for eight years, for example, told the *International Herald Tribune* that the East Europeans "have the same culture as Spain—that's what they tell us."

The EU reproduces at the supranational level some of the internal tensions of modern nation-states, while showing tendencies toward evolution along a different path. Common identity and the democratic understandings of the citizenry were fused together in the modern nation-state, where the citizen was socialized, schooled, and disciplined to embody a specific national identity. Of course, cultural homogeneity was more an ideal than an actual historical fact. Modern nation-states incorporated through annexation and oppression large cultural groups who were not given democratic voice. Yet contempo-

rary developments are splitting apart aspects of citizenship that modern nation-states usually bundled together.

Citizenship in the modern nation-state has three aspects: shared collective cultural identity; political rights and privileges; and social entitlements such as unemployment compensation, old age pensions, health care, educational subsidies, and so on. For EU citizens, both political rights and privileges (except those at the national level) and social entitlements, which in most cases accrue as a consequence of the wage-labor contract, are no longer dependent upon sharing a common national identity. Some commentators therefore view EU citizenship as a case of "postnational membership" heralding developments that will not remain confined to the EU. Postnational membership brings with it the dissociation of national identity from democratic rights, as well as the allocation of social entitlements on criteria other than those of national origin. But for the millions of third country residents of the EU, the classical model of national belonging is retained as a precondition for the exercise of political rights. Even so, insofar as the entitlement to social rights and benefits is dependent upon one's status as a wage laborer and not upon one's ethnic origin, the significance of nationality is waning.

Whether these developments presage the general decline of democratic citizenship and the emergence of a model of post-democratic governance or whether they can lead to a new form of citizenship, dissociated from nationality and closely tied to the local, regional, and transnational networks of a global civil society, is not easy to say. The disaggregation of citizenship carries danger as well as promise. For the EU's third country nationals, the danger is all too clear: despite the considerable social benefits enjoyed by those who have secured jobs and long-term residency in Europe's wealthy democracies, they remain culturally as well as politically "mere auxiliaries to the commonwealth," as Kant once called women, children, and servants. Their voices are not heard at the level of the newly emerging union. Many decisions—on family unification, for example—that deeply affect them are taken without their effective participation. As long as political participation rights are linked with nationality, many foreign residents of the EU will, in effect, trade political voice for social benefits.

These juridical discrepancies and political confusions can be seen in part as the growing pains of a new union. After September 11, however, they assume greater significance. As I have already pointed out, the majority of third country nationals who do not enjoy representation at the EU or local levels are Muslim (Turks, Kurds, Algerians, Moroccans, Albanians, Bosnians); a smaller number are Orthodox Slav in origin (Serbians, Bosnians, and Albanians); and so the institutional fault lines concerning rights and privileges perilously track ethnic and religious ones. Easing the naturalization process is certainly one way of dealing with this problem. Granting the right to participate in elections to the EU Parliament, as well as in local elections, according to some shared criteria across the EU, would be another. This political harmonization ought to be accompanied by the right to EU-wide mobility and employment for legal permanent residents.

A further question that needs to be addressed by the EU, the United States, and many other states and international organizations concerns the status of long-term refugees and asylees. At what point does the receiving state incur an obligation to incorporate these people? When and how can they assume immigrant status in legal fashion? There are no clear answers to these questions in either the theory or the practice of international law. The will of the national legislatures remains sovereign, despite continued lip service to human rights agreements.

As representatives of the fifteen member countries convene in an EU-wide constitutional convention this year, and as they negotiate the dialectic of identities and institutions, they will redraw the boundaries of their union. Whether the dream of the Euro-federalists to establish a multifaith, multinational, and multicultural Europe becomes a reality depends in large measure on the treatment of the foreigners in their midst. Given how closely the dividing line between those who enjoy full and complete citizenship status and those who do not corresponds to religious, ethnic, and class cleavages, it is important that a new European federation not perpetrate the historical divisions between Europe and its "others."

But political indicators since September 11 provide a different signal. In Hamburg during city-wide elections the Social Democratic Party was replaced by the conservative Christian Democratic Union; in Portugal a neoliberal has taken over from the socialists; in Denmark, the socialists have lost their hold on the government for the first time in eighty years. In the Netherlands, after the assassination of its leader, Pym Fortyn's anti-Muslim, anti-immigrant party picked up seats in the Parliament. The French Socialists lost the June 2002 elections; after scaring themselves and the world by giving Jean-Marie Le Pen a symbolic political victory, French voters provided President Jacques Chirac's rightists with an impressive majority in the National Assembly. With national elections pending in Germany this fall, which the Social Democrats seem likely to lose, Tony Blair's Labour Party may remain the only social democratic party in power in a major European country. At this juncture, the EU is turning sharply to the right, and in this continental shift, Europe's migrants are the first to lose.

---

* Ernest Renan, "What is a Nation?" in *Nation and Narration*, ed. by Homi Bhabha (Routledge, 1990), pp. 8–23.

SEYLA BENHABIB is the Eugene Meyer Professor of Political Science and Philosophy at Yale University and author of *The Claims of Culture, Equality and Diversity in the Global Era*.

From *Dissent*, Fall 2002, pp. 33-39. © 2002 by Dissent Magazine.

Letter from Poland

by David Ost

You know things have changed when you go to the historic Gdansk shipyard, where Solidarity was born, and find unemployed shipworkers hired out as ushers for a theater company renting part of the famed site. The company's doing a run of Brecht's *Happy End*, and these workers escort theatergoers from the factory gate to the theater, telling stories about the glory days. You thank them when you get there and wish them better luck, but then the curtain comes up and there they are, on stage, holding signs reading "UNEMPLOYED! WE WANT WORK!"

In other words: unemployed workers temping as former workers doubling as part-time actors playing unemployed workers. Right by the monument erected in 1980 to those "who died so that we might live in dignity."

Taken together, the pieces of the decline of the neoliberal model in Poland are all right here. The dire economic situation has created critics where once there were only boosters. The humbling of a powerful labor movement has led to the specter of an authoritarian populist backlash. And then there's Brecht. This Old Left master was purged from the repertoire after 1989. His revival here is a sign too, of the willingness of a new generation to think left alternatives again.

The success story so often told about Poland is not what you find when you get there. "When I go abroad," the leader of the Solidarity trade union in the Krakow region told me, "and everyone starts congratulating me on how well Poland is doing, all I'm thinking is, Are they talking about the place where unemployment is 18 percent, youth unemployment near 50 percent and hundreds of firms, both old and new, are this close to collapse?" It's not that the country has not had successes. It has a number of modernized plants, a sizable, if recently declining, middle and professional class, and exciting world-class cities in Warsaw and Krakow. But it has hit a wall, both economically and politically, that has people more frightened than they've been in quite some time. Unemployment is now higher than at any time since the fall of Communism, and hundreds of thousands of young people, a product of the baby boom following the imposition of martial law in 1981, are entering the labor market with no prospects whatsoever.

The country had a severe crisis after 1989 too, but while that was a crisis of the transition to capitalism, this is a crisis of the real thing. Whereas that one was expected to happen, this one was not. That it has happened seems to throw everything into disarray. Where once the TINA shibboleth—

"There is no alternative"—was on everyone's lips, now it seems all anyone can talk of is precisely that: alternatives.

Because this is post-Communism, however, the interest in alternatives first of all strengthens the radical right, which has been the chief opponent of capitalist transformation all along. While the former left-liberal oppositionists of Solidarity (Adam Michnik, Jacek Kuron, Bronislaw Geremek, Tadeusz Mazowiecki) saw marketization as the chance to "join Europe" and create an enlightened civil society, and the former Communists cheered them on in order to demonstrate their democratic bona fides, the religious-nationalist right denounced the post-1989 transformation as a betrayal of the nation, an assault on Christianity and a sellout to (a new set of) foreigners. One of the most dismaying things is to see the extremist right-wing newspaper *Nasz Dziennik* filled not only with authoritarian and anti-Semitic diatribes but with sympathetic coverage of the plight of the poor and powerful criticism of the ravages wrought by the new elite. Liberals have so focused on the positive sides of the transition that they have left the field of criticism wide open to the right. When things go so wrong, as they have now, it's no surprise the right is the first to benefit.

For now, that means "Self-Defense," the right-wing party that polled more than 10 percent of the vote in last year's parliamentary elections and has since emerged as the second-largest party in opinion polls. Its pugnacious leader, Andrzej Lepper, cultivates himself as a cross between Mussolini and Robin Hood, combining the former's bullying swagger with the latter's espousal of banditry for the people. Particularly strong among the impoverished rural population, still about a third of the total, Lepper looks increasingly like a Polish Le Pen, replete with tirades against liberals, bankers and foreigners (though the foreigners he opposes are the rich rather than the poor). He organizes road blockades, flouts the law with impunity and harbors private goon squads. When the governing party tried to "domesticate" Self-Defense by giving it some parliamentary authority, Lepper responded with a McCarthyite speech charging corruption throughout the political class, earning him sanction by Parliament and accolades from the dispossessed—exactly, of course, what he hoped to achieve.

All Self-Defense needs now, it would seem, is to piggyback onto a mass popular protest movement. And this past July such a movement emerged in Szczecin, following the bankruptcy of the city's Solidarity Shipyard, which left thousands without work. Named to evoke comparisons with the famous precursor of Solidarity, the Interfactory Protest Committee brought together labor representatives from more than 100 factories throughout the country that were facing bankruptcy. Besides protesting the government, however, the IPC attacked the main trade unions too, seeing them as part of the same cabal that brought about the mess.

The IPC is an embodiment of that peculiar post-Communist phenomenon, the right-wing labor movement. For while this was undoubtedly a workers' protest, a cry of the dispossessed, its rhetoric portrayed foreigners as the enemy and a strong state ready to punish the wrongdoers as the solution. It called for aid to "Polish banks, Polish culture and the Polish army," and for rejection of the European Union. It is less critical of official policy on unemployment than of the policy toward domestic capital (it says the government favors Western business interests over domestic ones). And its pugnacious style of politics, like Lepper's, can be seen in the team it sent to a nearby textile firm whose women workers had not been paid in months. With television cameras following along (or egging them on, though they were happy to oblige), about a dozen workers stormed the offices and roughed up the firm's director. While press headlines read "Lynch Mob!" Lepper volunteered to pay their bail.

Despite its growth, this nationalist right is not likely to come to power anytime soon. The reason is as simple as what one farmer told me: "Are we supposed to sell our goods to Russia instead?" While many Poles today, in contrast to a few years ago, are indeed aware that entering the EU has its costs, they just don't see an alternative. Russia hasn't paid its bills in years. And so, "even though I might not do so well in 'Europe,'" the farmer continued, "at least it might be better for my kids."

It is this gut antinationalism, along with the new distrust of capitalism, that has led to the growth of a democratic left for the first time since 1989. This goes far beyond the Democratic Left Alliance (heir to the Communist Party), now in power. Despite the party's name, its left-wing credentials are actually quite scanty. Apart from a recent bill forgiving the debts of large enterprises if they undergo restructuring, DLA representatives are usually overeager to support neoliberal politics. Indeed, business circles make up one of their core constituencies, along with critics of clericalism, voters fed up with the incompetence of other parties and those attracted by its slogans of social justice. Once in power, however, they seem to make sure not to offer any alternatives. My conversation with Tadeusz Iwinski, a party leader and secretary of state for international affairs, found him unable to articulate just what the leftness of the DLA entails, aside from a "sensitivity" to social injustice. In essence, the DLA is a pure vote-getting machine, refusing to confront the right over any serious issues. (It recently withdrew its commitment to abortion rights in return for the church's agreement not to oppose EU accession.)

And so it is chiefly outside the DLA that new left voices are emerging in Poland. The signs are everywhere, such as in the increased prominence of feminist discourse, or in the first real organizing effort of trade unions since 1989. Because of Solidarity, Poland has a reputation as a place of militant unionism. In fact, the Solidarity leadership has been so firmly on the side of market reform that not only has membership withered but workplace rights and opportunities for employee input have deteriorated dramatically. The situation is particularly severe in the large and growing private sector, which now makes up most of the economy. Because of an early post-Communist belief, repeated to me by Solidarity unionists with numbing regularity in the early 1990s, that private ownership means that "people who work hard get paid well," unions made no attempt to organize in new private firms and scaled back their involvement in privatized ones. The result, as the industrial sociologist Juliusz Gardawski explains, is that "labor has been marginalized while owners do whatever they want, without concern for rules." Hours are dictated, forced overtime common, safety concerns hushed up and, even though the law requires each firm to have a "social fund" for workplace improvement or employee assistance, employers regularly squander this on Christmas parties or managerial retreats. A popular way for employers to evade labor law entirely is to demand that employees register themselves as independent entrepreneurs, leading to a veritable boom in single-person firms of saleswomen, welders, food preparers and bus drivers. Besides boosting official statistics on the growth of private enterprise, this means that if, say, "self-employed" X-ray technicians (they have these too) "choose" to expose themselves to more radiation than the law allows, well, that's their free choice.

Not surprisingly, all this has led to a hemorrhaging of union membership (down to about 2.5 million total and 17 percent density, with Solidarity under 1 million, down nearly two-thirds from its 1989 level) and a widespread perception among workers that unions are simply irrelevant. Recently, however, things have begun to change. In direct response to experiences with "actually existing capitalism," Solidarity has set up a Union Development Office (UDO) targeting the private sector. Even the normally timid old official union federation is doing the same, via its new Confederation of Labor (created by former Solidarity activists disappointed with its pro-management and religious bent).

As it happens, retail has been at the cutting edge of this new organizing drive; in particular, the Western European-owned "hypermarkets" (think supermarket plus mini-mall, all in one store). Originally greeted as a symbol of the alluring, garish opulence of capitalism, with thousands lining up hopefully with job applications, they quickly became known as places of breakneck work pace, constantly changing job criteria, draconian supervision, mandatory unpaid overtime and immediate firing at the first sign of discontent. With workers themselves coming to the unions looking for help, the latter finally responded with an organizing drive filled with pickets, leaflets and press conferences—all hitherto unknown elements of Polish trade unionism.

If this sounds like something out of an American SEIU organizing campaign, it's because the latter conducted the training workshops that got it started. And this points to another promising development in Poland: the emergence of close international trade-union cooperation. Solidarity's UDO emerged out of a workshop organized by John Sweeney's SEIU, with more aid coming when Sweeney took over the AFL-CIO. (Unfortunately, US unions have not aided the Confederation of Labor, perhaps wrongly identifying it as a holdover from the old regime.) In private manufacturing plants, meanwhile, cooperation with European trade unions has been crucial. Stanislaw Ciepiera, Solidarity leader at General Motors' Opel plant in the depressed mining city of Gliwice, formed the local union there, thanks to contacts with a Polish Jesuit monk who had once worked at a German Opel plant and knew the head of its European Works Council. The monk arranged for his visit to Germany, where Ciepiera met with IG Metall unionists from Opel—"and we then felt we had someone behind us." This strategy soon spread to other companies. Ciepiera has contacts throughout Europe now, and even though he holds on to his conservative Catholic beliefs and considers himself antisocialist, he talks like a class-conscious social democrat when he says, "To have a united Europe, with a single, centralized, united union—this is my dream. When there's globalized capital, labor has no other way forward."

Liberal intellectuals are also starting to think about internationalism in a new way. Earlier this year the first sympathetic account of the "antiglobalization" movement appeared. *A World Not for Sale*, by Artur Domoslawski, a young journalist for Adam Michnik's liberal daily *Gazeta Wyborcza*, is a pathbreaking account that succeeds where many Western books do not, in that it begins with an understanding of how previous radical movements have degenerated into apologies for dictatorship, and then seeks to bring that awareness into this new movement. Domoslawski peppers activists he meets in Porto Alegre with questions about whether they understand the brutalities anticapitalism is capable of, and warns them not to ignore Eastern Europe's lessons (and thus lose Eastern European supporters). He admonishes Polish readers to stop thinking of Western leftists as crypto-Communists, and to recognize that their struggles against capitalist globalization constitute a large part of the hope for a better world in Poland too. It's hard to think of a better way to make "antiglobalization"—or, as Domoslawski

calls it, "alterglobalization"—a truly global movement. Moreover, by legitimizing a left critique, Domoslawski undercuts the appeal of the extreme right, which has hinged on its being the main critic of globalization.

Unlike in 1980, few in the West—or, for that matter, in Poland—seem to think the country has much to offer the rest of the world. Yet its experiences since 1989 do deserve to be mined more fully. With "privatization" still a globalization buzzword, Poland's experience with different types of employee-owned firms can be relevant not only to the search for effective alternatives but, with the bogus nature of some of them, as cautionary tales. And the budding "alterglobalization" awareness there needs to be cultivated as well. Ironically, Poland's traditional pro-Americanism is rather helpful here, for it means that the current search for alternatives need not pass through the facile anti-Americanism now in vogue in Western Europe. This search is already allowing thoughtful criticism of American policy toward Iraq, such as that of conservative theorist Aleksander Hall, who recently spoke out against "an international order in which the world superpower punishes and rewards sovereign states according to its own whims, even if that power represents our values and rendered great service in the defeat of Communism."

But all this needs to be nurtured. For if there's one thing not only Poland but all Eastern Europe has lacked since 1989, it's concerned engagement by Western progressives. Disappointed by the mad rush to capitalism (as if their own societies had not done that long before), and perhaps even by the fierce rejection of bankrupt "socialism," many progressives turned away, leaving concern for the region to the IMF-sanctioned privatizers and neoliberals, who made sure no alternatives would be recommended. As the labor sociologist Wlodzimierz Pankow once complained to me, "We don't have enough left anti-Communists discussing with us the real history of capitalism, so of course people believe in the imaginary kind instead." Recent Polish interest in alterglobalization and union internationalism lays the basis for changing all this, provided the Western left pays more attention.

A few years ago Boeing workers went on strike against outsourcing. Among the objects of their wrath was the contract given to a dying aircraft manufacturing plant in southeastern Poland to build doors for 767s, providing sixty jobs in a plant where about 10,000 were threatened. I still remember the words of the local union leader at the time: "Don't they know in Seattle that we're not their enemy?" They didn't know, of course, but more international cooperation along the lines of what has been happening lately could make a difference.

David Ost (ost@hws.edu), who teaches politics at Hobart and William Smith Colleges in Geneva, New York, has written widely on labor and democratization in Eastern Europe.

Ten Myths About Russia

Understanding and Dealing with Russia's Complexity and Ambiguity

Many characterizations of Russia don't get it right.

David Foglesong and Gordon M. Hahn

SINCE the collapse of the Soviet Union in 1991, American thinking about Russia has been distorted by at least ten major myths. Both conservatives and liberals, Russophobes and Russophiles, have clouded understanding of Russia by promoting unrealistic expectations about a rapid transformation, oversimplifications of Russia's history, essentialist ideas about its political culture, and exaggerated notions of a threat to American interests. The illusions that have clouded U.S.-Russian relations during the last decade must be dispelled if the present shaky cooperation against terrorism is to lead to a more stable partnership.

Myth 1
A Popular Revolution, Led by Liberal Democrats, Overthrew the Communist System and Launched Russia on a Speedy Journey to Democracy and a Free Market Economy

Early accounts of the demise of the Soviet Union depicted a miraculous transfiguration of the Russian people, who had suddenly cast off the fearful habits of the past, courageously resisted hard-line communist efforts to re-impose totalitarian oppression, and enthusiastically embraced the Western model of democracy and free enterprise.[1] Along with many politicians and journalists, political scientists were caught up in the early euphoria about the supposed victory of Russian civil society against an oppressive state. Many espoused the transitology approach, presuming that Russia had made a radical break with Soviet institutions and embarked on an inexorable "transition" to democracy. This "democratic teleology" became dogma for those who interpreted the dissolution of the Soviet communist regime as a struggle between state and society.[2] Even some critics of the transition paradigm joined in the widespread tendency to interpret the *perestroika* era as a long "struggle with state institutions" waged by an "insurgent political society" and "the organized, independent, revolutionary opposition."[3]

Although there are elements of truth in such portrayals, they greatly exaggerate the level of popular participation in the demise of the Soviet regime. In fact, prior to the August coup attempt, Mikhail Gorbachev and Boris Yeltsin had led efforts to dismantle the Soviet regime. Gorbachev's reforms and nascent transitional policies, combined with the powers Yeltsin gained as leader of the Russian Soviet Federated Socialist Republic (RSFSR), eroded the authority of the Communist Party of the Soviet Union (CPSU). From 1985 to 1991 the party-state was increasingly incapacitated as the regime split three ways: regime soft-liners like Gorbachev, opposition moderates like Yeltsin, and hard-line conservatives with considerable influence in the organs of coercion and the Party apparat.[4]

In 1990, Yeltsin and his allies took control of the Russian republic's Party machinery and used it to undermine the dominance of the CPSU. They expanded Gorbachev's efforts to partially separate the Party from the state and to decentralize the Union's relations with its republics, ultimately breaking the Soviet party-state's control over the Russian republic's bureaucracy, finances, and natural resources. These revolutionaries-from-above mobilized society for additional support, but the mobilization was minimal and society's resources were limited. Thus, society opposition played only a limited role in destroying the old order and building the new. Demonstrators in Moscow, St. Petersburg, and several other large cities, in relatively small numbers, actively resisted the attempted coup of August 1991, but across the country most Russians remained on the sidelines.[5] The coup's failure resulted from the three-way regime split, which by 1991 had extended to the party-state, the power ministries,[6] and the Party *apparat.* After the coup collapsed, the final destruction of the Soviet state and the construction of a new Russian regime were actually led by former Communist Party officials (including Yeltsin), opportunistic state bureaucrats, and younger members of the privileged *nomenklatura* class.[7] In sum, the revolution was a bureaucrat-led, state-based "revolution from above" far more than a popular revolution from below.[8]

Moreover, Yeltsin and his cohort were quick to demobilize societal opposition, restraining the development of civil society and a multi-party system in Russia. They soon cut a deal with the Soviet-era economic elite to co-opt the opposition emerging from the more partocratic element in the new ruling alliance against the domestic "neo-liberalism" and "pro-American" foreign policy of the young radicals.[9] Old apparatchiks and young members of the former *nomenklatura* divvied up Party and state property, excluding society from the great Soviet going-out-of-business sale.[10] In addition to the oligarchic-bureaucratic economy, the federal and political systems were constructed on the basis of intra-elite agreements. For example, the Russian Federation was built on the basis of bilateral treaties and agreements between the federal and regional executive branches that divided state property and finances among groups of bureaucrats. The political system was constructed in large part by incorporating Soviet state institutions (and apparatchiks) into the Russian state.[11]

The mistaken view of the revolution as one generated from below, and merely another case in a "third wave"[12] of global democratization, led to a cascade of unrealistic and false expectations, East and West, about the fate of Russia's third revolution in the twentieth century. The fall of the *ancien régime,* it was presumed, would lead almost inevitably to the consolidation of democracy and the market. This democratic teleology reinforced and sustained the view among decisionmakers that Russia could integrate into the West and the global economy with limited political and economic assistance. Like Estonia or Hungary, Russia, too, would find its way without anything akin to a Marshall Plan. The West could expand NATO without fear of provoking Moscow, because Russia was already on its way westward. If Moscow turned back, Russia and its culture were entirely to blame. The West would bear no responsibility for failure, which was unlikely anyway because a strong democrat was leading the transition.

Myth 2
Yeltsin Was a Democrat

Yeltsin has been lionized as the bold, white-haired leader who mobilized the Russian people from atop a tank.[13] In reality, he was a semi-democratic, semi-authoritarian personalistic ruler, schooled in the ways of bureaucratic intrigue by years of working in the Party machinery. Aside from those memorable three days in August 1991, Yeltsin fought the Soviet party-state more with presidential decrees, government instructions, and Russian state institutions than with demonstrations or general strikes. To be sure, he skillfully used the growing popular opposition to win concessions from Gorbachev's increasingly divided party-state. Deploying a tactical populism, Yeltsin appealed to the people when he needed to exert greater pressure on the regime to advance his revolutionary takeover of state institutions and Party resources.

However, after defeating the bumbling coup plotters, Yeltsin and his aides stifled the development of a multi-party system and civil society. Yeltsin refused to lead or even join a political party. He postponed promised regional elections and instead appointed regional governors until 1996. He co-opted any and all willing party-state apparatchiks into the state bureaucracy, regardless of their past records or attitudes toward developing democracy and a market economy. Few members of Yeltsin's administration—including Yeltsin himself—had more than a limited understanding of how a market economy functions. He made deals with former Soviet economic elites to reduce their opposition to the pro-American economic and foreign policies advocated by his more liberal advisers. This approach reached its logical conclusion in December 1992, when Prime Minister Egor Gaidar, the architect of market reforms, was replaced by the communist soft-liner Viktor Chernomyrdin, who had served Gorbachev as fuel and energy minister and a Central Committee member. Then, in 1993, Yeltsin forced the Russian legislature into a corner, abolished it, and ordered tanks to bombard the parliament building. After crushing the October 1993 rebellion, he closed down all the regional soviets. Although he finally held elections to a new federal parliament, the results of the simultaneous referendum on the new constitution may well have been falsified. When public approval of his government's painful and failing policies fell below 10 percent in 1996, Yeltsin came exceedingly close to canceling the scheduled presidential elections. He was able to secure victory only by buying votes with state funds and handing over the state's most valuable enterprises to oligarchs like Boris Berezovskii.[14]

While it is inaccurate to portray Yeltsin as a principled democratic leader, it is equally misleading to paint him as the embodiment of oppressive Russian authoritarianism. Despite his declining popularity, he refused to curb freedom of association, and he accepted the revived Communist Party of the Russian Federation. Although he sometimes manipulated and tried to intimidate the mass media, he tolerated substantial criticism of his policies from journalists. In short, Yeltsin was a hybrid figure—personalist and populist, authoritarian and democratic all at once. In terms of this internal contradiction, he was not unlike the country he ruled.

Myth 3
Russia Is Subject to Universal Laws of Development

Over the last decade, many policy advisers and scholars posited that Russia's inevitable destiny is to conform—or succumb—to the universal process of modernization. According to these arguments, Russia has no choice but to belatedly follow the paths to democracy and capitalism blazed decades or centuries ago by more advanced Western countries.[15]

In fact, Russia is not just another country to be plugged into preconceived formulas. It has a number of peculiarities that must be taken into account both to understand its "non-conformity" and to help transform it where possible. The main peculiarities include Russia's vast size, its geostrategic location, and the residual Soviet impression on its economic geography.

Russia's size has significant implications for both domestic and foreign policy that no other state can claim. By far the largest country in the world, Russia counts ten countries as neighbors. Its border with Kazakhstan alone is the same length as the boundaries of the continental United States. Russia's extensive borders and seacoasts require a large standing army and navy, which burden the budget and deplete economic manpower. These costs and the reality of a territorial expanse spanning eleven time zones would make it difficult for the federal government to build and maintain infrastructure (roads, railroads, bridges, power lines, etc.) even without the challenges of economic transformation. Russian officials and scholars now speak of a coming national techno-infrastructural catastrophe and of Russia's need to restore its "familiarization" with, and "possession" of, distant Siberia and the Far East.[16] The resources required to stave off the collapse of the country's infrastructure and develop Siberia and the Far East sufficiently to ensure their orientation toward Moscow would stretch the capacity of any economy, let alone Russia's weak post-communist one.

Geostrategically, Russia is the only country in the world that borders the European, Asian, and Muslim worlds. This places special burdens on its foreign and security policies. Russian national security strategists argue (sometimes with hyperbole) that the threat from each of these worlds is arguably growing.[17] In the east, the sleeping dragon is awake. In the south, the Muslim world is in turmoil, leading to terrorist jihads against the West and Russia, assistance for Chechen militants, and a threat to the stability of reasonably friendly secular regimes in Central Asia. In the west, NATO is expanding ever eastward, apparently to Russia's borders with the Baltic states, and eventually perhaps to Ukraine and Georgia. Any exacerbation of Russian security concerns in the three regions could set back progress on reforming the economy and post-Soviet institutions.

Russia's economic geography also hinders the conversion and modernization of its once heavily militarized industries. Russia has the only post-communist economy that consists of hundreds of one-company towns that, in many cases, dominate half the budgets of regions several times larger than medium-sized European countries. Closing, privatizing, or selling the company to foreigners will affect an entire region that is likely to be located hundreds of miles from any other population center. This constrains Russian willingness to engage in uncontrolled large-scale privatization, especially in the outlying regions. With the privatization of large enterprises, oligarchs came to dominate regional economies. Many are now parlaying their economic power into political power, becoming governors and senators. They seek office not to lobby for development aid for their regions, but to gain favors for their firms and immunity from prosecution.

These factors make it inadvisable to force a one-size-fits-all Western model on Russia. Transitology envisaged a rapid, almost automatic, transformation from hostile, autarchic Soviet totalitarianism to a Western-style Russian democracy and market. This mindset led to the belief that overhauling Russia's inefficient economy would not require massive Western financial assistance or new approaches tailored to Russian conditions.

Myth 4
Russia's Unique Culture Dooms It to Eternal Backwardness

When the illusions of sweeping overnight reforms failed to pan out, they gave way to disappointment, disenchantment, and disdain for Russia's alleged inability to change for the better. Bruce Clark, a British correspondent who stressed "Russia's sheer incomprehensibility," was one of the first to argue that the "Eastern Church" was a major obstacle to the Westernization. A little later, the political scientist Samuel Huntington defined Russia as the core of an inscrutable Orthodox civilization that was almost impossible to change. More recently, Matthew Brzezinski, another journalist, attributed the "loss" of the country to Russians' congenital corruption, their peculiar "Slavic soul," and their scheming, non-Western leaders.[18]

Such gloomy views were the opposite of the earlier euphoric universalism. While the zealous optimists had been overconfident about rapidly converting Russia, the pessimists wrongly disparaged Russians as irredeemably averse to Western values. As some pessimists exaggerated the influence of the Orthodox Church (despite seventy years of atheist persecution), others vented a racially tinged scorn for supposedly innate Russian traits (e.g., superstition, laziness, dishonesty). Overreacting to specific setbacks, especially the financial collapse of August 1998, the doomsayers prematurely wrote off Russia's ability to develop a prosperous economy.[19]

Myth 5
Russia Lacks the Cultural Requisites for Democracy and a Market Economy

After Russian voters elected an alarming number of communists and xenophobic nationalists to parliament in 1993 and 1995, many Western journalists and scholars began to voice gloomy appraisals of the incorrigible authoritarianism of "eternal Russia."[20] In 1993, they exaggerated the election outcome as a victory for the quirky quasi-fascist Vladimir Zhirinovskii's Liberal Democratic Party (63 deputies) and the communists.[21] In fact, the party of liberal pro-Western Egor Gaidar took a plurality of seats (76 deputies) in the Duma, and democratic and centrist parties took a majority of the Duma seats (51.7) after deputies elected in majoritarian single-member districts were factored in.[22] Such Russophobic pessimism faded in some circles when Yeltsin triumphed over his communist opponent in the 1996 presidential election and when the Russian stock market became bullish the following year. However, after Yeltsin handed over the presidency to former KGB officer Vladimir Putin at the end of 1999, there was a resurgence of scornful views of Russia as an impenetrable, irredeemable land of cruel masters and servile subjects. In the first days of Putin's presidency, for example, one relatively sophisticated correspondent declared: "Russians have been crushed for so long that they have learned to respond only to an iron fist."[23]

There have been numerous revolts against despotism and brief periods of quasi-democratic government that might have been more lasting had circumstances been more favorable.

In fact, there has been a recessive but nonetheless rich liberal-democratic sub-strain in Russian political culture that is too often ignored.[24] While Russian political history has indeed been dominated by authoritarianism and totalitarianism, there have been numerous revolts against despotism and brief periods of quasi-democratic government that might have been more lasting had circumstances been more favorable. The liberal Provisional Government of February–October 1917, in particular, might have been able to establish the foundations for democracy if Russia had not been entangled in World War I. Even in the darker periods of tsarist and Soviet rule, Russians formed revolutionary or dissident organizations, secretively circulated banned publications, and gained knowledge about the outside world from smuggled books or partially jammed radio broadcasts. Members of the "eternal Russia" school are fond of citing the Marquis de Custine's nineteenth-century indictment of Russians as obsequious Orientals, but like Custine, they miss the dynamic development of Russian society.[25]

Even as Russophobes in the West reproduce the myth that Russians are genetically antagonistic to democratic values, public opinion polls and in-depth interviews show that Russians have grown deeply attached to democratic processes and principles, despite their frequently acute disappointment with post-Soviet leaders and institutions.[26] Although the word *demokratiia* has acquired pejorative associations with corruption and foreign imposition, a recent in-depth survey conducted by the Carnegie Endowment for International Peace shows that the overwhelming majority of Russians treasure free elections (87 percent), freedom of expression (87 percent), freedom of the mass media (81 percent), freedom to choose place of residence (75 percent), and freedom of religion (70 percent).[27] Other recent polls show also a growing sense of economic well-being among Russians, an important prerequisite of middle-class democratic attitudes. According to one survey, over the last three years the number of survey respondents who regard the situation in Russia as catastrophic has fallen from 51 percent to 14 percent. Between 1995 and 2000, more than 50 percent of respondents felt that "life like this cannot go on any longer." By the end of 2001, only 27 percent claimed that life was intolerable. Although almost 42 percent believe they have suffered from the reforms, almost two-thirds view their current social status as "satisfactory," and 41 percent consider themselves to be middle-class.[28]

Contrary to the tendency of cultural essentialists to view Russians as passive, Russia now possesses a civil society that is a reasonably active, autonomous force. There are tens of thousands of non-governmental labor, business, environmental, anti-war, and other organizations that employ hundreds of thousands of citizens and represent the interests of around 20 million people. Some can already point to victories. Russia's trade unions recently forced the Duma to amend a draft Labor Code before passage. To be sure, Russian society could be more highly mobilized and better organized. But the enormous size of the country makes building nationwide organizations a difficult, expensive task, and with 80 percent of the capital concentrated in the city of Moscow, the overwhelming majority of Russians are too resource-starved for optimally effective self-organization. However, this is an argument not for dismissing the capacity of Russians for democratic activity, but for increasing Western aid to non-governmental organizations.

Even under current conditions, Russians manage to express their grievances and demand changes. On February 9, 2002, for example, 500 residents of Krasnoiarsk braved the Siberian winter to block a railroad used to import nuclear waste for processing in their region. At the same time, small business organizations protested tax hikes and other governmental decisions in regions across Russia.[29] In response, the federal government modified its tax policy to ease the burden on small businesses. There is also a strong social movement to institute alternatives to military service, and several regions began experimenting with such a system. Although the administration halted these illegal experiments, and stubborn military opposition forced the Putin administration to back, and the Duma to pass, an alternative service bill that requires a three and a half year commitment, the first step has been taken.[30] Moreover, the mayor of Nizhnii Novgorod recently reinstated his city's experiment after the Duma vote and vowed to support an NGO court challenge to the federal ban on regional versions of alternative service.

Myth 6
Putin Is a Dictator

Since the end of 1999, when he assumed the Russian presidency, Western commentators have asserted that the wellspring of Vladimir Putin's politics is his background as a KGB officer from the 1970s to 1980s and as head of the Federal Security Service (FSB) in the late 1990s. Simplistically labeled a "former KGB operative," Putin is accused of seeking to return Russia to a "police state" and "dictatorship" by centralizing political control, suppressing the independent media, and cracking down on dissent. In July 2000, for example, only months after his inauguration, two American national security analysts asserted that "Putin is now building a police state using primarily the police organs of the Federal Security Service, known as the FSB, and the army to seize all key power positions in Russia, eliminate dissent and attack both internal and external enemies."[31] Similarly, *New York Times* columnist William Safire alleged that Putin planned to follow China's model and crush all democratic tendencies, and he implied that Putin would make himself "president for life."[32]

Such nightmarish predictions are one-sided and ill-informed. An accurate portrait of Putin, like that of Yeltsin or of Russia as a whole, must see him in all his complexity. The simplistic assumption that anyone formerly associated with the KGB must possess the very worst totalitarian impulses of the old regime and be incapable of countenancing democratic reforms reflects an ignorance of history. For example, Gorbachev ascended to the Soviet leadership with support from a former KGB chief, Iurii Andropov, and key KGB leaders played critical roles in the defeat of the August 1991 putsch by refusing orders to assault democratic forces.[33]

In fact, there is some evidence that Putin himself showed mildly semi-nonconformist and democratic inclinations during his KGB career. As Putin has told Russian journalists, in the early 1980s agents in the intelligence service "were permitted to think differently. And we could say things that few ordinary citizens could allow themselves to say."[34] Putin seems to have thought and spoke quite freely during his tenure as a KGB operative in East Germany. According to one relatively unknown biography, he told German friends as early as 1987 that he thought Soviet leaders should be chosen by secret ballot in popular elections.[35]

More important, the cynical view of Putin as first and last a KGB man ignores his tenure in the democratic government of St. Petersburg, an experience that exerts considerable influence on his political makeup. Like many *apparatchiki* in the Gorbachev era, Putin soon shifted from being a supporter of the sinking Soviet regime to a moderate revolutionary. In 1990, he effectively left the KGB and returned to St. Petersburg State University, where he had earned a law degree. There he became an assistant to rector in charge of international liaison at St. Petersburg State University, where USSR People's Deputy Anatolii Sobchak was still a law professor a leading moderate democrat, was elected mayor of St. Petersburg later that year. During the attempted hard-line coup of August 1991, Putin reportedly played a key role by negotiating with the commander of the Baltic Military District to prevent troops from entering the city. After the Soviet collapse, the St. Petersburg administration, with Putin as Sobchak's top deputy, followed Yeltsin's lead in banning the CPSU, abolishing the Soviet Union, and privatizing state property. (This also meant that Putin became involved with the corruption that was part-and-parcel of the economic revolution from above.)

After Sobchak lost his re-election bid in 1996, Putin jumped to Yeltsin's presidential administration, where he eventually became intimately familiar with one of the leading alleged state inside traders of the Yeltsin era. As deputy to Kremlin property manager Pavel Borodin, Putin probably was privy to at least some of Borodin's financial and property machinations and the Kremlin's dirty dealings with oligarchs. Later, as chief of the administration's State Control Directorate, he monitored implementation of laws and presidential decrees. Putin saw first-hand the regions' disdain for federal law as well as the institutional chaos at the federal level created by the flood of presidential decrees, governmental orders, and other normative documents that were often self-contradictory and ignored by competing bodies. This is a source of Putin's efforts to re-centralize power in Moscow, harmonize regional law with federal law, and make federation institutions more efficient.

Putin and his cohort of pragmatic former Soviet officials are neither solely authoritarian nor purely democratic. Although Putin has condemned violations of the law by KGB officers in the Soviet era, he has also stated his opposition to declassifying files and his abhorrence at having a democrat, Vadim Bakatin, head the post-Soviet FSK after the 1991 coup.[36] While Putin and his associates respect the democratic processes (mainly free elections) established in the 1990s that serve to legitimate their power, they were disturbed by the drastic decline of federal authority in the Yeltsin era and the degeneration of Russia to near lawlessness.

Since his election as president in March 2000 with 53.44 percent of the vote, Putin has centralized federal power at the expense of the formerly wayward regions, consolidated several centrist parties into one large party, "United Russia," united factions in the Duma, and sought to co-opt into state-organized corporatist structures members and groups previously organized in autonomous associations. His authoritarian measures have been undertaken with a soft sleight of hand rather than an iron fist, as in the effort to remove the NTV and TV-6 television stations, respectively, from the control of the oligarchs Vladimir Gusinskii and Berezovskii. Putin has tolerated oligarchs as long as they limit their clandestine political activities, forgo building independent media empires, and perform economic tasks for the state. Here, he seems to be caught between two of his formative political experiences: his rise to power with the help of oligarchs like Borodin and Berezovskii, and his disdain for the oligarchs' corrupting effect on the state.

The more liberal Petersburg experience in Putin's political biography also informs his presidency. Putin has taken some quasi-democratic political positions, such as ignoring numerous calls, many from governors themselves, for regional governors and republic presidents to be appointed rather than elected. He has also twice quashed efforts to lengthen presidential terms from four to seven years. In economics, Putin has taken important steps to cut taxes and business regulations, encourage foreign investment, and begin reforms of the judiciary, procuracy, and military. In sum, neither Putin's pre-presidential background nor his policies as president match the caricature of him as an untrustworthy KGB spook turned would-be dictator.

Depictions of Yeltsin as a bold, heroic democrat and Putin as a sneaky, sinister autocrat are therefore seriously misleading and mask the important continuities between the Yeltsin and Putin eras. Both manipulated democratic processes and showed some authoritarian tendencies while blocking a totalitarian restoration. The worst-case outcome of Putin's likely eight years in power is probably a very soft authoritarian regime still plagued by high rates of crime, corruption, and rights violations—a situation not much worse than that left behind by Yeltsin. The best-case scenario is a somewhat better institutionalized democracy and market economy, with a slightly stronger civil society, considerable structural reform in the economy, less penetration of the state by business interests, somewhat greater horizontal accountability, and fewer violations of civil and political rights in the regions—a situation slightly better than that bequeathed by Yeltsin to Putin.

Myth 7
Russians Are Inherently Anti-Western and Anti-American

Outbursts of anger and bitterness by nationalist and communist demagogues because of harsh economic policies and Russia's declining global prestige have led many in the West to conclude that xenophobia is implanted in the bones of Russians like some long-lived radioactive isotope. However, most increases in Russian anti-Western sentiment have been provoked by Western policies and actions.

To some extent, the rise of anti-American feeling in the mid-1990s was a predictable counterpart to the naive idealization of the United States between 1989 and 1992. With the downfall of the Soviet Union, many urban Russians vaguely hoped that their country would magically become as prosperous as the United States, and they expected massive financial aid as a reward for overthrowing the "evil empire." When no Marshall Plan for Russia materialized and the economic reforms pushed by American advisers brought widespread hardship, many became disillusioned and embittered.[37]

While anti-American attitudes were held by roughly 30–40 percent of Russians in 1993, the figure doubled later in the decade in reaction to the expansion of NATO into Eastern Europe, the NATO bombing of Bosnian Serbs in 1994, and the NATO bombing of Serbia in 1999.[38] When 60–70 percent of Russian respondents say that the United States or NATO poses a threat to Russia, it should be understood as a reflection of the history of military invasions of Russia from the West and the emotional tribulations Russians have undergone over the last decade more than an inherited cultural paranoia. It is also not a completely irrational response to such Western policies as the expansion of NATO up to Russia's borders, the increase in the number of

Russian cities listed as potential targets of U.S. nuclear missiles, and the challenges to Russia's right to a sphere of influence in the Commonwealth of Independent States.

Unlike the rabidly anti-American extremists who have drawn disproportionate media coverage, an overwhelming majority of Russians have either a friendly or an ambivalent attitude toward the United States and the West. Among those who are ambivalent, opinion is subject to abrupt changes of attitude in response to specific events. For example, the terrorist attacks of 9/11 induced a wave of sympathy for America from Russians who believe their own country has been the victim of terrorist raids and bombings by Chechen rebels. Russians generally supported the U.S. effort to bring to justice al Qaeda and its Taliban supporters. An October 2001 public opinion survey conducted by the Russian Center for the Study of Public Opinion, for example, showed that 56 percent of Russians wished the United States success in its war against terrorism in Afghanistan.[39] In early 2002, anti-Americanism became more pronounced, partly because many believed that Russian competitors had been victimized by unfair judging and scapegoating at the Salt Lake City Olympic Games. However, the anger over Salt Lake soon faded, and anti-American sentiment again centered on the sizeable minority who are suspicious of NATO expansion and believe the United States is seeking to subordinate Russia to American interests rather than pursuing a respectful partnership.[40]

Like President Putin, who emphatically declares "we are Europeans," many Russians, especially in the younger generations, believe that Russia is or should be a part of Europe.[41] But if Russians feel humiliated, insulted, and excluded by the West, they will be more likely to look for allies in the East and to define themselves as Eurasian.[42]

Myth 8
Russia Is an Expansionist, Neo-Imperialist Menace

Despite the drastic decline of Russian power since 1991, Russophobes like the *New York Times* columnist William Safire have repeatedly charged Russia with harboring its "old imperialist urge." Even as Russia provided much valuable intelligence to assist the U.S. war in Afghanistan, one American think tank deployed its experts to denounce the Northern Alliance's occupation of Kabul as part of a grand Russian "military strategy" and an "ominous gambit" to expand Russian influence in South Asia.[43] Stratfor director George Friedman went a step further, warning that Russia's cooperation with the West in Afghanistan was paving the way for Russia's resurgence and the next war, which would pit Russia against the West.[44] Such views perpetuate reflexive cold war suspicions and wrongly draw a straight line from the nineteenth-century "Great Game" through the alleged Soviet quest for a warm-water port on the Indian Ocean to the new Russia's supposed expansionist aims in Central and South Asia. Proponents seem to have forgotten that Russia was but one of several players in the Great Game, as it was in the much older European game of partitioning Poland.

> *A long-range view of American-Russian relations thus suggests that collisions are more likely to stem from the expansion of U.S. commercial interests and security commitments than from rampant Russian imperialism.*

The projection of cold war antagonism into the post–cold war era rests, in part, on a shallow historical perspective. In more than 200 years of Russian-American relations, the two countries' vital interests rarely clashed before the cold war. When the United States expanded across the North American continent in the nineteenth century, Russia withdrew from settlements in the Pacific Northwest and then sold Alaska for pennies an acre. As American commerce expanded in Northeast Asia around 1900, Theodore Roosevelt and others briefly feared that Russia's prolonged occupation of Manchuria jeopardized the Open Door policy, but between the Japanese thrashing of Russia in 1904–5 and VJ Day in 1945, most U.S. leaders realized that Russia was actually a potential ally against the most formidable threat to U.S. interests across the Pacific. A long-range view of American-Russian relations thus suggests that collisions are more likely to stem from the expansion of U.S. commercial interests and security commitments than from rampant Russian imperialism.

In more recent years, the specters raised by Russophobic analysts have repeatedly failed to materialize. Putin's turn to the West after September 2001 was a ruse, they warned—Russia would use the "alliance" against terror to bolster its oil and gas pipeline dreams, and then exploit its resulting enhanced international status to challenge American hegemony. Despite the alarms raised by Russophobes, the deployment of Russian Emergency Ministry forces to build a high-tech field hospital and re-establish a Russian embassy in Kabul generated no challenge to U.S. policy in Afghanistan. Indeed, Putin later revealed that the Russian descent on Kabul was carried out with the aid of U.S. forces.

Beyond Afghanistan, there have been few major Russian challenges to U.S. initiatives. Although the two governments squabbled in the spring of 2002 over U.S. duties on Russian steel and a Russian ban on imports of American chicken, Putin calmly accepted the U.S. abandonment of the Antiballistic Missile Treaty, supported U.S. military aid to the Republic of Georgia against terrorists in the Pankisi Gorge, and bowed to Pentagon demands for flexibility to secure a nuclear weapons reduction treaty. Moscow's top priority has clearly been not to defy Washington, but to speed Russia's economic integration into the West.

Even if the Russian government wanted to pursue a sustained imperialist foreign policy, it lacks sufficient military and economic power to do so. An economy no larger than that of the Netherlands is barely capable of supporting imperialist aspira-

tions in Eurasia, much less beyond. Russia has been unable to invigorate the Commonwealth of Independent States (CIS) as a viable international organization, much less as a precursor to a renewed economic union. Only Belarus, Tajikistan, Kyrgyzstan, and Kazakhstan have joined the CIS Customs Union, and these are the states that are least viable and most dependent on Russia to begin with.

All of Russia's seeming neo-imperialist gambits in the post-Soviet era have been either exaggerated by Western analysts or episodic in implementation, intended to manipulate weak bordering states rather than re-incorporate them into a revived Soviet Union. Russia has played a clearly positive role by stationing the 201st Division in Tajikistan, thereby deterring Islamic incursions from Afghanistan and stabilizing the weak and corrupt—but secular—regime of Imomali Rokhmonov in Dushanbe. Western critics of the involvement of Russian forces in Georgia and Transdniestr have ignored the financial costs Russia will incur by withdrawing its troops and equipment, as well as the instability that might result. In Central Asia, where Russian national security really is threatened, weak regimes like Tajikistan, Kazakhstan, and Kyrgyzstan have not been pressured to join a political union with Russia. The so-called Russia-Belarus Union is largely a fiction, even as an economic union. The two sides cannot agree on a common currency, and even the customs agreement has been the subject of repeated disputes between the parties. Any prospects of a real Belarus-Russia Union are minimal until President Aleksandr Lukashenka leaves the scene, since the economies of the two states are vastly different, with Russia having implemented economic liberalization far beyond the virtually unreformed Soviet-style Belarusian economy.

Myth 9
Russia Is No Longer an Important International Player

Many so-called realists believe that Russia is so weakened that it is no longer a serious international player whose interests need to be taken into account when planning American foreign policy.[45] For example, Eugene B. Rumer of the National Defense University's Institute for National Strategic Studies advised the Bush administration that Russia "will not bounce back from its troubles anytime soon" and suggested "Its current decline may well continue indefinitely."[46] More colorfully, journalist Jeffrey Tayler called Russia "Zaire with Permafrost" and argued that its history doomed the country to shrink, decay, and disintegrate.[47]

Although Russia has experienced a breathtaking decline in its fortunes since the cold war, when the Soviet superpower confronted the United States around the world, it is not so weak that it no longer counts as a great power, and its problems are not necessarily permanent or irremediable. Russia's possession of thousands of nuclear weapons is not the only factor that explodes the myth of its insignificance. Besides the United States, Russia is the only country that is a major player in Europe, the Pacific, South and Central Asia, and the Middle East simultaneously. Because of its geostrategic position and relatively high level of technological development, Russia is a major player in the global energy market as well as in several other natural resource exports. It maintains a faltering but still major space program that is matched only by NASA.

To be sure, Russia's economy is small compared not only with other major powers in the Group of Seven (G-7), but also with many smaller states. However, Russia's vast natural resources, strong human capital, and potential for investment growth represented by the hundreds of billions of dollars secreted in foreign bank accounts suggest, taken together, that a fairly rapid revitalization is possible. With the right policies in these areas, including investors' rights, banking reform, and money-laundering, anti-corruption, and anti-crime laws, a Russian economic revival is quite conceivable. In the last three years, Russia's economy has experienced steady, substantial growth, and Moscow has taken important steps to reverse capital flight, encourage foreign investment, and overhaul its financial system. Russia recovered from its earlier "times of troubles" (in the seventeenth century, during the Crimean War, and during the civil war of 1917–21). It may now be on the way to recovery again.

Myth 10
Russia and the United States Are Strategic Allies

The newest myth is that the United States and Russia became strategic partners, even allies, after the events of September 11, 2001. To be sure, 9/11 reshuffled international affairs in general, and Russian-American relations in particular—at least temporarily. The terrorist attacks highlighted the previously ignored mutual interest in combating militant Islam and international terrorism that Washington and Moscow have shared since the end of the cold war. But there is no guarantee that this common interest will remain clear or paramount to Russian and American policymakers.

Some leaders on each side read developments in Afghanistan as justifying a suspicion that the other country is pursuing selfish gains at the expense of their own country. Thus, certain American actions reinforced the suspicions of some Russians that the United States is seeking to parlay the war against terror into a war for control of oil, gas, and pipeline routes. American special operations forces and marines were first deployed mainly in the south among the Pashtun, who make up the majority of the population of Pakistan, and the United States has had good relations with Pakistan since the cold war. The Pashtun also make up the bulk of the Taliban, who, Russian analysts have long suspected, were backed by Washington to counter Russian interests in Central Asia. The United States inserted Afghan Pashtun leader Abdul Haq into southern Afghanistan in order to entice local Pashtun leaders and Taliban commanders to defect from Osama bin Laden. This was viewed by Russian commentators as an effort to rally Pashtuns around a charismatic leader against the Afghan minorities of Uzbeks, Tajiks, and Khazaris that make up the Northern Alliance,

backed for years by Russia, Iran, and India. In addition, American bombing sorties around the town of Mazar i Sharif and the Baghram airport in the initial stage of the campaign in the north were regarded by many observers both East and West, including the Northern Alliance, as surprisingly tame. This fact, and later warnings by President Bush that the alliance should refrain from immediately entering Kabul, led some Russian officials to fear that Washington wanted to delay Kabul's capture so its southern allies could enter before the Northern Alliance.

Back in Washington, some experts claimed that Moscow's outward show of cooperation masked an effort to utilize American power for its own ulterior purposes. For example, Toby Gati, a State Department official in the Clinton Administration, declared that Putin "had the Americans doing his business in Afghanistan and he was fighting to the last American."[48] In a similar vein, Russia's dispatch of Emergency Ministry personnel to Kabul to set up a hospital was variously interpreted as a second Pristina,[49] the beginning of Russian troop deployments, and an intelligence operation.

As of the summer of 2002, potential ruptures have been averted or smoothed over by a division of labor. The Russians are working closely with the largely Tajik and Uzbek Northern Alliance, providing assistance for infrastructure and military development, while the United States maintains close ties to the Pashtuns and leads the military struggle against the terrorists in the south. However, there is no guarantee that there will be no friction in the future.

There is also a potential for conflict in the Republic of Georgia, where the U.S. military is training Georgian units for an operation against Taliban and al Qaeda forces holed up in Georgia's Pankisi Gorge. Despite Putin's tempered response, statements by foreign Minister Igor Ivanov, Defense Minister Sergei Ivanov, and others clearly indicate that many Russian leaders are dissatisfied with this American incursion into the post-Soviet space. The tension will only be exacerbated if the American-Georgian operation does not eliminate Chechen militants in the gorge.

Russian and American interests that coincided relatively well in destroying the Taliban will be less harmonious if and when the campaign shifts to Iraq.

Moreover, Russian and American interests that coincided relatively well in destroying the Taliban will be less harmonious if and when the campaign shifts to Iraq. Saddam Hussein's regime owes $7 billion to Russia and offers the potential for billions of dollars more in future oil and other contracts once sanctions are lifted. Russia also has economic interests in Iran, which is a major purchaser of Russian arms and a recipient of Russian nuclear technology. Moscow has already warned that it does not agree with Bush's categorization of Iraq, Iran, and North Korea as a new "axis of evil." When push comes to shove, Russia is likely to exercise its veto in the UN Security Council, forcing the Bush administration to act alone or at least with fewer allies. Tension over Iraq and Iran could complicate over pivotal issues in Russian-American relations, including Russian human rights violations in Chechnya, U.S. plans for a national missile defense system, and a second round of NATO expansion likely to reach Russia's western border.

Putin has brought Russia along so far, but expanding the anti-terrorism campaign to include Russian trading partners and debtors like Iran and Iraq could exhaust his political skills. Facing strong criticism of his cooperation with the United States from the Russian military, security forces, military-industrial complex, communists, and Muslims, Putin could buckle and revert to a Eurasian strategy of seeking much closer ties with China and Arab and Islamic states. Similarly, the Bush administration, split between militant unilateralists and moderate multilateralists, could tilt away from consultation and conciliation with Russia in order to pursue priority objectives unilaterally, some of which are believed to offer domestic political payoffs. In short, it is premature to be celebrating a Russian-American strategic partnership.

Beyond the Myths: Understanding and Dealing with Russia

To have a stable and positive relationship with Putin's Russia, the United States must move beyond the myths and polarized perspectives of the past decade. It is dangerous for both U.S.-Russian relations and international security for Washington to see Russia through monochromatic glasses, either dark or bright. Like the overly optimistic assessments of Russia's progress toward democracy and capitalism in the 1990s, the rosy views of a strategic partnership with the United States may produce a new round of disappointment and disdain. On the other hand, excessively pessimistic or alarmist views of Russia's supposedly failed democratization, innate authoritarians, and imperialism can undermine Russian-American cooperation and close off opportunities to influence Russia's political and social evolution.[50] To avoid falling into the over-reaction trap once more, we must have a clear, nuanced, and balanced view of Russia.

Russia is a kaleidoscope of interacting positive and negative trends. These must be detected and sorted out by way of objective analysis free of political science preconceptions, historical simplifications, and Russophobic prejudices. The contradictory trends in this sprawling country cannot be captured by crude stereotypes or rigid transition paradigms. Russia, like many other states, is stuck somewhere between a predominantly authoritarian and predominantly democratic order. It can be moving in two directions at once in different spheres, creating a hodge-podge of trends that is difficult to understand, much less model. Thus, Moscow's economic strategy involves greater openness to Western investment and deeper integration into the global economy, but the government's prosecution of critics and scientists for selling classified documents has discouraged open discussion and contacts with foreign colleagues. Russia

has adopted a new legal code with many amendments modeled on practices in the United States and Western Europe, yet Putin's vision of a "dictatorship of law" simultaneously entails moving away from Western conceptions of liberty and justice. Important electoral reforms have been implemented, but political parties have been stagnating or losing adherents. Russian judges have gained greater independence, but that independence has not dramatically improved the criminal justice system.[51] Not only have Putin's federal reforms re-centralized power in Moscow, they are also forcing the regions to rescind many of their undemocratic laws.[52] Given such complicated and surprising developments, Western analysts must consciously refrain from extrapolating disappointment over negative trends in one area onto the Russian government or people as a whole.

The pessimists and the optimists share a presumption that Russia's historically determined fate or natural evolutionary endpoint can be seen in advance. The first step in escaping the bipolar swings in American views of Russia is to abandon prophetic pretensions and jettison teleological hubris. Instead of focusing on forecasting the future and constructing (or tinkering with) abstract paradigms, students of post-communist Russia should concentrate on careful empirical study of developments and dynamics in its politics, business, culture, and society. Scholars should spend more time investigating what is really happening and less time judging how the transition measures up according to some predetermined finish line.

While Russophobic essentialists write as if cultural prerequisites were the key, if not sole, determinant for the development of democracy and markets, transitologists tend to eschew culture as an explanatory factor. Both are wrong. Cultural values are one of several important elements facilitating or obstructing democratic and market development. Contrary to the assumptions of Russophobes in the West and Slavophile nationalists in Russia, cultures are not monolithic. They are malleable under the influence of external forces, especially in the era of globalization. This does not mean that Americans can easily complete the cultural transformation and democratization of Russia by launching cold war–style propaganda programs to exploit the presumed gap between the supposedly pro-American Russian people and the obdurate Russian government. It does mean that Western (especially American) culture has strongly affected post-Soviet Russia, though often not in the ways or to the extent Westerners might wish.

Although propaganda campaigns based on an adversarial relationship to the Russian government are unlikely to be very successful (and may actually backfire), there are many ways that Westerners might exert a modest positive influence on Russia's development. This is not the place for a full set of proposals, but a few examples of practical initiatives can be mentioned. While being humbly cognizant of financial misconduct in Western businesses and governments, Western advisers (as Larry Diamond has suggested) can encourage and support the establishment and strengthening of corruption watchdog bodies in Russia, such as an Independent Counter-Corruption Commission and the Audit Chamber.[53] Western non-governmental organizations can promote the establishment of human rights ombudsmen in each of Russia's regions (at present they are set up in perhaps one-third of the regions) and the expansion of their powers so that they can more effectively investigate complaints regarding violations of press freedom and national minority rights.

Finally, the United States and American corporations can expand their cooperation in the development of energy resources and economic infrastructure in Siberia and the Far East, eventually including a trans-Bering rail tunnel for passenger and oil transport. This would simultaneously boost Russia's economic growth, earn the revenue its government needs for projects such as the modernization of schools and hospitals, and reduce Western dependence on energy resources from Arab and Muslim states.[54] To reinforce this strategy, Russia can be brought into the International Energy Association, and the IEA can be reformed to function as a counter to the OPEC cartel, as Ira Strauss has proposed.[55]

These prescriptions do not presume that Russia is already an ally because of Putin's demonstrated support for the United States in the war against Islamic terrorists. They do suggest some ways to assist the evolution of Russia's domestic institutions and to facilitate a closer international partnership. They should be complemented by other measures, such as gradually deepening Russia's relationship with NATO and its integration into the World Trade Organization, the Asia-Pacific Economic Community, and the Group of Eight (the Group of Seven since Russia's inclusion) to take advantage of the new opening for Russian-Western relations. Russian involvement in these international institutions will ease changes in its political culture, economy, and strategic thinking that will in turn alleviate Western fears and undermine Western stereotypes. Thus, a more stable basis for a Russian-American partnership can be established.

Notes

1. See, for example, James Billington, *Russia Transformed—Breakthrough to Hope: Moscow, August 1991* (New York: Free Press, 1992).

2. For an insightful critique of transitology's democratic teleology, see Thomas Carothers, "The End of the Transition Paradigm," *Journal of Democracy* 13, no. 1 (winter 2002): 3–21.

3. M. Steven Fish, *Democracy from Scratch: Opposition and Regime in the New Russian Revolution* (Princeton, NJ: Princeton University Press, 1995), p. 3. For Fish's critique of transitology, see idem, "Postcommunist Subversion: Social Science and Democratization in East Europe and Russia," *Slavic Review* 58, no. 4 (winter 1999): 798.

4. The *apparat* comprises the bureaucratic institutions and personnel of the Communist Party, as opposed to state institutions. Its personnel were known as *apparatchiki*.

5. On the relatively small proportion of the population that participated in the urban resistance, see, for example, Victoria Bonnell, Ann Cooper, and Gregory Freidin, eds., *Russia at the Barricades: Eyewitness Accounts of the August 1991 Coup* (Armonk, NY: M. E. Sharpe, 1994), pp. 13–14, 19.

6. The "power ministries" include the Ministry of Defense, the Ministry of Internal Affairs, and the KGB.

7. The *nomenklatura* were the elite members of the Communist Party, individuals who received privileges and promotions based on their rank.

8. See Gordon M. Hahn, *Russia's Revolution from Above, 1985–2000: Reform, Transition, and Revolution in the Fall of the Soviet Communist Regime* (New Brunswick, NJ: Transaction, 2002). For an illustration of the younger elites' approach to a revolution from above, see Egor Gaidar, *Dni porazhenii i pobed* (Days of Defeat and Victory) (Moscow: Vagrius, 1996).

9. On the politics of this grand compromise, see Gordon M. Hahn, "Opposition Politics in Russia," *Europe-Asia Studies* 46, no. 2 (1994): 305–35.

10. On the privatization scams, see Chrystia Freeland, *Sale of the Century: Russia's Wild Ride from Communism to Capitalism* (New York: Crown, 2000) and Janine Wedel, *Collision and Collusion: The Strange Case of Western Aid to Eastern Europe, 1989–1998* (New York: St. Martin's Press, 1998).

11. See Hahn, *Russia's Revolution from Above,* chaps. 10 and 11.

12. Larry Diamond and Marc Plattner, eds., *Consolidating the Third Wave of Democracies* (Baltimore: Johns Hopkins University Press, 1997).

13. Leon Aron, *Yeltsin: A Revolutionary Life* (New York: St. Martin's Press, 2000).

14. See Freeland, *Sale of the Century;* Paul Klebnikov, *Godfather of the Kremlin: Boris Berezovsky and the Looting of Russia* (New York: Harcourt, 2000).

15. Anders Åslund, *Building Capitalism: The Transformation of the Soviet Bloc* (New York: Cambridge University Press, 2001); Martin Malia, *Russia Under Western Eyes: From the Bronze Horseman to the Lenin Mausoleum* (Cambridge, MA: Belknap Press, 1999). On the imperative of modernization, see Jerry Hough, *Democratization and Revolution in the USSR, 1985–1991* (Washington, DC: Brookings Institution Press, 1997).

16. See *Novoe Osvoenie Sibiri i Dal'nego Vostoka* (Reclaiming Siberia and the Far East) (Moscow: Sovet po vneshnei i oboronnoi politike, 2002).

17. Soveta Voennoi i oboronnoi politike, *Rossiskaia vneshniaia politika perede vyzovami XXI veka* (Russian Foreign Policy Challenges for the 21st Century), esp. chap. 1, "Mir Vokrug Rossii" (The World Around Russia) (www.svop.tu/yuka/832.shtml); Aleksandr Dugin, *Osovy geopolitiki* (The Fundamentals of Geopolitics) (Moscow, 1997); A. S. Panarin, *History's Revenge* (Revansh istorii) (Moscow: Logos, 1998).

18. Bruce Clark, *An Empire's New Clothes: The End of Russia's Liberal Dream* (London: Vintage, 1995), esp. pp. 1, 93–94; Samuel Huntington, *The Clash of Civilizations and the Remaking of World Order* (New York: Simon & Schuster, 1996), esp. pp. 29, 142; Matthew Brzezinski, *Ca-*

sino Moscow: A Tale of Greed and Adventure on Capitalism's Wildest Frontier (New York: Free Press, 2001), esp. pp. 311, 268, 186. Matthew is a nephew of former U.S. national security advisor Zbigniew Brzezinski.

19. See, for example, Freeland, *Sale of the Century,* pp. 8, 22, 171. Ironically, the 1998 devaluation of the ruble that led many to give up on the dream of Russian capitalism actually helped to pave the way for a return to economic growth by the end of the century.

20. See Richard Pipes, "Russia's Past, Russia's Future," *Commentary* 101, no. 6 (June 1996): 30–38, esp. p. 32; Jonathan Steele, *Eternal Russia: Yeltsin, Gorbachev, and the Mirage of Democracy* (Cambridge: Harvard University Press, 1995); Clark, *Empire's New Clothes.*

21. Astrid S. Tuminez, "Russian Nationalism and the National Interest in Russian Foreign Policy," in *The Sources of Russian Foreign Policy After the Cold War,* ed. Celeste A. Wallander (Boulder, CO: Westview, 1996), p. 53.

22. Gordon M. Hahn, "Russia's Polarized Political Spectrum," *Problems of Post-Communism* 43, no. 3 (May/June 1996): 19.

23. Alessandra Stanley, "A Man Who Rode a Tank Became the Man on Horseback," *New York Times* (January 2, 2000): A3; see also Alison Smale, "Russia's Leaders Are Different. It's the People Who Are the Same," *New York Times* (January 6, 2002): A5.

24. See Nicolai Petro, *The Rebirth of Russian Democracy: An Interpretation of Political Culture* (Cambridge: Harvard University Press, 1995); V. V. Leontovich, *Istoriia Liberalizma v Rossii, 1762–1914* (A History of Liberalism in Russia, 1762–1914) (Moscow: Russkii Put, 1995).

25. For George F. Kennan's similar critique of Custine, see David S. Foglesong, "Roots of 'Liberation': American Images of the Future of Russia During the Early Cold War, 1948–1953," *International History Review* 21, no. 1 (March 1999): 63.

26. Ellen Carnaghan, "Thinking About Democracy: Interviews with Russian Citizens," *Slavic Review* 60, no. 2 (summer 2001): 336–67.

27. Timothy J. Colton and Michael McFaul, "Are Russians Undemocratic?" Carnegie Endowment for International Peace, Russian and Eurasian Program: Russian Domestic Politics Project, Working Paper No. 20, June 2001.

28. See the summary of the results of surveys conducted by the Russian Institute for Comprehensive Social Research, the Russian Independent Institute for Social and National problems, and Germany's Ebert Foundation, in Mikhail Gorshkov, Natalia Tikhonova, and Vladimir Petukhov, "Tak dal'she zhit' mozhno" (To Live This Way Anymore Is Impossible) *Obschaia gazeta,* no. 10 (March 7, 2002).

29. Gordon M. Hahn, "Growing Middle Class Reinforces Civil Society," *Russia Journal* 5, no. 5. (April 26–May 2, 2002): 10.

30. *New York Times* (June 29, 2002).

31. Mortimer B. Zuckerman, "A Great Step Backward," *U.S. News & World Report* (October 9, 2000); Stephen Blank and Theodore Karasik, "'Reforms' That Hark Back to Stalinist Times," *Los Angeles Times* (July 20, 2000).

32. William Safire, "Reading Putin's Mind," *New York Times* (July 23, 2001): A27 and (December 10, 2001): A29.

33. Their refusal was a consequence of the tripartite regime split noted earlier. On the KGB's behavior during the coup, see, for example, Bonnell, Cooper, and Freidin, *Russia at the Barricades,* pp. 18–19; Hahn, *Russia's Revolution from Above,* pp. 429–31.

34. Natalia Govorkian, Natalia Timakova, and Andrei Kolesnikov, *Ot pervogo litsa: razgovory s Vladimirom Putinym* (In the First Person: Conversations with Vladimir Putin) (Moscow: Vagrius, 2000), p. 61.

35. Iu. S. Bortsov, *Vladimir Putin* (Rostov: Feniks, 2001), p. 83.

36. Govorkian, Timakova, and Kolesnikov, *Ot pervogo litsa,* pp. 128–29.

37. Eric Shiraev and Vladislav Zubok, *Anti-Americanism in Russia: From Stalin to Putin* (New York: Palgrave, 2000), pp. 1, 18, 38, 43.

38. Ibid., pp. 145–47.

39. *Vremia MN* (October 26, 2001). See the VTsIOM survey showing an ambivalent attitude toward the United States in *Izvestiia* (September 28, 2001).

40. A survey conducted in May 2002 by the ROMIR agency found that 29 percent of Russians considered the United States "friendly," 28 percent thought it was "neutral," and 40 percent characterized it as "hostile." *San Jose Mercury News* (May 24, 2002): 10.

41. Govorkian, Timakova, and Kolesnikov, *Ot pervogo litsa,* pp. 156, 160.

42. For a classic reflection of this dynamic among Russia's Eurasianists, see Panarin, *History's Revenge.*

43. S. Frederick Starr, "Russia's Ominous Afghan Gambit," *Wall Street Journal* (December 11, 2001): 8; Glen Howard, "Moscow's Bid for Influence in Afghanistan: The Kiss of Death of a Broad-Based Government," *Central Asia–Caucasus Analyst* (November 21, 2001) (www.cacianalyst.org).

44. George Friedman, "The Geopolitical Price of War," (October 2, 2001) (www.Stratfor.com).

45. William E. Odom, "Realism About Russia," *National Interest,* no. 65 (fall 2001): 56–67.

46. Quoted in Michael Wines, "In Czar Peter's Capital, Putin Is Not a Great," *New York Times* (May 20, 2002): A7.

47. Jeffrey Tayler, "Russia Is Finished," *Atlantic Monthly* 287, no. 5 (May 2001): 35–52.

48. *New York Times* (December 16, 2001): A4.

49. At the end of the 1999 NATO campaign in Kosovo, Russian troops rushed to occupy the Pristina airport ahead of NATO forces, briefly triggering an international incident.

50. See, for example, Tayler, "Russia Is Finished."

51. See Todd Foglesong, "Lost in Translation: The Lessons of Russian Judicial Reform," (Carnegie Endowment for International Peace January 12, 2002); Peter H. Solomon and Todd S. Foglesong, *Courts and Transition in Russia: The Challenge of Judicial Reform* (Boulder, CO: Westview, 2000).

52. See Gordon M. Hahn, "Putin's Federal Reforms and Democratization in the Regions," *Russia Journal* 5, no. 22
(June 14–20, 2002); idem, "The Past, Present, and Future of
Russia's Federal State," *Demokratizatsiya* (fall 2002):
forthcoming.

53. Larry Diamond, "Winning the New Cold War on Terrorism: The Democratic-Governance Imperative," Institute for
Global Democracy, Policy Paper No. 1 (March 2002), p. 11.

54. For some specifics, see Gordon M. Hahn, "Russia's Far
East and U.S. National Security," *Russia Journal* 5, no. 24
(June 29–July 4, 2002): 11; Ronald R. Kotas, "The Linking
of Two Great Continents By Rail Connections under the
Bering Straits," *New Electric Railway Journal*, Free Congress Foundation Online (www.trolleycar.org/observations/
kotas010905.htm).

55. Ira Strauss, "How to Secure Russia's Place as an Oil Ally,"
Russia Journal 4, no. 47 (November 30–December 6,
2001): 12.

DAVID FOGLESONG, an associate professor of history at Rutgers
University, is completing a book on American dreams of remaking
Russia. GORDON M. HAHN, a visiting scholar at Stanford University's Hoover Institution and political analyst for the *Russia Journal*, is
the author of *Russia's Revolution from Above, 1985–2000* (2002).

From *Problems of Post-Communism,* Vol. 49, No. 6, November/December 2002, pp. 3-15. © 2002 by M.E. Sharpe, Inc. Reprinted by permission.

Russian Democracy Under Putin

Russians seem content with the current quasi-democratic, quasi-autocratic order.

Timothy J. Colton and Michael McFaul

Is Russia a democracy? Is democracy in Russia developing, eroding, or not changing—for either better or worse? The answers to these questions have tremendous implications for social scientists and policymakers. If Russia is a democracy, then theories that explain democratic transitions may provide a meaningful framework for understanding regime change in Russia. If Russia is not a democracy, then other metaphorical lenses may be more appropriate. If Russia is a democracy, then its entrance into Western multilateral institutions may be justified and Western aid for democracy assistance is no longer needed. If Russia is not a democracy, or if Russian democracy is eroding, then the exact opposite policy recommendations may be more appropriate—delayed membership in Western unions and more assistance that is democratic. If Russia is stuck in the middle—caught in the twilight zone between dictatorship and democracy—then this too has implications for theory development and policy-making.

The answers offered in this article to these difficult and politically charged questions are unlikely to please anyone. They are based upon a mixed and contradictory assessment. Although some might disagree, it is clear that some form of democracy emerged in Russia after the collapse of Soviet communism in 1991.[1] While not displaying the thick structures and norms typical of a mature "liberal democracy," the Russian regime that put down roots under Boris Yeltsin in the 1990s has many of the features of an "electoral democracy."[2] Especially after the enactment of Yeltsin's super-presidential constitution in 1993, mass-based interest groups were consigned to the fringes, pluralist interest intermediation became feeble, individual liberties began to be abridged by arbitrary practices, and institutions that could have helped to redress the imbalance—parliament, the party system, the judiciary—lost strength and independence. Nonetheless, the Russian state and Russian society displayed features of democratic development.[3] Elections took place under a set of rules recognized by all. The results of these elections were not entirely

certain beforehand, and no authority intervened after Election Day to reverse the outcome of the voting. The playing field for competitors in elections was never equal and has steadily become less so. Nonetheless, the rulers of Russia were selected in competitive elections. The regime that emerged in the 1990s was qualitatively different from the communist and tsarist dictatorships.

Since Vladimir Putin became president at the beginning of 2000, democratic institutions have eroded. When Yeltsin appointed Putin prime minister in the fall of 1999, the regime's uncertain and unconsolidated nature lowered the barriers for institutional change. Putin soon put his imprint not only on policy but on institutions. He has not amended or radically violated the 1993 constitution, and he has not upended the institutional configuration of Yeltsin's regime. Nor does he seem to have any coherent plan for doing so. He has, however, initiated or tolerated a series of discrete changes that have diminished the democratic legacy of the reform years. Yeltsin, in recruiting Putin from the closed world of the security agencies and announcing him as the "steel core" of a revitalized government, undoubtedly expected a course correction toward discipline and order. He now thinks that Putin has gone too far in certain respects. However, Yeltsin's feelings are irrelevant. What is important and worrisome is the cumulative impact of the changes.

Putin's innovations coincide with a spate of revisionist thinking about democratization in the contemporary world. Some say that autocracies are being replaced, as often as not, by hybrid regimes entwining democratic with authoritarian principles. Others go further, asserting that Russia and a series of other countries are best thought of as "competitive-authoritarian" systems, in which the authoritarian element has the upper hand.[4] Much ink has been spilled in recent years on the failure of the promising "third wave" of global democratization, which extended from the 1970s into the 1990s, and was capped by the fall of the Soviet dictatorship and its satellites in Eastern Europe. Although there have been democratic success stories in the former Soviet Union, there have been terrible failures and disappointments as well.[5]

It is premature to pigeonhole Russia into any of these autocratic categories. The phrase "managed democracy" will do as a marker for the current condition of its polity. If it is too early to sign the death certificate for democracy, it is too late to ignore tokens of a backing away from the liberal and democratic ideals in which name the Soviet regime was overthrown. Having begun on Yeltsin's watch, the retreat has gathered momentum under Putin. Russia's present rulers are modernizers in the economic and socioeconomic sphere and pro-Western realists in foreign policy. In the political domain, they take the electoral mechanism and the trappings of democracy for granted. They accept that they must periodically renew their popular mandate and that when they do, society must be afforded alternatives to the status quo. They are also reconciled to a limited diversity of opinions and interests within the state machinery. Without setting out to extinguish it, they aim to contain this diversity within boundaries they alone fix. For those at the rudder, democracy is neither good nor evil. It is an existential product of larger forces that, like gravity, cannot be stopped, yet, with the appropriate engineering, can be harnessed to one's own purpose. Institutional change under Putin has reflected this odd blend of preserving formal democratic practices and at the same time weakening the actual democratic content of these political rules and norms.

The New Balance of Power in the Duma

Putin took office bent on resuming the economic reforms that had been stymied by governmental disorganization and legislative resistance in Yeltsin's second term. Although he selected a face from the Yeltsin era, Mikhail Kasianov, to head his first cabinet, Putin inserted a team of market liberals into the next tier, most of them known to him from his St. Petersburg days. Key players were the new first deputy prime minister and minister of finance, Aleksei Kudrin (a fellow vice mayor with Putin under Anatolii Sobchak), the minister for economic development and trade, German Gref, and the president's personal adviser on economic affairs, the iconoclastic Andrei Illarionov. The team came in with an ambitious program encompassing tax reform, land privatization, deregulation, changes in labor and welfare policy, and incentives for foreign investors.

The 1999-2000 electoral cycle put in place a Duma and a president with the same basic political orientation, enabling rapid progress on this reform agenda. The Unity bloc, partnering with the People's Deputy faction (consisting of pro-Kremlin deputies from the districts) and Regions of Russia (which parted from Fatherland—All Russia [OVR] after the Duma election), materialized as the pivotal force in the Duma.[6] These political partners made a deal with the Communist Party of the Russian Federation (KPRF) to divide the chairs of major committees, cutting out OVR, the Union of Right Forces (SPS), Yabloko, and the Liberal Democrats (LDPR).[7] The pact gave the KPRF's Gennadii Seleznev a second term as speaker. Seleznev's subsequent departure from the communist hierarchy made it apparent that he now had a binding commitment to Putin and the Kremlin. Unity's alliance with the KPRF was purely tactical and unwound in the course of 2000 and 2001. Unity increasingly counted on rightist deputies to help it pursue its legislative agenda, leaving the jilted KPRF leader, Gennadii Ziuganov, to huff at Putin as a "liberal dictator."[8]

> For the first time since 1993, the balance of power in the Russian parliament is decisively anti-communist. The Duma has not indulged in squabbling with the president by debating impeachment and censure resolutions.

For the first time since 1993, the balance of power in the Russian parliament is decisively anti-communist. The Duma has not indulged in squabbling with the president by debating impeachment and censure resolutions. Pushed to act on the economy by Putin and his government, the Duma has enacted new sections of the Russian tax code, which had been in legislative limbo for years, putting in place a flat income tax of 13 percent and a lower profits tax.[9] It has gone along with a new labor code, considered very friendly to business interests, and a land code that allows for the ownership and sale of farms and urban land. Putin and the executive branch have also managed to work with the Duma to pass balanced and feasible budgets, a feat rarely accomplished in the Yeltsin years, when parliament and president were so bitterly estranged.[10] Putin has not yet sent the Duma draft legislation on some of the most painful structural changes, such as those touching on pensions and social assistance. Nevertheless, much has been accomplished since the polarization of executive and legislature was eased as a consequence of the 1999-2000 elections.[11]

The new relationship between the Duma and the president is not "anti-democratic." Every president around the world wants to work with a pliant parliament. Executives in liberal democracies most certainly spend considerable political and material resources to achieve a pro-presidential majority in their legislatures. The anti-democratic flavor of current executive-legislative relations in Russia comes from the way in which the new pro-presidential majority was achieved, that is, through an election in which the playing field was not level for all participants. Unlike any previous parliamentary election in Russia, the Kremlin intervened actively in the 1999 contest to assist Unity and destroy Fatherland—All Russia. The Kremlin relied on its allies in the country's two largest television networks, ORT and RTR, to unleash a negative assault against Fatherland—All russia. Although other factors contributed to Unity's strong finish and Fatherland-All Russia's disappointing showing in the 1999 parliamentary vote, the playing field for the two parties was not equal.[12]

Weakening the Federation Council

Putin has assembled super-majorities in the Duma—majorities capable of overriding vetoes of bills handed down by the Federation Council, the upper house of parliament. As a result, he has been able to transform the organization of the upper house and therefore the federal system. To everyone's surprise, Putin made reform of the Federation Council one of his top political goals in his first months in office.

The Russian constitution states that after an interim period during which members would be directly elected (1993-1995), each region of the federation was to send two deputies to the Federation Council: one representing the province's legislative assembly, and one representing its chief executive. The constitution did not specify how these representatives were to be selected. By the end of the two years, the regional governments had won agreement on a law mandating that all provincial leaders were to be popularly elected—until then, Yeltsin had appointed many governors—and that governors and legislative heads would henceforth sit *ex officio* in the Federation Council. This formulation gave the governors and their legislative colleagues increased local legitimacy and greater autonomy from Yeltsin and Moscow. By granting the governors and republic presidents a direct voice in the national parliament, it also created a constitutional anomaly in that these figures would be concurrently executives and legislators. The Federation Council functioned mostly as a lobby for regional interests.

Two weeks after he was sworn into office, Putin proposed a new recipe for the upper house that replaced the regional leaders with persons designated by them under an intricate formula.[13] The members of the Federation Council resisted tenaciously, knowing they would lose their apartments and offices in Moscow, their parliamentary immunity, and much of their clout with the federal government. After a heated battle, in which the Duma said it would override a Federation Council veto and the Kremlin allegedly threatened governors with criminal investigations if they did not support Putin's plan, the law was adopted in July 2000. As a sop, many governors and retired governors were appointed to a new presidential advisory body, the State Council.

The reform has emaciated a significant institutional counterweight to the president. Council members, being unelected, do not have the same authority as their predecessors. Many, in fact, are Muscovites with patronage ties to Putin—they obtained their seats with his administration's backing and have put the Kremlin's interests ahead of their constituents.[14] The new setup also makes it more difficult for regional leaders to take collective action vis-à-vis the central government. As the Duma deputy Vladimir Lysenko stated in 2001, "The president had managed to get rid of one of the strongest and most authoritative state bodies in the country. Under the old structure, the Federation Council provided somewhat of a check and balance on the other branches of power, especially the executive, which is fast evolving into an authoritarian regime."[15]

Putin's reforms of the Federation Council did not formally transgress the democratic rules of the game outlined in Russia's constitution. Moreover, the prior method of constituting the upper house was far from perfect, since it blurred the lines between executive and legislative authority. Putin's correction to this odd formation, however, was not the democratizing measure that many had proposed for years—that is, direct election of senators. Instead, his reform decreased the role of the citizenry in selecting its governmental representatives and thus weakened another check on the Kremlin's power.

Moscow Versus the Regions

Putin's clipping of the governors' wings was extended to their home turf by a decree enacted on May 13, 2000. The decree established seven super-regions ("federal districts"), accountable to Moscow, and super-imposed them on the eighty-nine units of the federation. Each super-region was to be headed by a plenipotentiary appointed by the president and sitting on his Security Council. Five of the seven envoys named in 2000 were from the Federal Security Service (FSB), the army, or the police.[16] Their writ extends to every federal agency in the regions other than the military forces, and thus they have access to officials in the politically most sensitive and influential agencies, such as the treasury, the tax inspectorate, the procuracy, the FSB, and the regular police. Their mission is to oversee the activities of the bureaucracy and report to the president's office on any regional noncompliance with the constitution or the law.

Three other changes accompanied the super-regions. First, a law passed in July 2000 authorizes the president to suspend elected governors accused of wrongdoing by the procurator-general's office. Inasmuch as criminal proceedings can drag on indefinitely (especially if it suits the president), the law is tantamount to a presidential right to fire governors. Putin has used the power only once, and indirectly at that (when he orchestrated the ouster of Governor Evgenii Nazdratenko of Primorskii Krai in 2001),[17] but the mere threat of it has had a chilling effect on gubernatorial initiative. Putin can also dismiss any regional legislature that passes laws contravening federal laws or the constitution. Second, Putin's government has stopped signing the bilateral agreements with the provinces that were one of Yeltsin's favorite instruments for winning their acquiescence. As of 2003, the division of labor among the national and subnational governments is to be governed by an omnibus law that in principle is to be applied uniformly across Russia. Third, Moscow has pushed through a more centralized allotment of tax receipts. As of 1999, roughly 45 percent of the revenues collected in the regions were supposed to be transferred to the central government, but the amount that reached it was often smaller. Under a law signed by Putin in 2000, about 55 percent is to go to Moscow and 45 percent to the regions, and the balance is to be reviewed regularly. Regions like Bashkortostan, which for years paid almost no federal taxes by a virtue of bilateral agreement, are once again contributing to the federal budget.

Party Fractures, Election Machinations

Russia's party system does not perform the role that party systems play in working democracies. Most of the country's parties lack a distinct identity or a stable following. They have little effect on the elections that count, the ones in which the president and the regional administrative heads are chosen. Russian electoral law assigns political parties a pivotal role in parliamentary elections, but non-partisans and weak party organizations continue to play a critical role. Finally, there is little internal cohesion within the parties that remain.

Fatherland—All Russia. The Fatherland—All Russia bloc (OVR), the founding of which initiated the electoral struggle, spoke for current and recent officeholders who sought control of the national government on the assumption that Yeltsin and his entourage were a spent force. Unity, the response to OVR's challenge, was initially created by some pro-Kremlin governors and businessmen like Boris Berezovskii who were concerned about the problems they would face if OVR and former prime minister Evgenii Primakov came to power.

Both founding groups miscalculated. OVR made the biggest blunder when it fumbled the Duma election and then concluded that it could not field a credible candidate for president. All Russia and the Regions of Russia caucus defected in January 2000 and mended fences with the Kremlin. In due course, the entire coalition followed abjectly into Putin's camp.

Unity. The original masterminds of Unity miscalculated in a different way. Unity achieved electoral success and incorporation into the power structure, but its architect, Berezovskii, did not survive as a political insider. Anticipating Putin's gratitude, Berezovskii got the back of his hand, because Putin feared that the "Family" group around Berezovskii and his business ventures had too much influence. He first ostracized Berezovskii and then

pushed him into exile in London in 2001. Unity thrived without Berezovskii, upgrading its legal status from electoral bloc to civic movement and then, in 2002, into a political party named Unified Russia. OVR agreed to a phased-in merger with Unified Russia that will be complete in time for the 2003 parliamentary election. Whereas Yeltsin discarded two consecutive parties of power, Russia's Choice and Our Home Is Russia, Putin favors strengthening Unity/Unified Russia as an organization and seems ready to endorse and assist it in the 2003 parliamentary elections.

Communists. A smoldering disagreement in the Communist Party of the Russian Federation (KPRF), the main opposition party, between the leader, Ziuganov, and the parliamentary speaker, Seleznev, burst into flame in 2002. Seleznev resigned from the party but, with Kremlin support, kept the speaker's job. He has formed his own political organization, Russia (*Rossiia*), and vows to battle the KPRF for leftist votes in the next elections. Many members are disgruntled with Ziuganov's inflexibility, and thus the KPRF may very well nominate a younger, less hidebound individual, such as Sergei Glazev, as its presidential standard bearer in 2004. Despite these internal battles, the KPRF is poised to benefit from its loyal and stable electorate. Compared to all of Russia's other parties, the KPRF has the most promising short-term future.

Union of Right Forces. On the right, the SPS has made the transition from a coalition of parties and movements to a political party. The head of its 1999 slate, Sergei Kirienko, withdrew from partisan activity when he became Putin's plenipotentiary in the Volga super-region. This left Boris Nemtsov as parliamentary chair, with Anatolii Chubais, Yeltsin's privatization tsar, lurking in the wings. Having cooperated with the government and seen it institute a liberal economic policy, SPS worries that it will not have a attractive platform to see to the electorate in 2003. Several veterans of the Russian democratic movement, most prominently human rights advocate Sergei Kovalev, have quit the party in disgust at its pro-war stance on Chechnya.[18] With Unity creeping to the right and the Kremlin ever more hostile to its leaders, SPS will have to fight hard to maintain its slightly right-of-center electoral base in the 2003 parliamentary elections.

Yabloko. SPS's liberal rival, Yabloko, suffered a number of defections after March 2000, including the manager of its 1999 campaign, Viacheslav Igrunov, who left to form his own boutique political movement.[19] Grigorii Yavlinskii remains at the helm and has firmed his relationship with Mikhail Khodorkovskii, the CEO of Yukos and the richest man in Russia. Sporadic negotiations with SPS about a common slate in 2003 or other forms of collaboration have been in vain.[20] After years of standoffishness toward the government, Yavlinskii has edged closer to Putin, perhaps aware of how much the president's blessings could help him in the next election. Putin's attitude toward the liberals was apparently influenced by their conduct during the crisis sparked by the seizure of hundreds of hostages in a Moscow theater by Chechen fighters in October 2002. He accused Nemtsov of exploiting the disaster for political gain and praised Yavlinskii for not doing so. His reaction fueled suspicion that Putin may back Yabloko as his liberal ally instead of SPS.[21]

Long-Term Effects. Whatever comes of these partisan intrigues and squabbles, there are two other changes underway that must be watched for their long-term effects. The first stems from the interest of the Russian leadership in revamping the rules for party formation and State Duma elections. Addressing Unity's convention in February 2000, Putin spoke in favor of a "workable" party system made up of "two, three, or four parties."[22] Streamlining was the main aim of a new law on parties passed in 2001, which stiffened the requirements for registration and stipulated that electoral blocs would now have to include one political party. In 1999, Unity called for an end to proportional representation and for all deputies to be elected in districts. Its motivations were not altruistic. Unity's poor showing in the districts in 1999 notwithstanding, its founders calculated that a party of power would do better in a districting-based system, especially if it could polarize the district races and then prevail in the runoff. Unity and its Duma allies have so far failed to institute such a change, but in 2002, they raised the threshold for the party list from 5 to 7 percent, effective in 2007 (they originally proposed 12.5 percent), which will decrease the number of parties that get into parliament. Putin's brain trust hopes eventually to push all parties other than Unified Russia and the KPRF to the sidelines.[23] If the communists and Unified Russia were to cooperate in getting rid of proportional representation altogether, Russia's proto-multiparty system might easily become a hegemonic party system dominated by Unified Russia.[24]

The second and more alarming trend is toward arbitrary interference by the central authorities in regional elections, usually with the connivance of local politicos, electoral commissions, and courts. The tone was set in November 2000, when Kremlin officials pressured a judge to remove the incumbent, Aleksandr Rutskoi, from the gubernatorial ballot in Kursk on the eve of the election. Rutskoi, a supporter of Unity in 1999 and Russia's vice president from 1991 to 1993, had, among other things, offended Putin during the controversy about the sinking of the submarine *Kursk* several months before.[25] In April 2002, the scenario was repeated with the front-runner for president of Ingushetiia, a republic bordering Chechnya.[26] The same year, Moscow intervened on behalf of clients in gubernatorial elections in Krasnoiarsk and Nizhnii Novgorod, and there were charges of fraud in the vote counting.[27] Such practices, whether or not they spread to the national level, compromise Russia's functioning even as an electoral democracy. As Andreas Shedler has ob-

served, the process of assessing electoral democracies is like multiplying by zero, as opposed to adding: "Partial compliance to democratic norms does not add up to partial democracy. Gross violation of any one condition invalidates the fulfillment of all the others. If the chain of democratic choice is broken anywhere, elections become not less democratic but undemocratic."[28]

■

> Putin's brain trust hopes eventually to push all parties other than Unified Russia and the KPRF to the sidelines.

■

The lack of strong opposition parties and the central state's ability to intervene in local elections underscore the weakness of the checks on the Kremlin's power. Rather than consolidating, these potential balancers of presidential power have weakened with time.

Chechnya and Civil Liberties

Putin's rise to power dovetailed with a cruel war in Chechnya, the second russia had fought there since 1994. In the 1999-2000 electoral cycle, voters saw Unity and then Putin as the political players who could best handle this tormenting issue. The initial use of force against the Chechen fighters making raids on nearby Dagestan in 1999 was justified. Russia also had a sovereign right to deal with the lawlessness that enveloped Chechnya after the Khasavyurt accord ended the first war in 1996, a plague whose barbarous manifestations included was a wave of kidnappings and the execution of hostages. The Russian government's response—full-scale reoccupation, bombardment by heavy weaponry, oppressive patrols and "filtration camps" for segregating and interrogating suspects—has not brought about the promised result. Putin has pledged military reform, as did Yeltsin before him, and appointed a civilian, Sergei Ivanov of the FSB, as defense minister in 2000, but this objective has taken a back seat to prosecuting the war with archaic military forces consisting of sullen conscripts led by a Soviet-era officer corps.[29]

Wars are always brutal, and Chechnya is no exception, but the violence of the guerrillas and the terrorists linked to them does not exonerate Russia's routinely inhumane actions. Human Rights Watch has documented atrocities that include summary shootings, the torching of villages, the rape of Chechen women, and the mistreatment of prisoners of war.[30] Experts reckon that the fighting has displaced 400,000 refugees.[31] Moscow has no strategy for either withdrawal or a negotiated settlement. The March 2003 referendum on Chechnya's status, in which more than 90 percent of its citizens supposedly endorsed all three of Moscow's questions, was a farce, emphasizing yet again the lack of a serious plan to end the bloodshed. To stanch the flow of information about human rights violations, Russia has expelled the observer mission of the Organization for Security and Cooperation in Europe from the republic.

President Putin has loosened the leash on the FSB, which he headed in 1998-1999 and which is now directed by his associate Nikolai Patrushev. The agency has stepped up its harassment of targeted human rights activists and environmentalists, Western non-governmental organizations, and religious groups affiliated with outside organizations.[32] New guidelines on foreign contacts for academics have been issued, and contacts with scientists in so-called closed nuclear cities are restricted. Several academics and environmentalists have been prosecuted for espionage, although the most conspicuous cases ended with acquittals or pardons.[33] At the end of 2002, the FSB became more aggressive about limiting contacts between Russian citizens and foreigners. The Ministry of the Interior must now review most visa invitations to non-Russians. In addition to evicting the OSCE from Chechnya, the Russian government canceled its agreement with the U.S. Peace Corps and refused reentry to Irene Stevenson, the long-time director of the AFL-CIO's Solidarity Center in Moscow.

Muzzling the Independent Media

Putin has also tightened the state's grip on the mass media, assigning priority to national television.[34] The commercial network NTV supported OVR in the Duma campaign and, though less warmly, Yavlinskii in the presidential campaign, and provided the most candid coverage of the two Chechen wars. Putin moved to settle scores in the spring of 2000. His Kremlin administration leaned on prosecutors to investigate alleged past misdeeds of Vladimir Gusinskii, president of the Media-Most company, which owned NTV. Gazprom, the natural gas conglomerate with strong ties to the Kremlin, then called in a large loan to NTV. In the space of several months, Gazprom's media holding company took control of the network, Gusinskii fled abroad, the staff of the weekly newsmagazine *Itogi* was fired, and most Media-Most ancillaries were shut down. Gazprom purged NTV a second time in January 2003, removing Boris Jordan, the Russian-American director it had appointed in 2000, due to NTV's critical coverage of the government's handling of the hostage crisis in a theater in downtown Moscow in the fall of 2002. Evgenii Kiselev and many of NTV's best journalists and producers migrated to TV-6, a much smaller station owned by Berezovskii, only to have the government close it. The former NTV employees got back on the air on a channel called TVS in 2002, but it has only a small fraction of the national audience. One of the original TVS board members, Evgenii Primakov, "called on editorial staff to exercise 'internal censorship' in order to keep the network 'responsible.'"[35] By the time Berezovskii relin-

quished TV-6, he had already ceded his large minority stake and editorial control in ORT, and Sergei Dorenko, the sarcastic newscaster who was his and the Kremlin's battering ram against OVR in 1999, had been sent packing. Governmental agencies have severely restricted access to Chechnya by Russian and foreign correspondents, and have arrested and intimidated several print journalists whose war stories they found inconvenient.[36]

The struggle about the media involves business and personality issues as well as questions of free speech. The losers to date are not blameless. Gusinskii's financial practices were questionable, and NTV did not offer equal access to all comers during the 1999-2000 elections. Nevertheless, the pluralism that comes from multiple owners and multiple biases is preferable to the monotone that would result from a total state monopoly of the news. In nationwide television broadcasting, Russia is closer to such a monopoly today than at any time since the establishment of NTV in 1993. In its Global Survey of Media Independence for 2003, Freedom House listed Russia as "not free" for the first time since the collapse of the Soviet Union. As the 2003-2004 round of elections approaches, even moderate opponents of Putin have many fewer outlets for delivering their message than in 1999-2000.[37]

Putin's Agenda and the Future of Russian Democracy

Putin and his statecraft cannot be appraised on one level or by one criterion. Enough is not yet known to make it possible to sort through the ellipses and contradictions in the thinking of the public man. The private man is hidden behind many veils.

Some of what is here called managed democracy is a pragmatic response to the trying circumstances Russia found itself in at the end of the 1990s. Boris Yeltsin, capable of flashes of imagination and boldness, was bored with the minutiae of government and preferred changing officials to rethinking policies. To buy support and stability in tumultuous times, he repeatedly made concessions to groups like the provincial governors and the new business elite, barely considering the costs. Putin inherited these arrangements, found many of them lacking, and set out to enforce or negotiate better terms. The particulars often reflect common sense more than ideology, and might very well have been implemented no matter who succeeded Yeltsin. Although the means have sometimes been suspect, there is nothing objectionable in Putin's ending the polarization of executive and legislature, removing the anomaly of governors sitting in the upper house of parliament, squeezing more tax revenues from the provinces, tinkering with the electoral system, putting one or two of the most arrogant oligarchs in their place, and retaliating against the Chechen incursion into Dagestan. In economic policy, Putin has listened to liberal advice and converted it into legislation more consistently and effectively than Yeltsin did. His reforms, along with the 1998 devaluation and the rise in world oil prices, have helped sustain an economic recovery now in its fifth year, a welcome respite after so long in the doldrums.

Prolonged economic growth should be conducive to democracy, for it will grow a middle class that will demand freedoms and accountable governance.[38] This could end up being Putin's most benign legacy to Russia. Nor should one ignore the institutional and political projects he supports that may ultimately strengthen democratic governance. To his credit, for example, Putin favors legal reforms that will pare the power of prosecutors, introduce jury trials nationwide, and lessen the incarceration rate. In 2002, he vetoed restrictive amendments to the law on the mass media passed by parliament after the Moscow hostage crisis. On occasion at least, Putin says the right things about democracy and human rights. In November 2001, he attended a Civic Forum sponsored by his administration with the purpose of bridging the chasm between state officials and grassroots activists. The sight of a former KGB agent, Putin, sitting at the same table as a former Soviet dissident and Helsinki Watch leader, Ludmila Alekseeva, was a stirring one, although some fretted that it was all a ploy to co-opt activists.[39] A year later, Putin met with a similar group on International Human Rights Day and proclaimed that his heart was with them:

> Protecting civil rights and freedoms is a highly relevant issue for Russia. You know that next year will see the tenth anniversary of our constitution. It declares the basic human rights and freedoms to be the highest value and it enshrines them as self-implementing standards. I must say that this is of course a great achievement.[40]

Unfortunately, Putin's actions are all too frequently at variance with his words. He has worked assiduously to weaken the ramshackle checks and balances built up during Yeltsin's tenure and to impose the tidy logic of the rationalizer and controller but not, as a rule, the logic of the democrat. Yeltsin loved adding pawns to the political chessboard. Putin is happier subtracting them, as he has with Fatherland—All Russia, the oligarchs who got too close to the throne (Berezovskii and Gusinskii), the governors who rashly meddled in Moscow politics, the parties he wants to limit to "two, three, or four," and the elected government of Chechnya. When the chips are down, Putin has shown himself to be, if not actively antagonistic to democratic values, indifferent to their application. In his pursuit of a strong state that can solve Russia's problems, he tends to forget what he said in his open letter to the electorate in February 2000—that a strong state, capable of promoting popular freedom and welfare, must itself be "bound by the laws." A presidential administration that schemes to have candidates whisked off the ballot hours before a gubernatorial election is not one bound by the law. Neither is a government that invokes phony legal ex-

cuses to seize control of an NTV or a TV-6 or that lets ill-trained troops run amok in the North Caucasus.

It is not the trees that one should dwell on here but the forest. Democracy as practiced by Putin is partly about practical problem-solving, but it is also about eliminating external checks on the power of the state and the leader without scrapping the constitutional framework bequeathed by Yeltsin. Russia's political institutions were never more than partly democratic and were not properly consolidated during the Yeltsin period. This makes it all the more deplorable that Putin has diverted the country further away from democratic development. After the critical set of elections in 1999-2000 and the first several years in office of the talented leader who triumphed in them, the future of Russian democracy is, in fact, more uncertain than before. Theorists and policymakers must come to grips with the regime trajectory in Russia today. The country is not following the democratic-transition script. Contrary to what some in the Bush administration believe, Russia is very unlikely to graduate to liberal democratic status by 2008.

The impact on the regime of Putin's rise to power suggests that the current political system has not consolidated. Russia's nascent democracy is on a negative trajectory, but the unconsolidated state of the regime gives some cause for hope. The regime has not become a total dictatorship.[41] Whether Putin even wants to create such a regime is an open question. Whether he could is also uncertain. Although weak throughout the 1990s and weaker today than just two years ago, democratic rules and procedures are still embedded in the regime, and democratic norms permeate society.[42] Above all else, every major political actor in Russia today believes that elections are the only legitimate way to choose national leaders. No serious leader or political force in Russia today has articulated an alternative model to democracy. For the near future, Putin and his advisers seem likely to manage a version of democracy that limits real political competition and blocks the strengthening of alternative sources of political power. During new crises or after unforeseen events, "managed democracy" can become unmanageable, and pseudo-democratic institutions may suddenly gain real democratic content. The experience of Slobodan Milošević in the former Yugoslavia and Leonid Kuchma in Ukraine demonstrates how formal democratic rules can suddenly and surprisingly undermine the best plans for "managing" democracy.

In Russia, though, the most likely outcome for the near future is neither more democracy nor more autocracy—neither liberal democracy nor dictatorship—but a stable regime somewhere in between. Putin has eroded democratic institutions and practices but has not destroyed them, nor has he articulated a plan for their further erosion. Russian society seems content with the current quasi-democratic, quasi-autocratic order. Russians value democracy but are too exhausted, from decades of turmoil, to fight for better democracy. Stability is the greater priority. Managed democracy could be around in Russia for a long time.

Notes

1. For more skeptical assessments, see Vladimir Brovkin, "The Emperor's New Clothes: Continuities of Soviet Political Culture in Contemporary Russia," *Problems of Post-Communism* 43, no. 2 (March/April 1996): 21–28; Peter Reddaway and Dmitri Glinski, *Market Bolshevism: The Tragedy of Russia's Reforms,* (Washington, DC: U.S. Institute of Peace Press, 1999); Stephen Cohen, "Russian Studies Without Russia," *Post-Soviet Affairs* 15, no. 1 (1999): 37–55; Lilia Shevstova, *Yeltsin's Russia: Myths and Realities* (Washington, DC: Carnegie Endowment for International Peace, 1999).

2. On the differences between electoral and liberal democracies, see Larry Diamond, *Developing Democracy: Toward Consolidation* (Baltimore: Johns Hopkins University Press, 1999).

3. For elaboration of the authors' views on this subject, see Timothy J. Colton, *Transitional Citizens: Voters and What Influences Them in the New Russia* (Cambridge: Harvard University Press, 2000); Michael McFaul, *Russia's Unfinished Revolution: Political Change from Gorbachev to Putin* (Ithaca: Cornell University Press, 2001).

4. See Larry Diamond, "Thinking About Hybrid Regimes," *Journal of Democracy* 13, no. 3 (July 2002): 21-35; Steen Levitsky and Lucan Way, "The Rise of Competitive Authoritarianism," *Journal of Democracy* 13, no. 3 (July 2002): 51–65; Larry Diamond and Marc F. Plattner, eds., *Democracy after Communism* (Baltimore: Johns Hopkins University Press, 2002).

5. Michael McFaul, "The Fourth Wave of Democracy *and* Dictatorship: Noncooperative Transitions in the Postcommunist World," *World Politics* 54, no. 2 (January 2002): 212–44.

6. See Thomas F. Remington, "Putin, the Duma, and Political Parties," in *Putin's Russia: Past Imperfect, Future Uncertain,* ed. Dale R. Herspring (Lanham, MD: Rowman & Littlefield, 2003), pp. 39–62.

7. The pact scrapped a rule of thumb that assigned committee chairs in proportion to the size of the respective fractions. OVR and the two liberal groups, SPS and Yabloko, boycotted Duma sessions for several weeks, to no end.

8. Quoted by Susan Glasser in the *Washington Post* (June 8, 2002): A14.

9. For details on the package, see Erika Weinthal and Pauline Jones Luong, "Resource Wealth and Institutional Change: The Political Economy of Tax Reform in Russia," Yale University, December 2002.

10. See Alexander Sokolowski, "Bankrupt Government: The Politics of Budgetary Irresponsibility in Yeltsin's Russia" (Ph.D. dissertation, Princeton University, 2002).

11. Political polarization generally results in bad economic policy. Polarization between institutions produces especially bad policy, as the 1998 financial crisis in Russia starkly demonstrated. On the first issue, see Timothy Frye, "The Perils of Polarization: Economic Performance in the Postcommunist World," *World Politics* 54, no. 3 (April 2002): 308–37. On the second issue, see Sokolowski, "Bankrupt Government"; Vladimir Mau, *Ekonomicheskaia reforma: skvoz prizmu konstitutsii i politiki* (Economic Reform: Through the Prism of Constitutionalism and Politics) (Moscow: Ad Marginem, 1999).

12. For details, see Timothy J. Colton and Michael McFaul, *Popular Choice and Managed Democracy: The Russian Elections of 1999 and 2000* (Washington, DC: Brookings Institution Press, 2003).

13. One representative is selected by the speaker of the regional assembly and confirmed by the assembly as a whole. The governor selects the second representative, but the assembly can veto the nominee with a two-thirds majority. Representatives serve at the pleasure of those who select them.

14. Aleksei Makarkin, "Sovet Federtsii: novyi sostav, novye problemy" (Federation Council: New Structure, New Problems), in *Politika v regionakh: gubernatory i gruppy vlianiia* (Politics in the Regions: Governors and Groups of Influence), ed. Rostislav Turovskii (Moscow: Tsentr politicheskikh tekhnologii, 2002), pp. 53–75.

15. Vladimir Lysenko, "The Federation Council Fails to Become a House of Lords," in *Russia on Russia: Administrative and State Reform in Russia,* ed. Yuri Senokosov and John Lloyd (Moscow: Moscow School of Political Studies, June 2002), p. 20.

16. Many of the "federal inspectors" reporting to them from the administrative regions also have backgrounds in the FSB/KGB and the uniformed police. Natalia Zybarevich, Nikolai Petrov, and Aleksei Titkov, "Federalyne okruga-2000" (Federal Districts—2000), in *Regiony Rossii v. 1999 g* (Russian Regions in 1999), ed. Nikolai Petrov (Moscow: Moscow Carnegie Center, 2001), p. 190.

17. Nazdratenko, who supported the Unity bloc in 1999, was removed mainly because his government was incapable of dealing with power outages in the region. He was allowed to resign and given the comfortable Moscow post of head of the national fisheries agency.

18. Viktor Pokhmelkin and Sergei Yushenkov also quit SPS, ostensibly for the same reason. They joined forces with Berezovskii in 2002 to form a new movement, Liberal Russia. They severed ties with him in 2003 and have demonstrated little appeal for voters.

19. Other defectors included the well-known Duma deputies Nikolai Travkin and Elena Mizulina.

20. In January 2003, SPS offered to support Yavlinskii as presidential candidate and to sever its ties to Anatolii Chubais, whom Yavlinskii abhors, but Yavlinskii rejected the proposition.

21. There were reports after the hostage crisis that Yavlinskii was considering taking a senior position in Putin's government. See Boris Sapozhnikov at www.gazeta.ru (December 23, 2002).

22. *RFE/RL Newsline* (February 28, 2000).

23. See the perceptive report by Olga Tropkina in *Nezavisimaia gazeta* (October 8, 2002).

24. Pointing in a more positive direction is the 2002 federal law mandating proportional representation for 50 percent of the seats in local and regional legislatures. The law creates incentives for party building at the subnational level, where it has gone at a snail's pace for the past decade. See the statement by Aleksandr Veshniakov of the Central Electoral Commission (www.cikrf.ru/_1_en/doc_2_1/).

25. The incident was widely reported at the time. See, for example, *Novosti Rossii* (November 9, 2000), available at www.newsru.com/russia/. Rutskoi confirmed the main elements of the story, but did not blame Putin personally, in an interview with Colton in Moscow on June 5, 2001.

26. *Novosti Rossii* (April 29, 2002).

27. See Anatolii Kostukov in *Nezavisimaia gazeta* (October 1, 2002).

28. Andreas Shedler, "The Menu of Manipulation," *Journal of Democracy* 13, no. 2 (April 2002): 41.

29. Some Russian observers speak of the "militarization" of civil government, as opposed to what Putin promised. See

Olga Kryshtanovskaia, "Rezhim Puitina: liberalnaia militokratiia?" (Putin's Regime: Liberal Military Rule?), unpublished manuscript, December 2002; "KGB vo vlasti," (KGB—There Is the Power), *Kommersant-Vlas*, (December 23, 2002), available at www.compromat.ru/main/fsb/kgbvovlastil/.

30. See, for instance, articles in the OSCE publication *Russia/Chechnya:* "Now Happiness Remains: Civilian Killings, Pillage, and Rape in Alkhan-Yurt," 12, no. 5 (April 2000): 1–33; "February 5: A Day of Slaughter in Novye Aldi," 12, no. 9 (June 2000): 1-43; "The 'Dirty War' in Chechnya: Forced Disappearances, Torture, and Summary Executions," 13, no. 1 (March 2001): 1–42; "Burying the Evidence: The Botched Investigation into a Mass Grave in Chechnya," 13, no. 3 (May 2001): 1–26. John Dunlop's *Chechnya Weekly*, published by the Jamestown Foundation, also provides full coverage of the war, including human rights violations. There is extensive discussion of the first and second wars in Matthew Evangelista, *The Chechen Wars: Will Russia Go the Way of the Soviet Union?* (Washington, DC: Brookings Institution Press, 2003).

31. This figure is cited in Sarah Mendelson, "Russia, Chechnya, and International Norms: The Power and Paucity of Human Rights?" working paper, National Council for Eurasian and East European Research, Washington, DC, 2001, p. 11.

32. Details may be found in the special issues on civil society in Russia in *Demokratizatsiya* 10, nos. 2–3 (spring and summer 2002).

33. Those involve Aleksandr Nikitin and Grigorii Pasko, who were accused of leaking classified information about the Russian navy's mismanagement of nuclear waste. Both were arrested when Yeltsin was still president.

34. For details, see Masha Lipman and Michael McFaul, "Putin and the Media," in Herspring, ed. *Putin's Russia*, pp. 63–84.

35. *RFE/RL Russian Political Weekly* (April 2, 2002).

36. Criminal prosecutions by the national and regional authorities have also been widely utilized. According to Oleg Panfilov, the director of the Center for Journalism in Extreme Situations, the number of criminal cases against journalists under Putin already exceeds the total under Yeltsin. Quoted in *RFE/RL Russian Political Weekly* (January 11, 2003).

37. The parties are thus devising new information strategies. These include expensive means for distributing programming to regional and cable stations.

38. See the argument in Adam Przeworski, Michael Alvarez, José Antonio Cheibub, and Fernando Limongi, *Democracy and Development: Political Institutions and Well-Being in the World, 1950–1990* (New York: Cambridge University Press, 2000).

39. Alexander Nikitin and Jane Buchanan, "The Kremlin's Civic Forum: Cooperation or Cooptation for Civil Society in Russia?" *Demokratizatsiya* 10, no. 2 (spring 2002): 147–65.

40. Remarks translated and circulated by Federal News Service (December 10, 2002).

41. On the differences between "politically close authoritarian," or full-blown dictatorship, and "competitive authoritarian," see Diamond, "Thinking About Hybrid Regimes"; Levitsky and Way, "Rise of Competitive Authoritarianism."

42. Timothy J. Colton and Michael McFaul, "Are Russians Undemocratic?" *Post-Soviet Affairs* 18, no. 2 (April/June 2002): 91-121.

TIMOTHY J. COLTON is the director of the Davis Center for Russian and Eurasian Studies at Harvard University. MICHAEL McFAUL is a Hoover Fellow and an associate professor of political science at Stanford University. This article is adapted from their forthcoming book, *Popular Choice and Managed Democracy: The Russian Elections of 1999 and 2000* (Washington, DC: Brookings Institution Press, 2003).

Putin's way

MOSCOW

Russia's experiment with parliamentary democracy, never full-hearted, is more or less dead. The country's wellbeing now depends more than ever on one man

"WE'VE become apolitical. And that's a good thing." Coming from Dmitri and Maria, a 31-year-old Moscow couple, these are chilling words. Twelve years ago they and their friends were on the streets, helping overthrow the Soviet Union. In elections they voted for either the social-democratic Yabloko or the pro-business Union of Right Forces (SPS), the self-appointed guardians of Russian liberalism. Since then they have turned into those parties' perfect target voters: a young middle-class family, jointly earning around $2,000 a month. But on December 7th, in the election for Russia's lower house of parliament, the Duma, they put their crosses next to the last of the 24 options on the ballot paper: Against All Candidates. Whoever won, they said, it would make no difference to their lives. "We came to vote just so as to keep out people like Zhirinovsky," said Dmitri with a chuckle.

The results have probably astounded even them. Vladimir Zhirinovsky and his ultra-nationalist, ultra-misnamed Liberal Democrats nearly doubled their vote over the last election in 1999. Yabloko and the SPS, on the other hand, were wiped out overnight: both fell short of the 5% needed to get their party-list candidates into the Duma, leaving them with just a few seats each from the single-mandate districts that make up half the Duma. Even Against All Candidates, at 4.8%, polled more.

Close behind the Liberal Democrats came Motherland, a Kremlin-backed party born only a few months ago. Led by Sergei Glazyev, an ex-Communist, and Dmitry Rogozin, a moderate nationalist, it did the job it was created for: snatching votes from the Communists, whose 12.7% vote was barely half what they won in 1999. The People's Party, United Russia, got 19 sin-

gle-mandate seats. The only non-surprise was that United Russia itself came first. Together with its single-mandate deputies, it has 222 seats, just shy of half the Duma.

The Duma that results is a democrat's nightmare: three parties whose only ideologies are an almost slavish loyalty to President Vladimir Putin and varying degrees of nationalism, plus one made of the dregs of seven decades of totalitarian rule. The two liberal parties were always small and their democratic credentials were often dubious; but, if ineffectual, they were at least loud. With so few seats, they will have even less influence; recovering it will be even harder; and blocking government legislation, good or bad, will be impossible. For the next four years, parliament belongs to Mr. Putin and to those around him.

Ture, that was nearly the case before. And the liberals are much to blame for their own defeat. The shock of it may trigger a needed renewal. But, given Russia's history, it is not a good sign for the future.

Autopsy of a defeat

The elections have overturned a big assumption about Russia's democratisation. This was that as a middle class emerged, it would to adopt democratic values and demand them from its leaders. A huge popular groundswell desired the fall of the Soviet Union, after all, and if those people were at first too busy surviving the aftermath to worry about democracy, prosperity would soon fix that. The 1990s did little to improve most Russians' lives, but under Mr. Putin stability has returned, the economy has grown and a true middle class is appearing. So why did they not vote as they were meant to?

The answer is complex. One reason, of course, is that United Russia was the state's party. Mr. Putin himself, defying the spirit, if never quite the letter, of the law, openly supported it. National, state-run TV stations blatantly ignored the law that requires equal media coverage for all candidates. In some regions the party polled more than double its national average of 37%, a strong sign of vote-fixing by zealous governors. In more remote areas especially, local bosses used strong-arm tactics such as making government workers campaign in their free time, on pain of being fired. Outside observers noted, and harshly criticised, all these things. Without them, say Yabloko leaders, their party would have cleared the 5% hurdle. The Communists are doing their own vote-count, which so far, they claim, gives both SPS and Ybloko more than 5%.

Recriminations are also flying within SPS and Yabloko. "There was a huge problem with the campaign strategy," says Lev Shlosberg, the Yabloko candidate in the western city of Pskov. "We were repeating what we've been saying for the past ten years, instead of coming up with a new formula for the 21st century." Alexander Barannikov, an SPS Duma member who has lost his seat, has similar misgivings: "We couldn't get our message across to the 15% or 20% of people who had started to live well. We couldn't explain to them that their good life today isn't a given." He thinks the campaign could have raised topics such as paying for health care and education—unpopular with most Russians, but something that the newly affluent might agree with. Indeed, Maria and Dmitri, who have a seven-year-old daughter, concurred: "None of the parties talked about health and education."

In any case, the problem goes back further. It may have slipped below the magic 5% this time, but Yabloko has never reached double figures in ten years of fighting elections. Its rival, SPS, was only created for the 1999 vote, when it got 8.5%; but on that occasion Mr. Putin, who was then prime minister, openly lent it his support. Without his help it collapsed. So why could the parties never tap their supposed core electorate?

Grigory Yavlinsky, the Yabloko leader, blames it on the fact that "When people saw what democracy looked like, they changed their minds about it." The reforms of the 1990s created not a middle class but a super-rich elite and a poverty-stricken mass. Post-Soviet devaluation robbed millions of their life savings. State companies were sold off to a few rich bankers at a fraction of their value, in a rigged scheme, in return for their supporting Boris Yeltsin's re-election in 1996. The fact that it was seen as necessary toward off the resurgence of communism didn't make it any less cynical. And the default and economic crash of 1998, just when things were starting to get better, only confirmed the average Russian's suspicions that it had all been for nothing. The fact that economic growth under Mr. Putin has come with more centralised control and less press freedom only proves to many that even more authority is needed.

Also, the party system is young and, as youngsters tend to be, weak and messy. In the 1995 election alone, 43 parties ran. The 5% Duma barrier was designed to weed out the just-for-fun contenders, but even the bigger ones have mutated, merged and divided like bacteria, leaving the voter bewildered. United Russia, for example, was a confederation formed in the Duma by Regions of Russia, which had never run in an election; Unity, which is nicknamed Bear; Fatherland-All Russia, which itself used to be two separate parties; and the People's Party, which has now split off.

In such a system, ideology matters little, and it is hard for opposition parties to convince anyone that they really are the opposition, except by opposing. Yabloko and SPS, though, more often than not backed the government's reforms. Indeed, SPS was often the source of them. That was enough to make them look like its cronies.

Instead, it is faces that voters latch on to. The liberals' chief faces are Yabloko's Mr. Yavlinksy, who after ten years as almost the sole front-man of Russia's social conscience resembles an embittered torch-singer; and SPS's Anatoly Chubais, who as

deputy prime minister in the mid-1990s oversaw the privatisations that made the oligarchs rich. The chief face of the pro-Kremlin parties is Mr. Putin, whose approval ratings still hover between 70% and 80%. No contest. Likewise, Motherland (fresh, young leaders) is thought to have lured voters from the Communists and Yabloko (old has-beens) thanks largely to Mr. Rogozin's performance on television.

Then there are other reasons. Under the old Soviet *propiska* system, Russians can vote only in their place of permanent residence, which is usually where they were born unless they have bought property elsewhere. Yabloko and SPS's upwardly and geographically mobile voters, the people most likely to be living and renting in a different city, fall foul of this. Another nail in the parties' coffin was their bitter campaign squabbles, which dragged both of them down.

The final one was the long-running investigation into Yukos, Russia, largest oil company. Like most big firms it funded SPS and Yabloko, as well as the Communists, and had several of its staff among their parliamentary candidates. When prosecutors launched an attack on Yukos, culminating in the arrest in October of its boss, Mikhail Khodorkovsky, all those associated with the firm were tainted. The jailing of Russia's richest man proved popular with the masses: particularly useful as the interior minister, Boris Gryzlov, is also the head of United Russia. And both Motherland and the Liberal Democrats capitalised on the public's distaste for Mr. Khordorkovsky by calling for increased taxes on natural-resources companies, a call that even some of SPS's members supported.

Power to the president

In short, fraud aside, the Russian people spoke on December 7th, and their message was that an all-powerful president is just fine with them. So what will Mr. Putin do with his new strength?

Answer: carry on as before, only more so. Having spent his first term securing the state's finances with the help of soaring oil prices, and with his re-election next March in effect guaranteed, he is now ready to push reforms that will spread wealth into the rest of the economy, says Chris Weafer, the chief strategist at Alfa-Bank in Moscow. These include closing tax loopholes that allowed the natural-resource companies to fill their wallets, while lightening the tax burden on everyone else; re-

inforcing the banking system to make it the driver of small business growth; investing in decaying infrastructure, especially the crumbling Soviet-era housing blocks and heating systems; putting more into education; streamlining the bureaucracy; overhauling the armed forces; and reforming the judicial system.

So it is no surprise that most foreign investors are pretty happy with the new Duma. Before, the government had to cobble a majority together from various hanger-on parties. Now United Russia is just four seats short of the simple majority needed to pass laws, and getting the extra votes will be no problem. Even if both Motherland and the Liberal Democrats say no, there are still 65 "independent" deputies, many of whom will happily freelance. Moreover, with the disappearance of SPS and Yabloko, big oil companies that had blocked the tax reforms—one reason, it is thought, why Mr. Khodorkovsky earned the Kremlin's ire—have lost a lot of the deputies they hoped to control.

But what if things go further? With all four of its puppet parties on board, the Kremlin will have the two-thirds majority needed to change the constitution. The Liberal Democrats' first step, says one of their spokesmen, will be to propose extending the presidential term to seven years. Mr. Putin has said that the constitution will stay untouched; in any case, changing it requires the approval of most of the regional legislatures too, a lengthy process. Yet two years from now, if he thinks he needs more time for his reforms, he may be tempted to accept—oh, so reluctantly—the pleas of his loyal acolytes. And other measures, such as further curbing the power of regional governors or the legislature, may appeal to him too.

All the same, events may not have played out quite as the president wants. "I think Putin wanted Ybloko in the Duma," says Michael McFaul of Stanford University, in California. It would have provided a symbolic balance and an appearance of pluralism to show the West. Ironically, almost all the parties in the new Duma are more left-wing than the president.

Which is why it may be less pliant than it seems. Motherland and the People's Party both represent the hard-line, security-services wing of the Kremlin elite. Their runaway success has emboldened their leaders. Motherland is already repeating its demands for even higher taxes on oil companies. With Mr. Zhirinovsky, they may try to obstruct the break-up or privatisation of the state-owned gas and banking behemoths, Gazprom and Sberbank, both of which stand in the way of other reforms that Mr. Putin wants.

They may also interfere in foreign policy, strengthening the hand of the Kremlin hawks against Mr. Putin's more westward-looking approach. Or they may just demand jobs, pressing the president to fulfil a vague promise he made earlier this year to form his next government on the basis of the Duma election. Mr. Putin must re-appoint his ministers after his re-election, and the prime minister, Mikhail Kasyanov, is reckoned to be ready for the chop; but the thought of shifty populists like Messrs Glazyev or Rogozin driving policy is not a happy one. The nationalists, says Nikolai Petrov of the Carnegie Endowment in Moscow, "could be a more serious enemy to the Kremlin than the Communists, who were a loyal opposition."

For the next few months, therefore, all eyes will be on Mr. Putin, to see whether he is as determined a reformer as he claims. But whatever the vagaries of the pro-Kremlin parties, and whatever the flaws of the anti-Kremlin ones, the emasculation of the Duma means one simple thing: politics will be less public than it was. And it is too enigmatic already.

The Yukos probes, for instance, bred a vast number of conspiracy theories about whether Mr. Putin ordered them, prompted by Mr. Khodorkovsky's political machinations, or whether it was his henchmen, trying to wrestle the company out of the oil baron's hands, and why. By the time of his arrest, most observers had swung towards the political interpretation, only to be left scratching their heads again when the

smaller Sibneft suspended a planned merger with Yukos at the last minute. This week, after reports that Sibneft had been trying to impose its own top management on the joint company, there were new reports that the deal was definitely off; but nobody is any clearer as to whether Roman Abramovich, the main Sibneft shareholder (and owner of England's Chelsea football club) was merely trying to get the most out of Yukos's weak position, or whether the Kremlin was using him as a lever to prise Mr. Khodorkovsky's shareholding away. Either way, five months of uncertainty have rocked investor confidence.

Another example is the war on Chechnya. Opinion polls show that displeasure at Mr. Putin's Chechnya policy is widespread. But public debate has been restricted to a couple of dogged newspapers and a handful of Duma deputies. Some of the most outspoken ones have been murdered; the rest are now outside. Yet, as another suicide bomb-killing five people right beside the Kremlin-reminded Muscovites this week, four years of having Russian troops bogged down in the rebellious republic has done nothing to end the conflict there, and has made ordinary Russians' lives more dangerous.

Death, yes; transfiguration, maybe

How can the opposition recover? Inevitably, there is much talk of phoenixes rising from ashes. Merger talks have started, for the umpteenth time, but many believe that Mr. Yavlinsky and Mr. Chubais have dis-

agreed too deeply for too long to come together now. "I think a united block would get about 6% or 6.5%, not more," says Mr. Shlosberg. The leaders could possibly be jettisoned: but almost everybody else in the parties is too unknown, and now that they are out of the Duma it will be harder still to raise their profile.

The parties' behind-the-scenes influence will continue. Mr. Yavlinsky and Mr. Putin are said to get on well; Mr. Chubais still heads the state electricity company, and his many protégés on the government's economic team. But becoming electable is another matter. "How we'll stay in the public eye for the next four years is something we'll have to decide," says Mr. Barannikov. "I don't see the way right now."

The Communists, for their part, face even tougher questions. Though they are still in parliament, they lost as great a share of their electorate as the smaller parties did. They are now little more than a Duma decoration—and not a pretty one, either.

To some, all this confirms the suspicions that rather than being a flowering of democracy, the 1990s were just a momentary lapse of Russia's normal authoritarianism. Certainly for the next few years the real power struggles—above all, the fight to succeed Mr. Putin—will take place within the pro-Kremlin factions, without serious challenges from outside. The new Duma does, therefore, have at least one advantage: it is reality. "Before, there was just an illusion of democracy," says Lilia Dubovaya of the SPS. "I honestly don't know if things aren't better this way."

UNIT 4

Political Diversity in the Developing World

Unit Selections

Key Points to Consider

- What have developing countries in common, and how are they diverse?

- How did the PRI maintain its dominance in Mexican politics for so long?

- What has caused the apparent impasse in Mexico's politics?

- Why do economic development and representative government run into such difficulties in most of Latin America and much of Africa?

- What are some of the major political, economic, and social problems that South Africa still has to face?

- How do you explain China's relative success in turning toward market reforms, as compared to the Soviet Union?

- How do you explain the apparent resilience of Indian democracy?

- What are some of the most common obstacles to the installation of a democracy in a country like Iraq or Afghanistan?

 **Links: www.dushkin.com/online/**
These sites are annotated in the World Wide Web pages.

Africa News Online
http://allafrica.com/
ArabNet
http://www.arab.net
ASEAN Web
http://www.aseansec.org/home.html
Inside China Today
http://www.einnews.com/china/
InterAction
http://www.interaction.org
Organization for Economic Cooperation and Development
http://www.oecd.org/home/
Sun SITE Singapore
http://sunsite.nus.edu.sg/noframe.html

Until recently, the **Third World** was a widely used umbrella term for a disparate group of states that are now more frequently called the **developing countries**. Their most important shared characteristic may well be that these countries have not become relatively modern industrial societies. Most of these developing nations also share the problems of poverty and, though now less frequently, rapid population growth.

In many other ways, the developing countries vary tremendously in their socio-cultural and political characteristics. Some of them have representative systems of government, and a few of these, such as India, even have an impressive record of political stability. Many of them have been governed by authoritarian regimes that normally claim to represent the best interests of the people. Closer examination will often reveal that the avowed determination of self-appointed leaders to improve their societies is frequently less significant than their determination to maintain and expand their own power and privilege.

In recent years, market-oriented development has gained in favor in many countries that previously subscribed to some version of heavy state regulation or socialist planning of the economy. Their renewed interest in markets resembles the strategic policy shift that has also occurred in former Communist-ruled nations as well as the more advanced industrial countries. It usually represents a pragmatic acceptance of a "mixed economy" rather than a doctrinaire espousal of laissez-faire capitalism. In other words, targeted state intervention continues to play a role in economic development, but it is no longer so pervasive, rigid or heavy-handed as often in the past.

In studying the attempts by developing countries to create institutions and policies that will promote their socioeconomic development, it is important not to leave out the international context. In the recent past, the political and intellectual leaders of these countries have often drawn upon some version of what is called **dependency theory** to explain their plight, sometimes combining it with demands for special treatment or compensation from the industrial world. In some of its forms, dependency theory is itself an outgrowth of the Marxist or Leninist theory of imperialism, according to which advanced capitalist countries have established exploitative relationships with the weaker economic systems of the less developed world. Such theories have often focused on **external factors** to explain a country's failure to generate self-sustained growth. They differ strikingly from explanations that give greater emphasis to a country's **internal obstacles** to development (whether socio-cultural, political, environmental, or a combination of these). Such theoretical disagreements are not merely of academic interest. The theories themselves are likely to provide the intellectual basis for strikingly different policy conclusions and development strategies. In other words, ideas and theory can have important consequences.

The debate has had some tangible consequences in recent years. It now appears that dependency theory, at least in its simplest and most direct form, has lost intellectual and political support. Instead of serving as an explanatory paradigm, it is now more frequently encountered as part of more pluralist explanations of lagging development that recognize the tangled complexity of both internal and external factors likely to affect economic

growth and change. There is much to be said for **middle-range theory** that pays greater attention to the contextual or situational aspects of each case of development. On the whole, multivariable explanations seem preferable to single-cause ones. Strategies of development that may work in one setting may come to naught in a different environment. One size rarely fits all.

Sometimes called the Group of 77, but eventually consisting of some 120 countries, the developing states used to link themselves together in the United Nations to promote whatever interests they may have had in common. They focused on promoting changes designed to improve their relative commercial position vis-à-vis the affluent industrialized nations of the North. Their common front, however, turned out to be more rhetorical than real. It would be a mistake to assume that there must be a necessary identity of interest among these countries or that they pursue complementary foreign policies.

Outside the United Nations, some of these same countries have occasionally tried to increase and control the price of industrially important primary exports through the building of cartel agreements among themselves. The result has sometimes been detrimental to other developing nations. The most successful of these cartels, the Organization of Petroleum Exporting Countries (OPEC), was established in 1973 and held sway for almost a decade. Its cohesion eventually eroded, resulting in drastic reductions in oil prices. While this latter development was welcomed in the oil-importing industrial world as well as in many developing countries, it left some oil-producing nations, such as Mexico, in economic disarray for a while. Moreover, the need to find outlets for the huge amounts of petrodollars, which had been deposited by some oil producers in Western banks during the period of cartel-induced high prices, led some financial institutions to make huge and often ill-considered loans to many developing nations. The frantic and often unsuccessful efforts to repay on schedule created new economic, social, and political dislocations, which hit particularly hard in Latin America during the 1980s.

Some of the poorer oil-producing nations recaptured a degree of economic leverage at the turn of the new century. In a reduced form, the situation resembled a déjà vu, as global energy consumption increased and the OPEC countries proved willing and able, at least for a while, to return to a coordinated policy of limiting the production and hence the supply of petroleum. As a result, energy prices rose rapidly, and the advanced industrial nations were once again made aware of their economic vulnerability, stemming from a dependence on a regular flow of relatively low-priced oil.

The problems of poverty, hunger, and malnutrition in much of the developing world are socially and politically explosive. In their fear of revolution and their opposition to meaningful reform, the privileged classes have often resorted to brutal repression as a means of preserving a status quo favorable to themselves. In Latin America, this led to a politicization during the 1970s of many lay persons and clergy of the Roman Catholic Church, who demanded social reform in the name of what was called **liberation theology**. For them, this variant of dependency theory filled a very practical ideological function by providing a relatively simple analytical and moral explanation of a complex reality. It also gave some strategic guidance for political activists who were determined to change this state of affairs. Their views on the inevitability of class struggle, and the need to take an active part in it, often clashed with the Vatican's far more conservative outlook. Like dependency theory, liberation theology today appears to have been effectively absorbed into more pluralist outlooks and pragmatic strategies for socioeconomic development.

The collapse of Communist rule in Europe has had a profound impact on the ideological explanation of the developing world's poverty and on the resulting strategies to overcome it. The Soviet model of modernization now appears to offer very little of practical value. The fact that even the Communists who remain in power in China have been eager to experiment widely with market reforms, including the private profit motive, has added to the general discredit of the centrally planned economy. Perhaps even more important, there seemed for a while to be a positive demonstration effect in some countries in Africa and Latin America that pursued more market-oriented strategies of development. On the whole, they appeared, at least until recently, to perform much better than some of their more statist neighbors tied to highly regulated and protected economies. This realization may help explain the intellectual journey of someone like the now-deceased Michael Manley, the former prime minister of Jamaica, who broke away from the combination of dependency theory and socialist strategies that he had once defended vigorously. During the 1980s, Manley made an intellectual U-turn as he gained a new respect for market-oriented economic approaches, without abandoning his interest in using reform politics to promote the interests of the poor. A similar political shift was taken by Fernando Henrique Cardoso, who came to embrace market economics before he became president of Brazil until 2002. In his youth, Cardoso had been exiled by the then-ruling military junta for having written a book on dependency and underdevelopment that became a primer of left-wing analysis in Latin America. More recently, the political scien-

tist and activist Jorge G. Castañeda called upon the Left in Latin America to abandon utopian goals and seek social reforms within "mixed" market economies. Until his resignation in 2003, he served as foreign minister of Mexico in President Fox's relatively market-friendly government.

Latin America illustrates the difficulty of establishing stable pluralist democracies in many parts of the developing world. Some authors have argued that its dominant political tradition is basically authoritarian and corporatist rather than competitively pluralist. They see the region's long tradition of centralized oligarchic governments, usually of the Right, as the result of an authoritarian "unitary" bias in the political culture. From this perspective, there would seem to be little hope for a lasting pluralist development, and the current trend toward democratization in much of Latin America would also appear unlikely to last. There are indeed signs pointing in that direction. Yet it is no mean accomplishment that one after the other dictatorship in the region has been replaced by an elected government. The demonstration effect of democratic governments in Spain and Portugal may well have played a role for the Latin American countries. Finally, the negative social, economic, and political experience with authoritarian rulers is one of the strongest cards held by their democratic successors.

In order to survive and develop, the democracies must meet the pragmatic test ("Does it work?"), by providing evidence of social and economic progress. They may yet turn out to have been short interludes between authoritarian regimes. Strife-torn Venezuela is a case in point. The even grimmer case of Argentina, which was one of the world's most prosperous countries at the beginning of the twentieth century, serves as a warning that both authoritarian-populist and neoliberal policy directions can end in social and political disaster. On the other hand, the new president of Brazil appears to have had a promising start. Right after winning office as a politician with left-wing credentials, he sought to calm the financial markets by announcing a policy orientation that seeks to strike a reasonable balance between the needs for greater social justice and efficiency.

In much of Latin America there seems to be a new questioning of the turn toward a greater emphasis on market economics that replaced the traditional commitment to strategies of statist interventions. It is too simple to explain this phenomenon as a product of impatience alone. A basic problem is that the benefits of economic growth do not "trickle down" as freely in practice as they do in economic theory. Instead, there are many instant losers in the economic dislocations that usually attend free market reforms.

There can be other serious problems as well, as shown in the attempt by former president Carlos Salinas of Mexico to move his country toward a more competitive form of market enterprise. His modernization strategy included Mexico's entry into the North American Free Trade Agreement (NAFTA) with the United States and Canada. In a time of enormous socioeconomic dislocations, however, Salinas showed considerable reluctance to move from an economic to a thorough political reform. Such a shift would have undermined the long-time hegemony of his own **Institutional Revolutionary Party** (PRI) and given new outlets for protest by self-perceived losers in the process. On the other hand, some observers criticized the market-oriented approach as too technocratic in its implicit assumption that economic modernization could be accomplished without a basic change of the political system. During his last year in office, Salinas was confronted by an armed peasant rebellion in the southern province of Chiapas, which gave voice to the demand for **land reform**

and economic redistribution. Mexican criticism of Salinas intensified after he left office in December 1994 and 3 months later sought political exile abroad. Soon after, some top Mexican officials and their associates were accused of having links to major drug traffickers with a sordid record of corruption and political assassination.

The successor to Salinas was elected in August 1994, in a competitive contest that was reported as not seriously distorted by fraud. The ruling party won with 51 percent of the vote. The PRI's first presidential candidate, Luis Donaldo Colosio, had been assassinated in the early part of the campaign. His place was taken by Ernesto Zedillo, an economist and former banker who fit the technocratic mold of recent Mexican leaders. As president, he continued the basic economic policies of Salinas, but Zedillo appeared far more willing to listen to demands for meaningful political reform as well. In other ways too, his governmental performance was remarkable. Shortly after he took office at the beginning of December 1994, the Mexican peso collapsed and brought the economy into disarray. A major factor was the country's huge trade deficit and the resultant loss of confidence in the peso. This setback could have paralyzed the new president. Instead, he dealt energetically and skillfully with the problem. By early 1997, the Mexican government was able to announce that it had paid back a huge relief loan provided by the United States. The overall economic prospect for the struggling country appeared to improve considerably.

The Mexican elections of July 1997 represented something of a political milestone in the country's recent history. In retrospect, they were an omen of things to come. The basic result was a considerable setback for the Institutional Revolutionary Party—an outcome that would have been unthinkable in earlier years. In the lower house of Congress, the two main opposition parties deprived the ruling PRI of its habitual controlling majority. They began to transform what had been regarded as a rubber stamp chamber into a political check on the president.

Some months before the new presidential elections were held in the summer of 2000, the PRI appeared to have recovered electoral support. Many observers thought it could once again win the country's highest political office, which the party had occupied for 72 years. This time, however, the election process appeared to be more democratic than in the past, beginning with a much-touted, first-ever selection of the PRI candidate in a contested "primary" race that differed from the traditional "handpicking" used in the past. Looked at more closely, the political reality was not so very different, for the party apparatus was geared to promote Francisco Labastida, who eventually won the nomination.

In the end, the PRI lost its grip on power when Labastida was defeated decisively by the charismatic businessman, Vicente Fox. The latter's center-right **National Action Party** (PAN) also became the leading force in both houses of Congress. As a result, Mexico has now experienced a major political turnover as the result of a general election. It is necessary to add that the great experiment with political and economic liberty in Mexico has coincided with political gridlock and economic setbacks, as analyzed in the article, "Mexico at an Impasse." Here, as in much of the rest of Latin America, the high expectations that accompanied long-awaited political changes have been followed by disappointments.

South Africa faces the monumental task of making democracy work in a multiracial society where the ruling white minority had never shared political or economic power with black Africans or Asian immigrants. A new transitional constitution was adopted in late 1993, followed by the first multiracial national elections in April 1994. Former president F. W. de Klerk may go into history as a late reformer, but his political work was bound to displease many members of South African society. If the reforms were judged to have gone much too far and too fast by many members of the privileged white minority, they clearly did not go sufficiently far or come quickly enough for many more people who demanded measures that went beyond formal racial equality.

Nelson Mandela, who succeeded de Klerk in the presidency, faced an even more difficult historical task. On the other hand, he possessed some strong political cards in addition to his undisputed leadership qualities. He represented the aspirations of a long-repressed majority, yet he was able to retain the respect of a large number of the white minority. It will be important that his successor continues to bridge the racial cleavages that otherwise threaten to ravage South African society. In an early interim constitution for post-apartheid South Africa, the reformers had sought political accommodation through an institutional form of power sharing. A new constitution, adopted in 1996, lays the foundation for creating simple majority-based governments that are bound to be dominated for now by the African National Congress (ANC), Mandela's political party. The new charter contains many guarantees of individual and group rights, but political prudence would seem to recommend some form of meaningful interracial coalition-building in South Africa's policy-making process.

The continued task of finding workable forms of power sharing is only one of many problems. In order for the democratic changes to have much meaning for the long-suppressed majority, it will be necessary to find policies that reduce the social and economic chasm separating the races. The politics of redistribution will be no simple or short-term task, and one may expect many conflicts in the future. There is a host of other social problems confronting the leaders of this multiracial democracy. Nevertheless, for the first time since the beginning of colonization, South Africa now offers some hope for an improvement in interracial relations.

In December 1997, Mandela stepped down from the leadership of the ANC as a first step in his eventual retirement from politics. His place was taken by Thabo Mbeki, the country's deputy president, who became president in June 1999, soon after the parliamentary elections in which the ANC won 266 of the 400 seats, or one short of a two-thirds majority. The new leaders appear to have done their best to provide for political continuity instead of a divisive power struggle after Mandela's departure. Mbeki (and everyone else) lacks Mandela's great moral authority. He is widely described as "businesslike" and competent, but Mbeki's dismissive and poorly informed views on the country's serious AIDS problem have caused international alarm. Recently Mandela has stepped back into the public limelight by announcing his intention to play a leading role in promoting policies that will seriously identify and confront this issue.

Nigeria will be another focus of attention. It covers a large area and has more than 100 million inhabitants, making it the most populous country in Africa. The former British colony has returned to electoral politics after 15 years of oppressive military rule that brought economic havoc to the potentially rich nation. The path toward democratic governance in this culturally diverse country will be long and difficult. Ethnic and religious conflicts threaten the emergence of both a well-functioning civil society and a stable form of representative government. Nigeria bears close watching by students of comparative politics.

China is the homeland of nearly 1.3 billion people, or about one-fifth of the world's population. Here the reform Communists, who took power after Mao Zedong's death in 1976, began much earlier than their Soviet counterparts to steer the country toward a relatively decontrolled market economy. They also introduced some political relaxation, by ending Mao's recurrent ideological campaigns to mobilize the masses. In their place came a domestic tranquillity such as China had not known for over half a century. But the regime encountered a basic dilemma: it wished to maintain tight controls over politics and society while freeing the economy. When a new openness began to emerge in Chinese society, comparable in some ways to the pluralism encouraged more actively by Gorbachev's glasnost policy of openness in the Soviet Union, it ran into determined opposition among hard-line Communist leaders. The aging reform leader, Deng Xiaoping, presided over a bloody crackdown on student demonstrations in Beijing's Tiananmen Square in May 1989. The regime has refused to let up on its tight political controls of society, but it continues to loosen the economic controls in the areas or zones designated for such reforms. In recent years, China has experienced a remarkable economic surge with growth rates that appear unmatched elsewhere in the world. A still unanswered question is whether the emerging market-oriented society can long coexist with a tightly controlled political system. In February 1997 Beijing announced the death of Deng Xiaoping.

Jiang Zemin, chosen by Deng as his successor in 1989, had been the country's president since 1993. As government and party leader, he appeared determined to continue the relatively pragmatic course adopted by Deng. It needs to be added that the regime has revived a hard line in dealing with real, imagined, or potential political dissidence, which includes some forms of religious expression. Moreover, there are familiar signs of social tension, as China's mixed economy leaves both "winners" and "losers" in its wake. With the country's undeniable problems and shortcomings, however, China's leaders have steered clear of the chaos that has plagued post-Soviet Russia. They seem determined to continue with their tight political controls, even as their economy becomes freer and more market-oriented. Some observers believe that the basic economic and political norms will eventually begin to converge, but that remains to be seen. A test case is the movement known as Falun Gong, which the ruling Communists see as a threat because of its effective organization and solidarity—qualities that no longer characterize the Communist Party to the same degree as earlier. It remains to be seen whether Hu Jintao, who was named party leader in the latter half of 2002, will turn out to move the country further in a technocratic direction, as many observers expect.

Globalization's Double Edge

Growing Market Offers Huge Potential—but Also Peril

By Robert J. Samuelson

Special to the International Herald Tribune

At the edge of a new century, globalization is a double-edged sword: a powerful vehicle that raises economic growth, spreads new technology and increases living standards in rich and poor countries alike, but also an immensely controversial process that assaults national sovereignty, erodes local culture and tradition and threatens economic and social instability.

A daunting question of the 21st century is whether nations will control this great upheaval or whether it will come to control them.

In some respects globalization is merely a trendy word for an old process. What we call the market is simply the joining of buyers and sellers, producers and consumers and savers and investors. Economic history consists largely of the story of the market's expansion: from farm to town, from region to nation and from nation to nation. In the 20th century, the Depression and two world wars retarded the market's growth. But after World War II ended, it reaccelerated, driven by political pressures and better technology.

The Cold War, from the late 1940s through the 1980s, caused the United States to champion trade liberalization and economic growth as a way of combating communism. A succession of major trade negotiations reduced average tariffs in industrialized countries to about 5 percent in 1990 from about 40 percent in 1946.

After two world wars, Europeans saw economic unification as an antidote to deadly nationalism. Technology complemented politics. Even before the Internet, declining costs for communication and transportation—from jet planes, better un-

dersea telephone cables and satellites—favored more global commerce. By the early 1990s, world exports (after adjusting for inflation) were nearly 10 times higher than they had been four decades earlier.

Globalization continues this process but also departs from it in at least one critical respect. Until recently, countries were viewed as distinct economic entities, connected mainly by trade. Now, this is becoming less true. Companies and financial markets increasingly disregard national borders when making production, marketing and investment decisions.

As recently as 1990, governments either individually or through such multilateral institutions as the World Bank provided half the loans and credits to 29 major developing countries (including Brazil, China, India, South Korea and Mexico), according to the Institute for International Finance, a banking industry research group in Washington.

A decade later, even after Asia's 1997–98 financial crisis, private capital flows dwarf governmental flows. In 1999, private flows (bank loans, bond financing, equity investment in local stock markets and direct investment by multinational companies) totaled an estimated $136 billion to these 29 countries, compared with government capital flows of $22 billion, according to the institute.

Meanwhile, multinational companies have gone on an international acquisition binge. In the first half of 1999 alone, the value of new cross-border mergers and acquisitions passed $500 billion in both advanced and developing countries.

The total roughly matched the amount for all 1998 ($544 billion) and was almost

seven times larger than the 1991 levels ($85 billion), according to the World Investment Report by the United Nations. The recent takeover struggle between British and German wireless giants—Vodafone AirTouch PLC and Mannesmann AG—is exceptional only for its size and bitterness.

Behind the merger boom lies the growing corporate conviction that many markets have become truly global. By trying to maximize their presence in as many nations as possible, companies seek to achieve economies of scale—that is, to lower costs through higher sales and production volumes—and to stay abreast of technological changes that can now occur almost anywhere.

In addition, companies increasingly organize production globally, dividing product design, component manufacturing and final assembly among many countries.

But it is not just multinational companies, seeking bigger sales and profits, that drive globalization. Governments do, too. In Europe, the relentless pursuit of the "single market" is one indicator. This reflects a widespread recognition that European companies will be hardpressed to compete in global markets if their local operations are hamstrung by fragmented national markets.

Among poorer countries, the best sign of support is the clamor to get into the World Trade Organization. Since 1995, seven countries—Bulgaria, Ecuador, Estonia, Kyrgyzstan, Latvia, Mongolia and Panama—have joined. And 32 (the largest being China) are seeking membership. There is a belief that global trade and investment can aid economic development by providing new products, technologies and management skills.

It's no myth. Countries succeed or fail mainly based on their own workers, investment and government policies. But engaging the wider world economy can help.

Consider Asia. Despite its financial crisis, rapid trade expansion and economic growth sharply cut the number of the desperately poor. From 1987 to 1998, those in the region, including China, with incomes of $1 or less a day dropped to 15 percent from 27 percent of the population, the World Bank estimates.

Meanwhile, Latin America and sub-Saharan Africa—whose embrace of the world economy has been late or limited—fared much less well. In Africa, for example, the World Bank reckons that 46 percent of the population lived on less than $1 a day in 1998, exactly what the percentage was in 1987.

Well, if globalization is so good, why is it also so risky? The answer is that two problems could neutralize its potential benefits.

The first is economic instability. The global economy may be prone to harsher boom-bust cycles than national economies individually. The theory that international trade and investment raise living standards works only if investment funds are well used and if trade flows do not become too lopsided.

The Asian financial crisis raised questions on both counts. In the early 1990s, most of Asia thrived because it received vast flows of foreign capital as bank loans, direct investment in factories or stock-market investment in local companies.

The ensuing spending boom in turn aided Europe, Japan and the United States by increasing imports from them. Then the boom abruptly halted in mid-1997 when it became apparent that as a result of "crony capitalism," inept government investment policies and excess optimism, much of the investment had been wasted on unneeded factories, office buildings and apartments.

What prevented the Asian crisis from becoming a full-scale global economic downturn has been the astonishing U.S. economy.

Its relentless growth helped the rest of the world by purchasing more and more of their exports. Since 1996, the U.S. current-account deficit in its balance of payments, the broadest measure of the country's international trade, has more than doubled, from $129 billion to an estimated total of $330 billion in 1999.

The world economy, as Treasury Secretary Lawrence Summers has repeatedly said, has been flying on one engine. The trouble is, as Mr. Summers has also warned, this cannot go on forever.

The great danger is that the world has become too dependent on American prosperity and that a slowdown or recession reflecting a decline in the stock market, a loss of consumer confidence or higher interest rates might snowball into a international slump.

By economic forecasts, Europe and Japan are going to do better. In 2000, the European Union's gross domestic product will grow 2.8 percent, up from 2.1 percent in 1999, according to projections by the Organization for Economic Cooperation and Development in Paris.

Japan is projected to grow 1.4 percent, the same as the OECD is predicting for 1999 but a big improvement from the 2.8 percent drop in 1998. If the forecasts materialize—and the OECD's growth estimates for Japan exceed most private forecasts—they will restore some balance to the world economy and relieve fears of a global recession.

Asia and Latin America can continue to recover without relying solely on exports to the United States. But until that happens, no one can be certain that Asia's financial crisis has truly ended. It remains possible that abrupt surges of global capital, first moving into Asia and then out, will have caused, with some delay, a larger instability.

Globalization's other problem is political, cultural and social. People feel threatened by any kind of economic change—and change from abroad naturally seems especially alien and menacing.

The street protesters at the Seattle meeting of the World Trade Organization in early December may have lacked a common agenda or even a coherent case against trade. But they accurately reflected the anxiety and anger that globalization often inspires. So do European fears of genetically modified food or nationalistic opposition to cross-border mergers.

What is local and familiar is suddenly being replaced or assaulted by something that is foreign and unfamiliar. And even if trade helps most people, it will usually create some losers. In the United States, workers in some high-cost industries—steel and autos, most conspicuously—suffered from intensified import competition.

Just because globalization is largely spontaneous—propelled by better communications and transportation—does not mean that it is inevitable or completely irreversible. Governments can, in subtle and not-so-subtle ways, shield local industries and workers against imports or discriminate against foreign investors. If only a few countries do, their actions will not matter much.

Global capital and trade will go where they are most welcome and productive. Indeed, it is precisely this logic that has persuaded so many countries to accept globalization. If they don't, someone else will. Judged by their behavior, most governments believe they have more to gain than to lose.

But this does not mean that a powerful popular backlash, with unpredictable consequences, is not possible. In a global recession, too many sellers will be chasing too few buyers. A plausible presumption is that practical politicians would try to protect their constituents from global gluts. If too many countries did, globalization could implode.

It's a scary prospect. Economic interdependence cuts both ways. Under favorable conditions, it helps everyone; under unfavorable conditions, it hurts everyone. Globalization's promise may exceed its peril but the peril is still real. Both await the new century. One of the great dramas will be to see which prevails.

From the *International Herald Tribune*, January 4, 2000, pp. 1, 3. © 2000 by Robert J. Samuelson. Reprinted by permission.

Mexico at an Impasse

M. Delal Baer

THE EXPECTATIONS REVOLUTION

THE JULY 2000 DEFEAT of Mexico's Institutional Revolutionary Party (PRI) after more than 70 years of rule sparked a revolution in expectations. There were celebrations in the streets, glowing editorials in foreign newspapers, and expressions of undiluted optimism in investment and policy circles. Newly elected president Vicente Fox projected a triumphant image of strength and confidence that inflated hopes at home and abroad: private investment would flood in, the rule of law would prevail, the sins of the past would be punished, and the U.S.–Mexico relationship would flower. More profoundly, Mexico would elude its existential condition as an underdeveloped nation.

Three years into Mexico's democratic transition, few of these dreams have been realized. Mexican politics are more democratic but less governable and are suffering from gridlock between the executive and legislative branches. The economy is stable, but growth and competitiveness are lagging as the next generation of reforms—tax, energy, and labor—falls prey to partisan bickering in Mexico's Congress. And the friendship between Fox and President George W. Bush has cooled over differences about immigration and policy toward Iraq. Mexico shows no signs of an imminent crisis, but its triple political, economic, and diplomatic impasse is taking a toll. The price of unreasonably high expectations has been premature disillusionment. A breakthrough in at least one area must come fairly soon—lest Mexico's grant experiment with economic and political liberty fail to fulfill its potential.

UNGOVERNABLE DEMOCRACY

THE PRINCIPAL CONCERN of Mexico's political elite today is how to build governing majorities and achieve consensus. After three years of stalemate in Congress, there is debate over whether Mexico's political paralysis is the result of a constitutional structure that makes it inherently ungovernable or of weak leadership on the part of President Fox. The answer to this question is not insignificant. If the logjam is due to weak leadership, the presidential elections of 2006 might resolve the problem. If the logjam,

however, is structural in nature, it will be much more difficult to overcome.

Fox's leadership style is unconventional and ideologically heterogeneous. Some commentators find him refreshing and authentic, whereas others complain that he has not established clear priorities or consistent legislative strategies. But whatever Fox's shortcomings, it is clear that any leader, no matter how gifted, would have struggled with the challenge of assuming the presidency at Mexico's singular moment of regime change. Fox won only 42.5 percent of the vote in the 2000 elections, and his National Action Party (PAN) controls just 30 percent of seats in the lower house of Congress (the Chamber of Deputies) and 38 percent in the Senate. In most instances of regime change, the old regime is defeated and dismantled definitively. In Mexico, the PRI was defeated but far from dismantled: it remains ensconced in Congress as a legitimate opposition party.

Many Mexicans believe that a democratic transition must include a punitive settling of accounts with the PRI. As a result, Fox has found himself on the horns of a dilemma: he needs a juicy corruption case from the PRI era to prosecute, but he also needs the PRI's support to form congressional majorities. Fox has failed to reconcile these competing demands. His cabinet is divided between pragmatists who see accommodation with the PRI as inescapable and confrontationists who think that the president's legitimacy depends on destroying the PRI, root and branch. Fox has oscillated between these two approaches, launching vituperative attacks on the PRI one day and calling for congressional unity the next. The result has been stalemate: the government launched investigations of the PRI that were aggressive enough to undermine the chance of legislative cooperation but not decisive enough to satisfy the appetite for vengeance.

Striking a balance between governability and historical reckoning is most difficult during the early years of a democratic transition, as was the case in Argentina and Chile. Some will inevitably complain that Mexico's democratic transition did not settle accounts in any spectacular fashion, despite the fact that a special prosecutor is investigating former President Luis Echeverría for his alleged role in the 1968 Tlatelolco student massacre. Others will argue that the PRI never committed human rights abuses on the scale of Chile's Augusto Pinochet or Argentina's Jorge Rafael Videla, making an expurgation of past sins less necessary. But what is most important is that the first three years of Mexico's transition have not seen a single serious threat to democracy. This success speaks well of both President Fox, who has emphasized stability, and the PRI, which accepted its defeat with at least a modicum of grace. To the extent that the stalemate of the past three years is attributable to the unique dilemma of regime change, it is a small price to pay for democratic survival. When such one-time tensions have faded, Mexico's parties may be able to put aside the past and cooperate on national business.

Today's gridlock, however, also stems from structural flaws that make Mexico particularly susceptible to the frustrations of a divided government and a limited presidency. Traditionally, governability was ensured only by the PRI's ability to deliver overwhelming majorities in both houses of Congress, as the politician Manuel Camacho has noted. There is no constitutional mechanism to guarantee that a president can successfully govern in the face of an opposition Congress. Without a majority in either house, therefore, the Fox presidency was instantly cut down to size by PRI legislators more than willing to exercise the constitutional prerogatives accorded to them in their new role as the opposition (the PRI's Senate leader recently declared that his party would govern from Congress).

It is improbable that any Mexican political party will be able to reconstruct the electoral majorities formerly enjoyed by the PRI. The historic 2000 elections did not produce realignment in favor of the PAN, nor did the 2003 midterm elections result in a PRI majority in Congress. Instead, three major parties of roughly equal strength vie for dominance: the PRI, the PAN, and the left-wing Democratic Revolutionary Party (PRD). Each party, moreover, is riven by personal and ideological faults that undermine the negotiating capacity of party leaders in Congress. The system is further divided by three small parties that survive thanks mostly to the use of proportional representation (based on a party's percentage of the national vote tally) to elect a portion of Congress.

Looking ahead to the 2006 presidential election, one can envision a scenario similar to that of the 2000 election: weak parties and strong candidates who lack electoral coattails. Mexico City Mayor Andres Manuel Lopez Obrador, one of the country's most popular potential presidential candidates, consistently polls in the neighborhood of 52 percent even though his party, the PRD, has never won more than 25 percent of the vote in a national election. In the event that a ticket-splitting Mexican electorate gives him a victory but only 17 percent of Congress to his party, forming a governing alliance would be immensely difficult. Similarly, a PRI or PAN candidate could win a weak victory in the presidential race while his or her party achieved a tepid plurality in Congress.

Some analysts have advocated a major constitutional overhaul to install a parliamentary regime and guarantee majority support for the executive. But many Mexicans, understandably disconcerted by the impasse between the president and the Congress and fearful for the viability of democracy, instead look back nostalgically on the days of a strong president. Accustomed to a pyramidal presidency so powerful that it was once described as a six-year Aztec monarchy, they are bewildered by this upside-down world. But the possibility of restoring an all-powerful presidency is remote, and reengineering the Mexican constitution to implant a parliamentary system is similarly unlikely.

Disillusionment with the political parties may account for historically low voter turnout (42 percent) in the 2003 midterm elections and could cause the electorate to seek out more charismatic figures. Jorge Castañeda, formerly Fox's foreign minister, launched an exploratory bid for the presidency on this logic, arguing that Mexican voters go to the polls only when presented with a charismatic individual who offers hope of change. As one senior Mexican diplomat has wryly commented, "In Mexico we have egos, not institutions." This trend toward personalism and weak parties may be nothing to worry about. Mexico might simply go the way of the United States: weak but persistent parties that field strong candidates. In a more ominous scenario, however, the decay of party institutions and congressional gridlock could restore the authoritarian temptation and pave the way for wild-card leadership.

Gridlock could restore the authoritarian temptation.

Under current conditions, there are only two ways to create majorities in Mexico: alliance building or modest political reform aimed at consolidating the party system. Without strong parties that can achieve electoral majorities across the board, the negotiating skills of future presidents will be crucial. Mexican political culture has little experience with compromise, and the road to democracy has been paved with insult and calumny. Give-and-take is central to a well-functioning democracy, but the spirit of retribution has bogged down relations between Fox and the PRI-dominated legislature. In time, the public may blame all parties for such gridlock, thereby creating incentives to compromise. The elimination of proportional representation, meanwhile, would encourage the gradual consolidation of the party system. Instituting campaign finance reform, congressional reelection, and "second round" provisions in presidential elections (to guarantee majority victories) would further enhance party legitimacy.

If there is hope for ending gridlock in the remaining three years of the Fox administration, it stems from the fact that all three major parties have a shot at winning the presidency in 2006. None wishes to inherit an ungovernable nation, and none wishes to be accused of obstructionism. The hunger for power, therefore, may encourage a flurry of congressional activity toward the end of Fox's tenure.

Mexican democracy is not fated to be dysfunctional. But without some reform, it may end up in a peculiar state of institutional limbo and semipermanent gridlock: a constitutionally mandated presidential system that operates more like a majority-less parliamentary system.

THE COMPETITIVENESS DEFICIT

THE 2000 PRESIDENTIAL ELECTION was the first in close to 30 years to take place unaccompanied by a massive devaluation of the Mexican peso—thanks to former President Ernesto Zedillo's commitment to fiscal discipline and a free-floating currency. Three years later, Mexican democracy has passed an important economic test: both Congress and President Fox have resisted the temptation to engage in deficit spending and foreign borrowing in the face of a stubborn, painful recession. In fact, Fox's economic team has achieved unprecedented price and monetary stability—treasury bond rates are below five percent, and inflation is around four percent. Meanwhile, the federal deficit has fallen to less than one percent of GDP, foreign debt represents less than 20 percent of GDP, and Mexico's balance of trade is stable. Macroeconomic stability has permitted real wages to rise for three consecutive years, and, if growth returns in a low-inflation environment, Mexico will increase its per capita GDP for the first time in nearly 30 years.

In the meantime, however, Mexico is caught in a grinding stagnation that has led to a net loss of 2.1 million jobs, average GDP growth of less than one percent in the first three years of the Fox administration, and a surge in illegal immigration to the United States. The onset of recession in the United States hit Mexico hard, especially in the manufacturing sector. But there are signs that the Mexican recession is the result of a growing competitiveness deficit, not simply a matter of bad luck to be solved by an uptick in the U.S. economy. Mexico faces pressures from Chinese exports in the U.S. market and from foreign assembly plants moving to the Caribbean, China, and other Latin American nations.

The current congressional impasse over economic reform is especially damaging in this context. The stalemate is not simply partisanship run amok; it is a symptom of regime change, of fundamental disagreement over how much to preserve from the older order. Many of Mexico's market reforms were imposed from above by the PRI's ruling technocracy in the 1990s. Ironically, opposition to them now comes not from President Fox and the PAN but from the PRI itself—the continuation of a long-simmering conflict within the party that has erupted into an open rebellion since the PRI lost the presidency. (Many PRI-istas, however, have started to push for early passage of some reforms to ease the task should the party recapture the presidency in 2006.) Although there is a cost to delaying reform, Mexico does need time to build a foundation of democratic support for its market economy. Competitiveness-enhancing reforms run headlong into taboos and have steep political costs.

Energy policy provides a good example of this deadlock. Energy has long served as a sacred symbol of Mexican sovereignty, and the constitution explicitly prohibits private ownership in energy sectors, even though the government does not have sufficient resources to finance its own oil and natural gas exploration. As a result, cheap energy does not offer the natural advantage to the Mexican economy that it should. Electricity costs there are, on average, higher than those in the United States, and there are frequent energy shortages that, among other things, keep investment away from many northern industrial parks. Although Mexico sits on one of the world's largest natural gas reserves, it has to import natural gas from the United States. (In fact, federal efforts to develop privately run, competitively priced electrical capacity have slowed to a crawl due to scarce gas supplies.) "A Mexican businessman can go to Texas and invest in natural gas production to sell to Mexico, but that businessman is unable to do the same at home in Mexico," one economic official has scoffed. Still, mustering the two-thirds congressional majority needed to change the constitution and liberalize the energy sector is a daunting task.

Reform of the judicial system, another crucial step in improving Mexico's economic situation, will not be easy either. Foreign investors are wary of wobbly courts (plagued by frivolous litigation and corrupt judges) and the capriciousness of the rule of law. The Dutch financial services company ING has been sued three times in three separate criminal courts for alleged underpayment on an insurance policy held by Fertinal, a nearly bankrupt company hoping to save itself with a huge reward. Senior ING executives have been arbitrarily jailed, and ING even saw its assets frozen on the order of a Mexico City court—a move that sent chills through the foreign financial community.

Raising taxes, also a necessary reform, is another political bombshell. Mexico's tax collection rate hovers around 11 percent of GDP—the lowest among the members of the Organization for Economic Cooperation and Development, which average collection rates of almost 27 percent. Future competitiveness depends on long-term investment in physical infrastructure and human capital, and Mexico's efforts in these areas will lag so long as its tax collection rate remains so low. Windfall resources from privatization and high oil prices have made it possible to postpone tax reform over the past two decades, but the moment of truth is fast approaching. Mexico is running out of public companies to privatize, oil prices are falling, and revenues derived from commercial tariffs have declined with the advent of free trade.

A coming demographic shift will only exacerbate these spending pressures. Although Mexico is typically considered a young country, the percentage of the population aged 65 and over is projected to increase to 13 percent in 2030 and to almost 25 percent by 2050 (from a low of 2.6 percent in 1930). In absolute terms, this means that there will be 17 million people older than 65 in 2030 and more than 30 million in 2050. The implications of this shift for health and pension costs are staggering. If Mexico cannot soon achieve economic modernity and tax efficiency, it will face a social catastrophe. As Richard Jackson, director of the Global Aging Initiative, puts it, Mexico must grow rich before it grows old.

Mexico has made enormous strides toward fiscal and monetary stability, but its economy cannot afford to idle while the rest of the world speeds ahead. Stalled reforms have dampened investor enthusiasm, costing Mexico $5 billion in direct foreign investment (which fell from $16 billion in 2000 to $11 billion in 2002). The failure to generate the more than one million jobs needed for new entrants into the labor market, meanwhile, could thrust hundreds of thousands of Mexicans out of their homes and toward the U.S. border. Still, some long-term investors are betting that the backlash against liberalization will fade as the wheels of generational change turn. Youthful Mexican politicians from all parties express positive convictions about the need for continued economic opening. Mexico may be closer than it seems to a true consensus on an open economy, but a breakthrough must occur soon if the competitiveness deficit is to be eliminated and the hemorrhage of Mexicans into the United States stanched.

BEYOND NAFTA

MEXICO'S DEMOCRATIC REVOLUTION raised hopes of a revolution in U.S.-Mexican relations. But ever since the North American Free Trade Agreement went into effect in 1994, the two countries have been searching for the next great advance in bilateral relations. Jorge Castaneda proposed transforming NAFTA into a European-style "North American Community," complete with free movement of labor and social development funds for poorer nations. Fox, enamored of Europe's success in helping to develop the formerly poor countries of Spain and Portugal, hoped that the United States might be willing to do the same for Mexico. He also asked that the Bush administration provide de jure recognition of the de facto residence of millions of Mexicans working illegally in the United States, the first step toward a free labor market.

A Mexican foreign policy that demanded sizeable amounts of aid and the legalization of millions of immigrants, however, was the last thing the Bush administration had expected. Washington tends to associate the European model with overregulation and excessive supranatural bureaucracy, and Mexico underestimated U.S. sensitivity to job competition and downward pressure on

wages in the face of looming recession. The free movement of labor remains unrealistic as long as Mexican wages are a fraction of wages in the United States. Plenty of U.S. policymakers remember that the last amnesty offered by Congress—the Simpson-Rodino Immigration Reform and Control Act of 1986—resulted in ever-larger waves of illegal immigration and undermined the credibility of U.S. law enforcement. Ultimately, the events of September 11 allowed the White House to gracefully sidestep the inconvenient requests of its southern neighbor.

Such setbacks do not mean that integration cannot continue or that nothing has been accomplished. Mexico has successfully broadened U.S. focus beyond its prior preoccupation with drug trafficking (thanks in part to the progress it has made in arresting cartel leaders, which allowed the U.S. Congress to modify its controversial certification process). The Partnership for Prosperity, a creative initiative launched by Bush and Fox in September 2001 to foster investment in Mexico's underdeveloped regions, has brought the Overseas Private Investment Corporation and the Peace Corps to Mexico for the first time. There is hope for coordination in developing border infrastructure and North American standards and certification procedures. Even in immigration policy, incremental progress is possible if care is taken to protect certain sensitive service and manufacturing sectors.

U.S.-Mexican relations are tied up in knots: each nation expects the impossible of the other.

Three lessons of enduring importance emerge from the experience of Bush and Fox thus far. The first is that it does not pay to hinge the success of the entire relationship on a single issue, as Mexico did when it defined success exclusively in terms of a comprehensive immigration accord. The second is the need for prior agreement when one partner seeks a sea change in relations. When the Fox administration announced its desire for changes in U.S. immigration policy without any prior negotiation, it created expectations that plague the relationship to this day. The third lesson is that issue linkage can prove fatal for bilateral harmony. With such a complex bilateral agenda, linking issues allows a fire in one area to spread to others, leading to multiple breakdowns in bilateral relations. Mexico tried to link the entire agenda to immigration; the United States has done the same with Iraq. As a result, U.S.-Mexican relations are tied up in knots: each nation expects the impossible of the other.

The next great shift in bilateral relations is within sight, but it awaits a more propitious moment. The United States and Mexico must first erect a new North American security architecture. Protection of the North American perimeter is essential to the security of both nations. (Consider the effects on Mexico of a contagious biological attack on Los Angeles or Dallas, or the economic costs should a terrorist attack on the United States be launched from Mexico.) Nonetheless, they have had no formal defense relations since the end of World War II, and, given Mexico's recent diplomatic choices, there is little chance that a strategic alliance will be forged in the short term. A few days before the first anniversary of September 11, Mexico withdrew from the Rio Pact, the western hemisphere equivalent of the NATO charter's provisions for collective self-defense. This move was a stunning blow from a neighbor presumed to be a friend. Mexico had taken to lambasting the pact as a militaristic relic of the Cold War, and the United States never actually expected that Mexican troops would participate in a Rio Pact—sponsored action. Nonetheless, Washington interpreted Mexico's withdrawal as a sign that the United States, in its darkest hour, could not expect even symbolic solidarity. So crippled was Mexico by its historic insecurity that, when confronted with the diplomatic challenges of September 11, it could not see the genuine vulnerability of its northern neighbor, let alone respond compassionately, without equating compassion with subordination.

Mexico's position in the run-up to the war on Iraq was also troubling. Its decision not to support the U.S. position can be attributed to domestic opposition and pressure from other allies, but it also had a tendency to indulge in what one senior U.S. official described as diplomatic "dancing in the end zone." Mexico may feel the need to burnish its anti-American credentials to play to a home audience upset by the lack of a new immigration accord. The result, however, has been a setback in bilateral relations.

Fortunately, U.S.-Mexican security cooperation is in better shape than such symbolic actions indicate. Mexico has pursued what one Mexican diplomat calls a "Janus-faced" policy: privately working to secure borders while publicly declaring diplomatic distance and issuing stern demands for immigration reform. In reality, a quiet revolution has begun. Both countries have stepped up efforts to secure the North American perimeter, sharing sensitive intelligence and jointly monitoring shared airspace. If there is anything to criticize, it is that the United States has not been quick enough to give Mexico the resources and technology it needs to upgrade its security infrastructure. Washington should grant Mexico observer status in the North American Aerospace Defense Command (NORAD, currently run with Canada's help) and create a joint bioterrorism task force to coordinate the epidemiological efforts and border health resources of both countries. Ultimately, the goal should be to build the institutional architecture necessary to turn bilateral relations into a strategic partnership, complementing the economic partnership established by NAFTA.

STOPPING THE DRIFT

THERE IS FRUSTRATINGLY LITTLE that the United States can do to enhance Mexico's economic competitiveness or to consolidate Mexican democracy; these are issues that Mexico must resolve on its own. But Washington can and should stop the drift in bilateral relations. The Bush administration must put Mexico back on its priority list, despite its recent disappointment with Mexican foreign policy.

President Bush should renew his commitment to the Partnership for Prosperity by naming a special envoy to marshal private investors and philanthropic interest to the high-migration regions of Mexico. Currently, less than one percent of foreign investment goes to rural Mexico; even a modest increase would make a meaningful difference for the almost 25 million Mexicans who live in these areas. The partnership is a bright spot in bilateral relations, but even it runs the risk of getting lost in the shuffle.

Washington should also take action on immigration policy, even though the interests of Mexico and the United States are not always perfectly aligned. Policymakers should begin with the agricultural sector, in which Mexican and U.S. workers do not compete. Mexican farm laborers should not have to face death in the desert to perform a vital function for the U.S. economy. Rather than wait for Congress to act on the politically thorny issue of immigration, Bush could increase the number of visas issued through the already existing agricultural worker program. The United States should also improve the consular services offered by its embassy in Mexico City. Consular and customs officers are the face of the United States to millions of Mexicans; too often, those faces are scowling and unfriendly, and demand for consular services far outstrips capacity. An infusion of money is necessary to increase the number and quality of officers.

As for Mexico, there is no better way to win the affection of the United States than to make it feel that it has a true partner in matters of mutual defense. Mexico should engage the security issue head-on as an equal partner, without hiding behind multilateral distractions and anachronistic shibboleths about losing national sovereignty.

Such steps, modest but not insignificant, will benefit both nations. The next three years will determine the outcome of Mexico's historic transition. Mexico and the United States, out of self-interest and mutual concern, must work to make the most of them.

M. DELAL BAER is Director of the Mexico Project at the Center for Strategic and International Studies and editor of *The NAFTA Debate*.

SOUTH AFRICA: DEMOCRACY WITHOUT THE PEOPLE?

Robert Mattes

Perhaps more than any other democratizing country, South Africa generates widely differing assessments of the present state and likely future prospects of its democracy. If one takes the long view—comparing South Africa today to where it was just 12 years ago—it is difficult not to be enthusiastic about its accomplishments and its future. South Africa successfully emerged from the shadow of apparently irreconcilable conflict and unavoidable racial civil war to create a common nation. It has negotiated two democratic constitutions and has held four successful nationwide elections for national and local government. On the economic front, it has avoided the triple-digit inflation that many feared would accompany a populist economic strategy of redistribution and government intervention. It has stabilized the expanding debt and reversed the double-digit inflation inherited from the apartheid-era government. There have been impressive gains in employment opportunities and income for the growing black middle class, and poor blacks have seen unprecedented improvements in access to basic necessities.

Yet if one looks at South Africa's new democracy in a comparative perspective, one's enthusiasm is greatly tempered, if not altogether removed. Crossnational analysis has highlighted three broad sets of factors crucial to democratic consolidation: a growing economy that steadily reduces inequality; stable and predictable political institutions; and a supportive political culture. In terms of these factors, an analysis of South Africa yields, at best, some reasons for guarded optimism and, at worst, many grounds for serious concern.

In each area, today's South Africa presents a paradox. In terms of political culture, South African society played a key role in achieving democracy through its widespread opposition to the apartheid regime. The country's numerous and diverse civil society organizations range from community grassroots groups to national trade unions and nongovernmental organizations. Yet citizens are not particularly supportive of democratic rule and now display low levels of community and political participation. Economically, macroeconomic stability, fiscal discipline, and low inflation sit alongside weak business confidence, low growth, massive unemployment, and rising intraracial inequality. Politically, an internationally praised constitution designed to promote multiparty competition and individual rights is overshadowed by one-party dominance and limited governmental accountability. Thus, seven years into its new dispensation, South Africa's democracy in form appears to be relatively healthy, but in substance shows signs of early decay.

Economic Development

South Africa's economic policy makers should be proud of a number of accomplishments. The national budget deficit has shrunk from 8 percent to around 2 percent of GDP. Public and private affirmative-action initiatives in education, business ownership, and hiring have created a sizeable black middle class.[1] Since 1995, more than a million low-cost houses have been built, and the poor now have access to free medicine and more than 700 additional healthcare clinics. More than 5 million needy children now get a fifth to a quarter of their daily nutritional needs through school-based programs. More than 2 million people have received access to electricity and 7 million to water.[2] Relatively low inflation, around 6 percent, means that working South Africans are able to keep up with the cost of living.

Yet the sluggish economy has actually shed 500,000 formal jobs over this period and deprived hundreds of thousands of households of the income needed to make ends meet. Broadly defined, unemployment now stands at 36 percent.[3] A lack of business confidence has stifled both domestic and foreign investment, thereby hampering growth. While growth has been running at approximately 3 percent annually since 1995, the government sees growth of 6 to 7 percent as a prerequisite to cutting unemployment and reducing inequality.

Interracial inequalities have been reduced as a result of increasing black incomes and the redistributive effects of government spending, but inequality within all race groups has increased. Among blacks the top one-fifth of all households have made impressive strides while the bottom two-fifths have moved backwards.[4]

Recently, a new specter has appeared on the economic horizon. In its September 1999 decision to move forward with a R29.9 billion package of arms purchases, the government appears to have ignored internal feasibility studies warning that any depreciation of the currency could increase cost significantly. This has in fact happened, and the full costs of the deal are now estimated to be at least R50 billion. Indeed, the costs of this deal threaten to spiral out of control and consume any future funds the government had intended for increased poverty alleviation.

Disappointing Institutions

South Africa's 1996 Constitution is the darling of both liberals and social democrats around the world. Widely seen as a "state of the art" document, it contains a wide array of classic political and socioeconomic rights, institutional innovations such as the National Council of Provinces, a range of independent watchdog agencies and commissions, and an activist Constitutional Court. The electoral system (pure proportional representation with no thresholds) has induced virtually all parts of political society to play the electoral game and has allowed the representation of a wide range of organized tendencies. Yet the constitutional framework is significantly flawed in several respects, particularly with regard to the interaction among party politics, voter representation, and legislative-executive relations.

First of all, various features of the Constitution limit voters' control over their elected representatives. While the electoral system provides for high degrees of "collective representation" (the overall balance among parties mirrors aggregate election results) and "descriptive representation" (the legislature tends to look like the electorate in terms of ideology, race, and ethnicity), it has created no direct link between legislators and voters. Constitutional provisions also eject from Parliament any member who leaves or is forced out of a political party, further reducing any incentive for MPs to represent public opinions running counter to the party line.

In addition, the Constitution does little to effect the separation of powers between the legislature and the executive; other than a formal vote of no confidence, few mechanisms exist with which the legislature may check executive action. Any rigorous parliamentary oversight by majority-party MPs places them in the difficult position of criticizing senior party leaders, who could eject them from the party and hence from Parliament. This ability to substitute loyal MPs for disloyal ones also potentially enables the governing party to preclude any vote of no confidence.

A minimalist theory of democracy would argue that, even with this constitutional framework, sufficient public influence over government can still be secured simply by holding regular free and fair elections. The threat of the next election forces the ruling party to "anticipate the voters' reactions" to current policy decisions and thus brings about an acceptable level of popular control and accountability. In South Africa, however, what is in theory a multiparty system is in fact completely dominated by one party. The ruling African National Congress (ANC) won 66 percent of the vote in 2000, up 4 percent from 1994, and is just one seat shy of the two-thirds majority necessary to amend the Constitution unilaterally. It also is the majority party in seven of the nine provincial governments—enjoying overwhelming dominance in at least five—and has decisive control in five of the country's six largest city governments. Part of this dominance is due to positive voter evaluations of its performance, but part of it is also thanks to the substantial number of dissatisfied black voters who do not identify with the ANC yet have thoroughly negative views of virtually all other parties.[5] For all intents and purposes, the ANC has few reasons to worry about future voter reactions to its current decisions.

Over the past five years, this constitutional and electoral landscape has resulted in several worrisome tendencies. First of all, there has been a trend toward centralism within the ANC. National party structures have increasingly extended their powers at the provincial and local levels; candidates for provincial premierships and local mayoralties are now nominated by a central committee rather than by provincial or local branches. Several provincial party structures have simply been dissolved and reformed by the national party, ostensibly because of "disunity" or "ill discipline," but critics have viewed these actions as attempts to head off grassroots movements critical of the president. The national party machinery has also deposed several provincial premiers, some of whom have been popular leaders widely seen as future challengers for party leadership.

The ANC's ability to eject people from Parliament by expelling them from the party was underscored in 1997 when it jettisoned one of its most popular figures, Bantu Holomisa, because he had publicly accused a sitting cabinet minister and former Bantustan ruler of apartheid-era corruption. Indeed, imposing party discipline has been an increasing preoccupation. At a 2000 national party meeting, Secretary-General Kgalema Motlanthe reminded members that "the principles of democratic centralism still guided party structures." New ANC members must promise to combat "any tendency toward disruption or factionalism."[6] Moreover, the interval between party conferences has been extended from three years to five, thereby limiting opportunities for the rank and file to elect senior party organs.

Very recently, the ANC suddenly dropped its steadfast opposition to legislators crossing the floor. This shift was prompted by a conflict that emerged between the key partners of the main opposition coalition, the Democratic Alliance (DA). As a result, the New National Party (the NNP is the direct heir of the architects of apartheid) decided to exit the coalition and enter into talks with the ANC. The ANC changed its position principally to enable NNP Cape Town city councilors to leave the DA and cross into an alliance with the ANC, thus giving it control of the only city government it did not already dominate. As this article went to press, it has tabled legislation that would allow the president to declare specific windows of time in which legislators at national, provincial, and municipal levels could cross the floor to new or existing parties and still keep their seats.[7] Apart from the naked political opportunism exhibited by these events, the ANC has yet to explain how it can allow members to switch parties and still observe the constitutional requirement that election results must result in proportional representation.

The increasing tendency of ANC central party bosses to stifle open debate and dissent perhaps explains how the government was able to impose one of its most important policies—the neoliberal "Growth, Employment and Reconstruction" (GEAR) program—over the strong objections of its alliance partners, the South African Communist Party (SACP) and the Congress of South African Trade Unions (COSATU). SACP and COSATU members complain that "consultations" over economic policy have amounted to little more than the ANC dictating what the policy will be.[8] COSATU and SACP MPs (who sit in Parliament as ANC members) have chafed under the traditions of collective cabinet decisions and "democratic centralism." These simmering internal differences finally exploded in August 2001 when union leaders, cabinet ministers, and the president publicly exchanged insults, and massive strikes were called in an effort to embarrass the government during the United Nations antiracism conference in Durban.

Problems of Governance

Beyond its handling of its own internal affairs, the manner in which the ANC has treated the institutions of governance is also a cause for concern. The governing party has failed to heed the 1996 Constitution's call that it pass legislation to enable Parliament to amend spending bills. (Currently, MPs only have the choice between accepting a bill or rejecting it altogether.) Additionally, the ANC has recently introduced two pieces of legislation containing seven separate amendments to the Constitution. The most important would reorder the relationship between the Appellate Court and Constitutional Court, scrap constitutional limits on the tenure of Constitutional Court justices, put their tenure in the hands of Parliament, enable the president to appoint two deputy ministers who are not MPs, allow national government intervention in municipal governments that do not comply with financial management standards, and broaden the finance minister's monopoly on introducing financial legislation. Not only does this rapid and far-reaching change have grave implications for the integrity of the Constitution, it is being attempted without giving other parties the opportunity to take positions on each provision separately.[9]

On several occasions, the ANC has invoked party loyalty to prevent Parliament from conducting effective oversight of executive action. In 1996, party leaders reportedly ordered members of the Portfolio Committee on Health to refrain from any tough questioning of the health minister during hearings on the unauthorized expenditure of R14 million for a dubious HIV/AIDS education musical called *Sarafina 11*.[10] And just recently, President Mbeki reportedly blocked internal party demands that Majority Whip Tony Yengeni appear before Parliament's Ethics Committee to explain why he received—but did not report—a discounted luxury truck from a European defense company that was bidding for an arms subcontract.

The most profound crisis in executive-legislative relations, however, originated in the R29.9 billion arms deal of 1999. In the second half of 2000, Parliament's Standing Committee on Public Accounts (SCOPA) began receiving allegations of nepotism, cronyism, and conflict of interest having to do with the negotiation of the deal. After an auditor general's report questioned the government's decision to select one of the more expensive sets of available options and highlighted deviations from accepted procurement practices, SCOPA (which traditionally operates on nonpartisan lines and is headed by an opposition party MP) launched its own inquiry, which included a high-profile anticorruption agency called the Special Investigating Unit (SIU). Although Parliament unanimously adopted a resolution in support of the inquiry, President Mbeki and other ANC leaders quickly attacked the process due to the inclusion of the SIU. The leader of the ANC delegation on SCOPA was replaced. Under pressure from party leaders, SCOPA's ANC members distanced themselves from the inclusion of the SIU, broke off communication with other investigators, and blocked efforts to obtain further information from the army and the government. The significance of this episode is hard to overstate. Parliament may continue to play an active role in developing and amending legislation in areas of no great interest to the executive, but when there is a difference of opinion on matters that are important to the executive, it will always prevail.

Perhaps no event better illustrates the troubling direction that South African politics has taken than what is now simply known as "the plot." When intra-ANC tensions began to surface in 2001, Minister of Safety and Security Steve Tshwete apparently took seriously charges that senior ANC officials were enlisting other party members and journalists in an anti-Mbeki campaign and (improbably) were spreading rumors implicating Mbeki in the 1992 murder of SACP leader Chris Hani. Operating on the strange assumption that the president's life would be endangered if these rumors were widely believed, Tshwete launched a police investigation into the matter and the possible involvement of former premiers Mathwes Phosa and Tokyo Sexwale, as well as Cyril Ramaphosa, the father of the 1993 and 1996 constitutions. Moreover, Tshwete went on national television to name the three as the subject of an official police investigation into a "plot" against Mbeki.

In short, a faction of the ruling party was using the police to deter what appeared to be legitimate canvassing, revealing that those in the highest positions of power are capable of conflating internal lobbying and caucusing with a treasonous "plot." On the positive side, however, both Mbeki and Tshwete quickly drew the wrath of CO-SATU, the SACP, and other key voices in civil society and the media. Mbeki did eventually say that Tshwete was "wrong" to publicly name the three, yet he chose not to fire the minister and went so far as to say that Tshwete was only doing his duty.[11]

Another worrying aspect of South Africa's institutional development is the gap between the government's aspirations and the state's capacity. While the government has demonstrated an impressive ability to use parastatal agencies to deliver water, electricity, and telephones, and to create government subsidies to allow people to purchase homes, the picture is not nearly so impressive in other areas. The most obvious is crime. Not only have most kinds of crime—especially violent crime—increased substantially since 1994, but the number of prosecutions launched and convictions attained has *declined*.[12] Law enforcement is so hard-pressed to fight ordinary crime that the national police commissioner recently refused the minister of health's request to commit personnel to enforce newly passed antismoking legislation. He also said that there were no resources available to enforce new legislation on domestic violence or on banning the use of cell phones by drivers.

One final problem of democratic governance in South Africa has less to do with political institutions than with the personality of President Thabo Mbeki and his stance on HIV/AIDS. In the face of one of the highest HIV infection rates in the world, Mbeki has consistently chosen to fritter away the considerable symbolic authority of his office by questioning the causal link between HIV and AIDS, investing time and resources in a presidential commission evenly divided between mainstream and "dissident" scientists. The government has stalled, if not blocked, funding for affordable anti-retroviral drugs and the distribution of available drugs that would drastically reduce the rates of mother-to-child transmission of HIV. Most recently, the government has moved to discredit and suppress a report by the country's Medical Research Council that directly contradicts Mbeki's attempts to minimize the impact of AIDS.[13]

Trends in Public Opinion

A country's political culture does not develop in a vacuum. Rather, it is against a background of economic and political trends and developments that public opinion about a democratic regime, a political system, and citizenship must be assessed and understood. A review of a range of public opinion indicators collected by the Institute for Democracy in South Africa (Idasa) since 1995 demonstrates that South African political culture is not yet mature enough to consolidate democratic practices.[14]

South Africans' support for democracy is lukewarm and has not grown in any substantial way over the past five years. With increasingly tenuous connections between the voters and their government and increasing policy disaffection, trust in government and satisfaction with economic and political performance are declining sharply. Perhaps most importantly, the web of organizations and the impressive tradition of popular participation that emerged to challenge the apartheid system have withered. Indeed, across almost all the key indicators of democratic political culture, South Africans compare quite poorly to their neighbors throughout southern Africa and elsewhere on the continent.

National identity. One area of political culture that does not appear to pose a major threat to democracy in South Africa, though it is often thought to do so, is the so-called "national question." The common view holds that, in deeply divided societies such as South Africa, people identify primarily with this or that component part—often their own racial, ethnic, or religious group—rather than with the multiethnic or multinational state. President Mbeki has entered this debate with his "two nations" thesis, which states that South Africa comprises "two nations," one relatively wealthy and largely white and the other relatively poor and overwhelmingly black. Although Mbeki's economic prognosis may still be largely correct, there is no evidence that the word "nation" ought to be applied to these economic divisions.

In fact, surveys since 1995 have revealed widespread popular consensus on the existence of a South African political community that transcends racial and economic divisions. Nationally, 90 percent or more are proud of being called South African, say it is a key part of how they see themselves, and want their children to think of themselves as South African. It is important to note, however, that there are some cracks in this consensus, as the proportions of white and Indian respondents agreeing with some of these items fell an average of 10 percent between 1995 and 2000.

To be sure, these high levels of self-identification with the nation exist alongside strong ties to subnational self-defined identity groups. Yet this may not be so much a contradiction as an indication that members of historically competing groups feel sufficiently comfortable to identify with a larger national community only when they have a strong sense of communal identity. And just as it is mistaken to assume that economic divisions necessarily translate into different visions of nationhood, it is also mistaken to assume that a strong sense of national community necessarily brings about domestic tranquility. Indeed, high levels of national identity coexist with significant levels of in-group chauvinism, out-group rejection, racism, and intolerance.[15]

Yet few South Africans cite racism or discrimination as a problem requiring government intervention. In 1994, six months after the first election, one in five respondents spontaneously cited problems of discrimination and the removal of apartheid as one of the three "most important problems facing this country that government ought to address." Since then, however, no more than 5 percent have mentioned this issue. A recent survey by the South African Institute of Race Relations found that racism was rated ninth on a list of "unresolved problems," with just 8 percent listing it as a priority matter. In fact, 48 percent of the total sample (and 49 percent of black respondents) said that race relations had improved in recent years, while 25 percent said they had deteriorated.[16]

Support for democracy. As of July—August 2000, 60 percent of South Africans said that democracy "is preferable to any other kind of government," and 55 percent said that democracy is always the best form of government "even if things are not working." Yet just 30 percent said they were "unwilling" to live under a nonelected government that was also able to "impose law and order, and deliver houses and jobs." On none of these items is there any evidence of increased support for democracy since 1995.

Yet South Africans are likely to reject authoritarian alternatives to liberal democracy when they are mentioned. Three-fourths would disapprove of abandoning multiparty elections for military rule, 66 percent would disapprove of a return to apartheid, but just 56 percent would disapprove of one-party rule. Moreover, only 40 percent reject all four alternatives.[17] South Africans' support for democracy and rejection of authoritarian rule are consistently lower than in most of the eight southern African countries where Afrobarometer surveys have been conducted (generally ahead only of Lesotho and sometimes Namibia); on those items that have been asked in 12 countries across the continent, South Africa ranks as one of the lowest.[18]

Many more South Africans give positive evaluations to the present political system (58 percent) than to the apartheid regime (25 percent). These figures, however, show a significant increase since 1995 in "nostalgia" for the way the country is perceived to have been governed under apartheid, especially among white, "colored," and Indian respondents. And while South Africans widely prefer their present form of government to what they had before, their optimism about how they will be governed in the future has declined noticeably.

An important aspect of South Africans' attitudes toward democracy is their highly economic and substantive understanding of the concept. When unprompted, South Africans spontaneously see democracy as the realization of individual rights and civil liberties. When provided with a list of constitutive elements of democracy, however, an average of 60 percent say that socioeconomic goods are "essential" for a country to be called democratic, while an average of just 35 percent say the same about procedural components like regular elections, multiparty competition, and freedom of speech. This 25-point "gap" between substantive and procedural understandings of democracy is by far the largest in southern Africa.

Evaluations of democratic performance. Although many international analysts place South Africa at the forefront of democratic development in Africa,[19] the country's own citizens are not so sanguine. In 2000, one year after the second successful democratic national election, nearly three-quarters thought the 1999 election had been either "completely free and fair" (42 percent) or "free and fair with some minor problems" (31 percent). Yet the citizens of Namibia (78 percent) and Botswana (83 percent) were even more optimistic when evaluating their recent elections. And when asked to assess the extent of democracy in their country, 60 percent of South Africans said the country was either "completely democratic" (26 percent) or "democratic with some minor exceptions" (34 percent). This figure placed South Africans parallel to Zambians and Malawians (62 percent), but behind Namibians (71 percent) and citizens of Botswana (83 percent), the region's oldest democracy. Finally, 52 percent are satisfied with "the way democracy works in South Africa," which is higher than the 41 percent registered in 1995 but down from the 63 percent of November 1998. It is also lower than the figure recorded in Botswana (75 percent), Namibia (64 percent), Zambia (59 percent), or Malawi (57 percent).

Views of political institutions. When assessing their political institutions, South Africans are becoming increasingly pessimistic. As of July—August 2000, trust in elected institutions, approval ratings of elected officials' job performances, and the extent to which people saw them as responsive to public opinion were all at the lowest levels yet measured under the new political system. Only 41 percent of respondents said they trusted President Mbeki, and 34 percent said they could trust Parliament. For such state institutions as the army, the courts, the police, and the criminal justice system, trust ranged from 35 to 44 percent. Fifty percent of South Africans approved of Mbeki's performance over the preceding 12 months, and 45 percent approved of Parliament.

A large part of this trend can be attributed to a general economic downturn and the accumulating political problems confronting the Mbeki government. For example, job creation has consistently been seen as the country's "most important problem," cited as such by 76 percent of all respondents in 2000. Yet just 10 percent approved of the government's efforts to create jobs. Sixty percent cited crime and security as a priority concern, yet just 18 percent approved of the way government has handled the problem. Indeed, surveys conducted by the Human Sciences Research Council showed that the proportion who said they felt "safe" or "very safe on most days" fell dramatically from 73 percent in 1994 to 44 percent in 1999.[20]

In addition, while public perceptions of corruption leveled off in 2000, they remain very high. Thus, even before the investigation of the arms deal, 50 percent of all South Africans felt that most or all government officials were involved in corruption. Two-thirds felt that the new government was at least as corrupt as the apartheid regime. How the ANC confronts the growing accusations of influence-buying and conflict of interest in the arms deal will tell us a great deal about the future course of public opinion.

Declining trust in government must also be attributed to the aforementioned flaws in South Africa's representative system. By 2000, only 54 percent of blacks and 46 percent of all respondents felt that the president was interested in their opinions; 48 percent and 42 percent, respectively, felt similarly toward Parliament; and only 33 and 31 percent said so about their local governments.

Economic evaluations. Individual evaluations of the economy have paralleled the country's macroeconomic trends. As recently as April 1999, more than half of all South Africans were optimistic about the country's economic future. By July—August 2000, however, just over one-quarter expected the economy to improve in the next year (the figure went from 63 to 35 percent among black respondents). Perceptions of relative deprivation have also increased sharply. Even in 1995, despite one of the highest rates of income inequality in the world, only 32 percent of South Africans said they were worse off than others. This was largely due to the fact that black South Africans tended to compare themselves to other blacks rather than to whites. By mid-2000, however, this figure had increased sharply to 50 percent. In the same survey, 31 percent of blacks said their lives were worse now than under apartheid, up sharply from 13 percent in 1997.

Citizenship and participation. The most troubling of the survey results are probably the data on citizen participation and interaction with government. South Africa now has one of the most passive citizenries in southern Africa. As of mid-2000, only 11 percent of South Africans said they "frequently" engaged in political discussion and 12 percent said they paid attention to government and public affairs "always" or "most of the time." Both figures were the lowest yet measured since 1995, and also the lowest out of seven southern African countries. South Africans are less likely to participate in community-level organizations (such as church or self-help groups) or political actions (such as attending election rallies or working for a party) than Zimbabweans, Zambians, Malawians, or Namibians.

Of even greater concern are South Africans' extremely low levels of actual contact with government leaders or other influential community leaders. Just 6 percent said they had contacted a government or party official in the previous year to give them their views, and only 10 percent had contacted any other community leader. Both figures are the lowest in southern Africa. Perhaps the most damning finding of the entire 2000 survey was that just 0.2 percent—that is, only four of the 2,200 respondents—said they had made contact with a sitting member of Parliament in 1999-2000. Absolutely no one in the sample said he had attended any hearing or meeting organized by Parliament or by an MP. This passivity cannot be traced to a lack of information, since South Africans actually have the highest rates of radio, television, and newspaper coverage in the region. Neither can it be traced to poverty, since South Africa's much poorer neighbors tend to have far higher rates of contact.

Fostering Citizenship

Although the public opinion data reviewed here are worrisome, they do not suggest a deeply held "culture" of norms, values, beliefs, or predispositions inhospitable to democracy. Rather, it would be more accurate to see the current contours of public opinion as *consequences* of, or even *reactions* to, the problems facing South Africa's economic and institutional development. South Africans' support for democracy is modest, in part, because they understand democracy to mean the delivery of a range of socioeconomic goods, and progress toward this goal had been slow.

Surveys show that, compared to other countries in the region, South Africans have had one of the highest rates of participation in protest action in the past and are among the most likely to resort to protest again, given the reason and the opportunity. This rules out any notion of an inherent "culture" of apathy or passivity. South Africans participate at low rates between elections because the system offers them few incentives to do so. They do not contact parliamentarians or attend parliamentary "outreach" hearings at least in part because they do not know who their parliamentarians are and because MPs have no incentive to reach out to people.

Afrobarometer results from southern Africa underscore the strong impact of constitutional design, especially the electoral system, on the degree of citizen-MP contact. In Namibia and South Africa, the two countries with proportional representation, the rate of contact with an MP or attendance at a parliamentary meeting or hearing is 1 percent and 0.2 percent, respectively. Among the five countries with first-past-the-post systems, contact rates are 7 percent in Zimbabwe and Zambia and 5 percent in Malawi and Lesotho. (Botswana is the "outlier" with a contact rate of 2 percent.) While all these figures may sound low, there is a huge difference between one out of every 10 or 20 people in each community having had contact with their elected national representatives and one out of every 100 or 200.

While South Africa is admired internationally for the negotiating skills and processes it has developed since 1990, as well as for its state-of-the-art Constitution, its citizens have been left behind by the past decade's preoccupation with elite bargaining and institutional design.

South Africans need to shift the focus onto problems of citizenship, representation, and participation. In the next decade, they need to put as much emphasis on building a grassroots culture of citizenship as they have already put on building a culture of elite accommodation. This requires renewed emphasis on civic education by schools and civil society organizations, in order to teach citizens the intrinsic value of democracy and equip them with the resources necessary to participate more fully in the political process.

Furthermore, this requires institutions that encourage meaningful participation. South African constitutional designers need to rethink their assumptions about how institutions interact with ordinary people, and they must abandon the view (implicit in the present constitution) that citizen participation emanates from a sense of duty rather than from incentives and self-interest. Therefore, public participation in democratic government should be encouraged not through special processes or forums but by giving citizens reasons to engage with their elected representatives nationally, provincially, and locally. This requires legislators and councilors who can listen to identifiable constituencies and be persuaded by them, and who can in turn act according to the wishes of the voters. This goal can be accomplished by a system of strong separation of powers with weak party discipline, but it can also be accomplished in a parliamentary system, as long as party caucuses are democratic and autonomous from the executive. Either way, more effective constituency representation is a necessary, though not sufficient, condition to bring about greater contact between citizens and representatives.

Indeed, the window for electoral reform in South Africa is now open, if only because existing electoral legislation has lapsed and the ANC has begun the process of amending related legislation in order to cooperate with the NNP. But simply creating single-member or multi-member districts will not be enough. Representatives must also be required to live in their districts, since if parties can "parachute" members into "safe districts" or "helicopter" them out when they face defeat, it will remove any incentive for MPs to anticipate voter reactions. Finally, lifting the ban on floor-crossing, as the ANC recently proposed, is misguided. Changing parties midterm is an undemocratic violation of the implicit contract under which a candidate stands for election, and it also disturbs the proportionality created by the voters. It would be better to amend the Constitution so that MPs have to give up their seats only if they *choose* to leave their political party, not if they are forced out. Mavericks who want to challenge party discipline will be less likely to be intimidated by party bosses if they know they can still keep their parliamentary seats if they are expelled from the party.

Together, these reforms should give legislators greater incentives to reach out to voters and to represent them, and give citizens and interest groups more reason to contact their representatives and interact with legislative bodies. In addition, they could help representatives more effectively oversee and check the actions of mayors, premiers, and presidents. Without such reforms, it is difficult to imagine the consolidation of South African democracy.

Notes

1. Andrew Whiteford and Dirk San Deventer, *Winners and Losers: South Africa's Changing Income Distribution in the 1990s* (Johannesburg: WEFA, 1999), 25–26.
2. Reg Rumney, "A Question of Perceptions," *Mail and Guardian* (Johannesburg), 3–9 August 2001, 15; Howard Barrell, "Back to the Future: Renaissance and South African Domestic Policy," *African Security Review* 9 (2000): 87; "Housing: A Good News Story," *RDP Monitor* 7 (May 2001): 2; "Electricity: Seeing Clearly Now," *RDP Monitor* 6 (July 2000): 2; and Josey Ballenger, "Troubled School Feeding Plan Is Still Essential," *Reconstruct*, 11 October 1998, 1.
3. John Daniel, "Discussion Paper on Socio-Economic Issues," presented to U. S. Department of State, Bureau of Intelligence and Research seminar on "South Africa: Future of Democratization" (Washington, D. C.: Meridian International Center, 5 April 2001); Jonathan Katzenellenbogen, "Jobless Figures Remain Over 25%," *Business Day* (Johannesburg), 27 January 2001, 3.
4. Andrew Whiteford and Dirk San Deventer, *Winners and Losers*, 11–19; Debbie Budlender, "Earnings Inequality in South Africa, 1995–1998," *Measuring Poverty In South Africa* (Pretoria: Statistics South Africa, 2000).
5. Robert Mattes and Jessica Piombo, "Opposition Parties and the Voters in South Africa's 1999 General Election," *Democratization* 8 (Autumn 2001): 101–28.
6. Cited in Tom Lodge, "Romantic Aspiration," *Mail and Guardian* (Johannesburg), 10–16 August 2001, 17.
7. "Loss or Retention of Membership of National and Provincial Legislatures Bill," (Republic of South Africa) Draft Document: 12 November 2001; and Wyndham Hartley, "President in Driving Seat for Defections," *Business Day* (Johannesburg), 13 November 2001, 1.
8. See the interview with COSATU president Willie Mdasha in Howard Barrell and Sipho Seephe, *Mail and Guardian* (Johannesburg), 31 August–6 September 2001.
9. Patrick Laurence, "Debate These Changes One at a Time," *Focus* 23 (September 2001): 13–15.
10. Richard Calland, ed., *The First Five Years: A Review of South Africa's Democratic Parliament* (Cape Town: Idasa, 1999), 36.
11. Barry Streek, "Tshwete Was 'Wrong' to Name Plotters, Says Mbeki," *Mail and Guardian* (Johannesburg), 1–7 June 2001, 1.
12. David Bruce, "Suspect Crime Statistics Cannot Obscure rim Truth," *Sunday Independent* (Johannesburg), 10 June 2001, 9; Michael Dynes, "South Africa's Huge Steps on Long Walk to Prosperity," *Sunday Independent* (Johannesburg), 26 August 2001, 4; S. Pedrag, "Crime out of Control in South Africa," *MSNBC News*, 29 May 2000, available at *www.msnbc.com*; *Economist*, 24 February 2001, cited in John Daniel, "Discussion Paper on Socio-Economic Issues."
13. Nicoli Nattrass, *Ethics, Economics and AIDS Policy in South Africa*, CSSR Working Paper No. 1 (Cape Town: Centre for Social Science Research, University of Cape Town, August 2001); Howard Barrell and Jaspreet Kandra, "Shocking Aids Report Leaked," *Mail and Guardian* (Johannesburg), 5–11 October 2001, 2. For a detailed review of Mbeki's statements on the disease, see Drew For-

rest, "Behind the Smokescreen," *Weekly Mail & Guardian* (Johannesburg), 26 October to 1 November 2001, 25.

14. For the most comprehensive summary of these findings, see Robert Mattes, Yul Derek Davids, and Cherrel Africa, "Views of Democracy in South Africa and the Region: Trends and Comparisons," *Afrobarometer Working Papers Series*, No. 8 (Cape Town, Accra, and East Lansing: Afrobarometer, 2000); available at *www.afrobarometer.org*.

15. Robert Mattes, Donald Taylor, and Abigail Poore, "The Role of National Identity in Building a Democratic Culture in South Africa," paper presented at the Conference of the International Sociological Association's Research Group on Ethnic, Race and Minority Relations on "Multicultural Citizenship in the New South Africa" (Cape Town: Idasa Cape Town Democracy Centre, 15–17 December 1997).

16. "Racism 9th on Country's List of Problems," *Cape Times* (Cape Town), 24 August 2001, 5.

17. Michael Bratton, "Wide but Shallow: Measuring Popular Support for Democracy in Africa," paper presented at a workshop on "Democracy in Africa in Comparative Perspective," Stanford University, 27 April 2001.

18. The eight southern African states are Botswana, Lesotho, Malawi, Namibia, South Africa, Tanzania, Zambia, and Zimbabwe; the four not in southern Africa are Ghana, Mali, Nigeria, and Uganda.

19. Freedom House, for example, awards South Africa the highest score in southern Africa for 2000–2001 in terms of political rights. Larry Diamond has named it one of the four "liberal democracies" in the region (along with only Botswana, Namibia, and Malawi). See Larry Diamond, "Introduction," in Larry Diamond and Marc F. Plattner, eds., *Democratization in Africa* (Baltimore: Johns Hopkins University Press, 1999), ix-xxvi.

20. Nedbank/ISSS, "Criminal Justice Monitor," *Crime Index* 4 (January–February 2000).

Robert Mattes is associate professor in the department of political studies and director of the Democracy in Africa Research Unit in the Centre for Social Studies at the University of Cape Town. He is also an associate with the Institute for Democracy in South Africa (Idasa), and a co-founder and co-director of the Afrobarometer, a regular 12-country survey of Africans' attitudes toward democracy, markets, and civil society.

China
The Quiet Revolution
The Emergence of Capitalism

Doug Guthrie

When Deng Xiaoping unveiled his vision of economic reform to the Third Plenum of the 11th Central Committee of the Chinese Communist Party in December 1978, the Chinese economy was faltering. Reeling from a decade of stagnation during the Cultural Revolution and already falling short of the projections set forth in the 1976 10-year plan, China needed more than a new plan and the Soviet-style economic vision of Deng's political rival, Hua Guofeng, to improve the economy. Deng's plan was to lead the country down a road of gradual and incremental economic reform, leaving the state apparatus intact, while slowly unleashing market forces. Since that time, the most common image of China, promulgated by members of the US Congress and media, is of an unbending authoritarian regime that has grown economically but seen little substantive change.

There is often a sense that China remains an entrenched and decaying authoritarian government run by corrupt Party officials; extreme accounts depict it as an economy on the verge of collapse. However, this vision simply does not square with reality. While it is true that China remains an authoritarian one-party system, it is also the most successful case of economic reform among communist planned economy in the 20th century. Today, it is fast emerging as one of the most dynamic market economies and has grown to be the world's sixth largest. Understanding how this change has come about requires an examination of three broad changes that have come together to shape China's transition to capitalism: the state's gradual recession from control over the economy, which caused a shift in economic control without privatization; the steady growth of foreign investment; and the gradual emergence of a legal-rational system to support these economic changes.

Reform Without Privatization

During the 1980s and 1990s, economists and institutional advisors from the West advocated a rapid transition to market insti-

tutions as the necessary medicine for transforming communist societies. Scholars argued that private property provides the institutional foundation of a market economy and that, therefore, communist societies making the transition to a market economy must privatize industry and other public goods. The radical members of this school argued that rapid privatization—the so-called "shock therapy" or "big bang" approach to economic reforms—was the only way to avoid costly abuses in these transitional systems.

The Chinese path has been very different. While countries like Russia have followed Western advice, such as rapidly constructing market institutions, immediately removing the state from control over the economy, and hastily privatizing property, China has taken its time in implementing institutional change. The state has gradually receded from control over the economy, cautiously experimenting with new institutions and implementing them incrementally within existing institutional arrangements. Through this gradual process of reform, China has achieved in 20 years what many developing states have taken over 50 to accomplish.

The success of gradual reform in China can be attributed to two factors. First, the gradual reforms allowed the government to retain its role as a stabilizing force in the midst of the turbulence accompanying the transition from a planned to a market economy. Institutions such as the "dual-track" system kept large state-owned enterprises partially on the plan and gave them incentives to generate extra income by selling what they could produce above the plan in China's nascent markets. Over time, as market economic practices became more successful, the "plan" part of an enterprise's portfolio was reduced and the "market" part grew. Enterprises were thus given the stability of a continued but gradually diminishing planned economy system as well as the time to learn to set prices, compete for contracts, and produce efficiently. Second, the government has gradually promoted ownership-like control down the government administrative hierarchy to the localities. As a result, the central government was able to give economic control to local administrators without privatization. But with economic control came accountability, and local administrators became very invested in the successful economic reform of the villages, townships, and municipalities under their jurisdictions. In a sense, as Professor Andrew Walder of Stanford University has argued, pushing economic responsibilities onto local administrators created an incentive structure much like those experienced by managers of large industrial firms.

Change From Above

Even as economic reform has proceeded gradually, the cumulative changes over two decades have been nothing short of radical. These reforms have proceeded on four levels: institutional changes instigated by the highest levels of government; firm-level institutions that reflect the legal-rational system emerging at the state level; a budding legal system that allows workers institutional backing outside of the factory and is heavily influenced by relationships with foreign investors; and the emergence of new labor markets, which allow workers the freedom and mobility to find new employment when necessary. The result of these changes has been the emergence of a legal-rational regime of labor, where the economy increasingly rests upon an infrastructure of ordered laws that workers can invoke when necessary.

Under Deng Xiaoping, Zhao Ziyang brought about radical change in China by pushing the country toward constitutionality and the rule of law to create rational economic processes. These changes, set forth ideologically as a package of reforms necessary for economic development, fundamentally altered the role of politics and the Communist Party in Chinese society. The early years of reform not only gave a great deal of autonomy to enterprise managers and small-scale entrepreneurs, but also emphasized the legal reforms that would undergird this process of change. However, by creating a body of civil and economic law, such as the 1994 Labor Law and Company Law and the 1995 National Compensation Law upon which the transforming economy would be based, the Party elites held themselves to the standards of these legal changes. Thus the rationalization of the economy led to a decline in the Party's ability to rule over the working population.

In recent years, this process has been continued by global integration and the tendency to adopt the norms of the international community. While championing global integration and the Rule of Law, Zhu Rongji also brought about broader political and social change, just as Zhao Ziyang did in China's first decade of economic reform. Zhu's strategy has been to ignore questions of political reform and concentrate instead on the need to adopt economic and legal systems that will allow the country to integrate smoothly into the international community. From rhetoric on "linking up with the international community" to laws such as the 2000 Patent Law to institutions such as the State Intellectual Property Office and the Chinese International Economic Trade and Arbitration Commission, this phase of reform has been oriented toward enforcing the standards and norms of the international investment community. Thus, Zhu's

objective is to deepen all of the reforms that have been discussed above, while holding these changes to the standards of the international community.

After two decades of transition, the architects of the reforms have established about 700 new national laws and more than 2,000 new local laws. These legal changes, added regulations, and experiments with new economic institutions have driven the reform process. A number of laws and policies in the 1980s laid the groundwork for a new set of policies that would redefine labor relations in fundamental ways. For example, the policies that set in motion the emergence of labor contracts in China were first introduced in an experimental way in 1983, further codified in 1986, and eventually institutionalized with the Labor Law in 1994. While there are economic incentives behind Chinese firms' willingness to embrace labor contracts, including the end of lifetime employment, these institutional changes have gradually rationalized the labor relationship, eventually providing a guarantee of due process in the event of unfair treatment and placing workers' rights at the center of the labor relationship. Incremental changes such as these have been crucial to the evolution of individual rights in China.

The obvious and most common response to these changes is that they are symbolic rather than substantive, that a changing legal and policy framework has little meaning when an authoritarian government still sits at the helm. Yet the scholarship that has looked extensively at the impact of these legal changes largely belies this view. Workers and managers take the new institutions seriously and recognize that the institutions have had a dramatic impact on the structure of authority relations and on the conception of rights within the workplace.

Other research shows that legal and policy changes that emphasize individual civil liberties are also significant. In the most systematic and exhaustive study to date of the prison system, research shows that changes in the treatment of prisoners have indeed resulted in the wake of the Prison Reform Law. And although no scholarship has been completed on the National Compensation Law, it is noteworthy that 97,569 suits were filed under this law against the government in 1999, a proportional increase of over 12,000 percent since the beginning of the economic reforms. These institutions guarantee that, for the first time in the history of the People's Republic of China, individuals can have their day in court, even at the government's expense.

The 1994 Labor Law and the Labor Arbitration Commission (LAC), which has branches in every urban district, work hand-in-hand to guarantee workers their individual rights as laborers. Chapter 10 of the Labor Law, entitled "Labor Disputes," is specifically devoted to articulating due process, which laborers are legally guaranteed, should a dispute arise in the workplace. The law explicitly explains the rights of the worker to take disputes to outside arbitration (the district's LAC) should the resolution in the workplace be unsatisfactory to the worker. Further, many state-owned enterprises have placed all of their workers on fixed-term labor contracts, which significantly rationalize the labor relationships beyond the personalized labor relations of the past. This

An Age of Jurisprudence

Lawyers

Legal Cases

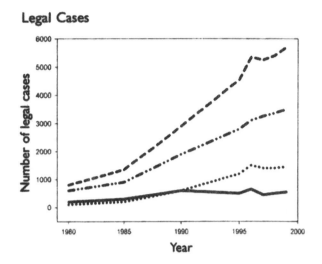

The above graphs depict two recent trends in China: a growing body of lawyers and an increasing number of legal cases. As the graph at left indicates, the number of lawyers in China has increased dramatically in the past 20 years, rising from fewer than 10,000 in 1980 to over 100,000 in 2000. The graph at right shows the growth in various types of legal cases over the same period. In particular, there have been significant increases in civil, economic, and first-trial cases.

2002 Statistical Yearbook of China

bundle of changes has fundamentally altered the nature of the labor relationship and the mechanisms through which authority can be challenged. For more than a decade, it has been possible for workers to file grievances against superiors and have those grievances heard at the LACs. In 1999, 52 percent of the 120,191 labor disputes settled by arbitration or mediation were decided wholly in favor of the workers filing the suits. These are official statistics from the Chinese government, and therefore should be viewed skeptically. However, even if the magnitude is incorrect, these numbers illuminate an important trend toward legal activity regarding workers' rights.

Many of these changes in labor practices were not originally adopted with workers' rights in mind, but the unintended consequence of the changes has been the construction of a regime of labor relations that emphasizes the rights of workers. For instance, extending the example of labor contracts that were being experimented with as early as 1983, these were originally intended as a form of economic protection for ailing enterprises, allowing a formal method of ending lifetime employment. However, workers began using the terms of employment codified in the contracts as the vehicle for filing grievances when contractual agreements were not honored. With the emergence of the LACs in the late 1980s and the further codification of these institutions in the Labor Law, the changes that were in progress became formalized in a set of institutions that ultimately benefited workers in the realm of rights. In a similar way, workers' representative committees were formed in the

state's interest, but became an institution workers claimed as their own. These institutions, which many managers refer to as "our own little democracy," were adopted early in the reforms to co-opt the agitation for independent labor unions. These committees do not have the same power or status as independent labor unions in the West, but workers have made them much more significant in factories today than they were originally intended to be.

Foreign Investment's Impact

At the firm level, there is a process of rationalization in which firms are adopting a number of rational bureaucratic systems, such as grievance filing procedures, mediation committees, and formal organizational processes, that are more often found in Western organizations. In my own work on these issues, I have found that joint venture relationships encourage foreign joint ventures to push their partner organizations to adopt stable legal-rational structures and systems in their organizations. These stable, legal-rational systems are adopted to attract foreign investors, but have radical implications for the structure of authority relations and the lives of individual Chinese citizens. Chinese factories that have formal relationships with foreign, and particularly Western, firms are significantly more likely to have institutionalized formal organizational rules, 20 times more likely to have formal grievance filing procedures, five times

177

more likely to have worker representative committee meetings, and about two times more likely to have institutionalized formal hiring procedures. They also pay about 50 percent higher wages than other factories and are more likely to adopt China's new Company Law, which binds them to abide by the norms of the international community and to respect international legal institutions such as the Chinese International Economic Arbitration and Trade Commission. Many managers openly acknowledge that the changes they have set in place have little to do with their own ideas of efficient business practices and much more to do with pressure brought on them by their foreign partners. Thus, there is strong evidence that foreign investment matters for on-the-ground change in China.

> Foreign investors and Chinese firms are not interested in human rights
> per se, but the negotiations in the marketplace lead to transformed
> workplaces, which affect millions of Chinese citizens on a daily basis.

Given the common image of multinational corporations seeking weak institutional environments to capitalize on cheap labor, why would joint venture relationships with Western multinationals have a more positive impact in the Chinese case? The answer has to do with the complex reasons for foreign investment there. Corporations are rarely the leading advocates of civil liberties and labor reform, but many foreign investors in China are more interested in long-term investments that position them to capture market share than they are in cheap labor. They generally seek Chinese partners that are predictable, stable, and knowledgeable about Western-style business practices and negotiations. Chinese factories desperately want to land these partnerships and position themselves as suitable investment partners by adopting a number of the practices that Western partners will recognize as stable and reform-minded. Among the basic reforms they adopt to show their fitness for "linking up" with the international community are labor reforms. Thus, the signaling of a commitment to stable Western-style business practices through commitments to labor reform has led to fundamental changes in Chinese workplace labor relations. Foreign investors and Chinese firms are not interested in human rights per se, but the negotiations in the marketplace lead to transformed workplaces, which affect millions of Chinese citizens on a daily basis.

However, changes at the firm level are not meaningful if they lack the legal infrastructure upon which a legal-rational system of labor is built. The construction of a legal system is a process that takes time; it requires the training of lawyers and judges, and the emergence of a culture in which individuals who are part of the legal system come to process claims. This process of change is difficult to assess because it relies on soft variables about the reform process, such as, for example, how judges think about suits and whether a legal-rational culture is emerging. But we can look at some aspects of fundamental shifts in society. All of these changes, in turn, rest upon a legal-rational system that is slowly but surely emerging in China.

Finally, beyond the legal and institutional changes that have begun to transform Chinese society fundamentally, workers are no longer tied to workplaces in the way that they once were. In the pre-reform system, there was very little mobility of labor, because workers were generally bound to their "work units" for life. The system created a great deal of stability for workers, but it also became one of the primary means through which citizens were controlled. Individuals were members of their work units, which they were dependent on for a variety of fundamental goods and services.

This manufactured dependence was one of the basic ways that the Party exercised control over the population. Writing about the social uprisings that occurred in 1989, Walder points out that the erosion of this system is what allowed citizens to protest with impunity on a scale never before observed in communist China: "[W]hat changed in these regimes in the last decade was not their economic difficulties, widespread cynicism or corruption, but that the institutional mechanisms that served to promote order in the past—despite these long-standing problems—lost their capacity to do so." It is precisely because labor markets have opened up that workers are no longer absolutely dependent upon the government for job placements; they now have much more leverage to assert the importance of their own rights in the workplace. And while the private sector was nonexistent when the economic reforms began, the country has seen this sector, which includes both private enterprises and household businesses, grow to more than 30 million individuals. With the growth of the private sector, there is much greater movement and autonomy among laborers in the economy. This change has afforded workers alternative paths to status attainment, paths that were once solely controlled by the government.

Quiet Revolution

Much like the advocates of rapid economic reform, those demanding immediate political and social reform often take for granted the learning that must occur in the face of new institutions. The assumption most often seems that, given certain institutional arrangements, individuals will naturally know how to carry out the practices of capitalism. Yet these assumptions reflect a neoclassical view of human nature in which rational man will thrive in his natural environment—free markets. Completely absent from this view are the roles of history, culture, and pre-existing institutions; it is a vision that is far too simplistic to comprehend the challenge of making rational economic and legal systems work in the absence of stable institutions and a history to which they can be linked. The transition from a command economy to a market economy can be a wrenching experience, not only at the institutional level but also at the level of individual practice. Individuals must learn the rules of the market and new institutions must be in place long enough to gain stability and legitimacy.

The PRC government's methodical experimentation with different institutional forms and the Party's gradual relinquishing of control over the economy has brought about a "quiet revolution." It is impossible to create a history of a legal-rational economic system in a dramatic moment of institutional change. The architects of China's transition to capitalism have had success in reforming the economy because they have recognized that the transition to a radically different type of economic system must occur gradually, allowing for the maximum possible institutional stability as economic actors slowly learn the rules of capitalism. Capitalism has indeed arrived in China, and it has done so via gradual institutional reform under the communist mantle.

DOUG GUTHRIE is Associate Professor of Sociology at New York University.

The Emperor Is Far Away

Understanding the Challenges Faced By the New Leadership

A Conversation with Ezra Vogel

HARVARD INTERNATIONAL REVIEW:

China enjoyed remarkable growth rates in the last 20 years. What accounts for this accelerated rate of development, and how has China's economic liberalization affected its attitude toward the West?

China's opening to the West began in 1970, when the Chinese leadership decided that the biggest risk was no longer the United States but the Soviet Union. Practically no Westerners had had direct contact with China, and initial progress was slow. China remained a relatively closed country until 1978, when its leadership decided to adopt an official policy of foreign opening. By the mid-1980s, China began to grow quite rapidly and continued at an ever greater rate in the early 1990s. The average per capita annual income is now about US$1,000, so China remains relatively undeveloped, though many countries are much poorer. This process of opening and growth has allowed the Chinese government to prepare its people to take their place in world affairs.

Historically, China has been the dominant power in the region, but it was never a global power. China began to take part in world affairs for the first time in the 19th century. For the subsequent 150 years, it was much weaker than other world powers and suffered oppression from the outside world. But once China opened in the early 1980s, it was able to take part in the world system. One of my favorite Chinese expressions is "linking tracks." In the 1930s, some of the Chinese warlords had no railroads because they had a narrower gauge than the national railway, leaving a wider distance between the rails. The warlords had to design a way to make the tracks compatible in order to form a national railway system. Now, China uses "linking tracks" to describe the process of adjusting various traditional practices so that they can interface with the global system.

This is an enormous change, and on the whole, China has done remarkably well. China today has become one of the world's leading trading states with a substantial trade surplus. This development marks extraordinary progress over a short period of time from the backward, isolated country that China once was. Furthermore, this is a much more exciting period within China than the outside world realizes. The 1989 Tiananmen protest and response received so much attention that even today China is often thought of as one big jail. But some of the most exciting cultural and intellectual growth in the world is taking place in China right now. There are a lot of smart people thinking about how to combine diverse Western influences with Chinese history. There are extraordinarily creative programs being conducted in every field on the grand scale—it is truly a renaissance. China can be criticized for being too repressive, but the change for the average person in China has been overwhelming.

Do you ascribe the opening of China to structural change, individual action, or a combination of factors?

I think there were three reasons for the opening. The first is that in its basic foreign policy strategy, China first identifies its greatest foreign adversary and then seeks allies against it. After the late 1940s, China saw the United States as the major enemy. By 1970, when it decided that the Soviet Union was the greatest enemy, China sought cooperation with the West. That decision had a serious impact on the re-organization that began China's entrance to the world system. Second, the Cultural Revolution ruined the country and was extremely painful to many people. There was real chaos because so many of the leaders had been in jail for an extended period of time. Then, after Mao Tsetung died in 1976, the new leadership began to think, "What should we do?" The timing was right, and the West was receptive to an opening from China. The third factor is individual leadership, and China has been very lucky in this regard. There were a number of circumstances that made it possible for Deng Xiaoping to become the paramount leader after Mao. He guided the country through an extremely difficult time and achieved rapid growth and openness in the midst of extreme poverty, corruption, and chaos. To be able to manage that process took extraordinary skill and good sense.

Do you think that subsequent leaders like Jiang Zemin have followed in Deng's success?

Mao united the country and became such an icon that it was almost impossible to say anything critical about him. Deng had a kind of revolutionary background that made him an especially strong figure. The situation with Jiang is quite different. The pattern of liberalization under his rule reminds me of a company that is tightly controlled by its owner and that later gets taken over by a corporation with an administrative system that makes it impossible for a single individual to control the business.

The key variable is not the type of person in charge. Instead, it is the whole situation surrounding the decision to change. Jiang Zemin was brought in as a compromise after Tiananmen. He was acceptable to those who wanted a crackdown as well as to more radical interests. He did not have much experience in central party politics. His rise in government is analogous in the United States to a governor who is elected president and installed in the White House with no prior experience in Washington. Although Jiang was at one time a minister, that post was very different from being in a position of genuine power. Heading a ministry is a very technical job compared with running the Chinese Communist Party, and I think Jiang proved to have greater strength and sounder judgment about international affairs and many local interests than people would have expected. Jiang did not know the details of running the Party headquarters, but I think he managed the process quite well. China flourished under him. He provided a very

different kind of leadership—much less dramatic than Deng or Mao, who, it can be argued, had problems in their later years. Jiang was a good leader for his time.

A great deal of Hu Jintao's experience is from his time in the western provinces, particularly in Tibet. What do you think of China's future regarding ethnic minorities like the Tibetans or the Uighurs of Xianjiang?

Hu had a very tough problem when he was in Tibet. People in the United States think "the more freedom the better." In the 1980s, some top Beijing leaders felt the same way and took measures that increased popular expectations and hopes. This led to chaos and demonstrations. Hu took part in leading a crackdown in response, but Hu did it without alienating the local community. In his attention to root problems, he demonstrated concern for the issues of the local population. I think minorities feel that Hu is a person they can deal with, someone who understands them.

Minorities compose roughly eight percent of China's population. When Jiang visited Harvard University in 1997, some responsible for his security were less concerned with the thousands of demonstrators for the Tibetan movement and more worried about the small number of Uighurs, who have demonstrated a willingness to resort to violence. In contrast, Tibetan Buddhists have generally avoided violence since their uprising in 1959. The United States itself no longer considers the Uighurs "freedom fighters;" after September 11, they became Islamic terrorists. The current US attitude is now closer to the Chinese view that some Uighurs present a problem to social order. Xinjiang is officially led by a Uighur government and Uighur officials, and they use their traditional language. The Uighurs have not assimilated as much as the Hui, another Muslim minority in Xingiang.

The minority populations of China include very different kinds of people, and the diversity among the

groups extends to their grievances. On one hand, there are the Koreans, who have a higher level of education and income than the average Chinese and, as a result, form a kind of privileged minority. Then there are a number of groups, particularly in southwest China and mountainous regions, who have been pushed back by the advancing Chinese in a way similar to the experience of Native Americans in the United States.

The Chinese government will make an effort to bring aid to backward areas, but there will still be far more investment in the area near the eastern coast because capital flows are now governed by a free market, and investors will make more money in the east. The amount of money the government will put in the west will not be nearly enough to counterbalance that lure. Nonetheless, the Chinese government will do quite a bit to build infrastructure and transport links to the western part of the country. They will also try to build schools and universities in the region. You can argue about whether this is enough or not, but at least there will be some national program of assistance.

But even this approach can be complicated when minority issues are at stake. In the 1990s, for instance, as money began to flow into Tibet and the government began its construction projects, many merchants, such as the Hui, moved from nearby areas in search of profit. Many outsiders came to Lhasa, the Tibetan capital, because the government gave financial aid. These people are working to respond to market opportunities, not because of official assignments.

When discussing economic modernization, what do you think of the internal changes in the way the domestic Chinese economy is run? How does this impact China's foreign trade?

China was a planned economy when it began to open in 1978. The big factories were all entirely state owned. The government dreaded having private enterprises, which were only allowed on a small scale. After 1978, private enterprises were gradually allowed to exist and grow. In the last decade, the government has allowed foreign companies and their subsidiaries to develop infrastructure in the country. During its liberalization period, the former Soviet Union was under the influence of the World Bank, so it tried to privatize right away. In contrast, China felt—I think rightly—that this would not be a good policy. In China, there were no private investors and no real experience with the free market. The unemployment situation was so severe in China that privatization could have led to massive social unrest. What China wanted was to build up enterprises first and then gradually put more pressure on the state enterprises to become competitive, a process that continues today.

But in the last decade, foreign investment has become the cutting edge of the export market. There were few foreign companies in China in the early years of reform, and generally they were required to have Chinese partners. As more foreign companies were allowed in, the vast portion of Chinese exports are now produced by more competitive foreign companies. Other countries at comparable stages of development, like Japan, were far more restrictive in allowing foreign enterprises to enter. For China, that policy means ceding a certain portion of profits to foreign countries, but it also means that China grows and acquires modern technology. China is now modernizing fairly rapidly, moving up the chain from the handicraft industry of the 1970s to a labor-intensive light industry and toward higher technology production. China cannot yet compete with Japan or Korea in terms of high technology products, but there has been notable progress. One example of this progress is that Chinese businesses are beginning to make memory chips and computer parts.

This industrial evolution will only accelerate in coming years as China's World Trade Organization (WTO) membership forces it to allow more foreign firms into the country. China has learned from the Japanese Ministry of International Trade and Industry how to manage the process of slowing the entry of foreign firms while simultaneously telling local companies that they must get ready for the transition. The officials supervising the Chinese auto industry have decided that the only way to manage the coming competition is to allow many foreign companies to have joint ventures in China. Modern foreign industries are coming in, and the Chinese who are operating their plants are learning very quickly. So the Chinese auto industry is rapidly developing labor and management skills as well as higher levels of technology. After all, if they do not adapt, these businesses will be pushed out. On the other hand, the pressure from WTO membership will inevitably lead to problems with copyrights and patents. There will also be other internal issues with admission to the WTO , but they will not stop China from continuing to catch up with the industrialized world.

Is this a rosy picture of Chinese industrialization? Does the Chinese government still face problems with industrialization, urbanization, and a migrant population of workers?

To say that the picture is rosy is too simple and ignores a host of issues. Certainly the picture for China is rosier than for some, but there are many problems. In the 1980s, when farmers began to produce more because individual households received profits for the first time, farm incomes increased rapidly. Then agricultural productivity improved, so agricultural prices did not keep pace with the rise in price of industrial goods. As a result, agricultural wages stagnated. As Chinese agricultural production becomes more efficient, the country will need fewer agricultural laborers. There are people in need of employment leaving rural areas, and there are urban factories that require work-

ers. So it follows that there will continue to be massive migration to urban centers.

Migrants face great problems in the cities. The 700 million people currently involved in agriculture must undergo huge adjustments. Consider that in Japan in 1947, agriculture workers represented around 50 percent of the workforce; today, they are less than three percent. China will go through a similar process. The question is whether cities can expand fast enough to provide sufficient opportunities to accommodate this influx of workers. Factories are not going to be enough. There also has to be a large service sector. Nonetheless, factories can do a great deal to generate wealth and provide income for local governments to build infrastructure.

Migration poses many problems. If you were an employer and were getting almost unlimited workers coming into a place, how high a wage would you pay? Probably what the market would bear, with labor standards high enough for the workers to be willing to stay. That is typical of the free market. The important companies in China, because of foreign pressures and because of their knowledge, provide marginally better wages and circumstances for their workers. But there is a wide range of wages and working conditions. There are some local entrepreneurs, from places like Taiwan and Southeast Asia, who believe that cheaper is better. They tolerate minimal working conditions and incur many injuries among their employees. This system promotes exploitation, but it is how the market functions.

On the other hand, life in some of the factories I visited in the coastal areas reminds me of small college life in the United States. Many of the workers in these factories are young men and women who live together in a dormitory setting. They have clean, modern products, and the factory atmosphere even functions like a campus. These workers have a new kind of life, including compensation in the form of a salary, a good part of which they often send back home. In some isolated rural communities, the average income from the migrants is higher than the total locally generated income. Many of these workers return to their homes after a few years of factory work.

Do you think that Hu Jintao will continue the positive trends initiated by his predecessors? Is there reason to have confidence in his ability to address the challenges facing China?

Hu Jintao is a product of his generation. Like Jiang, he graduated in engineering around the time of the revolution. But Hu combined a high-technology background with very high positions in the western provinces of Gansu, Guizhou, and Tibet. Because Beijing thought he handled the situations there quite well, he was brought into the premier leadership group. China's Standing Committee of the Politburo functions like a corporation of overseers. There are now nine members, but previously there were seven. Hu has been a member of that select group for the past decade, the only member of his age group to have that experience, and is therefore thoroughly familiar with all major decisions for the past decade. Hu is like a Washington insider, and his ascent in government is analogous to the elevation of a corporation's vice-president to the top post.

Hu is a bright, cosmopolitan person with strong natural talents and 10 years of friendship with top officials. This latter characteristic is truly remarkable because it demonstrates that he can get along with all kinds of different people. This is the first time since Mao that China has successfully prepared for a transfer of power. Mao selected all kinds of successors who failed, but now China has someone who has been intimately involved in the highest levels of Chinese politics for a decade. In my opinion, Hu is not in a big hurry. He knows that he has a lot of talent and support. I think the chances are that Hu will have a very promising future.

Reprinted with permission from *Harvard International Review*, Summer 2003, pp. 38-41. © 2003 by the President of Harvard College. All rights reserved.

In March Toward Capitalism, China Has Avoided Russia's Path

Asia: Unlike its onetime idol, Beijing has used a gradual approach to developing a market-oriented economy.

By HENRY CHU
TIMES STAFF WRITER

BEIJING—If the Soviet Union always seemed like the terrifying embodiment of Big Brother to the West, then for years it was something of a big brother to China toward the south.

Inspired by the same Marxist-Leninist ideals that first took root in Russia, Beijing alternately held up Moscow as its role model and, in times of disillusionment, its nemesis.

But since the Soviet Union's collapse, China has come to regard Russia as one thing only: its worst nightmare—a country with a political system in disarray; a society in sometimes violent flux; and, now, an economy in free fall.

In attempting to remake itself from a Communist behemoth into a capitalist beacon, China has studiously tried to avoid the path of its onetime idol, preferring a more gradual approach to change. Over the last 20 years, the result has been shaky but mostly upward progress: steady economic growth, an emerging middle class, a new breed of entrepreneurs.

As world leaders and economists reassess the wisdom of free markets amid today's global turmoil, the China model—from the perspective of Russia's collapse and the pain in lesser Asian countries that wholeheartedly embraced capitalism—looks wise enough.

Yet even as Beijing silently congratulates itself on the wisdom of its go-slow approach, analysts say that historical conditions here have been nearly as big

a contributor to China's improvement as current policy.

And as in Russia, major domestic reforms—especially China's latest efforts to shed its money-losing state enterprises and streamline its bloated bureaucracy—have brought about a whole new set of problems, making the final outcome of one of the most ambitious economic transitions in history far from certain.

"It is too soon to say whether China's reforms will succeed," Nicholas Lardy, an economist with the Brookings Institution in Washington, wrote recently.

Like Russia, China has struggled to redesign a planned economy into a market-oriented one. But even though both were Communist in name, the two countries launched their modernization drives at very different stages in their development.

"The Communist revolution in the former Soviet Union was over 70 years old; the Communist revolution in China was 30," said Harry Harding, a Sinologist at George Washington University. "The former Soviet Union was more industrialized; China was still an agricultural, rural society."

China embarked on its transformation when Deng Xiaoping, the nation's late "paramount leader," officially ended Beijing's isolation in 1978 with a series of measures designed to open up and liberalize the world's most populous country.

The enormous rural communes set up by Mao Tse-tung were dismantled. Peasant farmers were permitted to sell food on the private market. Two years later, the doors to foreign investment were thrown open in specially designated zones along the southern coast.

Setting the Stage

Radical Maoism was dead, discredited after the 1966–76 Cultural Revolution, one of China's darkest periods, during which hundreds of thousands of citizens were killed.

Ironically, however, many scholars now argue that some of Mao's wrongheaded policies actually fostered the political climate and infrastructure necessary for the success of China's long march toward capitalism—or, in Deng's wordplay, "socialism with Chinese characteristics." Fanaticism was replaced by pragmatism and a thirst for a new national direction.

"The Cultural Revolution deinstitutionalized the political system and de-legitimized the Communist Party in ways that made reform both necessary and more possible," Harding said.

Under Mao, much of China's economic decision-making and planning had already devolved to local authorities. After Deng's reforms began, local officials used their knowledge and the fledgling industrial development across China to push for rapid industrialization of the countryside through a combination of tax breaks and enterprising schemes.

Labor was cheap—and plentiful. Three of every four Chinese toiled in the fields and could be redirected into industrial jobs and big, capital-intensive projects. In the Soviet Union, by contrast, industrialization was largely complete when the Soviet empire collapsed, leaving 75% of workers scrambling for hard-to-find jobs in new sectors of the economy.

Chinese cities such as Shenzhen, the first of the special economic zones, mushroomed with activity.

Shiny new skyscrapers now rise from a robust manufacturing base. Millions of Barbie dolls roll off assembly lines into the eager hands of children worldwide. The population of Shenzhen, a onetime fishing village with 30,000 inhabitants across from the Hong Kong border, skyrocketed a hundredfold to 3 million.

Traders work the Shenzhen stock market. This year, foreign investment through July totaled an impressive $1.6 billion.

Much of the investment in Shenzhen and throughout the rest of China comes from a natural resource that Russia does not have: the ethnic Chinese around the world who still feel strong ties with "the motherland" and who have become one of China's primary engines for growth.

Whereas the Soviet Union splintered along nationalist and ethnic lines after its breakup, overseas Chinese, about 55 million in all, have remained remarkably unified through their common cultural heritage across boundaries of state and time.

"Hong Kong, Taiwan, Singapore and the Chinese diaspora in South [and] East Asia and North America are filled with ethnic Chinese entrepreneurs who have proved to be valuable sources of knowledge and investment and who have served as important bridges to the world economy," Andrew G. Walder, sociologist and specialist in China market reforms at Stanford University, observed in the China Quarterly magazine.

Amazingly, between 75% and 80% of all foreign investment in China (including money from Hong Kong) comes out of the pockets of ethnic Chinese across the globe, whose ranks boasted three dozen billionaires in East Asia in 1994.

Although the regional financial crisis has pinched some of the capital flow from the outside, economists say that money keeps pouring in at a fast clip.

In addition to abundant foreign investment, a comparatively low foreign debt—thanks to Mao's insistence on national self-sufficiency—has been crucial to China's revival as one of the world's major economies.

In stark contrast to Russia, China has not had to resort to crushing bailout packages by the International Monetary Fund to shore up its economy. While the government is struggling to keep expenditures in check as central tax revenue dwindles, Beijing does not need to devote huge resources to servicing short-term foreign debt; 80% of its debt is long-term, according to Hu Biliang, a senior economist with a French securities firm here.

Moscow, meanwhile, has buckled under the weight of $31.2 billion in IMF cash since 1992. And those loans have invariably come with political strings attached, reflecting one of the widest and most important divergences between China and Russia on the way to the free market: their different political systems.

For Russia, economic reform has gone hand in hand with political restructuring. At about the same time that Moscow relinquished its stranglehold on the economy, the Russian people also flung off the totalitarian Communist regime in one violent shudder.

Since then, prescriptions for a free market have been intertwined with efforts to build a free society. Economic shock treatment and the massive unloading of nationalized industries in Russia are bound up with ending the political monopoly of the Communist Party and building a raucous, but functional democracy.

Beijing, on the other hand, represents the last great bastion of Communist control, a one-party dictatorship that oversees one-fifth of humanity. Its authoritarian rule has greatly loosened over the last two decades—some detect the signs of a civil society emerging—but the one-party Communist regime remains China's government.

As such, China's leaders can still rule by fiat, pushing through relatively unpopular measures when necessary, although the regime is careful not to push too hard lest it provoke a popular uprising such as the 1989 Tiananmen Square demonstrations. Even the ensuing massacre that year put only a temporary crimp in the economy, which flagged until Deng launched a "southern tour" of China in 1992 to jump-start greater economic liberalization.

Now many Chinese appear content to ignore the government so long as it allows some personal freedom, such as easier internal movement within China, and the liberty to pursue a higher living standard.

Beijing knows its legitimacy increasingly rests on its handling of the economy, and it has tried to help its citizens discover the truth of Deng's famous maxim: "To get rich is glorious." China's leaders are hoping that an economic overhaul is enough, without knitting it together with a political one, as happened in the former Soviet bloc.

"Where in Eastern Europe [economic] shock therapy and mass privatization are designed in part to dismantle communism and strip former Communists of power and privilege," Walder wrote, "in China gradual reform is intended to allow the party to survive as an instrument of economic development."

As a multi-party state, Russia is now full of vested interests jockeying for position. Politicians, elected by popular vote, must cater to them to stay in power.

The result has been a crony capitalism and democracy stage-managed by a handful of "oligarchs" behind the scenes, who have gobbled up the wealth and used it to wrest favors from Moscow.

So far, China has stayed largely immune to such stresses. But it has spawned a crony capitalism of its own that threatens the stability that the government is obsessed with maintaining.

Among those who have enriched themselves the most from Beijing's market reforms are not the *laobaixing,* or common people, but the families of high officials, who have used their connections to gain control of some of the most lucrative businesses in China.

Indeed, such corruption was one of the main grievances that drove the *laobaixing* to Tiananmen Square in 1989, marching for an end to Communist Party privilege and nepotism.

Fighting Corruption

The issue still ranks as China's No. 1 public beef. Frustrated locals and foreigners alike complain that preferential treatment for party "princelings" or through money passed under the table kills competition and undermines their ability to do honest business.

The Asian financial crisis has put enormous pressure on the government as exports have slowed and the economy tightens. Production surpluses in industries such as steel sit untouched in huge stockpiles. Devastating flooding across China has made government promises of an 8% economic growth rate this year ring hollow.

Unemployment, officially at 3.5% but probably higher, is rising as local authorities eagerly shed their small and medium-sized state-owned enterprises at a speed the government was evidently not prepared for. In some cases, the enterprises were sold for pennies on the dollar to friends and relatives of local officials, though not on the scale of the "false" privatization in Russia that concentrated assets in just a few hands, analysts say.

"There are as yet no media moguls like [Boris] Berezovsky or energy czars like [Viktor] Chernomyrdin, but localities are seething with resentment against those who appropriated local collective enterprises over the past five to 10 years," said Douglas Paal, president of the Asia Pacific Policy Center in Washington and former National Security Council senior staffer under Presidents Reagan and Bush.

Last month, in a sign of growing alarm, the Communist regime issued an official editorial calling for a halt to "blind selling of state-owned firms."

"Leaders in some localities have simplified these serious and complicated reforms, and have taken them to mean merely selling such enterprises," the New China News Agency said. Local authorities should "carefully study" the proper guidelines regulating such sales, it added.

With joblessness on the rise, Beijing has backed off from ambitious plans to make residents buy their own homes and to slash China's bureaucracy in half, a potential loss of 4 million jobs.

Worker protests have already broken out, from Sichuan province in central China to Heilongjiang in the northeast, but are not reported in the official media.

These days, no one is willing to write off China as a potential economic success story, but pessimism hangs in the air among economists and some citizens here over the current state of China's gradual, multi-pronged reform program. It seems clear, however, that the Russian strategy is not an alternative.

"There probably are no panaceas in this world," said Harding. "Neither the Russian model nor the Chinese model is perfect. Or, as the cynic once said, 'The grass is brown on both sides of the fence.'"

NEW DIMENSIONS OF INDIAN DEMOCRACY

South Asia Faces the Future

Susanne Hoeber Rudolph and Lloyd I. Rudolph

Conventional wisdom has it that India is the world's largest democracy, but few have recognized that it is so against the odds. The Indian experience runs against the widely held view that rich societies are much more likely to be democratic than poor ones, and that societies with large minority populations are prone to ethnic cleansing and civil war. Democracy in India, a poor and notoriously diverse country, has succeeded for more than half the twentieth century and seems likely to succeed as well in the twenty-first. India's democracy has proved substantial as well as durable. Electoral participation has been higher than in the United States, elections have been free and fair, governments have alternated at the center and in the states, and free speech and association are constitutionally protected and widely practiced. But democracy is subject to challenge and change. This essay examines why and how democracy in India during the 1990s responded to a variety of challenges. These may be summarized under seven headings:

1) A more prominent role for federal states in India's political system. The states are making themselves heard and felt politically and economically more than they ever have in the half-century since India gained its independence from Britain.

2) The transformation of the party system. The era of dominance by the Indian National Congress has ended. Congress remains a major party, but it now must operate within a multiparty system that includes not only the nationally influential Bharatiya Janata Party (BJP) but a host of significant regional and state-based parties as well.

3) Coalition government. Stable central governments based on parliamentary majorities have given way to coalition governments that must depend on constellations of regional parties. India has become in this regard like Italy or Israel, both places where small parties can make or break governments and thereby affect the whole nation.

4) A federal market economy. Economic liberalization has been marked by a decline in public investment and a rise in private investment, the displacement of the federal Planning Commission by the market, and the emergence of the states as critical actors in economic reform and growth. The result has contributed to a transformation of India's federal system.

5) The central government as regulator. Despite what the foregoing might suggest, India's central government is not fading away. The center is holding, but its role has changed. The center had acted as an intervenor. Now it acts as a regulator. In the economic realm, it monitors the initiatives of the several states. It tries (albeit mostly without success) to enforce fiscal discipline. In the political realm, the center acts—through regulatory institutions such as the Supreme Court, the presidency, and the Election Commission—to ensure fairness and accountability. Since the emergence of the first coalition government in 1989, this role as "policeman" or honest broker has grown, while the interventionist institutions, the cabinet and parliament, have waned in significance.

6) A social revolution. In most states, and to a significant extent at the center as well, there has been a net flow of power from the upper to the lower castes. Indian politics has experienced a sociopolitical revolution that, in *varna* terms, has meant a move from a Brahman (priests, intellectuals) toward a Shudra (toilers) raj.

7) Centrism has held against extremism. The imperatives of centrist politics have checked the momentum of Hindu fundamentalism. India's diverse and pluralist society, the rise of coalition politics, and the need to gain the support of the median voter have transformed the Hindu-nationalist BJP from an extremist to a centrist party.

1) The rise of the states. In recent years, the 28 states of India's federal system have played a more prominent role in India's public life. Not least has been their contribution to helping India live peacefully with difference. In a world where armed strife has increasingly taken the form of civil war and ethnic cleansing—of the 96 recorded conflicts between 1989 and 1996, only five were between sovereign states—India's federal system has helped to keep cultural and ethnic differences within relatively peaceful bounds.

Forty years ago, there seemed good reason to fear that India's "fissiparous tendencies" would soon lead to Balkanization or dictatorship. Today such worries seem unpersuasive.

In thinking about something with which to compare India's federalism, the multilingual European Union seems more appropriate than does the United States. Much like the English and the Indians, the Hindi speakers of Bihar state in the shadow of the Himalayas and the Tamil speakers of Tamil Nadu at the subcontinent's southern tip speak quite distinct languages. They share little history and few points of contact. Their traditional rulers, legends, and folk cultures are distinct from one another. Their socioeconomic profiles are as different as those of Sweden and Portugal. Bihar is poor and mostly illiterate. Tamil Nadu is prosperous and advanced. No contrast between any two of the 50 U.S. states comes anywhere close. Forty years ago, there seemed good reason to fear that Selig Harrison was right to warn that India's "fissiparous tendencies," particularly its linguistic differences, would soon lead to Balkanization or dictatorship. Today such worries seem unpersuasive. The federal system has helped India to live peacefully with its marked difference.

How anomalous is a multinational federal state? India reminds us that the nation-state as we know it is a relative historical newcomer, with roots in the post-Revolutionary, post-Napoleonic Europe of the nineteenth century. The nation-state reached its apogee after the two world wars. Before 1914, the numbers of people and extent of territory ruled by nation-states were dwarfed by those which lay under the sway of multinational entities such as the Habsburg, Ottoman, and Romanov empires, or the maritime dominions of Britain and other European colonial powers. After 1945, the working out of Woodrow Wilson's doctrine of self-determination had seemingly conferred sovereignty on enough aspiring "nations" to bring the era of the multinational state to a decisive end. The nation-state, said many scholars, stood revealed as the natural end toward which the history of state formation had been tending.

This claim was soon belied, however, by the formation of the European Community and its successor, the European Union. On 1 May 2001, the *New York Times* reported the proposal by German chancellor Gerhard Schroeder's Social Democratic Party of "a far-reaching plan… to turn the European Union into a more centralized federal system." The EU was becoming more like the sovereignty-sharing Holy Roman Empire than the warring nation-states of the First World War. Had the Holy Roman Empire become the dominant polity in the twelfth century, the process of state formation in Europe would have conformed more closely to the world norm. The path that marks the rise of India's federal, multinational state since 1947 also tracks the emergence of an alternative to the increasingly outmoded nation-state.

By promoting peace among their constituent parts, both the EU and the vast federal republic that is India are saving the world from a great deal of trouble and strife. If it has done nothing else, the EU, the creation of a Europe bloodied, exhausted, and chastened by two gigantic and terrible wars, has radically reduced the prospect of conflict among its member states. Something similar is true of India. Each of its 28 federal states could well be a nation-state unto itself. The largest, Uttar Pradesh, has more people than Germany and France combined, and is nearly as populous as Russia. If Uttar Pradesh and its neighbors were sovereign nation-states, there would be that many more countries living in the Hobbesian world of anarchy and self-help. Instead of ending in domestic arbitration, the dispute between Tamil Nadu and Karnataka over Krishna River water rights could have led to war. The internal conflicts within Punjab and Assam, like the civil wars that roiled Congo-Kinshasa during the 1990s, could have been made worse by outside forces seeking strategic gain. As it is, the international community has quite enough to occupy it as a result of the longstanding dispute between India and Pakistan over the fate of Kashmir, India's northernmost and only Muslim-majority state.

The story of India's state formation since independence has included a story of rising influence on the part of the federal states. At independence in 1947, India inherited the British-brokered constitution of 1935. It embodied two possibilities, a centralized authoritarian "vice-regal" state and a decentralized, or federal, parliamentary state. Mohammad Ali Jinnah, the "great leader" of Pakistan, chose the former option, in effect acting as the successor to Lord Louis Mountbatten, the British raj's last viceroy and governor-general of India. Jawaharlal Nehru, despite his personal penchant for centralized rationalization, selected the latter course and became the prime minister of a parliamentary government in a federal system.

Each choice was a fateful one. Pakistan has known parliamentary democracy for barely half of its five decades as an independent country. The rest of the time, it has been run by generals and authoritarian bureaucrats. Its civilian political landscape has been profoundly troubled, and its unsteady constitutional mixture of unitary and federal features contributed to the violent secession of East Pakistan (present-day Bangladesh) and a related war with India in 1971. India reinforced the federal character of its constitution in 1956 by implementing a sweeping "states reorganization" that redrew state boundaries on the basis of language. Mohandas K. Gandhi had set the stage for this as early as 1920, when he reformed the Indian National Congress by creating 20 Provincial Congress Committees (PCCs) based on regional languages. Arguably, Gandhi's far-seeing decision to provide a form of political expression for ethnocultural identities such as Hindustani, Tamil, and Bengali opened the way for greater popular participation under conditions of democratic pluralism.

Gandhi's linguistic reforms, like his strong support of Muslim causes, flowed from his inclusive understanding of what Indian nationalism should mean. Inclusive nationalism is reflected in the opening years of the twenty-first century by Indians' capacity to live with dual and overlapping national identities, regional and transregional. As one Tamil writer has put it, "Tamil is my mother, India is my father," a gendered metaphor that captures how the linguistic-cultural "home space" fosters a "subjective" sense of care and affection while the national "civil space" promotes a due respect for the "objective" virtues of security, discipline, and the rule of law. In an era of ethnic cleansing and civil war, this kind of federalism has powerfully enhanced a diverse India's capacity to live with difference.

2) The party system transformed. The dominant-party system of the Nehru-Gandhi era that led to the formation of Congress majority governments was replaced after the ninth parliamentary election in 1989 by a regionalized multiparty system and coalition governments. The 1989 elections resulted in India's first hung parliament. V.P. Singh's Janata Party, which held the largest bloc of seats in the 545-member Lok Sabha, became the nucleus of India's first coalition government. Each of the four national elections since the watershed has led to a coalition government in which parties based in single states have been key. Today, for instance, the coalition government that came out of the 1999 elections is led by Prime Minister Atul Behari Vajpayee of the BJP, but includes in its 300-seat majority fully 120 members from single-state parties.

According to the Election Commission's classification of parties (national, state, registered, and independents) and its declared election results, the four national ballotings held from 1991 to 1999 saw national-level parties' vote share drop from 77 to 67 percent, while the proportion of seats they controlled slid from 78 to 68 percent. By contrast, parties based in single states went from 17 percent of the votes and 16 percent of the seats to 27 and 29 percent, respectively.

The shift from dominant-party to multiparty politics and the rise of state parties at the expense of national parties have undone the centralizing thrust of the 1950 Con-

stitution. One telling sign of this is the reduced use of Article 356, the "president's rule" clause which was used—some would say misused—by majority-party governments at the center to remove irksome state governments. With state-based parties now holding the balance of power in New Delhi, freewheeling invocations of Article 356 are a thing of the past.

3) Coalition government. The third major feature of contemporary Indian democracy, the rise of coalition government, is implicit in what we have said about the transformation of the party system from a dominant to a multiparty system. Strong central governments based on sturdy one-party majorities in the Lok Sabha have given way to precarious coalitions that must cater to state parties in order to survive. Since the era of coalition government began in 1989, coalitions have differed in their ideological make-up and caste composition, but all have depended on subnational parties, particularly those form the southern states of Tamil Nadu and Andhra Pradesh. Following Indian politics since 1989 has become rather like following Italian or Israeli politics, where smaller parties can and do hold national governments hostage in order to advance narrow partisan agendas.

In the 32 years from 1947 to 1989, India had a total of five prime ministers. There have already been six in the 12 years since coalition government began. But perhaps the suggestion of instability carried by these numbers is deceptive. The Narasimha Rao government lasted five years (1991–96), longer than a U.S. presidential term. Until a corruption scandal threatened to trip it up in March 2001, the second government under A.B. Vajpayee seemed likely to complete its five-year term. And at the time of this writing in November 2001, it is still carrying on. Even the combined burden of scandal, Vajpayee's poor health, and dissension in the ranks could not overcome the absence of any viable alternative to him as a national leader.

Now that coalition governments are the order of the day, how are we to judge them? If we think of India as analogous to a potential EU federal government, composed of 15 former nation-states, each with its own identity and interests, we might appreciate the fact that coalition governments can give federal units weight and voice. Coalitions can soften extremism. The BJP, for instance, began as a predominantly north Indian party dedicated to Hindutva (Hindu nationalism), but has had to shelve that agenda in order to accommodate key coalition partners, especially secular state parties from south India that care little for anti-Muslim "communalism."

But this happy outcome is not the only possible result of coalition politics. The unedifying tale of Jayalalitha Jayaram, the corrupt and vindictive chief minister of the ruling AIADMK party in Tamil Nadu, seems to provide a lesson in how coalitions can be hijacked. For years, she shamelessly used the threat of bringing down the Rao and Vajpayee governments to shield herself from the legal consequences of the abuses that she committed while chief minister of Tamil Nadu between 1991 and 1996. Re-elected to that post in May 2001 and sworn in by a faint-hearted governor after she brushed aside the Election Commission's ruling that her criminal convictions disqualified her from office, she was turned out only after the Indian Supreme Court upheld the Commission in a landmark September 2001 ruling.

While the final deposition of the Jayalalitha case may have reduced the danger that state parties will blackmail coalition governments, there are other exigencies that can undermine or threaten coalition governments. One is the bloated, ineffective cabinets that are the byproduct of efforts to cobble together ruling coalitions by handing out ministerial appointments. Another is legislative gridlock as coalition partners and their constituencies jockey for advantage and block ministerial initiatives. The Vajpayee government's difficulties in keeping economic liberalization moving owe something to this effect. The cabinet is committed to privatizing more public-sector undertakings, to enacting an exit policy for labor, and to promoting new initiatives in energy, telecommunications, and transport-infrastructure policy, but political conflicts among ministers have stymied its efforts.

It is clear that coalition government based on a region-favoring multiparty system is a mixed blessing. It has made it possible to avoid ethnic cleansing, civil war, and extremist politics by facilitating the country's capacity to live with difference and to support centrist politics. At the same time, however, coalition government has weakened the country's ability to pursue economic liberalization or achieve vigorous economic growth.

4) A federal market economy.

When you opened your daily copy of the *Times of India* back in the 1950s or 1960s, you could read all about the big dams, steel mills, and other megaprojects that master planner P.C. Mahalanobis and his colleagues were launching at the national Planning Commission. The celebrities of the command economy and the "permit-license raj" were the bureaucrats, administrators, economists, and other experts who were helping Prime Minister Nehru build a modern industrial economy of which government held the commanding heights. Today, a decade after the turn toward economic liberalization, newspapers and magazines feature stories about state chief ministers such as Chandrababu Naidu of Andhra, A.M. Krishna of Karnataka, and surprisingly, Jyoti Basu, who until recently headed the Communist government of Bengal state. These stories describe how the chief ministers of various Indian states are traveling the world to meet with business leaders, woo investors, and persuade the likes of Bill Clinton or Bill Gates to endorse the idea of investing in the future of Kerala, Karnataka, or Tamil Nadu.

Economic liberalization, the dismantling of the permit-license raj, and an increasing reliance on markets have fostered the emergence of the "federal market economy." But economic liberalization is only part of the story.

Equally important has been the marked decline in centrally directed public investment, which has reduced the central government's financial leverage and opened up new fields of initiative for enterprising state governments.

In the 1990s, India's deficit-ridden central government found that it could no longer afford planned investment. The center's gross assistance to states' capital formation declined from 27 percent of the center's revenue expenditure in 1990–91 to 12 percent in 1998–99. The more alert state governments have moved in to fill the gap by securing private investment and multilateral assistance. The decline of central public investment and the growth of private investment have given the federal states a greatly expanded role in economic liberalization and in promoting investment and economic growth.

Our use of the term "federal market economy" is meant to draw attention not only to the decentralization of the market and the shift to a region- and state-based multiparty system but also to new patterns of shared sovereignty between the states and the center for economic and financial decision making. This increased sharing shifts India's federal system well beyond the economic provisions of its formal Constitution. Over the past decade, it has become ever more clear that if economic liberalization is to prevail, state governments and their chief ministers must break through the barriers that are holding back economic growth.

5) The central government as regulator.

Despite the fading of Nehru's vision of a strongly centralized, development-guiding state, the center is holding. But it is holding in a different way. Regulation is replacing direct intervention as the center's preferred mode of affecting both the polity and the economy. Since 1991, economic liberalization has meant the abandonment of the permit-license raj and central planning. But federal regulatory agencies remain active in monitoring markets for goods, services, and capital to ensure that they perform competitively and effectively. Politically, the shift form one-party dominance to fragile coalition governments has changed the balance among institutions at the center. The cabinet and parliament, the traditional initiators of intervention, have ceded pride of place to regulatory institutions such as the presidency, the Supreme Court, and the Election Commission—enforcers of rules that safeguard the democratic legitimacy of the political system.

The role of regulatory institutions is more procedural than substantive, more about enforcing rules than making law and policies. Regulatory institutions are needed not only to create, sustain, and perfect markets but also to ensure procedural fairness in elections, in the operation of a multiparty system, and in the formation of coalition governments. The travails that many countries around the world are now experiencing as they strive to establish democracy and markets show how vital the rule of law and a viable state are to both. Russia and some other post-Soviet and East European states suffer from what Max

Weber called "political capitalism," meaning the accumulation of wealth through political power (often wielded deceitfully and coercively) rather than economic enterprise and open competition. Transitions to a market economy and to democracy require more than privatization and liberty. They require fair regulatory mechanisms.

The Supreme Court, the presidency, and the Election Commission became more visible and effective in the 1990s as the reputations and authority of ministers, cabinets, and legislatures suffered.

Although India's case is far less dramatic, a similar logic applies. In the economic arena, the role of the center as regulator has been to monitor the states in the name of fiscal discipline. For a few years after 1991 the center backed state-level economic initiatives with sovereign guarantees, but it is now reluctant to do so. Under Article 293 of the Constitution, the center must approve all foreign loans contracted by the states, and has de facto veto power over all domestic borrowing as well. In the spirit of "Do as I say, not as I do," the center tries to make the states accept fiscal discipline by imposing conditions that look suspiciously like those which the International Monetary Fund demands of faltering national economies—and enforces them with a similarly wide latitude of discretion.

The political front has seen a parallel decline of interventionist institutions and an enhancement of regulatory ones. The Supreme Court, the presidency, and the Election Commission became more visible and effective in the 1990s as the reputations and authority of ministers, cabinets, and legislatures suffered. During the Congress party's heyday, executives and legislatures had benefited from association with the Congress-dominated party system, the (declining) political capital left over form the independence struggle, and the authority and resources made available to politicians by the existence of a command economy.

Today, all this has changed. The complexity and fragility of the coalition governments, their rapid turnover, and their dependence on region- and state-based parties have sapped the executive capacity of governments. As ministerial executives and legislatures have receded, they have made room for judges, presidents, and election commissioners to act in ways that highlight their constitutional roles as regulators who make democratic politics possible by ensuring that the game is not rigged.

Structural conditions alone do not tell the whole story of this shift. National prime ministers, state chief ministers, legislators, and civil servants have discredited themselves in the eyes of India's growing, well-educated, and increasingly influential middle classes. As taxpayers, investors, producers, consumers, and citizens, middle-class Indians care a great deal about the reliability and security than cannot be had apart from good governance and the rule of law. In the mid-1980s, they responded to Rajiv Gandhi's promises to provide clean government and a high-tech, environmentally friendly economy that could carry India into the twenty-first century. Rajiv disappointed them, leaving office under a cloud in 1989 after a scandal involving an arms deal with the Swedish Bofors company. The early 1990s saw an unprecedented number of state and national ministers indicted for taking bribes, and the BJP's carefully cultivated reputation for probity will not recover quickly from the Tehelka scandal of March 2001, which was blown wide open by hidden-camera videotapes showing top figure sin that party taking bribes. Amid this atmosphere of public disillusionment and hunger for integrity, the symbolic and practical words and deeds of the Supreme Court, the president, and the Election Commission have taken on a new significance. These institutions, despite weaknesses of their own, are now the repositories of middle-class hopes and aspirations for steady, transparent, and honest government.

The Supreme Court's judicial activism marks a particularly novel turn for a body that spent the first four decades after independence mostly defending the rights of property owners against land redistribution. The Court's decision in the 1980s to begin taking a stand against rights abuses against the poor and powerless and to hear cases based on public-interest legislation—the Indian equivalent of the U.S. class-action lawsuit—paved the way for the judicial activism of the 1990s. With executive power slipping and wobbly coalition governments the order of the day, the Court's activism emphasizes lawfulness and predictability, often in the face of state abuses. Despite overloaded dockets and an often-glacial pace of adjudication, the Court has had some success in protecting citizens' rights, limiting police brutality and inhuman treatment in jails, and safeguarding environmental and other public goods.

In the mid-1990s, coincident with a marked increase in ministerial-level corruption, the Supreme Court moved to assert the independence of the Central Bureau of Investigation (CBI), the Union government's principal investigative agency. That such a proceeding should have achieved even partial success highlights the relative shift in the balance between the executive and regulatory functions of the central government. The CBI had been barred from investigating a department or its minister without prior consultation with and the concurrence of the secretary-to-government of the ministry concerned. "Prior consultation" and "government concurrence" meant that prime ministers, who also controlled CBI appointments, promotions, and transfers, dominated CBI initiatives and actions. In a landmark judgment, the Court removed the requirement of government concurrence that governed CBI investigations and gave the CBI director a minimum two-year term of office. These actions left the CBI somewhat freer to investigate on its own cognizance ministerial cases.

India does not lack environmental legislation, but neither does it lack powerful interests ready to block the enforcement of such laws. In the late 1980s and early 1990s, the Supreme Court—prompted in some cases by assertive NGOs—began to redress the balance by acting to protect such public goods as clean air and water and safe blood supplies. At stake in some of these cases were two of India's greatest assets, the Taj Mahal and the Ganges River. To protect the sixteenth-century mausoleum from further damage by air pollution, the Court had by 1992 closed 212 nearby businesses for chronic violations of environmental regulations. Almost two hundred polluters along the banks of the Ganges found themselves similarly shuttered by Court order. In 1996 and 1997, the Court began beefing up enforcement of clean air and water laws in the heavily polluted Delhi area. By early 2000, the Court had ordered polluting buses and cars off the roads and shut down enterprises that were emitting pollutants into the Yamuna River. When the environmental minister and industry minister of the National Capital Territory defied the Court by trying to keep the outlets open, the Court countered by threatening to jail noncomplying local officials for contempt.

The transformation of the party system and the rise of coalition government have also opened the way for the president to play a regulatory role. In the era of Congress party majorities, presidents had little to do beyond the pro forma duty of asking Congress's leader to form a government. Since 1989, however, the exercise of presidential discretion has become crucial in determining the make-up of governments. Presidents in turn have leveraged this newfound influence into a bigger regulatory role for their office.

Although Article 53 vests the "executive power of the Union" in the president, the president, like modern British monarchs, is expected to act at the behest of the cabinet rather than as a principal. As a constitutional head of state indirectly elected through a weighted voting system in which all federal and state-level elected legislators participate, the president retains a separate and potentially highly prestigious identity as a steward of the nation's interests. He stands apart from and above mere partisan or bureaucratic politics. In the 1990s, presidents Shankar Dayal Sharma and K.R. Narayanan acted in ways that stressed the autonomy of their office. This was most striking when each resisted political pressure to invoke Article 356, the "president's rule" clause, as part of a plan to unseat a state government for partisan advantage. President Narayanan also delivered a remarkable address on the fiftieth anniversary of independence (27 January 2000), in which he questioned the BJP-led government's efforts to change the Constitution by replacing an executive responsible to parliament with a directly elected president

and protecting parliament against dissolution by fixing its term.

Unlike in other national contexts where presidential powers have been used to undermine or destroy democratic institutions, in India recent presidents have exercised their powers on behalf of democratic transparency and accountability.

Starting in 1991 with the tenure of T.N. Sheshan as its chief, the Election Commission joined the Supreme Court and the president in strengthening constitutional government and democratic participation. The Commission is a constitutionally mandated central body whose fixed terms make it independent of the political executive. While the Commission had been a bulwark of free and fair elections in India before 1991, its task became more difficult in the 1990s as India's sprawling electoral process came under well-publicized threats from terrorists and criminal gangs bent on using force to impede or distort the expression of the people's will. The Election Commission gained national fame as a restorer and defender of free and fair voting. Polls indicate that the public trusts it more than any other political institution. When the Supreme Court backed the Commission by removing Jayalalitha from office in September 2001, it enhanced the Commission's role as the guardian par excellence of the democratic process in India. Like the Court and the presidency, the Commission draws enthusiastic support from the educated, urban middle classes, who are eager for solutions to the problem of official corruption and lawlessness. It is not too much to say that the Commission, the Court, and the presidency are the three vital pillars of the new regulatory state in India.

6) A social revolution. Since 1947, Indian society has experienced a social revolution with massive political consequences. Political power in the states, and to a significant extent at the center, has moved from the hands of the so-called twice-born upper castes into the hands of lower-caste groups, known in Indian parlance as the "other backward castes" (OBC) and the *dalits* (former "untouchables").

In early postindependence elections, social prestige translated readily into political power. Upper-caste patrons—coming from a social stratum that contained about a fifth of the populace—could tell their lower-caste dependents how to vote, and elections produced state and national cabinets dominated by officials from upper-caste backgrounds. In the 54 years since independence, the OBCs and *dalits*—together about two-thirds of the population—have displaced the upper castes in the seats of power in many state cabinets. At the turn of the twenty-first century, lower-caste chief ministers are no longer rare, and at least one national cabinet—the one that headed the National and Left Front governments of Deve Gowda and I.K. Gujral in the mid-1990s—had almost no upper-caste members. The logic of "one person, one vote" in free and fair elections has put power in the hands of the more numerous lower castes.

Analysts of developing countries often stress the importance of economic growth for political stability and legitimacy. What they notice less often is the contribution that social mobility can make to political stability and legitimacy. Status as well as income matter for both. In India, the "status growth" enjoyed by members of the once-reviled lower castes has been rapid, and this seems to have palliated much discontent with the relatively slow pace of economic growth.

7) *The center holds.* In the early 1990s, the BJP and its Hindu nationalism appeared to be on the march. Today, centrist structural constraints, coalition politics, and the ideological moderation imposed by the need to attract the median voter have forced the BJP gradually to abandon communalist extremism in favor of a position much nearer the middle of the spectrum.

In 1992, such an outcome seemed unlikely. Two years earlier, BJP leader L.K. Advani had completed an all-India *yatra* or pilgrimage featuring an image of a martial but caged Lord Ram, the site of whose birthplace at Ayodhya in Uttar Pradesh was said to have been usurped by a six-teenth-century Muslim mosque known as the Babri Masjid. Everywhere it went Advani's *yatra* had drawn large crowds, seemingly galvanizing Hindu militants and swelling the BJP's electorate: BJP support jumped from a mere 9 percent of the vote and 2 seats in the 1984 general election to 11 percent and 86 seats five years later, and then to 20 percent and 117 seats—more than a fifth of the Lok Sabha—in 1991. On 6 December 1992, young Hindu extremists acting in the presence of BJP leaders and before the eyes of a global television audience stormed the Babri Masjid and tore it down stone by stone. Hindu-versus-Muslim communal violence exploded across northern and western India. Observers split over the likely impact of this episode, with some claiming that this assault on a prominent Muslim place of worship would fuel the rise of Hindu nationalist politics and others maintaining that it would discredit them. The future was more complex than either group expected.

In retrospect, it appears that the destruction of the Babri Masjid, instead of being the harbinger of a new BJP surge, was the crest of a wave. The violence of the assault and its wanton indifference to life and property shocked many of the moderate Hindus who had been providing the BJP with the bulk of its support. In the 1993 state assembly elections, the BJP lost heavily in four states, especially in its core state of Uttar Pradesh—India's largest state and the heart of the populous "Hindi Belt" across the north-central part of the subcontinent.

Yet the BJP did not collapse, and even gained ground. In the 1996 election it took 20 percent of the vote and 161 seats, though it could not form a government because no other party would join it. In 1998, the BJP garnered 25 percent of the vote and 182 seats—its best showing ever. (In the 1999 balloting, the party held on to its seat share but saw its voter support drop slightly to 24 percent.) Having absorbed the lesson of 1996, the party turned decisively toward moderation two years later. Led by the avuncular and moderate A.B. Vajpayee, it managed to put together a governing coalition, known as the National Democratic Alliance (NDA), by working mostly with regional parties. Conspicuously absent from the NDA's preelection program were such divisive Hindu-nationalist agenda items as calls for stripping Kashmir of its special constitutional status, demands that a Hindu temple be raised on the site of the Babri Masjid, and promises to override Muslim personal law via a uniform civil code.

In recent years the BJP's upper-class leadership has realized that electoral success depends on lower-caste support and living with difference. This explains the party's about-face on the Mandal Report, a government white paper that recommends set-asides for OBCs in school admissions and civil-service employment. The BJP, it would seem, is now seeking to exploit the very social revolution it once bitterly criticized. Whatever maneuvering the leadership may be doing, however, it would be going too far to suggest that the center of gravity of the entire BJP now lies stably in the middle of the Indian political spectrum, or that Indian voters now believe it does. Important organizations affiliated with the party such as the Hindu-extremist Vishva Hindu Parishad (Universal Hindu Organization) are showing signs of serious alienation from what they see as the BJP's excessive centrism. The Swadeshi Jagran Manch (Homemade-Products Promotion Council) continues to challenge economic liberalization. Vajpayee is still shutting the extremists out of the central advisory positions they crave, but his health is failing. The Tehelka tapes have taken a terrible toll on the BJP's good name. State assembly elections as well as by-elections for the Lok Sabha have lately gone badly for both the BJP and its coalition partners. The successful efforts by the BJP family of "saffron" organizations to infiltrate India's cultural organizations and activities and to rewrite the history texts used in schools in order to paint Muslims as invaders and foreigners have produced a backlash. Hindu extremists have turned from seemingly politically counterproductive and more dangerous Muslim targets to the softer targets of India's far smaller Sikh and Christian minorities.

After Vajpayee?

What can we say about the prospects for democracy in India? We take as given the prior consolidations of democracy—for example, the realization of free and fair elections; alternating governments; freedoms of speech, press, and association; and the more or less successful transition from an interventionist to a regulatory state.

Our story of new dimensions suggests that democracy in India has proved resilient and adaptable. Absent an exogenous shock, centrist politics and coalition governments seem capable of providing stable if not always effective government. With the BJP vote share peaking at 24 percent, upper-caste Hindu extremist politics seems to have slowed. To remain viable as a contender for national office, the BJP will have to continue to reach out to lower castes and minorities and be able to form coalitions with secularist state parties. Judging by its wins and performance at the state level, the Congress seems to be regaining its capacity to practice centrist, inclusivist politics.

The problem for the future is that A.B. Vajpayee has become physically weak and psychologically weary and there is no comparable alternative to him. Congress leader Sonia Gandhi's dynastic legitimacy does not compensate adequately for her political inexperience and foreign provenance, but to date, no one can challenge her.

Business as usual may not be good enough; the country needs to gain, not lose, momentum. A viable regulatory state may have displaced a failing interventionist state, but if India is to prove its mettle, the country's political and economic life needs to be revitalized.

Susanne Hoeber Rudolph is professor of political science at the University of Chicago. Lloyd I. Rudolph is professor of political science at the University of Chicago. Their numerous published works on South Asia and India include In Pursuit of Lakshmi: The Political Economy of the Indian State (1987) and Reversing the Gaze: The Amar Singh Diary—A Colonial Subject's Narrative of Imperial India (2002).

From *Journal of Democracy*, January 2002, pp. 52-66. © by the National Endowment for Democracy and The Johns Hopkins University Press. Reprinted with permission of The Johns Hopkins Univeristy Press.

Iran's Crumbling Revolution

Jahangir Amuzegar

WESTERN REPORTERS tend to describe the current situation in Iran in alarmist terms, suggesting that the people are near revolt, the regime faces collapse, and the country is prone to political upheaval. Even if these assessments are premature or extreme, the relentless confrontations between the "reformist" *Majles* (national assembly) and the "conservative" Council of Guardians (which has veto power over *Majles* legislation and vets all candidates for elective office) augur a turbulent political future. The 1979 revolution faces a profound challenge from a new and disenchanted generation, widely known in Iran as "the Third Force." For this broad swath of society born after 1979, Ayatollah Ruhollah Khomeini's promise of a just and free Islamic society has proven a sham. After nearly a quarter-century of theocratic rule, Iran is now by all accounts politically repressed, economically troubled, and socially restless. And the ruling clerical oligarchy lacks any effective solutions for these ills.

The changes wrought by this turmoil call for a new and nuanced U.S. policy toward the Islamic Republic—particularly if the United States goes to war against Iraq. Since the high-profile inclusion of Iran in President George W. Bush's "axis of evil," proposals to deal with that "rogue" state have run the gamut from a preemptive military strike to the pursuit of diplomatic engagement. Between these two extremes, suggestions have included covert action to destabilize the ruling regime, assistance to internal and external opposition groups, financial aid for foreign-based Iranian media, and a call for international condemnation of the ayatollahs. To know what shape U.S. policy should take, however, it is necessary to understand how Iran arrived at its current parlous state.

THE BEST OF ENEMIES

AFTER THE SEIZURE of the U.S. embassy in Tehran in November 1979 by a radical group calling themselves "Students Following the Imam Line," the United States suspended diplomatic relations with Iran. But this "absence" of diplomatic ties has always been somewhat unreal. Mutual demonization has gone hand in hand with participation by the two countries in venues such as the claims tribunal set up in The Hague to arbitrate U.S.-Iran financial disputes. Formal encounters and even coopera-

tion have taken place in the context of multilateral conferences on the future of Afghanistan and on antidrug efforts. The United States had maintained unilateral sanctions on trade and investment with Iran but also carried out clandestine arms-for-hostages deals. There are even reports of joint efforts to combat al Qaeda terrorists and Iraqi oil smugglers, as well as other forms of bilateral cooperation. But neither party has been willing to publicize these supposed contacts.

In fact, despite occasional signs of rapprochement in the last quarter-century, the relationship has remained stalled. Informal polls in both countries have shown no strong domestic opposition to resuming ties, but the influence of powerful hard-line minorities in each country and a number of outstanding disputes that push domestic political buttons have held back all efforts at conciliation. At the same time, Tehran's perception of Washington's eagerness to improve ties has encouraged Iranian foreign-policy makers to increase their demands.

> ## U.S. policy apparently calls for regime change in Iran but trusts the Iranian people to do it themselves.

Washington initially pointed to five major obstacles to the resumption of relations: Iran's state sponsorship of international terrorism, its pursuit of weapons of mass destruction, its opposition to the Arab-Israeli peace process, its threats to neighbors in the Persian Gulf, and its regime's violations of human rights at home. In recent years, the last two issues seem to have lost some of their potency and are now only infrequently raised. On the other hand, a new accusation of Iran's harboring of al Qaeda operatives has recently been added to the list.

The Islamic Republic, for its part, originally demanded that the United States accept the legitimacy of the 1979 revolution, not interfere in Iran's internal affairs, and deal with the Iranian regime on the basis of "respect and equality," As Tehran became more secure domestically and reduced its international isolation, further conditions were added: lifting U.S. economic sanctions, releasing frozen Iranian assets in the United States, and removing the U.S. Navy from the Persian Gulf. The Clinton administration's mildly conciliatory gestures emboldened the ruling clerics to demand even more: an end to one-sided support for Israel and a formal apology for Washington's past misdeeds. Some of these demands have been emphasized more than others, depending on domestic politics within Iran.

After the election of President Muhammad Khatami in 1997 and his subsequent suggestion that "the wall of mistrust" between the two countries be torn down, reconciliation once more began to seem possible, particularly toward the end of Bill Clinton's administration. But mutual hostility was suddenly raised to a new high under George W. Bush. Lumping Iran with Iraq and North Korea in an "axis of evil." Bush castigated Iran for a series of wrongdoings. In particular the pursuit of weapons of mass destruction. This announcement was presumably designed to please hawks at home, garner international support for the war on terror, and warn Tehran of the consequences of any new mischief.

The message, not surprisingly, backfired. The implied threat in downgrading Iran from "rogue" to "evil" status pleased the Iranian opposition in exile but invoked a fiery response from the regime. Government officials dismissed the accusation as another brutish manifestation of the United States' "global arrogance," and many Iranians took it as a deep insult to their national dignity. Significantly, the conflict also caused considerable unease among U.S. allies in Europe and Japan. Ironically enough, the U.S. move also led to increased official contacts between Iran and Iraq.

In an apparent attempt to control the damage and separate good from evil, Washington subsequently drew a distinction between the powerless "elected" reformers in the *Majles* and the relatively weak local councils, and the "unelected" clerics who hold the levers of power. A White House press release on July 12, 2002, assured all Iranians who sought freedom and human rights that they had no better friend than the United States. This communiqué, however, which was apparently timed to coincide with the third anniversary of the prodemocracy student uprisings at Tehran University, again caused a backlash.

The unelected rulers whom Bush sought to condemn used the message to arouse public anger against the United States. Supreme Leader Ali Khamenei (who is backed by hard-line fundamentalists), Khatami (who spearheads the elected reformists), and former president Hashemi Rafsanjani (who leads the modern technocrats) joined together to denounce Bush's statement as interference in Iran's domestic politics. Even Ayatollah Jalaleddin Taheri—a leading dissident who had chastised the theocracy days earlier and was expected to welcome U.S. support—joined the three in asking for anti-American demonstration. Indeed, many reformers, eager to prove their patriotic bona fides, were more vehement than were conservatives in repudiating the White House's message. As a result of this united front, government-sponsored demonstrations in Tehran and other major cities became a forum for a brand of virulent anti-Americanism rarely witnessed during Khatami's presidency.

Meanwhile, rumors circulated in Tehran that in response to the U.S. pressure, conservative hard-liners were planning to declare a state of emergency, dissolve the *Majles*, and dismiss the Khatami government. Although this crackdown did not happen, the conservative-led judiciary did close newspapers, harass and jail dissidents, forbid the teaching of Western music, insist that shops and restaurants close at midnight, and in general suppress domestic opposition—all in the name of social order.

Noting the failure of its proreform effort, the Bush administration articulated a new "dual track" approach based on "moral clarity." Zalmay Khalilzd a senior National Security Council staff member, unveiled the latest U.S. policy at an influential Washington think tank. The United States now would not seek to impose change in Iran but would instead support the Iranian people in their own quest for democracy. A literal interpretation of this dual-track policy is that the United States finds the Islamic Republic's behavior destructive and unacceptable and is thus calling for the regime change—but that Washington trusts the Iranian people to do it themselves. Subsequent calls in mid-November 2002 by State Department officials and Voice of America broadcasts for the Islamic Republic to "listen to its people" who were demanding "a change in the way they are being governed" were again strongly rejected by Khatami's government as interference in Iran's internal affairs.

THE ROAD TO TEHRAN

To FIND a truly effective policy within this new dual-track posture will require an understanding of what makes Iran tick—a combination of a fierce sense of national independence, the Byzantine dynamics of Iran's domestic politics, the freewheeling character of Shi'a theology and the emergence of the Third Force. A look at the interplay of these four factors reveal why past U.S. strategies (such as sanctions, containment, and diplomatic pressure) have not been able to change the Islamic Republic's behavior.

Iranian's fierce nationalism is characterized by intense suspicion and outright resentment of outside influences. For example, Ayatollah Khomeini climbed to the Peacock Throne not on the wings of Koranic angels but mainly by championing freedom from U.S. interference. Khomeini's portrayal of the shah as Washington's stooge drew wide appeal because it channeled resentment about British and Russian influence during the previous 200 years of Iranian history. Indeed. The well-publicized chants of "Death to America" by government-organized demonstrators resonate much less with the vast majority of Iranians than does Khomeini's famous comment in the wake of the revolution that "America cannot do a damn thing." Thus any U.S. strategy that even remotely raises the specter of foreign interference in Iran is doomed to fail.

Beyond looking at this yearning for independence, outside observers must also take into account the state of Iran's domestic politics. Contrary to the popular caricature, both the "reformers" and the "conservatives" in Iran are cut from the same cloth. Both camps are byproducts of the same revolution, and both are sworn to abide by the basically undemocratic and even subtly xenophobic 1979 constitution. Few of the current reformers are Jeffersonian democrats; in fact, they are firmly committed to the union of mosque and state. Neither they nor their conservative opponents share America's human rights culture. Consequently, any U.S. policy that favors one group over the other will have little chance of success. Overt support for the opposition abroad or dissidents at home will enable the conservative power-holders to brand the reformers as American lackeys. Similarly, any compromise with the conservatives will likewise be interpreted by the reformers as a sellout by Washington.

Third, it would be a major strategic mistake to treat the Shi'a clerics in Iran as a unified force that rejects modernization or even Westernization. The highly unstructured hierarchy of the Shi'a sect allows Iran's ten or so grand ayatollahs to have not only their own disciples and private financing but also to independently issue religious edicts, or *fatwas*. Khatami's "politics of inclusion" and his plea for a "dialogue among civilization," both rooted in his view of Islamic scripture, can be understood in the same terms. Any successful U.S. strategy, therefore, should harness the positive influence of Iran's internal religious diversity and seek to direct it toward political change.

Finally, the government-encouraged baby boom of the early 1980s has now spawned a new generation, the Third Force, which sees neither the fundamentalists' concept of *velayat-e faqih* (the supremacy of Shi'a jurists) nor Khatami's "Islamic democracy" as the answer to Iran's current predicament. This highly politicized generation has no recollection of the 1979 revolution and no particular reverence for the eight-year "holy war" between Iran and Iraq. Rather, they focus on their frustrated ambitions for a better future. This group includes almost everyone who is not in power and a few who are, representing a wide swath of Iranian society. The common bond among these disparate groups is their disenchantment with the revolution and its aftermath and their distrust of the clerics' ability to cope with Iran's many problems. The Third Force, although still lacking resolute leadership and a specific platform, is united by a common goal of an independent, free, and prosperous Iran blessed by the rule of law. Indeed, some members have proposed a new constitution separating mosque and state, to be established by an internationally observed referendum.

RELIGION AND RECESSION

THE UNITED STATES should seize this moment to plan for Iran's political endgame because the regime's particular brand of politics and religion is in a state of ferment. At the same time, the government has been further weakened because it has failed to deliver on its promises of economic development.

The Iranian public and the press openly question the role of Islam in the country.

Ayatollah Khomeini built a governing ideology on concepts of independence, freedom, and the *velayat-e faqih*. This fusion of statecraft with piety through the absolute power of a supreme leader (the *rahbar*) is now beginning to crumble. The first crack appeared in 1997 when the philosophy's principal architect, Grand Ayatollah Hossein Ali Montazeri, rejected the unquestioned power of the *rahbar* on the grounds that Islam forbids the supremacy of fallible humans. Emboldened by this attack on Khomeini's orthodoxy, a number of mid-ranking clerics and seminarians have subsequently denounced theocratic intrusion into daily life, refusing to accept the inviolability of the *rahbar*'s religious edicts and even allowing fresh interpretations of the Koran itself. The new generation of clerics, taking their cue from older theologians such as Montazeri, now openly questions the legitimacy of absolutist religious power and even speaks of the need for an Islamic reformation. Some young seminarians in the holy city of Qom are now even questioning whether the unity of mosque and state is in their interest, since the unpopularity of the Islamic regime has reduced the number of clerics in the *Majles* and local councils and has also shrunk sources of private funding.

The latest condemnation of the regime came from Ayatollah Taheri, who in July 2002, while resigning from his post as the leader of Friday prayers in Isfahan, lambasted the religious hard-liners for incompetence and corruption. The cleric, formerly a devoted Khomeini follower and an early revolutionary during the shah's time, bemoaned the host of social, political, and economic woes afflicting the country—from rising unemployment to growing drug addiction to increasing disregard for the law. No previous internal criticism of the theocratic regime had ever been this scathing. The response by the leadership was mostly dismissive. However, Supreme Leader Khamenei, while complaining that this type of dissent would only embolden the regime's enemies, did acknowledge that he himself had pointed to some of the same shortcomings.

Trust in the power of Islamist ideology has declined even more profoundly as Khomeini's mixture of religion and politics has failed to deliver its promised rewards of prosperity and social justice. Despite a 100 percent rise in average annual oil income since the revolution, most indicators of economic welfare have steadily deteriorated. The so-called misery index (a combination of inflation and unemployment) has reached new highs. Average inflation in the years after the revolution has been at least twice as high as during the 1970s, unemployment has been three times higher, and economic growth is two-thirds lower. As a result, Iran's per capita income has declined by at least 30 percent since 1979. By official admission, more than 15 percent of the population now lives below the absolute poverty line, and private estimates run as high as 40 percent.

A combination of slow growth, double-digit unemployment, high inflation, declining labor productivity, and increasing dependence on oil revenue has thus defied almost all government efforts to put the economy back on track. Although the alarming rate of population growth in the first decade after the revolution has been brought under control, both per capita income and domestic income distribution lag behind official targets. In short, the ailing economy has helped bring the regime's legitimacy further into question. A recent study leaked from Iran's Interior Ministry revealed that nearly 90 percent of the public is dissatisfied with the present government. Of this total 28 percent wants "fundamental" changes in the regime's structure, and 66 percent desires "gradual reforms." Less than 11 percent—most probably those on the government dole—is satisfied with the status quo. Other private polls show an even greater degree of unhappiness with the government.

The combination of these two phenomena—the bankruptcy of Iran's ideology and the failure of its economy—now confronts the Islamic Republic with the worst challenge to its legitimacy yet. The public and the press now openly question the role of Islam—and especially the concept of the *velayat-e faqih*—in a society where people want greater freedom and the rule of law.

A TEHRAN SPRING?

IRAN'S CONSERVATIVE CLERICS are now helplessly witnessing a slow but steady drive toward democratization. Despite the political crackdown, legislative deadlock, and rumors of a coup, two provocative and parallel developments are challenging the mullahs' hegemony and paving the way for the regime's eventual collapse.

The first development relates to the expansion of civil society and the use of civil disobedience to loosen the theocracy's grip on national institutions. Nongovernmental organizations are being formed by the thousands, with and without official permission, to deal with ongoing problems ranging from family planning to drug addiction to pollution. Workers have formed informal (and extralegal) trade unions, and students have organized both Islamic and secular unions of their own. Despite a wave of newspaper closings and press repression, there are now 22 percent more licensed publications than there were in 1998. Furthermore, journalists have found a new haven in cyberspace beyond the authorities' reach. Currently, more than 1.75 million Iranians reportedly have access to the Internet. Even some nonestablishment aya-

tollahs have set up their own Web sites to connect with their flock. Their *fatwas* are now used by dissidents to counter the positions of the ruling clerics.

Street demonstrations, labor strikes, teacher's boycotts, and other forms of civil disobedience (such as taunting the morals police with un-Islamic attire) are increasingly common. For instance, thousands of workers demonstrating against poor working conditions managed to increase this year's official minimum wage. Strikes by teachers resulted in a substantial increase in this year's education budget. Human rights activists have also pushed the authorities to respond to foreign public opinion. According to the latest report by Human Rights Watch, the Islamic Republic may now start cooperating with foreign monitors for the first time. And in a noteworthy victory, the government shelved a bizarre, religiously sanctioned scheme to set up "temporary weddings" after women's groups, politicians, and some clerics denounced it as legalized prostitution. Most recently, several consecutive days of nationwide student protest in mid-November 2002 forced the supreme leader and the head of the judiciary to order an appeals court to expedite review of the death sentence imposed on reformist scholar Hashem Aghajari. The *rahbar* also recommended to judges that they avoid opening themselves up to public criticism in their rulings.

The second important change in Iran is a series of small but significant economic measures that are likely to reduce the oligarchs' economic power and help integrate Iran's oil-dependent economy with the global marketplace. The reduction of the hard-liners' financial support is a critical factor in their declining political clout. Indeed, more than any ideological or religious factor, it is control of the nation's economic resources that has allowed Iran's ruling clerics to hold on to power. Donations by devout Muslims, public and private monopolies in key sectors, special business licenses dispensed through patronage, privileged access to cheap credit and foreign exchange, and even widely reported bank fraud have all helped fund the clerics.

Crucial economic reforms, repeatedly promised by Khatami in the last five years, have partially taken shape in the last few months. This change has occurred largely in response to pressure from foreign institutions such as the International Monetary Fund, the World Bank, and the European Commission, whose approval is necessary for the government's continued access to foreign credit. Although these reforms will not dry up all the hard-liner's sources of funding overnight, they can affect them in critical areas. For instance, the legalization of private banking and insurance since early 2000 has opened up new venues for the mobilization and allocation of national savings—and removed them from potential political uses by state banks. The government's efforts to consolidate the country's multiple exchange rates since March 2002 has also bottled up corruption stemming from access to cheaper dollars by privileged institutions or favored cronies. Fiscal reform in late 2001 aimed at lowering corporate income taxes and eliminating tax exemption for so-called religious charitable foundations is expected to increase private investment and level the playing field for potential investors. The government's new law to protect foreign investment and enforce some copyrights may reduce dependence on oil revenue. A successful euro bond issue this past summer has opened up another source of foreign exchange to counter volatility in oil prices.

The government has promised to take a number of further steps in the coming months to privatize state enterprises and further diminish the hard-liners' control of the economy. Replacing the inefficient subsidy system (which takes up some 20 percent of GDP and benefits mostly the urban rich) with a means-tested social safety net would substantially lighten the government's fiscal burden. In addition, further consolidation of the tax code should reduce the more than 50 different fees that various ministries and agencies impose on production and imports, thus cutting collection costs and special sources of finance for pork-barrel projects. The government's plan to enact a value-added tax in lieu of the current uncollected (and uncollectable) income taxes would likely diminish reliance on oil income and also shrink the bureaucracy.

Replacing the current system of quotas and special licenses on imports with tariffs would eliminate the monopolies enjoyed by politically favorite business interests. A comprehensive overhaul of the outdated 1968 commercial code would encourage more transparent and productive ventures, particularly in the small business sector. A revision of the current anti business labor law, enacted when leftist ideologues controlled the Fourth *Majles* in 1990, would encourage new employment. Downsizing the bloated bureaucracy may stop oil income from being invested in politically favored but economically unsound projects. Turning the Tehran Stock Exchange into a self-regulated but politically supervised institution would promote the establishment of mutual funds to attract both domestic and foreign capital.

Finally, Iran's entry into the World Trade Organization (so far blocked by the United States) and the conclusion of a comprehensive trade and cooperation accord with the European Union would shake the entrenched economic mafia to its roots and revolutionize the Iranian economy. The WTO's mantra of free markets is anathema to the Islamic Republic's state-dominated and highly politicized economic system. To qualify for full membership, Iran must make a host of economic changes, ranging from trade liberalization to financial deregulation to copyright protection. These new reforms will undoubtedly meet with severe resistance from vested interests. But the urgent need to find jobs for the millions of unemployed—combined with the paucity of domestic investment, sluggish non-oil exports, and weak foreign-exchange reserves—makes turning to the global economy inevitable.

And this shift will not be possible without fundamental reform.

THE IRAQ CARD

THE INTERNAL CURRENTS shaping Iran's future will undoubtedly be affected by events in the region, particularly the fate of Saddam Hussein's regime in Iraq. At present official Iranian policy, under a principle of "active neutrality", opposes U.S. preemptive action without a United Nations mandate as a "dangerous precedent." In part, the government objects out of a scarcely concealed concern that it could face a similar U.S. challenge one day. Although Tehran would certainly be happy to see Saddam go, Iran's government also worries that the establishment of a pro-American regime in Baghdad would leave Iran encircled by U.S. allies. The ruling clerics are similarly not enthusiastic about the prospect of a free and democratic Iraq, which would surely encourage the Third Force to intensify its reform efforts.

Virtually all Iranians oppose Iraq's partition or potential disintegration for fear that Iraqi Kurds may incite their counterparts in Iran to rise up and agitate for an independent state. Additionally, Iran does not wish to see a long-term decline in the price of oil as Iraq again pumps at full capacity. There is also concern that major international oil companies may invest in Iraqi oil fields at Iran's expense. It is impossible to know at this stage how these various forces will interact.

THE TIPPING POINT

THE ONGOING POLITICAL IMPASSE, economic distress, and social turmoil (not to mention a possible invasion of Iraq) all threaten the survival of the Islamic state. The discontent of the Third Force in particular has created a seemingly unstoppable momentum toward change. In its post revolutionary history, Iran has never been as politically polarized or ideologically divided as it is today.

Khatami's recent belated attempt to reclaim his authority has raised the political temperature several degrees. His open suggestion that he might resign if further stymied by the Council of Guardians or the judiciary, as well as threats of mass resignation from members of the Islamic Participation Front (the largest bloc in the *Majles*), is an ominous warning of a looming constitutional crisis or worse in coming months. Two bills submitted by Khatami to the *Majles* in September 2002, which are now undergoing the long process of ratification, would curb the veto power of the Council of Guardians and give the president legal authority to force hard-line Islamic courts to abide by the constitution. The renewed crackdown by the judiciary on reformist groups is reported to be an attempt to pressure the president to withdraw these bills. Regardless of the ultimate fate of this controversial legislation, its very introduction marks a major turning point in Iran's domestic political dynamics.

Temporary reversals of democratization nevertheless remain likely. But the Iranian people have sown the seeds of change and the country's theocratic rulers cannot postpone their harvest forever. The autocratic and dubiously Islamic concept of the *velayat-e faqih* is clearly in retreat and the oligarchs know that if they do not bend, they will break. A recent open letter signed by more than 125 former *Majles* deputies lambasting the hard-liners made this point abundantly clear.

These developments should not suggest, however, that Washington can determine or even affect the outcome of Iran's political ferment. Events within Iran will dictate the U.S. posture rather than the other way around. Clerical dogmatism cannot be defeated from afar—particularly given Iranians' profound mistrust of outside meddling.

If the United States truly wishes to see a modern, democratic, and peaceful Iran, Washington must follow a calculated "wait and see" policy. Neither Bush's anger, nor his empathy, nor even his promise of friendship with democratic forces will be enough to change Iran. Thus as long as U.S. vital national interests are not seriously threatened and Iran is not clearly implicated in anti-American terrorist acts, the United States should refrain from both unsubstantiated accusations and implied threats against the Islamic Republic. Washington would be best served by letting the currently accelerating process of democratization run its course. The theocracy's days are numbered—Iran's own internal currents assure this.

JAHANGIR AMUZEGAR is an international economic consultant. He was Finance Minister and Economic Ambassador in Iran's pre-1979 government.

Bin Laden, the Arab "Street," and the Middle East's Democracy Deficit

"Bin Laden speaks in the vivid language of popular Islamic preachers, and builds on a deep and widespread resentment against the West and local ruling elites identified with it. The lack of formal outlets to express opinion on public concerns has created [a] democracy deficit in much of the Arab world, and this makes it easier for terrorists such as bin Laden, asserting that they act in the name of religion, to hijack the Arab street."

DALE F. EICKELMAN

In the years ahead, the role of public diplomacy and open communications will play an increasingly significant role in countering the image that the Al Qaeda terrorist network and Osama bin Laden assert for themselves as guardians of Islamic values. In the fight against terrorism for which bin Laden is the photogenic icon, the first step is to recognize that he is as thoroughly a part of the modern world as was Cambodia's French-educated Pol Pot. Bin Laden's videotaped presentation of self intends to convey a traditional Islamic warrior brought up-to-date, but this sense of the past is a completely invented one. The language and content of his videotaped appeals convey more of his participation in the modern world than his camouflage jacket, Kalashnikov, and Timex watch.

Take the two-hour Al Qaeda recruitment videotape in Arabic that has made its way to many Middle Eastern video shops and Western news media.[1] It is a skillful production, as fast paced and gripping as any Hindu fundamentalist video justifying the destruction in 1992 of the Ayodhya mosque in India, or the political attack videos so heavily used in American presidential campaigning. The 1988 "Willie Horton" campaign video of Republican presidential candidate George H. W. Bush—in which an off-screen announcer portrayed Democratic presidential candidate Michael Dukakis as "soft" on crime while showing a mug shot of a convicted African-American rapist who had committed a second rape during a weekend furlough from a Massachusetts prison—was a propaganda masterpiece that combined an explicit although conventional message with a menacing, underlying one intended to motivate undecided voters. The Al Qaeda video, directed at a different audience—presumably alienated Arab youth, unemployed and often living in desperate conditions—shows an equal mastery of modern propaganda.

The Al Qaeda producers could have graduated from one of the best film schools in the United States or Europe. The fast-moving recruitment video begins with the bombing of the USS *Cole* in Yemen, but then shows a montage implying a seemingly coordinated worldwide aggression against Muslims in Palestine, Jerusalem, Lebanon, Chechnya, Kashmir, and Indonesia (but not Muslim violence against Christians and Chinese in the last). It also shows United States generals received by Saudi princes, intimating the collusion of local regimes with the West and challenging the legitimacy of many regimes, including Saudi Arabia. The sufferings of the Iraqi people are attributed to American brutality against Muslims, but Saddam Hussein is assimilated to the category of infidel ruler.

Osama bin Laden… is thoroughly imbued with the values of the modern world, even if only to reject them.

Many of the images are taken from the daily staple of Western video news—the BBC and CNN logos add to the videos' authenticity, just as Qatar's al-Jazeera satellite television logo rebroadcast by CNN and the BBC has added authenticity to Western coverage of Osama bin Laden.

Alternating with these scenes of devastation and oppression of Muslims are images of Osama bin Laden: posing in front of bookshelves or seated on the ground like a religious scholar, holding the Koran in his hand. Bin Laden radiates charismatic authority and control as he narrates the Prophet Mohammed's flight from Mecca to Medina, when the early Islamic movement was threatened by the idolaters, but returning to conquer them. Bin Laden also stresses the need for jihad, or struggle for the cause of Islam, against the "crusaders" and "Zionists." Later images show military training in Afghanistan (including target practice at a poster of Bill Clinton), and a final sequence—the word "solution" flashes across the screen—captures an Israeli soldier in full riot gear retreating from a Palestinian boy throwing stones, and a reading of the Koran.

THE THOROUGHLY MODERN ISLAMIST

Osama bin Laden, like many of his associates, is imbued with the values of the modern world, even if only to reject them. A 1971 photograph shows him on family holiday in Oxford at the age of 14, posing with two of his half-brothers and Spanish girls their own age. English was their common language of communication. Bin Laden studied English at a private school in Jidda, and English was also useful for his civil engineering courses at Jidda's King Abdul Aziz University. Unlike many of his estranged half-brothers, educated in Saudi Arabia, Europe, and the United States, Osama's education was only in Saudi Arabia, but he was also familiar with Arab and European society.

The organizational skills he learned in Saudi Arabia came in to play when he joined the mujahideen (guerrilla) struggle against the 1979 Soviet invasion of Afghanistan. He may not have directly met United States intelligence officers in the field, but they, like their Saudi and Pakistani counterparts, were delighted to have him participate in their fight against Soviet troops and recruit willing Arab fighters. Likewise, his many business enterprises flourished under highly adverse conditions. Bin Laden skillfully sustained a flexible multinational organization in the face of enemies, especially state authorities, moving cash, people, and supplies almost undetected across international frontiers.

The organizational skills of bin Laden and his associates were never underestimated. Neither should be their skills in conveying a message that appeals to some Muslims. Bin Laden lacks the credentials of an established Islamic scholar, but this does not diminish his appeal. As Sudan's Sorbonne-educated Hasan al-Turabi, the leader of his country's Muslim Brotherhood and its former attorney general and speaker of parliament, explained two decades ago, "Because all knowledge is divine and religious, a chemist, an engineer, an economist, or a jurist" are all men of learning.[2] Civil engineer bin Laden exemplifies Turabi's point. His audience judges him not by his ability to cite authoritative texts, but by his apparent skill in applying generally accepted religious tenets to current political and social issues.

THE MESSAGE ON THE ARAB "STREET"

Bin Laden's lectures circulate in book form in the Arab world, but video is the main vehicle of communication. The use of CNN-like "zippers"—the ribbons of words that stream beneath the images in many newscasts and documentaries—shows that Al Qaeda takes the Arab world's rising levels of education for granted. Increasingly, this audience is also saturated with both conventional media and new media, such as the Internet.[3] The Middle East has entered an era of mass education and this also implies an Arabic lingua franca. In Morocco in the early 1970s, rural people sometimes asked me to "translate" newscasts from the standard transnational Arabic of the state radio into colloquial Arabic. Today this is no longer required. Mass education and new communications technologies enable large numbers of Arabs to hear—and see—Al Qaeda's message directly.

Bin Laden's message does not depend on religious themes alone. Like the Ayatollah Ruhollah Khomeini, his message contains many secular elements. Khomeini often alluded to the "wretched of the earth." At least for a time, his language appealed equally to Iran's religiously minded and to the secular left. For bin Laden, the equivalent themes are the oppression and corruption of many Arab governments, and he lays the blame for the violence and oppression in Palestine, Kashmir, Chechnya, and elsewhere at the door of the West. One need not be religious to rally to some of these themes. A poll taken in Morocco in late September 2001 showed that a majority of Moroccans condemned the September 11 bombings, but 41 percent sympathized with bin Laden's message. A British poll taken at about the same time showed similar results.

Osama bin Laden and the Al Qaeda terrorist movement are thus reaching at least part of the Arab "street." Earlier this year, before the September terrorist attacks, United States policymakers considered this "street" a "new phenomenon of public accountability, which we have seldom had to factor into our projections of Arab behavior in the past. The information revolution, and particularly the daily dose of uncensored television coming out of local TV stations like al-Jazeera and international coverage by CNN and others, is shaping public opinion, which, in turn, is pushing Arab governments to respond. We don't know, and the leaders themselves don't know, how that pressure will impact on Arab policy in the future."[4]

Director of Central Intelligence George J. Tenet was even more cautionary on the nature of the "Arab street." In testimony before the Senate Select Committee on Intelligence in February 2001, he explained that the "right catalyst—such as the outbreak of Israeli-Palestinian violence—can move people to act. Through access to the Internet and other means of communication, a restive public is increasingly capable of taking action without any identifiable leadership or organizational structure."

Because many governments in the Middle East are deeply suspicious of an open press, nongovernmental organizations, and open expression, it is no surprise that the "restive" public, increasingly educated and influenced by hard-to-censor new media, can take action "without any identifiable leadership or organized structure." The Middle East in general has a democracy deficit, in which "unauthorized" leaders or critics, such as Egyptian academic Saad Eddin Ibrahim—founder and director of the Ibn Khaldun Center for Development Studies, a nongovernmental organization that promotes democracy in Egypt—suffer harassment or prison terms.

One consequence of this democracy deficit is to magnify the power of the street in the Arab world. Bin Laden speaks in the vivid language of popular Islamic preachers, and builds on a deep and widespread resentment against the West and local ruling elites identified with it. The lack of formal outlets to express opinion on public concerns has created the democracy deficit in much of the Arab world, and this makes it easier for terrorists such as bin Ladin, asserting that they act in the name of religion, to hijack the Arab street.

The immediate response is to learn to speak directly to this street. This task has already begun. Obscure to all except specialists until September 11, Qatar's al-Jazeera satellite television is a premier source in the Arab world for uncensored news and opinion. It is more, however, than the Arab equivalent of CNN. Uncensored news and opinions increasingly shape "public opinion"—a term without the pejorative overtones of "the street"—even in places like Damascus and Algiers. This public opinion in turn pushes Arab governments to be more responsive to their citizens, or at least to say that they are.

Rather than seek to censor al-Jazeera or limit Al Qaeda's access to the Western media—an unfortunate first response of the United States government after the September terror attacks—we should avoid censorship. Al Qaeda statements should be treated with the same caution as any other news source. Replacing Sinn Fein leader Gerry Adams' voice and image in the British media in the 1980s with an Irish-accented actor appearing in silhouette only highlighted what he had to say, and it is unlikely that the British public would tolerate the same restrictions on the media today.

Ironically, at almost the same time that national security adviser Condoleezza Rice asked the American television networks not to air Al Qaeda videos unedited, a former senior CIA officer, Graham Fuller, was explaining in Arabic on al-Jazeera how United States policymaking works. His appearance on al-Jazeera made a significant impact, as did Secretary of State Colin Powell's presence on a later al-Jazeera program and former United States Ambassador Christopher Ross, who speaks fluent Arabic. Likewise, the timing and content of British Prime Minister Tony Blair's response to an earlier bin Laden tape suggests how to take the emerging Arab public seriously. The day after al-Jazeera broadcast the bin Laden tape, Blair asked for and received an opportunity to respond. In his reply, Blair—in a first for a Western leader—directly addressed the Arab public through the Arab media, explaining coalition goals in attacking Al Qaeda and the Taliban and challenging bin Laden's claim to speak in the name of Islam.

PUTTING PUBLIC DIPLOMACY TO WORK

Such appearances enhance the West's ability to communicate a primary message: that the war against terrorism is not that of one civilization against another, but against terrorism and fanaticism in all societies. Western policies and actions are subject to public scrutiny and will often be misunderstood. Public diplomacy can significantly diminish this misapprehension. It may, however, involve some uncomfortable policy decisions. For instance, America may be forced to exert more diplomatic pressure on Israel to alter its methods of dealing with Palestinians.

Western public diplomacy in the Middle East also involves uncharted waters. As Oxford University social linguist Clive Holes has noted, the linguistic genius who thought up the first name for the campaign to oust the Taliban, "Operation Infinite Justice," did a major disservice to the Western goal. The expression was literally and accurately translated into Arabic as *adala ghayr mutanahiya,* implying that an earthly power arrogated to itself the task of divine retribution. Likewise, President George W. Bush's inadvertent and unscripted use of the word "crusade" gave Al Qaeda spokesmen an opportunity to attack Bush and Western intentions.

Mistakes will be made, but information and arguments that reach the Arab street, including on al-Jazeera, will eventually have an impact. Some Westerners might condemn al-Jazeera as biased, and it may well be in terms of making assumptions about its audience. However, it has broken a taboo by regularly inviting official Israeli spokespersons to comment live on current issues. Muslim religious scholars, both in the Middle East and in the West, have already spoken out against Al Qaeda's claim to act in the name of Islam. Other courageous voices, such as Egyptian playwright Ali Salem, have even employed humor for the same purpose.[5]

We must recognize that the best way to mitigate the continuing threat of terrorism is to encourage Middle Eastern states to be more responsive to participatory demands, and to aid local nongovernmental organizations working toward this goal. As with the case of Egypt's Saad Eddin Ibrahim, some countries may see such activities as subversive. Whether Arab states like it or not, increasing levels of education, greater ease of travel, and the rise of new communications media are turning the Arab street into a public sphere in which greater numbers of people, and not just a political and economic elite, will have a say in governance and public issues.

NOTES

1. It is now available on-line with explanatory notes in English. See <http://www.ciaonet.org/cbr/cbr00/video/excerpts_index.html>.

2. Hasan al-Turabi, "The Islamic State," in *Voices of Resurgent Islam,* John L. Esposito, ed. (New York: Oxford University Press, 1983), p. 245.

3. On the importance of rising levels of education and the new media, see Dale F. Eickelman, "The Coming Transformation in the Muslim World," *Current History,* January 2000.

4. Edward S. Walker, "The New US Administration's Middle East Policy Speech," *Middle East Economic Survey,* vol. 44, no. 26 (June 25, 2001). Available at <http://www.mees.com/news/a44n26d01.htm>.

5. See his article in Arabic, "I Want to Start a Kindergarten for Extremism," *Al-Hayat* (London), November 5, 2001. This is translated into English by the Middle East Media Research Institute as Special Dispatch no. 298, Jihad and Terrorism Studies, November 8, 2001, at <http://www.memri.org>.

DALE F. EICKELMAN *is Ralph and Richard Lazarus Professor of Anthropology and Human Relations at Dartmouth College. His most recent book is* The Middle East and Central Asia: An Anthropological Approach, *4th ed. (Englewood Cliffs, N. J.: Prentice Hall, 2002). An earlier version of this article appeared as "The West Should Speak to the Arab in the Street,"* Daily Telegraph *(London), October 27, 2001.*

Reprinted from *Current History,* January 2002, pp. 36-39. © 2002 by Current History, Inc. Reprinted by permission.

There Is No Crash Course In Democracy

By JOHN F. BURNS

HILLA, Iraq

AMERICANS have set out to teach Iraqis about democracy, and the way it is going says much about the differing cultures and histories and aspirations of the teachers and the students. It is another matter whether the American effort can succeed: Whether President Bush will be able to make Iraq a torch of democracy capable of lighting a fire among the autocracies and dictatorships of the Arab world, or will end up resembling Woodrow Wilson with his belief that the League of Nations would make the world safe for Jeffersonian values after World War I.

The venue for the "democracy training" classes run by American occupation authorities at Hilla, 80 miles south of Baghdad, could scarcely have been more apt for the transition the Americans hope to achieve before the deadline they have set for handing sovereignty back to an Iraqi provisional government next June. The Iraqis who take power then, according to the accelerated timetable approved by Mr. Bush last month, will lead the country as it adopts a constitution with American-style rights and moves to popular elections for a full-fledged new government by the end of 2005.

Overhanging everything here is the shadow of Saddam Hussein, his tyranny and mass murder. So it was apt that James Mayfield, the 70-year-old emeritus professor of the University of Utah who has led the classes, an expert in local government in the Middle East, should find himself addressing Iraqi tribal leaders and stern-faced Shiite clerics in a crypt-like room at the rear of a huge mosque that Mr. Hussein built to his own glory in the closing passage of his 24-year rule.

For the Americans, the tribal leaders and the clerics are crucial constituencies. Many in this country of 25 million give their first and overriding loyalty to their tribal families, and to the men who control

their mosques. It was a fact acknowledged by Mr. Hussein, who accompanied his terror with a policy of buying and compromising tribesmen and clerics alike. The Americans too need their backing if they are to work their way back to anything approaching broad support after the months of erosion following the invasion.

An American talks of law and divided government, but an Iraqi can't translate.

At Hilla, it was a tough sell, presaging the problems in forging anything like a consensus on the government that will emerge from the occupation. Tribal and religious leaders, after all, are among those who stand to lose the most if Iraq adopts the broader civic principles preached by Mr. Mayfield. The men who came to Hilla are, for the most part, schooled in the arts of subterfuge and maneuver that find no place in the democratic handbook. "We are chameleons," one of them boasted, after acknowledging that a year ago he could have been found at the mosque limning the praises of Mr. Hussein and celebrating his re-election as Iraq's president by a claimed 100 percent of the vote.

The man who said that, Sayed Farqad Al-Qiswini, is president of the theological college that took over the mosque after Mr. Hussein's downfall, stripping the marble entranceways of plaques that had reminded the dangerously absent-minded or suicidally irreverent that they were stepping into a place of worship not of God alone, but of Mr. Hussein. A senior cleric, Mr. Qiswini had the merit of candor, at least, when discussing his erstwhile fealty to Mr. Hussein. "If you said anything against Saddam, you might as well have jumped into a boiling sea." He

said. "I had no intention of jumping into the sea."

This pliability, essential to survival under Mr. Hussein, is a problem now for the Americans, who are arguing for a politics of principle in a country that has had no legitimacy save the gun for most of its existence, under the British after World War I, under the monarchy that was overthrown in 1958, and under the Baathists who paved Mr. Hussein's path to power. If principle were all, America would have little problem in persuading Iraqis of the merit of the formulas brought by the new rulers, focused on the need for a government that can be held accountable to the people.

Listening to Mr. Qiswini, it was possible at times to think him a stalwart advocate of everything in the Mayfield handbook. After the democracy class adjourned, he led a visitor out to a monument in the mosque's parking lot in memory of the thousands of Iraqis, mostly Shiites, who were buried in the largest mass grave discovered since April, at Mahawel, a few miles up the road. Standing there, it was easy to believe him when he said Iraqis had learned a bitter lesson from the dictatorship, that no man should ever again be allowed to concentrate power like Mr. Hussein.

"Saddam Hussein stripped Iraqis of all morality, of all conscience, and left us like a blank sheet of paper, ready for the writing of a new creed," he said as fellow graduates gathered. "We would rather eat dirt than have somebody like Saddam back in power again. All Iraqis have resolved never to allow the tyranny to be restored. So we will construct a new society that will be a model for all the countries in the Middle East."

'We are chameleons,' said an Iraqi in a class on government.

But it was striking how he avoided mention of the word democracy, the keystone of everything the American lecturer had said. Mr. Qiswini is a local strongman for Muqtada Sadr, the 30-year-old cleric who issues edicts from a Shiite slum in northeast Baghdad and is the son of an ayatollah assassinated on Mr. Hussein's orders in 1999.

Mr. Sadr has come out defiantly against the American occupation, and has devoted himself to street politics that emphasize the demand for a swift transition to an elected government, which in an Iraq with a 60 percent Shiite majority would mean, with certainty, an end to rule by the Sunni minority that has ruled since 1921. Briefly, in the fall, Mr. Sadr declared his movement to be the rightful government, suggesting that he, at least, is not an ardent student of the subtleties of constitutions and minority rights.

Finding ways to mitigate the effects of handing Iraq over to a Shiite-dominated government that might mistreat the Sunnis or simply dominate them is at the heart of the debate among the Americans and Britains who are working on a schedule for a constitution and elections.

At the core, this involves keeping promises made before the invasion that tyrannical centralism would be replaced by a federal system, with a bill of rights protecting minorities and other features to shape a working political relationship among the rival Sunnis, Shiites and Christians, as between Arabs, Kurds and Assyrians.

Nothing like this has ever been tried in Iraq before, and nothing like it, at least on more than paper, has been seen elsewhere in the Arab world. Still, the Americans are betting that Mr. Hussein's ultimate legacy will be, in effect, that past nightmares will draw Iraqis on a path of entrenched individual and group rights, of a firewall separation between church and state, of independence for the executive, legislative and judicial branches, and above all, of tolerance for minorities. In other words, the core of a civil society as understood in the West.

The vision is not shared by all Americans here. As they struggle to make sense of the volatile moods here, some senior officers have lowered their benchmarks for an American withdrawal. Now, they say, a stable pro-American government capable of defending itself against overthrow by Hussein irredentists would constitute a success. To hear some American officers and many ordinary Iraqis talk, the country's need is for a pro-Western strongman of the kind that govern in many other Arab countries.

Mr. Mayfield, the lecturer of Hilla, had a more ambitious view. In the gaps between power failures and a chorus of imprecations to Allah, he spoke of his epiphanies. He said he had met a 12-year-old boy who asked him. "Will this democracy you speak of give me a job?" In one way or another, that is the view of many Iraqis, impatient of political process but desperate to the point of rebellion for work, for electricity, for schools and hospitals that function as efficiently as they did under Mr. Hussein—and for law and order.

But Mr. Mayfield took an optimistic view: "I realized that a year ago if this young boy had stood and asked a question of that kind of Saddam Hussein, he would have been shot. And when the neighbors of this young boy started to clap, I took it as evidence that the people of Iraq want democracy."

The lecturer, however, ran onto stony ground when he tried to explain the importance of the separation of powers. "That's why a constitution is so important, so that they cannot take your property, they cannot put you in jail, they cannot force you to be tortured, because the courts are controlled by the government," he said. The interpreter, otherwise fluent in English, was stumped by the concept of divided government, and made several false starts in attempts to convey the idea before giving up.

Otherwise, the reaction of the class was polite, but hardly enthusiastic.

Something closer to a bottom line emerged when they were asked if it wasn't presumptuous to teach basic political principles to the citizens of a land long hailed as the cradle of civilization. Several men said Mr. Mayfield had said nothing new to Iraqis, because it was all written in the Koran anyway. Saddam Hussein, like Iraqi leaders for centuries, they said, was an aberration from Koranic principles, but that didn't mean Islam was at fault, only that it hadn't been properly applied since the Caliphs ruled in Baghdad nearly 1,000 years ago.

To travelers in the Muslim world, this sealed argument, attractive as it is, is unconvincing. The democratic possibilities in the Koran are most intensively studied at Islamic studies centers in Europe and the United States, not in the many Arab states where the propagation of democratic ideas can lead swiftly to prison. If Iraq can prove the exception, against all odds, the American venture here may et be the landmark its backers have hoped it will be.

UNIT 5

Comparative Politics: Some Major Trends, Issues, and Prospects

Unit Selections

Key Points to Consider

- What is meant by the first, second, and third waves of democratization?

- Discuss the reversals that followed the first two.

- Where are most of the countries affected by the third wave located?

- What factors appear to have contributed to their democratization?

- What are the signs that the third wave may be over?

- What are some main problems and dilemmas of old and new democracies, according to Larry Diamond?

- In what ways can market capitalism and liberal democracy be said to be mutually supportive, according to Gabriel Almond?

- What is the implication of the argument that in economics, one model or "size" is unlikely to "fit all"?

- What does Benjamin Barber mean when he warns that democracy is threatened by globalism and tribalism?

 **Links: www.dushkin.com/online/**
These sites are annotated in the World Wide Web pages.

Commission on Global Governance
http://www.sovereignty.net/p/gov/gganalysis.htm

IISDnet
http://www.iisd.org/default.asp

ISN International Relations and Security Network
http://www.isn.ethz.ch

United Nations Environment Program
http://www.unep.ch/

Virtual Seminar in Global Political Economy/Global Cities & Social Movements
http://csf.colorado.edu/gpe/gpe95b/resources.html

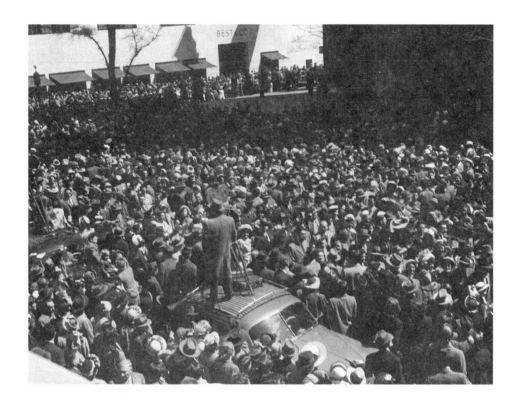

The articles in this unit deal with three major political trends or patterns of development that can be observed in much of the contemporary world. It is important at the outset to stress that, with the possible exception of Benjamin Barber, none of the authors predict some form of global convergence in which all political systems would become alike in major respects. On closer examination, even Barber turns out to argue that a strong tendency toward global homogenization is offset by a concurrent tendency toward intensified group differentiation and fragmentation.

Thus the trends or patterns discussed here are neither unidirectional nor universal. They are situationally defined, and therefore come in a great variety. They may well turn out to be temporary and partly reversible. Moreover, they do not always reinforce one another, but show considerable mutual tension. Indeed, their different forms of development are the very stuff of comparative politics, which seeks an informed understanding of the political dimension of social life by making careful comparisons across time and space.

After such cautionary preliminaries, we can proceed to identify three recent developments that singly and together have had a very important role in changing the political world in which we live. One is the *democratic revolution*, which has been sweeping much of the world. This refers to a widespread trend toward some form of **popular government** that often, but not always, takes the form of a search for representative, pluralist democracy in countries that were previously ruled by some form of authoritarian oligarchy or dictatorship.

Another trend, sometimes labeled the *capitalist revolution*, is the even more widespread shift toward some form of *market economy*. It includes a greater reliance on private enterprise and the profit motive, and involves a concurrent move away from strong regulation, central planning, and state ownership. The "social market economy," found in much of Western Europe, remains a form of capitalism, but one which includes a major role for the state in providing services, redistributing income, and setting overall societal goals. In some of the Asian Communist-ruled countries, above all China, we have become used to seeing self-proclaimed revolutionary socialists introduce a considerable degree of capitalist practices into their formerly planned economies.

The third major trend could be called the *revival of ethnic or cultural politics*. This refers to a growing emphasis on some form of an **exclusive group identity** as the primary basis for political expression. In modern times, it has been common for a group to identify itself by its special ethnic, religious, linguistic, or other cultural traits and to make this identity the basis for a claim to rule by and for itself.

The article that makes up the first section covers democratization as the first of these trends, that is, the startling growth in the number of representative governments in recent years. Even if this development is often fragile and likely to be reversed in some countries, we need to remember how remarkable it has been in the first place. Using very different criteria and data, skeptics on both right and left for a long time doubted whether representative government was sufficiently efficient, attractive or legitimate to spread or even survive in the modern world.

Samuel Huntington's widely discussed thesis concerning a recent wave of democratization is usefully summarized and car-

207

ried further by Larry Diamond. Huntington is one of the best-known observers of democratization, who in the past emphasized the existence of cultural, social, economic, and political obstacles to representative government in most of the world. Even before the collapse of the communist regimes in Europe, however, he had begun to identify a broad pattern of democratization that had started in the mid-1970s, when three dictatorships in southern Europe came to an end (in Greece, Portugal, and Spain). In the following decade, democratization spread to most of Latin America. Central and Eastern Europe then followed, and the trend has also reached some states in East and South Asia like Taiwan or South Korea as well as some parts of Africa, above all South Africa and now, tentatively, Nigeria. The recent transfer of political power in Mexico, after more than seven decades of one-party hegemony, can also be seen in this context.

In a widely adopted phrase, Huntington identified this widespread trend as the "third" in a series of successive "waves" of democratization in modern history. The "**first wave**" of democratization had been slow to develop but long in its reach. It began in the 1820s and lasted about one century, until the 1920s, a period during which first the United States and subsequently 28 other countries established governments based on a wide and eventually universal suffrage. In the 1920s, however, Mussolini's capture and consolidation of power in Italy began a period of democratic setbacks—a "reverse wave," as it were—that lasted until the mid-1940s. During two decades, the number of democracies plunged from 29 to 12, as many became victims of dictatorial takeovers or subsequent military conquests.

A "**second wave**" of democratization started with the Allied victory in World War II and continued during the early postwar years of decolonization. This trend lasted until the early 1960s and resulted in the conversion of about 2 dozen previous authoritarian systems into democracies or quasi-democracies, sometimes of very short duration. There followed a second "reverse wave" that lasted a little over a decade until 1974. During this period of democratic setbacks, the number of democracies fell from 36 to 30 and the number of non-democracies rose from 75 to 95, as various former colonies or newly minted democracies fell under authoritarian or dictatorial rule.

Then, in the mid-1970s, the important "**third wave**" of democratization got its start. It was more sweeping and universal than its predecessors. Already by the beginning of the 1990s, Huntington counted about 60 democracies in the world. That is an impressive change, amounting to a doubling of their number in less than two decades, even though there are now signs of another reversal in a number of the new and unstable democracies. Both Huntington and Diamond's findings lend support to the conclusion that democracy's advance has been at best a "two steps forward, one step back" kind of process.

The expectations associated with the coming of democracy are in some countries so high that disappointments are bound to follow. Already the earlier "third wave" democratic advances in countries like the Sudan, Algeria and Peru have been followed by authoritarian reversals. Haiti (like Nigeria) has gone through its own double wave. The prospects for democracy on that poverty-stricken Caribbean island do not seem bright. There are ominous signs of authoritarian revivals elsewhere in the world.

What are the general conditions that inhibit or encourage the spread and stabilization of democracy? Huntington and other scholars have identified some specific historical factors that appear to have contributed to the third wave. One important factor is the loss of legitimacy by both right- and left-wing authoritarian regimes, as they have become discredited by failures. Another factor is the expansion in some developing countries of an urban middle class, with a strong interest in representative government and the rule of law. In Latin America, especially, the influence of a recently more liberal Catholic Church has been important. There have also been various forms of external influence by the United States and the European Community, as they have tried, however tentatively, to promote a human rights agenda. A different but crucial instance of external influence took the form of Mikhail Gorbachev's shift toward nonintervention by the Soviet Union in the late 1980s, when he abandoned the Brezhnev Doctrine's commitment to defend established communist rulers in Central and Eastern Europe and elsewhere against "counterrevolution." Finally, there is the "snowballing" or demonstration effect with the successful early transitions to democracy in countries like Spain or Poland, which served as models for other countries in similar circumstances.

Huntington's rule of thumb is that a democratic form of government can be considered to have become stable when a country has had at least two successive peaceful turnovers of power. Such a development may take a generation or longer to complete, even under fortunate circumstances. Many of the new democracies have little historical experience with a democratic way of life. Where there has been such an experience, it may have been spotty and not very positive. There may be important cultural or socioeconomic obstacles to democratization, according to Huntington. Like most other observers, he sees extreme poverty as a principal obstacle to successful democratization.

Germany provides a valuable case study for testing some of these interpretations of democracy. After World War I, antidemocratic forces in Germany identified its democratic Weimar Republic with international disaster, socioeconomic ruin, and political weakness and instability. In the wake of the Great Depression, they supported Adolf Hitler's Nazi movement that came to power in January 1933 and abolished the fledgling constitutional democracy. After World War II, by contrast, the Federal Republic of Germany became increasingly credited with stability and growing prosperity. At first accepted passively, the West German democratic system soon generated an increasing measure of pragmatic support from its citizenry, based primarily on its widely perceived effectiveness. In time, the new republic also appeared to gain a deeper affection from much of the population. Careful observers, like David Conradt, detected a transformation of German values in a liberal democratic direction already in the early 1970s. The Federal Republic faced another test after Germany's unification with its accompanying wrenching changes and inevitable disappointments for many people in eastern Germany. For many of them, national unification had been linked to unrealistic expectations of almost immediate socioeconomic alignment with the prosperous West. When the new order failed to deliver quite as promptly or bountifully as they had expected, some East Germans used their new freedom to protest. In dealing with this challenge, the Federal Republic is fortunate in having a stable set of institutions, a well-developed democratic tradition, and a solid economic structure.

The second section of this unit covers the trend toward capitalism or, better, some form of **market economy**. Here Gabriel Almond explores the connections between capitalism and democracy in an article that draws upon both theory and empirical studies. His systematic discussion shows that there are ways in which capitalism and democracy support each other, and ways in which they tend to undermine each other. Is it possible to have the best of both? Almond answers at length that there is a non-utopian manner in which capitalism and democracy can be reconciled, namely in democratic welfare capitalism.

Almond's discussion can be linked to a theme emphasized by some contemporary political economists. They point out that the economic competition between capitalism and socialism, at least in the latter's traditional meaning of state ownership and centralized planning, has become a largely closed chapter in contemporary history. The central question now is which form of capitalism or market economy will be more successful. A similar argument has been made by the French theorist, Michel Albert, who also distinguished between the British-American and the continental "Rhineland" models of capitalism. The former is more individualistic, antigovernmental, and characterized by such traits as high employee turnovers and short-term profit-maximizing. It differs considerably from what the Germans themselves like to call their "**social market economy**." The latter is more team-oriented, emphasizes cooperation between management and organized labor, and leaves a considerable role for government in the setting of general economic strategy, the training of an educated labor force, and the provision of social welfare services.

These different conceptions of capitalism can be linked to different histories. Both Britain and the United States experienced a head start in their industrial revolutions and felt no great need for deliberate government efforts to encourage growth. By contrast, Germany and Japan both played the role of latecomers, who looked to government protection in their attempts to catch up. To be sure, governments were also swayed by military considerations to promote German and Japanese industrialization. But the emergence of a kind of "social capitalism" in other continental countries of Europe suggests that cultural and institutional rather than military factors played a major role in this development. We should continue to expect very differently mixed economies, because one economic model or size is unlikely ever to fit all.

A crucial question is whether the relative prosperity and social security associated with this kind of mixed economy can be maintained in a time of technological breakthroughs and global competition. Those who expected a practical answer to come from the policies and strategies adopted by the "red-green" government in Germany have been largely disappointed. In 1999, Gerhard Schröder issued a joint statement with Tony Blair, in which the two Europeans distinguished between "a market economy" and "a market society." They supported the former but not the latter, without really clarifying the intriguing distinction. More than five years after it assumed office, the German government has presented a major reform project, "Agenda 2010."

The third section deals with the revival of **the ethnic and cultural dimension in politics**. Until recently, relatively few observers foresaw that this element would play such a divisive role in the contemporary world. There were forewarnings, such as the ethnonationalist stirrings in the late 1960s and early 1970s in peripheral areas of such countries as Britain, Canada, or Spain. It also lay behind many of the conflicts in the newly independent countries of the developing world. But most Western observers seem to have been poorly prepared for the task of anticipating or understanding the resurgence of politicized religious, ethnic, or other cultural forces. Many non-Westerners were taken by surprise as well. Mikhail Gorbachev, for example, grossly underestimated the centrifugal force of the nationality question in his own country.

The politicization of religion in many parts of the world falls into this development of a "**politics of identity**." In recent years, religious groups in parts of Latin America, Asia, the Middle East, sub-Saharan Africa, Asia, and southern Europe have variously set out on the political road in the name of their faith. As Max Weber warned in a classic lecture shortly before his death, it can be dangerous to seek "the salvation of souls" along the path of politics. The coexistence of people of divergent faiths is possible only because religious conviction need not fully determine or direct a person's or a group's politics. Where absolute and fervent convictions take over, they make it difficult to compromise pragmatically and live harmoniously with people who believe differently. Pluralist democracy requires an element of tolerance, which for many takes the form of a casual "live and let live" attitude.

There is an important debate among political scientists concerning the sources and scope of politics based on ethnic, religious, and cultural differences. Samuel Huntington argues forcefully that our most important and dangerous future conflicts will be based on clashes of civilizations. In his view, they will be far more difficult to resolve than those rooted in socioeconomic or even ideological differences. His critics, including the German Josef Joffe, argue that Huntington distorts the differences *among* civilizations and trivializes the differences *within* civilizations as sources of political conflict. Chandra Muzaffar, a Malaysian commentator, goes further by contending that Huntington's thesis provides a rationalization for a Western policy goal of dominating the developing world. Others have pointed out that ethnic conflicts are in fact often the result of political choices made by elites. This can turn out to be a hopeful thesis because it would logically follow that such conflicts are avoidable if other political choices were made.

In a widely discussed article, Benjamin Barber brings a broad perspective to the discussion of identity politics in the contemporary world. He sees two major tendencies that threaten democracy. One is the force of **globalism**, brought about by modern technology, communications, and commerce. Its logical end station is what he calls a "McWorld," in which human diversity, individuality, and meaningful identity are erased. The second tendency works in the opposite direction. It is the force of **tribalism**, which drives human beings to exacerbate their group differences and engage in holy wars or "jihads" against each other. Barber argues that globalism is at best indifferent to liberal democracy, while militant tribalism is deeply antithetical to it. He argues in favor of seeking a confederal solution, based on democratic civil societies, which could provide human beings with a nonmilitant, parochial communitarianism as well as a framework that suits the global market economy fairly well.

209

The Global State of Democracy

"The progress of democracy in the world over the last quarter-century has been nothing less than remarkable.... But if the reach of democracy is greater than ever, it is also thinner and more vulnerable."

LARRY DIAMOND

Historians and philosophers already see the twentieth century as the bloodiest and the most destructive and brutal century in human history. But a parallel fact is less often noted: the twentieth century witnessed a profound transformation in the way societies are governed. As Freedom House pointed out in its January 2000 annual survey of freedom in the world, not a single country in 1900 would qualify as a democracy by today's standards.[1] By 1950, only 22 of the 80 sovereign political systems in the world (about 28 percent) were democratic. When the most recent wave of global democratization began in 1974, 39 countries were governed by democracies, but the percentage of democracies in the world was about the same, only 27 percent.

By January 2000, Freedom House counted 120 democracies, the highest number and the greatest percentage (62.5) in world history. This represents a dramatic change even from 1990, when less than half the world's independent states were democracies. Freedom House's assessment of the number of "free" states—those that "maintain a high degree of political and economic freedom and respect basic civil liberties"—also is near a recent historic high, with 85 states (44 percent) "free" at the end of 1999.

Since the fall of the Berlin Wall and the collapse of Soviet communism, democracy has been the dominant form of government. It is not difficult to infer from this dramatic expansion a nearly universal legitimacy for democracy—a global hegemony. Indeed, in its most recent Country Reports on Human Rights Practices, the United States Department of State went so far as to identify democracy and human rights as a third "universal language" (after money and the Internet).[2] The State Department's report envisions the emerging transnational network of human rights actors (both public and private) becoming an "international civil society... that will support democracy worldwide and promote the standards embodied in the Universal Declaration of Human Rights."

The globalization of democracy is indeed one of the most historic and profound global changes of the past several decades. In its duration and scope, this third global wave of democratization also stands in sharp contrast to the "second wave" of democratization that began at the end of World War II and expired in less than 20 years. That movement gave way to a "second reverse wave" in which democracy broke down in more than 20 developing countries and military rulers and civilian autocrats brutalized human rights and the rule of law.[3]

Remarkably, a quarter-century after the inception of democratization's third wave in 1974, the world still has not yet entered a "third reverse wave." Not only do more democracies exist than ever before, but very few high-profile democratic reversals have occurred. In fact, during the third wave's first 25 years, only three blatant reversals of democracy took place in countries with more than 20 million people: the military coup in Nigeria at the end of 1983, the 1989 military coup in Sudan, and the 1991 military coup in Thailand. The former two coups occurred in Africa before the third wave of democratization reached the continent in 1991. The Thai coup was a major setback for democracy in Southeast Asia, but it did not last. In little more than a year, the country's military leaders felt compelled to convene national elections to legitimize their rule, and their insistence on installing a nonelected army commander as prime minister triggered massive demonstrations that brought down the authoritarian project. Just 17 months after the February 1991 coup, democracy was restored to Thailand with the election of the first nonmilitary prime minister since the mid-1970s.

If we understand that the military coups in Nigeria and Sudan (and in Ghana in 1981) came before the third wave reached Africa, then, prior to October 1999, democratic reversals during the third wave had been of only three types. First were democratic breakdowns during the 1990s in small, relatively marginal states such as the Republic of Congo (Brazzaville), Gambia, Lesotho, Niger, and Sierra Leone. Second, democratic transitions or possibilities for democratic transitions were reversed or aborted in countries such as Cambodia, Lebanon, Kenya, Nigeria, and several post-Soviet states. And finally, democracy was mangled by elected presidents in Peru and Zambia, but in ways that preserved the framework of competitive, multiparty politics and thus at least some possibility of displacing the autocratic presidents in a future election.

The October 1999 military coup in Pakistan, however, may portend a more ominous trend; Pakistan is a truly strategic country, a regional power with nuclear weapons and a long-running, precarious conflict with India over the disputed territory of Kashmir. The principal causes of democratic breakdown in

Pakistan—the abuse of executive power, human rights, and the rule of law; growing ethnic and religious sectarian violence; and profound economic failure and injustice stemming from structural distortions and administrative incapacity—are not unique to Pakistan. Increasingly, these problems afflict many other large, strategic, emerging democracies in the world, such as Russia, Brazil, Turkey, Nigeria, and the Philippines.

THE VARIED STATES OF DEMOCRACY

If we look only at the aggregate picture of democracy in the world, we can be cheered. More democracies exist than ever before, and the average level of freedom is also the highest ever recorded in the Freedom House annual survey of political rights and civil liberties. To comprehend the true state of democracy worldwide, however, we must analyze global trends.

Democracies—in the minimal sense, "electoral" democracies—share at least one broad essential requirement. The principal positions of political power in the country are filled through regular, free, and fair elections between competing parties, and an incumbent government can be defeated in those elections. The standard for electoral democracy—what constitutes "free and fair"—is more ambiguous than is often appreciated. As a result of the dubious conduct of recent national elections, such prominent multiparty states as Russia, Ukraine, Nigeria, and Indonesia fall into a gray area that is neither clearly democratic nor clearly undemocratic, even in the minimal electoral sense. Indeed, there is growing evidence of outright fraud in the March 2000 election that confirmed Vladimir Putin in the presidency of Russia.[4] Even short of fraud, Putin had such massive advantages of incumbency and support from crony capitalists that opposition parties virtually conceded his election in advance.

Russia is not unique. Freedom House laudably resists classifying as democracies such countries as Malaysia, Singapore, Peru, and Kenya, where electoral competition has been blatantly tilted in favor of the ruling party or president. But some of Freedom House's "democracies," such as Nigeria, Liberia, Indonesia, and the Kyrgyz Republic, suffer such widespread electoral fraud or systematic unfairness as to render the outcomes dubiously democratic at best. In fact, five of the states classified by Freedom House as democracies in 1999 (Djibouti, the Kyrgyz Republic, Liberia, Niger, and Sierra Leone) suffer from too much fraud, intimidation, or abridgment of free electoral choice to justify that classification. Yet even if we move these states, along with Russia, Ukraine, Nigeria, and Indonesia, out of the category of electoral democracy—while recognizing that Mexico and Senegal became electoral democracies in 2000 as a result of reforms in electoral administration that allowed the opposition finally to capture the presidency—we still find that almost 60 percent of the world's states are democracies. In the long sweep of world history, this is an extraordinary proportion.

However we judge them, elections are only one dimension of democracy. The quality of democracy also depends on its levels of freedom, pluralism, justice, and accountability. The deeper level of liberal democracy requires these conditions:

- Freedom of belief, expression, organization, demonstration, and other civil liberties, including protection from political terror and unjustified imprisonment;
- A rule of law under which all citizens are treated equally and due process is secure;
- Political independence and neutrality of the judiciary and of other institutions of "horizontal accountability" that check the abuse of power, such as electoral administration, audits, and a central bank;
- An open, pluralistic civil society, including not only associational life but the mass media as well;
- Civilian control of the military.[5]

These various dimensions of democratic quality constitute a continuum, and determining exactly when a regime has sufficient freedom, pluralism, lawfulness, accountability, and institutional strength to be considered a liberal democracy is difficult. For some years, I took as a rough indicator the Freedom House designation of a country as "free." Generally, these are countries that receive an average rating of between 1 and 2.5 on the two scales of political rights and civil liberties. (Each scale ranges from 1 to 7, with 1 being "most free" and 7 "least free.") However, countries with average scores of 2.5 have civil liberties scores of 3 on the 7-point scale, indicating serious deficiencies in the rule of law and the protection for individual rights. Typically in such countries (for example, the Philippines, El Salvador, and recently India), the judiciary is weak and ineffectual, if not politically compromised; corruption is widespread; and police and other security forces abuse citizens' rights with impunity. Therefore, we should only consider as minimally "liberal" those countries with an average score of 2.0 or better (that is, lower) on the Freedom House combined scale of political rights and civil liberties. By this standard, only 37 percent of the world's states were liberal democracies at the beginning of 2000.

We also need to consider the stability and rootedness of democracies. For political scientists, democracies are "consolidated" when all significant political elites, parties, and organizations, as well as an overwhelming majority of the public, are firmly committed to the democratic constitutional system and regularly comply with its rules and constraints. Strikingly, the third wave of democratization that began in 1974 has progressed only slowly toward consolidation. Except for the new democracies of southern Europe (Spain, Portugal, and Greece) and a few scattered others, the third-wave democracies have not taken firm root, although they are progressing more rapidly in Central and Eastern Europe.

Global assessments of the state of democracy and freedom in the world mask large differences among groups of countries. This is clearly true with respect to the level of development. The 30 "core" countries of Western Europe, along with the United States, Canada, Australia, New Zealand, Japan, and Israel, are all liberal, consolidated democracies. In fact, these core states account for the clear majority of all liberal democracies with populations over one million. Size also matters in the following respect. "Microstates" (those with populations under 1 million) are overwhelmingly democratic and liberal; and aside from the 30 core countries (eight

Democracy, Liberal Democracy, and "Free" States by Region (and Cultural Grouping), 1999–2000

Region	Number of Countries	Number of Democracies (percent of total)	"Free" States (percent of total)	Liberal Democracies (percent of total)
Western Europe and Anglophone states	28	28 (100%)	28 (100%)	28 (100%)
Latin America and Caribbean	33	29 (88%)	20 (70%)	16 (48%)
South America	12	11 (92%)	6 (50%)	4 (33%)
East Central Europe and Baltic States	15	14 (93%)	10 (67%)	9 (60%)
Former Soviet Union (less Baltics)	12	5 (42%) 4 (33%)*	0	0
Asia (East, SE, South)	26	12 (46%)	8 (31%)	3 (12%)
Pacific Island	11	10 (91%)	9 (82%)	9 (82%)
Africa (Sub-Sahara)	48	20 (42%) 16 (33%)*	8 (17%)	5 (10%)
Middle East-North Africa	19	2 (11%)	1 (5%)	1 (5%)
Total	192	120 (63%) 115 (69%)*	85 (44%)	71 (37%)
Arab Countries	16	0	0	0
Predominantly Muslim Countries	41	8 (20%) 5 (12%)*	1 (2%)	0

Source: The 1999 Freedom House Survey; *Journal of Democracy,* January 2000, pp. 187-200.

*Indicates a regime classification of the author that differs from that of Freedom House (FH). Freedom House rates Djibouti, the Kyrgyz Republic, Liberia, Niger, and Sierra Leone as electoral democracies, but all five have levels of coercion and fraud that make the electoral process less than free and fair. Other countries rated as electoral democracies have only dubiously democratic elections, including Russia, Nigeria, and Indonesia.

of which are microstates), no other group of countries in the world has so much political and civil freedom on average. Of the 41 countries with populations under 1 million, two-thirds are liberal democracies and almost four-fifths are democracies. However, these microstates have little scope to influence the direction of many other countries. (Indeed, two-thirds are island states, and hence share no land border with any country.)

As can be seen in the table above, electoral democracy stretches into nearly every major world region, although it is much more prevalent in some areas than in others. Liberal democracy is another story. The fragility and limited reach of liberal democracy is indicated by the fact that 54 of the 71 liberal democracies are either the 30 core countries or other states with populations of less than 1 million. If we set aside the 30 core countries and the other 33 microstates, we have 129 states. Only 13 percent of these 129 states in Asia, Africa, Latin America, the Middle East, and postcommunist Europe are liberal democracies.

Also striking are the differences in the distributions of regimes within regions. The 15 postcommunist states of Central and Eastern Europe (including the Baltic states) are moving to-

ward the liberal democratic West in their levels of freedom; the majority of these states are now liberal democracies, and many are progressing toward democratic consolidation. Of the remaining 12 states of the former Soviet Union, none is a liberal democracy, and less than half are democracies.

Just under half of the 26 states of Asia (East, Southeast, and South) are democracies, and only three are liberal democracies, but we see the effect of size when we compare this group with the 11 Pacific Island states, which are mainly liberal democracies. Similarly, while half the states of Latin America and the Caribbean are liberal democracies, these are mainly clustered in the Caribbean region. Only a third of the 12 South American states are liberal democracies. Liberal democracy is scarcely present (10 percent) among the 48 states of sub-Saharan Africa (the liberal democracies of Africa are again disproportionately microstates), but at least a third of these 48 states are now electoral democracies, a much greater figure than just a decade ago.

In contrast, not a single Arab democracy or majority Muslim country is a liberal democracy; indeed, only slightly more than

10 percent of the states with predominantly Muslim populations are even electoral democracies.

VARIED PROGRESS TOWARD CONSOLIDATION

If we set aside the core states and the microstates, surprisingly few other democracies in the world are clearly "consolidated" (a democracy is consolidated when all politically significant elites and organizations, as well as the overwhelming majority of the mass public, believe that democracy is the best form of government and comply with its rules and restraints). Among the long-standing democracies in the developing world, India (with all its troubles), Costa Rica, Mauritius, and Botswana could be seen as consolidated. Venezuela and Colombia were considered consolidated democracies in the 1970s and 1980s but have become destabilized and seriously threatened in the past decade by economic mismanagement, corruption, and state decay as established parties and politicians grew complacent and distant from popular concerns. Indeed, the entire Andean region of South America now suffers a deep crisis of governance, sharply eroding the authority and capacity of the state and public confidence in democratic institutions. Like Colombia, Sri Lanka's long-established democracy has also sunk into illiberal and unstable status as a result of protracted internal violence, in this case an ethnic civil war. In Latin America, only Uruguay shows the levels of both elite and popular commitment to democracy that mark consolidation, although the recent presidential elections in Argentina and Chile (as well as the growing readiness of Chile to confront the crimes of the authoritarian past) indicate progress toward consolidation.

Significantly, the region where the most rapid, visible, and frequent strides toward democratic consolidation are being made is Central and Eastern Europe. In that area (including the Baltic states but not much of the Balkans), former communist countries are entrenching democratic practices and norms. Electoral returns, elite behavior, and mass attitudes and values (as revealed in public opinion surveys) show a deepening commitment to democracy in the Czech Republic, Poland, Hungary, Slovenia, Estonia, Latvia, and Lithuania, and progress as well in Slovakia, Bulgaria, and Romania. Popular commitment to democracy is particularly strong among younger people; hence the political culture and party system will become more democratic as voters who have come of age in the postcommunist era become more numerous. Within a decade or two, almost all of Europe from the Atlantic to the former Soviet border will likely consist of consolidated liberal democracies as integration into the expanding architectures of the European Union and the North Atlantic Treaty Organization helps lock the new democracies into place.

It is difficult for people living amid a profound but slow-moving transformation to recognize its historical significance. But the creation of a new, enlarged, unified, and entirely democratic Europe will be seen by historians a few decades hence as one of the truly great and lasting changes in the political character of the world.

Levels of freedom, democratic quality, and mass support for democracy are all considerably weaker in the non-Baltic former Soviet countries. In 1998, for example, Richard Rose of the University of Strathclyde in Glasgow found that 41 percent of Russians and 51 percent of Ukrainians favored the restoration of Communist rule (and only slightly lower percentages said they would approve suspending parliament and having strong single-leader rule). By contrast, only one in five respondents from Central and Eastern Europe supported either alternative. In Russia and Ukraine, as well as in other post-Soviet electoral "democracies," power is wielded much more roughly, elections are less fair, the rule of law is much more tenuous, and thus people are much more cynical about their politics and government.

The key question for the European community of democracies is whether this postcommunist divide can be overcome. In particular, will the new Europe include Russia? Will Russia gravitate, economically and politically, to the democratic West, or will it fall back on some version of its authoritarian and imperial tradition? As former national security adviser Zbigniew Brzezinski argued in the Fall 2000 *National Interest*, the United States and its European allies, in their ongoing engagement with Russia, should hold open the option of a "truly democratic Russia" becoming closely associated with both the European Union and NATO. At the same time, however, they should move forward vigorously with expanding both organizations to include ultimately all the former communist states of Central Europe. Such a strategy would cement the construction of an enlarged and democratically unified Europe while creating the context for a truly post-Soviet generation of Russian leaders to realize "that in order to recover Russia must opt for the West."

THE FUTURE OF THE "SWING" STATES

The future of democracy in the world will be heavily determined by the political trajectory of the most powerful and the most populous states outside the wealthy, liberal democratic core. Depending on where the line is drawn (a population of 100 million or 50 million, or a GNP of $100 billion or $50 billion), 20 or 30 such states can be identified. Because of their political, economic, and demographic weight, these states will have a disproportionate influence on the democratic prospects of their regions. Among the most influential, troubled, and changeable are China, India, Russia, Brazil, Colombia, Mexico, Turkey, Pakistan, the Philippines, Iran, Nigeria, South Africa, and Indonesia. Because few of these states have stable consolidated regimes (whether democratic or authoritarian), they are "strategic swing states."[6] Only a few of this group of 30 influential states—South Korea, Taiwan, Chile, Poland, and the Czech Republic—might be considered liberal and in some respects consolidated democracies, and even some of these states have flawed democratic functioning. India's democracy is consolidated, but it faces serious problems with respect to entrenching good government and the rule of law.

Most of the 30 strategic swing states are much more deeply troubled and unstable than India. Their instability stems from three interrelated crises of governance, all of which were dramatically manifested in Pakistan as its democracy reeled toward collapse in the 1990s. First, they suffer a pervasive lack of accountability and a weak rule of law that permits endemic corruption, smuggling, violence, personalization of power, and abuse of human rights. Second, they have not been able to find workable, credible institutional formulas and civic codes to manage regional and ethnic divisions peacefully and give all citizens an inclusive stake in the political system. Third, they have faced economic crisis, stagnation, or instability because they have not sufficiently liberalized their economies, reduced state ownership and control, or rationalized and strengthened their corrupt, swollen state bureaucracies.

These crises of governance are not unique to large strategic states of the developing and postcommunist worlds. They afflict the smaller states as well. They represent the core problems that inhibit sustainable democratic progress and that threaten either the complete breakdown of democracy, as in Pakistan, or the kind of progressive erosion that has been occurring for a decade in Colombia and Venezuela.

None of the governance challenges confronting the swing states is more serious and pervasive than controlling corruption. Probably not a single threatened and vulnerable democracy in the world today has dilemmas that do not stem from rampant political corruption, rent-seeking behavior, and, more broadly, the weakness of the rule of law. In the next decade the prospects for sustainable democratic progress in the world will be heavily shaped by one question: Will emerging democracies and transitional regimes adopt the institutional reforms to control corruption and ensure a predictable, fair, credible, accessible, and efficient administration of justice?

To a great extent, we now know what must be done. Judiciaries must be modernized and professionalized, and their independence must be rigorously protected through reforms that insulate the appointment, remuneration, administration, and supervision of judges and prosecutors from partisan political influence. A wide range of other independent institutions of horizontal accountability must not only be established but given similar constitutional autonomy, substantial resources, and capable, dedicated leadership. These include:

- A countercorruption commission for receiving and monitoring the declared assets of public officials and for investigating corruption charges;
- A human rights commission to receive and investigate citizen complaints about violations of constitutional rights, and to educate people about their rights and obligations as democratic citizens;
- An independent, supreme auditing agency to audit the accounts of any state agency on a regular basis and on suspicion of specific wrongdoing;
- An ombudsman's office to provide citizens an outlet for grievances about unfair treatment and abuse of power by government agencies; and
- A truly independent electoral commission, which would ensure that abusive and corrupt elected officials can be removed from office in free and fair elections, and that all parties and officials can be disciplined in advance of elections.

The progress of democracy in the world over the last quarter-century has been nothing less than remarkable. No period in world history has seen a wider expansion of the democratic form of government and of the ability of citizens, armed with universal suffrage, to change their political leaders in relatively free and fair elections. But if the reach of democracy is greater than ever, it is also thinner and more vulnerable. The great challenge of the next decade is to deepen, stabilize, and consolidate the many emerging and struggling democracies outside the core. To do that, most will have to address seriously the triple crisis of governance outlined here. Most important, if they are to win the permanent and unconditional support of their citizens, these troubled democracies must make dramatic progress in controlling corruption and strengthening the rule of law.

It is too often forgotten that the challenge of building democracy heavily overlaps that of establishing the authority and capacity of a viable but restrained state. Whether this broad challenge can be effectively addressed, especially through legal, institutional, and economic reforms of the state's structure and role, will determine whether democracy continues to prosper in the world or gives way to a third "reverse wave" of democratic breakdowns.

NOTES

1. Freedom House is an independent nongovernmental organization based in New York that advocates for democracy and human rights worldwide. Its annual survey of freedom in the world, which it has conducted for the past 30 years, is available on its website, www.freedomhouse.org.

2. *1999 Country Reports on Human Rights Practices* (Washington, D.C.: United States Department of State, Bureau of Democracy, Human Rights, and Labor, February 25, 2000).

3. Samuel P. Huntington, *The Third Wave: Democratization in the Late Twentieth Century* (Norman: University of Oklahoma Press, 1991).

4. For extensive documentation of fraud in Russia's March 2000 presidential election—sufficient to question its legitimacy—see the special report in *The Moscow Times*, September 11, 2000 (www.themoscowtimes.com).

5. For a fuller description, see Larry Diamond, *Developing Democracy: Toward Consolidation* (Baltimore: Johns Hopkins University Press, 1999), 10–12.

6. Larry Diamond, "Is Pakistan the (Reverse) Wave of the Future?" *Journal of Democracy*, July 2000.

LARRY DIAMOND *is a senior research fellow at the Hoover Institution, coeditor of the* Journal of Democracy, *and codirector of the National Endowment for Democracy's International Forum for Democratic Studies.*

Capitalism and Democracy*

Gabriel A. Almond

Joseph Schumpeter, a great econo-mist and social scientist of the last generation, whose career was almost equally divided between Central Eu-ropean and American universities, and who lived close to the crises of the 1930s and '40s, published a book in 1942 under the title, *Capitalism, Socialism, and Democracy*. The book has had great influence, and can be read today with profit. It was written in the aftergloom of the great depres-sion, during the early triumphs of Fascism and Nazism in 1940 and 1941, when the future of capitalism, socialism, and democracy all were in doubt. Schumpeter projected a fu-ture of declining capitalism, and ris-ing socialism. He thought that democracy under socialism might be no more impaired and problematic than it was under capitalism.

He wrote a concluding chapter in the second edition which appeared in 1946, and which took into account the political-economic situation at the end of the war, with the Soviet Union then astride a devastated Eu-rope. In this last chapter he argues that we should not identify the fu-ture of socialism with that of the So-viet Union, that what we had observed and were observing in the first three decades of Soviet exist-ence was not a necessary expression of socialism. There was a lot of Czar-ist Russia in the mix. If Schumpeter were writing today, I don't believe he would argue that socialism has a brighter future than capitalism. The relationship between the two has turned out to be a good deal more complex and intertwined than Schumpeter anticipated. But I am sure that he would still urge us to separate the future of socialism from

that of Soviet and Eastern European Communism.

Unlike Schumpeter I do not in-clude Socialism in my title, since its future as a distinct ideology and pro-gram of action is unclear at best. Western Marxism and the moderate socialist movements seem to have settled for social democratic solu-tions, for adaptations of both capital-ism and democracy producing acceptable mixes of market competi-tion, political pluralism, participa-tion, and welfare. I deal with these modifications of capitalism, as a con-sequence of the impact of democracy on capitalism in the last half century.

At the time that Adam Smith wrote *The Wealth of Nations*, the world of government, politics and the state that he knew—pre-Reform Act England, the French government of Louis XV and XVI—was riddled with special privileges, monopolies, inter-ferences with trade. With my tongue only half way in my check I believe the discipline of economics may have been traumatized by this condition of political life at its birth. Typically, economists speak of the state and gov-ernment instrumentally, as a kind of secondary service mechanism.

I do not believe that politics can be treated in this purely instrumental and reductive way without losing our analytic grip on the social and histor-ical process. The economy and the polity are the main problem solving mechanisms of human society. They each have their distinctive means, and they each have their "goods" or ends. They necessarily interact with each other, and transform each other in the process. Democracy in particu-lar generates goals and programs. You cannot give people the suffrage,

and let them form organizations, run for office, and the like, without their developing all kinds of ideas as to how to improve things. And some-times some of these ideas are adopted, implemented and are pro-ductive, and improve our lives, al-though many economists are reluctant to concede this much to the state.

My lecture deals with this interac-tion of politics and economics in the Western World in the course of the last couple of centuries, in the era during which capitalism and democ-racy emerged as the dominant prob-lem solving institutions of modern civilization. I am going to discuss some of the theoretical and empirical literature dealing with the themes of the positive and negative interaction between capitalism and democracy. There are those who say that capital-ism supports democracy, and those who say that capitalism subverts de-mocracy. And there are those who say that democracy subverts capital-ism, and those who say that it sup-ports it.

The relation between capitalism and democracy dominates the politi-cal theory of the last two centuries. All the logically possible points of view are represented in a rich liter-ature. It is this ambivalence and di-alectic, this tension between the two major problem solving sectors of modern society—the political and the economic —that is the topic of my lecture.

Capitalism Supports Democracy

Let me begin with the argument that capitalism is positively linked with democracy, shares its values and culture, and facilitates its development. This case has been made in historical, logical, and statistical terms.

Albert Hirschman in his *Rival Views of Market Society* (1986) examines the values, manners and morals of capitalism, and their effects on the larger society and culture as these have been described by the philosophers of the 17th, 18th, and 19th centuries. He shows how the interpretation of the impact of capitalism has changed from the enlightenment view of Montesquieu, Condorcet, Adam Smith and others, who stressed the *douceur* of commerce, its "gentling," civilizing effect on behavior and interpersonal relations, to that of the 19th and 20th century conservative and radical writers who described the culture of capitalism as crassly materialistic, destructively competitive, corrosive of morality, and hence self-destructive. This sharp almost 180-degree shift in point of view among political theorists is partly explained by the transformation from the commerce and small-scale industry of early capitalism, to the smoke blackened industrial districts, the demonic and exploitive entrepreneurs, and exploited laboring classes of the second half of the nineteenth century. Unfortunately for our purposes, Hirschman doesn't deal explicitly with the capitalism–democracy connection, but rather with culture and with manners. His argument, however, implies an early positive connection and a later negative one.

Joseph Schumpeter in *Capitalism, Socialism, and Democracy* (1942) states flatly, "History clearly confirms… [that]… modern democracy rose along with capitalism, and in causal connection with it… modern democracy is a product of the capitalist process." He has a whole chapter entitled "The Civilization of Capitalism," democracy being a part of that civilization. Schumpeter also makes the point that democracy was historically supportive of capitalism. He states, "… the bourgeoisie reshaped, and from its own point of view rationalized, the social and political structure that preceded its ascendancy…" (that is to say, feudalism). "The democratic method

was the political tool of that reconstruction." According to Schumpeter capitalism and democracy were mutually causal historically, mutually supportive parts of a rising modern civilization, although as we shall show below, he also recognized their antagonisms.

Barrington Moore's historical investigation (1966) with its long title, *The Social Origins of Dictatorship and Democracy; Lord and Peasant in the Making of the Modern World*, argues that there have been three historical routes to industrial modernization. The first of these followed by Britain, France, and the United States, involved the subordination and transformation of the agricultural sector by the rising commercial bourgeoisie, producing the democratic capitalism of the 19th and 20th centuries. The second route followed by Germany and Japan, where the landed aristocracy was able to contain and dominate the rising commercial classes, produced an authoritarian and fascist version of industrial modernization, a system of capitalism encased in a feudal authoritarian framework, dominated by a military aristocracy, and an authoritarian monarchy. The third route, followed in Russia where the commercial bourgeoisie was too weak to give content and direction to the modernizing process, took the form of a revolutionary process drawing on the frustration and resources of the peasantry, and created a mobilized authoritarian Communist regime along with a state-controlled industrialized economy. Successful capitalism dominating and transforming the rural agricultural sector, according to Barrington Moore, is the creator and sustainer of the emerging democracies of the nineteenth century.

Robert A. Dahl, the leading American democratic theorist, in the new edition of his book (1990) *After the Revolution? Authority in a Good Society*, has included a new chapter entitled "Democracy and Markets." In the opening paragraph of that chapter, he says:

It is an historical fact that modern democratic institutions… have existed only in countries with predominantly privately owned, market-oriented economies, or

capitalism if you prefer that name. It is also a fact that all "socialist" countries with predominantly state-owned centrally directed economic orders—command economies—have not enjoyed democratic governments, but have in fact been ruled by authoritarian dictatorships. It is also an historical fact that some "capitalist" countries have also been, and are, ruled by authoritarian dictatorships.

To put it more formally, it looks to be the case that market-oriented economies are necessary (in the logical sense) to democratic institutions, though they are certainly not sufficient. And it looks to be the case that state-owned centrally directed economic orders are strictly associated with authoritarian regimes, though authoritarianism definitely does not require them. We have something very much like an historical experiment, so it would appear, that leaves these conclusions in no great doubt. (Dahl 1990)

Peter Berger in his book *The Capitalist Revolution* (1986) presents four propositions on the relation between capitalism and democracy:

Capitalism is a necessary but not sufficient condition of democracy under modern conditions.

If a capitalist economy is subjected to increasing degrees of state control, a point (not precisely specifiable at this time) will be reached at which democratic governance becomes impossible.

If a socialist economy is opened up to increasing degrees of market forces, a point (not precisely specifiable at this time) will be reached at which democratic governance becomes a possibility.

If capitalist development is successful in generating economic growth from which a sizable proportion of the population benefits, pressures toward democracy are likely to appear.

This positive relationship between capitalism and democracy has also been sustained by statistical studies. The "Social Mobilization" theorists of the 1950s and 1960s which included

Daniel Lerner (1958), Karl Deutsch (1961), S. M. Lipset (1959) among others, demonstrated a strong statistical association between GNP per capita and democratic political institutions. This is more than simple statistical association. There is a logic in the relation between level of economic development and democratic institutions. Level of economic development has been shown to be associated with education and literacy, exposure to mass media, and democratic psychological propensities such as subjective efficacy, participatory aspirations and skills. In a major investigation of the social psychology of industrialization and modernization, a research team led by the sociologist Alex Inkeles (1974) interviewed several thousand workers in the modern industrial and the traditional economic sectors of six countries of differing culture. Inkeles found empathetic, efficacious, participatory and activist propensities much more frequently among the modern industrial workers, and to a much lesser extent in the traditional sector in each one of these countries regardless of cultural differences.

The historical, the logical, and the statistical evidence for this positive relation between capitalism and democracy is quite persuasive.

Capitalism Subverts Democracy

But the opposite case is also made, that capitalism subverts or undermines democracy. Already in John Stuart Mill (1848) we encounter a view of existing systems of private property as unjust, and of the free market as destructively competitive—aesthetically and morally repugnant. The case he was making was a normative rather than a political one. He wanted a less competitive society, ultimately socialist, which would still respect individuality. He advocated limitations on the inheritance of property and the improvement of the property system so that everyone shared in its benefits, the limitation of population growth, and the improvement of the quality of the labor force through the provision of high quality education for all by the state. On the eve of the emergence of the modern democratic capitalist order John Staurt Mill wanted to control the excesses of both the market economy and the majoritarian polity, by the education of consumers and producers, citizens and politicians, in the interest of producing morally improved free market and democratic orders. But in contrast to Marx, he did not thoroughly discount the possibilities of improving the capitalist and democratic order.

Marx argued that as long as capitalism and private property existed there could be no genuine democracy, that democracy under capitalism was bourgeois democracy, which is to say not democracy at all. While it would be in the interest of the working classes to enter a coalition with the bourgeoisie in supporting this form of democracy in order to eliminate feudalism, this would be a tactical maneuver. Capitalist democracy could only result in the increasing exploitation of the working classes. Only the elimination of capitalism and private property could result in the emancipation of the working classes and the attainment of true democracy. Once socialism was attained the basic political problems of humanity would have been solved through the elimination of classes. Under socialism there would be no distinctive democratic organization, no need for institutions to resolve conflicts, since there would be no conflicts. There is not much democratic or political theory to be found in Marx's writings. The basic reality is the mode of economic production and the consequent class structure from which other institutions follow.

For the followers of Marx up to the present day there continues to be a negative tension between capitalism, however reformed, and democracy. But the integral Marxist and Leninist rejection of the possibility of an autonomous, bourgeois democratic state has been left behind for most Western Marxists. In the thinking of Poulantzas, Offe, Bobbio, Habermas and others, the bourgeois democratic state is now viewed as a class struggle state, rather than an unambiguously bourgeois state. The working class has access to it; it can struggle for its interests, and can attain partial benefits from it. The state is now viewed as autonomous, or as relatively autonomous, and it can be re-formed in a progressive direction by working class and other popular movements. The bourgeois democratic state can be moved in the direction of a socialist state by political action short of violence and institutional destruction.

Schumpeter (1942) appreciated the tension between capitalism and democracy. While he saw a causal connection between competition in the economic and the political order, he points out "… that there are some deviations from the principle of democracy which link up with the presence of organized capitalist interests…. [T]he statement is true both from the standpoint of the classical and from the standpoint of our own theory of democracy. From the first standpoint, the result reads that the means at the disposal of private interests are often used in order to thwart the will of the people. From the second standpoint, the result reads that those private means are often used in order to interfere with the working of the mechanism of competitive leadership." He refers to some countries and situations in which "… political life all but resolved itself into a struggle of pressure groups and in many cases practices that failed to conform to the spirit of the democratic method." But he rejects the notion that there cannot be political democracy in a capitalist society. For Schumpeter full democracy in the sense of the informed participation of all adults in the selection of political leaders and consequently the making of public policy, was an impossibility because of the number and complexity of the issues confronting modern electorates. The democracy which was realistically possible was one in which people could choose among competing leaders, and consequently exercise some direction over political decisions. This kind of democracy was possible in a capitalist society, though some of its propensities impaired its performance. Writing in the early years of World War II, when the future of democracy and of capitalism were uncertain, he leaves unresolved the questions of "… Whether or not democracy is one of those products of capitalism which are to die out with it…" or "… how well or ill capitalist society qualifies for the task of working the democratic method it evolved."

Non-Marxist political theorists have contributed to this questioning of the reconcilability of capitalism and democracy. Robert A. Dahl, who makes the point that capitalism historically has been a necessary precondition of democracy, views contemporary democracy in the United States as seriously compromised, impaired by the inequality in resources among the citizens. But Dahl stresses the variety in distributive patterns, and in politico-economic relations among contemporary democracies. "The category of capitalist democracies" he writes, "includes an extraordinary variety... from nineteenth century, laissez faire, early industrial systems to twentieth century, highly regulated, social welfare, late or postindustrial systems. Even late twentieth century 'welfare state' orders vary all the way from the Scandinavian systems, which are redistributive, heavily taxed, comprehensive in their social security, and neocorporatist in their collective bargaining arrangements to the faintly redistributive, moderately taxed, limited social security, weak collective bargaining systems of the United States and Japan" (1989).

In *Democracy and Its Critics* (1989) Dahl argues that the normative growth of democracy to what he calls its "third transformation" (the first being the direct city-state democracy of classic times, and the second, the indirect, representative inegalitarian democracy of the contemporary world) will require democratization of the economic order. In other words, modern corporate capitalism needs to be transformed. Since government control and/or ownership of the economy would be destructive of the pluralism which is an essential requirement of democracy, his preferred solution to the problem of the mega-corporation is employee control of corporate industry. An economy so organized, according to Dahl, would improve the distribution of political resources without at the same time destroying the pluralism which democratic competition requires. To those who question the realism of Dahl's solution to the problem of inequality, he replies that history is full of surprises.

Charles E. Lindblom in his book, *Politics and Markets* (1977), concludes his comparative analysis of the political economy of modern capitalism and socialism, with an essentially pessimistic conclusion about contemporary market-oriented democracy. He says

We therefore come back to the corporation. It is possible that the rise of the corporation has offset or more than offset the decline of class as an instrument of indoctrination.... That it creates a new core of wealth and power for a newly constructed upper class, as well as an overpowering loud voice, is also reasonably clear. The executive of the large corporation is, on many counts, the contemporary counterpart to the landed gentry of an earlier era, his voice amplified by the technology of mass communication.... [T]he major institutional barrier to fuller democracy may therefore be the autonomy of the private corporation.

Lindblom concludes, "The large private corporation fits oddly into democratic theory and vision. Indeed it does not fit.

There is then a widely shared agreement, from the Marxists and neo-Marxists, to Schumpeter, Dahl, Lindblom, and other liberal political theorists, that modern capitalism with the dominance of the large corporation, produces a defective or an impaired form of democracy.

Democracy Subverts Capitalism

If we change our perspective now and look at the way democracy is said to affect capitalism, one of the dominant traditions of economics from Adam Smith until the present day stresses the importance for productivity and welfare of an economy that is relatively free of intervention by the state. In this doctrine of minimal government there is still a place for a framework of rules and services essential to the productive and efficient performance of the economy. In part the government has to protect the market from itself. Left to their own devices, according to Smith, businessmen were prone to corner the market in order to exact the highest possible price. And according to Smith businessmen were prone to bribe public officials in order to gain special privileges, and legal monopolies. For Smith good capitalism was competitive capitalism, and good government provided just those goods and services which the market needed to flourish, could not itself provide, or would not provide. A good government according to Adam Smith was a minimal government, providing for the national defense, and domestic order. Particularly important for the economy were the rules pertaining to commercial life such as the regulation of weights and measures, setting and enforcing building standards, providing for the protection of persons and property, and the like.

For Milton Friedman (1961, 1981), the leading contemporary advocate of the free market and free government, and of the interdependence of the two, the principal threat to the survival of capitalism and democracy is the assumption of the responsibility for welfare on the part of the modern democratic state. He lays down a set of functions appropriate to government in the positive interplay between economy and polity, and then enumerates many of the ways in which the modern welfare, regulatory state has deviated from these criteria.

A good Friedmanesque, democratic government would be one "... which maintained law and order, defended property rights, served as a means whereby we could modify property rights and other rules of the economic game, adjudicated disputes about the interpretation of the rules, enforced contracts, promoted competition, provided a monetary framework, engaged in activities to counter technical monopolies and to overcome neighborhood effects widely regarded as sufficiently important to justify government intervention, and which supplemented private charity and the private family in protecting the irresponsible, whether madman or child ...."
Against this list of proper activities for a free government, Friedman pinpointed more than a dozen activities

of contemporary democratic governments which might better be performed through the private sector, or not at all. These included setting and maintaining price supports, tariffs, import and export quotas and controls, rents, interest rates, wage rates, and the like, regulating industries and banking, radio and television, licensing professions and occupations, providing social security and medical care programs, providing public housing, national parks, guaranteeing mortgages, and much else.

Friedman concludes that this steady encroachment on the private sector has been slowly but surely converting our free government and market system into a collective monster, compromising both freedom and productivity in the outcome. The tax and expenditure revolts and regulatory rebellions of the 1980s have temporarily stemmed this trend, but the threat continues. "It is the internal threat coming from men of good intentions and good will who wish to reform us. Impatient with the slowness of persuasion and example to achieve the great social changes they envision, they are anxious to use the power of the state to achieve their ends, and confident of their own ability to do so." The threat to political and economic freedom, according to Milton Friedman and others who argue the same position, arises out of democratic politics. It may only be defeated by political action.

In the last decades a school, or rather several schools, of economists and political scientists have turned the theoretical models of economics to use in analyzing political processes. Variously called public choice theorists, rational choice theorists, or positive political theorists, and employing such models as market exchange and bargaining, rational self interest, game theory, and the like, these theorists have produced a substantial literature throwing new and often controversial light on democratic political phenomena such as elections, decisions of political party leaders, interest group behavior, legislative and committee decisions, bureaucratic, and judicial behavior, lobbying activity, and substantive public policy areas such as constitutional arrangements, health and en-

vironment policy, regulatory policy, national security and foreign policy, and the like. Hardly a field of politics and public policy has been left untouched by this inventive and productive group of scholars.

The institutions and names with which this movement is associated in the United States include Virginia State University, the University of Virginia, the George Mason University, the University of Rochester, the University of Chicago, the California Institute of Technology, the Carnegie Mellon University, among others. And the most prominent names are those of the leaders of the two principal schools: James Buchanan, the Nobel Laureate leader of the Virginia "Public Choice" school, and William Riker, the leader of the Rochester "Positive Theory" school. Other prominent scholars associated with this work are Gary Becker of the University of Chicago, Kenneth Shepsle and Morris Fiorina of Harvard, John Ferejohn of Stanford, Charles Plott of the California Institute of Technology, and many others.

One writer summarizing the ideological bent of much of this work, but by no means all of it (William Mitchell of the University of Washington), describes it as fiscally conservative, sharing a conviction that the "... private economy is far more robust, efficient, and perhaps, equitable than other economies, and much more successful than political processes in efficiently allocating resources...." Much of what has been produced "... by James Buchanan and the leaders of this school can best be described as contributions to a theory of the failure of political processes." These failures of political performance are said to be inherent properties of the democratic political process. "Inequity, inefficiency, and coercion are the most general results of democratic policy formation." In a democracy the demand for publicly provided services seems to be insatiable. It ultimately turns into a special interest, "rent seeking" society. Their remedies take the form of proposed constitutional limits on spending power and checks and balances to limit legislative majorities.

One of the most visible products of this pessimistic economic analysis of democratic politics is the book by

Mancur Olson, *The Rise and Decline of Nations* (1982). He makes a strong argument for the negative democracy–capitalism connection. His thesis is that the behavior of individuals and firms in stable societies inevitably leads to the formation of dense networks of collusive, cartelistic, and lobbying organizations that make economies less efficient and dynamic and polities less governable. "The longer a society goes without an upheaval, the more powerful such organizations become and the more they slow down economic expansion. Societies in which these narrow interest groups have been destroyed, by war or revolution, for example, enjoy the greatest gains in growth." His prize cases are Britain on the one hand and Germany and Japan on the other.

The logic of the argument implies that countries that have had democratic freedom of organization without upheaval or invasion the longest will suffer the most from growth-repressing organizations and combinations. This helps explain why Great Britain, the major nation with the longest immunity from dictatorship, invasion, and revolution, has had in this century a lower rate of growth than other large, developed democracies. Britain has precisely the powerful network of special interest organization that the argument developed here would lead us to expect in a country with its record of military security and democratic stability. The number and power of its trade unions need no description. The venerability and power of its professional associations is also striking.... In short, with age British society has acquired so many strong organizations and collusions that it suffers from an institutional sclerosis that slows its adaptation to changing circumstances and technologies. (Olson 1982)

By contrast, post-World War II Germany and Japan started organizationally from scratch. The organizations that led them to defeat were all dissolved, and under the occupation inclusive organizations like the general trade union movement and general organizations of the industrial and commercial community were first formed. These inclusive organizations had more regard for the general national interest and exercised some discipline on the narrower interest organizations. And both countries in the post-war decades experienced "miracles" of economic growth under democratic conditions.

The Olson theory of the subversion of capitalism through the propensities of democratic societies to foster special interest groups has not gone without challenge. There can be little question that there is logic in his argument. But empirical research testing this pressure group hypothesis thus far has produced mixed findings. Olson has hopes that a public educated to the harmful consequences of special interests to economic growth, full employment, coherent government, equal opportunity, and social mobility will resist special interest behavior, and enact legislation imposing anti-trust, and anti-monopoly controls to mitigate and contain these threats. It is somewhat of an irony that the solution to this special interest disease of democracy, according to Olson, is a democratic state with sufficient regulatory authority to control the growth of special interest organizations.

Democracy Fosters Capitalism

My fourth theme, democracy as fostering and sustaining capitalism, is not as straightforward as the first three. Historically there can be little doubt that as the suffrage was extended in the last century, and as mass political parties developed, democratic development impinged significantly on capitalist institutions and practices. Since successful capitalism requires risk-taking entrepreneurs with access to investment capital, the democratic propensity for redistributive and regulative policy tends to reduce the incentives and the resources available for risk-taking and creativity. Thus it can be argued that propensities inevitably resulting from democratic politics, as Friedman, Olson and many

others argue, tend to reduce productivity, and hence welfare.

But precisely the opposite argument can be made on the basis of the historical experience of literally all of the advanced capitalist democracies in existence. All of them without exception are now welfare states with some form and degree of social insurance, health and welfare nets, and regulatory frameworks designed to mitigate the harmful impacts and shortfalls of capitalism. Indeed, the welfare state is accepted all across the political spectrum. Controversy takes place around the edges. One might make the argument that had capitalism not been modified in this welfare direction, it is doubtful that it would have survived.

This history of the interplay between democracy and capitalism is clearly laid out in a major study involving European and American scholars, entitled *The Development of Welfare States in Western Europe and America* (Flora and Heidenheimer 1981). The book lays out the relationship between the development and spread of capitalist industry, democratization in the sense of an expanding suffrage and the emergence of trade unions and left-wing political parties, and the gradual introduction of the institutions and practices of the welfare state. The early adoption of the institutions of the welfare state in Bismarck Germany, Sweden, and Great Britain were all associated with the rise of trade unions and socialist parties in those countries. The decisions made by the upper and middle class leaders and political movements to introduce welfare measures such as accident, old age, and unemployment insurance, were strategic decisions. They were increasingly confronted by trade union movements with the capacity of bringing industrial production to a halt, and by political parties with growing parliamentary representation favoring fundamental modifications in, or the abolition of capitalism. As the calculations of the upper and middle class leaders led them to conclude that the costs of suppression exceeded the costs of concession, the various parts of the welfare state began to be put in place—accident, sickness, unemployment insurance, old age insurance,

and the like. The problem of maintaining the loyalty of the working classes through two world wars resulted in additional concessions to working class demands: the filling out of the social security system, free public education to higher levels, family allowances, housing benefits, and the like.

Social conditions, historical factors, political processes and decisions produced different versions of the welfare state. In the United States, manhood suffrage came quite early, the later bargaining process emphasized free land and free education to the secondary level, an equality of opportunity version of the welfare state. The Disraeli bargain in Britain resulted in relatively early manhood suffrage and the full attainment of parliamentary government, while the Lloyd George bargain on the eve of World War I brought the beginnings of a welfare system to Britain. The Bismarck bargain in Germany produced an early welfare state, a postponement of electoral equality and parliamentary government. While there were all of these differences in historical encounters with democratization and "welfarization," the important outcome was that little more than a century after the process began all of the advanced capitalist democracies had similar versions of the welfare state, smaller in scale in the case of the United States and Japan, more substantial in Britain and the continental European countries.

We can consequently make out a strong case for the argument that democracy has been supportive of capitalism in this strategic sense. Without this welfare adaptation it is doubtful that capitalism would have survived, or rather, its survival, "unwelfarized," would have required a substantial repressive apparatus. The choice then would seem to have been between democratic welfare capitalism, and repressive undemocratic capitalism. I am inclined to believe that capitalism as such thrives more with the democratic welfare adaptation than with the repressive one. It is in that sense that we can argue that there is a clear positive impact of democracy on capitalism.

We have to recognize, in conclusion, that democracy and capitalism are both positively and negatively related, that they both support and subvert each other. My colleague, Moses Abramovitz, described this dialectic more surely than most in his presidential address to the American Economic Association in 1980, on the eve of the "Reagan Revolution." Noting the decline in productivity in the American economy during the latter 1960s and '70s, and recognizing that this decline might in part be attributable to the "tax, transfer, and regulatory" tendencies of the welfare state, he observes,

The rationale supporting the development of our mixed economy sees it as a pragmatic compromise between the competing virtues and defects of decentralized market capitalism and encompassing socialism. Its goal is to obtain a measure of distributive justice, security, and social guidance of economic life without losing too much of the allocative efficiency and dynamism of private enterprise and market organization. And it is a pragmatic compromise in another sense. It seeks to retain for most people that measure of personal protection from the state which private property and a private job market confer, while obtaining for the disadvantaged minority of people through the state that measure of support without which their lack of property or personal endowment would amount to a denial of individual freedom and capacity to function as full members of the community. (Abramovitz 1981)

Democratic welfare capitalism produces that reconciliation of opposing and complementary elements which makes possible the survival, even enhancement of both of these sets of institutions. It is not a static accommodation, but rather one which fluctuates over time, with capitalism being compromised by the tax-transfer-regulatory action of the state at one point, and then correcting in the direction of the reduction of the intervention of the state at another point, and with a learning process over time that may reduce the amplitude of the curves.

The case for this resolution of the capitalism-democracy quandary is made quite movingly by Jacob Viner who is quoted in the concluding paragraph of Abramovitz's paper, "... If... I nevertheless conclude that I believe that the welfare state, like old Siwash, is really worth fighting for and even dying for as compared to any rival system, it is because, despite its imperfection in theory and practice, in the aggregate it provides more promise of preserving and enlarging human freedoms, temporal prosperity, the extinction of mass misery, and the dignity of man and his moral improvement than any other social system which has previously prevailed, which prevails elsewhere today or which outside Utopia, the mind of man has been able to provide a blueprint for" (Abramovitz 1981).

References

Abramovitz, Moses. 1981. "Welfare Quandaries and Productivity Concerns." *American Economic Review*, March.

Berger, Peter. 1986. *The Capitalist Revolution*. New York: Basic Books.

Dahl, Robert A. 1989. *Democracy and Its Critics*. New Haven: Yale University Press.

_____. 1990. *After the Revolution: Authority in a Good Society*. New Haven: Yale University Press.

Deutsch, Karl. 1961. "Social Mobilization and Political Development." *American Political Science Review*, 55 (Sept.).

Flora, Peter, and Arnold Heidenheimer. 1981. *The Development of Welfare States in Western Europe and America*. New Brunswick, NJ: Transaction Press.

Friedman, Milton. 1981. *Capitalism and Freedom*. Chicago: University of Chicago Press.

Hirschman, Albert. 1986. *Rival Views of Market Society*. New York: Viking.

Inkeles, Alex, and David Smith. 1974. *Becoming Modern: Individual Change in Six Developing Countries*. Cambridge, MA: Harvard University Press.

Lerner, Daniel. 1958. *The Passing of Traditional Society*. New York: Free Press.

Lindblom, Charles E. 1977. *Politics and Markets*. New York: Basic Books.

Lipset, Seymour M. 1959. "Some Social Requisites of Democracy." *American Political Science Review*, 53 (September).

Mill, John Stuart. 1848, 1965. *Principles of Political Economy*, 2 vols. Toronto: University of Toronto Press.

Mitchell, William. 1988. "Virginia, Rochester, and Bloomington: Twenty-Five Years of Public Choice and Political Science." *Public Choice*, 56: 101–119.

Moore, Barrington. 1966. *The Social Origins of Dictatorship and Democracy*. New York: Beacon Press.

Olson, Mancur. 1982. *The Rise and Decline of Nations*. New Haven: Yale University Press.

Schumpeter, Joseph. 1946. *Capitalism, Socialism, and Democracy*. New York: Harper.

*Lecture presented at Seminar on the Market, sponsored by the Ford Foundation and the Research Institute on International Change of Columbia University, Moscow, October 29—November 2.

Gabriel A. Almond, professor of political science emeritus at Stanford University, is a former president of the American Political Science Association.

From *PS: Political Science and Politics*, September 1991, pp. 467–474. © 1991 by The American Political Science Association. Reprinted by permission.

CULTURAL EXPLANATIONS

The man in the Baghdad café

Which "civilisation" you belong to matters less than you might think

GOERING, it was said, growled that every time he heard the word culture he reached for his revolver. His hand would ache today. Since the end of the cold war, "culture" has been everywhere—not the opera-house or gallery kind, but the sort that claims to be the basic driving force behind human behaviour. All over the world, scholars and politicians seek to explain economics, politics and diplomacy in terms of "culture-areas" rather than, say, policies or ideas, economic interests, personalities or plain cock-ups.

Perhaps the best-known example is the notion that "Asian values" explain the success of the tiger economies of South-East Asia. Other accounts have it that international conflict is—or will be—caused by a clash of civilisations; or that different sorts of business organisation can be explained by how much people in different countries trust one [an]other. These four pages review the varying types of cultural explanation. They conclude that culture is so imprecise and changeable a phenomenon that it explains less than most people realise.

To see how complex the issue is, begin by considering the telling image with which Bernard Lewis opens his history of the Middle East. A man sits at a table in a coffee house in some Middle Eastern city, "drinking a cup of coffee or tea, perhaps smoking a cigarette, reading a newspaper, playing a board game, and listening with half an ear to whatever is coming out of the radio or the television installed in the corner." Undoubtedly Arab, almost certainly

Muslim, the man would clearly identify himself as a member of these cultural groups. He would also, if asked, be likely to say that "western culture" was alien, even hostile to them.

Look closer, though, and the cultural contrasts blur. This coffee-house man probably wears western-style clothes—sneakers, jeans, a T-shirt. The chair and table at which he sits, the coffee he drinks, the tobacco he smokes, the newspaper he reads, all are western imports. The radio and television are western inventions. If our relaxing friend is a member of his nation's army, he probably operates western or Soviet weapons and trains according to western standards; if he belongs to the government, both his bureaucratic surroundings and the constitutional trappings of his regime may owe their origins to western influence.

The upshot, for Mr Lewis, is clear enough. "In modern times," he writes, "the dominating factor in the consciousness of most Middle Easterners has been the impact of Europe, later of the West more generally, and the transformation—some would say dislocation—which it has brought." Mr Lewis has put his finger on the most important and least studied aspect of cultural identity: how it changes. It would be wise to keep that in mind during the upsurge of debate about culture that is likely to follow the publication of Samuel Huntington's new book, "The Clash of Civilisations and the Remaking of World Order".

The clash of civilisations

A professor of international politics at Harvard and the chairman of Harvard's Institute for Strategic Planning, Mr Huntington published in 1993, in *Foreign Affairs*, an essay which that quarterly's editors said generated more discussion than any since George Kennan's article (under the by-line "x") which argued in July 1947 for the need to contain the Soviet threat. Henry Kissinger, a former secretary of state, called Mr Huntington's book-length version of the article "one of the most important books... since the end of the cold war."

The article, "The Clash of Civilisation?", belied the question-mark in its title by predicting wars of culture. "It is my hypothesis", Mr Huntington wrote, "that the fundamental source of conflict in this new world will not be primarily ideological or primarily economic. The great division among humankind and the dominating source of conflict will be cultural."

After the cold war, ideology seemed less important as an organising principle of foreign policy. Culture seemed a plausible candidate to fill the gap. So future wars, Mr Huntington claimed, would occur "between nations and groups of different civilisations"—western, Confucian, Japanese, Islamic, Hindu, Orthodox and Latin American, perhaps African and Buddhist. Their disputes would "dominate global politics" and the battle-lines of the future would follow the fault-lines between these cultures.

No mincing words there, and equally few in his new book:

> Culture and cultural identities... are shaping the patterns of cohesion, disintegration and conflict in the post-cold war world... Global politics is being reconfigured along cultural lines.

Mr Huntington is only one of an increasing number of writers placing stress on the importance of cultural values and institutions in the confusion left in the wake of the cold war. He looked at the influence of culture on international conflict. Three other schools of thought find cultural influences at work in different ways.

• **Culture and the economy**. Perhaps the oldest school holds that cultural values and norms equip people—and, by extension, countries—either poorly or well for economic success. The archetypal modern pronouncement of this view was Max Weber's investigation of the Protestant work ethic. This, he claimed, was the reason why the Protestant parts of Germany and Switzerland were more successful economically than the Catholic areas. In the recent upsurge of interest in issues cultural, a handful of writers have returned to the theme.

It is "values and attitudes—culture", claims Lawrence Harrison, that are "mainly responsible for such phenomena as Latin America's persistent instability and inequity, Taiwan's and Korea's economic 'miracles', and the achievements of the Japanese." Thomas Sowell offers other examples in "Race and Culture: A World View". "A disdain for commerce and industry", he argues, "has... been common for centuries among the Hispanic elite, both in Spain and in Latin America." Academics, though, have played a relatively small part in this debate: the best-known exponent of the thesis that "Asian values"—a kind of Confucian work ethic—aid economic development has been Singapore's former prime minister, Lee Kuan Yew.

• **Culture as social blueprint**. A second group of analysts has looked at the connections between cultural factors and political systems. Robert Putnam, another Harvard professor, traced Italy's social and political institutions to its "civic culture", or lack thereof. He claimed that, even today, the parts of Italy where democratic institutions are most fully developed are similar to the areas which first began to generate these institutions in the 14th century. His conclusion is that democracy is not something

that can be put on like a coat; it is part of a country's social fabric and takes decades, even centuries, to develop.

Francis Fukuyama, of George Mason University, takes a slightly different approach. In a recent book which is not about the end of history, he focuses on one particular social trait, "trust". "A nation's well-being, as well as its ability to compete, is conditioned by a single, pervasive cultural characteristic: the level of trust inherent in the society," he says. Mr Fukuyama argues that "low-trust" societies such as China, France and Italy—where close relations between people do not extend much beyond the family—are poor at generating large, complex social institutions like multinational corporations; so they are at a competitive disadvantage compared with "high-trust" nations such as Germany, Japan and the United States.

• **Culture and decision-making**. The final group of scholars has looked at the way in which cultural assumptions act like blinkers. Politicians from different countries see the same issue in different ways because of their differing cultural backgrounds. Their electorates or nations do, too. As a result, they claim, culture acts as an international barrier. As Ole Elgstrom puts it: "When a Japanese prime minister says that he will 'do his best' to implement a certain policy," Americans applaud a victory but "what the prime minister really meant was 'no'." There are dozens of examples of misperception in international relations, ranging from Japanese-American trade disputes to the misreading of Saddam Hussein's intentions in the weeks before he attacked Kuwait.

What are they talking about?

All of this is intriguing, and much of it is provocative. It has certainly provoked a host of arguments. For example, is Mr Huntington right to lump together all European countries into one culture, though they speak different languages, while separating Spain and Mexico, which speak the same one? Is the Catholic Philippines western or Asian? Or: if it is true (as Mr Fukuyama claims) that the ability to produce multinational firms is vital to economic success, why has "low-trust" China, which has few such companies, grown so fast? And why has yet-more successful "low-trust" South Korea been able to create big firms?

This is nit-picking, of course. But such questions of detail matter because behind

them lurks the first of two fundamental doubts that plague all these cultural explanations: how do you define what a culture is?

In their attempts to define what cultures are (and hence what they are talking about), most "culture" writers rely partly on self definition: cultures are what people think of themselves as part of. In Mr Huntington's words, civilisation "is the broadest level of identification with which [a person] intensely identifies."

The trouble is that relatively few people identify "intensely" with broad cultural groups. They tend to identify with something narrower: nations or ethnic groups. Europe is a case in point. A poll done last year for the European Commission found that half the people of Britain, Portugal and Greece thought of themselves in purely national terms; so did a third of the Germans, Spaniards and Dutch. And this was in a part of the world where there is an institution—the EU itself—explicitly devoted to the encouragement of "Europeanness".

The same poll found that in every EU country, 70% or more thought of themselves either purely in national terms, or primarily as part of a nation and only secondly as Europeans. Clearly, national loyalty can coexist with wider cultural identification. But, even then, the narrower loyalty can blunt the wider one because national characteristics often are—or at least are often thought to be—peculiar or unique. Seymour Martin Lipset, a sociologist who recently published a book about national characteristics in the United States, called it "American Exceptionalism". David Willetts, a British Conservative member of Parliament, recently claimed that the policies espoused by the opposition Labour Party would go against the grain of "English exceptionalism". And these are the two components of western culture supposedly most like one another.

In Islamic countries, the balance between cultural and national identification may be tilted towards the culture. But even here the sense of, say, Egyptian or Iraqi or Palestinian nationhood remains strong. (Consider the competing national feelings unleashed during the Iran-Iraq war.) In other cultures, national loyalty seems preeminent: in Mr Huntington's classification, Thailand, Tibet and Mongolia all count as "Buddhist". It is hard to imagine that a Thai, a Tibetan and a Mongolian really have that much in common.

So the test of subjective identification is hard to apply. That apart, the writers define

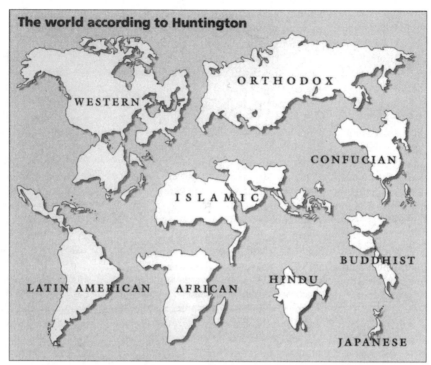

The world according to Huntington

WESTERN

ORTHODOX

CONFUCIAN

ISLAMIC

BUDDHIST

LATIN AMERICAN　　AFRICAN　　HINDU

JAPANESE

Source: Adapted by The Economist from "The Clash of Civilisations and the Remaking of World Order"
by Samuel Huntington

a culture in the usual terms: language, religion, history, customs and institutions and so on. Such multiple definitions ring true. As Bernard Lewis's man in the Levantine café suggests, cultures are not singular things: they are bundles of characteristics.

The trouble is that such characteristics are highly ambiguous. Some push one way, some another.

Culture as muddle

Islamic values, for instance, are routinely assumed to be the antithesis of modernising western ones. In Islam, tradition is good; departure from tradition is presumed to be bad until proven otherwise. Yet, at the same time, Islam is also a monotheistic religion which encourages rationalism and science. Some historians have plausibly argued that it was the Islamic universities of medieval Spain that kept science and rationalism alive during Europe's Dark Ages, and that Islam was a vital medieval link between the ancient world of Greece and Rome and the Renaissance. The scientific-rationalist aspect of Islam could well come to the fore again.

If you doubt it, consider the case of China and the "Confucian tradition" (a sort of proxy for Asian values). China has been

at various times the world's most prosperous country and also one of its poorest. It has had periods of great scientific innovation and times of technological backwardness and isolation. Accounts of the Confucian tradition have tracked this path. Nowadays, what seems important about the tradition is its encouragement of hard work, savings and investment for the future, plus its emphasis on co-operation towards a single end. All these features have been adduced to explain why the tradition has helped Asian growth.

To Max Weber, however, the same tradition seemed entirely different. He argued that the Confucian insistence on obedience to parental authority discouraged competition and innovation and hence inhibited economic success. And China is not the only country to have been systematically misdiagnosed in this way. In countries as varied as Japan, India, Ghana and South Korea, notions of cultural determination of economic performance have been proved routinely wrong (in 1945, India and Ghana were expected to do best of the four—partly because of their supposed cultural inheritance).

If you take an extreme position, you could argue from this that cultures are so complicated that they can never be used to explain behaviour accurately. Even if you

do not go that far, the lesson must be that the same culture embraces such conflicting features that it can produce wholly different effects at different times.

That is hard enough for the schools of culture to get to grips with. But there is worse to come. For cultures never operate in isolation. When affecting how people behave, they are always part of a wider mix. That mix includes government policies, personal leadership, technological or economic change and so on. For any one effect, there are always multiple causes. Which raises the second fundamental doubt about cultural explanations: how do you know whether it is culture—and not something else—that has caused some effect? You cannot. The problem of causation seems insoluble. The best you can do is work out whether, within the mix, culture is becoming more or less important.

Culture as passenger

Of the many alternative explanations for events, three stand out: the influence of ideas, of government and what might be called the "knowledge era" (shorthand for globalisation, the growth of service-based industries and so forth). Of these, the influence of ideas as a giant organising principle is clearly not what it was when the cold war divided the world between communists and capitalists. We are all capitalists now. To that extent, it is fair to say that the ideological part of the mix has become somewhat less important—though not, as a few people have suggested, insignificant.

As for the government, it is a central thesis of the cultural writers that its influence is falling while that of culture is rising: cultures are in some ways replacing states. To quote Mr Huntington again "peoples and countries with similar cultures are coming together. Peoples and countries with different cultures are coming apart."

In several respects, that is counter-intuitive. Governments still control what is usually the single most powerful force in any country, the army. And, in all but the poorest places, governments tax and spend a large chunk of GDP—indeed, a larger chunk, in most places, than 50 years ago.

Hardly surprising, then, that governments influence cultures as much as the other way around. To take a couple of examples. Why does South Korea (a low-trust culture, remember) have so many internationally competitive large firms? The answer is that the government decided that it should. Or another case: since 1945 German politicians of every stripe have been insisting that they want to "save Germany from itself"—an attempt to assert political control over cultural identity.

South Korea and Germany are examples of governments acting positively to create something new. But governments can act upon cultures negatively: ie, they can destroy a culture when they collapse. Robert Kaplan, of an American magazine *Atlantic Monthly*, begins his book, "The Ends of the Earth", in Sierra Leone: "I had assumed that the random crime and social chaos of West Africa were the result of an already-fragile cultural base." Yet by the time he reaches Cambodia at the end of what he calls "a journey at the dawn of the 21st century" he is forced to reconsider that assumption:

Here I was… in a land where the written script was one thousand two hundred years old, and every surrounding country was in some stage of impressive economic growth. Yet Cambodia was eerily similar to Sierra Leone: with random crime, mosquito-borne disease, a government army that was more like a mob and a countryside that was ungovernable.

His conclusion is that "The effect of culture was more a mystery to me near the end of my planetary journey than at its beginning." He might have gone further: the collapse of governments causes cultural turbulence just as much as cultural turbulence causes the collapse of governments.

Culture as processed data

Then there is the "knowledge era". Here is a powerful and growing phenomenon. The culture writers do not claim anything different. Like the Industrial Revolution before it, the knowledge era—in which the creation, storage and use of knowledge becomes the basic economic activity—is generating huge change. Emphasising as it does rapid, even chaotic, transformation, it is anti-traditional and anti-authoritarian.

Yet the cultural exponents still claim that, even in the knowledge era, culture remains a primary engine of change. They do so for two quite different reasons. Some claim that the new era has the makings of a world culture. There is a universal language, English. There are the beginnings of an international professional class that cuts across cultural and national boundaries: increasingly, bankers, computer programmers, executives, even military officers are said to have as much in common with their opposite numbers in other countries as with their next-door neighbors. As Mr Fukuyama wrote in his more famous book: the "unfolding of modern natural science… guarantees an increasing homogenisation of all human societies." Others doubt that technology and the rest of it are producing a genuinely new world order. To them, all this is just modern western culture.

Either way, the notion that modernity is set on a collision course with culture lies near the heart of several of the culture writers' books. Summing them up is the title of Benjamin Barber's "Jihad versus McWorld". In other words, he argues that the main conflicts now and in future will be between tribal, local "cultural" values (Jihad) and a McWorld of technology and democracy.

It would be pointless to deny that globalisation is causing large changes in every society. It is also clear that such influences act on different cultures differently, enforcing a kind of natural selection between those cultures which rise to the challenge and those which do not.

But it is more doubtful that these powerful forces are primarily cultural or even western. Of course, they have a cultural component: the artefacts of American culture are usually the first things to come along in the wake of a new road, or new television networks. But the disruptive force itself is primarily economic and has been adopted as enthusiastically in Japan, Singapore and China as in America. The world market is not a cultural concept.

Moreover, to suggest that trade, globalisation and the rest of it tend to cause conflict, and then leave the argument there, is not enough. When you boil the argument down, much of its seems to be saying that the more countries trade with each other, the more likely they are to go to war. That seems implausible. Trade—indeed, any sort of link—is just as likely to reduce the potential for violent conflict as to increase it. The same goes for the spread of democracy, another feature which is supposed to encourage civilisations to clash with each other. This might well cause ructions within countries. It might well provoke complaints from dictators about "outside interference". But serious international conflict is a different matter. And if democracy really did spread round the world, it might tend to reduce violence; wealthy democracies, at any rate, are usually reluctant to go to war (though poor or angrily nationalist ones may, as history has shown, be much less reluctant).

In short, the "knowledge era" is spreading economic ideas. And these ideas have three cultural effects, not one. They make cultures rub against each other, causing international friction. They also tie different cultures closer together, which offsets the first effect. And they may well increase tensions within a culture-area as some groups accommodate themselves to the new world while others turn their back on it. And all this can be true at the same time because cultures are so varied and ambiguous that they are capable of virtually any transformation.

The conclusion must be that while culture will continue to exercise an important influence on both countries and individuals, it has not suddenly become more important than, say, governments or impersonal economic forces. Nor does it play the all-embracing defining role that ideology played during the cold war. Much of its influence is secondary, ie, it comes about partly as a reaction to the "knowledge era". And within the overall mix of what influences people's behaviour, culture's role may well be declining, rather than rising, squeezed between the greedy expansion of the government on one side, and globalisation on the other.

The books mentioned in this article are:

Benjamin Barber. Jihad versus McWorld (Random House; 1995; 400 pages; $12.95).

Francis Fukuyama. The End of History and the Last Man (Free Press; 1992; 419 pages; $24.95. Hamish Hamilton; £20.) and Trust: The Social Virtues and the Creation of Prosperity (Free Press; 1995; 480 pages; $25. Hamish Hamilton; £25).

Lawrence E. Harrison. Who Prospers? How Cultural Values Shape Economic and Political Success (Basic Books; 1992; 288 pages; $14).

Samuel Huntington. The Clash of Civilisations? *Foreign Affairs* Vol. 72 (Summer 1993) and The Clash of Civilisations and the Remaking of World Order (Simon & Schuster; 1996; 367 pages; $26).

Robert Kaplan. The Ends of the Earth (Random House; 1996; 475 pages; $27.50. Papermac; £10).

Bernard Lewis. The Middle East (Wiedenfeld & Nicolson; 1995; 433 pages; £20. Simon & Schuster; $29.50).

Seymour Martin Lipset. American Exceptionalism (Norton; 1996; 352 pages; $27.50 and £19.95).

Robert Putnam. Making Democracy Work: Civic Traditions in Modern Italy (Princeton; 1993; 288 pages; $24.95 and £18.95).

Thomas Sowell. Race and Culture: A World View (Basic Books; 1994; 331 pages; $14).

Jihad vs. McWorld

The two axial principles of our age—tribalism and globalism—clash at every point except one: they may both be threatening to democracy

Benjamin R. Barber

Just beyond the horizon of current events lie two possible political figures—both bleak, neither democratic. The first is a retribalization of large swaths of humankind by war and bloodshed: a threatened Lebanonization of national states in which culture is pitted against culture, people against people, tribe against tribe—a Jihad in the name of a hundred narrowly conceived faiths against every kind of interdependence, every kind of artificial social cooperation and civic mutuality. The second is being borne in on us by the onrush of economic and ecological forces that demand integration and uniformity and that mesmerize the world with fast music, fast computers, and fast food—with MTV, Macintosh, and McDonald's, pressing nations into one commercially homogenous global network: one McWorld tied together by technology, ecology, communications, and commerce. The planet is falling precipitantly apart and coming reluctantly together at the very same moment.

These two tendencies are sometimes visible in the same countries at the same instant: thus Yugoslavia, clamoring just recently to join the New Europe, is exploding into fragments; India is trying to live up to its reputation as the world's largest integral democracy while powerful new fundamentalist parties like the Hindu nationalist Bharatiya Janta Party, along with nationalist assassins, are imperiling its hard-won unity. States are breaking up or joining up: the Soviet Union has disap-

peared almost overnight, its parts forming new unions with one another or with like-minded nationalities in neighboring states. The old interwar national state based on territory and political sovereignty looks to be a mere transitional development.

The tendencies of what I am here calling the forces of Jihad and the forces of McWorld operate with equal strength in opposite directions, the one driven by parochial hatreds, the other by universalizing markets, the one re-creating ancient subnational and ethnic borders from within, the other making national borders porous from without. They have one thing in common: neither offers much hope to citizens looking for practical ways to govern themselves democratically. If the global future is to pit Jihad's centrifugal whirlwind against McWorld's centripetal black hole, the outcome is unlikely to be democratic—or so I will argue.

McWORLD, OR THE GLOBALIZATION OF POLITICS

Four imperatives make up the dynamic of McWorld: a market imperative, a resource imperative, an information-technology imperative, and an ecological imperative. By shrinking the world and diminishing the salience of national borders, these imperatives have in combination achieved a considerable victory over factiousness and

particularism, and not least of all over their most virulent traditional form—nationalism. It is the realists who are now Europeans, the utopians who dream nostalgically of a resurgent England or Germany, perhaps even a resurgent Wales or Saxony. Yesterday's wishful cry for one world has yielded to the reality of McWorld.

The market imperative. Marxist and Leninist theories of imperialism assumed that the quest for ever-expanding markets would in time compel nation-based capitalist economies to push against national boundaries in search of an international economic imperium. Whatever else has happened to the scientist predictions of Marxism, in this domain they have proved farsighted. All national economies are now vulnerable to the inroads of larger, transnational markets within which trade is free, currencies are convertible, access to banking is open, and contracts are enforceable under law. In Europe, Asia, Africa, the South Pacific, and the Americas such markets are eroding national sovereignty and giving rise to entities—international banks, trade associations, transnational lobbies like OPEC and Greenpeace, world news services like CNN and the BBC, and multinational corporations that increasingly lack a meaningful national identity—that neither reflect nor respect nationhood as an organizing or regulative principle.

The market imperative has also reinforced the quest for international peace and stability, requisites of an efficient international economy. Markets are enemies of parochialism, isolation, fractiousness, war. Market psychology attenuates the psychology of ideological and religious cleavages and assumes a concord among producers and consumers—categories that ill fit narrowly conceived national or religious cultures. Shopping has little tolerance for blue laws, whether dictated by pub-closing British paternalism, Sabbath-observing Jewish Orthodox fundamentalism, or no-Sunday-liquor-sales Massachusetts puritanism. In the context of common markets, international law ceases to be a vision of justice and becomes a workaday framework for getting things done—enforcing contracts, ensuring that governments abide by deals, regulating trade and currency relations, and so forth.

Common markets demand a common language, as well as a common currency, and they produce common behaviors of the kind bred by cosmopolitan city life everywhere. Commercial pilots, computer programmers, international bankers, media specialists, oil riggers, entertainment celebrities, ecology experts, demographers, accountants, professors, athletes—these compose a new breed of men and women for whom religion, culture, and nationality can seem only marginal elements in a working identity. Although sociologists of everyday life will no doubt continue to distinguish a Japanese from an American mode, shopping has a common signature throughout the world. Cynics might even say that some of the recent revolutions in Eastern Europe have had as their true goal not liberty and the right to vote but well-paying jobs and the right to shop (although the vote is proving easier to acquire than consumer goods). The market imperative is, then, plenty powerful; but, notwithstanding some of the claims made for "democratic capitalism," it is not identical with the democratic imperative.

The resource imperative. Democrats once dreamed of societies whose political autonomy rested firmly on economic independence. The Athenians idealized what they called autarky, and tried for a while to create a way of life simple and austere enough to make the polis genuinely self-sufficient. To be free meant to be independent of any other community or polis. Not even the Athenians were able to achieve autarky, however: human nature, it turns out, is dependency. By the time of Pericles, Athenian politics was inextricably bound up with a flowering empire held together by naval power and commerce—an empire that, even as it appeared to enhance Athenian might, ate away at Athenian independence and autarky. Master and slave, it turned out, were bound together by mutual insufficiency.

The dream of autarky briefly engrossed nineteenth-century America as well, for the underpopulated, endlessly bountiful land, the cornucopia of natural resources, and the natural barriers of a continent walled in by two great seas led many to believe that America could be a world unto itself. Given this past, it has been harder for Americans than for most to accept the inevitability of interdependence. But the rapid depletion of resources even in a country like ours, where they once seemed inexhaustible, and the maldistribution of arable soil and mineral resources on the planet, leave even the wealthiest societies ever more resource-dependent and many other nations in permanently desperate straits.

Every nation, it turns out, needs something another nation has; some nations have almost nothing they need.

The information-technology imperative. Enlightenment science and the technologies derived from it are inherently universalizing. They entail a quest for descriptive principles of general application, a search for universal solutions to particular problems, and an unswerving embrace of objectivity and impartiality.

Scientific progress embodies and depends on open communication, a common discourse rooted in rationality, collaboration, and an easy and regular flow and exchange of information. Such ideals can be hypocritical covers for power-mongering by elites, and they may be shown to be wanting in many other ways, but they are entailed by the very idea of science and they make science and globalization practical allies.

Business, banking, and commerce all depend on information flow and are facilitated by new communication technologies. The hardware of these technologies tends to be systemic and integrated—computer, television, cable, satellite, laser, fiber-optic, and microchip technologies combining to create a vast interactive communications and information network that can potentially give every person on earth access to every other person, and make every datum, every byte, available to every set of eyes. If the automobile was, as George Ball once said (when he gave his blessing to a Fiat factory in the Soviet Union during the Cold War), "an ideology on four wheels," then electronic telecommunication and information systems are an ideology at 186,000 miles per second—which makes for a very small planet in a very big hurry. Individual cultures speak particular languages; commerce and science increasingly speak English; the whole world speaks logarithms and binary mathematics.

Moreover, the pursuit of science and technology asks for, even compels, open societies. Satellite footprints do not respect national borders; telephone wires penetrate the most closed societies. With photocopying and then fax machines having infiltrated Soviet universities and *samizdat* literary circles in the eighties, and computer modems having multiplied like rabbits in communism's bureaucratic warrens thereafter, *glasnost* could not be far behind. In their social requisites, secrecy and science are enemies.

The new technology's software is perhaps even more globalizing than its hardware. The information arm of international commerce's sprawling body reaches out and touches distinct nations and parochial cultures, and gives them a common face chiseled in Hollywood, on Madison Avenue, and in Silicon Valley. Throughout the 1980s one of the most-watched television programs in South Africa was *The Cosby Show*. The demise of apartheid was already in production. Exhibitors at the 1991 Cannes film festival expressed growing anxiety over the "homogenization" and "Americanization" of the global film industry when, for the third year running, American films dominated the awards ceremonies. America has dominated the world's popular culture for much longer, and much more decisively. In November of 1991 Switzerland's once insular culture boasted best-seller lists featuring *Terminator 2* as the No. 1 movie, *Scarlett* as the No. 1 book, and Prince's *Diamonds and Pearls* as the No. 1 record album. No wonder the Japanese are buying Hollywood film studios even faster than Americans are buying Japanese television sets. This kind of software supremacy may in the long term be far more important than hardware superiority, because culture has become more potent than armaments. What is the power of the Pentagon compared with Disneyland? Can the Sixth Fleet keep up with CNN? McDonald's in Moscow and Coke in China will do more to create a global culture than military colonization ever could. It is less the goods than the brand names that do the work, for they convey lifestyle images that alter perception and challenge behavior. They make up the seductive software of McWorld's common (at times much too common) soul.

Yet in all this high-tech commercial world there is nothing that looks particularly democratic. It lends itself to surveillance as well as liberty, to new forms of manipulation and covert control as well as new kinds of participation, to skewed, unjust market outcomes as well as greater productivity. The consumer society and the open society are not quite synonymous. Capitalism and democracy have a relationship, but it is something less than a marriage. An efficient free market after all requires that consumers be free to vote their dollars on competing goods, not that citizens be free to vote their values and beliefs on competing political candidates and programs. The free market flourished in junta-run Chile, in military-governed Taiwan and Korea, and, earlier, in a variety of autocratic European empires as well as their colonial possessions.

The *ecological imperative*. The impact of globalization on ecology is a cliché even to world leaders who ignore it. We know well enough that the German forests can be destroyed by Swiss and Italians driving gas-guzzlers fueled by leaded gas. We also know that the planet can be asphyxiated by greenhouse gases because Brazilian farmers want to be part of the twentieth century and are burning down tropical rain forests to clear a little land to plough, and because Indonesians make a living out of converting their lush jungle into toothpicks for fastidious Japanese diners, upsetting the delicate oxygen balance and in effect puncturing our global lungs. Yet this ecological consciousness has meant not only greater awareness but also greater inequality, as modernized nations try to slam the door behind them, saying to developing nations, "The world cannot afford your modernization; ours has wrung it dry!"

Each of the four imperatives just cited is transnational, transideological, and transcultural. Each applies impartially to Catholics, Jews, Muslims, Hindus, and Buddhists; to democrats and totalitarians; to capitalists and socialists. The Enlightenment dream of a universal rational society has to a remarkable degree been realized—but in a form that is commercialized, homogenized, depoliticized, bureaucratized, and, of course, radically incomplete, for the movement toward McWorld is in competition with forces of global breakdown, national dissolution, and centrifugal corruption. These forces, working in the opposite direction, are the essence of what I call Jihad.

JIHAD, OR THE LEBANONIZATION OF THE WORLD

OPEC, the World Bank, the United Nations, the International Red Cross, the multinational corporation… there are scores of institutions that reflect globalization. But they often appear as ineffective reactors to the world's real actors: national states and, to an ever greater degree, subnational factions in permanent rebellion against uniformity and integration—even the kind represented by universal law and justice. The headlines feature these players regularly: they are cultures, not countries; parts, not wholes; sects, not religions; rebellious factions and dissenting minorities at war not just with globalism but with the traditional nation-state. Kurds, Basques, Puerto Ricans, Ossetians, East Timoreans, Quebecois, the Catholics of Northern Ireland, Abkhasians, Kurile Islander Japanese, the Zulus of Inkatha, Catalonians, Tamils, and, of course, Palestinians—people without countries, inhabiting nations not their own, seeking smaller worlds within borders that will seal them off from modernity.

A powerful irony is at work here. Nationalism was once a force of integration and unification, a movement aimed at bringing together disparate clans, tribes, and cultural fragments under new, assimilationist flags. But as Ortega y Gasset noted more than sixty years ago, having won its victories, nationalism changed its strategy. In the 1920s, and again today, it is more often a reactionary and divisive force, pulverizing the very nations it once helped cement together. The force that creates nations is "inclusive," Ortega wrote in *The Revolt of the Masses*. "In periods of consolidation, nationalism has a positive value, and is a lofty standard. But in Europe everything is more than consolidated, and nationalism is nothing but a mania.…"

This mania has left the post-Cold War world smothering with hot wars; the international scene is little more unified than it was at the end of the Great War, in Ortega's own time. There were more than thirty wars in progress last year, most of them ethnic, racial, tribal, or religious in character, and the list of unsafe regions doesn't seem to be getting any shorter. Some new world order!

The aim of many of these small-scale wars is to redraw boundaries, to implode states and resecure parochial identities: to escape McWorld's dully insistent impera-

tives. The mood is that of Jihad: war not as an instrument of policy but as an emblem of identity, an expression of community, an end in itself. Even where there is no shooting war, there is fractiousness, secession, and the quest for ever smaller communities. Add to the list of dangerous countries those at risk: In Switzerland and Spain, Jurassian and Basque separatists still argue the virtues of ancient identities, sometimes in the language of bombs. Hyperdisintegration in the former Soviet Union may well continue unabated—not just a Ukraine independent from the Soviet Union but a Bessarabian Ukraine independent from the Ukrainian republic; not just Russia severed from the defunct union but Tatarstan severed from Russia. Yugoslavia makes even the disunited, ex-Soviet, non-socialist republics that were once the Soviet Union look integrated, its sectarian fatherlands springing up within factional motherlands like weeds within weeds within weeds. Kurdish independence would threaten the territorial integrity of four Middle Eastern nations. Well before the current cataclysm Soviet Georgia made a claim for autonomy from the Soviet Union, only to be faced with its Ossetians (164,000 in a republic of 5.5 million) demanding their own self-determination within Georgia. The Abkhasian minority in Georgia has followed suit. Even the good will established by Canada's once promising Meech Lake protocols is in danger, with Francophone Quebec again threatening the dissolution of the federation. In South Africa the emergence from apartheid was hardly achieved when friction between Inkatha's Zulus and the African National Congress's tribally identified members threatened to replace Europeans' racism with an indigenous tribal war. After thirty years of attempted integration using the colonial language (English) as a unifier, Nigeria is now playing with the idea of linguistic multiculturalism—which could mean the cultural breakup of the nation into hundreds of tribal fragments. Even Saddam Hussein has benefited from the threat of internal Jihad, having used renewed tribal and religious warfare to turn last season's mortal enemies into reluctant allies of an Iraqi nationhood that he nearly destroyed.

The passing of communism has torn away the thin veneer of internationalism (workers of the world unite!) to reveal ethnic prejudices that are not only ugly and deep-seated but increasingly murderous. Europe's old scourge, anti-Semitism, is back with a vengeance, but it is only one of many antagonisms. It appears all too easy to throw the historical gears into reverse and pass from a Communist dictatorship back into a tribal state.

Among the tribes, religion is also a battlefield. ("Jihad" is a rich world whose generic meaning is "struggle"—usually the struggle of the soul to avert evil. Strictly applied to religious war, it is used only in reference to battles where the faith is under assault, or battles against a government that denies the practice of Islam. My use here is rhetorical, but does follow both journalistic practice and history.) Remember the Thirty Years War? Whatever forms of Enlightenment universalism might once have come to grace such historically related forms of monotheism as Judaism, Christianity, and Islam, in many of their modern incarnations they are parochial rather than cosmopolitan, angry rather than loving, proselytizing rather than ecumenical, zealous rather than rationalist, sectarian rather than deistic, ethnocentric rather than universalizing. As a result, like the new forms of hypernationalism, the new expressions of religious fundamentalism are fractious and pulverizing, never integrating. This is religion as the Crusaders knew it: a battle to the death for souls that if not saved will be forever lost.

The atmospherics of Jihad have resulted in a breakdown of civility in the name of identity, of comity in the name of community. International relations have sometimes taken on the aspect of gang war—cultural turf battles featuring tribal factions that were supposed to be sublimated as integral parts of large national, economic, postcolonial, and constitutional entities.

THE DARKENING FUTURE OF DEMOCRACY

These rather melodramatic tableaux vivants do not tell the whole story, however. For all their defects, Jihad and McWorld have their attractions. Yet, to repeat and insist, the attractions are unrelated to democracy. Neither McWorld nor Jihad is remotely democratic in impulse. Neither needs democracy; neither promotes democracy.

McWorld does manage to look pretty seductive in a world obsessed with Jihad. It delivers peace, prosperity, and relative unity—if at the cost of independence, community, and identity (which is generally based on difference). The primary political values required by the global market are order and tranquility, and freedom—as in the phrases "free trade," "free press," and "free love." Human rights are needed to a degree, but not citizenship or participation—and no more social justice and equality than are necessary to promote efficient economic production and consumption. Multinational corporations sometimes seem to prefer doing business with local oligarchs, inasmuch as they can take confidence from dealing with the boss on all crucial matters. Despots who slaughter their own populations are no problem, so long as they leave markets in place and refrain from making war on their neighbors (Saddam Hussein's fatal mistake). In trading partners, predictability is of more value than justice.

The Eastern European revolutions that seemed to arise out of concern for global democratic values quickly deteriorated into a stampede in the general direction of free markets and their ubiquitous, television-promoted shopping malls. East Germany's Neues Forum, that courageous gathering of intellectuals, students, and workers which overturned the Stalinist regime in Berlin in 1989, lasted only six months in Germany's mini-version of McWorld. Then it gave way to money and markets and monopolies from the West. By the time of the first all-German elections, it could scarcely manage to secure three percent of the vote. Elsewhere there is growing evidence that *glasnost* will go and *perestroika*—defined as privatization and an opening of markets to Western bidders—will stay. So understandably anxious are the new rulers of Eastern Europe and whatever entities are forged from the residues of the Soviet Union to gain access to credit and markets and technology—McWorld's flourishing new currencies—that they have shown themselves willing to trade away democratic prospects in pursuit of them: not just old totalitarian ideologies and command-economy production models but some possible indigenous experiments with a third way between capitalism and socialism, such as economic cooperatives and employee stock-ownership plans, both of which have their ardent supporters in the East.

Jihad delivers a different set of virtues: a vibrant local identity, a sense of community, solidarity among kinsmen, neighbors, and countrymen, narrowly conceived. But it also guarantees parochialism and is grounded in exclusion. Solidarity is secured through war against outsiders. And solidarity often means obedience to a hierarchy in governance, fanaticism in beliefs, and the obliteration of individual selves in the name of the group. Deference to leaders and intolerance toward outsiders (and toward "enemies within") are hallmarks of tribalism—hardly the attitudes required for the cultivation of new democratic women and men capable of governing themselves. Where new democratic experiments have been conducted in retribalizing societies, in both Europe and the Third World, the result has often been anarchy, repression, persecution, and the coming of new, noncommunist forms of very old kinds of despotism. During the past year, Havel's velvet revolution in Czechoslovakia was imperiled by partisans of "Czechland" and of Slovakia as independent entities. India seemed little less rent by Sikh, Hindu, Muslim, and Tamil infighting than it was immediately after the British pulled out, more than forty years ago.

To the extent that either McWorld or Jihad has a *natural* politics, it has turned out to be more of an antipolitics. For McWorld, it is the antipolitics of globalism: bureaucratic, technocratic, and meritocratic, focused (as Marx predicted it would be) on the administration of things—with people, however, among the chief things to be administered. In its politico-economic imperatives McWorld has been guided by laissez-faire market principles that privilege efficiency, productivity, and beneficence at the expense of civic liberty and self-government.

For Jihad, the antipolitics of tribalization has been explicitly antidemocratic: one-party dictatorship, government by military junta, theocratic fundamentalism—often associated with a version of the *Führerprinzip* that empowers an individual to rule on behalf of a people. Even the government of India, struggling for decades to model democracy for a people who will soon number a billion, longs for great leaders; and for every Mahatma Gandhi, Indira Gandhi, or Rajiv Gandhi taken from them by zealous assassins, the Indians appear to seek a replacement who will deliver them from the lengthy travail of their freedom.

THE CONFEDERAL OPTION

How can democracy be secured and spread in a world whose primary tendencies are at best indifferent to it (McWorld) and at worst deeply antithetical to it (Jihad)? My guess is that globalization will eventually vanquish retribalization. The ethos of material "civilization" has not yet encountered an obstacle it has been unable to thrust aside. Ortega may have grasped in the 1920s a clue to our own future in the coming millennium.

Everyone sees the need of a new principle of life. But as always happens in similar crises—some people attempt to save the situation by an artificial intensification of the very principle which has led to decay. This is the meaning of the "nationalist" outburst of recent years... things have always gone that way. The last flare, the longest; the last sigh, the deepest. On the very eve of their disappearance there is an intensification of frontiers—military and economic.

Jihad may be a last deep sigh before the eternal yawn of McWorld. On the other hand, Ortega was not exactly prescient; his prophecy of peace and internationalism came just before blitzkrieg, world war, and the Holocaust tore the old order to bits. Yet democracy is how we remonstrate with reality, the rebuke our aspirations offer to history. And if retribalization is inhospitable to democracy, there is nonetheless a form of democratic government that can accommodate parochialism and communitarianism, one that can even save them from their defects and make them more tolerant and participatory: decentralized participatory democracy. And if McWorld is indifferent to democracy, there is nonetheless a form of democratic government that suits global markets passably well—representative government in its federal or, better still, confederal variation.

With its concern for accountability, the protection of minorities, and the universal rule of law, a confederalized representative system would serve the political needs of McWorld as well as oligarchic bureaucratism or meritocratic elitism is currently doing. As we are already beginning to see, many nations may survive in the long term only as confederations that afford local regions smaller than "nations" extensive jurisdiction. Recommended reading for democrats of the twenty-first century is not the U.S. Constitution or the French Declaration of Rights of Man and Citizen but the Articles of Confederation, that suddenly pertinent document that stitched together the thirteen American colonies into what then seemed a too loose confederation of independent states but now appears a new form of political realism, as veterans of Yeltsin's new Russia and the new Europe created at Maastricht will attest.

By the same token, the participatory and direct form of democracy that engages citizens in civic activity and civic judgment and goes well beyond just voting and accountability—the system I have called "strong democracy"—suits the political needs of decentralized communities as well as theocratic and nationalist party dictatorships have done. Local neighborhoods need not be democratic, but they can be. Real democracy has flourished in diminutive settings: the spirit of liberty, Tocqueville said, is local. Participatory democracy, if not naturally apposite to tribalism, has an undeniable attractiveness under conditions of parochialism.

Democracy in any of these variations will, however, continue to be obstructed by the undemocratic and antidemocratic trends toward uniformitarian globalism and intolerant retribalization which I have portrayed here. For democracy to persist in our brave new McWorld, we will have to commit acts of conscious political will—a possibility, but hardly a probability, under these conditions. Political will requires much more than the quick fix of the transfer of institutions. Like technology transfer, institution transfer rests on foolish assumptions about a uniform world of the kind that once fired the imagination of colonial administrators. Spread English justice to the colonies by exporting wigs. Let an East Indian trading company act as the vanguard to Britain's free parliamentary institutions. Today's well-intentioned quick-fixers in the National Endowment for Democracy and the Kennedy School of Government, in the unions and foundations and universities zealously nurturing contacts in Eastern Europe and the Third World, are hoping to democratize by long distance. Post Bulgaria a parliament by first-class mail. Fed Ex the Bill of Rights to Sri Lanka. Cable Cambodia some common law.

Yet Eastern Europe has already demonstrated that importing free political parties, parliaments, and presses cannot establish a democratic civil society; imposing a free market may even have the opposite effect. Democracy grows from the bottom up and cannot be imposed from the top down. Civil society has to be built from the inside out. The institutional superstructure comes last. Poland may become democratic, but then again it may heed the Pope, and prefer to found its politics on its Catholicism, with uncertain consequences for democracy. Bulgaria may become democratic, but it may prefer tribal war. The former Soviet Union may become a democratic confederation, or it may just grow into an anarchic and weak conglomeration of markets for other nations' goods and services.

Democrats need to seek out indigenous democratic impulses. There is always a desire for self-government, always some expression of participation, accountability, consent, and representation, even in traditional hierarchical societies. These need to be identified, tapped, modified, and incorporated into new democratic practices with an indigenous flavor. The tortoises among the democratizers may ultimately outlive or outpace the hares, for they will have the time and patience to explore conditions along the way, and to adapt their gait to changing circumstances. Tragically, democracy in a hurry often looks something like France in 1794 or China in 1989.

It certainly seems possible that the most attractive democratic ideal in the face of the brutal realities of Jihad and the dull realities of McWorld will be a confederal union of semi-autonomous communities smaller than nation-states, tied together into regional economic associations and markets larger than nation-states—participatory and self-determining in local matters at the bottom, representative and accountable at the top. The nation-state would play a diminished role, and sovereignty would lose some of its political potency. The Green movement adage "Think globally, act locally" would actually come to describe the conduct of politics.

This vision reflects only an ideal, however—one that is not terribly likely to be realized. Freedom, Jean-Jacques Rousseau once wrote, is a food easy to eat but hard to digest. Still, democracy has always played itself out against the odds. And democracy remains both a form of coherence as binding as McWorld and a secular faith potentially as inspiring as Jihad.

Benjamin R. Barber is the Whitman Professor of Political Science at Rutgers University. Barber's most recent books are Strong Democracy *(1984),* The Conquest of Politics *(1988), and* An Aristocracy of Everyone.

From *The Atlantic Monthly*, March 1992, pp. 53–55, 58–63. © 1992 by Benjamin R. Barber. Reprinted by permission.

Index

Index

Le Pen, Jean-Marie, 33, 34-35, 48, 127
leaders, democratic, public confidence in, 64, 65
Lebanonization, 227, 229-230
Lehmbruch, Gerhard, 50
Lenin, Vladimir, 72, 227
Lepper, Andrzej, 128
Liberal Democrat Party, in Britain, 16, 17, 20; in Russia, 152, 153
Lindblom, Charles E., 218
Livingstone, Ken, 18
Logic of Collective Action, The (Olson), 70
London, mayor of, 16

M

Maastricht Treaty, 19, 26, 124-125
macroeconomics, Japan and, 57
Madison, James, 91
Majiles, 195, 196, 199, 200
majoritarian voting, 87
majoritarianism, 107
majority rule, and democracy, 91, 94
"managed democracy," 149
mandatory referendums, 101
Mao Tsetung, 180, 181
Marbury v. Madison, 97
market imperative, as a dynamic of Mc-World, 227-228
Marx, Karl, 72, 217, 227
Mbeki, Thabo, 169, 170
McAvan, Linda, 89
McWorld, 227-231
media: and the demise of political parties, 67-68; Vladimir Putin and, 148
Mexico, democracy in, 162-166
Michelin Corporation, in France, 46
migration: China and, 182; and immigration in the EU constitution, 123-127
Mill, John Stuart, 217
misery index, 197-198
Mitterand, Francois, 34, 40-41
monarchy, British, 16
Moroccans, in France, 125
Morris, Dick, 73
Mueller, John, 72
multi-party parliamentary system, 103-111
Muslims: in the European Union, 126; in India, 189

N

National Action Party (PAN), 162, 163
National Compensation Law, 176
National Front, in France, 35, 48. *See also* Le Pen, Jean-Marie
National Republican Movement, in France, 35
Nehru, Jawaharlal, 188, 190
neocorporatism, in democracies, 92
neoliberal model, in Poland, 128-130
New Labour Party. *See* Labour Pary
New National Party (NNP), 168-169, 173
New Zealand, voters of, 100
nomenklatura, 132
North American Free Trade Agreement (NAFTA), 165-166

North Atlantic Treaty Organization (NATO), 136, 139; Russia and, 132, 133
Northern Alliance, 136
Northern Ireland, 12; devolution and, 17-18, 20
Norton, Philip, 20
Norway, women in politics in, 87

O

oligrachs, 198; Russian, 132, 135
Olson, Mancur, 70, 71, 72, 219-220
On Democracy (Dahl), 76
Organization for Economic Cooperation and Development (OECD), 73, 164
Ortega y Gassett, José, 229, 231

P

Pakistan, 188-189; democracy in, 210-211
Papon, Maurice, 35
parliamentary sovereignty, in democracies, 94
participation, in democracies, 94
"partisan dealignment, of mature democracies, 67
Partnership for Prosperity, 166
party government, in democracies, 94
pastoral myth, in France, 40
Patent Law of 2000, 176
People's Deputy faction, 144
perestroika, 131
Perot, Ross, 68, 69
Perry, Matthew, 57
personalized proportional representation, 110
pluralism, in democracies, 94
Poland: European Union and, 120, 122; post-communist developments in, 128-130
Political Parties in Advanced Industrial Democracies (Webb), 69
political parties: demise of, 67-69; in democracies, 94; South African, 167-170; political rights, of citizens in the European Union, 126
Politics and Markets (Lindblom), 218
polls: of EU voters, 223; of Russian voters, 134; in South Africa, 170-171
"polyarchy," 90, 93
Portugal, and the Revolution of the Carnations, 90
positive political theorists, 219
post-communism, in central and eastern Europe, 128-130
Powell, Colin, 203
PR voting systems, 109, 110
presidential election of 2000, 103
presidentialism, in democracies, 94
Prime Ministers, powers of, in parliamentary system, 104-105
privacy, and the demise of political parties, 67
privatization, in China, 175
procedural norms, in democracies, 92-93
propiska system, 153
proportional representation, 87, 109-110
Proposition 13, of California 102

public choice theorists, 219
public realm, 91
Pushtuns, 138
Putin, Vladimir, 134, 139; authoritarianism of, 135-136; Russian democracy and, 143-151, 152-154
Putnam, Robert, 65, 223

Q

quotas, for women in politics, 88

R

race, politics of, in France, 35
racial purity, German theories on, 58
Raffarin, Jean-Pierre, 33, 35, 37-38, 39
rational choice theorists 219
Reagan, Ronald, 69
Rees-Mogg, William, 20
Referendums Around the World (Butler and Ranney), 101
referendums, 68, 75, 77; voters and,100-102
reform, constitutional, in Britain, 16-21
regimes, democracy and, 90-91
regulatory institutions, federal, in India, 187, 190-191
religion: and recession, 197-198; tribalism and, 230
Renan, Ernest, 123
representative democracy, 74; criteria for, 76-77
representatives, democracy and, 92
Republican Party, in the United States, 69
resource imperative, as a dynamic of Mc-World, 228
responsiveness, of rulers, in democracies, 94
Revolt of the Masses, The (Ortega y Gassett), 229
Revolution of 1688, 24
Rice, Condoleezza, 203
Rise and Decline of Nations, The (Olson), 219
Rival Views of Market Society (Hirschman), 216
Royal Commission on the House of Lords. *See* Wakeham Commission
Rule of Law, 176
Rumsfeld, Donald, 49
Russia: capitalism in, 184-186; economic growth in, 149; myths about, 131-142
Russian Orthodox Church, as an obstacle to Westernization, 133
Russophobes, 131, 134, 137, 139

S

"safe seats" phenomenon, 105-108
Safire, William, on Russia, 135, 136
Sarkozy, Nicolas, 35, 43, 45
Schengen accord, 118-120, 124
Schrameck, Olivier, 34
Schröder, Gerhard: coalition government of, 47-49, 69; on economic reforms in Germany, 52-54, 55; war in Iraq and, 49
Schumpeter, Joseph, 215, 216, 217

Test Your Knowledge Form

We encourage you to photocopy and use this page as a tool to assess how the articles in *Annual Editions* expand on the information in your textbook. By reflecting on the articles you will gain enhanced text information. You can also access this useful form on a product's book support Web site at *http://www.dushkin.com/online/*.

NAME: DATE:

_____

TITLE AND NUMBER OF ARTICLE:

_____

BRIEFLY STATE THE MAIN IDEA OF THIS ARTICLE:

_____

LIST THREE IMPORTANT FACTS THAT THE AUTHOR USES TO SUPPORT THE MAIN IDEA:

_____

WHAT INFORMATION OR IDEAS DISCUSSED IN THIS ARTICLE ARE ALSO DISCUSSED IN YOUR TEXTBOOK OR OTHER READINGS THAT YOU HAVE DONE? LIST THE TEXTBOOK CHAPTERS AND PAGE NUMBERS:

_____

LIST ANY EXAMPLES OF BIAS OR FAULTY REASONING THAT YOU FOUND IN THE ARTICLE:

_____

LIST ANY NEW TERMS/CONCEPTS THAT WERE DISCUSSED IN THE ARTICLE, AND WRITE A SHORT DEFINITION:

We Want Your Advice

ANNUAL EDITIONS revisions depend on two major opinion sources: one is our Advisory Board, listed in the front of this volume, which works with us in scanning the thousands of articles published in the public press each year; the other is you—the person actually using the book. Please help us and the users of the next edition by completing the prepaid article rating form on this page and returning it to us. Thank you for your help!

ANNUAL EDITIONS: Comparative Politics 04/05

ARTICLE RATING FORM

Here is an opportunity for you to have direct input into the next revision of this volume.
We would like you to rate each of the articles listed below, using the following scale:

1. **Excellent: should definitely be retained**
2. **Above average: should probably be retained**
3. **Below average: should probably be deleted**
4. **Poor: should definitely be deleted**

Your ratings will play a vital part in the next revision.
Please mail this prepaid form to us as soon as possible.
Thanks for your help!

RATING	ARTICLE	RATING	ARTICLE
	1. A Constitutional Revolution in Britain?		28. Russian Democracy Under Putin
	2. The Blair Moment		29. Putin's Way
	3. Coming Out Smiling: Blair Survives His Biggest Test as Prime Minister and Promises No Wavering on Bold Policies		30. Globalization's Double Edge
			31. Mexico at an Impasse
	4. Tories, Even With a New Leader, See Little to Hope For		32. South Africa: Democracy Without the People?
			33. China: The Quiet Revolution
	5. A Divided Self: A Survey of France		34. The Emperor is Far Away
	6. French Secularism Unwraps Far More than Headscarves in the Classroom		35. In March Toward Capitalism, China Has Avoided Russia's Path
	7. Iraq Aside, French View the U.S. With a Mixture of Attraction and Repulsion		36. New Dimensions of Indian Democracy
			37. Iran's Crumbling Revolution
	8. Gerhard Schröeder Clings On		38. Bin Laden, the Arab "Street," and the Middle East's Democracy Deficit
	9. Untangling the System		
	10. Schröeder's Unfinished Business: Why the Reforms Agreed for Germany's Ailing Economy Leave the Job Half-done		39. There is No Crash Course in Democracy
			40. The Global State of Democracy
			41. Capitalism and Democracy
	11. The Vices and Virtues of Old Germany's 'Model' Economy		42. Cultural Explanations: The Man in the Baghdad Cafe
			43. Jihad vs. McWorld
	12. Japanese Spirit, Western Things		
	13. Public Opinion: Is There a Crisis?		
	14. Political Parties: Empty Vessels?		
	15. Interest Groups: Ex Uno, Plures		
	16. Advanced Democracies and the New Politics		
	17. Women in National Parliaments		
	18. Europe Crawls Ahead …		
	19. What Democracy Is … and Is Not		
	20. Judicial Review: The Gavel and the Robe		
	21. Referendums: The People's Voice		
	22. The Case for a Multi-Party U.S. Parliament? American Politics in Comparative Perspective		
	23. When East Meets West		
	24. The European Union Cannot Reach Deal on Constitution		
	25. In Search of Europe's Borders: The Politics of Migration in the European Union		
	26. Letter From Poland		
	27. Ten Myths About Russia: Understanding and Dealing With Russia's Complexity and Ambiguity		

(Continued on next page)

BUSINESS REPLY MAIL

FIRST CLASS MAIL PERMIT NO. 551 DUBUQUE IA

POSTAGE WILL BE PAID BY ADDRESEE

McGraw-Hill/Dushkin
2460 KERPER BLVD
DUBUQUE, IA 52001-9902

NO POSTAGE
NECESSARY
IF MAILED
IN THE
UNITED STATES

ABOUT YOU

Name _____ Date _____

Are you a teacher? ❑   A student? ❑
Your school's name _____

Department _____

Address _____ City _____ State _____ Zip _____

School telephone # _____

YOUR COMMENTS ARE IMPORTANT TO US!

Please fill in the following information:
For which course did you use this book?
_____

Did you use a text with this ANNUAL EDITION? ❑ yes ❑ no
What was the title of the text?
_____

What are your general reactions to the *Annual Editions* concept?
_____

Have you read any pertinent articles recently that you think should be included in the next edition? Explain.
_____

Are there any articles that you feel should be replaced in the next edition? Why?
_____

Are there any World Wide Web sites that you feel should be included in the next edition? Please annotate.
_____

May we contact you for editorial input? ❑ yes ❑ no
May we quote your comments? ❑ yes ❑ no